FORM AND FUNCTION IN A LEGAL SYSTEM —
A GENERAL STUDY

This book addresses three major questions about law and legal systems: (1) What are the defining and organizing forms of legal institutions, legal rules, interpretive methodologies, and other legal phenomena? (2) How does frontal and systematic focus on these forms advance understanding of such phenomena? (3) What credit should the functions of forms have when such phenomena serve policy and related purposes, rule of law values, and fundamental political values, such as democracy, liberty, and justice? This is the first book that seeks to offer general answers to these questions and thus give form in the law its due. The answers not only provide articulate conversancy with the subject, but also reveal insights into the nature of law itself, the oldest and foremost problem in legal theory and allied subjects.

Robert S. Summers is the William G. McRoberts Professor of Research in the Administration of Law at Cornell Law School. He has won international acclaim for his work in contracts, commercial law, jurisprudence, and legal theory. He has authored and coauthored multiple works in these fields for which he has received honorary degrees and other recognition. His treatise on the Uniform Commercial Code, coauthored with James White, is the most widely cited on the subject by courts and scholars. Professor Summers has served as official advisor both to the Drafting Commission for the Russian Civil Code and to the Drafting Commission for the Egyptian Civil Code. He lectures annually on jurisprudence and legal theory in the United States, Britain, Scandinavia, and Europe.

A SELECTION OF OTHER BOOKS BY THE AUTHOR

Form and Substance in Anglo-American Law, coauthored with Patrick S. Atiyah (Oxford University Press, third reprinting with minor revisions, 2002).

Contract and Related Obligation: Theory, Doctrine and Practice (4th ed.), coauthored and coedited with Robert A. Hillman (West Group, 2001).

La Naturaleza Formal del Derecho (Mexico City, Fontamara, 2001, in Spanish).

Collected Essays in Legal Theory (Amsterdam, Kluwer Academic Publshers, 2000).

The Uniform Commerical Code, coauthored with James J. White (West Group, 5th ed. of 1 vol. ed. of multi-volume treatise, 2000).

Interpreting Precedent – A Comparative Study, coedited and coauthored with members of the Bielefelder Kreis (Dartmouth Press, 1997).

The Uniform Commercial Code, 4 vols., coauthored with James J. White (West Group, 4th ed., 1995, with annual supplement).

Essays on the Nature of Law and Legal Reasoning (Berlin, Duncker and Humblot, 1992).

Interpreting Statutes – A Comparative Study, coedited and coauthored with members of the Bielefelder Kreis (Dartmouth Press, 1991).

Law: Its Nature, Functions, and Limits (3rd ed.), coauthored and coedited with several others (West Pub. Co., 1986).

Lon L. Fuller (Stanford University Press, 1984).

Pragmatischer Instrumentalismus (Karl Alber, Freiburg, 1983, German translation of next item below).

Instrumentalism and American Legal Theory (Cornell University Press, 1982).

Collective Bargaining and Public Benefit Conferral – A Jurisprudential Critique (Cornell University, ILR Monograph Series, 1976).

More Essays in Legal Philosophy (University of California Press, and Blackwells, Oxford, 1971).

Essays in Legal Philosophy (University of California Press, and Blackwells, Oxford, 1968).

FORM AND FUNCTION IN A LEGAL SYSTEM – A GENERAL STUDY

ROBERT S. SUMMERS

William G. McRoberts Professor of Research in the
Administration of Law, Cornell Law School, and
Arthur L. Goodhart Visiting Professor of Legal Science,
Cambridge University, 1991–2

B.S. 1955, University of Oregon; LL.B. 1959, Harvard Law School;
Doctor of Laws, Honoris Causa, University of Helsinki, 1990;
Doctor of Laws, Honoris Causa, University of Göttingen, 1994

CAMBRIDGE
UNIVERSITY PRESS

32 Avenue of the Americas, New York NY 10013-2473, USA

Cambridge University Press is part of the University of Cambridge.

It furthers the University's mission by disseminating knowledge in the pursuit of education, learning and research at the highest international levels of excellence.

www.cambridge.org
Information on this title: www.cambridge.org/9780521857659

© Robert S. Summers 2006

This publication is in copyright. Subject to statutory exception and to the provisions of relevant collective licensing agreements, no reproduction of any part may take place without the written permission of Cambridge University Press.

First published 2006

A catalogue record for this publication is available from the British Library

Library of Congress Cataloguing in Publication data

Summers, Robert S.
Form and function in a legal system : a general study / Robert S. Summers.
   p. cm.
Includes bibliographical references and index.
ISBN-13: 978-0-521-85765-9 (hardback)
ISBN-10: 0-521-85765-1 (hardback)
1. Law – Philosophy.   2. Law – Methodology.   I. Title.
K237.S86   2006
340'.1 – dc22   2005020120

ISBN 978-0-521-85765-9 Hardback
ISBN 978-0-521-12388-4 Paperback

Cambridge University Press has no responsibility for the persistence or accuracy of URLs for external or third-party internet websites referred to in this publication, and does not guarantee that any content on such websites is, or will remain, accurate or appropriate.

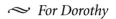 *For Dorothy*

GENERAL TABLE OF CONTENTS

PART ONE: INTRODUCTION, BASIC CONCEPTS AND DEFINITIONS,
AND A GENERAL APPROACH

1	Introduction	3
2	Basic Concepts and Definitions	37
3	A General Approach	64

PART TWO: THE FORMS OF FUNCTIONAL LEGAL UNITS

4	Forms of Institutions – Legislative	91
5	Forms of Precepts – Rules	136
6	Form and Content within a Rule – Continued	182
7	Forms of Nonpreceptual Law – Contracts and Related Property Interests	211
8	Forms of Legal Methodologies – Statutory Interpretation	241
9	Forms of Sanctions and Remedies	283

PART THREE: THE OVERALL FORM OF A LEGAL SYSTEM
AND ITS OPERATION

10	The Overall Form of a Legal System as a Whole	305
11	Cumulative and Synergistic Effects of Legal Forms – A Schematic Practical Application	351

DETAILED TABLE OF CONTENTS

Preface	*page* xiii
Acknowledgments	xv

PART ONE: INTRODUCTION, BASIC CONCEPTS AND DEFINITIONS, AND A GENERAL APPROACH

1 Introduction 3

Section One: Preliminary Overview	3
Section Two: Importance of Legal Form	17
Section Three: The Neglect of Form	24
Section Four: Protests Against Misunderstanding	33

2 Basic Concepts and Definitions 37

Section One: Introduction	37
Section Two: A Selection of Functional Legal Units and Their Overall Forms	37
Section Three: The Overall Form of a Functional Legal Unit – A General Definition and Refinements	39
Section Four: Types of Purposes That Overall Form Is to Serve – A More Extended Account	42
Section Five: Rationales for the General Definition of Overall Form Adopted Here	47
Section Six: Differentiation of the Overall Form From Material or Other Components of a Functional Legal Unit	57
Section Seven: The "Form v. Substance" Contrast	61

3 A General Approach 64

Section One: Introduction	64
Section Two: Advancing Understanding through Study of Form	64
Section Three: Attributing Credit to Form for Purposes Served	66
Section Four: A Form-Oriented Approach as Primary, with a Rule-Oriented One Secondary	72

ix

x   Detailed Table of Contents

PART TWO: THE FORMS OF FUNCTIONAL LEGAL UNITS

4   Forms of Institutions – Legislative **91**

Section One: Introduction   91
Section Two: Overall Legislative Form and Its Constituent Features   97
Section Three: The Compositional Feature   101
Section Four: The Jurisdictional Feature   108
Section Five: The Structural Feature   112
Section Six: The Procedural Feature   116
Section Seven: The Preceptual Feature   126
Section Eight: Form and the Unity of the Legislature   127
Section Nine: Skepticism about Institutional and Other Form,
  and Responses Thereto   131

5   Forms of Precepts – Rules **136**

Section One: Introduction   136
Section Two: Internal Formal Features of Rules   141
Section Three: The Feature of Prescriptiveness   143
Section Four: The Feature of Completeness   147
Section Five: The Feature of Definiteness   155
Section Six: The Feature of Generality   161
Section Seven: The Feature of Structure   164
Section Eight: The Encapsulatory Feature   170
Section Nine: The Expressional Feature   176
Section Ten: Responses to Objections   179

6   Form and Content within a Rule – Continued **182**

Section One: Introduction   182
Section Two: General Purposes of the Form and Content of
  Rules – A Summary   183
Section Three: Initial Choices of Policy or Other Content and of
  Formal Features in a Projected Rule   188
Section Four: Further Initial Choices of Formal Features   190
Section Five: Final Choices of Form and Final Choices of Policy
  and Other Content   199
Section Six: General Interactions and Other Inter-relations Between
  Choices of Form and Choices of Content   203
Section Seven: Further Responses to Objections   207

**7   Forms of Nonpreceptual Law – Contracts and Related
    Property Interests** **211**

Section One: Introduction   211
Section Two: Choices of Form and of Complementary Material or
  Other Components of Content in a Contract   215
Section Three: Due Credit to Form   221
Section Four: Formal *Prima-Facie* Validity and Further Credit Due to
  Form   228

Detailed Table of Contents

Section Five: Contractual Form and Related Property Interests – Still
Further Credit to Form — 232

Section Six: Implementation of Contractual and Related Property
Law – Credit to Form Continued — 236

Section Seven: Responses to Form-Skeptics and Law-Is-Policy
Reductionists — 238

8 Forms of Legal Methodologies – Statutory Interpretation — 241

Section One: Introduction — 241

Section Two: Sources of Needs for a Well-Designed Methodology to
Interpret Statutes — 245

Section Three: Study of the Overall Form of a Particular Interpretive
Methodology As an Avenue for Advancing Understanding — 250

Section Four: The General Credit That May Be Due the Overall Form
of an Interpretive Methodology for Statutes — 266

Section Five: Other Related Factors of Form — 273

Section Six: Formalistic Statutory Interpretation — 275

Section Seven: Methodological Forms and Other Forms — 282

9 Forms of Sanctions and Remedies — 283

Section One: Introduction — 283

Section Two: The Forms of Enforcive Functional Units – General — 287

Section Three: The Sanction of State Imprisonment for Criminal
Offenses — 289

Section Four: Remedies for the Private Wrong of Breach of Contract — 295

PART THREE: THE OVERALL FORM OF A LEGAL SYSTEM AND ITS OPERATION

10 The Overall Form of a Legal System as a Whole — 305

Section One: Introduction — 305

Section Two: Systematization of Institutions and Entities –
Centralized and Hierarchical Ordering *within* Each Main Type of
Jurisdictional Sphere: Legislative, Judicial, Administrative, and
Private-Ordering — 311

Section Three: Systematization *as between* Jurisdictional Spheres of
Institutions and Private Entities – Prioritization — 315

Section Four: Systematization of Valid Laws within Discrete Fields — 319

Section Five: Systematization through Uniformity of Interpretive and
Other Methodologies, and in Regard to Sanctions and Remedies — 323

Section Six: Further Systemization of Functional Legal Units through
Basic Operational Techniques — 326

Section Seven: Operation of Basic Techniques in Conformity with
Principles of the Rule of Law — 332

Section Eight: The Roles of Further Systematizing Factors — 344

Section Nine: Formalness As One Major Characteristic of a Legal
System As a Whole — 345

xii   **Detailed Table of Contents**

11   **Cumulative and Synergistic Effects of Legal Forms – A Schematic
     Practical Application** 351

   Section One: Introduction   351
   Section Two: Choices of Forms of Basic Operational Techniques   363
   Section Three: Choices of Forms in Legislatures, Administrative
      Bodies, or Other Entities   367
   Section Four: Choices of Preceptual and Related Forms at the
      Law-Making Stage   369
   Section Five: Choices of Form at the Stage of Public Promulgation   377
   Section Six: Form and the Stage of Addressee Self-Application   379
   Section Seven: An Exceptional yet Important Stage – Administrative
      Intervention   381
   Section Eight: Ultra-Exceptional Stage – Trial and Appellate Court
      Action   383
   Section Nine: Choices of Form – Summary of Major Cumulative and
      Synergistic Effects   386
   Section Ten: The Roles of Form and Information in a Linear
      Progression   387
   Section Eleven: The Limits of Form and Also Its General Potency   390

Name Index   393
Subject Index   395

PREFACE

I first lectured on themes here while I was the Arthur L. Goodhart Visiting Professor of Legal Science at Cambridge University in 1991–2, and began the book a number of years later.[1] I have written it not only for those with academic interests in law and legal systems, such as law students, professors of law, legal theorists, and other scholars, but for lawyers and judges as well.[2] The scope of the book is not confined to Anglo-American systems. It is addressed more generally to the forms and functions of legal phenomena in developed Western societies, and its central themes apply still more widely. I now offer the book as an ambitious yet unhurried attempt to develop systematic ways of giving form in law its due, both as an avenue of understanding and as a means of serving a variety of purposes: policy and related ends, rule of law values, and fundamental political values.

I focus here on paradigms of the forms of a varied selection of functional legal units: legislatures and courts; statutory and other rules; species of law besides rules, such as contracts and property interests; legal methodologies, such as those for interpreting statutes; and enforcive devices, such as sanctions and remedies. In addressing the make-up, unity, instrumental capacity, distinct identity, and other attributes of these functional legal units with focus on their forms, the book provides a new way of viewing the familiar. These functional units, and the system as a whole, are subjected to a special mode of analysis that I introduce here and call "form-oriented." It is so named because it focuses frontally, systematically, and holistically on how paradigms of the overall forms of such units are generally defined and organized, and also on how a paradigmatic version of the overall form of a developed Western legal system is generally defined and organized, all to serve

---

[1] See R. S. Summers, "The Formal Character of Law," 51 *Cambridge L. J.* 242 (1992).

[2] Many American lawyers and judges will recognize this work as highly compatible with a treatise that I coauthored: J. White and R. Summers, *The Uniform Commercial Code*, 4 vols. (4th ed., West Group, St. Paul, Minn. 1995, with annual supplements). Indeed, Chapter Seven of the present book applies the theory of form set forth here to the fields of contract and commercial law.

purposes. Readers so disposed can make this form-oriented mode of analysis part of their own general intellectual equipment and will find they can apply it to any functional legal unit and not merely to those selected for analysis here. Form-oriented analysis goes beyond analysis of functional legal units in terms of the contents of those legal rules that are reinforcive or constitutive of such units, analysis prominent in the works of major legal thinkers, such as H. L. A. Hart and Hans Kelsen.

Here, each paradigm of an overall form of a functional legal unit is defined and differentiated from the complementary material and other components of the unit. These overall forms and their constituent features are then analyzed to advance understanding of the whole. In this way, we can see that well-designed forms of functional legal units are not formalistic or bare and thin; instead, they are intrinsically purposive and value-laden and can, along with the complementary material and other components of such units, even be highly efficacious. We can also see how formal devices systematize the various functional legal units into a coherent and effective operational system.

This study also enables the reader to see how well-designed form can merit much credit for purposes served through the functioning of the various legal units within an operational system. Indeed, it is a central thesis of this book that significant credit for purposes served through deployment of functional legal units should go to well-designed form and not merely to the material or other components of these units, such as physical facilities and trained personnel. The frontal and systematic study of form is important, as well, for those who would construct functional legal units anew or improve upon existing units within particular systems, all the better to serve various ends.

There are still further reasons to study legal form. The subject itself is conceptually rich, wide-ranging, and absorbing. Also, because law is of great social importance, and form is intrinsic to law, legal form, too, is of great importance. Yet the subject has been neglected. Indeed, the subject has not yet been fully recognized as a discrete subject, let alone one for systematic study. Some American legal scholars and theorists have even treated aspects of form in law in unqualifiedly pejorative and dismissive terms. If I am right, this makes the need for such a book as this all the more pressing, although it is certain to be controversial in those quarters.

Robert S. Summers
February 17, 2005

ACKNOWLEDGMENTS

I wish to thank first my diligent research assistants, and the students in my annual seminars on American Legal Theory at Cornell Law School. All of these have contributed in various ways to the final version of this book.

I owe a deep debt of gratitude to my former administrative assistant, Mrs. Pamela F. Finnigan who has worked with me on this book from the beginning. Without her dedicated and highly effective assistance, it is certain the book would not yet be completed. I also wish to thank my current administrative assistant, Anne Cahanin.

I wish to record a special debt to an earlier coauthor, Professor Patrick S. Atiyah with whom, in the 1980s, I had many productive discussions of the related subject "form and substance" in law and legal reasoning.[1] The present book is a very different book from the one we coauthored; however, it is unlikely that I would have written the present one had the earlier one not preceded it.

Of my former teachers, I single out two for their tutelage, insight, and inspiration: the late H. L. A. Hart of Oxford University and the late Lon L. Fuller of Harvard University. Only the work of the great nineteenth-century German jurist, Rudolf von Jhering, has been more of a source of inspiration in the writing of this book.

I wish to thank numerous colleagues and friends who read part or all of the manuscript and made numerous helpful comments: Professor Okko Behrends of the University of Göttingen, Professor D. Neil MacCormick of the University of Edinburgh, Professor Philip Soper of the University of Michigan, Professor William Ewald of the University of Pennsylvania, the late Dr. Geoffrey Marshall formerly Provost of the Queen's College, Oxford University, Professor Pedro Alemán Láin of the University Complutense in Madrid, Professor Manuel Atienza of the University of Alicante, Professor Glenn Altschuler of Cornell

---

[1] P. S. Atiyah and R. S. Summers, *Form and Substance in Anglo-American Law* (Clarendon Press, Oxford, 1987).

University, and Mr. Paul Markwick. I am also indebted to an anonymous reviewer of the manuscript for Cambridge University Press for various helpful suggestions.

I am grateful as well to numerous hosts and audiences at various universities in the United States and in Europe for comments and discussions following lectures I was invited to present over the years on the various themes I take up in this book. In the United States, I am indebted to hosts and lecture audiences at the Universities of Chicago, Cornell, Florida, Georgia, and Oregon. Abroad, I am indebted to hosts and lecture audiences at the Universities of Cambridge, Oxford, London, and Bristol in England; the Universities of Edinburgh and St. Andrews in Scotland; the Universities of Göttingen, Hamburg, Heidelberg, Münster, Bielefeld, Freiburg, Tübingen, and Kiel in Germany; the Universities of Bologna, Ferrara, and Pavia in Italy; the Universities of Helsinki and Tampere in Finland; the Universities of Madrid, Alicante, and Mallorca in Spain; the Universities of Groningen and Utrecht in the Netherlands; the University of Paris (Sorbonne and also Nanterre), the University of Brussels, the University of Lund, and the University of Vienna.

I am also grateful to several deans of the Cornell Law School: Russell Osgood, the late Lee Teitelbaum, and Stewart Schwab, for research and other support.

Finally, I wish to thank my spouse, Dorothy Kopp Summers for all those many special forms of support and assistance that have always counted for so much in my book writing and other academic endeavors, and without which this particular prolonged effort simply could not have come to fruition.

Robert S. Summers
Cornell Law School
Ithaca, New York
February 17, 2005

PART ONE ∾

Introduction, Basic Concepts and Definitions, and A General Approach

1 ∼ INTRODUCTION

"Theory is the most important part of . . . the law, as the architect is the most important . . . in the building of a house."   – O. W. Holmes, Jr.[1]

"[Die Form] . . . ist im innersten Wesen des Rechts begründet."

"Form is rooted in the innermost essence of law."   – Rudolf von Jhering[2]

SECTION ONE: PRELIMINARY OVERVIEW

Given the unfamiliar nature of this study, an extended preliminary overview is called for. The most fundamental question of law and legal theory is: What is the nature of a legal system? Many leading scholars and theorists of law in the twentieth century, including H. L. A. Hart[3] and Hans Kelsen,[4] viewed a legal system as essentially a system of rules. In developed Western societies, however, a legal system is far more than this. It is made up of diverse functional units only one major variety of which consists of rules. These diverse units are, in turn, duly organized in complex ways to form a system. To grasp the nature of a legal system, it is first necessary to understand the diverse functional units of the system. These include institutions, such as legislatures and courts,[5] legal precepts, such as rules and principles,[6] nonpreceptual species of law, such as contracts and

---

[1] Oliver Wendell Holmes, Jr., *Collected Legal Papers*, 200 (Harcourt Brace and Co., New York, 1921).

[2] R. Jhering, *Geist des Römischen Rechts: auf den verschiedenen Stufen seiner Entwicklung*, vol. 2, at 479 (Scientia Verlag, Aalen, 1993) and see also R. Jhering, *Zweck im Recht*, (Breitkopf and Hartel, Wiesbaden, 1970) translated as *Law As a Means to an End* (I. Husik trans., The Boston Book Co., Boston, 1913). I am also indebted to Professor Okko Behrends here.

[3] H. L. A. Hart, *The Concept of Law*, 8 (2nd ed., Clarendon Press, Oxford, 1994). See further *infra* n. 60 and accompanying text. See also Chapter Three at 72.

[4] H. Kelsen, *Introduction to the Problems of Legal Theory*, 55–6 (B. Paulson and S. Paulson trans., Clarendon Press, Oxford, 1992). See also Chapter Three, at 72.

[5] See *infra* Chapter Four.

[6] See *infra* Chapters Five and Six.

property interests,[7] interpretive and other legal methodologies,[8] sanctions and remedies,[9] and more. A discrete legal unit does not function independently. It must be combined and integrated with other units.[10]

Although in developed Western societies, functional legal units of the same general variety vary somewhat from system to system and even within systems, those of a given variety do not, for the most part, differ fundamentally. Here, I address paradigms of a selection of major varieties. Each paradigmatic unit has its own attributes – its own purposes, makeup, unity, mode of operation, instrumental capacity, and distinct identity.

According to Hart, Kelsen, and their adherents, functional legal units are generally reducible to one variety, namely rules, although of various types. Some of these rules are what I call regulative. That is, they regulate primary conduct and thus, for example, proscribe crimes and rule out tortious behavior. There are many other rules, too. Many of these other rules do not regulate primary conduct, but rather are what I call "reinforcive." They prescribe and otherwise reinforce facets of the purposes, makeup, unity, instrumental capacity, and other attributes of what in my view are major functional legal units in no way reducible to rules or analyzable solely as rules. However, on a general view such as that of Hart, and to an extent also Kelsen, these other major functional units such as legislatures and courts, nonpreceptual species of law, such as contracts and property interests, interpretive and other legal methodologies, and sanctions and remedies, for example, are to be elucidated largely by "unpacking" the contents of those reinforcive rules that purport to prescribe facets of such units. For scholars and theorists, such as Hart and Kelsen, then, it may be said that a legal system is largely reducible to a system of regulative, reinforcive, or other rules.

For introductory purposes, one schematic example will suffice briefly to illustrate the most general version of what might be called the "Hart-Kelsen" mode of analysis in which, regulative rules aside, functional legal units are to be reduced to, and analyzed in accord with, the contents of reinforcive rules. I will call this mode of analysis "rule-oriented." Consider a functional legal unit that is institutional in nature, such as, a court. Important rules of a reinforcive nature (Hart's "rules of adjudication") prescribe, for example, facets of judicial makeup, unity, and mode of operation. Thus, we may study the contents of what Hart would call "rules of composition" and learn such things as how many judges there are to be and what qualifications they are to have. We may study "rules of jurisdiction" and learn about the powers of a court. We may also study "rules of procedure" and learn something about how the body is to function, and so on. Plainly, such rules

---

[7] See *infra* Chapter Seven.
[8] See *infra* Chapter Eight.
[9] See *infra* Chapter Nine.
[10] See *infra* Chapter Ten.

Section One: Preliminary Overview

reinforce the functional legal unit of a court and are even necessary to its very existence.

Here, I do not seek to elucidate a court, a legislature, or any other functional unit mainly via an analysis of the contents of reinforcive rules, although I concede a significant role for such rules. Rather, I introduce and apply what I call a "form-oriented" mode of analysis as the main method for elucidating the nature of functional legal units and of the legal system as a whole. Each variety of unit is conceived in terms of its purposes, its overall form, constituent features thereof, and complementary material or other components. This overall form is defined here as the purposive systematic arrangement of the unit as a whole – its "organizational essence," and is to be further analyzed in terms of its constituent features, and their inter-relations. The overall form of a unit and its constituent formal features does not include, and is to be differentiated from, complementary material and other components, such as, in a court, physical facilities, the actual judges, support personnel, and various resources, although overall form does specify such complementary components as well.

It is true that the overall form of a functional legal unit as a whole, its constituent features, and the complementary material or other components of the unit are partly prescribed, though not explicitly in these terms, in the contents of reinforcive legal rules or other positive law. However, these rules could not even have been drafted in the first place without first formulating the purposes, desired form, features, and complementary components.

The overall form of a unit – its purposive systematic arrangement – has a reality of its own that, in varying degrees, is both explicit in general social agreement, such as "blueprints" and other sources, and implicit in existing practices, as well as prescribed to some extent, though seldom expressly in terms of form, in the contents of rules reinforcive of the functional unit. The organizational reality of a functional unit, such as a court or a legislature, is identifiable and describable apart from its actual complementary components, such as its personnel and material resources. The distinct organizational reality of the overall form of a functional unit, and the constituent features of this form, can be detailed, dense, and complex.

The constituent formal features of the overall form of a functional unit, such as a court or a legislature, are also inter-related and unified in various ways. Together, they coherently organize who is to do what, when, how, and by what means. As already noted, the overall form of a court and its constituent formal features are to be differentiated from material components of the whole, such as physical facilities, personnel, and technology.[11]

---

[11] The individuation of discrete units can be done on the basis of the distinctiveness of both the overall form of the whole, and the complementary components of each. Different varieties of units do not overlap very much.

The purposes, overall forms, and constituent features of units differ greatly as between different units. Thus, for example, the purposes, overall form, and the constituent features of a court are designed, defined, and organized very differently from those of a legislature. The purposes, overall form, and constituent features of a regulative rule are designed, defined, and organized very differently from a contract. The purposes and overall forms and constituent features of all the foregoing differ greatly from those of an interpretive methodology, and so on.

The overall form of any functional legal unit in a particular system is a response of responsible participants to perceived needs to serve a special cluster of purposes through definitive organization. First, a conception of the overall form of the whole of a functional unit is needed to serve the founding purpose of defining, specifying, and organizing the *makeup* of such a unit so that it can be brought into being and can fulfill its own distinctive role along with other units in serving ends. For example, as we have seen, the overall form of a court or a legislature must have such features as those defining, specifying, and organizing the composition of its membership, its jurisdiction, and its various procedures.

Secondly, a conception of the overall form of the whole is needed for the purpose of organizing the internal *unity* of relations between various formal features of a functional unit and between each formal feature and the complementary components of the whole unit. For example, the two chambers of a bicameral legislature each take a form and these chambers and their members must be organized to function together.

Thirdly, and relatedly, a conception of the overall form of the whole functional unit is needed to organize further the *mode of operation* and the *instrumental capacity* of the unit. For example, internal committee structures and operational procedures within a legislature must be designed and internally coordinated to facilitate the study, debate, and adoption or rejection of proposed statutes.

Fourthly, no legal unit is independently functional. That is, no unit can alone serve the ends and values in view. For example, a legislature can pass a regulatory statute, but without other implementive units in operation, the statute would become a dead letter. Even a simple rule, as signified by an isolated stop sign positioned along a roadway on a lonely prairie must, to be effective, operate together with other functional units, including the organized public facility of the roadway itself, other rules of the road, and an official agency of enforcement. A conception of the overall form of an operational technique (here, mainly what may be called the "administrative-regulatory") is required to combine, integrate, and coordinate the relations between different functional units so that together they can effectively create and implement law to serve the ends in view.

Once the overall form and the constituent features of a functional legal unit are duly defined, organized, and put in place, what keeps the unit "on track?" That is, what holds these organized realities in place so that they generally operate more or less as designed? The quality of the original formal design is a major

Section One: Preliminary Overview

factor. For example, well-designed features of overall legislative form simply work better than ill-designed features, and what works tends to survive. The quality of training of the personnel responsible for the workings of the unit is another major factor. The evolution of well-defined customary practices supportive of the unit can be significant, too. Also, rule-minded theorists would stress the existence of legal rules the contents of which, in effect, reinforce features of overall form.

Where have all the numerous overall forms of functional legal units recognized today in Western legal systems come from? In part, they have been inherited from predecessor systems. In part, they have been borrowed from other systems. In part, they have evolved over time in response to felt needs. Few have been invented totally *de novo*, at least in modern times. Various factors have played roles in shaping these forms, but purposive and reasoned means-end analysis has doubtless been most prominent.

The overall forms of functional legal units, as manifest in duly constructed wholes, stand as tributes to the organizational inventiveness of developed Western societies. The realization of humanistic values of Western civilization, including justice, order, liberty, democracy, rationality, the rule of law, and more, has been heavily dependent on this inventiveness.

Surprising as it may seem, especially given the importance of law and the extensive study of forms, as forms, in other major fields of human learning and endeavor, the overall forms – purposive systematic arrangements – of most functional legal units have seldom in the course of Western legal theory been explicitly conceived as objects of frontal and systematic theoretical inquiry of the kind preferred here. As a result, these forms and their constituent features have not received their due either as avenues for advancing understanding of the nature of functional legal units or as contributing to the efficacy of such units as means to ends.

Even the overall form of that most common of all major varieties of functional legal units – that of a legal rule – has not yet received its due. Yet if rules are to be understood, the overall form of a rule and its constituent formal features, namely, prescriptiveness, completeness, definiteness, generality, internal structure, manner of expression, and mode of encapsulation, must be objects of concentrated attention. Complementary components of a rule include policy or other contents, and these must be studied as well. In all this, the effects of overall form, including the "imprints" of constituent formal features on each other and on components of content in a rule, must be a central focus.[12] As will be demonstrated, rules and all

---

[12] The word "imprint" may, to some, not seem strong enough here to do justice to the effects of well-designed form on material or other components of content. However, an imprint can be "deep" and "indelible." "Imprint" may, therefore, even be too strong in a particular use! Jhering used a different metaphor: he said that what I call the imprints of form on content, or on other nonformal elements of a legal unit, comprise the "most sharply etched characteristic of law" *supra* n. 2, *Geist*, vol. 2, at 470. The famed American judge, Benjamin N. Cardozo used still another metaphor when he said form can be "closely knit to substance" *Old Company's Lehigh, Inc. v. Meeker*, Receiver, et. al. 294 US 227, 230 (1935).

other varieties of functional legal units simply cannot be adequately understood without intensive focus on their forms, formal features, specifications of material and other components, and the effects and imprints of form on other formal features and on material components.

Without its overall form, a functional legal unit simply could not exist and serve ends.[13] Even if minimally organized in form sufficient to exist, such a unit could still be far less than optimally efficacious. Moreover, ill-designed form can itself wreak havoc via confusion, arbitrariness, and inefficacy. The credit due to well-designed form for purposes served can be considerable.

Furthermore, to grasp the nature of a legal system and the purposes it can serve, it is not enough to understand the functional units of the system. Even if these were all optimally designed, they could not, without more, constitute a legal system, and could not serve ends well, if at all. These units must also be combined and integrated within an operational system to be duly functional. Various systematizing devices are required for this. Some of these devices centralize and hierarchically order the relations between legal institutions as, for example, with the general prioritization of a legislature over a court in the making of law. Other such devices specify and order system-wide criteria for identifying valid rules and other species of law of the system in the first place. Hart and Kelsen sought to capture these in a "rule of recognition"[14] or "Grundnorm"[15] specifying criteria for identifying a valid law of the system. Other devices consist of basic operational techniques that integrate and coordinate institutions, precepts, methodologies, sanctions, and other functional units. As we will see, these techniques consist mainly of penal, grievance-remedial, private-ordering, administrative-regulatory, and public-benefit conferring techniques. Each technique is a formal organizational modality of wide-ranging significance.[16] Systematizing devices are in part formal, and the resulting organized system is a highly complex whole that is formal in a variety of important ways, also to be explained here.[17]

From systematic study of the nature and roles of legal form, form itself can be clarified, functional legal units and the legal system as a whole can be better understood, general credit can be given to form for serving ends, and the modeling of functional legal units and of the system as a whole can be improved.

In this book, I introduce and develop what may be called a general theory of legal form. In the next chapter, I clarify, analyze, and refine my general definition of the overall form of a functional legal unit as its purposive systematic arrangement.

---

[13] For a very different account of types of functional legal units, see the illuminating discussion of R. Alexy, "The Nature of Legal Philosophy," 7 *Associations* 63 (2003).

[14] H. L. A. Hart, *supra* n. 3, at 94.

[15] H. Kelsen, *supra* n. 4, at 55–64.

[16] See R. Summers, "The Technique Element in Law," 59 *Calif. L. Rev.* 733 (1971). The five main operational techniques of law are treated in Chapter Ten.

[17] See *infra* Chapter Ten.

Section One: Preliminary Overview

The required conceptual analysis, clarification, and refinement is itself a major task of this book, given the complexities of form, and given that the word "form" has many meanings in Western languages, including various pejorative meanings at odds with my general definition and its refinements here. I seek to introduce a coherent vocabulary and terminology of form. Also, I seek to show that this vocabulary and terminology is not only felicitous, but is usually grounded in certain well-recognized English usages.

My general definition of the overall form of a functional legal unit is that this form is the purposive systematic arrangement of the unit as a whole. Later, I expound upon and provide major rationales for this general definition. I also refine and apply this definition to a *selection* of major functional legal units necessary to or salient within Western legal systems, including legislatures, rules, contracts, interpretive methodologies, and sanctions.

Also, I seek to advance and to render more articulate our general understanding of the distinctive nature of each selected functional legal unit as a whole through a frontal and systematic focus on its overall form, the constituent features of this form, and the complementary material or other components within the whole. The key questions here are these: What purposes is the unit designed to serve? What is its makeup? That is, what is its overall form, constituent features thereof, and complementary components within the whole? What is the unity of the whole? That is, how is it purposively and systematically arranged to unify the whole? What imprints or other effects does form leave? What is the mode of operation and the instrumental capacity of the unit? Its distinct identity? Its systematic integration with other functional units to serve ends? In what reinforcive rules, other species of positive law, or still other sources are the facets of the unit at least partially prescribed? Throughout I attempt to show how the overall form and constituent formal features of a functional legal unit should share credit with its material or other components for ends realized.

I also seek to show how focus on the form and formal features of a legal system as a whole advances understanding of its nature. I concentrate on how one of the general characteristics of a legal system can be said to be its overall formalness and on how this general characteristic has a claim to special primacy. I also attempt to demonstrate the credit due to formal systematizing devices and the resulting formal features of the system as a whole, insofar as these contribute to serving ends. At various intervals, I will also strive to explain how the frontal and systematic study of form casts light on certain traditional problems of law, jurisprudence, and legal theory in addition to the nature of functional legal units and the nature of a legal system as a whole.

The understanding I seek to advance in this book does not generally require discovery and presentation of new facts. Rather, it requires that we reconceive, reorder, and reclassify much of the subject matter of a legal system in terms of a variety of functional legal units and that we focus on familiar yet frequently unnoticed formal facets of these units, as well as formulate felicitous concepts and terminology to portray these facets and render explicit and thus lay bare much that is often left implicit and so goes unnoticed. Such efforts can yield insights into each functional unit considered, provide a clearer view of the whole of each, and reveal important inter-relations between the units within a legal system as duly systematized.

Moreover, the attribution of general credit to overall form and to constituent features thereof for the ends realized through creation and deployment of individual functional units in the operations of a legal system, does not, as I treat the subject here, require empirical studies of a social scientific nature. As I later explain, it is usually sufficient for my purposes to rely on necessary truths, on general facts already known, on highly plausible supporting assumptions, and on tried and true modes of argument.[18]

This book seeks to shift the emphasis in one major tradition of Western legal scholarship and theory not only away from regulative rules, but also and more emphatically, away from analyses of the contents of those reinforcive rules that are taken to prescribe the facets of functional legal units generally. Instead, form-oriented analysis is introduced and is focused upon the overall forms of functional legal units, and on the overall form of a legal system as a whole, as major avenues for advancing understanding. "Form-oriented" analysis[19] is applied here to a wide range of selected functional legal units operative within a legal system. This fundamental shift in emphasis entails intensive concentration on the overall forms of such units and on the overall form of a legal system as a whole. Here we study a wide range of functional legal units in addition to rules, and we study these mainly via a direct and frontal focus on the overall forms of such units and their complementary components and not merely indirectly through the study of the contents of legal rules reinforcive of such units. Instead of, for example, studying the functional unit of a legislature or a court obliquely through the contents of any rules purportedly reinforcive of its composition, jurisdiction, structure, and procedure, as in the fashion of Hart, Kelsen, and others, we frontally address the features of the overall form of the institution.

Moreover, in stressing the credit due to form, this book introduces still another shift of emphasis. What law achieves is not to be credited solely to the policy or other contents of regulative rules. Nor is what law achieves to be credited solely to any rules the contents of which are purportedly reinforcive of functional units.

---

[18] See *infra* Chapter Three. See also Lon L. Fuller, *The Morality of Law* (Rev. ed., Yale University Press, New Haven, 1969).

[19] Form-oriented analysis is discussed in detail, *infra* Chapters Two and Three, and is systematically contrasted with rule-oriented analysis in Section Four of Chapter Three. As we will see, form-oriented analysis distinctively advances understanding of the rules themselves. Among other things, reinforcive rules purporting to prescribe facets of functional legal units are rarely explicit about form.

Section One: Preliminary Overview

Nor is what law achieves to be credited solely to material and other components of the makeup of functional legal units, such as the trained personnel and material resources of institutions, or the sheer "force" of a sanction. Major credit must also be given to the overall forms of functional legal units as such and to the constituent features of these forms.

That legal scholars and theorists have not yet given form sufficient credit for ends realized is attributable to a variety of related factors. The factors include: (1) the lack of an adequate general definition of overall form as the purposive systematic arrangement of a functional unit as a whole, (2) the failure to differentiate the overall form of a unit from the material and other components of the unit as objects of credit, (3) a tendency to over-emphasize the material and other components of a unit when attributing credit, (4) the fact that some varieties of overall form and its features are too obvious to be noticed, or are hidden or overshadowed, even when in front of our very eyes, (5) the fact that the roles of many overall forms and features thereof, because of their seeming simplicity and familiarity, tend to be taken for granted, (6) the failure of legal theorists and other scholars to develop the concepts and terminology required to sharpen general awareness of form and formal features, (7) excessive skepticism about the reality and efficacy of "mere" form, skepticism borne partly of various antiformal tendencies of academics and others in some systems – tendencies that may even derive from salutary reactions to the over-formal and the formalistic in legal analysis, and (8) a predisposition to rule-oriented analysis, especially its over-emphasis on rules reinforcive of functional legal units to the neglect of their forms.

As I will show, the overall form of a discrete functional unit purposively and systematically arranges the unit as a whole. Rudolf von Jhering, the nineteenth-century German jurist of the University of Göttingen, whose later work was one major source of inspiration for this book, might have said that this overall form is the "organizational essence" of the unit. This form and its constituent features are dictated largely by the special purposes of the functional unit within the system. Those who would create such a unit must design or choose an overall form appropriate to it in order to organize the unit to fulfill its special role in serving purposes together with other units.

As I will show, the general definition of the overall form of a functional legal unit as the purposive systematic arrangement of the whole can be felicitously refined to fit the highly varied functional legal units selected for consideration in this book. In Chapter Two, I will explain how this definition also conforms in important respects to certain technical and ordinary uses of the word "form," in English. These uses give a nonpejorative meaning to "form."

Often the overall forms of functional legal units are taken for granted, without even being recognized as formal. Some who do recognize forms at work may still be skeptical of their overall significance. Matters are still worse. Some schools of

12   Introduction

legal theory have been hostile to form, and some theorists often use the words "form" and "formal" pejoratively. For example, according to certain American legal realists and neo-realists, the forms of at least some (perhaps many) rules, and of certain other functional legal units are in decided tendency "rigid," "formalistic," to be applied "mechanically," or similarly objectionable.[20] Yet even in America, with its continuing antiformal realist tradition in some academic circles, many academics concerned with the law have been highly respectful of form, even though they may not use the word "form" to express this. Also, many judges and lawyers have also been, and are, highly respectful of form.[21]

Deeply antiformal attitudes have not been confined to the American academic scene, however. For example, the nineteenth-century German "free-law" movement known as "Freierechtslehre" could certainly be characterized as antiformal.[22] The jurist, Rudolf von Jhering, opposed this.[23] He explicitly singled out form in functional legal units as a fertile and important subject both for theory and practice, even if he did not himself address the subject very systematically. I will shortly identify the specific sources of inspiration I have found in Jhering's work.

This book is an extended plea for a more open and sympathetic recognition of the overall forms of functional legal units and their significance.[24] Chapters Four through Eight of this book are organized around overall forms of selected units: legislatures, statutory rules, contracts and related proprietary interests, methodologies of statutory interpretation, and sanctions and remedies. Although this selection is hardly exhaustive of the functional units of a system of law, this is not a random selection. I have selected these units because they are salient in all such systems, reveal how varied such units are, and demonstrate the versatility of form-oriented analysis. I have also selected them because of what may be called their overall functional representativeness: one unit of a law-creating nature (a legislature), two units representative of law duly created (statutory rules and contracts),

---

[20] See, e.g., D. Kennedy, "Legal Formality," 2 *J. Legal Stud.* 351, 358–9, 378 (1973); R. Posner, *The Problems of Jurisprudence* (Harvard University Press, Cambridge, 1990). For an extended survey see R. Summers, *Instrumentalism and American Legal Theory*, Chapter 6 (Cornell University Press, Ithaca, 1982). See further *infra*, at 259. Some well-known scholars and theorists have sometimes appeared to assume that form is largely confined to rules and to reasoning from rules, almost as if other legal units could exist without form! See, e.g., D. Kennedy, "Form and Substance in Private Law Adjudication," 89 *Harv. L. Rev.* 1685, 1687 (1976).

[21] The opinion of Judge Bleckley in *Cochran v. State*, 62 Ga. 731, 732 (1879) is a good example. I have used a quote from this opinion to introduce Chapter Two. Many English judges are highly respectful of form, although they are also duly critical of the formalistic in legal reasoning. See generally S. Waddams, *Dimensions of Private Law*, 2 (Cambridge University Press, Cambridge, 2003).

[22] See, e.g., E. Ehrlich, *Freierechtsfinding und Freierechtswissenschaft* (L. Hirschfeld, Leipzig, 1903); H. Kantorowicz, *Der Kampf um die Rechtswissenschaft* (C. Winter's Buchhandlung, Heidelberg, 1906); see also O. Behrends, "Von der Freierechtsschule zum konkreten Ordnungsdenken," in *Recht und Justiz im Dritten Reich*, 34–80 (R. Dreier and W. Sellert eds., Surhkamp, Frankfurt am Main, 1989).

[23] See R. Jhering, books cited *supra* n. 2.

[24] I am indebted to the late Geoffrey Marshall for this articulation.

Section One: Preliminary Overview

one unit of an applicational nature (an interpretive methodology for statutes), and two different enforcive units (imprisonment for crime and expectancy damages for breach of contract). Treatment of the foregoing selection is sufficient to sustain my central theses that study of the overall forms and constituent formal features of functional legal units is itself rich in conceptual and other terms, can distinctively advance understanding of these units, and reveals that well-designed form deserves major credit for any ends realized.[25]

A leading tenet of the general theory of form set forth here is that well-designed forms of functional units are sturdy and robust. They are not "bare and thin," as Jhering once put it when mocking critics of form.[26] A "bare and thin" form would be relatively devoid of purpose and structure and thus could not sufficiently define and organize an effective functional unit, let alone define and organize a legal system as a whole.

Although I concentrate here on form, this does not mean that my focus is merely on anatomical facets of functional units or that I conceive of these units merely in static terms. Instead, my approach may be said to be physiological and dynamic. Functional legal units and their forms are treated as units to be integrated and coordinated within operational techniques for creating and implementing law. I present such units as functional, and I conceive of legal ordering as a dynamic activity.[27]

In the remainder of this preliminary overview, I identify some more specific sources of inspiration I have found in the work of Rudolf von Jhering. I then summarize my main rationales for writing this book. Jhering often focused on the overall forms of wills, contracts, and other "legal transactions" and seldom conceptualized form quite as broadly as here. Nevertheless, he asserted that form is rooted in the "innermost essence" of law.[28] He would have agreed that the study of form is an essential avenue for advancing understanding of a functional legal unit. Jhering would also have agreed that the overall form of a functional legal unit, when well-designed, defines and organizes the makeup and unity of the unit, renders it determinate and organizationally efficacious, and gives it its distinctive identity. Jhering even said that form is to the identity of such a unit as "the mark of the mint is to coinage."[29]

---

[25] I am indebted to Philip Soper here.

[26] R. Jhering, *supra* n. 2, *Geist*, vol. 2, at 478. He stressed purpose in law throughout his book *Law As a Means to an End*. R. Jhering, *supra* n. 2. The German title of this book is more faithful to its contents: R. Jhering, *Zweck im Recht* (Breitkopf and Härtel, Wiesbaden, 1970), which translated means "Purpose in the Law." See generally R. Summers, "Rudolf von Jhering's Influence on American Legal Theory – A Selective Account," in *Jherings Rechtsdenken: Theorie und Pragmatik im Dienste evolutionärer Rechtsethik* (O. Behrends ed., Vandenhoeck & Ruprecht, Göttingen, 1996).

[27] I am indebted to Manuel Atienza for this articulation.

[28] R. Jhering, *supra* n. 2, *Geist*, vol. 2, at 479.

[29] *Id.*, at 494.

14   Introduction

According to Jhering, the overall form of a functional legal unit is highly purposive. For example, those who would create a judicial institution must arrange
it purposively and systematically so that it has a definitive makeup and unity
capable of fulfilling the instrumental purposes of a court. Those who would create such a body must define, organize, and integrate the constituent features of
overall judicial form: compositional, jurisdictional, structural, procedural, and
preceptual.

Jhering would have agreed, as well, that those who would create an institution
must provide for and integrate any material and other components complementary to its overall form and formal features. In the case of a court, the purposes
of this systematic arrangement require certain personnel, material resources, and
other components, which as duly organized, also bear imprints of the overall form
of a court.

Although he did not develop these themes or state them precisely in these
terms, Jhering saw the study of form as a major key to practical and theoretical
understanding of functional legal units. Jhering also saw how well-designed forms
are entitled to major credit for the ends served. He recognized that legal transactions cannot even occur without recognized forms for their valid creation,[30] that
there can be no "legal content" without form,[31] and that definitiveness of form
is required to fix the relations between conflicting policies or other ends, i.e., "to
fix fluid substance" in a law.[32] He also emphasized that form is the "twin sister of
liberty."[33] For example, without the legally recognized overall form that a valid
contract must take, liberty of contract simply could not exist.

Jhering also championed the relation between form and rationality. He stressed
that well-designed form is the "sworn enemy of the arbitrary."[34] The forms – the
purposive systematic arrangements – of institutions, legal rules, contracts and
property interests, interpretive methodologies, sanctions, and other functional
legal units, manifest a profound commitment to reason. This commitment is not
only revealed in the creation of legal units in due form as *means* to external policy
ends, that is, in "instrumental" reason. It is also revealed in the very creation of
certain units, such as democratic electoral arrangements as themselves *ends* to
be pursued, that is, in "constitutive" reason. Indeed, if a legal system is to have
functional units well-designed in form, it must resort to reason throughout – in
the creation of institutional units, in the creation of rules and other species of law,
in determinations of the validity of putative law, in interpreting and applying law
to construct reasons for action or decision, in the rational finding of facts relevant
to the creation or application of law, and more. Each type of functional unit has its

[30] R. Jhering, *supra* n. 2, *Geist*, vol. 2, at 494.
[31] *Id.*, at 473.
[32] *Id.*, at 471.
[33] *Ibid.*
[34] *Ibid.*

Section One: Preliminary Overview

own primary founding purposes and must be rationally designed to fulfill these purposes if it, along with other functional units is to serve purposes of policy, the rule of law, and other values.[35]

I have three general rationales for writing this book, each of which I will now briefly summarize. In upcoming sections, I will elaborate on each. My first rationale is implicit in what I have said so far. The overall forms of functional legal units and the overall form of a legal system as a whole are, as Jhering plainly saw, of major theoretical and practical importance. Study of the forms of such units itself qualifies as a discrete and full-fledged branch of legal study, although not yet recognized as such. The study of such forms, either in particular systems or in more abstract terms, as here, is a major avenue to theoretical and practical understanding of the nature of functional legal units, and of the nature of a system of law as a whole – the latter being the central topic in the whole field of legal theory. As I will show, the study of such forms also casts light, directly or tangentially, on various special topics of law and legal theory including the nature of institutional and other sources of law, criteria of legal validity, legal rules, the relation between law and morals, and the rule of law.

Because form can contribute to the realization of valuable ends, the study of how this is so is also of immense practical significance, as I will explain. Apart from advancing understanding of functional legal units and apart from according due credit to form, a theory of form, with appropriate concepts and terminology, can also facilitate the modeling and improved construction of functional legal units.

Some might conclude that some of the truths I seek to substantiate here about the theoretical and practical importance of the overall forms of functional legal units are obvious. For example, it might be thought quite obvious that addressees of a rule cannot determine what action the rule calls for if the rule lacks an appropriately formal feature, such as definiteness. Even if this is conceded, many still might not realize that the feature of definiteness that is entitled to major credit is itself a formal feature and, therefore, fail to see that form merits some credit here. One might fail to recognize definiteness as formal for lack of felicitous concepts of the overall form of a rule and its constituent features.[36] Even with such concepts, one still might fail to recognize what is before one's very eyes. The philosopher, Ludwig Wittgenstein, had no difficulty explaining why this occurs. He emphasized that:[37] "The aspects of things that are important for us are hidden because of their simplicity and familiarity. (One is unable to notice

---

[35] Jhering develops the intimacy between purpose and reason in *Zweck im Recht, supra* n. 2.

[36] See Chapter Five *infra*.

[37] L. Wittgenstein, *Philosophical Investigations*, 129, at 50 (G. E. M. Anscombe trans., The MacMillan Co., New York, 1953). See also Wittgenstein's related remark: "Philosophical problems can be compared to locks on safes, which can be opened by dialing a certain word or number, so that no force can open the door until just this word has been hit upon, and once hit upon any child can open it" L. Wittgenstein, *Philosophical Occasions*, 175 (J. Klagge and A. Nordmann eds., Hackett Publishing Co., Indianapolis, 1993).

something – because it is always before one's eyes.)" In the same vein, the noted American justice of the United States Supreme Court, Oliver Wendell Holmes, Jr., once stressed that what we often need is "education in the obvious" rather than "investigation of the obscure."[38] Not all that may seem obvious to some is generally so. For example, as is shown in Chapters Five and Six, it is not generally obvious that there are six major constituent features of the overall form of a legal rule, or that there are various complex inter-relations between these formal features, and between these features and the material or other components of the rule.

Even though the theoretical and the practical importance of the overall forms of functional legal units is very great, Western legal theorists and other scholars have generally neglected this subject. This is a second rationale for this book. Legal theorists and other scholars have seldom explicitly recognized *the forms* of functional legal units as a general subject for study, let alone as a subject for a general theory. This is not to say these units have been totally neglected. There are many studies, including ones focused on the contents of reinforcive rules specifying facets of a legal unit, such as, for example, the contents of the rules designating the personnel and the procedures of courts. Few theorists and other legal scholars have, however, studied either reinforcive or regulative rules with explicit focus on their overall form and constituent formal features. Thus, even if some of the truths I identify with respect to forms ultimately emerge as obvious, many students of the law have yet to be educated in them in any extended fashion, and many may not enjoy an articulate conversancy with these truths. It is symptomatic of the neglect of the subject I now seek to demarcate and develop that Western legal theorists do not today even have an agreed general definition of the overall form of a functional unit and do not have an accepted typology of legal units and their forms.

The third rationale for this book is that the subject poses important challenges of its own. The aims of any book that introduces a "form-oriented" approach and seeks to develop a general theory of legal form are necessarily ambitious. It is by no means certain that all I assert and argue for here will, in the end, prove to be "obvious" in the spirit of Wittgenstein's remark. Also, the subject is not easily treated. One is even reminded of Bentham's statement that some truths of law "grow among thorns; and are not to be plucked, like daisies."[39] Doubtless

---

[38] O. W. Holmes, Jr., *Collected Legal Papers*, 292–3 (Harcourt, Brace and Co., New York, 1921). Karl N. Llewellyn once emphasized that: "Inquiry into the obvious . . . is a fruitful labor" see Llewellyn, "The Effect of Legal Institutions upon Economics," 15 *Economic Review* 665, 665 (1925). See also G. C. Homans: "But why cannot we take the obvious seriously?" in *The Philosophy of Social Explanation* at 64 (A. Ryan ed., Oxford University Press, London, 1973). T. J. Reed has written that "To see and state the obvious . . . [can be] a creative achievement" see T. J. Reed, *Göethe*, 14 (Oxford University Press, Oxford, 1984). H. L. A. Hart once wrote that unity in a legal order can be worth thinking about "because it sharpens our awareness of what is often too obvious to be noticed" Hart, *supra* n. 3, at 116.

[39] H. L. A. Hart, *Essays on Bentham: Studies in Jurisprudence and Political Theory*, 125 (Clarendon Press, Oxford, 1982).

Section Two: Importance of Legal Form

other theorists, including some respectful of form, will disagree with some of my conclusions. It is gratifying to contemplate that this disagreement may advance the subject beyond where I have had to leave it.

SECTION TWO: IMPORTANCE OF LEGAL FORM

I will now elaborate upon my first rationale for writing this book, namely, that the study of overall forms of functional legal units and the overall form of a legal system in its entirety can advance theoretical and practical understanding. Such study can provide comprehensive and synoptic theoretical understanding of a fundamental characteristic of a system of law – its formal nature. As I will show, it can lead to the formulation and clarification of concepts and terminology for the perspicuous representation of any functional legal unit and its form. It can explicate the distinctive makeup and unity of such a unit, and thus fit its disparate formal features and complementary components into a coherent whole. It can render explicit the organizational basis of the instrumental capacity of any functional unit. It can portray the distinct identity of any unit. It can identify the purposes and values at stake and clarify both the instrumental and the constitutive relations between form and the realization of ends.

The study of form can be of immense practical importance, too. It is familiar that functional legal units such as rules and sanctions, when duly formed and put to use, not only can curb violence, fraud, promise-breaking, and other wrongs, but can also serve as great affirmative forces for good. It is not only that well-designed form in such units better serves ends. It can also incorporate, express, enshrine, symbolize, radiate, and reinforce values of the society. For example, the values of fairness to persons accused of a crime are not only implemented in, but are also expressed and symbolized in, a duly defined and organized judicial procedure, which is a major constituent of overall adjudicative form.[40] Certainly these values are not expressed merely through actions of the person who happens to be the judge. The study of legal form thus reveals how humanistic values of Western civilization are at stake in legal ordering and reveals the power of legal inventiveness in serving these values. I will now elaborate on the foregoing truths, but only selectively and in an introductory fashion. In later chapters, I treat these truths more fully.

Form Required for Existence and Efficacy of Functional Legal Units. Form is necessary for the very existence of an institution, a rule or other precept, a nonpreceptual species of law, such as a contract, a methodology for interpreting

---

[40] E. Cassirer, *The Philosophy of Symbolic Forms* (R. Manheim trans., Yale University Press, New Haven, 1953).

statutes, a penal sanction, or any individual legal unit. Form is also necessary for the very existence of a system of law as a whole in which individual units are, among other things, systematized within operational techniques for the creation and implementation of law. Without the purposive systematic arrangement of each unit in some degree, there simply could be no such units and no legal system anywhere. As Jhering stressed, a functional legal unit simply cannot exist as totally formless.[41] Without due recognition of the forms of the relevant functional legal units, people could not even formulate the intention to create a statutory rule, or to create a contract, or to make a will, or to set up a corporation, and on and on.

Let us illustratively consider an institution such as a court. To exist, to function, and to be identifiable as a court, it must be duly organized as such, that is, take the overall form of a court. An incipient society could be rich in the components required for a functioning court, such as personnel, judicial "know-how," and material resources. However, the mere coexistence of all this unorganized richness in one locale at the same time could hardly signify the existence of a court.[42] For a court to exist, the society must have an apt conception of the overall form of a court and of the constituent features of such a form. The society may inherit or may import such a conception or it may construct the conception in light of its own means-end analyses. The society must sufficiently implement the conception and thereby integrate the personnel, material resources, and other components into an organized functional whole, which is a purposive systematic arrangement of the makeup, unity, mode of operation, and instrumental capacity of a judicial institution.

The contributions of institutional forms to the creation of legal rules and other law are not confined to what is required for courts to exist and thus create precedents. Without the required overall form of a legislature having authority to create statutes, a society could have no bodies of statute law either. Without the required overall form of an administrative agency with power to make binding regulations, a society could not have administrative regulations as we know them. Without institutional and other recognized sources of law, there could be no legal rules or other law, and therefore no rule of law at all.

Furthermore, in order for a system of law to be effective, officials and the laity, with any required assistance of lawyers, must be able to identify valid law. This requires the existence of accepted general criteria that citizens, officials, and others can invoke to identify valid law and differentiate it from nonlaw. Such criteria, another traditional subject of legal theory, include specified sources of valid law, such as "enacted by the legislature," "adjudicated by a court," and "laid down by an authorized administrative body." Source-oriented criteria of validity of

---

[41] R. Jhering, *supra* n. 2, *Geist*, vol. 2, at 478. See also *supra* n. 2, *Zweck*, passim.
[42] Compare *infra* Chapter Four with respect to a legislature.

Section Two: Importance of Legal Form

this nature presuppose the existence of an institutional source, which, in turn, presupposes the complex overall form required for the very existence of such a source. For example, without reference to the internal operations of the formal compositional, jurisdictional, structural, and procedural features of the overall form of a legislature (including its "decision-rule," e.g., majority vote), officials and others simply could not tell when such a body had exercised its authority to create a statute and thus could not determine whether law assertedly deriving from the relevant authoritative source, i.e. "enacted by the legislature," is thus valid by this criterion.

It is one thing for a functional legal unit to exist at all, and another for it to be optimally designed to serve ends. For example, a legislature ill-designed in form could exist, yet be relatively ineffective, or a statutory rule might take sufficient form merely to exist, yet lack due definiteness – a formal feature – and thus not be effectively administrable.

Form as an Avenue for Advancing Understanding of Functional Legal Units. Functional legal units, and the legal system as a whole must be understood, both for the sake of understanding as such, and in order for officials, citizens, and others to deploy them effectively to serve ends. No legal unit can be adequately understood without grasping its form. It will be sufficient for now merely to provide two schematic examples concerned with regulative statutory rules.

First, the makeup of a regulative statutory or other rule is something more than its component of policy or other content. A rule cannot, for example, be "all content and no form." A rule must take a special overall form to be a rule at all. To understand a rule fully, it is necessary to grasp how this form defines and organizes it and how this gives the unit a distinct identity. The overall form of the most common type of statutory rule prescribes that a class of addressees must, may, or may not act in a described fashion in recurrent circumstances over time. This overall form is, itself, plainly very different from that of an order or that of a contract. A rule is not merely an embodiment of policy or other content, but is a combination of such content with prescriptiveness, generality, definiteness, internal structure, completeness, due expression, and a mode of encapsulation, which are all constituent features of the overall form of a rule. No rule is ever created with labels on it identifying these various formal features. In this book, I introduce concepts and vocabulary to clarify and designate all of the foregoing formal features of typical rules. These concepts and vocabulary sharpen awareness of such features and invite focus on them and their inter-relations, as well as their relations with complementary policy or other content.

Second, study of the overall form and constituent features of the form of a regulative statutory rule, reveals *how* this form embraces content in order, with other functional units, to serve ends of policy and other values, including those of the rule of law such as fair notice and equal treatment, and those of fundamental political values, such as rationality, freedom, justice, security, and democracy. It enhances understanding of the makeup, unity, and instrumental capacity of a rule to grasp how its formal features harness the content of the rule in a specified prescriptive modality, at one level of generality rather than another, with a given degree of definiteness rather than another, and so on, with each such feature penetrating, and definitively shaping, components of content. For example, a rule that says "Retire at age 65," incorporates a formal feature of high definiteness. Although this feature of high definiteness retains its distinct identity as a formal feature, it nonetheless leaves a deep imprint on the complementary component of policy content in the rule, which is an imprint very different from that left by a rule with low definiteness that says: "Retire when no longer fit." Without formulating and comparing alternative versions of the same formal feature of a rule as manifest in different complementary content it is not possible adequately to understand the important imprints and other harnessing effects of such features on content and thus not possible to design the form and content of the rule optimally.

Credit Due to Form for Values Realized. Let us assume (1) that a functional legal unit exists, (2) that along with other units, it serves purposes, (3) that the purposes served are valuable, and (4) that the overall form of the unit and its constituent features have been identified and differentiated from complementary material and other components of the unit. In these circumstances, some of the credit for ends realized partially through the unit plainly should be accorded to form. Moreover, in general, the better designed this form, the more credit due it.

Let us briefly review several examples. Within the overall form required for the very existence of a legislative institution, there are structural features such as committees and other internal structures through which the institution functions. There are also procedures of operation and decision-rules, such as adoption by majority vote. Such structures, procedures, and decision-rules are features of overall legislative form. These constituent formal features, along with complementary material and other components, such as personnel, buildings for offices and meetings, research materials, and other resources, make the enactment of valid statutory rules possible. When well-designed, features of overall legislative form also focus rational scrutiny on proposed laws and tend to beget laws good in form and content. Thus, a procedural feature requiring that all proposed statutes be referred to committees for study and subjected to floor debate tends to beget statutes good in form and content. Also, a proposed rule that is definite and clearly expressed in form is a more fit object for committee scrutiny and general debate than a vague and unclear rule. David Hume once put this more generally and rather strongly: "So great is the force of... particular forms of government, and so little dependence have they on the humors and tempers of men, that

Section Two: Importance of Legal Form

consequences almost as general and certain may sometimes be deduced from them, as any which the mathematical sciences afford us."[43]

Even though a statute be legally valid, it may still not be very effective in serving values. This may be because of deficiencies in its overall form and their effects on complementary content. For example, a proposed state policy, such as that of having "potable drinking water" free of the potential for cholera and related diseases, cannot become a meaningful legal policy unless it is formulated in rules having formal features duly embracing this policy content. Among other things, this content must be set forth in a sufficiently definite measurement indicating what relevantly qualifies as potable water, such as "coliform concentrations must be less than 200 colonies per 100 milliliters." This formal feature of definiteness greatly facilitates implementation of the rule. That is, under such a rule, officials and other addressees can measure for potability, and act accordingly, thus constructing faithful reasons for action under the rule.[44] Although, as we will see, other formal features of rules are of major import, Plato singled out due definiteness as a special hallmark of effective law.[45]

When a legislature exists and adopts valid and effective statutory rules, much credit must go to the forms of functional units involved. Of course, form can be ill-designed, too. For example, a rule may be too indefinite. As Roscoe Pound stressed, "irrationality of form" can even breed "irrationality of substance."[46] This, however, further underscores the importance of purposively well-designed and thus rational form.

In addition, forms and the functional units that they define and organize, can extend and enrich the very menu of possible *ends* to be pursued. Form in such units is not solely instrumental; it is not solely a means to external and independently existent ends, such as in my speed limit example (timeliness and safety of roadway travel) or my potable water supply example (public health). Form can be constitutive of certain ends, as well as instrumental to their very realization. For example, the forms of democratic governance, as manifest in duly constructed units of electoral, legislative, and related institutions and processes designed to serve the very value of self-governance, may even be said to *add* a further possible end for inhabitants of a society to pursue. Such forms define, organize, and thus

---

[43] D. Hume, *Political Writings*, 102 (S. Warner and D. Livingston eds., Hackett Publishing Co., Indianapolis/Cambridge, 1994).

[44] On law and authoritative reasons for action, see further Chapters Five and Nine.

[45] Plato said that "unless you are definite, you must not suppose that you are speaking a language that can become law" *The Dialogues of Plato*, vol. 2, 491 (B. Jowett trans., Random House, New York, 1937). Roman lawyers also had an important maxim for definiteness: Ius finitum et debet esse et potest – "The law can and should be definite" O. Behrends, "Formality and Substance in Classical Roman Law," in *Prescriptive Formality and Normative Rationality in Modern Legal Systems*, 207, 215 (W. Krawietz et. al. eds., Duncker & Humblot, Berlin, 1994). See also J. Lucas, *The Principles of Politics*, 237 (Clarendon Press, Oxford, 1966).

[46] R. Pound, *Jurisprudence*, vol. 3, 735–6 (West Publishing Co., St. Paul, 1959).

22   Introduction

are partially constitutive of, the very end of democracy itself. It is not enough to subscribe merely to the abstract end of democratic self-governance. Without electoral forms that are duly implemented, there could be no concrete end of democratic governance susceptible of meaningful pursuit. Here, form is partially constitutive of, as well as instrumental to, the end to be pursued.

There are many more examples; some are grand, whereas others are prosaic. Let us consider an example of the prosaic, yet one involving a fundamental freedom. Without due form, free and efficient movement of persons on highways, as known in developed Western societies, would simply not be possible. A modern highway is not merely asphalt laid in linear fashion. Those who choose to drive along a highway utilize a highly organized public facility, which is a functional legal unit that takes its own special form with its own material components. The freedom highway users exercise is coordinative in nature and thus dependent on rules in due form that organize who may do what, when, and how, all to the knowledge of concurrent users. Without such organized form duly prescribed in rules themselves sufficiently formal to be determinate and followable, the resultant free and efficient movement on highways in populous areas simply could not exist as a viable end. Here, too, form is partially constitutive of the end as well as instrumental to that end.[47]

The credit due to form for ends and values realized is profound and wide-ranging. Functional legal units and their forms, in the foregoing examples and in many other ways, thus extend and enrich the range of possible ends and means of social life. The extension and enrichment of possible individual and collective ends and means that well-designed form in functional legal units can, along with material and other components, add to the menu of social choices and social realizations must be counted among the most fundamental of all contributions to civilization from any source.

Form and the Work of Lawyers. Members of an organized legal profession (itself another functional legal unit) are trained to participate in the creation and administration of public and private law. As Lon L. Fuller stressed, good lawyers understand what is required for the workability and fitness of legal institutions and view themselves as special custodians of these very institutions.[48] Even though many lawyers do not use the terminology of form explicitly, good lawyers implicitly understand how forms define and organize functional legal units and understand how such forms differ from, yet relate to and interact with, material and other components of the overall forms of legal units. A lawyer who understands little of form

---

[47] See further Chapter Six.
[48] R. Summers, *Lon Fuller*, Chapter 11, 137–50 (Stanford University Press, Stanford, 1984).

Section Two: Importance of Legal Form

simply cannot be a good drafter, interpreter, or advisor. Good lawyers understand, at least implicitly, how form figures in the very identification of valid law and in its differentiation from nonlaw. As we saw, form even defines and organizes the authoritative institutional and other sources of valid law. Good lawyers are also aware that well-designed features of form in rules and in other law are generally required to serve policy and principle, to serve general legal values associated with the rule of law, and to serve fundamental political values.

Again, although many good lawyers do not use the terminology of form explicitly, they in fact regularly construct arguments in support of what are choices of form when participating in the creation of law. They exercise sound judgment in deciding that one overall form or one formal feature serves the ends at stake better than another, as when faced, for example, with a choice between a definite rule or a rule incorporating an indefinite standard. Good lawyers can criticize readily an actual or proposed choice of form as inferior to an alternative, and when advising clients on the law, are able to see how a formal feature does, or does not, contribute to the determinateness of a law. Good lawyers are sensitive to form when interpreting and applying law as well. In all this, and more, they combine the formal with complementary material or other components in legal analysis. They are aware, too, of what, in an actual or potential legal achievement, should be credited at least partly to an appropriately formal feature of a rule, such as its definiteness, its generality, or its mode of expression, rather than solely to components of content, such as policy or the like.

Lawyers have some responsibility for the quality of law. The frontal and systematic study of form, and the understanding this generates, can sharpen awareness of deficiencies in one's own legal system and foster practical proposals for improvements. Many deficiencies cannot be clearly seen, let alone fully understood, without study of the forms involved. For example, such focused study might lead one to the view that, in one's own system, legislators have created "mixed institutional forms" that unduly sacrifice important values, as in the case of administrative agencies that have jurisdictional and structural features in which adjudicative and administrative functions are not sufficiently separated. Or, for example, such form-focused study might also lead one to the view that in one's own system, legislators have generally tended to create indefinite statutory rules that leave too much unstructured discretion to officials or other addressees of those rules.[49] Form-focused analysis might even lead one to the view that in one's own system, some judges not infrequently depart from statute law in the guise of interpretation, which often violates important methodological canons that are

---

[49] P. Atiyah and R. Summers, *Form and Substance in Anglo-American Law*, 75–88 (Clarendon Press, Oxford, 1987).

formal in nature.[50] Such judicial action reduces the determinateness of statutes, undermines predictability, and offends canons of judicial candor.

The serious study of form could also lead some professors of law to conclude that they have been guilty of an antiformal animus, and lead them to see that the formal in functional legal units is not to be equated with the formalistic – with mechanical adherence to rigid rules, with wooden literalism in interpretation,[51] or the like. Some might even come to see that the terms "form" and "formal" can be used nonpejoratively to designate features that define and organize functional legal units to serve good ends! Such study might also lead some professors of law to be more evenhanded in their criticism of judicial reasoning and thus be mindful not only of the formalistic, but also of the substantivistic in such reasoning.[52]

SECTION THREE: THE NEGLECT OF FORM

I will now elaborate on the second principal rationale for this book. Given that the overall forms of functional legal units have profound theoretical and practical importance, one might assume that these forms have long been the subject of intensive study. Yet, Western legal theorists have taken little interest in developing a systematic general theory of legal form.

This is highly anomalous, especially given that numerous varieties of social and other forms have long been central subjects within other major humanistic disciplines, some of which even overlap with law. Forms of government, such as autocracy and democracy,[53] forms of economic and social organization,[54] forms of architectural constructions,[55] forms of literary compositions,[56] forms of musical

---

[50] In the United States, for example, some judges in fact depart from statutes, and they sometimes do so in the guise of interpretation. Here are several illustrative examples from the American system: *Welsh v. United States*, 398 US 333 (1970) (holding that a personal moral code was a religion within the meaning of the statute despite statutory language expressly to the contrary); *Markham v. Cabell*, 326 US 404 (1945) (permitting claim for debt arising during World War II despite language barring claims after 1917); *Friends of Mammoth v. Board of Supervisors*, 502 P. 2d 1049 (Ca. 1972) (holding the California Environmental Quality Act applicable to private development despite clear language to the contrary). Two scholars have remarked that: "[J]udicial departures [by American judges] from the obligation to decide in accordance with the established rules has become a deeply ingrained and characteristic feature of the judicial process, a feature sustained by the milieu in which judges operate" M. Kadish and S. Kadish, *Discretion to Disobey*, 91 (Stanford University Press, Stanford, 1973).

[51] See *infra* Chapter Eight, at Section Six.

[52] *Supra* n. 50.

[53] See, e.g., *The Dialogues of Plato, supra* n. 45, at 283 et. seq. Of course, there is some overlap here with legal forms.

[54] See, e.g., A. Smith, *The Wealth of Nations* (Knopf, New York, 1991).

[55] See, e.g., M. Trachenburg and I. Hyman, *Architecture from Prehistory to Post-Modernism* (Prentice Hall, Englewood Cliffs, 1986).

[56] See, e.g., *The Basic Works of Aristotle*, 1455 (R. McKeon ed., Random House, New York, 1941).

Section Three: The Neglect of Form

composition,[57] and forms of artistic creation,[58] among many others, have long been subjects of frontal and systematic studies, and these studies have advanced understanding of the relevant forms and have accorded due credit to form. Well-designed overall forms are just as essential to functional legal units as well-designed other varieties of form are in these other realms of human endeavor and learning. In functional legal units, form does not represent less of what there is to understand or less of what is worthy of credit than form represents in these other realms.

The neglect of legal form has not been total, however, even in the United States, despite its realist tradition in legal theory, and despite a somewhat indiscriminate antiformal animus in some academic quarters.[59] Some American theorists and other scholars have addressed particular topics that would qualify as contributions to particular branches of a general theory of legal form. I will now identify representative examples without attempting to be at all comprehensive. Thus, today there is a body of theory on rules and on "rule v. discretion."[60] Even here, most have not addressed the subject in the concepts and terminology of form, even though the issue is, in major part, one of due prescriptiveness, due completeness, due generality, due definiteness, and due structure, that is, due design of formal features of a rule.[61] There is also a vast literature on the principles of the rule of law.[62] Work on the principles of the rule of law is generally not set forth in the concepts and terminology of form; however, most of these principles are formal in major ways, as I will show.[63] Some scholars have devoted thoughtful attention to aspects of what they sometimes call institutional form.[64] Some have also written illuminatingly on form in private law with emphasis on the law of torts and contracts.[65] Others have written on aspects of form in the creation of statute law.[66]

---

[57] See, e.g., S. Macpherson, *Form in Music* (Joseph Williams, Ltd., London, 1940); see also *The Oxford Companion to Music*, 473–8 (A. Latham ed., Oxford University Press, Oxford, 2002).

[58] See, e.g., D. Pole, "The Excellence of Form in Works of Art," in *Proceedings of the Aristotelian Society*, 13 (Methuen & Co. Ltd., London, 1972).

[59] See, e.g., D. Kennedy, *supra* n. 20; R. Posner, *supra* n. 20.

[60] See, e.g., K. Davis, *Discretionary Justice: A Preliminary Inquiry* (University of Illinois Press, Urbana, 1971). See also F. Schauer, *Playing by the Rules: A Philosophical Examination of Rule-Based Decision-Making in Law and in Life* (Clarendon Press, Oxford, 1991); and L. Alexander and E. Sherwin, *The Rule of Rules* (Duke University Press, Durham and London, 2001). "Rule v. discretion" is in part shorthand for the choice between high definiteness and low definiteness in a rule – a choice of a formal feature with complementary content.

[61] In Chapters Five and Six of this book, I will show in detail how this can make a difference.

[62] See, e.g., L. Fuller, *The Morality of Law* (Revised ed., Yale University Press, New Haven, 1969).

[63] See *infra* Chapter Nine.

[64] See, e.g., L. Fuller, "The Forms and Limits of Adjudication," 92 *Harv. L. Rev.* 353 (1978). For a European work, see D. N. MacCormick and O. Weinberger, *An Institutional Theory of Law: New Approaches to Legal Positivism* (D. Reidel Publishing Co., Dordrecht, 1986).

[65] See, e.g., E. Weinrib, *The Idea of Private Law* (Harvard University Press, Cambridge, 1995), and Lon L. Fuller, "Consideration and Form," 41 *Colum. L. Rev.* 799 (1941).

[66] See, e.g., P. Atiyah and R. Summers, *supra* n. 49, Chapters Four and Eleven; J. Waldron, *Law and Disagreement*, Chapter Four (Clarendon Press, Oxford, 1999).

American scholars of procedure have regularly addressed some problems of form, although seldom explicitly in terms of form. Yet their writings are relevant to a general theory of form.[67] Many others, including scholars of constitutional law, have addressed aspects of the forms of certain legal institutions and the inter-relations between such institutions, which are major realms of structural form, although many would probably claim that they have not been writing about "mere form."[68] Some constitutional and other scholars have written on the principles of the rule of law and have suggested that these are, at least partly, formal.[69] Some have written on the methodologies of constitutional and statutory interpretation, although this is seldom done in terms of form.[70] Scholars of legislation have written on the formal methodologies for drafting statutory rules, although again usually not in the concepts and terminology of form.[71] It is true that form and formalities in the law of contracts and wills have been the subject of extensive study by scholars of positive law in these fields, and here the work has frequently been in the idiom of form.[72] Comparative lawyers, American and other, have also, in effect, done work on form while comparing legal systems or basic facets of legal systems.[73]

Even so, no legal theorist or other scholar has, to my knowledge, sought to work out a systematic general theory of the overall forms of a wide and representative selection of functional legal units, as here. It might be thought that, of the participants in modern schools of legal theory, those writing in the tradition of legal positivism[74] would be most likely to develop a general theory of legal form.[75] Yet, a close examination reveals that neither H. L. A. Hart[76] nor Hans Kelsen,[77] the leading positivists of the twentieth century, systematically treated

---

[67] See, e.g., B. Kaplan, "Civil Procedure – Reflections on the Comparison of Systems," 9 *Buff. L. Rev.* 409 (1960).

[68] A classic early treatment is J. Madison, "The Federalist No. 47," in A. Hamilton et. al, *The Federalist: A Commentary on the Constitution of the United States*, 312 (Random House, New York, 1950).

[69] See e.g., R. Fallon, Jr., "The Rule of Law as a Concept in Constitutional Discourse," 97 *Colum. L. Rev.* 1 (1997).

[70] See, e.g., K. Greenawalt, "Constitutional and Statutory Interpretation," in *The Oxford Handbook of Jurisprudence and Philosophy of Law*, 268 (J. Coleman and S. Shapiro eds., Oxford University Press, Oxford, 2002).

[71] See, e.g., *Professionalizing Legislative Drafting: The Federal Experience* (R. Dickerson ed., American Bar Association, 1973).

[72] See e.g., Fuller, *supra* n. 65. B. Mann, "Self-Proving Affidavits and Formalism in Wills Adjudication," 63 *Wash. U. L.Q.* 39 (1985).

[73] For example, the forms of interpretive methodologies in Western legal systems are compared in D. N. MacCormick and R. S. Summers, eds. *Interpreting Statutes–A Comparative Study* (Dartmouth, Aldershot 1991).

[74] Lon L. Fuller once stated that, "all forms of legal positivism . . . deal not with the content of the law but with its form . . . " L. Fuller, *The Law in Quest of Itself*, 132 (Beacon Press, Boston, 1940).

[75] Let me add I am not a positivist in any of the usual uses of that much abused word. That I am a positivist is sometimes asserted. See, e.g., R. Fallon, *supra* n. 69, at 2 n. 6.

[76] See H. L. A. Hart, *supra* n. 3.

[77] See H. Kelsen, *supra* n. 4.

Section Three: The Neglect of Form

the major overall forms of functional legal units and their significance as such. Hart, in his justly famous book, *The Concept of Law*, analyzed legal institutions, such as courts, largely in terms of the contents of rules said to be "constitutive" (I say "reinforcive") of their composition, jurisdiction, and procedure. Hart often did so almost as if the overall forms and the material and other components of courts could be illuminatingly reduced to the aggregate contents of such rules.[78]

Neither Hart nor Kelsen provided systematic and comprehensive analyses of the overall forms of any legal institutions. They did not provide such analyses of the preceptual forms of legal rules and principles. Nor did they so treat the forms of nonpreceptual species of law, such as contracts and property interests. They did not systematically address the forms of interpretive and other legal methodologies. Nor did they systematically consider the forms of sanctions and remedies. Although both were very interested in what unifies rules of law into a system, they did not do justice to the variety of systematizing devices that account for the formal systemic unity of a legal system overall. As I will show in Chapter Ten, there is far more to these devices than either Hart's "rule of recognition" or Kelsen's "Grundnorm" can possibly tell. For example, neither Hart nor Kelsen dealt at all comprehensively with how the forms of law's major operational techniques – the penal, the grievance-remedial, the administrative-regulatory, the public-benefit conferring, and the private-arranging – integrate, coordinate, and thus systematize various types of legal units in differing ways, all in order to create and implement law.[79]

A major nonpositivist jurist of the twentieth century, Lon L. Fuller, did address what he called basic "forms of social order," especially adjudication, legislation, and private contract. He stressed the relations between means and ends with some explicit attention to form and the purposes of form.[80] Although Fuller's works are illuminating, they do not qualify as a systematic general theory of the forms of functional legal units and their integration within a legal system.

As I have indicated, although the great German jurist, Rudolf von Jhering, did not develop a general theory of legal forms, he did scatter numerous insightful remarks on form throughout his two major works.[81] Jhering may have actually conceived of legal forms as a major subject worthy of a general theory. Certainly he had great respect for the forms of many functional legal units.[82] At the same time, he was highly critical of formalistic legal reasoning, such as wooden literalism in

---

[78] H. L. A. Hart, *supra* n. 3, Chapter 5. As I argue in Chapter Three, what is needed here is primarily a form-oriented analysis rather than one that is primarily rule-oriented. See R. Summers, "Professor H. L. A. Hart's Concept of Law," 1963 *Duke L. J.* 629, 638–45 (1963).

[79] See *infra* Chapter Ten.

[80] See especially the essays on this subject in *The Principles of Social Order: Selected Essays of Lon L. Fuller* (K. Winston ed., Duke University Press, 1981).

[81] See R. Jhering, *supra* n. 2.

[82] R. Jhering, *supra* n. 29–34.

28 Introduction

the interpretation of statutes.[83] However, quite unlike some American theorists, he did not appear to assume that whatever is formal must also be formalistic and, therefore, bad. He acknowledged the general neglect of form in his day and suggested that the subject may be "too abstract for the lawyers" and "too concrete for philosophers."[84] Another German scholar, Max Weber, manifested high respect for form as such, although he, too, failed to develop a general theory.[85]

Given the profound importance of legal forms, and given the extensive studies of forms in fields outside the law, it is natural and also instructive to inquire why legal theorists and other scholars have not gone beyond isolated treatments and developed a general theory of form. This inquiry may be viewed as all the more pressing especially in light of the great efflorescence of Western legal theory in the last seventy-five years led by such figures as Roscoe Pound, Gustav Radbruch, Hans Kelsen, H. L. A. Hart, Torstein Eckhoff, Karl N. Llewellyn, Lon L. Fuller, Alf Ross, Norberto Bobbio, and others. Given the unavailability of specific evidence as to what failed to motivate prior thinkers here, the explanations I now offer for the relative neglect of form must be an exercise in rational speculation.

In some Western legal systems, such as the English and the German, it may be that the importance of form has, for the most part, been so taken for granted that theorists and others have not felt moved to take up the subject in a frontal, systematic, and relatively comprehensive fashion.[86] On the other hand, in some systems, one encounters in some quarters a dismissiveness of form born, I believe, mainly of hostility to the formalistic in judicial and other legal analysis. This may go far to explain why what has been perceived as formal in the law of those systems has often been viewed in some quarters as an object of ridicule rather than as a subject worthy of study. In the modern era, the most deeply antiformal movement was that of the American legal realists led by the *early* Karl N. Llewellyn.[87] Many antiformal pronouncements of the early Llewellyn were largely salutary reactions to formalistic interpretive and other applicational methodologies of some late-nineteenth- and early-twentieth-century American judges.[88] Llewellyn sometimes

---

[83] R. Jhering, *Scherz und Ernst in der Jurisprudenz* (9th ed. Breitkopf & Härtel, Leipzig, 1900). See also H. L. A. Hart, "Jhering's Heaven of Concepts and Modern Analytical Jurisprudence," *Jhering's Erbe*, 68 (F. Wieacker and C. Wollschläger eds., Vandenhoek & Ruprecht, Göttingen, 1970). For further discussion, see *infra* Chapter Eight, at Section Six.

[84] R. Jhering, *supra* n. 2, *Geist*, vol. 2, at 472.

[85] See M. Weber, *Economy and Society: An Outline of Interpretive Sociology*, vols. 1–2 (G. Roth and C. Wittich eds., E. Fischoff et. al trans., University of California Press, Berkeley, 1978). Other Europeans interested in form, yet whose work does not qualify as a general theory, include G. del Vecchio, *The Formal Bases of Law* (J. Lisle trans., The Boston Book Co., Boston, 1914) and H. Kopp, *Inhalt und Form der Gesetze als ein Problem der Rechtstheorie* (Polygraphischer Verlag, A. G., Zurich, 1958).

[86] Jhering noted a special English respect for form. See R. Jhering, *supra* n. 2, *Geist*, vol. 2, at 503.

[87] See especially K. Llewellyn, *The Bramble Bush* (Rev. ed., Oceana Publications, New York, 1960). With the American realists who are said to have reacted to "formalists," compare the German development in which Interessenjurisprudenz is said to have arisen in response to Begriffsjurisprudenz.

[88] R. Summers, *supra* n. 20, Chapter Six. See also *infra* Chapter Eight, Section Six.

Section Three: The Neglect of Form

went well beyond this, however. The early Llewellyn famously ridiculed the functional unit of a rule, including its form by referring to it as a "pretty plaything."[89] The early Llewellyn (and others) also manifested a behavioralist tendency hostile to institutional and preceptual forms. According to this view, law is reducible to little more than behavior patterns of officials, which of course, are not the same as, and may diverge from, form in rules.

Modern American successors of the legal realists on the right, such as Richard Posner,[90] and on the left, such as Duncan Kennedy,[91] and their various adherents have, in some of their writings, manifested intense hostility at least to certain varieties of form and the formal. These and other neo-realists have, in some of their writings, even tended to identify the formal with some versions of the formalistic, including mechanical adherence to rigid rules and wooden literalism in interpretation. Any such general identification converts "form" and "formal" into pejoratives. In equating the formal with the formalistic, such theorists sometimes even seem to assume we could dispense with form in functional legal units altogether and still have a viable legal system! To judge from the tone of some of the writings of some of these theorists, far from acknowledging scope for serious study of form, some might dismiss the very idea of a general theory of legal form as little more than nonsense upon stilts.[92]

In some systems, including the United States, legislatures and courts sometimes do create formalistic legal rules, such as those with contents that embody distinctions without real differences or those with contents that conflate real differences. It is true, as well, that some judges sometimes mechanically apply rules or treat rules as rigid. It is also true that some judges sometimes interpret statutes in a woodenly literal, i.e. formalistic, way. It is true, as well, that some judges have sometimes made a fetish of formalities, such as those required for the valid execution of contracts and wills.

The term "formalistic" can be used to condemn each of the foregoing and certain related vices, but it hardly follows that the overall forms of functional legal units are inherently formalistic. For example, nothing in the overall form of a rule inherently incorporates distinctions without differences or inherently conflates real differences. Nothing inherent in the forms of common law rules or the formal methodology for their application calls for "mechanical" or

---

[89] See, e.g., K. Llewellyn, *supra* n. 87, at 14.

[90] See, e.g., R. Posner, *supra* n. 20. On this book, and especially its treatment of form, see R. Summers, "Judge Richard Posner's Jurisprudence," 89 *Mich. L. Rev.* 1302 (1991).

[91] D. Kennedy, "Legal Formality," *supra* n. 20, 351. Although highly critical of the formalistic, neither Professor Posner nor Professor Kennedy is even-handedly critical of the substantivistic; yet the American legal system provides more than its share of examples. See, e.g., *supra* n. 50.

[92] One further possible explanation may be a tendency of those hostile to form to equate respect for form with conservative intransigence. This explanation does not seem plausible, however. Again, theorists broadly hostile to form include not only thinkers from the left, but also ones from the right. Compare R. Posner, *supra* n. 20 with D. Kennedy, *supra* n. 20.

conceptualistic reasoning. A formal methodology for the interpretation of statutes does not inherently require wooden interpretations.[93] Yet such fallacious leaps as the foregoing may help to explain failures to treat form in positive terms.

The neglect of the overall form and constituent features of rules may also be traceable in part to an assumption that only the policy or other "substantive" content of a rule can truly serve ends. On such an assumption, the formal in a rule, for example, its definiteness, cannot itself have any real end-serving significance. Yet this is plainly false. If a formal feature of a rule is well-designed as such, and also in light of its complementary content, then this formal feature, too, will help to serve the relevant policy or other content of the rule. For example, the initial choice of a quite definite rule rather than one that incorporates an indefinite standard may be essential to effective realization of a given policy. Thus, a formally definite rule with complementary content on eligibility to vote, e.g., age eighteen rather than an indefinite rule, e.g., "age of mature judgment," may adequately serve the policy that the young voter not be too young and also avoid the excessive costs of administering a "mature judgment" standard voter by voter. We can see in this and many other examples that there is nothing formalistic about the formal feature of definiteness as such. Indeed, all other constituent features of the overall form of rules such as completeness, generality, and manner of expression contribute, along with complementary contents, to the realization of policies and values. Well-designed form in a rule is often no less "substantive" in its effect than well-designed policy content. This is also true with respect to form in institutional, methodological, enforcive, and other varieties of functional legal units.[94]

Those who neglect form may assume there is a deep, pervasive, and irreconcileable opposition between form in a legal rule and its policy or other content. Yet, form and good policy content in well-designed rules work together. Instead of being opposites, they are complementaries. For example, a highly definite speed limit rule not only has this formal feature, and still other formal features, but also has complementary policy content – a stated rate of speed.[95] Such form and content together serve policies of safe and efficient traffic flow. Moreover, as I will show, means to ends simply cannot be incorporated in the content of a law, and be satisfactorily implemented, without due form in that law. A well-designed law cannot be "all substance and no form."[96]

---

[93] For extended discussion of wooden literalism, see *infra* Chapter Eight, at Section Six.

[94] Justice Cardozo, however, may have overstated matters: "The strength that is born of form and the feebleness that is born of the lack of form are in truth qualities of the substance. They are the tokens of the thing's identity. They make it what it is." B. Cardozo, *Law and Literature: And Other Essays and Addresses*, 6 (Harcourt, Brace and Co., New York, 1931). Compare Cardozo's earlier metaphor in *supra* n. 12 when he wrote of form merely as "closely knit to substance."

[95] The formal feature of definiteness here is readily separable from any particular rate, a matter of policy content. See *infra* Chapter Five.

[96] Judges and practicing lawyers know this.

Section Three: The Neglect of Form

The formal features of a rule such as due prescriptiveness, due generality, and due definiteness, are essential to optimal realization of policy or other content. Also, the formal feature of due expression is required to set forth the policy content of a rule.[97] An antiformalist might consider manner of expression to be least important. Due expression, however, is required to communicate the form and content of the rule. Moreover, whether the law should be written (i.e., printed) rather than oral also pertains to form of expression. That a choice of written (i.e., printed) expression is often taken for granted does not render it unimportant. If all of our law had to be oral, we simply could not have the complex legal systems of modern societies.[98]

Institutional form, too, contributes to the quality and efficacy of the rules that institutions create and administer. For example, well-designed form in legislative procedures that require committee study of draft rules on due advance notice tends to induce legislators to bring reason to bear. This also tends to beget good content in the rules ultimately adopted.[99] Yet, of equal import, this procedurally formal feature has significance independently of its contributions to the quality and efficacy of particular laws thereby created. Procedural and other features of form are constitutive of the very legislative process whereby democratic participation becomes realizable. Such participation is itself a "process value" – a value realized in the course of the workings of a formal process – and worth having, apart from and in addition to, the form and contents of whatever laws are adopted or rejected.[100] Even if two different legislative processes were to adopt identical and highly effective laws, the form of one of these processes could be highly preferable as serving more fully process values such as fair notice and opportunity to participate. Similarly, procedural fairness of the workings of an adjudicative or an administrative process is also a "process value." Contributions to the realization of policy or to other outcomes, that is, to "outcome substance," although of great import, are not the be-all and end-all of legal ordering.

There are other sources of hostility to form and the formal that may help explain why so many theorists have neglected it. One of these is partly linguistic. As already noted, some theorists who are antiformal have frequently used the nouns "formality" and "formalism" pejoratively, and this also sometimes occurs in general usage.[101] It may, therefore, be natural for such theorists to use what

---

[97] See *infra* Chapters Five and Six.

[98] See *infra* Chapter Five.

[99] See *infra* Chapter Four.

[100] R. Summers, "Evaluating and Improving Legal Processes – A Plea for 'Process Values,'" 60 *Cornell L. Rev.* 1 (1974).

[101] See *The Oxford English Dictionary*, vol. 6, at "formality" and "formalism" (2nd ed., J. Simpson and E. Weiner, eds., Clarendon Press, Oxford, 1989). The radical ambiguity of "formalism" is canvassed in M. Stone, "Formalism" in J. Coleman and M. Shapiro eds., *Jurisprudence and Philosophy of Law* 166–205 (Oxford University Press, Oxford, 2002).

32   Introduction

may seem to them to be the corresponding adjective "formal" pejoratively. Yet, once the relevant clarification is made, this linguistic source of hostility cannot rationally survive. In general usage, "formal" is far more often used as adjectival for the noun "form" rather than for the nouns "formality" and "formalism" (even assuming these are sometimes used correctly as pejoratives). Yet the noun "form" is *itself* not pejorative in nearly all of its uses.[102] Hence, when "formal" is properly used as adjectival for "form" in nearly all uses of "form," the term "formal," as so used, is nonpejorative.

Another related source of confusion that may breed hostility to form is the tendency of antiformalists to equate emphasis on form in functional legal units with advocacy of a general approach to law that is "formal," where such an approach is taken to exclude due concern for the quality of complementary policy or other content of rules. Yet it is wrong to equate these. There is no inconsistency whatever in advocating both due form and due content in a legal rule, for example.

Beyond dismissiveness borne of misguided hostility to form, and beyond the foregoing fallacies and confusions about form, there are still other explanations for the failure of some legal theorists and other academics to take form seriously. I will treat but one. When it is said that a functional legal unit takes an overall form or that law is formal, the reaction may simply be: "Ah, that is tautologous," and the conclusion then be drawn that nothing further can be said about the subject that is nontautological or nontrivial. Yet much remains here for study.

It is true that functional legal units necessarily take overall forms, but exactly how? Exactly what about a given unit is a matter of its form? What is not and why? What more is there to the overall form of a functional unit than the mere sum of its constituent formal features? In what respects may the overall form of such a unit be well-designed? What imprints or other effects do the features of the overall form of a unit leave on the material or other components of the unit? What are the major contrasts between form and content in rules and other preceptual law, and between form and the material or other components in still other legal units? What are the interactions between form and other facets of a unit? How do answers to these questions advance understanding of functional legal units? What light does a general theory of form cast on the nature of a legal system and traditional problems of legal theory? What credit should form have for what functional legal units contribute to the realization of ends? How can form affect the performances of the law's addressees? What may be said in answer to these and further related questions is not generally tautological or trivial. It is often informative and significant, as I will seek to show here.[103]

---

[102] *Id.*, at "form." I am indebted to the late Geoffrey Marshall here.

[103] For still other major explanations possibly accounting for the neglect of form, see *infra* pp. 62–63.

Section Four: Protests Against Misunderstanding

At this juncture, a contrary minded critic might pose a seeming paradox. If most Western legal theorists have been so neglectful of form or have failed to understand it very well, the question may be posed: how is it that so many of the overall forms of different legal units in many developed Western systems of law today appear to be at least tolerably well-designed and organized? There are several major responses to this question.

First, many Western systems have evolved over long periods. Hence the relatively high quality today of their functional units, which we will postulate for the moment, might be due to many small yet salutary improvements over time in the quality of the design and organization of the overall forms of legal units – accretions derived from lessons of trial and error, special insight, cumulative wisdom, imaginative borrowing, and luck. However, had these systems been launched initially with more informed theoretical and practical attention to the design and organization of the overall forms of these units, the time required to achieve such high quality might well have been far shorter.

Second, it is possible that legal theorists and other scholars in a given society might be generally neglectful or dismissive of form. However, lawyers, judges, legislators, and others nevertheless could still be well-practiced in the art of form and thus able to design and organize overall legal forms tolerably well without the aid of a body of theory or other scholarly treatment. If one assumes so, it still would not follow that attempts to advance theoretical and scholarly sophistication in matters of legal form would be unimportant. Not all societies can count on continuing to have personnel well-practiced in the art of form or count on borrowing from those that do. Also, even though a practical art could be highly developed in a particular society at a particular time, this art might later be lost because of general social decay or other causes. Consider, for example, the decay in post-classical Rome in matters of law! Moreover, well-formulated theoretical and practical understanding of legal form and articulate conversancy with its optimal design, are worth having for their own sake anyway. Here legal theorists and other scholars have special educative roles.

Third, can we be so certain that legal forms, even in developed Western systems today, are all in optimal shape and really cannot be significantly improved over what they now are? It is implausible to suppose that the overall forms of all functional legal units in these systems are today more or less perfect. What if these systems were to undergo revision at the hands of sophisticated reformers with a thorough grasp of optimal design and organization?

SECTION FOUR: PROTESTS AGAINST MISUNDERSTANDING

The theory offered here is a general theory addressed not to the overall forms of particular functional units in a given system, but mainly to general paradigms or exemplars of the overall forms of a selection of functional legal units in developed Western societies. In applying the theory to any particular Western society, adjustments will be called for. Also, although the theory is addressed to Western legal systems, as systems of functional units, the theory is not frontally addressed to all characteristics of a system of law. Rather, it is addressed to only one relatively neglected yet fundamental and complex characteristic of such a system, namely, its formalness.

The theory of legal forms I set forth here is not a "positivist" theory. It is true that many legal positivists have evinced interest in legal form. Yet, insofar as a legal positivist is one who believes that whatever the "law-giver" purports to lay down as "law" necessarily qualifies as law, regardless of its form and content, then plainly the theory of legal form set forth here is not positivistic. For one thing, a purported "law" may be so deficient in form as to be profoundly dysfunctional, and thus be at best a highly degenerate specimen of law, and, if deficient enough, not law at all, even though officially "laid down." For example, the expressional feature of the overall form of an enacted statutory rule otherwise in due form may be such that what the rule means is quite unclear to all of its addressees! On my view, such a "rule" would fail to qualify as law at all.[104]

Merely in virtue of being an overall form, or a constituent feature of the overall form of any functional legal unit, it does not necessarily follow that this form or feature is itself good or well-used. A form, or a feature of form, might be well-designed as a facet of an efficacious means, but be used to a bad end. In that event, form though an efficacious means as such, would plainly not be well-used. If efficaciously used as a means to a good end, form so used would at least be instrumentally good. Also, a form or a feature of form might be ill-designed, and whether used for a bad or a good end, instrumentally deficient. Further, an overall form, as we have seen, may be required to define and organize a good end such as democratic governance.[105] Here we may say the form as such is constitutively as well as instrumentally good. Plainly, as I generally use the phrase "X is formal," I do not use it pejoratively. However, from "X is formal" it does not necessarily follow that X is well-designed as a means. Nor does it necessarily follow that the end to which X is put is good, even when form is in part constitutive of the end.

---

[104] Nor is my theory positivistic in embracing the doctrine that there is no necessary connection whatsoever between a duly formed system of law and moral goodness. I do not embrace this doctrine. A brilliant critique of positivism, one with which I am in sympathy, is R. Alexy, *Begriff und Geltung des Rechts* (Karl Alber, Freiburg/München, 1992). This book has now been translated into English. See R. Alexy, *The Argument from Injustice – A Reply to Legal Positivism* (B. L. Paulson and S. L. Paulson, trans., Clarendon Press, Oxford, 2002).

[105] On how form can be constitutive of ends, which if valuable, are good when realized, see *supra* at p. 20.

Section Four: Protests Against Misunderstanding

An overall form is not necessarily politically conservative, politically liberal, or "middle of the road." Often it is relatively neutral. It is true that due form in a rule, for example, may be said to conserve content. This content, however, may itself be either conservative or liberal. At the same time, the duly designed form of a rule renders its content a more fit object for critical scrutiny. Moreover, legislative and other institutional forms explicitly provide for open public criticism of existing laws and provide ways to change their content or even repeal them entirely. Such changes in content may be politically liberal or politically conservative. The many overall forms of implementive legal units such as rules, sanctions, and remedies can be used to serve ends that are either liberal or conservative.

Some thinkers unsympathetic to form tend to assume that if what is treated as the overall form of, or as a formal feature of, a functional legal unit can be shown to serve as a means to the realization of a policy or other valuable end in some way, it cannot be formal. Rather, it can only be "substantive" or something else that we should embrace enthusiastically, but only in these other terms. On such a view, the overall form or a formal feature of a legal institution or other functional unit can never receive any share of the credit for what law achieves. Instead, its contribution is defined away. In this book, I seek to demonstrate the error of this way of thinking about form.

In concentrating on the overall forms of legal institutions, rules and other species of law, methodologies, sanctions, remedies and other implementive devices, and the legal system as a whole, I most emphatically do not intend to downplay the importance of the material or other components of such functional units. It is plain that there is much more to a functional legal unit than form. More than form is required for such a unit to be effective and good.

I also concede that there is much more than form to a developed Western legal system as a whole. Such a legal system requires a territory, an informed population, trained personnel, material resources, knowledge of physical causation, knowledge of means-end relations, a language, systems of communication, and various other components. Substantive policy and principles, fundamental political values, general values of the rule of law, and private autonomous choice must also inform the content and form of law. Societal attitudes of agreement with, acceptance of, and acquiescence in a system's apparatus for creating and implementing law are essential. So, too, is coercive capacity.

Reason should permeate and shape the purposive design of overall form, its constituent features, and the complementary material or other components of each functional legal unit. Without duly designed forms, even the potentially most proficient of such components could avail us relatively little. Although these components must have their due, this requires form as well. If one who emphasizes the formal in such units is to be called a formalist, such a person can, without inconsistency, at the same time be a nonformalist, too – a "substantivist," a champion of material or other components, and a proponent of value and of all else that must and should figure together with well-designed form in a system of law that is good and effective.

Again, what I advocate in the name of the overall forms of functional legal units is not at bottom either an elaborate version of pre-realist formalism[106] or a reincarnation of the conceptualist's "Heaven of Juristic Concepts" so colorfully ridiculed by that major figure whose respect for form in law was a real source of inspiration for this book, namely, Rudolf von Jhering himself.[107] In the spirit of Jhering, I, too, reject conceptualistic deductivism in legal reasoning and all other versions of the formalistic. Nor do I embrace that version of "legal formalism" according to which the functional units of a legal system consist only of rules to be applied rigidly, mechanically, or in woodenly literal fashion. In earlier published writings, I have subjected pre-realist formalism to elaborate and extended criticism, and I have not changed my mind.[108]

The general theory I offer here does not purport to provide optimally efficacious designs for, or models of, the overall forms of functional legal units. Nor does this theory purport to provide a universally applicable calculus for determining the optimal design of such forms. The theses that I seek to advance in this book do not require that I undertake these tasks, and these theses are quite enough for one book.

---

[106] Yet my rejection of pre-realist formalism is not at all clear from some representations of my views, as for example, in L. Lidsky, "Defensor Fidei: The Travails of a Post-Realist Formalist," 47 *Fla. L. Rev.* 815 (1995).

[107] R. Jhering, *supra* n. 2, *Geist*, vol. 3, 321. See also Chapter Eight, Section Six.

[108] R. Summers, *supra* n. 20.

2 ∼ BASIC CONCEPTS AND DEFINITIONS

"Those who are impatient with the forms of law ought to reflect that it is through form that all organization is reached. Matter without form is chaos; power without form is anarchy."

– Bleckley, J.[1]

SECTION ONE: INTRODUCTION

This chapter opens with a general account of, and rationale for, the selection of functional legal units to be treated in this book. Thereafter I develop and refine my general definition of the overall form of any such unit as the purposive systematic arrangement of the makeup, unity, instrumental capacity, distinct identity, and other attributes of that unit. I then set forth the justifications for adopting this general definition of form.

Next, I turn to the varied types of general purposes that determine the systematic arrangement of any functional legal unit. I then clarify the main difference between the overall form and constituent formal features of a legal unit and the complementary material or other components of that unit. I also explain why I have not adopted the perhaps more familiar "form v. substance" contrast as central. Along the way, I explain how my uses of "form" and "formal" are similar to, or different from, certain ordinary uses of these words in English and also similar to, or different from, certain technical uses of these words by legal theorists and other scholars.

SECTION TWO: A SELECTION OF FUNCTIONAL LEGAL UNITS AND THEIR OVERALL FORMS

As we have seen, a functional legal unit may be institutional in nature, such as a legislature, or preceptual, such as a statutory rule, or a nonpreceptual species of law, such as a contract, or a methodological unit, such as an interpretive methodology

---

[1] *Cochran v. State,* 62 Ga. 731, 732 (1879).

for statutes, or an enforcive unit, such as a sanction of imprisonment. A functional legal unit is constructed according to the design of its own overall form. For example, a legislative institution is defined and organized differently from a judicial institution and thus takes its own overall form – its own purposive systematic arrangement. Institutions are, in turn, very different from precepts. A statutory rule takes its own overall form and is defined and organized very differently from other preceptual units, such as a principle, maxim, or general order. A nonpreceptual species of law, such as a contract, takes its own overall form and is defined and organized very differently from a rule or principle. All the foregoing forms, in turn, differ greatly from interpretive and other methodological units, as well as enforcive units, such as sanctions and remedies. The typology of forms of functional legal units selected for consideration here is not merely taxonomic or classificatory. It also incorporates concepts and terminology for the faithful and perspicuous representation of the ways paradigmatic exemplars of various units are defined and organized.

The overall forms of functional legal units within Western legal systems vary in their approximations to what may be ideal. Yet these forms define and organize the units to serve purposes. When the purposes to be served are valuable, and these forms and their complementary material and other components are sufficiently well-designed, then some value will ordinarily be realized when the units are duly put to use.

The first major type of functional legal unit considered here is institutional. This type includes such units as legislatures, courts, administrative agencies, corporate entities, and more. In Chapter Four, we concentrate on the overall form of a legislature as an exemplar of one major institutional form. There are basic similarities in the overall forms of legislatures in developed Western systems. The constituents of the overall forms of legislatures include compositional, jurisdictional, structural, and procedural features. Although there are variations, these features are similarly organized in many Western systems.

The second major type of functional legal unit to be considered is preceptual, and thus consists of rules, principles, maxims, and general orders. In Chapters Five and Six, we concentrate on the overall form of rules as one exemplar of preceptual form. Although there are variations, the overall form of rules is highly similar from system to system.

A third major type of functional unit to be considered consists of nonpreceptual species of law. These include private contracts and various property interests. Private contracts depend for their existence on the overall form they take to be validly created, and on pre-existing frameworks for their creation. The most common overall form of a valid contract in Western systems provides for the agreed bilateral exchange as between two parties. Such an exchange is considered in Chapter Seven as an exemplar of this category.

Section Three: The Overall Form of a Functional Legal Unit   39

The fourth major type of functional legal unit to be considered in this book is methodological. Recognized legal methodologies include those for the interpretation of statutes, contracts, and wills, as well as for the application of precedent, drafting, and adjudicative fact-finding. Although there are significant variations, all developed Western systems have a generally recognized methodology for interpreting statutes. Such a methodology is treated in Chapter Eight as an exemplar of one major variety of basic methodological form.

The fifth major type of functional legal unit to be considered here consists of the means for direct enforcement and implementation of law. This category includes sanctions and remedies. Overall forms of exemplars of these are treated in Chapter Nine.

We then turn to the legal system as a whole with its highly complex overall form, its systematizing devices, and the resulting systematized features that are constituents of the overall form of a legal system as a whole. Formal systematizing devices organize functional legal units into a system. For example, one systematizing device centralizes and hierarchically orders institutions. A related device specifies system-wide criteria for identifying purported law as legally valid within the system.

The primary structure of this book, then, is organized around the foregoing exemplars of overall forms of functional legal units. This is not an exhaustive selection of overall forms of functional units. Yet they represent the range and variety of such forms. That my general definition of overall form as the purposive systematic arrangement of a functional unit can be refined to fit felicitously this range and variety itself goes far to demonstrate the adequacy of this definition. Moreover, an analysis of the overall forms, constituent formal features, and the material and other components of this selection of exemplars sufficiently demonstrates how it is possible to advance understanding of the makeup, unity, mode of operation, instrumental capacity, and distinct identity of each type of functional unit. In addition, study of these exemplars is sufficient to reveal how overall form should share credit for the ends served. By extrapolation and analogy, one can also readily see how to advance understanding of, and how to accord credit to, the overall forms of other functional legal units not considered here.

SECTION THREE: THE OVERALL FORM OF A FUNCTIONAL LEGAL UNIT — A GENERAL DEFINITION AND REFINEMENTS

A general definition of overall form such as I adopt here – the purposive systematic arrangement of a functional legal unit – is required for several reasons. First, because any functional unit not only takes an overall form, but also consists of various complementary material or other components, a general definition of what counts as the overall form of the unit is required if the reader is to grasp what is referred to when claims are asserted on behalf of such a form as distinguished from the material or other components of the unit.

Second, a general definition is also required to clarify and differentiate what I mean by overall form in contrast with other familiar meanings of "form" not only in legal theory and law, but also in the English language generally[2] and in other Western languages. In view of all this variety, it is especially important to single out the meaning of "form" that I adopt here.[3]

Third, a general definition of overall form is required as the basic point of departure for the refinements necessary to take account of the distinctive nature of the overall forms of sub-types within types of functional legal units: the overall form of the legislative sub-type within the institutional type, the overall form of the sub-type of a rule within the preceptual type, the overall form of the contractual sub-type within nonpreceptual types of law, the overall form of the interpretive sub-type within the methodological type, and so on. All such refinements presuppose a general definition of form here as the point of departure for the refinements.

I will now clarify key terms of the general definition. The overall form of a functional legal unit is "purpose-built," that is, it is designed to serve the purposes of the functional unit.[4] It follows that the overall form of an efficacious functional unit is necessarily *purposive*. If not designedly purposive, it simply could not be efficacious. It could serve ends only by happenstance and thus should not be termed purposive at all. Consider, for example, the overall form of the centralized legislative institution in a developed Western society. This form purposively arranges the makeup, unity, instrumental capacity, and other attributes of the legislature as a multi-member entity designed for the legitimate, democratic, rational, and procedurally fair creation of general and efficacious written law, and for the conduct of various other related activities, such as oversight of administration and education of the public on governmental issues of the day. These founding and other purposes in turn require various constituent features of overall legislative form. For example, the purpose of securing legitimacy and democracy requires elected legislators, the central facet of the compositional feature of the overall form of

---

[2] Although I have consulted various dictionaries in doing this work and also several historical and etymological works, insofar as I rely to a limited extent here on general usages, I rely mainly on *The Oxford English Dictionary*, vols. 1–27 (2nd ed., J. Simpson and E. Weiner eds., Clarendon Press, Oxford, 1989), hereinafter *OED*.

[3] Form and its derivatives have multiple meanings in other languages, too. As the Italian theorist del Vecchio once wrote, "No word is understood in so many ways as the word form" G. del Vecchio, *The Formal Bases of Law*, 113 (J. Lisle trans., The Boston Book Co., Boston, 1914). Relatedly, the German theorist Max Weber wrote: "As everyone knows, there is no expression more ambiguous than the word 'formal' . . ." M. Weber, *Critique of Stammler*, 79 (G. Oakes trans., Free Press, New York, 1977).

[4] Legal theorists who have stressed the defining purposes in what are, in effect, the overall forms of functional legal units include R. Jhering, *Zweck im Recht*, vols. 1–2 (Breitkopf and Härtel, Wiesbaden, 1970) and L. Fuller, *The Law in Quest of Itself* (Beacon Press, Boston, 1940).

Section Three: The Overall Form of a Functional Legal Unit 41

a legislature. The purpose of securing rational deliberation requires appropriate procedural and structural features of the overall form of the institution.

The purposive overall form of a functional unit is also to be analyzed in terms of constituent formal features and complementary material or other components that are *systematically arranged in coherent union with each other*. For example, the law-making authority of a legislature – a formal jurisdictional feature – itself presupposes a formal procedural feature for exercise of authority to adopt statutes. Without a formal procedure for adoption of valid statutes, we could not know what action of the body constitutes the exercise of jurisdiction to adopt statutes. At the same time, without formal jurisdiction to adopt statutes, any set procedure for such an action would be pointless. These formal features of jurisdiction and procedure are thus interdependent features of overall legislative form that, along with complementary material and other components of personnel and physical facilities, are coherently arranged within a unified whole.

In the previous example, the foregoing formal jurisdictional and procedural features presuppose a third feature of the systematic arrangement, namely, a compositional feature specifying the makeup of the legislature. Only duly designated personnel can exercise jurisdiction in accord with the procedure. A fourth formal feature within the set – that of internal structure – organizes and differentiates the roles of participating members within committees and within the whole. Who is to do what, when, and how is thus purposively and systematically arranged. Complementary components, such as personnel and physical facilities, are duly regimented in accord with these features so that the functional unit operates as a unitary whole.

A constituent feature of the overall form of a functional legal unit may be a necessary feature or merely a salient feature. In the case of a legislature, for example, some agreed procedure for the adoption of legally valid statutes would be a feature necessary to the very existence of a legislature, whereas an internal structure with two chambers would be merely a salient feature.

The key concepts in the general definition of overall form, namely, arrangement, systematic arrangement, and purposive systematic arrangement, are independently significant. For a functional unit to be purposively arranged, that is, to be duly defined and organized, it must be sufficiently ordered. A less than adequately arranged unit would not be duly ordered. For example, in the case of a legislature, the compositional feature of overall form might be arranged only in part, such as when the mode of selection is specified, with qualifications for members left unspecified. In the event of truly significant organizational gaps, it might be said that the unit is not systematically arranged overall to serve purposes.

Although a functional unit is arranged, that is, ordered in some fashion, and although all of its parts are ordered so that there are no organizational gaps in the arrangement, its various parts still might not be systematically arranged in a

42 Basic Concepts and Definitions

further way. That is, they might not be ordered consistently in relation to each other to serve relevant purposes. For example, the composition of a legislature might be too large and unwieldy for its procedures to operate efficiently.

From the foregoing, we can see that the overall form of a functional legal unit as a whole must be systematically arranged to serve the purposes of such a unit within the system. Appropriate purposes determine the design of the arrangement, the constituent features of this arrangement, the inter-relations between these features, the complementary material or other components, and the inter-relations between formal features and components.

This can be readily seen if we merely construct the beginnings of a fictitious "system" of law not appropriately purposive in major respects. Suppose we imagine a newly emerging society being inhabited for the first time or imagine one recently freed from foreign dominance. Assume that the inhabitants agree on who is to count as a member of the society, but that they have not yet established a legislature, although they have agreed that the primary purpose of any such legislature would be to adopt general written law binding on all members of the society. Now, let us imagine that some inhabitant comes forward and says to a few members remaining after a casual meeting of the whole: "O.K., any of you who so wish should gather tomorrow at my place where we will sit around and make some laws for everybody." Imagine that several then meet. Assume they do not even agree on what procedural steps the "body" is to take to enact law, and that they do not provide for notice to those absent of any possible law-making activity. Yet, assume that after some general talk, some of them claim to adopt several laws and seek to impose them on all others by posting general notices on centrally located trees.

In the absence of the special conditions sustaining dictatorship or oligarchy, attempts such as the foregoing to adopt and impose legislative law would fail. These simply could not succeed (1) without some purpose widely shared among members that what any such self-appointed few do on behalf of all by way of law-making is to be authoritative for all, and (2) without some shared purpose, at least among the "law-makers," as to what procedural and other steps are to count as adopting laws on behalf of all. Without sufficient purposiveness, in at least the foregoing two major respects, the resulting legal "unit" simply could not serve the primary end for which it exists, namely, the creation of general written law on behalf of all that is authoritative for all.

SECTION FOUR: TYPES OF PURPOSES THAT OVERALL FORM
IS TO SERVE — A MORE EXTENDED ACCOUNT

The overall form of a functional legal unit as a whole must be designed to serve purposes. That is, it must be "purpose-built." The purposes may be numerous,

Section Four: Types of Purposes that Overall Form is to Serve 43

varied, and complex. As we have seen, the primary purposes of the overall form of a legislature in a developed Western society include the purpose of providing for the creation of general written law. Some of the further primary purposes of this overall form pertain to *how* such law is to be created: democratically, legitimately, fairly, and rationally. Insofar as a legislature is well-designed, such purposes shape and permeate its overall form, its constituent formal features, its material and other components, and the various inter-relations of all these.[5]

A unit's overall form and constituent features simply could not be designed at all, let alone well-designed, without reference to what purposes the unit is to serve and how it is to serve them. Also, the required complementary material or other components of the whole could not even be identified without reference to the purposes to be served. The relations between formal features and complementary components within the whole could not be duly specified without reference to purposes. When the purposes to be served are valuable, when the overall form, its constituents, and its complementary components are well-designed to serve these purposes, when the unit is integrated and coordinated with other units and duly deployed, the realization of purposes will serve values. In these circumstances, overall form and its constituents, and not merely material or other components of the whole, such as personnel and material resources, must receive a share of the credit. A grasp of form is also essential to understanding the whole unit.

When officials, citizens, and others responsible for the creation of a functional unit choose to define and organize it and thus give it an overall form designed to serve some purposes rather than others, this has profound significance. For example, the purposes of a well-designed procedural feature of overall legislative form include the provision of avenues for rational and democratic influence on the content of proposed statutes. A choice of a formal procedural feature here that is not well-designed may foreclose entire avenues of potentially rational and democratic influence. Imagine an ill-designed legislature with a formal procedural feature that fails to provide any stage in the process whereby legislators may debate and amend proposed statutes prior to final vote!

I will now identify several major categories of overlapping purposes to be served partly through well-designed overall forms. (Of course, complementary material or other components are also required to serve these purposes.) One major category might be called "founding" purposes. Without sufficiently purposive and systematically arranged overall forms, the very founding of legal units duly suited to their functions would simply not be possible. To exist at all, a functional legal unit must be sufficiently defined and organized to serve its characteristic founding purpose or purposes. We have illustrated founding purposes of a legislature. Consider, as a further example, the founding purpose of one typical variety of a

---

[5] These and their inter-relations are treated extensively in Chapter Four.

rule. To use Collingwood's rough formulation, this purpose is to create an overall form with complementary content consisting of "a generalized decision to do many things of a specific kind on occasions of a specific kind."[6]

A second major category of purposes to be realized partly through well-designed overall forms of most functional legal units is concerned with the internal requirements essential to the mode of operation of the unit. For example, one procedurally formal constituent of the overall form of a legislature is a "decision-rule," such as adoption by majority vote. This rule enables the body authoritatively and democratically to resolve differences over, for example, the terms of a proposed statute and, thus, effectively make law. A purpose of such a procedural rule is that of securing the "decisiveness" required for law-making fecundity and for realization of values dependent on the creation of statute law. Most functional legal units have their own internal operational purposes. As a further example, consider one of the modes of operation of legal rules. To be effective, many rules must be applied by lay addressees. Thus, it is a major purpose of many rules that they be sufficiently clear and definite – formal features – so that addressees can apply them on their own. Or consider contracts. It is a major purpose of contracts that they be clear and definite enough for the parties to know how to perform them.

A third major category of purposes to be served consists of the full range of public policies incorporated in statutory rules adopted by legislatures, in precedents created by courts, in regulations adopted by administrative bodies, and more. This vast category of policies includes public health, highway safety, the prevention of crime, and the regulation of business activity. As incorporated in a rule or other law, policy content is a component complementary to the overall form of the rule. This policy component instantiates a purpose that shapes the defining and organizing form of the functional legal unit of a rule, as when a traffic regulation policy leads to adoption of a speed limit with a highly definite feature.

Functional legal units, if purposively well-designed in overall form and in complementary components, afford vast scope not merely for realization of public policies and other public ends, but also for realization of private ends of individuals, including socially significant achievements of individuals acting freely within their own protected spaces. In many societies, individuals in the course of their own more or less private activities make major scientific, technological, medical, or other discoveries, or create significant musical, artistic, literary, architectural, or other cultural works. Without policies of contractual and other freedoms, and of protection of persons and property, as secured through well-designed forms and complementary components of the relevant functional legal units, such creations of private individuals that benefit all would occur far less often.

---

[6] R. Collingwood, *The New Leviathan*, 216 (Rev. ed., D. Boucher ed., Clarendon Press, Oxford, 1992).

Section Four: Types of Purposes that Overall Form is to Serve

A fourth major category of purposes to be realized partly through units well-designed in form with appropriate complementary components consists of fundamental political values. This category includes legitimacy, rationality, democracy, justice, and basic freedoms. Well-crafted purposive systematic arrangements of units, along with their complementary components, are required for the realization of such values. Plainly, "governance" through the sheer force of autocracy could not be legitimate, rational, democratic, or just. To serve the purpose of realizing fundamental political values, well-formed institutional and other legal units, as duly integrated and coordinated within operational techniques, are essential.[7] We have seen, for example, that democratic legislatures require a "compositional" feature of overall form providing for elected law-makers. As a noninstitutional example consider freedom of contract. To serve the purposes of this freedom, the overall form of a valid contract itself must be recognized and implemented.

An important subset of fundamental political values relevant here consists of "process values."[8] Such values are realized in the course of the very workings of well-designed legal processes, as distinguished through the outcomes of such processes. For example, democratic participation in a law-making process is a major process value. It could not be realized without duly formal and thus purposive procedural and structural features, in addition to democratic composition of legislative membership.

A fifth major category of purposes to be realized partly through well-designed forms of functional legal units consists of general values of the rule of law. These values include fair advance notice of the law's requirements, predictability of law, equality before the law, the dignity of citizen self-direction under law, and freedom from official arbitrariness. (These values might also be viewed as a sub-set of fundamental political values.) General values of the rule of law are realized in virtue of the ways in which officials, citizens, and other inhabitants function within operational techniques to create and implement law. For example, principles of the rule of law require that rules have duly designed formal features of definiteness, generality, and clarity of expression.

Indeed, it is a striking fact that the main requirements of nearly all the various types of functional legal units and thus also of their overall forms are largely deducible from widely accepted general principles of the rule of law. The most fundamental such principle is that there be law governing human relations. To have law at all, there must be duly formed law-creating institutions, such as legislatures and courts, which is the first category in the typology of forms treated here. Another fundamental principle of the rule of law is that the law should be, in general, determinate and knowable in advance. It follows that at least much of the

---

[7] R. Summers, "The Technique Element in Law," 59 *Calif. L. Rev.* 733 (1971), and Chapter Eleven, *infra.*

[8] R. Summers, "Evaluating and Improving Legal Processes – A Plea for 'Process Values,'" 60 *Cornell L. Rev.* 1 (1974).

law must take the overall form of rules well-designed in form and content, which is another leading category in the typology of functional legal units considered here. Indeed, the rule of law is heavily dependent on the overall form of rules with their complementary contents. The principles of the rule of law requiring fair notice and equal treatment under the law call not only for rules, but also for uniform methodologies of interpretation and application, which is another basic category in our typology. Principles of the rule of law also require that the law be enforcible. It follows that sanctions, remedies, and other enforcive devices are a necessity, which is a further major category in our typology of forms. Moreover, an unsystematized "system" of operative functional units would be a contradiction in terms and grossly dysfunctional. This topic is covered, along with more on the rule of law, in Chapter Ten.

I have so far identified rationality as one of the values to be realized partly through the forms of some functional legal units. Rationality is also required for the effective realization of all other values through legal units and their forms. A well-designed legal system, with its own functional units and their forms, is a monument to countless reasoned choices (1) in constructing formal features and complementary components of law-making and law-administering institutions, (2) in constructing the form and content of preceptual and nonpreceptual species of law, (3) in constructing the various formal features and complementary components of law-making and law-applying methodologies, (4) in constructing the forms and complementary components for sanctions, remedies, and other enforcive devices, (5) in constructing all other functional legal units, and (6) in integrating and coordinating such units within a duly systematized operational system. Form and the formal in functional legal units, and in a legal system as a whole, simply cannot be equated with rigid rules mechanically applied.[9]

Occasions for the deployment of sound moral, political, economic, and institutional reasons – purposive rationality – thus constantly arise in the course of constructing and operating a well-designed system of law. In this book, I differentiate such reasons from reasons of a second kind that may be called authoritative reasons for action or decision. Authoritative reasons are those that arise under a legal rule or other species of law. Two schematic examples of common authoritative reasons are: "Because, properly interpreted, the statute requires it," and "Because a precedent so holding requires as much." Of course, authoritative reasons may be entirely sound in their own way, too! Such reasons are denominated in this book as legal reasons for action or decision. Sound moral, political, economic, and institutional reasons are not, as such, legal reasons for an action or decision and have no authoritative force until adopted by a court or other authority. Yet

---

[9] For what, at various points, may be interpreted as a view to the contrary, see D. Kennedy, "Legal Formality," 2 *J. Legal Stud.* 351 (1973). See further Section Six of Chapter Eight.

Section Five: Rationales for the General Definition of Overall Form   47

when sound, such reasons do have justificatory force.[10] In a well-designed system, such reasons – purposes – directly and immediately determine many choices of formal features and of complementary components in functional legal units and continuously determine how these features and components are to be deployed to serve purposes and values. A well-designed system of functional legal units is thus a monument to form and to the rationality that shapes form. This rationality requires purposive reasons. As Jhering might have put it, to deploy such reasons aptly is to "express rational purposes."[11]

SECTION FIVE: RATIONALES FOR THE GENERAL DEFINITION OF OVERALL FORM ADOPTED HERE

Several rationales justify the choice of my general definition of the overall form of a functional legal unit as the purposive systematic arrangement of the unit as a whole. First, this general definition goes far to capture the defining function of form. It is therefore also aligned relatively closely with one major *technical* meaning of the word "form" recognized in English (and in several other major Western languages). This major technical meaning is a traditional philosophical meaning of "form," namely, "that which makes anything . . . a determinate species or kind of being."[12] As we will see, the overall form, that is, the duly refined purposive systematic arrangement of, for example, a legislature, or a statutory rule, or an interpretive methodology, or a sanction goes far to make the functional unit involved a "determinate species or kind of being," thereby giving it a distinct identity. This signifies that my general definition not only goes far to capture the defining function of form but is in this respect also generally faithful to one major technical usage of form in English. The foregoing also signifies that my general definition is not lexically arbitrary. Without its own overall form, a functional legal unit would not be intelligible as a determinate legal unit with its own distinct identity. In later chapters of this book, when identifying an overall form of a functional unit, I will sometimes argue from, or appeal to, the foregoing philosophical usage. As we have seen, this line of argument would have appealed to Jhering, who concluded that form is to a legal unit as the mark of the mint is to a coin.

I do not, however, unqualifiedly espouse the foregoing technical philosophical usage of form recognized in English. An initial qualification is this: According to the general definition of overall form adopted here, although such form arranges

---

[10] R. Summers, "Two Types of Substantive Reasons – The Core of a Theory of Common Law Justification," 63 *Cornell L. Rev.* 707 (1978).

[11] R. Jhering, *Law As A Means To An End*, 10 et. seq. (I. Husik trans., The Boston Book Co., Boston 1913).

[12] *OED*, supra n. 2, vol. 6, at "form" I.4. I am indebted to Paul Markwick here. See also *The Basic Works of Aristotle, Metaphysics*, Bk VIII (Random House, New York, 1941). Plato's theory of forms is quite different.

a functional legal unit (purposively and systematically), and although this distinctive arrangement, as further refined to fit a unit, may go far to define it as a "determinate species or kind of being," the resulting overall form does not alone make the unit *as a whole* determinate. Complementary material or other components also contribute to making such an entity the determinate species that it is. A particular institution, such as a legislature, is a distinctive integrated whole – a unity of form and complementary components – as is a rule or other precept, an interpretive methodology, an enforcive device, or any other legal unit. When the complementary material or other components of two discrete units are highly similar, but the overall forms thereof significantly different, as is possible with a given administrative agency and a given court, we still have two distinct species.

A further qualification is this. The foregoing technical philosophical meaning of form may be construed as somewhat narrower than my general definition of the overall form of a unit in the following way. According to my general definition, a given formal feature of the purposive systematic arrangement of a functional legal unit may not contribute to the determinateness and identity of the unit as a distinct "species or kind of being," yet still qualify as a salient formal feature of its arrangement. For example, a merely salient feature of many complex statutory rules is that they include cross-references to related rules. Such a feature may be quite important, yet it is hardly a necessary feature in a rule. Even given the two foregoing qualifications, the general definition of overall form I adopt here is relatively closely aligned with the foregoing technical philosophical usage recognized in English.

A second rationale for adopting as the general definition of the overall form of a functional legal unit, the purposive systematic arrangement of the whole unit, is that this general definition aligns with one widely recognized *ordinary* English usage. That is, the organizational emphasis in this general definition is largely faithful to that major ordinary use of "form" in which the word means the "orderly arrangement of parts"[13] of an abstract or a concrete object. The general definition adopted here is not lexically arbitrary for this further reason. Indeed, this organizational emphasis is also recognized in the specialized discourse of many jurists and judges. Indeed, as one oft quoted American judge stressed: "it is through form that all organization is reached. Matter without form is chaos; power without form is anarchy."[14]

A third rationale that indirectly supports the general definition adopted here is this. When we turn to the various constituent features of overall form, as refined to fit a given functional unit, it commonly transpires that some such features are themselves recognized more specifically as formal in ordinary English usage, too. For example, a procedural feature, which figures as a constituent of the overall

---

[13] *OED, supra* n. 2, vol. 6, at "form" I.8.
[14] *Cochran v. State*, 62 Ga. 731, 732 (1879) (Bleckley J.).

Section Five: Rationales for the General Definition of Overall Form 49

form of an institution such as a legislature or court, is more specifically recognized as formal.[15] So, too, is the structural feature of the form of an institution, of a rule, or of a methodology, and so on.[16] To the extent that this is so, it follows that the general definition is also faithful to a more specific recognized usage in English and is not lexically arbitrary for this reason, as well.

In light of the foregoing alignment of the general definition with at least one major technical, one major ordinary, one judicial, and various more specific usages of "form" recognized in English, it also follows that this definition is not vulnerable to the charge that the concept and the terminology of form adopted in this book are simply being made up out of whole cloth, or to the charge that the conceptual and terminological universe developed here is idiosyncratic, or to the charge that meanings of "form" are simply being picked here at will from an array of diverse usages to suit whatever happens to be the theoretical purpose at hand.

Fourth, and as the late Oxford philosopher, J. L. Austin, would have stressed, in thus faithfully and consistently using the word "form," and its derivative "formal," we are "looking . . . not merely at words . . . but also at the realities we use the words to talk about."[17] As I will demonstrate, the general definition adopted here of the overall form of a functional legal unit as its purposive systematic arrangement can be refined to fit felicitously the functional realities of the organized forms of all the varied legal units and their complementary material or other components that I treat in this book.

Thus, for example, the general definition of the overall form of a functional unit can be refined not only to fit the institutional type of unit as such, but more relevantly here, can also be refined further to fit more concrete sub-types such as legislatures or courts. Similarly, the general definition can be refined not only to fit the preceptual type of unit, but can also be further refined to fit its more concrete sub-types such as rules or principles. Further, the general definition can also be refined to fit nonpreceptual types of law, including its more concrete sub-types such as contracts or proprietary interests. Moreover, the general definition can also be refined to fit the methodological type, and as further refined, to fit its concrete sub-types such as interpretive and other methodologies. All of these units can thus be seen to be purposively and systematically arranged in their own ways.

---

[15] *OED, supra* n. 2, vol. 6, at "form" I.11.a.

[16] *Id.*, at "form" I.5.a.

[17] [O]ur common stock of words embodies all the distinctions men have found worth drawing, and the connexions they have found worth marking, in the lifetimes of many generations: these surely are likely to be more numerous, more sound, since they have stood up to the long test of the survival of the fittest, and more subtle, at least in all ordinary and reasonably practical matters, than any you and I are likely to think up in our arm-chairs of an afternoon – the most favored alternative method.

    . . . When we examine what we should say when, what words we should use in what situations, we are looking again not *merely* at words (or 'meanings,' whatever they may be) but also at the realities we use the words to talk about: we are using a sharpened awareness of words to sharpen our perception of, though not as the final arbiter of, the phenomena. J. L. Austin, *Philosophical Papers*, 130 (J. Urmson and G. Warnock eds., Clarendon Press, Oxford, 1961).

Later, I demonstrate such refined "phenomenological fit" in detail. Because, as I will demonstrate, the general definition of overall form can be felicitously refined to fit such detail and also to fit so widely, this further confirms its faithfulness to the realities of functional legal units. The extent and coherence of this wide-ranging fit, together with the considerable conformity of the general definition to wide-ranging and long established usages, further supports adoption of this general definition.

Finally, the foregoing duly refineable, definitionally and organizationally functional, lexically legitimate, and phenomenologically felicitous general definition of overall form aptly serves the theoretical and practical aims of this book. The general definition, as duly refined to apply to sub-types of functional legal units, allows for the characterization of such a unit as taking an overall form with its own constituent formal features, and allows for differentiation of complementary material or other components of the unit. This makes it possible: (1) to focus on how the frontal and systematic study of a given overall form and of its formal features advances understanding of the functional legal unit involved as having its own makeup, unity, instrumental capacity, distinct identity, and other attributes, and (2) to demonstrate how such form and formal features are entitled to a share of the credit, along with complementary material and other components, for realization of purposes through deployment of the functional unit. Because the general definition does not swallow up the material or other components and, indeed, fully preserves, as I later show, the essential contrast between the formal and other components of a particular unit, this also reduces the risk that overall form or a formal feature will be over-credited.

To clarify further my conceptualization and general definition of the overall form of a functional legal unit, it is useful to compare and contrast this definition with various other common meanings of the word "form" widely recognized in English but not adopted here. In the course of this, I will also explain briefly why I have not adopted these other meanings. It is worthwhile to do this for two reasons. First, because the word "form" still has these other defined meanings in English (and in other languages), it is well to explain why I prefer the one I adopt here over at least those that might also seem to be candidates. Second, some of the meanings not adopted should be explicitly differentiated from the general definition I adopt here, given that some of those not adopted can be fertile sources of confusion for readers. Several common meanings of the word "form" in English may at first seem close to my definition, yet, as I will show, they are different in important ways.

In perhaps the most common use of the word in English, "form" means the visible contours or shape of a physical thing.[18] Thus, we speak and write of wood

---

[18] The wide use of form as meaning the visible contours or shape of a physical thing appears as the very first *OED* entry for "form" see *OED*, *supra* n. 2, vol. 6, at "form" I.1.a.

Section Five: Rationales for the General Definition of Overall Form 51

"in the form of" a table, or of a building "in the form of" a citadel. Although I do not adopt this usage as such, my general definition of "overall form" as the purposive systematic arrangement of a functional legal unit is analogous. Just as the form of a table may be said to arrange and shape the wood, and the form of a citadel may be said to arrange and shape the building materials, and just as both can also be said to be so arranged and shaped purposively and systematically, the form of a legislative institution, for example, can similarly be said to arrange and shape this type of body, including its components such as material resources, personnel, and so on. So, too, the form of a rule can be said to arrange this unit including its components of policy or other content. Likewise, the form of a sanction or remedy. And so on.

There are, however, at least two general disanalogies here, as well, and these explain why the foregoing common meaning of form as "the visible contours or shape of a physical thing" is not apposite as a general definition of overall form here. The first disanalogy is that the overall form of a functional legal unit as a whole is not itself a form of a physical thing such as a table or a citadel (although physical artifacts and the like often do figure as components in the overall makeup of a legal unit, as with a building to house a court or a legislature). It follows that the overall form of a functional unit as a whole, such as a legislature, a rule, a contract, an interpretive methodology, or an enforcive device, does not, as with physical things, such as buildings or human beings, have contours or shapes, except metaphorically. The second and related disanalogy is that the overall forms and formal features of functional legal units (except perhaps the expressional feature of rules or other law set forth in writing or in print) are not visibly manifest in the fashion of the forms of physical things such as tables or citadels. In applying the term "overall form" to the purposive systematic arrangement of a functional unit, we should not look for physical shape. Whenever, as in the general theory of legal forms as set forth here, "form" is used to refer to the overall form of a legislature, a rule, a contract, or an interpretive methodology, there is simply no corresponding physical object the shape of which may be visualized as the overall form of the functional legal unit.

Whereas it is true that we can, for example, see words on paper expressing a rule, and whereas mode of expression is one of the formal features of a rule, seeing these words is still not equivalent to seeing the overall form of a rule. Yet it is to see *manifestations* of a rule. Indeed, these and other manifestations of rules and of certain other functional units are visible. This, in part, enables persons to "manage" legal rules and other units, and to operate with, or in regard to, such units.[19] Persons can visibly discern manifestations of procedures, such

---

[19] I am indebted to Okko Behrends here. See O. Behrends, "Struktur und Wert," in *Rechtsdogmatik und praktische Vernunft* (Göttingen Academie der Wissenschaften, O. Behrends, M. Disselhorst, and R. Dreier, eds., 1989).

as legislative debating, the operations of a court in letting only one side talk at a time, the following of a rule by driving to the right, activities constituting contractual performances, interpretational activities, and so on. Persons can also discern formal patterns manifest in these activities, as in legislative debating the form of which takes a certain sequential order, or as with litigants acting out the form of a dialogic procedure, or as with a citizen interpreting and following a rule of the road in a car, and so on. Even so, these manifestations are not, as such, *equivalent* to the overall forms that define and organize the functional units involved. The forms are more complex. These manifestations are also of material or other components of the whole unit, such as the behavior of official personnel and the like. Thus, the overall form of the unit makes possible, and figures in, what is in part a visibly discernable reality that is legally ordered. Of course, persons bring to this reality conceptions of the overall form, and of the material or other components of, the functional units involved, and identify and construe these manifestations in accord with these conceptions.

Another common usage of the word "form" might be called the "container" conception.[20] According to one pejorative version of this usage, form is empty – nothing more than a mere container for possible content or the like. This conception also has some vague nonpejorative analogs in the law as reflected in such expressions as "the common law form" or the "statutory form" of a rule. Generally, in the analysis here, I use such expressions as these nonpejoratively to refer not to the overall form of a unit but rather to a constituent feature of its form. I call this the encapsulatory feature of the overall form of a rule (or other species of law). This feature is only one of the constituents of the overall form of one type of functional legal unit and is, therefore, not sufficiently generic to serve as a general definition, even as a nonpejorative one.

In law, in legal theory, and in lay usage the "container" conception of form is sometimes utilized pejoratively to signify that form is empty in the more specific sense that it is devoid of purpose and so has no shaping effects on constituent features or on the material or other components of a whole unit. The general definition of overall form I develop here, however, is highly purposive. It follows that it is quite unlike the empty container conception, which Lon L. Fuller once disparaged as the legal positivist's concept of law as an "empty wheelbarrow." As Fuller said, this empty "wheelbarrow" is devoid of purpose, can be filled with any content and pushed "in any direction."[21] Any such conception is also highly misleading insofar as it suggests that overall form is infinitely pliable, and has no continuous shaping effects on "content" or other components. The shaping effects of overall legal form is not like the shaping effects of the form of a bucket

---

[20] *OED, supra* n. 2, vol. 6, at "form" II.18.a-b.

[21] L. Fuller, *supra* n. 4, at 114–15.

Section Five: Rationales for the General Definition of Overall Form 53

full of water, effects lost when the water is poured out. Overall form with its constituent features usually has continuous shaping effects upon, and even leaves major imprints on, the material or other components of a functional legal unit, as when the formal feature of definiteness sharply etches the contents of a rule. Overall form also leaves imprints on constituent features, as we will see.

Further, my general definition of overall form as the purposive systematic arrangement of the make-up, unity, instrumental capacity, and distinct identity of a functional legal unit differs from those common uses of "form" and "formal," by lay persons, legal theorists, and legal scholars simply to refer to an authority or to whatever is authoritative.[22] For example, the authors of an earlier work often used "formal" to refer to those *reasons* recognized as legally authoritative, in contrast merely to moral, economic, social, or other "substantive" considerations that may nonetheless figure in a legal decision or action.[23] Plainly, the overall form of a given functional legal unit as a whole, for example, that of a rule must be authoritative in some way. Yet as I have shown, the overall form of such a unit and its constituent features embrace much more than this. They define and organize the unit as a whole. Whatever authoritativeness the unit may have is not equivalent to, or reducible to, the purposively and systematically arranged character of the whole unit, which is itself typically multi-featured and complex in its own ways.

Plainly, the general definition of overall form adopted here, with its derivative, "formal," also applies more widely than those common technical uses of "form" and "formal" to refer to a certain type of legal formality, such as the two witnesses required for valid wills or testaments, or the "consideration" or "causa" required for the validity of contracts.[24] Such requirements, when satisfied, may be a feature or features of the resulting purposive systematic arrangement of the functional unit involved, such as a valid will or a valid contract, but such units are themselves unified wholes taking their own forms with still further constituent features that go beyond any such required formalities. For example, in Anglo-American systems, the overall form of a valid will generally also includes the formal features of provision for testamentary disposition (whatever the subject matter), for due expression thereof by the testator, and for authentic signature of the testator, as well as for the formality of witness attestation.

Similarly, the general definition of the overall form of a unit adopted here includes much more than formal "mode of expression" or the like as used in ordinary or in legal discourse. Also, whereas a formal expressional feature does figure in the overall form of some functional legal units, it does not figure in

---

[22] *OED, supra* n. 2, vol. 6, at "form" I.13; *id.*, vol. 6, at "formal" A.3.a.

[23] P. Atiyah and R. Summers, *Form and Substance in Anglo-American Law: A Comparative Study of Legal Reasoning, Legal Theory, and Legal Institutions* (Clarendon Press, Oxford, 1987).

[24] *OED, supra* n. 2, vol. 6, at "form" I.12.a.

the form of all. It figures in the form of a rule and includes choices of degree of explicitness, of lay versus technical vocabulary, of simplicity or complexity of sentence structure, and whether oral, in writing, or in print. These expressional facets are likewise to be contrasted with the component of content that is expressed. The general definition of overall form also encompasses far more than whatever constituent feature it may have that pertains to mode of expression or the like. As we have seen, the overall form of a rule, for example, includes prescriptiveness, generality, definiteness, and more.

I will now explicitly identify major refinements of my general definition of the overall form of a functional unit. These refinements will be a central focus of this book. The selection of general types of overall forms of functional legal units, and, more importantly, of illustrative sub-types thereof to be treated here, can be schematically (although inexhaustively) summarized as follows:

Institutional type:

legislatures
courts
administrative bodies
corporate and other private entitites

Preceptual type of law:

rules
principles
maxims
general orders

Nonpreceptual type of law:

contracts
certain property interests
wills

Methodological type:

interpretive
drafting
fact-finding

Enforcive or implementive type:

sanctions
remedies
others

In the foregoing overall scheme of analysis, our general definition of overall form as the purposive systematic arrangement of any functional unit will be characterized

Section Five: Rationales for the General Definition of Overall Form

as the "top level" definition. In the overall scheme, this top-level definition is presupposed rather than explicitly stated. It is formulated at the highest level of generality and is applicable generically not only to the preceding selection, but to all units. In the framework just presented, two levels of refinement appear below this presupposed top-level general definition. At what might be called the "middle level" of refinement, the general definition may (a) be refined to *fit* one type of legal form, for example, the institutional, or the preceptual, or the methodological, and so on, and (b) be formulated to *differentiate* this one type from other such types at this level, for example, the institutional from the preceptual, or from the methodological.

Hereafter, I narrow my general focus. I do not focus on the "top level" at all. That is, I give no further consideration to the general definition as such. Nor do I focus on refinements of that definition at the "middle level": the institutional, preceptual, etc. Rather, I focus on refinements of the general definition only at what I will call the "bottom level." There, I refine the general top level definition of overall form (a) to fit a selected sub-type of form within a type, for example, the legislative sub-type within the institutional type, or the "rule" sub-type within the preceptual type, etc. and (b) to differentiate a selected sub-type from another sub-type, for example, the legislative sub-type from the judicial sub-type within the institutional type, and the "rule" sub-type from the "principle" sub-type within the preceptual type, and so on.

Overall forms of the same sub-type of functional units are not identical even in developed Western societies. That is, the same sub-type of functional legal unit can vary, at least in salient features of overall form, from society to society. For example, overall legislative form in one society may incorporate the executive, such as in the British Parliament; yet in another society, overall legislative form may separate the legislature from the executive, such as in the United States. Although the overall form of a given sub-type of functional unit is not identical in all developed Western societies, paradigms of these forms do share what I will call necessary features.[25] Yet even a necessary formal feature of a unit such as the compositional feature of a legislature, may vary in its instantiation in significant ways from society to society. One society may, for example, have a very large legislative membership, whereas another society of the same size may have a very small membership.

Refinements of the general definition of overall form at the bottom level are required to advance understanding of the makeup, unity, instrumental capacity, and distinct identity of the functional legal unit at hand. How the general definition can be refined at the bottom level to fit sub-types of overall form, and how the explicit differentiations required can together advance understanding of the unit

---

[25] Hart even contended that a *system* of law as a whole, "in spite of many variations in different cultures and in different times, has taken the same general form and structure . . ." H. L. A. Hart, *The Concept of Law*, 240 (2nd ed., Clarendon Press, Oxford, 1994).

will be demonstrated in Part Two of this book in which a selection of sub-types of overall forms are analyzed in detail. Likewise, refinements of the general definition at the bottom level will enable us to identify overall forms and constituent formal features to which credit may be due for ends served. Indeed, most often in this book, we proceed at the bottom level.

To illustrate what I am claiming, it will be enough for now to provide one simple example. It is illuminating to consider at the bottom level how the same variety of constituent features within two different overall forms, even of the same sub-type, reflects the differing purposes that these forms serve and for which they are entitled to credit. For example, a procedural feature is a complex constituent of both the overall form of a court and of the overall form of a legislature – two leading institutional sub-types. Yet, when duly designed, the procedural feature of a court is fundamentally different from that of a legislature largely because of their different founding purposes.

One major aspect of this fundamental difference can be readily illustrated as follows. The complex feature of a trial court procedure in many Western systems typically provides for the dialogic definition and resolution of disputed issues of fact and law arising out of discrete episodes in the past. That is, opposing sides assert positions and respond thereto, and the judge (or jury) resolves the issues in light of the results of these exchanges and of who has the burden of persuasion. The corresponding feature of a legislative procedure, however, is not essentially dialogic and provides for the introduction, study, amendment, and adoption (or rejection) of proposed written laws for the future. Many of the differences between these two basic procedural features are to be understood and explained largely in terms of the different purposes informing the overall form of each institution as a whole, including their procedural as well as other features. These different purposes dictate the different designs and organized realities of each formal feature.

Thus, the main purposes of the procedure of a court include a rational finding of the disputed facts of a past episode, fair opportunity of the litigants to be heard and to respond to each other with respect to evidence and legal argument, and the faithful application of law to the facts, all in the course of resolving a dispute between litigants. To serve these purposes, the procedure must be dialogic to an extent. The purposes of a legislative procedure are very different. One primary purpose of a legislature is that of considering and adopting laws for the future. This does not require a dialogic procedure. Because of such differences of primary purpose, these two procedurally formal features differ greatly even though they are both institutional. The relevant purposes of legislation and of adjudication simply could not be satisfactorily realized through the same procedural features. Differences in the purposes of the overall forms and their constituent features thus explain such procedural differences. In concentrating on form, as refined at

Section Six: Differentiation of the Overall Form 57

the "bottom level" in our framework, we can thus advance understanding of the functional legal units involved. We can also see better what credit the overall form of the whole and its constituent features should have for any values realized.

To provide (1) an account of the overall form of a sub-type of a functional legal unit or (2) an account of what is distinctive about the overall form of such a sub-type, one must plainly acquire knowledge of the general nature and purposes of the unit under study. My attention heretofore to standard dictionaries and other lexicons should not be taken to indicate a contrary view. At the bottom level of refinement of our general definition, a lexicon may provide little guidance. Certainly we need far more than what dictionaries report to be general meanings of words such as "legislature," "rule," "interpretive methodology," or "sanction." The lexicons of a given language do provide some guidance that is of value in giving a very general account of the overall form of a given sub-type of a functional legal unit. Yet lexicons do not explicitly identify and differentiate forms. Also, lexicons cannot provide adequate accounts of how overall forms define and organize functional units. One must study the general functional realities of the sub-type of phenomenon involved to provide an analytical-descriptive account of the purposive and systematic nature of the arrangement at hand, and an account of what is special about it. In our example, we must consider how a legislature is one institutional sub-type with general functional realities of its own. We must consider how these realities are to be differentiated from the other institutional sub-type being compared – that of a court in our example. Plainly, this requires that we draw on special knowledge and insight seldom revealed merely in reports on general meanings of words as set forth in general lexicons of a natural language. Inquiry is required into the defining and organizing features of the sub-types of paradigm arrangements, such as for example, the differing procedural features of legislatures and courts, including the contrast between nondialogic and dialogic procedure, as previously mentioned.

SECTION SIX: DIFFERENTIATION OF THE OVERALL FORM FROM MATERIAL OR OTHER COMPONENTS OF A FUNCTIONAL LEGAL UNIT

Throughout this book, a distinction is drawn between the overall form of a functional legal unit as a whole and the material or other components of the unit.[26] The material or other components of the unit do not themselves purposively and systematically arrange the unit as a whole, yet they figure in the makeup of the whole. Examples are the material resources and the personnel of a legislative body, the courthouse and judicial personnel, the policy or other content of a rule, the subject matter of a contract of sale, the materials of legislative history that may

---

[26] I do not use the phrase "nonformal" here. The expression can mean formless and it is often pejorative.

figure in an interpretive methodology, or the coercive force that may be brought to bear in a sanction. This contrast between the overall form of the whole unit and its material or other components is essential (1) to secure the intelligibility and credibility of my account of what is formal in legal units, for these units plainly include material or other components that are not formal, (2) to sharpen the focus on, and to exploit, overall form and its constituent features as a distinct avenue for advancing understanding of a unit, and (3) to attribute a share of credit to overall form and its constituent features for purposes served. At the same time, the overall form of a functional legal unit and its material or other components are hardly separate worlds. In most units, overall form and these other components are complementaries, and form leaves its effects and imprints on such components.

I will now differentiate more explicitly between the nature and function of the overall form of a functional legal unit as a whole, such as a court or a rule or an interpretive methodology on the one hand and the material or other components of the unit on the other. As we will see, in my analysis, overall form does not swallow up the material or other components of the unit. Hence, the analysis here should not over-credit form for what role it plays in advancing understanding or in serving ends.

We may readily differentiate, in functional terms, between the overall form (and features thereof) of a functional unit as a whole on the one hand and the material or other components of such a unit on the other hand. The overall form and its features purposively and systematically arrange the whole of the functional unit. This is true, for example, of the overall form and constituent features of a court. This unit takes the overall form of a tripartite adjudicative body. This whole unit is thus defined and organized in accord with its overall form and features of this form, such as composition, structure, and procedure. This form and these features also specify requisite material or other components of the whole. These material or other components include a courthouse and judicial personnel. However, such components as these cannot be similarly said to define and organize the functional unit of a court as a whole. Nor can these components *themselves* specify that they are requisites of the functional unit as a whole. Overall form must do this and merits credit accordingly. A similar analysis applies to other functional units besides courts and thus also differentiates form and the formal in such units from their material or other components.

There is one qualification, but in the end it cuts in favor rather than against crediting form. Some of the material or other components that figure in the makeup of a functional legal unit, and thus are here differentiated from the overall form and constituent features of the unit, are themselves duly defined and organized to serve relevant purposes. Hence they may be said to take what I will call a "component form" in contrast to the "overall form" of the whole unit. This is true,

Section Six: Differentiation of the Overall Form

for example, of a courthouse, which consists of more than physical facilities. As a component of a court, it typically takes its own form as well. That is, the physical facility of a courthouse is organized in various ways to serve special functions of the institution as a whole.[27]

The foregoing qualification or concession in the end cuts in favor rather than against crediting form, however. Instead of merely crediting the unit's overall form (and constituents thereof), we now also recognize and credit any "component form," that is, whatever special form any material or other component of the whole unit takes, provided this form defines and organizes this component.[28]

It is also true that although some components of a whole functional unit may not be appropriately said to take a component form, nonetheless, the unit's overall form (and its constituent features) may be said to leave important formal imprints on its components. Consider, for example, the component of judicial personnel within the makeup of a court. Judges are not merely human beings but are duly trained and qualified. Here we see the imprints of overall form. The individual person of the judge is thus an *object* of organization within the court as a whole. The required general training and qualifications of a person who is to serve as a judge thus satisfy the formal compositional feature of a court. This does not, however, render a court in this regard "all form and nothing else." Here, the "personnel-element" – that is, the individual person of the judge – remains a material component of the whole unit. The foregoing imprints of compositional form do not swallow up this "personnel-element" of a court.[29]

Let us turn to a further type of example, noninstitutional in nature. Rules divide at least into overall form on the one hand, and complementary content and addressees on the other. The constituent features of the overall form of a rule include its prescriptiveness, completeness, generality, and definiteness. These formal features are readily differentiated from the policy or other content of the rule – which is typically some type of prescribed action of addressees that must, or may, or may not occur, in specified circumstances, all to serve policy or other ends.[30] It might be argued, however, that when the features classified as formal, such as prescriptiveness, completeness, generality, and definiteness, appear within complementary policy content of a rule, as they must, the imprints of these features will be so deep and indelible that this policy content loses its own identity and becomes entirely formal. For example, it may be argued that once the policy

---

[27] Not all material or other components of functional legal units are physical. For example, the policy content of a rule is not.

[28] For an insightful account of how special architectural form can serve the purposes of legislative form, see K. Wheare, *Legislatures*, Chapter One (Oxford University Press, London, 1963).

[29] I am indebted to Okko Behrends here.

[30] See *infra* Chapter Five, at 143 et. seq, where I explain further the distinction between formal prescriptiveness in contrast to descriptiveness, and to the merely hortatory, and in contrast to the subject matter in which this is expressed.

content comes to bear the formal imprint of definiteness in a 75 mph speed limit rule, this policy content becomes "all form and no complementary content."

Such imprints of form on complementary policy content of the rule, however deep and indelible, still do not convert this content into form. The formal imprints remain only that, and content, as the bearer of these imprints, retains its distinct identity. This identity remains characterizeable as the rule's regulatory content in which policies of safety, efficient traffic flow, and driver free choice are operationally expressed or implicated. Moreover, on my analysis, a rule simply cannot be all form and no content. To be a rule, it must have some policy or other content, and this content, unlike form, does not define and organize the whole.

The distinctness of the overall form of a functional legal unit from the material or other components of that unit may be further clarified as follows. The one might exist without the other. Thus, for example, there might be no recognized overall adjudicative form and thus no courts in the territory, yet there might be persons who could serve as judges, and buildings that might serve as courthouses. Likewise, the overall form of a given functional unit and the features thereof might actually subsist, even when the components required for that very unit to be operational do not exist at all. For example, in a new state being created within a territory, an authorized "blueprint" of the institutional form of a legislature might be created by a constitutional assembly well prior to when personnel are selected for the institution or prior to when material resources are marshaled for use by legislators. This form might even be "mapped out" and specified to some extent in the contents of reinforcive rules of constitutional, statutory, or other law, in anticipation of selection of personnel. Or, more commonly, a fully formed institution might cease to operate for an interval, such as with a court that has adjourned awaiting a new term. In such instances, we may correctly say that the relevant overall form and its constituent formal features exist, even though the legal unit involved is simply not operational.

The separateness of overall form and complementary material or other components of a functional unit may be further elucidated as follows. We may readily imagine that if we were to change the overall form of the unit, yet keep its material or other components more or less the same, we could even create a different functional unit. Suppose that the overall form of a functioning court is changed to that of an administrative agency, yet the material or other components are kept more or less the same – the material resources, the personnel, and so on. We might thus convert an operational court into an administrative agency! If, however, we were to keep the overall form the same, for example, keep the form that of a court with its tripartite structure, dialogic procedure, etc., and if we were to substitute for the component of personnel, persons without the full qualifications of judges, this would not necessarily yield a different type of institution, although it would certainly impair its efficacy. Without more, we could still have a court, at least marginally.[31] This holds similarly for many types of functional legal units.

SECTION SEVEN: THE "FORM V. SUBSTANCE" CONTRAST

For some, a still more felicitous conceptualization here might be a contrast between the "form" of a functional legal unit on the one hand and the "substance" of that unit on the other. Let us consider claims on behalf of this contrast, because it is widely adopted for some purposes in modern legal scholarship.[32]

First, one might argue that a factor favoring a "form v. substance" contrast here is that "form v. material or other components" is sharply "on-off," whereas form is not always sharply separable from material or other components and sometimes shades off along a continuum into "substance." If a continuum be the reality, and if the form v. substance contrast is not sharply on-off, but is instead more hospitable to a continuum, then, so the argument goes, a form v. substance contrast would be more felicitous here.

My view, however, is that it is usually possible to differentiate relatively sharply between the overall form of a functional legal unit and its material or other components. Consider a court, for example. Adjudicative form, in its compositional, structural, and procedural features, can be readily distinguished from the personnel and physical facilities of a court. So, too, the form of a rule in its generality and definiteness from its complementary policy or other content. And so on. This is not, however, to say that the purposive nature, or the systematically arranged nature of the overall form of a functional legal unit, is never a matter of degree. It is to say that whether any purported legal unit is purposively and systematically arranged in some degree, rather than not at all, is ordinarily sufficiently "on-off" to be readily determinable as such. If, as I claim, a relatively sharp differentiation here is generally faithful to the realities, then my two primary purposes of advancing understanding and according due credit can be more readily served than if a continuum were more faithful. This is because the overall form (and constituent features) of a functional legal unit can be more clearly identified both as a distinct avenue for advancing understanding of the unit as a whole and as a distinct object worthy of credit for realization of ends.

---

[31] See further R. Summers, "The Place of Form in the Fundamentals of Law," 14 *Ratio Juris* 106, 109–10 (2001).

[32] For example, P. Atiyah and R. Summers, *supra* n. 23, invoked this contrast. The primary version of this contrast in the Atiyah and Summers book was between types of reasons, and the "form v. substance" distinction can do this work, largely because these contrasting terms can serve readily as stand-ins for "formal," i.e., authoritative, legal reasons, and for "substantive," i.e., moral, economic, and other such reasons. This approach is far less appropriate when the functional units that are the central focus extend beyond reasons as in the present book.

Adoption of the "form v. substance" contrast also might lead one to use "form" and "formal" in misleading ways. For example, it might be thought that "substance" designates all things substantial within this contrasting pair, with the result that form is not substantial.[33] This, in turn, may even invite the assumption that "form" itself can have no affirmative general meaning of its own, but, as is true with many contrasting pairs of words, is merely a term to be used in contradistinction to "substance" to exclude or to rule out one or more varieties of substance.[34] Yet, in the analysis set forth here, the term "form" does have a general meaning of its own, namely, the purposive systematic arrangement of a functional legal unit. Such overall form, as refined to fit any sub-type of a functional legal unit, can be affirmatively characterized, often robustly, as defining and organizing the whole of that unit. Moreover, as we saw, the rationales for adopting this general meaning are several. It is not only faithful to the relevant realities. It largely conforms to one technical philosophical usage of form, largely conforms to one major ordinary usage of "form," is functionally apt, and does not threaten the basic contrast between overall form and material or other components, and can be refined to fit felicitously the wide-ranging and representative typology of forms treated here.[35]

Another common "form v. substance" contrast, as often drawn, at least impliedly restricts the extent, density, and significance of the overall form of a functional legal unit. This contrast exalts substance as the "real" subject matter incorporated within "mere form."[36] Yet overall form, defined here as a purposive systematic arrangement of a functional legal unit as a whole, is itself a robust defining and organizing conception and, thus, does not imply that the extent and density of form is quite restricted.

Indeed, the "form v. substance" contrast, as it is invoked in several ordinary English usages that recur in legal discourse, may imply that only the "substance" and not the "form" could contribute either to the advancement of understanding or to the realization of ends and values. One such ordinary usage is that substance is "essential," and this may imply that, by contrast, form and the formal must not be essential to a functional legal unit.[37] Still another usage has it that substance

---

[33] For lexical confirmation of this particular implication, see *OED, supra* n. 2, vol. 17, at "substance" 5.a-b, and vol. 6 at "formal" A.7.

[34] On "excluder terms," see J. L. Austin, *Sense and Sensibilia*, 70–1 (G. Warnock ed., Clarendon Press, Oxford, 1962).

[35] See Section Five, *supra*. I reject Weber's general position insofar as he implies that no real sense can be made of usage here: "As everyone knows there is no expression more ambiguous than the word 'formal' and no dichotomy more ambiguous than the distinction between form and content" M. Weber, *supra* n. 3, at 79. Sense can be made of English usage in the fashion I have shown. It is almost certain that Weber was referring only to German usage and his position may not stand up there either.

[36] This contrast is drawn in one technical legal usage, too. See, e.g., R. Pound, *Jurisprudence*, vol. 3, Chapter Sixteen (West Publishing Co., St. Paul, 1959).

[37] *OED, supra* n. 2, vol. 17, at "substance" 13.a.

Section Seven: The "Form v. Substance" Contrast

is "real" whereas form and the formal are not, and can at most be "mere appearance."[38] On such views as these, which are embedded in an even wider range of English usages, substance is not merely superordinate with form subordinate, but the implication is that form is hardly significant at all. Indeed, it may be that form cannot be efficacious at all and cannot contribute to the realization of ends. In fact, form may not even exist. Instead, it may only be mere appearance! Again, the differentiation between the overall form and the material or other components of a functional unit adopted here does not suggest any of these things. Moreover, this differentiation lends no support to the assumption that form is in tension with material or other components of the whole. Rather, a grasp of form contributes, jointly with material or other components of the whole, to the advancement of understanding and to the realization of ends. It follows, too, that well-designed form is not value neutral.

The English language also harbors some technical uses of "form" and "substance" and their adjectival counterparts that, in juxtaposition, diminish or marginalize form. Indeed, matters are even worse. As indicated in Chapter One, embedded within technical legal usages in English are several uses of "form" and "formal" that equate it with the formalistic, or with the conceptualistic, or with mechanical reasoning, or with rigidity, or with still other pejoratives.[39] The influence of these usages can prejudice from the very start any claim that the overall forms of functional legal units have, either as a key to understanding such units or as contributing to the realization of ends.

Some of the many uses of the term "formalism" also require brief consideration. In one well-recognized use in some quarters, this term means respect for forms and a disposition to use them.[40] This is a nonpejorative use congenial to the general theory of form in this book. There are, however, various pejorative uses of "formalism," too, both in ordinary discourse and in the discourse of legal theorists and other scholars. According to some, "formalism" is the doctrine that the law consists solely of rules that bind like fetters and never leave scope for any choice by the applier of the rule.[41] Another common pejorative use of "formalism" is to refer to the well-known vice in legal analysis or legal reasoning called conceptualism or "deductivism."[42] I treat this use in Chapter Eight, Section Six. In this book I do not adopt these or other pejorative uses, although I do condemn the doctrine and the practices so labeled.

---

[38] *Id.*, vol. 17, at "substance" 10.a.; *Id.*, vol. 6, at "form" I.3.

[39] These are discussed further *infra* Chapter Eight at 275.

[40] H. Fowler, *A Dictionary of Modern English Usage*, 208 (2nd ed., Oxford University Press, New York, 1965).

[41] H. L. A. Hart, *supra* n. 25, 129.

[42] For an inventory of uses of "formalism," see M. Stone, "Formalism," in *The Oxford Handbook of Jurisprudence and Philosophy of Law*, 166 (J. Coleman and S. Shapiro eds., Oxford University Press, Oxford, 2002).

3 ∼ A GENERAL APPROACH

"[M]odern . . . thought . . . emphasize[s] the importance of method. . . . "

– M R. Cohen[1]

"[I]t is possible to be interested in a phenomenon in a variety of ways [and some are] . . . not empirical. . . ." – L. Wittgenstein[2]

"There is no necessity of thought with which we can dispense so little as the division of things into content and form. . . ." – G. Simmel[3]

SECTION ONE: INTRODUCTION

In the preceding chapter, I defined and clarified central concepts and terminology in the general theory of legal form set forth in this book. The present chapter is also broadly methodological, but differently so. Section Two is devoted in summary terms to general questions of approach that arise in seeking to advance understanding of functional legal units by focusing on their overall forms. Section Three treats possible empirical and other methodological issues that may arise in attributing credit to forms for ends realized through such legal units. Section Four explains the major differences between a Hartian "rule-oriented" approach to the problems addressed in this book, and what I deploy here as a "form-oriented" approach.

SECTION TWO: ADVANCING UNDERSTANDING THROUGH
STUDY OF FORM

Through study of the overall form of a functional legal unit, of constituent features of this form, and of any forms of component parts of a unit, it is possible

---

[1] Morris R. Cohen, *Law and the Social Order*, 128 (Transaction Books, New Brunswick, N.J., 1982).

[2] L. Wittgenstein, *Philosophical Investigations*, 47e (G. E. M. Anscombe trans., MacMillan & Co., N.Y., 1953).

[3] G. Simmel, "On the Nature of Philosophy," in *Essays on Sociology, Philosophy and Aesthetics*, 288 (Harper Torchbooks, New York, n.d.).

Section Two: Advancing Understanding Through Study of Form 65

to advance understanding of the unit as a whole. Such understanding is worth having for its own sake, as well as for its instrumental value.[4] What, then, is it to understand a functional legal unit? How is it possible to advance understanding of the unit through study of form? Is there a general method or approach here? I will now briefly recapitulate the very general answers to these questions I have so far suggested. In later chapters, I treat these questions in depth with regard to a representative selection of functional legal units.

To understand a functional legal unit, it is at least necessary to understand its attributes. All, or nearly all, such units have the following general attributes:

a. makeup
b. unity
c. determinateness
d. continuity of existence
e. mode of operation
f. instrumental capacity
g. intelligibility and distinct identity
h. ordered inter-relations with other units

Institutions, precepts, nonpreceptual species of law, methodologies, sanctions and remedies, and other functional legal units all have their own versions of the foregoing general attributes, although the nature of these attributes varies markedly from unit to unit. To understand a functional unit, one must grasp the versions of such attributes peculiar to the unit in question. Among other things, this requires focus on the relevant special purposes at work.

If one is ignorant of one or more attributes of a unit or if one encounters what seem to be erroneous assumptions about one or more such attributes, it becomes necessary to consider how to advance understanding of the attribute or attributes in question. Ignorance of the attributes of functional legal units is commonplace. For this and other reasons, erroneous assumptions about attributes are also commonplace. For example, ignorance and error with respect to the formal makeup of that most common of functional legal units, namely, legal rules, is widespread. As I show in Chapters Five and Six, the constituents of the overall form of a rule are numerous and complex, and they extend well beyond generality and definiteness. As will be seen, the inter-relations between these constituents and thus their essential unity comprise still another complex attribute.

Even today, legal theorists and other scholars have not yet developed a systematic general account of functional legal units in terms of their attributes. A central thesis here is that one major avenue for advancing understanding of a unit is to study the

---

[4] Jhering stressed the importance of the savings in havoc that misunderstanding can wreak here. R. Jhering, *Geist des Römischen Rechts: auf den verschiedenen Stufen seiner Entwicklung*, vol. 2, at 480 (Scientia Verlag, Aalen, 1993).

overall form of the unit as a whole, the constituent features thereof, and any forms of component parts of the unit. Such study, in relation to complementary material or other components, illuminates the makeup, unity, instrumental capacity, and other attributes of the unit.

Study of the overall form of a rule, for example, reveals how this form purposively defines, specifies, and organizes the attribute of the *makeup* of a rule. Constituent features of the overall form of a rule, such as prescriptiveness, completeness, generality, definiteness, and internal structure, purposively permeate the very makeup of a rule, as we see in Chapters Five and Six. Such features explicitly or implicitly specify the addressees of the rule and specify the actions they are to take to serve the policy or other ends of the rule. Imprints or other effects of formal features are manifest in the content of the rule. For example, a given rule may bear the imprint of high definiteness, such as in a highway speed limit rule.

Study of form reveals how it purposively organizes the general attribute of the *unity* of a functional unit as well. For example, such features of the form of a rule as prescriptiveness, internal structure, and due definiteness integrate the facets of a rule into a unified whole.

A form-oriented approach not only can advance understanding of the various attributes of a given functional legal unit, but can also reveal other more general truths as well. We will ultimately see how form is not purposeless, not bare and thin, not airy, and not intangible or impalpable. Indeed, we will grasp the general purposive nature of form and its robust organizing potency. The resulting attribute of the *instrumental capacity* of the whole of a given unit can even be striking, as we will see. The form-oriented approach deployed here also reveals that form is not confined to defining and organizing the various functional legal units in isolation. This role extends to what is another general attribute of legal units, namely, their ordered *inter-relations* with other units, especially as *integrated and coordinated* within operational techniques: the penal, the grievance remedial, the administrative regulatory, the public-benefit conferring, and the private-ordering.

SECTION THREE: ATTRIBUTING CREDIT TO FORM
FOR PURPOSES SERVED

Other matters of method arise when some credit is to be accorded to the overall form of a functional legal unit for purposes served in part through the unit. As already explained, without its overall form, a functional legal unit could not exist at all. Hence, some credit is due to form insofar as legal units exist at all and serve valuable purposes. Moreover, when the overall forms and complementary components of existing units are well-designed and effectively deployed to serve valuable purposes, even more credit will be due form.

Section Three: Attributing Credit to Form for Purposes Served 67

Credit may also be due form for realization of "process" values. Such values are those realized in the course of the operations of legal processes of well-designed legal units, quite apart from whether the outcomes of these processes also serve values.[5] This can be readily seen with regard to the role of form in institutional processes. For example, participants in a legislative process may, in the course of its purposive workings, realize such process values as fair and democratic participation, rationality in the scrutiny of statutory proposals, and overall legitimacy. Here, some credit can be due to a well-designed formal feature of composition providing for democratically elected legislators, to a well-designed formal structure providing for committees to study proposals, and to a well-designed formal procedure providing for scrutiny of draft laws, and for debate of them. Important "process" values can even be realized when a proposed statute is considered but not ultimately adopted.

When a statute or other law is created and implemented, and when the purposes it serves are valuable, the credit for this should not be attributed solely to a valuable policy or other content of the law, or solely to wise personnel, or solely to necessary resources, or solely to other material components complementary to form. A form-skeptic or law-is-policy reductionist may fail to see that significant credit should always go to well-designed forms of the functional legal units deployed. It is important to focus on the actual or possible credit due form for three reasons. First, there is a tendency to under-credit form and over-credit material and other components of a unit. Second, to the extent a unit fails to serve purposes, this often calls for improvements in the design of form. Third, the diverse, complex, and detailed functional roles of form in serving purposes comprise a neglected branch of legal study.

The attribution of credit is frequently a complex matter. Various issues of method may arise. Yet, empirical or sociological research is often not required to attribute significant credit to form for purposes served. To illustrate, let us now schematically consider the legislative adoption and implementation of a statutory rule to serve valuable ends. Assume that a primary rule imposing a major duty is created. If we plausibly assume that this primary rule is, along with auxiliary units such as sanctions, effective to serve valuable purposes, the *possible* objects of credit could be numerous and complex. These would usually include:

(1) the very existence, quality, and efficacy of the institutional and other functional legal units required for creation of such a primary rule in the first place;

(2) the quality of the purposes chosen at the outset that the rule is to serve, the extent to which these ends are realistically susceptible of being served

---

[5] See R. Summers, "Evaluating and Improving Legal Processes – A Plea for Process Values," 60 *Cornell L. Rev.* 1 (1974).

through such a rule, and the existence of any required auxiliary functional units implementive in nature such as sanctions or remedies;

(3) the soundness of the hypothesis of the law-makers that the actions of addressees of the rule, as prescribed in the policy or other content of the rule, will effectively serve as means to chosen purposes when the actions are carried out;

(4) the extent to which the overall form and complementary content in the rule itself are well-designed, including (a) the overall preceptual form of the rule, (b) the constituent formal features, including prescriptiveness, completeness, generality, definiteness, and internal structure, (c) the formal expressional features, such as vocabulary and syntax, and (d) the formal encapsulatory feature, for example, statutory law, administrative regulation, common law, or other law;

(5) the quality and efficacy of the overall forms, and the forms and other facets of the complementary components of the auxiliary functional legal units simultaneously deployed, as integrated and coordinated within an overall operational technique to serve the purposes of the primary rule, including any official institutions or agencies charged with disseminating and administering the rule, the personnel required to staff and support these entities and to deploy any sanctions, remedies, or other implementive devices;

(6) the capacities of addressees of the primary rule, including officials, private citizens, other inhabitants, and corporate and any noncorporate entities; and

(7) material and other resources required for any of the foregoing.

Again, there are three types of claims that may justifiably be made in attributing credit to form and its constituent formal features for the purposes served: (1) claims the truth of which is not contingent upon empirical proof, (2) claims the truth of which is so contingent, but that are still not really controversial even without empirical research, and (3) claims the truth of which is so contingent and that would be controversial without empirical proof, yet are not controversial either because the facts are already in or because highly plausible assumptions can be made.

Let us consider an example of a primary rule imposing a duty implemented pursuant to what I will call the administrative-regulatory technique.[6] Assume that under legislative authority embodied in a statute, an already existing administrative body created and promulgated a definite and clear rule imposing a duty on manufacturers of canned foodstuffs to disclose fully on all containers the nature and proportions of ingredients. Assume this rule was to serve the ends of providing

---

[6] For an extended summary of this technique, see *infra* Chapter Ten, at 329.

Section Three: Attributing Credit to Form for Purposes Served

opportunities for informed consumer choice and for improved consumer health. Assume this same administrative body and its local branches also had responsibility to inspect containers for compliance and to enforce this duty. Let us also plausibly assume that manufacturers learned of, and generally complied with, the rule. This general compliance could be explained partly by reference to each of the foregoing seven possible objects of due credit identified earlier. Moreover, choices of form very likely figured significantly in each of the first five. It is enough to explain briefly how.[7]

First, with well-designed choices of form and of complementary material and other components, the very existence of the required law-creating institution – a duly defined and organized administrative agency – became possible, and when instituted, this body could then consider and adopt a regulatory rule, such as the foregoing. Second, with a law-creating institution in existence, the overall form of which was well-designed, and with constituent formal structures and procedures calling for scrutiny of the proposed form and content of the rule, it became more likely that the general ends adopted for the rule to serve would be good, and would be susceptible of effective implementation. Third, it also became more likely that law-makers would adopt a rule with form and complementary content prescribing actions having effects that would serve the purposes of the rule. Fourth, it became more likely that the formal features of this rule would be well-designed. Had the rule been insufficiently prescriptive, incomplete, insufficiently general, indefinite, or had it been faulty in formal manner of expression or mode of encapsulation, the primary addressees of the law – the manufacturers – simply could not know what actions or decisions were expected of them and could not comply, except perhaps by chance. Fifth, had an auxiliary functional unit, such as an agency with personnel and material resources concerned with promulgating, publicizing, and enforcing the rule, not been formally well-designed, levels of compliance would have been lower or possibly minimal. It is evident that the overall credit due to well-designed forms in such an effective use of law would be considerable. This is not to say the relative credit to be apportioned as between form and the nonformal could be, or needs to be, precisely measured.

Now, let us consider the general nature of some of the foregoing claims to credit for form here. The first thing to stress is that some of these claims are *nonempirical*, or at least require no empirical research. One major type of claim to credit on behalf of the overall form of a functional legal unit is simply that without some such overall form, the use of law that has occurred simply would not have been possible. For example, without sufficiently well-designed overall forms here, neither the relevant law-making institution, nor the primary rule prescribing the relevant actions of manufacturers could *exist at all*. Even assuming that at least

---

[7] A much more extended account appears in Chapter Eleven.

the minimally formal features conceptually required for the rule to exist at all are in being, it hardly follows that this minimal form would serve the quality and efficacy of the rule at all well. The required further form could be entitled to much credit.

Further, sufficiently well-designed form is frequently necessary to the authoritative refinement and definition of policy or other ends, if they are to serve as purposes of legal rules and duly shape the form and content of those rules. This, too, is an important type of claim that requires no empirical research. Many refined policy ends embodied in law are necessarily legal constructions that definitively reconcile and synthesize various competing policy and other considerations. For example, the necessary information on canned foodstuffs to be specified in a well-formed legal rule may have to be determined in light of cost-benefit analysis and prescribed accordingly in the form and content of the rule, which must in turn be duly publicized.

I now turn to a second common type of claim that can frequently be justifiably made in according due credit to form for purposes served. Although empirical, and thus dependent on factual contingencies, this second type of claim is not very controversial or not controversial at all, even without specific empirical proof. Beyond surmounting the minimum threshold required for the very existence of a functional legal unit, the quality of the design of its overall form can make major differences to the efficacy of the unit. Returning to our foodstuff labels illustration, let us assume that in fact all, or nearly all, manufacturers do read and come to understand the requirements of the primary rule here. That is, the form and complementary content of the rule are straightforward and duly inform manufacturers. Hence, manufacturers generally take the rule as the source of a legal reason for determinate action and thereafter provide the required information on the labels, and this in turn ultimately serves the purposes of securing opportunities of consumers for informed choice and improved health. Assume now that I also make an affirmative claim to credit on behalf of the overall form of the rule to the effect that the manufacturers' understanding of the rule requiring that they provide the legally required information on labels is attributable partly to the high quality of the design of the formal features of the rule, including its prescriptiveness, completeness, definiteness, generality, and expressional clarity. These formal features, then, figure in conveying to addressees what compliance requires. Indeed, manufacturers could not even be said to have complied with the rule requiring information on labels of foodstuff containers if they did not know of, or could not understand, the contents of the rule.

Assume that I offer no specific empirical proof that the foregoing particular features of the overall form of the rule actually caused, or played a role in, the cognitive, psychological, and other processes whereby particular manufacturers came to know and understand the requirements of the rule. Even so, my claim that

Section Three: Attributing Credit to Form for Purposes Served

the foregoing features of form actually so contributed would not be controversial at all. It is simply common knowledge, when we focus on it, that such well-designed formal features of prescriptiveness, completeness, definiteness, generality, and expressional clarity in a rule go far to enable literate addressees who are notified of the existence of the rule to know and understand what actions the rule requires. Again, well-designed form and complementary content largely account for this.[8] Many similar contingent claims that, for a variety of reasons, engender little or no controversy can be made when according credit to form for ends and values realized.[9]

A third category of contingent claims would plainly be controversial without empirical proof, yet such proof may be available in abundance. Assume it is claimed that many manufacturers not only learned of, but complied with, labeling requirements. It is plausible that proof of compliance could be available in abundance with no need for empirical studies. For example, manufacturers might have been required to fill out official documents reporting compliance with labeling requirements, which official inspectors then reviewed. One might explain this compliance on the ground that manufacturers were motivated by their view of the rule itself as a source of a determinate and preemptive *legal* reason for so acting.

Here, some credit should plainly go to form for this compliance and the purposes thereby served, namely, the securing of opportunities of consumers for informed choice and improved health. This is not only because formal promulgation of the rule and well-designed features of the form of the rule indisputably go far to enable manufacturers to learn of and to understand what actions the rule requires. It is also because, according to my claim, manufacturers are motivated to act on such a well-formed rule as a source of a determinate and preemptive legal reason for such action. This further claim to credit on behalf of form is contingent, because it is a claim about what in fact motivated compliance. Yet actions consistent with the rule should not be explained as merely random unknowing action here. A further highly plausible assumption is that, in a tolerably well-ordered society, addressees, such as foodstuff manufacturers, generally take seriously and thus are motivated by, preemptive legal reasons for determinate action that they can see to arise under well-formed law, given at least that these addressees, as persons selling directly or indirectly to the public, wish or wish to be seen to be, law-abiding. This highly plausible assumption also applies widely beyond the present context involving manufacturers of foodstuffs.

---

[8] Moreover, without such formal features in some degree, addressees could not even learn the contents of the rule when promulgated. Indeed, without such features in some degree, such a rule could not even exist.

[9] Note that I have used the same factual context to illustrate (1) a nonempirical claim and (2) a noncontroversial empirical claim. The main thrust of the nonempirical claim is that without form, the relevant use of law could not even occur. The empirical claim is that due form enables addressees of the rule to know and understand what actions the rule requires. I am indebted to Paul Markwick here.

72 A General Approach

My contingent claim that a preemptive reason for determinate action arising under a well-formed rule or other law is also a motivating reason for action here, can be further substantiated by reference to still other factors in which form plays a role. For example, the known prospect of official inspections and of the possible imposition of sanctions for noncompliance, such as revocation of a license to manufacture foodstuffs in our illustration, can also reinforce motivation to act in accord with a preemptive legal reason. Such a sanction, as a functional legal unit, also takes a form.[10]

Admittedly, it is possible to overstate the credit due to forms for what is achieved through law. A society could even be rich in well-designed forms of functional legal units, yet widely fail to serve purposes through uses of law. Form is limited, a matter to which I return later in this book.

SECTION FOUR: A FORM-ORIENTED APPROACH AS PRIMARY, WITH A RULE-ORIENTED ONE SECONDARY

The most fundamental questions arising in the general theory of legal form may now be stated more fully as follows: What purposes is the functional legal unit at hand designed to serve? What is its makeup? That is, what is its overall form, the constituent features thereof, and its material or other components? How are these purposively and systematically arranged to form an integrated unity? What is the resulting instrumental capacity of this unit? Its distinct identity? Its manner of integration with other units? How can focused study of the overall form and its features serve as an avenue for advancing understanding of the attributes of a unit? What credit may be due to the form of a functional legal unit for what is achieved? How can the study of form improve the modeling of such units and the performances of participants in the system? What roles do forms play in the systematization of a legal system as such? How can an understanding of forms cast light on the general nature of law and on other traditional problems of law and legal theory?

What I call a "form-oriented" approach to the foregoing questions is needed, and I will adopt it as primary. I will now explain this approach more systematically than heretofore, and I will contrast it in general terms with the "rule-oriented" approach that H. L. A. Hart generally applied in *The Concept of Law*, the leading work of legal theory in the modern analytical tradition.[11] Hart's rule-oriented approach has been highly influential in law and in legal theory and is akin to

---

[10] See Chapter Nine. Jhering once observed that because duly designed form itself seldom fails, its benefits are taken for granted, whereas when ill-designed form wreaks havoc, as it easily can, form gets a bad name overall, without regard to its benefits when it is duly designed. See R. Jhering, *supra* n. 4, 480.

[11] See H. L. A. Hart, *The Concept of Law* (2nd ed., Clarendon Press, Oxford, 1994). Still a third approach might be called "behavior-oriented." Various American legal realists, including the early Karl Llewellyn, often advocated this approach. It has been discredited, and will not be considered here. For criticisms,

Section Four: A Form-Oriented Approach as Primary

what might be called the "norm-oriented" method of Hans Kelsen. Both thinkers ended up in similar places. Hart concluded, with some modifications, that a legal system is a system of rules.[12] Kelsen concluded that a legal system is a system of legal norms.[13] Today, a rule-oriented approach is dominant in many circles of law and legal theory. It is also the primary approach in many law schools in Western systems.[14] I do not urge its abandonment. However, I argue here that, for many purposes, what I call a form-oriented approach to the study of functional legal units, and of a legal system as a whole, should be primary with a rule-oriented one secondary and supplemental.

The approach of Hart, Kelsen, and those of like mind may be said to be rule-oriented in two major respects. First, this approach to the foregoing questions focuses primarily on legal rules to the relative neglect of other types of functional legal units, such as institutions, contractual arrangements, interpretive and other methodologies, sanctions, and remedies. Second, insofar as Hart and Kelsen do address other types of units, this is often obliquely via a focus on the contents of what I will call "reinforcive" rules that prescribe facets of these other types of units rather than frontally on the overall forms of these units and their constituent features.[15] I here define a reinforcive rule as one belonging to that special class of rules that prescribes a facet or facets of the makeup, unity, instrumental capacity, or other attributes of a functional legal unit. An example of such a rule is one specifying, and thus reinforcing, a procedural feature of a court. This type of rule is to be differentiated from rules that are largely regulative of primary behavior, such as those prohibiting crimes or imposing liability for torts.

It is not difficult to explain the attractions of what I will call Hartian rule-oriented analysis. All or nearly all major varieties of functional legal units already exist in developed Western systems and are reinforced at least partly by legal rules prescribing the facets of these units. The contents of such reinforcive rules are also generally reliable sources. Thus, it seems natural to assume that these contents must be a key avenue to understanding the makeup, unity, instrumental capacity, distinct identity, and other attributes of any discrete functional unit of a legal system.

---

see, e.g., R. Summers, *Instrumentalism and American Legal Theory*, Chapters Three and Four (Cornell University Press, Ithaca, 1982). I am indebted to Manuel Atienza for discussion of these approaches.

[12] H. L. A. Hart, *supra* n. 11, 117.

[13] H. Kelsen, *Introduction to the Problems of Legal Theory*, 55 (B. Paulson and S. Paulson trans., Clarendon Press, Oxford, 1992).

[14] Many professors of law in America tend to focus, often in highly sophisticated fashion, primarily on the contents of any relevant rules, whatever the nature of the functional unit to be elucidated, whether it be preceptual, institutional, methodological, enforcive, or other.

[15] The word "constitutive" although often used here, is not as apt as "reinforcive." "Constitutive" may imply that the contents of rules constitute the whole of the phenomenon, yet rarely do they, even together, specify all of the overall form, features thereof, complementary or other components, and their inter-relations.

On a form-oriented approach, however, functional legal units are the primary objects of analysis. It is true that regulative rules comprise one type of such unit, take their own form, and thus qualify as primary objects of analysis on a form-oriented approach here, along with other varieties of functional legal units. Reinforcive rules, however, do not qualify as primary objects of analysis on a form-oriented approach. Rather, the units that reinforcive rules reinforce qualify as the primary objects of analysis: institutions, such as legislatures and courts, precepts, such as regulative rules and principles,[16] nonpreceptual law, such as contracts and property interests, interpretive and other methodologies, and sanctions and remedies. The attributes of such units to be understood are to be elucidated mainly through form-oriented analysis, and this may also be supplemented fruitfully with analysis of the contents of relevant reinforcive rules.

Some facets of overall forms, some constituent formal features, and some complementary components of functional legal units are often to some extent prescribed in the contents of those rules that Hart in effect treated as reinforcive of such functional units. For example, the qualifications of the membership of a legislature are specified in reinforcive rules and this is one facet of the formal compositional feature of the overall form of a legislative institution. Even so, this should not lead us thus to focus obliquely on the contents of such rules and divert us from focusing frontally on the overall form, constituent features, and complementary components of such a functional legal unit. Actually, in no system with which I am familiar, do reinforcive rules prescribe in explicit terms or at all fully the overall forms and constituent formal features of *any* functional legal units. Indeed, in no developed Western system of which I am aware are there even reinforcive legal rules the contents of which themselves purport to prescribe the overall form and constituent features of *regulative* legal rules – even of those that prohibit crimes! Yet, as I will show, a form-oriented approach fully applies to all rules, as well as to all other varieties of functional legal units.

Even if legal systems generally include reinforcive rules that fully and explicitly prescribe overall forms and constituent features of all functional legal units, it would still be my view that a frontal form-oriented analysis of such units would advance understanding of such units more fully than a merely rule-oriented one. The two approaches, however, are not mutually exclusive. Although I seek to demonstrate the generally superior virtues of a form-oriented over a merely rule-oriented approach, I recognize an important place for reinforcive rules. In this

---

[16] Here, I concur in part with Professor Dworkin to the extent that he criticized Hart's focus on regulative rules to the exclusion of principles. See R. Dworkin, "Is Law a System of Rules?," in *Essays in Legal Philosophy*, 25 (R. Summers ed., Basil Blackwell, Oxford, 1970). But I also stress the importance of entirely nonpreceptual legal units and their forms, too. This emphasis has some ancient antecedents. See O. Behrends, "Die Gewohnheit des Rechts und das Gewohnheitsrecht," in *Die Begründung des Rechts als historisches Problem* (D. Willoweit ed., Schriften des Historichen Kollegs, München, 2000).

Section Four: A Form-Oriented Approach as Primary

book, I treat form-oriented and rule-oriented analysis as complementary with a primary focus on form-oriented analysis.

Here, I present a legal system not, in the fashion of Hart and Kelsen, as ultimately reducible to a system consisting of regulative, reinforcive, and other kinds of rules, but as a system with a wide variety of functional legal units, including rules, as duly integrated with other units. Moreover, unlike Hart and Kelsen, I emphasize that functional legal units take distinctive overall forms – purposive systematic arrangements – with their own constituent formal features and complementary material or other components. I thus present such functional units as dependent on their forms and on their other components. I emphasize that these units are systematized within a legal system as a whole. These units are, among other things, duly integrated and coordinated with other units organized into operational techniques for the creation and implementation of law to serve ends.[17]

Let us consider Hart more fully as a proponent of rule-oriented analysis. In Hart's terms, a legal system is essentially a system of rules consisting mainly of primary (duty-imposing) and secondary (power-conferring) rules. He said it is the "union" of these two types of rule that deserves, if anything does, to be called the "key to the science of jurisprudence."[18] Yet, Hart failed to address frontally, systematically, and comprehensively the overall form of a rule itself, even though it is this form and its constituent features that define and organize such a unit. In addition, Hart did not frontally address the overall forms of institutional, nonpreceptual, methodological, enforcive, and other major varieties of functional legal units that exist in a Western legal system. In my view, if there is such a thing as the key to the science of jurisprudence, that key consists of the overall forms that define and organize discrete functional legal units and the overall form that defines and organizes a legal system as a whole.

Hart did recognize other functional units such as legislatures, courts, nonpreceptual law, methodologies, sanctions, and so on. However, instead of focusing frontally on the overall forms of these units, on the constituent features of these forms, and on the forms of complementary components, such as those for physical facilities, he generally tended to analyze such units obliquely in terms of the contents of what I call reinforcive rules that prescribe some facets of these units and not explicitly in terms of any forms and complementary components so prescribed. Thus, for example, he analyzed the institutional unit of a court in terms of what he called rules of composition, jurisdiction, and procedure. He did not, however, explicitly address the overall form of a court, its constituent features, and the formal and other facets of complementary components of a court, such as

---

[17] For extended treatment of these systematizing operational techniques, and of still other major systematizing devices, see Chapter Ten.

[18] H. L. A. Hart, *supra* n. 11, at 81.

the courthouse and qualified personnel. Nor did he consider how courts are integrated and coordinated within various overall forms of operational techniques for the creation and implementation of law.[19] According to Hart, the functional legal unit of a court is to be understood primarily in terms of the contents of its rules of composition, jurisdiction, and procedure that, as he put it, "lie behind the operation of a law court."[20] He sometimes said that the contents of these rules are "constitutive" (in my terms, reinforcive) of such an institution, and that such rules are required for a court to have authority to adjudicate and thus to exist at all.[21]

The rules that I here call "reinforcive" also provide, according to Hart, what might be called the "normative cement" required to hold the institution of a court together.[22] That is, the judge is bound by these rules and accepts them as common public standards for the conduct of judicial activity. At the same time, the litigants before the court measure the judge's actions by these reinforcive rules, which are standards to be followed. Accordingly, the litigants insist that the judge follow them. In Hart's view, if the judges did not take such an "internal point of view" toward the reinforcive rules of composition, jurisdiction, and procedure, and treat themselves as bound by them, such an institution would fall apart.[23] When judges follow such rules, the operations of a court have law-like constancy and regularity over time. Hart added that the contents of such rules "define a group of important concepts . . . [including] the concepts of judge or court, jurisdiction and judgment."[24] From the contents of these rules, we can also get some sense of what is distinctive about courts, for example, as compared to legislatures.

Given Hart's more or less exclusive methodological emphasis on unpacking the contents of reinforcive rules to elucidate the makeup, unity, instrumental capacity, and other attributes of courts and of still other functional legal units it may be worthwhile to pause and attempt to identify some factors that may explain his emphasis. Hart practiced law full time as a barrister for over eight years, and like many lawyers, he seems to have come to view courts and many other types of functional units mainly or exclusively through the lens of any rules that pertain to such a unit. Hart later was an academic philosopher at Oxford University in the 1950s and 1960s. At that time, and for an extended period, the nature of rules of various kinds, including especially rules "constitutive" of games, were central topics of discussion in Oxford philosophical circles.[25] Hart was also

---

[19] See R. Summers, "Professor H. L. A. Hart's Concept of Law," 1963 *Duke L. J.* 629, 640–5 (1963).

[20] H. L. A. Hart, *supra* n. 11, at 29.

[21] *Id.*, at 5, 29, 116. See also, R. Guastini, "Six Concepts of Constitutive Rule," Beiheft 10 *Rechtstheorie* 261 (T. Eckhoff et. al. eds., Duncker and Humblot, Berlin, 1986).

[22] H. L. A. Hart, *supra* n. 11, at 138. I am indebted to Peter Hacker for this expression.

[23] *Id.*, Chapter Five.

[24] *Id.*, at 97.

[25] P. Hacker, *Wittgenstein's Place in Twentieth-Century Analytic Philosophy*, 151 (Blackwell Publishing, Oxford, 1996).

Section Four: A Form-Oriented Approach as Primary

influenced by the philosophy of Ludwig Wittgenstein who sometimes stressed that we are to understand many of the concepts we have through rules, especially rules of language governing how the relevant words for expressing the concept in question are used.

I will now contrast Hart's rule-oriented approach with the main tenets of the form-oriented approach to the study of functional legal units that I deploy in this book. I will also treat the main advantages of this form-oriented approach as the primary means for advancing understanding of functional legal units and for according credit to the forms of such units for purposes served. It is true that Hart's own aims did not explicitly include the crediting of form. Even so, this is an important aim. I will contend throughout that a form-oriented approach should be primary overall with any rule-oriented analysis ancillary and supplemental. In my view, Hart's rule-oriented analysis "inverts ancillary and principal," to use his own expression.[26]

Here are the main steps in what would be a systematic and comprehensive form-oriented analysis, as schematically and illustratively addressed to a given functional legal unit of an institutional nature, such as a legislature or a court:

(1) Identify a paradigmatic exemplar of the unit to be studied, and isolate its overall form and constituent features – the purposive systematic arrangement of the unit;

(2) Identify the founding and other purposes that permeate and determine the overall form and the constituent features of this form (and any elaborations thereof);

(3) Describe the overall form and the major constituent features of the form of the unit;

(4) Consider and explain how the major constituent features of the overall form are related to each other and how they are unified in the whole of the functional unit;

(5) Determine the complementary material or other components that figure importantly in the unit;

(6) Determine whether, and if so how, each major constituent feature of overall form has, or shares, a facet or facets of a complementary material or other component of the organized whole;

(7) Consider how the overall form of the unit, and each constituent feature thereof defines, specifies, organizes, and leaves imprints or other effects on other features and on complementary components of the unit;

(8) Along the way, explicate how a grasp of overall form and formal features advances understanding of attributes of the unit, such as its makeup, unity, mode of operation, instrumental capacity, determinateness, and distinct

---

[26] H. L. A. Hart, *supra* n. 11, 40–1.

identity, and how the unit may be systematically integrated and coordinated with other units;

(9) Treat how, in projected operation, duly designed overall form and its major features can contribute to the realization of relevant purposes and corresponding values through the existence, operation, and functions of the unit together with other units, and thus identify in general terms the share of credit to be given to well-designed form for any ends realized partly through the unit; and

(10) Characterize what is distinctive about the overall form of the unit under study in comparison with other related units. A legal system as a whole may also be subjected to form-oriented analysis, as demonstrated in Chapter Ten.

In ensuing chapters, I apply the foregoing form-oriented approach to a selection of functional legal units with more emphasis on some steps than on others. My *immediate aims* in adopting this approach are numerous and complex and may be summarized as follows: (1) to identify and demarcate discrete units such as legislatures, statutory and other rules, contracts, interpretive methodologies, sanctions, and so on; (2) to provide general descriptive accounts of paradigmatic exemplars of the overall forms of such units, along with accounts of the constituent features of these forms, and accounts of complementary material or other components of the units on which these features leave imprints or other effects; (3) to sharpen awareness of these formally organized realities and lay bare and do justice to their complexities; (4) to represent these realities perspicuously through use of the concepts and terminology of overall form as a purposive systematic arrangement, with its own constituent features and their inter-relations, all as duly refined to fit the unit or units under study; (5) to identify choices of form in the overall design of such units and in their components, and thereby foster a wider recognition of the functional significance of such choices and their bearing through formal imprints and effects on other formal features and on complementary components of the units; (6) to identify general factors that rationally affect choices of form in such units; and (7) to elucidate the distinctiveness of, and the relations between, discrete functional legal units.

My more *ultimate* aims in deploying such form-oriented analysis are first, to demonstrate how a systematic and in-depth study of forms can advance understanding of the attributes of functional legal units such as makeup, unity, and instrumental capacity; second, to attribute credit to the forms of such units as means to ends; third, to reveal the form of a legal system as a duly systematized whole, and fourth, to achieve a clearer and more synoptic view of the parts, and of the whole of a system of law, and in this and related ways, cast special light on

Section Four: A Form-Oriented Approach as Primary

discrete functional units, on the nature of a legal system, and on other traditional topics of law, legal theory, and jurisprudence.

In my view, Hart's rule-oriented approach (and that of Kelsen) cannot, as a primary approach, be as adequate to the foregoing aims as a form-oriented approach. I will now provide a general and systematic statement of major reasons why I think this to be so. In later chapters, I will demonstrate in detail the virtues of adopting a form-oriented approach as primary with rule-oriented analysis secondary. In what follows in this chapter, I will illustrate my general points most often through institutional examples, but these points apply, *mutatis mutandis*, to preceptual, methodological, enforcive, and other types of discrete functional legal units, too.

First, a study of a functional legal unit primarily through analysis of the contents of reinforcive legal rules prescribing facets of the unit is a study of those facets *by indirection* without frontal focus on the overall form, on constituent formal features and their inter-relations, and on the material or other components of the unit complementary to its form and formal features. The contents of such reinforcive rules never explicitly identify the overall form as such and differentiate it from the material or other components of the unit. Hence, these rules fail to focus specifically on how overall form and its constituent features define, specify, and organize such attributes of the unit as its makeup, unity, mode of operation, and instrumental capacity. For example, it is typical that the contents of reinforcive rules pertaining to a court do not explicitly spell out in terms of form the overall tripartite structural feature of a court, or spell out the inter-relations between the parts of this structure. It is true that some if not most of this formal framework can be inferred from the contents of several reinforcive legal rules taken together. Yet study of these contents alone cannot be adequate to give overall form its due either as an avenue of understanding or as an object of credit for purposes served.

It is also true that the contents of reinforcive rules prescribing facets of a court may prescribe the qualifications of judges, the mode of selecting judges, the location of the courthouse, types of nonjudicial personnel, such as bailiffs and court reporters, court procedures, courtroom equipment, dates of court terms, and much more. But in order to capitalize on the study of form as the major avenue for advancement of understanding that it is, and in order for form itself to be the important object of credit for realization of ends that it is, the forms and formal features of functional legal units must be *explicitly* identified as such, duly differentiated, and then subjected to frontal analysis. This means there must be frontal focus on overall form and its constituent features such as, for example, the structural and procedural features of a court, and also on any forms of components within a functional unit such as, for example, the form of a duly designed courthouse. An explicit general theory of what counts as overall form, with its constituent features, is required for this. A form-oriented analysis provides such a theory, whereas a mere analysis of the contents of reinforcive rules does not.

It must be conceded that the contents of those reinforcive legal rules figuring in a rule-oriented analysis do prescribe some features of functional legal units that, according to a theory of legal form, can *also* be explicitly classified as formal. Such rules do prescribe, although not in these terms, the formal tripartite structure of a court, for example. Also, rules in effect prescribe formal procedure. Insofar as the contents of such reinforcive rules do prescribe features independently classifiable as formal, the contents of these rules do afford at least the beginnings of a basis for constructing the overall form of a functional legal unit, for identifying the features of this form, and for identifying any features of component parts of the unit that are formal. To so classify and then construct the overall form of the unit, however, not only also requires a theory of what counts as formal in the first place, but much more, as we will now see.

The contents of reinforcive rules that do, in effect, prescribe facets of a functional legal unit independently classifiable as formal not only fail explicitly to so classify these facets. These contents also usually fail to go far enough to provide a sufficient basis for constructing and describing the overall form, constituent features thereof, and any forms of complementary material or other components within the unit as a whole. The contents of actual reinforcive rules seldom, even taken together, provide a sufficient basis for providing a holistic account of the overall form of the functional legal unit at hand. Yet the overall form, its constituents, and complementary components must be put together and understood as a whole. Mere study of the contents of reinforcive rules either individually or together, cannot, as can form-oriented analysis, lay bare and elucidate the *makeup, unitary* nature, and complex *inter-relatedness* of formal features of the unit as a whole, and thus cannot adequately advance understanding here. For example, the contents of reinforcive rules that in effect prescribe facets of a court's tripartite structure merely so prescribe. These contents do not go into how this formal structure also coheres with a formal procedure that is dialogic as between the two parties, with a judge duly presiding neutrally between these parties.[27] To grasp such "fit" and thereby advance understanding of these vital attributes of make-up, unity, and instrumental capacity, a more comprehensive form-oriented mode of analysis is required. Such analysis must begin with a faithful account of the accepted holistic conception of such a unit as a whole.

As will be demonstrated at length in Chapter Four, a systematic account oriented to the overall form of a functional legal unit and its constituent formal features not only reveals *how related parts of the whole fit together*, but also enables us to see in holistic terms that the *whole is more than the sum of its parts*. To return

---

[27] See further *supra* p. 56.

Section Four: A Form-Oriented Approach as Primary

to my example, in regard to an institution such as a court, the relevant reinforcive rules themselves are usually silent about the relational "fit" between a given formal feature of structure and a separate formal feature of procedure in the same institution. Thus, for example, a rule securing judicial independence and impartiality vis-a-vis the parties may preclude a party from separately contacting the judge – a formal feature of internal structure. Quite a different rule may require that a party always have a chance to respond to the other – a feature of dialogic procedural form. A holistic form-oriented account would focus on the important "relational" fit here: these two rules are closely related precisely in the respect that each in its own way serves the purposes of securing a duly informed and impartial judge in circumstances in which the parties both have fair access to the judge and fair opportunity to respond to what each presents to the judge in front of the other.

Similarly, the contents of reinforcive rules may themselves be silent, for example, on how form affirmatively specifies, organizes, or otherwise affects material or other components of the unit in some further important way. For example, formal features of external structure providing for the independence of judges from political branches of government, and also from the litigating parties, are designed partly to influence and inspire the very personnel who occupy the judicial role to rise to this role and adopt a more objective and impartial frame of mind overall than they otherwise might – a major effect or imprint of formal structure on the component of judicial personnel. Yet, the contents of reinforcive rules with respect to judicial independence are seldom explicit about inspiring judicial objectivity and impartiality overall as a central attribute of *mode of operation* of the functional legal unit of a court. Indeed, many rules of relevance here merely appear to proscribe various types of impermissible influences. A form-oriented analysis focuses frontally on these structural features and their purposive rationales, and thus promises a deeper and more comprehensive understanding of the functional legal unit of a court.

At the same time, study merely of the contents of a reinforcive legal rule, either individually or together with other rules, cannot reveal the general nature of the credit due to well-designed form for purposes served partly through the functional legal unit under study. The attribution of credit to form requires independent and frontal form-oriented analysis that identifies what is formal in the unit, and treats the *relations* between this form (or forms) and any resulting realization of purposes. For example, as we saw in the preceding section of this chapter, study merely of the contents of a rule requiring manufacturers of foodstuffs to disclose ingredients on boxes cannot, by itself, reveal the effects of any particular *formal* features of the rule on its addressees by way of contributing to their grasp of the rule itself so they can apply it. At the very least, what is formal in the content of the rule must be explicitly identified and differentiated from other content before any effects can be attributed to *form*. Although formal features are manifest in the material or other complementary content of a rule, and leave imprints on that content, frontal form-oriented analysis of such features of a rule as prescriptiveness, generality, definiteness, and mode of expression, as so manifest, is required. Only after such formal features are identified is it even possible to consider how these features contribute, or might contribute, to the realization of the ends at stake. For example, in appropriate circumstances, credit can be seen to be attributable to due definiteness in a highway speed limit rule: "Drive no faster than 70 mph." To classify the feature of definiteness as formal requires a theory of form. An analysis oriented merely to the general undifferentiated contents of reinforcive rules simply does not go far enough as to any functional unit.

Second, as Hart deployed his rule-oriented approach, he did not sufficiently isolate and separate the paradigm of the functional legal unit in the foreground under study, for example, the institution of a court, from any reinforcive rules in the background that, as he once put it, "lie behind" the operation of a court.[28] Such a unit is not the same as, and remains plainly distinct from, any reinforcive rules that purport to prescribe some or all of the facets of the unit. The functional unit in the foreground – its overall form, constituent features thereof, and complementary material or other components – should be the primary focus of analysis with the contents of reinforcive rules in some statutory rule or book of rules addressed to this unit merely secondary and supplemental. We can have access to the realities of a unit such as a court through, among other things, accepted general concepts, their manifestations in practices, and the expressed critical attitudes of personnel, as well as through the contents of reinforcive rules. This independent access, along with study of the contents of reinforcive rules, enables us to deploy form-oriented analysis to represent the relevant contours of the reality of a court or other functional unit.

An existing instance of a paradigmatic version of a functional legal unit such as an operational legislature or court, is thus susceptible to a frontal analysis and description in terms of its attributes of makeup, unity, mode of operation, instrumental capacity, and distinct identity. The actual operational form of such a unit – its purposive systematic arrangement – is the primary avenue of understanding here. Such a unit, in operation, is not, itself, the same as a set of reinforcive rules. That is, the operational form of a unit, such as that of a legislature or a court, is not the same as, and is not reducible to, the particular contents of a set of rules prescribing composition, powers, and procedures, however faithful to the contents of such rules the operations of the unit may be. Moreover, the operational material or other components of any institutional unit, such as physical facilities or personnel, are plainly not the same as, and not reducible to the contents of any rules dealing with these components. The reality of an ongoing institution,

---

[28] H. L. A. Hart, *supra* n. 11, 29.

Section Four: A Form-Oriented Approach as Primary

or of any other functional legal unit, cannot be reduced to the contents of a set of reinforcive rules. Indeed, the actual overall form of an operational unit is not reducible to and is simply not equivalent to the contents even of any reinforcive rules that, in effect, happen to prescribe all of the features of the overall form of that unit.

Third, the contents of a set of purportedly reinforcive rules could even misconceive the intended functional legal unit and its overall form in some major respect. A court, for example, is plainly not merely whatever is prescribed in rules that on the surface may recite that a court is being set up. To establish this, it is enough to hypothesize an extreme case in which the imagined contents of purportedly reinforcive rules plainly misconceive features of the overall form of a court. Suppose that a book labeled "Court Procedure" has in it only rules on "introduction of bills," "procedure for debate of bills," "amendment of bills," and the like. It would be plain that the drafter of these rules had a fundamentally erroneous conception of the overall form of a court! I inject this possibility not because it has occurred, or because it is at all likely, but simply to underscore the logic of the matter. That is, to know in the first place that the contents of a set of reinforcive rules prescribe facets of what a court truly is, we must first have a prior understanding of the overall form of a court. Form-oriented analysis is required to provide this. Form is the primary key to the very identity of a functional legal unit. Plainly, the form of a court – its purposive systematic arrangement – is simply not equivalent to whatever may be prescribed in any book of rules reciting that it is about "courts."

In one major respect, Hart erred in suggesting that the contents of legal rules "define the concept" of an institution such as a court in the first place.[29] Before any reinforcive rule or rules can even be drafted to prescribe facets of what is to be a court, the overall form of a court, the constituent features of this form, and the material and other components of a court, must first be defined, specified, and delineated. This may be done on the basis of generally accepted concepts and purposes, general historical experience with the type of institution at hand including knowledge of customary practice, and a constructivist analysis of what such an institution necessarily requires by way of overall form, constituent features thereof, and material and other components in order to fulfill its projected purposes. The same is true not merely of the form of a legal institution. It is true as well of the forms of all other types of functional legal units.

---

[29] H. L. A. Hart, *supra* n. 11, at 97. He had good company. Wittgenstein seems to have assumed that rules, more fundamentally than forms, put the concept of an institution "in order". Yet it is just the reverse. We cannot even know how to draft the content of the rules until we have determined what the form of the functional legal unit is to be, and it is this form that "puts things in order" in the first place. Rules can then come in to provide "normative cement" for this "order." The passage in which this error appears is in *The Wittgenstein Reader*, 268 (A. Kenny ed., Blackwells, Oxford, 1994); see also A. Kenny, *The Legacy of Wittgenstein*, 42 (Basil Blackwell, Oxford, 1984).

Thus, if there be no pre-existing "blueprint" or any models from elsewhere, those who would create a functional legal unit must first think out, or learn of, the purposes to be served, and think out, or learn how the unit should be systematically arranged, i.e., think out, or learn the overall form it should take to serve those purposes. This will call for important choices of form. For example, a projected structural feature of a legislature, such as whether it is to be unicameral or bicameral, would plainly have to be settled upon prior to drafting rules with content prescribing this feature.

Any Hartian account of an institution or other functional legal unit in terms of the contents of reinforcive rules that purports, in effect, to prescribe the overall form of the unit, presupposes a drafter of those very rules who had access to a *prior* and *apposite conceptualization* and description *of the relevant form* in the first place. It must be possible to conceptualize and describe overall form and its constituents independently of any rules that purport to prescribe these. Indeed, we can for example, conceptualize and describe facets of the procedural feature of the overall form of a court such as taking evidence, hearing argument, weighing and balancing evidence or argument, and so on, without resort to the contents of any rules prescribing these features, even when these features are to be regular and consistent, from case to case. It is not even true that such descriptions, to be informative and accurate, must somehow "implicitly" invoke the contents of actual or projected reinforcive rules. Again, this is not to say rules are superfluous. Also, something rule-like may even be said to enter the description of the form and complementary components of a functional unit, because the unit must have regularity of operation and continuity of existence. Rules add normative cement, as well.

Thus, one must at least know what the relevant overall form and its constituent features are to be *before* one can even begin to draft the contents of any reinforcive rules that prescribe these. Indeed, one must know far more to draft such rules well. One must also know of any material or other complementary components of the whole, how form is to shape these, and how overall form is to shape, organize, and leave imprints or other effects upon constituent features of form and on components of the whole, how such components are to be integrated in the whole, what any interplay between formal and other facets of the unit are to be, what the role of the unit is to be as combined and integrated within an overall operational technique, and how all of this would bear on the realization of the relevant ends and values. When we arrive at the stage of drafting the relevant rules, those responsible for this drafting must have already informed themselves and either have thought all this through or have learned it from existing models or other sources.

Fourth, in a Hartian rule-oriented analysis, there is little or no frontal focus on the purposive means-end *rationales* for the contents of reinforcive rules. This

Section Four: A Form-Oriented Approach as Primary

is not surprising given that the usual contents of such legal rules seldom themselves incorporate any such rationales explicitly. Yet the duly designed overall form of a functional legal unit, institutional or other, is a *purposive* systematic arrangement of the whole unit. Form is designed and organized for a purpose or purposes. It follows that a form-oriented analysis must also frontally address the relevant purposes, that is, the rationales.[30] The conception of form embedded in a form-oriented analysis is therefore more holistic in this respect, too, than is a rule-oriented analysis. That is, it explicitly encompasses the rationales – means-end relations including purposes and corresponding values – that make the overall form appropriate for such a well-designed unit as a whole. This also invites illuminating comparison of the differing rationales for the different overall forms of different functional units. As we will see, a full-fledged form-oriented analysis thus promises a fuller understanding *of the unit in question* than a rule-oriented analysis, given that reinforcive rules usually do not express any rationales at all. Indeed, a grasp of the purposive rationales of overall form advances understanding of all major attributes of the unit: makeup, unity, mode of operation, instrumental capacity, and distinct identity.

A form-oriented analysis with its holistic emphasis on the rationales intrinsic to overall form also promises to advance understanding of the very contents of the *reinforcive rules* themselves and in this respect also goes beyond what a merely rule-oriented account typically provides. For example, consider the rule in many Anglo-American systems that requires the judge to abstain from investigating possible evidence to be presented at trial, and instead requires the opposing parties to do all this. What is the rationale for such a rule? An approach focused merely on the contents of rules themselves devoid of any stated rationales cannot sufficiently advance understanding of this. Yet, a form-oriented analysis can, given that it also embraces the purposive rationale for these structural and procedural features of form. This tripartite division of labor is an internal structural feature of form in which only the parties and not the judge are to investigate possible evidence. One rationale for this is that, were the judge to do these things, the judge might pre-judge the case by coming to identify with one of the parties prior to the trial based on evidence the judge uncovered while preparing. To avoid this, the parties are usually called upon to do all pre-trial investigation on their own, with the judge being kept ignorant of the results of this until the parties present evidence later at the public trial.

Again, this purposive rationale cannot be gleaned from the contents of the usual reinforcive rules here, whereas a full-fledged form-oriented analysis requires inquiry into this. Form-oriented analysis facilitates the drafting of reinforcive

---

[30] Of course, a rule-oriented analysis could be expanded beyond ordinary rule content to include rationales, although Hart and Kelsen seldom did so.

rules in the first place. The drafter studies possible means-end relations between purposive forms, possible actions, and ends to be realized, and prescribes action in the rule accordingly. Although rules are typically drafted without explicitly incorporating means-end rationales, a drafter can hardly draft well if unaware of these possible purposive rationales and how they mediate between form, action, and value. Moreover, addressees who understand the rationale for a rule are likely to be more disposed to take what Hart calls an internal point of view toward it and view it as a binding standard.

Fifth, readers of the words and phrases appearing in the contents of actual reinforcive rules prescribing features of institutions and other functional legal units frequently cannot satisfactorily understand some of these very words and phrases without prior understanding of the form and features of form to which these words and phrases merely refer. Such specific words and phrases, even in well-drafted rules, often cry out for further clarification by reference to the very forms of the organized legal units to which these words and phrases merely allude. A robust and explicit form-oriented analysis can satisfactorily provide this clarification. For example, and as I explain in Chapter Eight, prescribed modes of interpretive argument comprise one formal feature (along with complementary content), of the overall form of a major functional legal unit, namely, an interpretive methodology for statutes. Assume that one reinforcive methodological rule prescribes very generally: "Courts shall interpret ordinary (nontechnical) words in statutes in accord with the standard ordinary meanings of the words used, unless the context otherwise clearly requires." Extensive further study, including form-oriented analysis of this simple sounding yet complex mode of interpretive argument, is required here if its true makeup is to be satisfactorily understood.[31] Merely to consider one of several complex aspects of this mode of argument, what is meant by "context?" The general context of enactment? The linguistic context? The general circumstantial context of the envisioned addressees of the statute? And why?

These various possible elaborations of merely one facet of one key formal feature (with complementary content) of an interpretive methodology could be quite different in their implications for resolution of interpretive issues. The typically succinct terminology of a reinforcive rule merely authorizing appeal to ordinary meaning in light of context, cannot *itself* advance understanding in the foregoing important respect of what "context" means in the makeup of such argumentation. A frontal and in depth form-oriented analysis elaborating on the methodologically relevant type of context and its rationale is required, and this would take us well beyond the words in the rule (as Chapter Eight makes clear).

---

[31] R. Summers and G. Marshall, "The Argument From Ordinary Meaning in Statutory Interpretation," 43 *N. Ireland L.Q.* 213 (1992).

Section Four: A Form-Oriented Approach as Primary

The terms of many other reinforcive rules that purport to prescribe a feature of the form of a functional legal unit are, standing alone, just as fragmentary and uninformative as the one in the above example. Consider, as another example, a set of rules that, in one way or another, addresses one facet of the procedural feature of the overall form of an institution – its mode of operation. The terms of many such rules, even very important ones, can often be adequately understood only by a person who brings to the rules a *prior* understanding of the overall form and constituent formal features, including relevant rationales, for the procedural set up to which the rules are addressed. The terms of individual rules of, for example, court procedures that prescribe pleading and pre-trial discovery in a particular system cannot be satisfactorily understood without regard to the overall form of the procedural set up that these individual rules contemplate. Once it is understood, for example, that a given system is so organized that disputants are to define issues of fact mainly through a pre-trial conference after pre-trial discovery rather than through the exchange of detailed pleadings, these pleadings take on much less importance, even though explicitly provided for in reinforcive rules, and even though the exchange of pleadings, from the contents of those rules, may even seem to occur earlier in the overall procedural process than a pre-trial conference, and from this alone would appear to have primacy. Indeed, here the reinforcive rules alone might even be quite misleading.

Sixth, a primary aim of form-oriented analysis is to lay bare, do justice to, and advance understanding of, the internal complexities of the highly variegated overall forms of discrete functional units. This is an especially important aim with regard to the internalities of complex attributes of makeup, unity, mode of operation, and instrumental capacity of institutions. A rule-oriented analysis is not frontally addressed to the elucidation of these complexities. Hart, in practicing rule-oriented analysis, neglected these complexities in the first edition of his book. Later, he admitted this neglect in the Postscript to the second edition (in relation to courts).[32] At the least, what is needed is a recognition of the purposes and organizational norms that shape the overall forms of institutions, their constituent features, and their complementary material and other components. I provide an illustrative account in Chapter Four.

Seventh, on a rule-oriented approach, there is often a temptation to conceive of a functional legal unit as static rather than dynamic. A form-oriented approach, however, conceives of such a unit as combined, integrated, and coordinated with other units within an operational technique for the conduct of law-making and law-implementing *activities*. An operational technique, such as the penal or the grievance-remedial, is not static but dynamic.[33]

---

[32] H. L. A. Hart, *supra* n. 11, at 259.
[33] See, on these and other techniques, *infra* pp. 326–332.

Eighth, a form-oriented rather than a rule-oriented approach should have primacy for a related reason. On a form-oriented approach, one can better advance understanding of another major attribute of such a unit, namely, its functional inter-relations with other units. For example, both a legislature, and a proposed statutory rule in process of creation for projected use, figure in the activity of legislative law-making. So, too, does a methodology of legislative drafting. Also, statutes cannot be well-drafted without regard to the accepted general methodology of interpretation. A form-oriented approach is oriented to the dynamic, integrative, and systematized nature of law-making and law-implementing activities that always involve diverse functional units. Thus, a form-oriented approach is in this major respect also more holistic than a rule-oriented approach.

Finally, a rule-oriented approach, at least in the hands of some scholars and others tends to be merely descriptive of the contents of reinforcive rules. A form-oriented approach is not merely descriptive of form in functional units, but also encompasses evaluative analysis of the design of overall form and its constituent features. Such analysis is highly relevant to any effort to give form due credit for ends served. Addressed as it is to the purposive systematic arrangements of units combined and integrated within operational techniques for the creation and implementation of law, a form-oriented approach conceives such units and their forms as designed to serve ends, and thus subject to evaluation for means-end efficacy. Form-oriented analysis must be evaluative as well as descriptive. Also, insofar as descriptive, it is not narrowly so in the way many rule-oriented analyses in the positivist tradition have tended to be.

It must be conceded that a particular legal system *could* include many reinforcive rules the contents of which (1) explicitly so identify and prescribe the overall forms of virtually all functional units and all the constituent features of these forms, (2) explicitly delineate the relations between constituent formal features, and between those features and complementary material or other components of all units, (3) set forth the purposive rationales for these forms, features, and components, and (4) include specifications of the combination and integration of different units into operational wholes. To my knowledge no legal system in developed Western societies has ever had very many such reinforcive rules.

In sum, a form-oriented approach is required as the primary approach to advancing understanding of functional legal units and to attributing due credit to their forms for ends realized. This approach should also be supplemented by rule-oriented analysis insofar as relevant, both as a source of information, and in accounting for the normative cement of functional legal units. In Chapters Four through Nine, I will demonstrate the foregoing in detail as we study the forms of a selection of paradigms of major functional legal units in developed Western systems. In Chapter Ten, I extrapolate and apply form-oriented analysis to the legal system as a whole.

PART TWO ～

The Forms of Functional
Legal Units

4 ∼ FORMS OF INSTITUTIONS – LEGISLATIVE

"[T]here must be some sort of organization for making the laws. It cannot just be left to a large public meeting."
— K. C. Wheare[1]

SECTION ONE: INTRODUCTION

In this and in the next five chapters, we will systematically concentrate on a selection of paradigms of functional legal units in developed Western legal systems. One general type of unit is institutional, and includes: legislatures, courts, administrative agencies, other entities such as state corporations, and special bodies that administer sanctions, and deploy other enforcive devices.[2] To demonstrate how it is possible to advance understanding of legal institutions through the study of their overall forms and the imprints and other effects of these forms and to reveal the types of credit that may be due such forms when well-designed, we will illustratively analyze the overall form of a single major variety of institution – that of the centralized legislature with substantial nationwide jurisdiction. Although the analysis that follows is addressed generally to an abstract paradigm of centralized legislatures in developed Western systems and although there are variations in how these legislatures converge on this paradigm, the analysis here can be readily applied, by extrapolation, to particular legislative institutions in these systems.[3]

---

[1] K. C. Wheare, *Legislatures*, 167 (Oxford University Press, London, 1963). I am indebted to the late Dr. Geoffrey Marshall for assistance here.

[2] Of course, there are also important "private" frameworks for creating and implementing private contracts. See *infra* Chapter Seven.

[3] See, e.g., P. Norton ed., *Legislatures* (Oxford University Press, Oxford, 1990). Norton observes that "material on legislatures as a particular genus of institution is sparse" and that "[o]nly infrequently have writings appeared which have affected perceptions of and added significantly to our understanding of legislatures, as opposed to a particular legislature...." *Id.*, at 2–3. One of the major exceptions is K. C. Wheare, *Legislatures* (Oxford University Press, Oxford, 1963). Both Norton and Wheare treat the British parliament, among others. On the French Parliament, see A. Stevens, *Government and Politics in France* (3rd ed., Palgrave MacMillan, New York, 2003). See also J. Bell, French Constitutional Law (Clarendon Press, Oxford, 1992). On the German federal parliament, see U. Thaysen, R. Davidson and R. Livingston, eds. *The U.S. Congress and the German Bundestag* (Westview Press, Inc., Oxford, 1990),

The analysis can also be readily applied, *mutatis mutandis* to courts, administrative agencies, and still other institutions. Much of what may already be familiar will be presented anew here in the idiom of form and formal.

The key questions to be addressed are: (1) What basic purposes determine how centralized legislative institutions are defined and organized, i.e., formed, in developed Western societies? (2) What may be viewed as the paradigmatic overall form – the purposive systematic arrangement – of centralized legislative institutions in developed Western societies? (3) What are the constituent features of this overall form and how are they inter-related? (4) What are the complementary material and other components of legislatures such as physical facilities, personnel, and the like, and how does form affect these? (5) How can study of overall legislative form advance understanding of the attributes of legislative makeup, unity, mode of operation, instrumental capacity, and integration and coordination with other functional legal units? (6) What general share of credit can be due well-designed legislative form and its constituent features for realization of ends? All credit ought not to go to material or other components of the institution such as facilities and personnel. Nor should all credit go to reinforcive rules. Well-designed form is essential, and the quality of its design can make major differences to the efficacy of the functional unit. Also, focus on form can lead to the articulation of standards for criticism and for improvement of existing forms and the units involved.

Given the founding purpose to create a legislature, reason dictates that a society adopt the relevant overall form, constituent features, and complementary material and other components. Here I treat a paradigm of the modern centralized legislature in developed Western societies from two perspectives. First, I seek to advance understanding of such a legislature viewed from the outside as a body taking a duly designed overall form in order to serve the characteristic purposes of such a body as a special functional unit within a legal system. So viewed from the outside, given its overall form – its purposive systematic arrangement – the legislature can be described and understood as a determinate and intelligible body with distinct functions and identity.

The second perspective adopted here is more internal. I also address the overall form, constituent formal features, and complementary material and other components (such as physical facilities and personnel) of modern centralized legislatures from the inside, with emphasis on the purposive and dense "inner order" of such a legislature, as Jhering might have put it. This inner order consists mainly of the makeup of constituent formal features, their complementary material and other components, and the formal features and components as duly unified within a coherent whole.

and Klaus von Behme, *The Legislator: German Parliament as a Centre of Political Decision-Making* (Ashgate, Aldershot U.K., 1998). An early comparative study of considerable interest is C. Ilbert, *Legislative Methods and Forms* (Clarendon Press, Oxford, 1901).

Section One: Introduction   93

From the foregoing perspectives, one can also see that there is more to the overall form of such a functional legal unit beyond its constituent formal features. As I will explain, this more consists of (a) the inter-relations between such features and (b) an all-embracing conception of the form of the unit as a whole, including these features and their inter-relations.

Given the vast academic literature on legislatures in political and in legal studies, and also in comparative institutional research, one may well ask whether anything is left here for an analyst concentrating on overall legislative form to add, especially if no new empirical findings about legislatures are to be presented? Much is left. First, the academic literature in systems with which I am familiar consists mainly of studies of particular legislatures, and these do not frontally and systematically address duly designed overall legislative form and its constituent features, the defining and organizing purposes of this form, the complementary material and other components, such as physical facilities and personnel, and the imprints and other effects of formal features on each other and on such components.[4] The form-oriented analysis I apply here not only differs from and goes beyond the rule-oriented approaches of legal theorists, such as Hart and Kelsen,[5] but also generally differs from behaviorist, empiricist, and other social-scientific approaches.

Form-oriented analysis identifies, characterizes, and underscores the purposes that define and organize, i.e., form, the legislative institution, sharpens awareness of duly designed legislative form and its constituent features, reveals much as formal that is often not so recognized, lays bare the complexities of form, and treats the relations between formal features and between form and complementary components. Form-oriented analysis addresses the imprints and effects of formal features on each other and on complementary components. Such analysis also treats what might be called the "inner logic" of the original construction of such a legislative functional unit from the ground up. In the end, form-oriented analysis can advance understanding of the makeup, unity, mode of operation, instrumental capacity, and other leading attributes of such an institution. Much empirical and other academic literature takes overall legislative form and its constituent features for granted and does not focus frontally upon the purposes, concepts, and terminology of form as applied to legislatures.

Second, I seek to identify the general nature of the types of credit due to well-designed legislative form for the realization of purposes. In so doing, I apply a methodology quite different from the empiricist methodology that many social

---

[4] See generally, Norton, *Legislatures, supra* n. 3, and the literature there cited. On the parliamentary model, see also T. Koopmans, *Courts and Political Institutions – A Comparative View* esp. Chapters 2 and 3 (Cambridge University Press, Cambridge, 2003). I do not treat the vast literature that generally disparages the functioning of legislatures. For a review of this literature, see J. Waldron, *Law and Disagreement*, Chapter 4 (Oxford University Press, Oxford, 1999).

[5] H. L. A. Hart, *The Concept of Law* (2nd ed., Clarendon Press, Oxford, 1994); H. Kelsen, *General Theory of Law and State* (A. Wedberg trans., Harvard University Press, Cambridge, 1945).

scientists so fruitfully use in their own ways. The form-oriented approach adopted here requires reasoned analysis of how the overall form of a functional unit, when well-designed in light of relevant purposes, can contribute, along with complementary material and other components of the unit, to the realization of these purposes. On this approach, legal theorists and other scholars can attribute a major share of credit in general terms to the overall form and formal features of a functional unit for purposes served without engaging in empirical or social science research. This is so at least insofar as the credit claimed on behalf of form is confined to:

(1) claims the truth of which is not contingent on findings of fact, examples of which (among many) are that:
  (a) "without duly designed form, there could be no legislature, and thus no purposes served through statutes"
  (b) "duly designed form is necessarily required to add major purposes to the socio-legal menu, such as democratic representation in a legislature, which itself must be duly constituted through electoral and other features of form,"
  (c) "formal provisions for notice of the introduction of a bill, and for its careful consideration in committee and on the floor, are valuable,"
  (d) "form can serve and symbolize important values as, for example, in a well-designed formal procedure that fairly allows affected interests to be heard,"
  (e) "the law-making fecundity of a legislature necessarily requires a formal decision rule that is determinate, for example, adoption by majority vote,"
(2) claims the truth of which are contingent on findings of fact, yet are still not controversial even without empirical research, given general knowledge and experience, examples of which (among many) are that:
  (a) "well-designed form in formal procedures tends to beget good content in laws adopted,"
  (b) "a well-designed formal feature of definiteness in a statutory rule facilitates self-direction on the part of addressees of the rule, for it contributes to the determinateness of the rule as a source of reasons for addressees to act thereunder,"
(3) claims the truth of which are contingent on factual findings for which sufficient supporting evidence already exists,
(4) claims the truth of which are contingent on findings of fact that are not controversial given appropriate qualifications, for example, "referral of a proposed bill to a well-designed legislative committee for study (procedural form) is likely to lead to improvements in the bill, provided the subject

Section One: Introduction 95

> matter of the bill is important and the committee agenda is not already overcrowded with matters of higher priority."

The general theory of legal form, as conceived here, does not consist essentially of answers to questions about particular institutions in any particular society,[6] nor does it require concrete comparisons of such institutions with their counterparts in other societies. Rather, I address in general and abstract terms the necessary and salient features of the overall form of a paradigm of the centralized legislative institution found in developed Western societies.[7]

Beyond what a study of such form might add to existing literature of interest to scholars in other fields, it is possible also to add here to legal scholarship and especially to legal theory. Institutions comprise one major type of functional unit in a legal system. Legal theorists have largely neglected institutional forms (except those for courts). Even H. L. A. Hart,[8] the leading legal theorist in the modern analytic tradition, seldom focused frontally on institutions, and when he did, he generally adopted a rule-oriented approach and tended to reduce institutions to the contents of reinforcive rules – rules that purport to prescribe facets of institutions.

On a Hartian rule-oriented approach, a legislature is to be understood largely through study of the particular contents of reinforcive legal rules – rules that include, without explicit differentiation, form-prescriptive contents and other contents that specify material and other components of the legislature. On my form-oriented analysis, such rules are important, but not primary. Hart himself, as a rule-oriented theorist acknowledged that so called reinforcive rules merely "lie behind" such an institution.[9] Yet the more important question is what lies in the forefront, and the answer is form duly designed to serve relevant purposes. Those who would create a legal institution such as a legislature could not even know what overall form and features thereof to prescribe in the contents of reinforcive rules without first conceiving and agreeing upon the founding and other purposes that determine the overall form of the institution, its constituent features, and its complementary and other components. A legal institution such as a legislature cannot be defined and organized, i.e., formed, in a purposeless or value-free vacuum.

---

[6] Cf. Norton, *Legislatures, supra* n. 3.

[7] What I offer here, therefore, does not consist of sociological inquiries of an empirical nature into particular legislative institutions in particular systems. Of course, such inquiries would be quite unmanageable in the confines of a single book. They are also quite unnecessary given my main aims: (1) the provision of an account of what is formal about a paradigm of such a functional legal unit, (2) the advancement of general understanding of such units through study of form, and (3) the general attribution of credit to well-designed form for purposes served. See also Waldron, *supra* n. 4.

[8] See H. L. A. Hart, *supra* n. 5.

[9] H. L. A. Hart, *supra* n. 5, at 29.

A legislative institution consists of (1) its founding and other purposes, (2) its overall form as duly designed to serve these purposes, (3) the constituent features of this overall form and their inter-relations, (4) complementary material and other components such as facilities and personnel, (5) the inter-relations between all of the foregoing, and (6) such resulting attributes as makeup, unity, mode of operation, and instrumental capacity. Legislative form may be manifest in a variety of ways: in institutional "blueprints," in activities of institutional participants as duly organized, in accepted standards for evaluating such activities, in the contents of reinforcive rules and other law, and in still other ways. It is true that a determinate and stable institution could not exist without some rules prescribing some of its features and thus providing essential normative cement.[10]

Some legal scholars and theorists, including the early Karl Llewellyn and other American legal realists of the twentieth century, certain American neo-realists of today, and still others of a behavioralist bent (who focus mainly on judicial institutions), have concentrated not on the overall forms of institutional units, and not even on the contents of reinforcive rules, but mainly on the component of institutional personnel and their activities. As the early Llewellyn once put it, mainly with regard to courts, "What officials do about disputes is, to my mind, the law itself."[11] Such an approach reduces overall form simply to the behavior of officials, and more or less takes for granted what an official is, what empowers officials to act, how they are to proceed, the very nature of their activities, and the purposes to be served. Yet an official is a person whose job it is to act out an institutional role. This role cannot be adequately explicated without a form-oriented analysis revealing how the role is conceived, defined, and organized to serve purposes. (Behavioralist reductionism even obliterates the distinction between a correct and a mistaken application of a law.)

Although this chapter plows some familiar ground, the aim is to turn up the sod of form and reveal its distinctive fertility. We will see how a paradigm of the centralized legislature in developed Western systems is not merely a "creature" of reinforcive rules, and that it certainly cannot be reduced to behavior patterns of legislators.[12] Rather, it takes a complex overall form with various constituent formal features. When duly designed, these features leave deep and indelible imprints and other effects not only on the organization of the institution but also on complementary material and other components of the institution. Some components, such as legislative buildings and other facilities, may take their own special forms as well.

---

[10] Again, I am indebted to Peter Hacker for the concept of "normative cement."

[11] K. Llewellyn, *The Bramble Bush*, 8 (Oceana Publications, New York, 1960). For extended discussion, see R. Summers, *Instrumentalism and American Legal Theory*, Chapter 9 (Cornell University Press, Ithaca, 1982).

[12] H. L. A. Hart, *supra* n. 5, at 5, 31.

SECTION TWO: OVERALL LEGISLATIVE FORM AND ITS CONSTITUENT FEATURES

Here, I report no new facts about legislatures. Rather, my approach is to call attention to and describe familiar general facts about a legislative paradigm, and then present these facts in light of form-oriented analysis. The centralized legislature in developed Western societies is a body that is usually designed to serve several major purposes, including democratic representation and operation, adoption of legislation, provision of a forum for public debate of major issues of the day, oversight of administration, participation in foreign policy, and treatment of budgetary matters. In the English system and others modeled on it, the legislature also selects and holds directly accountable the government of the day – the executive.

A centralized multi-member legislative body is an essential institution of government in these societies. As a socially constructed entity, it consists of far more than its material components of facilities, personnel, and the like. To have its makeup and unity, determinateness, a recognizable identity of its own, and the instrumental capacity required effectively to carry out institutional activities in its name, this entity must take a stable overall form that duly defines and organizes its existence and operations to serve its general purposes. In developed Western societies in which such a legislature has long been in place, most of its overall form and constituent features tend to be taken for granted and generally tend not to be objects of explicit focus.

The legislative institution thus takes the overall form of a duly composed official body with system-wide jurisdiction not only to make binding written law democratically, but to serve other important purposes as well, all in accord with recognized structures and procedures. Its overall form and the constituent features of this form are to be differentiated from its subordinate organizational details. Such details are extensive and vary greatly from system to system. In developed Western societies, the main constituent features of the overall form of the paradigm of a centralized legislative body are much less variable. These features are familiar and may be described in general terms as consisting of:

- an appropriately organized compositional feature – provision for determination of the membership of the body, including democratic representation
- an appropriately organized jurisdictional feature – powers duly conferred on the body to make general written law and to conduct other activities on behalf of members of the society
- an appropriately organized structural feature – internal organization of the membership into committees and into a committee of the whole or the like enabling it to transact legislative business as a body, along with specified external organization defining the relation of the legislature to other governmental institutions

- an appropriately organized procedural feature – procedures for formulating, considering, and democratically adopting general written law, and for the conduct of other activities in exercise of its jurisdiction
- an appropriately organized preceptual feature – precepts, that is, reinforcive rules and principles prescribing at least some of the foregoing features of institutional form

As we will see, each of the foregoing features leaves major imprints on, and has still other effects on other formal features, on complementary material and other components such as personnel and physical facilities, and on the whole of the institution. Such an institutional makeup – organized features and their complementary components – are inter-related in various ways. This makeup forms a coherent whole having its own inner order and unity. Without any one of the foregoing features, as duly designed, a legislature would be significantly dysfunctional. Without a grasp of the relevant overall form, its constituent features, any component forms, material and other components, and the effects of the foregoing on each other, it simply would not be possible adequately to understand a legislative institution.

The very existence of legislatures in complex centralized form in developed Western societies is itself a standing tribute to human capacity for purposive organizational rationality – for reasoned construction of institutional arrangements to serve purposes. A body of this nature is usually constructed over time, or all at once, in accord with purposive reasons of two basic kinds. First, it is constructed in accord with purposive reasons that justify choices of those features that duly define and organize such a body. For example, the democratic compositional feature requires provision for elections and the rational and efficient dispatch of legislative business calls for and justifies adoption of the structural feature of a committee system, as well as a well-designed procedural feature. Second, such a body is usually also constructed partly in accord with any relevant *legal* reasons such as those that arise from antecedent constitutional requirements. For example, the U.S. Constitution requires that the American federal legislature have a specified membership.

Overall legislative form with its determining purposes, its constituent features, and its complementary material and other components, together comprises an integrated whole. As we have seen, social reality of this nature can hardly be reduced to the contents of reinforcive rules. Thus, for example, the formal structure of a legislative committee system is simply not reducible to the set of rules prescribing this structure. Rather, this structure, as operational, resides primarily in actual, ongoing, activities of authorized personnel. The complementary material and other components of these structured activities include buildings in use, communicative devices, other material resources, and actual personnel. These, too, and how they are used, can hardly be reduced to the contents of reinforcive rules.

Section Two: Overall Legislative Form and Its Constituent Features   99

Without the overall form of a legislative institution duly defined and organized, i.e., formed to serve its purposes, there could be no specified membership, no defined jurisdiction, no internal structure, no procedure for the creation of valid law (or for conduct of other institutional activities), no drafting methodologies, and no reinforcive rules prescribing facets of the foregoing. Plainly a legislature does not consist merely of material and other components such as personnel, available material resources, and shared knowledge of legal means-end relations all located or available in a discrete vicinity. Well-designed overall form, with its constituent features, is required to define and organize a legislature as an operational whole to serve characteristic purposes. Much of what a legislature is, in a developed Western society, consists of densely specified, inter-related, and unified features of form that define and organize the makeup, unity, modes of operation, instrumental capacity, and distinct identity of the legislature. Through a frontal and systematic focus on overall form and its constituents, it is possible to advance understanding of all these attributes.

That duly designed form is essential to the very existence of workable versions of these attributes can be seen from many lessons of historical experience. Great flaws of form plagued legislative bodies in earlier eras. For example, the compositional feature of some early Greek legislatures provided for far too many members. Other legislatures had no definitive internal structure. Still others had only haphazard procedures. Although legislative form, duly designed to serve characteristic purposes, tends to be taken for granted today, the modern centralized legislature in developed Western societies has not sprung fully formed from the foreheads of socio-legal architects. Many facets of its features have been "hard won" from long experience.

There is more to the overall form of an institution such as a legislature than the mere sum of its constituent formal features. These features of composition, jurisdiction, structure, procedure, reinforcive rules and other precepts, and complementary material and other components are also integrated within a unified whole. The very existence of these coherent inter-relations between parts itself signifies that this whole is more than the mere sum of its parts.

Nor can the unified whole here be reduced, without remainder, merely to the aggregate contents of all the reinforcive rules purporting to prescribe particular features of the body.[13] For example, a duly designed legislative mode of operation provides for debate of proposed statutes. The actual legislative activity of debate is hardly identical with the contents of any reinforcive rules prescribing it, nor is it reducible to the contents of those rules. It is true that a procedural rule purportedly reinforcive of the process may, as is usual, provide in a few words for "debate." Other procedural rules may specify how debate is to be carried out. The nature of debate, however, is a highly complex form of legislative activity, only

---

[13] See *supra* Chapter Three, Section Four.

partly revealed in the contents of such rules. It usually presupposes internal structures, including the two "sides" that may debate. The concepts and vocabulary for description of debate are much richer than the language of typical procedural and structural rules would indicate. Suppose someone asked: "What do legislative debaters typically do?" That is, just what is this institutional activity? Suppose the answer was: "Debaters are following rules that allow for discussion of the merits and demerits of a bill." Even if more detailed, this answer would advance understanding far less than a form-oriented analysis, which would include treatment of the form of debate, its significant varieties, the dependencies of debate on structure, specification of where debate fits in overall procedural form, and rationales for prescribing debate, including due deliberation, fair participation of those affected, democratic input and representation, improvement of bills, and more. Indeed, an adequate account of such formal features and their complementary components necessarily requires analyses of their purposive rationales. As I have stressed, reinforcive rules typically do not include formulations of their rationales.[14]

Consider this analogy. In an ongoing game, far more is supposed to occur than is usually captured in the rules purporting to prescribe facets of the game. For example, the distinctive skills of such players are not so captured, nor are important mental attitudes or "mind-sets" of players, nor are the tactics of good play, nor are even general strategies for winning. The overall form of the game itself thus cannot be fully captured in any single rule or set of rules. Similarly, there is much more to the activities of a particular ongoing institution than is captured in the contents of its typical reinforcive rules. A first-hand descriptive account can be given, for example, of the formal structural feature and complementary components of a particular legislature such as whether it is subdivided into committees and whether political parties play major roles in this structure. The main outlines of formal structure (or other formal features) in a particular institution can usually be determined more or less noncontroversially from general observations and reports without full scale empirical inquiry. A similar account of these outlines cannot, however, be adequately pieced together merely by drawing inferences from the specific contents of a number of the usual reinforcive rules. It is necessary to determine and provide an account of the main facets of institutional form as it generally operates and bring to this account adequate concepts of formal features, their complementary components, and the purposes to be served.

It is true that legislative form, as manifest in practices of institutional participants, might, at some points, diverge from what is prescribed in applicable reinforcive rules. When these practices prevail despite such divergence, the true

---

[14] I do not claim that a rule-oriented analysis necessarily omits all reference to rationales, only that rules often do not incorporate such rationales explicitly.

Section Three: The Compositional Feature

form is not the form prescribed in the rules, but the form generally manifest in institutional operations, except insofar as meaningfully subject to invalidation under the rules.

A fundamental claim to credit due form is simply that without duly designed overall form, we could not have an institution such as a legislature at all and so could not have statutory law as we know it. This is not, however, a contingent claim the truth of which is dependent on finding and assessing facts. It is simply a claim to the effect that without X, Y would not be possible. To refute such a claim, it would be necessary to show that a legislative body could exist without any overall form – without any purposive systematic arrangement of the whole, which is simply not possible. As Jhering would have said, such a body cannot be "formless" and still exist.[15] Some overall form is necessary for the very existence of a functional legislature, although still hardly sufficient by itself. This same type of general claim to credit for form can be validly made with respect to the dependency of all functional legal units on their forms. Moreover, a further important claim here is that, in general, the better designed the form, the better the unit, and the worse the form, the worse the unit. Although this claim is, in part, empirical, it can be readily substantiated and so is not really controversial.

Without a grasp of overall legislative form and of its constituent features, it is simply not possible to understand what a legislature is. The same is true of any purported governmental institution.[16] Also it advances understanding of such a functional unit to focus not merely on its overall form and the constituent features thereof but also on any forms of material or other components of the whole. Plainly, some of these components take forms, too. For example, well-designed physical facilities of a legislature can take a distinctive form highly facilitative of legislative activities.

SECTION THREE: THE COMPOSITIONAL FEATURE

One feature of the overall form of any legal institution is compositional. The effects and imprints of this feature are deep and indelible. This feature defines and organizes the determinate makeup of the complementary component of personnel, including the legislators. Without this feature, a legislative institution could not exist, and its purposes therefore could not be served. In the case of a legislature, the compositional issues pertaining to legislators that require definitive resolution

---

[15] R. Jhering, *Geist des Römischen Rechts: auf den verschiedenen Stufen seiner Entwicklung*, vol. 2, at 478 (Scientia Verlag, Aalen, 1993).

[16] Of course, those who in fact advance their own grasp of the nature of a legislature partly through an improved understanding of its form, are not necessarily conscious that something classifiable as form is at work. And when they do become aware, they may exclaim "Ah, but that is obvious!" This does not, however, diminish the importance of form. On alleged "obviousness," see, again, n. 36, 37, and 38 of Chapter One, at pp. 15–16.

include: (1) the number of members, (2) any geographical or other distribution of members, (3) their eligibility and qualifications, (4) their mode of selection, (5) their term of office, and (6) their periodic replacement. Organized provision for, and definitive specification of, legislative personnel is frequently set forth to some extent in the contents of reinforcive rules in a constitution.

The make up of legislative membership is plainly of profound importance. Except for such laws as those prohibiting crimes, protecting public health, regulating traffic and the like, many people do not really understand, care about, or have time to think about, the form and contents of laws that a modern legislature adopts. Rather, they generally assume that if the "right people," that is, people duly elected, with their various qualifications, make the laws, and if those people adhere in their activities to appropriate legislative form, then most of the laws so made will at least be acceptable.

Two rationales sustain my characterization of duly defined and organized composition as a feature of the overall form of the legislative institution in developed Western societies. First, some provision for such composition is a necessary feature of this form. Some arrangement has to be made for *who* is to legislate and *who* is to conduct other legislative activities. This compositional feature is one of several that together satisfy the general definition of overall form as the purposive systematic arrangement of a functional unit, a general definition introduced and defended in Chapter Two, and here refined to fit the legislative institution. Second, the definition and organization of compositional makeup, as such, is also generally recognized in English (and in other) lexicons as "formal."[17] This also supports my characterization of the definition and organization of composition as formal. This is not to say that the attribute of overall institutional *makeup* is solely a matter of form. This attribute also encompasses complementary components of personnel, physical facilities, and other resources.

The attribute of makeup here encompasses, as well, the purposes implicit in a legislature. These purposes permeate compositional form. That is, if such form is well-designed, it will define and organize the compositional feature to serve the purposes of a democratic legislature. It is not possible to define and organize such a feature of form in a purposeless vacuum. Compositional form is necessarily purposive, and when those purposes are good, form is value-laden.

In designing Western legislatures, institutional architects have made various basic choices here. These profoundly affect what institutional personnel can achieve, and it advances understanding to see how this is so. Let us consider the possible consequences of some bad choices.[18] For example, the total number of members might be ill-designed with the result that there might be too many

---

[17] *The Oxford English Dictionary*, vol. 6, at "form," I.5.a (2nd ed., J. Simpson and E. Weiner eds., Clarendon Press, Oxford, 1989), hereinafter *OED*.

[18] See R. Jhering, *supra* n. 15, at 480.

Section Three: The Compositional Feature

legislators for the body to function effectively. The qualifications for legislators might be ill-designed and, for example, be set too low for legislators to be able to do their work well. Provision for distribution of members in the legislature might be ill-designed, with quite disproportionate membership from less populous areas, thereby undermining democratic values. Terms of office might be so short that legislators could not learn to do their work sufficiently well or might be so long that legislators lose their sense of accountability to the electorate. If members are to be elected, the very definition of what constitutes the casting of a vote for a legislative candidate in an election might even be left imprecise and indeterminate. In turn, this could make it difficult to determine who received a majority, thereby undermining the very legitimacy of those designated as elected.[19]

From the foregoing, we can also see how some choices of compositional form can be entitled to much credit for the realization of democratic and other values. Simple comparisons of choices in different systems also make this clear. For example, if we compare the traditional composition of the English upper house of Parliament with the American Senate, we see that the former is simply not democratically composed, whereas the latter is.

Every major constituent feature of the overall form of a legislature has, or at least shares, some complementary material or other component within the makeup of the whole. Complementary to the formal compositional feature of a legislature is the component of individual personnel who become legislators. As duly qualified and selected, such personnel bear imprints of compositional form. Yet, the contrast is preserved here between the formal compositional feature and complementary material and other components of the whole such as duly elected personnel. This contrast further legitimizes my characterization of composition as a distinct formal feature that is less than the whole, yet susceptible of its own affirmative characterization.

Well-designed compositional form defines and organizes who can be legislators, and thus tends to beget good legislators, although it hardly guarantees them.[20] In this way, form defines and shapes its complementary component of personnel, and the two together affect the operation and functions of the body as a whole. Because of the imprints and other effects of well-designed form on these components, form must have major credit here.

The overall form of a democratic and effective legislature, then, requires a defined and organized membership, duly designed to serve these purposes. Different systems elaborate in various ways beyond the minimum required here. For example, there are various ways of elaborating on democratic selection, one of

---

[19] Cf. *Bush v. Gore: The Court Cases and the Commentary* (E. Dionne Jr. and W. Kristol eds., Brookings Institution Press, Washington, D.C., 2001).

[20] Cf. Fuller, "Positivism and Fidelity to Law: – A Reply to Professor Hart," 71 *Harv. L. Rev.* 630 (1958).

which is proportional representation. The existence of multiple political parties may also call for other special elaborations.

The formal feature of composition is highly purposive. Democratic purposes and purposes of legislative rationality are the primary determinants. The representational mode of composition serves a fundamental political value, one that also contributes legitimacy to the legislative body. As John Locke stressed, those chosen as legislators should also be among those affected by at least some of the very laws they make, as under democratic composition, for those persons will have special incentive to bring reason to bear on any proposed laws.[21] Also, the general purpose of securing rational law-making influences compositional choices of minimum qualifications.

Insofar as such purposes as democracy, legitimacy, and rationality in law-making are served here, some credit is due well-designed compositional form. That some provision must be made for *who* is to legislate is also a matter of necessity and not an empirical claim to credit for form. Moreover, if democratic selection were not provided for, then the legitimacy that derives from this would be forfeited. All these purposes are ones that can, to some extent, be realized merely "processually," that is, in the course of the very operations of the legislative process itself.

The effective rule of law and the values served thereby also require *determinate* sources of valid law. Such sources give rise to formal "source-oriented" criteria of valid law such as "enacted by the legislature." A legislature that is duly defined and organized, i.e., formed, is both a determinate and an authoritative source of law. This facilitates efforts of officials, citizens, and others readily to identify as valid any law emanating from such a source, and to take action accordingly. To the extent this is an empirical claim, it, too, is not controversial. Determinateness and authoritativeness of source also require that the procedural feature of legislative form specify with definiteness a "decision-rule," e.g., "a majority of those present," for valid adoption of statutes. (This is not to say a legal system should have no content-oriented criteria of valid law as well.)

A further type of general claim to credit on behalf of compositional form, one that is not empirical, is this. In all developed Western societies, legislative composition is not merely a way of staffing the body with personnel who make law and discharge the other functions of a legislature. It is also a way of defining and thus furthering the purpose of democratic representation in law-making. Form is not merely an instrumental means here. It is also essential to the very definition of, and thus at least partly constitutive of, the very end to be pursued. A purpose such as democratic representation through periodic election of legislators

---

[21] J. Locke, *The Second Treatise of Government*, 82 (T. Peardon ed., The Bobbs-Merrill Co., Indianapolis, 1952).

Section Three: The Compositional Feature

is not a "natural" pre-legal or a-legal purpose like physical security of person – an end that would still be an end entirely independently of all law and legal form. Rather, democracy is partly the creation of law and legal form. It is true that democracy also captures some version of a pre-legal or a-legal democratic value, namely that of due participation by those affected. However, this ideal conception – "democratic representation in law-making" – is, as such, insufficiently defined and organized to be susceptible of implementation. To be susceptible, it must take a duly designed and specified form in which a variety of definitional and organizational, i.e., formal, issues are resolved. For example, an electoral process has to be set up. When are elections to be held? What qualifications must candidates have? How should constituencies be defined? Who is to vote? What counts as casting a vote? How are votes for and against to be aggregated? All this and more must be duly defined and organized so that election results can be accurate and clearly discernable and thus serve the purpose of democratic representation.

Not until an electoral functional unit is duly defined and organized through form, can it even be said that the purpose of having a democratically composed legislature has itself come into being as a viable socio-legal purpose meaningfully susceptible of implementation. Here, form is, in major part, constitutive of this very end. In defining and organizing the required electoral arrangements, form adds the highly complex purpose of democratic governance to the socio-legal menu. A claim that compositional form merits credit here is not solely an empirical claim. It is also at least a claim that without such duly defined and organized form, the purpose of democratic representation could not be meaningfully pursued. Many purposes are like democracy and thus require some defined and duly organized legal form to be susceptible of meaningful pursuit. In the foregoing and other examples, there is usually scope for rather different choices of form. An electoral process must be duly defined and organized. Hence the credit to form here can be considerable. This is not to say good choices of form and value in an electoral process itself will alone be enough. Among other things, electoral processes, however formally well-designed on their own, and however democratic, have to be protected against intimidation, fraud, bribery, and other vices. Something similar is true of many other important ends.

Once the compositional feature is duly designed and put in place, and once the contents of any required rules reinforcive of composition are set forth, it might be assumed that the scholar who wishes to advance understanding of the composition of such an institution – its authoritative participants, their mode of selection, their terms of office, and so on – need only recommend that we read the reinforcive rules on these subjects.[22] It is certainly true that the contents of rules of composition for a particular legislature will usually provide significant information, even though

---

[22] H. L. A. Hart, *supra* n. 5.

they fail to identify the formal explicitly. However, to understand what is formal about composition, to understand complementary components, such as elected personnel, and to understand how all these are defined and organized to serve relevant purposes, a form-oriented approach promises more here, too.

Thus, the contents of reinforcive rules of composition in Western systems themselves typically say little about *why* legislators should be elected – about why this type of compositional feature of form is well-designed. If we go beyond the rules to identify rationales, we can often advance understanding of the possible appropriateness of the design of form beyond what mere study of the contents of such rules can provide. On a form-oriented approach, we look to the purposive rationales that the form is to serve, and to the imprints and other effects of form on, for example, the duly elected personnel. Again, to illustrate from the eighteenth-century American example, the Federalists followed Locke in favoring an elected legislature. Their rationales were that such a body creates between the rulers and the people a "common interest" and an "intimate sympathy."[23] The Federalists held that elected legislators "can make no law which will not have its full operation on themselves and their friends as well as on the mass of society."[24] Also, elected legislators "will enter upon public service under circumstances which cannot fail to produce a temporary affection at least to their constituents. There is in every breast a sensibility to marks of honor, of favor, of esteem, and of confidence, which apart from all the considerations of interest, is some pledge for grateful and benevolent returns."[25] To grasp such purposive rationales for democratic composition is to advance one's understanding of the very form adopted – of the very purposive systematic arrangement adopted – and thus also of attributes of makeup, unity, and instrumental capacity of the legislature.

Also, the contents of many reinforcive rules prescribing compositional form and related facets may be compatible with different purposive rationales. For example, consider the contents of the rule requiring that members of the U.S. House of Representatives be elected every two years. Why this? Again, study of the contents of such a reinforcive rule via rule-oriented analysis will usually not reveal the purposive rationale. Here, the rule prescribes election at two year intervals, but is silent as to rationale. The language is also compatible with several rationales. For example, one rationale might be the belief that many qualified citizens would feel they could afford no more than two years of such public service. On a form-oriented analysis, we would identify the actual purpose to be served by this feature of compositional form. We would find that the founders believed that frequent elections secure the likelihood that representatives will have "an immediate dependence upon, and

[23] "The Federalist No. 52," in A. Hamilton et. al, *The Federalist: A Commentary on the Constitution of the United States*, 341–6, esp. 343 (Random House, New York, 1950).
[24] *Ibid.*
[25] See n. 23, "The Federalist No. 57," at 370–6, esp. 372.

Section Three: The Compositional Feature

an intimate sympathy with the people."[26] Given the two foregoing possible rationales, knowledge of actual rationale would advance understanding of this facet of composition in the particular system involved. Again, such analysis could also be generalized beyond a particular legislature to cast light on features of legislative form generally and their possible rationales.

Similarly, let us consider the content of a reinforcive rule that specifies the number of members the legislative body is to have. Such content usually tells us little or nothing about the rationale for the rule, yet a grasp of rationale, pursuant to a form-oriented analysis, would advance understanding here as well. Again, the formal compositional feature of the U.S. House of Representatives provides an example. Reinforcive rules provide the formula for the number of members. The Federalist Papers, but not the rules themselves, provided a partial rationale for this compositional feature: the number should be that which is "necessary to secure the benefits of free consultation and discussion, and to guard against too easy a combination for improper purposes."[27] This rationale in itself furthers understanding of this formal feature of legislative composition.

A mode of analysis focusing merely on the contents of reinforcive rules may be limited in still another major way. The content of a particular reinforcive rule may only prescribe a fragment of the relevant purposive systematic arrangement. Even a reading of all related rules of composition may not enable us to comprehend fully either the fragment at hand or the organized form as a whole within which this fragment is supposed to fit. This is because the prescribed feature of who the institutional members are to be – the compositional feature of legislative form – is determined also in light of what they are to do, how, when, by what means, and with what effects. We can understand and see all of this only through a holistic analysis of further formal features, of the inter-relations between such further features, and of the complementary components that make up and unify the whole.

To put this another way, to recognize that the contents of a reinforcive rule duly prescribe a compositional feature, and to understand the particulars of that feature fully, it is usually necessary to understand other related features of the overall form of the institution as a whole. For example, a specified number of members of a legislative body in a given society might, on its own, appear to be sufficiently representative. Yet, given the need for enough persons annually to fulfill various roles in considering proposed bills – further structural and procedural features of overall legislative form – the number of legislators may need to be higher. A holistic form-oriented approach would be more likely to reveal as much.

---

[26] See n. 23, "The Federalist No. 52," at 341–6, esp. 343.
[27] See n. 23, "The Federalist No. 55," 359–65, esp. 361.

The contents of reinforcive rules purporting to prescribe facets of composition may even be silent about some important types of participants in a legislature in a democracy. Thus, in some societies, reinforcive rules do not address, or address far less than fully, what the relations are to be between elected legislators on the one hand, and various types of participants in the process such as political parties and their leaders, pressure groups, and lobbyists on the other hand. Yet all these might actually participate regularly in major ways in a legislative process, if not when it is initially organized and launched, then later and continuously. A faithful and comprehensive form-oriented account of the compositional and related features would extend to all modes of important participation in the legislative institution, and would thus address the formal structural and procedural relations between elected legislators and the foregoing other participants, too.

A rule-oriented analysis usually stops with an account of the contents of existing rules purporting to prescribe facets of the functional legal unit under consideration. It does not inquire explicitly into form or inquire into the general credit that the relevant overall form at hand and its constituent features should have for purposes served through organized institutional action. The contents of reinforcive rules do not themselves even differentiate explicitly between form and complementary material and other components of a functional legal unit. Yet credit cannot be attributed without such differentiation, and this requires a theory of form. Well-designed compositional form, along with its complementary components, tends to contribute not only to such ends as the realization of policy through statutes adopted and implemented, but also to the realization of various important "process values," such as democratic participation, legitimacy, and procedural fairness, which are values realized in the course of the very operations of the legislative process. Without due compositional form, none of these purposes could be adequately realized, nor could the instrumental capacity of the legislature be understood. This is not an empirical claim, but a necessary truth. Moreover, with well-designed compositional form, the realization of such ends is certainly more likely. Although this is an empirical claim, it is not controversial.

SECTION FOUR: THE JURISDICTIONAL FEATURE

Another constituent feature of the overall form of a legislative institution is jurisdictional. In general, each major type of legal institution in developed Western societies has distinct yet limited authority to act. In the case of a legislature, this formal feature defines and organizes the conferral and limitation of authority, among other things, to make statute law, to commandeer resources, to conduct oversight of administrators, to provide a forum for public discussion, and, in some systems, even to install the executive branch. This formal jurisdictional feature and its complementary subject matters are part of the makeup of the legislative

Section Four: The Jurisdictional Feature

institution, and account for important facets of its mode of operation and instrumental capacity.

Of the foregoing types of jurisdictional authority, the most important is the power to create general written law in a chosen set of words in fixed verbal sequence. The authority to legislate is often conferred in terms of various complementary subject matter categories of legislative action to meet major types of needs. These categories may or may not be specified in rules of a written constitution. The jurisdiction to legislate is also often limited in terms of specified subject matter. For example, in a federal system the federal legislature may have no general authority to adopt ordinary criminal law, this being left to state or regional legislatures. Legislative jurisdiction may also be limited by a constitutional Bill of Rights or the like. Such limits require general rules well-designed in form. Legislative jurisdiction may be limited not only in terms of subject matter. It is familiar that legislatures generally have no authority to adjudicate disputes between citizens or between citizens and officials, and constitutions may specifically forbid this.[28] The usual legislature does not itself have a formal structural feature securing the independence and impartiality appropriate to an adjudicative role, nor a compositional feature with complementary personnel having requisite judicial qualifications, nor the appropriate feature of dialogic procedure, nor still other formal features required for due discharge of adjudicative functions.

The definition and specification of the jurisdiction of a legal institution, such as a legislature, is a necessary feature of its overall form – of the purposive systematic arrangement of the whole.[29] Again, this feature is one of several that together here satisfy the general definition of overall form introduced and defended in Chapter Two, and here refined to fit legislative form. "Formal," in one of its relevant uses in English, and in other languages, also refers to an authoritative source. This reinforces characterization of the definition and specification of jurisdiction as formal, for such conferral of jurisdiction goes far to determine what legislative action is authoritative.[30]

If the jurisdictional feature of overall legislative form is well-designed, it will define and organize the nature and scope of legislative jurisdiction to serve the characteristic purposes of such a body. Thus, this feature, too, cannot be defined and organized in a purposeless vacuum. Jurisdictional form is necessarily purposive, and when the purposes are good, such form is value-laden.

A form-oriented analysis also reveals how formal features presuppose and cohere with other constituent features of overall legislative form. This coherence

---

[28] U.S. Const. art. I, §9.

[29] This has been put more generally: authority to shape a community's actions by directing individual conduct is conditional "on criteria of form (source, scope, or vires)." J. Finnis, *Oxford Companion to Philosophy*, 469 (T. Honderich ed., Oxford University Press, Oxford, 1995).

[30] *OED, supra* n. 17, vol. 6, at "formal," A.2, A.3.a, A.5.

is one type of internal relation between formal features that accounts for the inner order and unity of overall legislative form. For example, the jurisdictional feature presupposes a procedural feature. It would make little sense, for example, to confer authority to legislate on an entity without organized procedures for consideration and adoption of valid legislation. At the same time, appropriate procedural form also presupposes a certain type of jurisdictional form. The nondialogic procedure appropriate for the exercise of legislative jurisdiction could not be appropriate for the exercise of adjudicative jurisdiction.[31]

Legislatures in many systems, then, are empowered to enact statutes, provided the particular subject matters of these statutes fall within formally defined and specified grants of legislative jurisdiction. Without some such conferral of jurisdiction, the body would be relatively formless in this major respect and thus lack determinateness, unless, of course, the body can be assumed to have power to do anything, which is not usual. The formal feature of appropriately designed conferral of jurisdiction is entitled to some credit here when statutes are duly adopted, although such statutes must also be adopted by duly elected legislators in accord with specified procedures, and pursuant to any required executive assent.

The formal jurisdictional feature and its complementary subject matter confers upon legislators the power, among other things, to create entirely new law, and to change existing law, with any separate executive assent if necessary, all via the peaceful and orderly processes of democratic legislative activities.[32] Without the compositional, jurisdictional, procedural, structural, and preceptual features of legislative form, which together duly channel social forces for and against legal change, the very orderliness of civil society under the rule of law would itself be at risk. This overall form and its constituent features here also serve legal certainty and other values of the rule of law through duly specified conferral of law-making power, subject to limits. In general, the more clearly citizens can see *what*, even in general terms, legislators are, and are not, empowered to do, and the more clearly citizens can determine *whether* legislators have stayed within their powers, the more legitimate their authority will be seen to be. Democracy is served as well, because legislators can be held accountable if they exceed their jurisdiction. These claims to credit on behalf of definitive jurisdictional form are not really controversial.

Public acceptance, acquiescence, and assent are major sources of institutional legitimacy as well, and the formal feature of jurisdiction is relevant here, too. When power to legislate is explicitly granted in general terms subject to specified

---

[31] On dialogic v. nondialogic, see *supra* Chapter Two, at 56. For extended treatment of the unity of the whole legislative institution, see Section Eight of this Chapter.

[32] The very great value of such a peaceful and orderly mode of change in laws is stressed in R. Collingwood, *The New Leviathan or Man, Society, Civilization and Barbarism* (Revised ed., D. Boucher ed., Clarendon Press, Oxford, 1992).

Section Four: The Jurisdictional Feature

limits, is located in duly circumscribed institutional roles, and is duly exercised procedurally over time, these exercises of power are also more likely to become the object of genuine public acceptance, acquiescence, and assent. It is an advance in understanding to see that the legitimate exercise of legislative authority over time simply cannot be an ad hoc, unorganized, and formless affair. Duly designed jurisdictional and other form merit much credit.

The rule of law requires that officials and the people have capacity to determine whether statutes assertedly valid are truly valid according to the general criterion: "duly adopted by the legislature." It advances understanding to see how the formal definitiveness of jurisdictional grants of power contribute to this capacity to determine validity. Assertedly valid statutes can be identified as valid or not by reference to such grants, to the acts of a determinate and authoritative formal source – the legislature itself, and by reference to objectively datable and formally recorded past events of due enactment, in accord with requisite procedures. In general, such references to objectively datable and duly recorded past events of enactment can be relatively free of dispute. This, too, contributes legitimacy.[33] Again, much credit is due here to duly defined and well-organized form, even though usually taken for granted.

Here, a merely rule-oriented analysis of the contents of reinforcive rules would simply address the contents of jurisdictional rules,[34] especially those conferring and limiting power to legislate. It is true that legislative jurisdiction is conferred in many systems via rules in written constitutions, and the contents of such rules are plainly important. Yet a form-oriented analysis goes further. It concentrates, as indicated previously, on the definition and organization of the formal feature of jurisdiction. In addition, form-oriented analysis holistically treats this feature as duly integrated with other related features of overall legislative form. Unlike rule-oriented analysis as such, form-oriented analysis also addresses rationales for the *conferral* of legislative jurisdiction, and addresses rationales for the *denial* to legislatures of adjudicative and certain other powers as well. There are, for example, good reasons why legislatures should not seek to adjudicate.

A form-oriented analysis is required to identify and specify any desired formal feature to be incorporated in a reinforcive rule or rules in the first place. Reinforcive rules cannot be drafted to confer jurisdiction until this has been done. Furthermore, an analysis of the very *form* of general jurisdictional rules themselves casts further light on jurisdictional form, because it reveals the essential contributions here of formal features of such rules, including the prescriptiveness, generality, definiteness, completeness, and clarity of expression in these rules, as they bear on the definitiveness of jurisdictional grants of power, and related matters. A

---

[33] J. Finnis, *supra* n. 29, at 269.
[34] H. L. A. Hart, *supra* n. 5, at 29, 68.

form-oriented analysis also addresses, as indicated here, the overall credit due well-designed jurisdictional form separately, and jointly with, other formal features, for purposes served. A rule-oriented account is silent with respect to credit as such.

SECTION FIVE: THE STRUCTURAL FEATURE

A structural feature of a functional legal unit defines and organizes relations between parts within the whole. A legislative body, like most major legal institutions, must have an organized internal structure in order for it to have the make-up and unity required for its instrumental capacity. As with other formal features, this does not mean all legislatures have the same formal feature here. Thus, in parliamentary systems, such as in Great Britain and various Commonwealth countries, members of the executive are also members of the legislature and assume the managerial role in that body. In systems such as the United States in which the executive and the legislative powers are separated, the makeup of internal legislative structure is very different. The executive does not manage that body as in Great Britain.

The formal feature of internal structure in a legislative body is complex and specifies who is to preside over the whole body when it transacts business, who is to prepare the legislative and other agendas for the whole body, what bills and other matters are to be referred to what committees of the body, who is to sit on and chair committees, who is to determine the order in which bills or other matters are to be considered by the whole body, and so on. Legislatures in all Western systems are typically subdivided into standing and special committees that have varying relations to the whole and to each other. Because political parties figure prominently in the modern Western legislature, they, too, must be factored into the overall structure. Internal structure is a pragmatic necessity. It defines and organizes relations between parts within what can be a highly complex division of legal labor.

Structure is justifiably characterized as formal for the following reasons. First, internal structure is a necessary feature of the overall form of any legislature – of its purposive systematic arrangement. Thus, internal structure, together with other formal features, satisfies the general definition of overall form introduced and defended in Chapter Two, and here refined to fit overall legislative form. Second, the ordering of relations between parts within a whole is recognized in English and other lexicons as "structural," and such ordering is, in turn, recognized in standard lexicons as "formal".[35] These usages also support my characterization of this feature as formal.

---

[35] *OED, supra* n. 17, vol. 6, at "form," I. 5.a. See also *OED, supra* n. 17, vol. 16, at "structural," 3 ("of or pertaining to the arrangement and mutual relations of parts of any complex unity").

Section Five: The Structural Feature

If the internal structural feature of overall legislative form is well-designed, it will define and organize the nature and scope of legislative structure to serve the characteristic purposes of such a body. Thus, this feature, too, cannot be defined and organized in a purposeless vacuum. Structural form is necessarily purposive, and when the purposes are good, such form is value-laden.

The formal feature of internal legislative structure defines and organizes various complementary components. These include designated legislative members who are to officiate in meetings of the whole, members who chair or otherwise participate on committees, various materials required for committee study of the contents of draft legislation, relevant bodies of means-end knowledge, lawmaking expertise and advice, and physical facilities. Internal structural and still other formal features, in organizing such components, leave formal imprints. For example, a major imprint consists of the effects of a focused committee study on the policy or other contents of draft statutes, as revealed in revisions of these very draft statutes. Despite such imprints, form-oriented analysis here preserves the basic contrast between internal formal structure and the foregoing complementary components. This further legitimizes my characterization of structure as formal. Such structure is something less than the whole and remains a distinct feature that organizes complementary components.

A legislature is not merely internally structured into committees and subcommittees requiring organization, and not merely organized to act also as a whole body. It is familiar that a legislature may also be subdivided into two chambers, with each to act in cooperation with the other and to check the other. When so, the internal structure must also provide for reconciliation of differences between the two chambers. These and other matters of internal structure can be organized well or poorly. The credit that may be due to choices of form here, can be considerable.

As already indicated, in developed Western societies, there is a "great division" in basic structure between (1) the British system and ones like it in which the "cabinet" (the executive government of the day) sits in the legislature and takes the lead in making the laws, with the advice and consent of the legislative body, and (2) systems like the American and various others where a separate legislature makes the laws, subject to veto (over-ridable) by an independent executive.[36] Such a basic difference of structural form plainly has profound effects on attributes of makeup, unity, mode of operation, and instrumental capacity. It has long been argued that where the legislature and the executive are separate, as in the American system, the two can more effectively check each other and thereby secure freedoms and limit abuses. To the extent this is so, we may say credit is due external structural form. On the other hand, the English form has its advantages, too. For example, debate in the English House of Commons, with the Cabinet present and required

---

[36] K. Wheare, *supra* n. 1, at 162–3.

on the spot to respond to organized opposition may provide a more thorough airing of pros and cons prior to vote by legislators.

Major credit is also due external structural features, and due jurisdictional features whereby legislative and executive powers on the one hand, are separated from judicial powers on the other, as in nearly all developed Western systems. This credit has long been recognized, even though not always seen to be formal. Again, structural form, and the reasons behind this form – the purposive rationality of such form – have been highly influential. Such separation preserves the independence of the judiciary from the political forces of the legislative and executive branches. In some systems, it also invites and enables the judiciary to check, in light of conferred jurisdiction, bills of rights, and the like, purported exercising of powers by the legislature and the executive. Separation of the legislature from the executive invites, and enables, the legislature to check the executive, as well. Such separations of powers also facilitate specialization and accumulation of experience in the overall division of legal labor between different institutions. All the foregoing advantages and others are widely recognized today, though still not sufficiently seen to be partly attributable to choices of structural form.

The internal structural feature of a committee system with complementary legislative personnel generally affords legislators deliberative opportunities to measure the form and the content of proposed laws against jurisdictional grants conferring and limiting the power to legislate, against bills of rights, and against the various requirements of form embodied in principles of the rule of law. Also, a structured process that is systematically attentive to the requirements of bills of rights, and the rule of law in the drafting of bills, is far more legitimate than one that fails in those respects. If this be construed as an empirical claim to credit for form, it is one that is not really controversial. It is also a claim on behalf of structural effects that serve ends, such as rationality and legitimacy processually, that is, in the course of the very operations of the legislative process itself.

Further choices of internal structural form in a legislature can also serve various fundamental political values such as democracy, legitimacy, rationality, and orderly legal change. When these values are served, this occurs to a large extent in the course of the very workings of legislative processes and thus also depends on well-designed internal structure and complementary material and other components. It is familiar that by channeling proposed legislation to specialized committees for study, well-designed structural form can help regularize legislative activity, bring reason to bear, and facilitate efficient dispatch of legislative business. This instrumental legislative capacity also contributes to institutional determinateness and stability. Together, these tend to beget legislative fecundity, including creation of statutes susceptible to effective implementation. In turn, this contributes to the rule of law, as well. Again, the credit due choices of well-designed form here can be very great.

Section Five: The Structural Feature

It is also familiar that a legislative body subdivided into specialized committees can accumulate expertise about given fields of law and of law-making rather better than can a legislature functioning solely as a committee of the whole. Through division and specialization of labor, the different committees and their staffs can find facts and bring specialized experience, knowledge, expertise, and reason to bear in order to improve the content of proposed laws, and the content of existing laws. Committee structures can also provide some protection against the undue influence of pressure groups on individual legislators. Such well-designed structural form tends to beget good policy content in statutes, and tends to beget effective schemes of implementation, thereby serving policy ends. These claims on behalf of form are empirical. That is, their truth is contingent on the occurrence of relevant effects in particular instances. It is also the case that even the best of structural and other form can hardly guarantee that statutes will have good content. It is even true that a committee system can be abused, as when committee chairs wield excessive power, and utilize committee referrals to bottle up good bills and prevent their consideration on the floor of the whole body. Yet, there is much truth in the foregoing claims on behalf of internal structural form, and these claims are generally not controversial. There is little evidence of sentiment for abandonment of formal committee structures in developed Western societies.

It is true that political parties are prominent and they can fail to function congruently with some of the rationales for the various structural, procedural, and other formal features so far treated in this chapter. In some systems, individual legislators may become subservient to a political party. Committee chairs may be selected by majority party affiliation in accord with seniority rather than merit. Committees may hold hearings on bills, but blindly reject quite justified bills or quite justified proposals for modification because they are contrary to majority party positions. Floor debate on bills may occur, but without passage even of entirely sound amendments because the majority party opposes them. Thus, a price is paid for the forms in place here.

At the same time, incongruent as the foregoing may sometimes be with rationales for certain features of legislative form, a strong party system may still serve democracy well overall and still adequately facilitate an efficient flow of "party-blessed" legislative business within existing forms. In many developed Western systems, a majority political party controls the leadership position in a legislature and controls its committee system, which are both structural features. Insofar as these structural features enable citizens and others, with the aid of the media, to perceive which parties are responsible for what legislative successes and failures, this serves democratic accountability. Certainly without some such structure, the lines of political accountability would very likely be far less discernible. Here, too, structural form merits significant credit.

Again, any assumption that a merely rule-oriented analysis should also have primacy here is highly dubious. The contents of the reinforcive rules of a particular system prescribing the structural feature of the overall form of a legislature simply could not have been drafted without prior understanding of the structure to be prescribed. For example, the structure of the desired committee system and its integration within overall law-making procedure would have to be thought through before any rules prescribing these features could be drafted. Also, once drafted and in place, it would not follow that study merely of the contents of these reinforcive rules would be the best avenue to understanding legislative structure. The contents of such rules might only be uncertainly pieced together and thus not provide a faithful and holistic account of overall operational form. Reinforcive rules might even omit features of structure. It is familiar that such rules often have many gaps. For example, in some systems the contents of reinforcive rules purporting to prescribe internal structure are relatively silent with respect to the role and procedures of political parties, yet the majority party may, in practice, determine the composition of committees, the internal relations between committees, and the legislative agenda! A form-oriented account addresses all significant aspects of legislative structure, even when not prescribed in rules.

Even if the contents of the relevant reinforcive rules were to specify all significant relations between parts within the whole, i.e., the structure, the contents of these rules would, if typical, still fail explicitly to incorporate the purposive rationales for those structures. A form-oriented account, with its focus on form as a purposive systematic arrangement, and thus on its appropriateness to serve relevant purposes, would render explicit the rationales. This would further advance understanding of the institution as a whole.

Even if, on a merely rule-oriented account, we could faithfully discern general operational structure on the basis of piecing together the contents of various reinforcive rules, and even if we were able to go outside the rules and identify the purposive rationales for this structure, such an account would still fail to address what general credit this formal feature, in particular, should have for ends realized. A merely rule-oriented account is virtually silent here. A form-oriented analysis of legislative activities and their general effects, as defined and organized by structural and other formal features, is required to determine the contributions of such form, and thus accord due credit.

SECTION SIX: THE PROCEDURAL FEATURE

A legislature is procedural in its makeup, too. There are several reasons to characterize the defining and organizing feature of procedure as formal. Together with other features, it satisfies the general definition of form introduced and defended in Chapter Two. The purposive systematic arrangement of a legislative institution

Section Six: The Procedural Feature

necessarily includes a procedural feature that goes far to define and organize the mode of operation of the body. A legislature without regularized procedures for rational and democratic creation of valid law, and for conduct of its other important activities, would be grossly dysfunctional, and simply could not have required instrumental capacity. Furthermore, the specification and organization of the steps in a linear sequence required for the conduct of an activity such as the creation of valid statutes, is also standardly recognized in English and other lexicons as "procedural" and as "formal."[37]

If the procedural feature of overall legislative form is well-designed, it will define and organize legislative procedure to serve the characteristic purposes of such a body. Thus, this feature, too, cannot be defined and organized in a purposeless vacuum. Procedural form is necessarily purposive, and when the purposes are good, such form is value-laden, too.

The history of progress in the governance of developed Western societies has been, in major part, a history of the development of well-designed procedures and of related forms for the conduct of institutional activities. How such activities are conducted has importance beyond any effects by way of particular ultimate outcomes in terms of laws adopted or rejected. Yet, there is often a tendency for participants and observers to focus solely on ultimate outcomes and to undervalue *how* things are done. Important qualities of the legislative process, including the realization of certain values that occurs in the course of the very workings of the process – "process-values" – depend heavily on the internal formal feature of procedure and its design. Among such values are democratic participation in law-making and other activities, rational scrutiny of proposed laws, procedural fairness, legitimacy, and peaceful and orderly legal change.

I will concentrate illustratively on law-making procedures. Plainly, a legislature simply could not bring democratic participation and rational scrutiny duly to bear on the form and content of proposed statutes without procedures requiring advanced notice to other legislators and to the public of a timetable for consideration of proposed statutes. This consideration must in turn provide a sufficient opportunity to apply "legislative" fact-finding and drafting methodologies to the proposals, provide for committee research and study of the contents of proposals for policy or other efficacy and for conformity to principles of the rule of law, provide for debate, collective deliberation, and amendment of proposals, and provide opportunity to educate the public as to proposals. Formal procedures so providing, along with complementary material and other components of personnel, research materials, physical facilities, and the like, tend to improve the form and content of statutes in the course of adoption, and tend to lead participants to reject bad proposals. Such procedures also tend to serve participatory and other

---

[37] *OED, supra* n. 17, vol. 6, at "form," I 11.a.

process values. Again, whereas these claims on behalf of well-designed form are, to some extent, empirical, they are not really controversial. Of course, procedures can afford opportunities for special interests to exert undue influence, too.

A well-designed procedural feature, along with complementary material and other components, can contribute in major ways to the quality of the final form and content of statutes. This occurs perhaps most dramatically when the fruits of intensive committee study and subsequent floor debate indisputably lead to improvements in bills. Sound reasons of policy and principle may go far here to determine final statutory form and content, and thus affect both ends and means. Here, due credit must be given to procedural form.

Yet, issues of law-making commonly arise on which reasons of policy and principle, and reasons of still other kinds, may not weigh heavily one way rather than another. Here, and in regard to many proposed laws the content of which is not fully determinable by reason, the existence of a procedural "decision-rule," that is, adoption by a bare majority, takes on added importance, especially in legislatures not dominated by a majority political party. Such a procedural "decision-rule" makes it possible to adopt statutes, even when reason cannot be brought to bear to determine their form and content in full. For example, it becomes possible to adopt statutes such as those providing effective dates for retirement of public employees, dates that inherently impose relatively arbitrary cut-offs. When a statute incorporating such relatively arbitrary distinctions is called for, which is not uncommon, and is duly enacted, it may be said that procedural form contributes "justified fiat" to content. Fiat of this nature is justified as a response to the social need for a highly definitive rule even though neither policy nor principle can fully dictate its content. Here, adopted content pays special homage to form. The very existence of formal decision-making procedures for the creation of valid law makes it possible for complementary personnel – law-makers – to fill "gaps in reasoned content" with justified fiat. David Hume would have approved: "When natural reason, therefore, points out no fixed view of public utility . . . positive laws are often framed to supply its place. . . . "[38] Procedural form, and the formal feature of high definiteness in a rule, plainly merit credit here.

Within a legislature, the material and other components complementary to the procedural and related features of overall legislative form include personnel such as law-makers and administrative staff, the subject matter of proposed legislation, testimonial, documentary, and various other materials supporting or opposing bills, and, of course, required physical facilities. Personnel participate in procedural steps at each stage. The ready contrast here between procedural form and the

---

[38] D. Hume, *An Enquiry Concerning the Principles of Morals*, 173 (T. Beauchamp ed., Oxford University Press, Oxford, 1998).

Section Six: The Procedural Feature

foregoing material and other components further legitimizes my characterization of procedure as a distinct formal feature within the legislative whole. This procedural feature is also susceptible of its own affirmative characterization apart from such components.

Various material and other components, including especially the very policy or other content of proposed laws, bear the imprints and other effects of the procedural form through which legislators introduce and process proposed statutes at committee hearings, in committee deliberations, in floor debates, and so on. The workings of the procedural feature may even lead to modifications contrary to the initial views of a majority political party, yet no one to my knowledge has ever advocated total abandonment of such key procedures.

The feature of procedure is susceptible to elaboration well beyond a bare minimum. A minimal procedure would not go much beyond requirements for introduction of a bill, some opportunity for debate and amendment, and a majority vote for passage. But one usually finds more elaborate procedures for how the legislature is to operate from inception of a bill until final vote, for how different chambers of a two-chamber legislature are to interact, and for how a legislature is to interact with any independent executive branch in regard to an adopted bill.

In most developed Western systems, the general mode of operation is familiar and proceeds as follows: proposed bills are introduced, referred to committees, and thereafter considered in accord with procedures of the relevant committees and of the body as a whole. When a bill is to be considered by the legislature as a whole, procedures usually require notice of introduction of the bill, presentation of committee reports, debate, deliberation, any amendment, and adoption or rejection. Most procedures define, specify, and organize steps from one stage to another in a projected and known linear sequence. This affords proponents and opponents opportunity to prepare in advance for consideration and for debate of bills. Of course, matters do not always go according to plan, and even well-designed procedures can also be turned into "roadblocks." In a legislature dominated by a majority political party, that party may prevent amendments, for example. In some systems, a minority may even talk a bill to death, if there is no provision for cloture of debate.

Many procedural matters will be set forth in the contents of a set of reinforcive procedural rules that the body itself has adopted. Some of major import may even be prescribed in a written constitution. Still others may merely be matters of customary practice or tradition. Some special rules of procedure may include safeguards against secret laws, hastily made laws, "special" laws (favoring special interests), and so on. Even so, procedures can be abused, circumvented, or even disregarded. Form cannot guarantee against such things, though it can help forfend against them.

The procedural and the other constituent features of overall legislative form are interdependent. To see how this is so also advances understanding. Without at least a procedural feature and a jurisdictional feature, it would not be possible for a legislature to make *valid* law at all, even with well-designed features of compositional and structural form. This is a claim to credit on behalf of formal procedural and jurisdictional features, and it is not an empirical claim. Without at least features of legislative form that are jurisdictional and procedural, it follows that officials, citizens, and other inhabitants simply could not know what action would count as enactment of a valid statute. Even assuming jurisdiction to adopt a statute, the legislature would still need to have procedures required for enactment, and these would require compliance with a decision-rule such as "adoption by majority vote." Duly designed procedural form is indispensable to the instrumental capacity to make statutory law.

I have so far treated the features of structure and procedure separately. Although each feature has its own independent significance, it is important to understand how these formal features operate together. Structure presupposes procedure, and procedure presupposes structure. Structure pertains to relations between parts within the whole legislature – how they are integrated, coordinated, subordinated, and the like. Procedure pertains to the nature and sequence of the various steps to be taken in the conduct of legislative activities, including lawmaking. Together, structure and procedure can synergistically interact. Structure can enhance procedure, as, for example, when a committee structure intensifies rational scrutiny at a stage in the procedure for considering a bill, and procedure can likewise enhance structure in providing opportunity for advanced preparation of committee members for committee hearings. In such synergistic interactions, complementary physical facilities and personnel are essential, too.

As with many such distinctions, it is possible here to identify aspects that are plainly structural yet not procedural, such as the existence and relations between committees in a legislature, and the existence and relations between two legislative chambers. It is also possible to identify aspects that are procedural but not structural, as with the requirement that a proposed law be published and distributed to legislators. Yet there are overlapping matters that may be characterized both as procedural and as structural. This is true, for example, of the work of "conference committees" in some systems. These are set up to resolve differences between two bills on the same matter passed by two chambers of the same legislature. Such a committee is part of the structure that mediates the relation between two chambers. Yet, the practice of referring bills to such a committee (made up of members from both chambers) is one major type of step in an overall procedure for composing such differences. Such overlap, which is hardly confined to this example, does not undermine my thesis that several distinct features of overall form figure in such an institution, and merit important credit for what the

Section Six: The Procedural Feature

institution achieves. Form remains no less pervasive when its varieties overlap, all the more so, when form overlaps with form.

I have so far assumed that the legislative procedure includes a collective "decision- rule" defining what counts as an authoritative decision to adopt a proposed statute. In democracies, the most widely applicable such decision-rule requires passage of proposed legislation by majority vote. This is really a formal rule of legislative procedure, with democratic content. The rule may actually consist of several rules. The formal inner order here can be quite complex.

Thus, the procedural provision for collective decision via a decision-rule, such as passage by majority vote, must necessarily specify what is to count as a vote for, and a vote against, a bill, and must provide for how votes for, and against, are to be summed up. This requires that, at the time the voting takes place, the proposed statute, which typically purports to reconcile conflicting interests, be drafted in a chosen set of words in fixed verbal sequence that, in definiteness and in mode of expression, fix what would otherwise be unduly "fluid substance."[39] Votes of legislators purportedly in favor of a statute cannot be properly added together unless they are voting "for the same thing," nor can purportedly opposing votes be tallied as opposed, unless these legislators are voting "against the same thing." Nor can the sum of the votes "for," and the sum of the votes "against," be properly netted against each other unless one side is voting for, and the other against, "the same thing."

This "thing," this proposed statute, is very likely not going to be the same thing for different legislators if it is not expressed in the same, and continuously the same, chosen set of words in fixed sequence, when voted upon, but is instead presented in different verbal formulations for different voters when voting. This is not to say a chosen set of words in fixed sequence guarantees sameness of meaning for different legislators. Legislators, when voting, may erroneously "read in" meanings that are not there, or "read out" meanings that are there. But the formal feature of fixity of verbal formulation goes as far as possible to secure sameness of meaning here. A proposed bill, with any amendments, will therefore be reduced to a chosen set of words in fixed sequence before voting takes place.

Possible differences of understanding among legislators as to the "thing" they are voting on can be even further reduced through formal choices of modes of expression in a proposed rule. Such choices may eliminate ambiguity, vagueness, confusing ellipses, and the like. Even with clarity of expression, if the proposal is not also in a chosen set of words in fixed sequence, sameness of form and content in the eyes of different legislators voting on the proposal would often be

---

[39] R. Jhering, *supra* n. 15, vol. 2, at 471. Here formal features are required to "fix fluid substance" and in so doing prioritize as between conflicting interests.

impossible. It might be that votes could not even be reliably taken as counting for one side rather than the other side, and so could not be added together on each side to determine a majority. Hence, to adopt a valid statute, it is necessary to have a procedural decision-rule providing for decision by majority vote on a proposal set forth in a chosen set of words in fixed sequence and with due clarity of expression. Yet many take matters of form for granted here, and are not articulately conversant with the foregoing necessities. As a result, sufficient credit is not attributed to the procedurally formal feature of the institution, including fixity of verbal formulation of proposed statutes. Much credit is also due the formal features of definiteness and mode of expression in draft rules, for making democratic legislation possible. In the foregoing ways, realization of the very end of democracy is heavily dependent on features of legislative and preceptual form.[40] Although usually taken for granted, duly designed form here goes far to account for the mode of operation and the instrumental capacity of a legislature, and thus advances understanding of the very requisites of majority rule. Form also merits credit for what it contributes here to institutional legitimacy, decisiveness, and law-making fecundity. Empirical research is not required to ground these conclusions.

The credit due to form extends even further. Legislative enactments of statutes cumulate over time. Formal features, in having, as emphasized earlier, made the democratic enactment of legislation possible in past instances, also enable present-day addressees of the law – officials, judges, lawyers, citizens, and other inhabitants of the society – to determine with high certainty whether the legislature, in any such particular past instance, actually did adopt an asserted statute and did so validly within its law-making jurisdiction. That is, today's addressees of a law said to have been adopted in the past can determine what action the legislature actually took, even very long in the past, by consulting (as necessary) faithful records of the relevant compositional, jurisdictional, structural, procedural, and preceptual features of form operative on the relevant prior occasions, and by consulting faithful records of the relevant prior enacting events then formally recorded in print or in writing.

For the democratic rule of law to be possible and continuous, it must be possible for elected law-makers to create valid law, and for subsequent addressees of the law, even many years later, to tell with high certainty whether a law then claimed to be valid was validly created years earlier. If officials and others could not usually, and with high certainty, identify valid statutory law as previously adopted in accord with official records, and differentiate this from nonlaw, the rule of law simply could not prevail over time. Moreover, certainty, fair notice, and equal treatment

---

[40] See R. Summers, 'Statutes and Contracts as Founts of Formal Reasoning,' in *Essays for Patrick Atiyah*, 71 (P. Cane and J. Stapleton eds., Clarendon Press, Oxford, 1991); see also J. Waldron, *supra* n. 4.

Section Six: The Procedural Feature

under law could not be realized. Thus, the credit to form here is large. This includes credit to printed and duly recorded form made possible by procedural and also preceptual form. Again, the fundamental claims I make here by way of credit to form do not require empirical research. A grasp of form at work, as above, also advances understanding of law-making processes, and of the continuity of a legal system.

In sum, appropriate procedural steps provide for careful drafting of bills in the form of rules or other preceptual form, the study and evaluation of the factual, policy or other bases of bills, debate and any amendment of bills, due enactment pursuant to a collective decision-rule, and faithful recording of those events in written or printed form. These procedural steps, together with features of structure, afford opportunities to bring evidence, reasoned analysis, and standards of good drafting to bear on the content and form of proposed bills. Formal procedures also provide an open forum within which publicity can be brought to bear on proposals, and on the arguments for and against. Material and other components, private as well as public, play major roles, too. These components include conscientious legislative personnel, informed legislative advisors, well-gathered data on the factual premises of bills, policy studies, general knowledge of legal means-end relations, required physical facilities, and more. Without well-designed formal procedures, these complementary components could not be sufficiently effective. Above all, the actions of conscientious legislators operating pursuant to well-designed procedures reflect many effects of form. Indeed, even the private media may be said to bear imprints of legislative form.

A series of procedural steps extended in time, and known in advance to legislators and other participants, enables all to learn what they must do to prepare to take positions on statutory proposals in accord with a known timetable. These steps can provide fair opportunity for democratic participation, and fair opportunity for rational deliberation on ends and means. Also, such a procedure known in advance can also inspire the trust and confidence of participants and of observant third parties. This serves democracy, because it enables elected legislators to exercise informed and rational judgment when voting. Well-designed procedure also enables citizens and other inhabitants to follow public debates as reported in the media, and to learn how their representatives vote. As a result, they can hold legislators accountable at election time. Again, much credit is due formal procedure.

Duly designed procedures also afford legislators opportunities to evaluate the very form and content of proposed statutes in light of bills of rights and of binding principles of the rule of law which may, in turn, require amendments. For example, in the American system, legislators participating in well-designed legislative processes may come to see that a proposed law would be void for vagueness, that is, be insufficiently definite to provide fair notice, or would fail to accord "equal

124 Forms of Institutions – Legislative

protection" to similarly situated persons. As a result, legislators might then redraft, or even abandon, a proposed law.

Procedural form, together with other formal features and complementary components, can go far to secure an inner legislative order that serves numerous ends "internally" in the course of the very workings of legislative processes, including such "process values" as democracy, legitimacy, rationality, procedural fairness, and peaceful and orderly modes of legal change. Ends of policy and the like can, in turn, be "externally" realized subsequently through outcomes of processes in which laws are adopted and ultimately implemented. Some ends, such as democracy, legitimacy, and the rule of law, can be realized both internally and externally.

Enactment of a valid statute usually takes place at a final stage of the procedure. Here, too, formal features have complementary material and other components that are at work. As we have seen, valid enactment involves far more than printed and duly recorded adoption of a "performative" use of language in fixed verbal sequence, such as "Be it enacted that...," by a majority of legislators acting pursuant to a well-formed decision-rule. Here, in order to advance overall understanding of form and its complements, a holistic analysis is necessary. In many systems, enactment of a valid statute presupposes a formal compositional feature specifying who can legislate, a formal jurisdictional feature authorizing legislation of the type at hand, a formal structural feature specifying required actions of the body including any committee study, and a formal procedural feature consisting of the steps to be taken for legislative action, including consideration of bills, debate, amendment, and valid enactment through voting and application of a collective decision-rule. Through such steps a majority of legislators, as the duly designated few in the society, act, and can be seen to act, as the lawful agency of all others in creating a statute. A valid statute is therefore far more than a precept with a certain form and content. It is a highly complex legal creation with a multi-faceted formal and other history of its own. A valid statute is brought into being by a duly composed entity acting pursuant to a grant of jurisdiction and acting in accord with specified structures, procedures, and methodologies of law-making – all in major respects matters of form. Duly designed form thus goes far to define and organize the makeup, unity, mode of operation, and instrumental capacity of the legislature.

A merely rule-oriented analysis of procedural and related features of overall legislative form cannot advance understanding as fully as a form-oriented account. It is true that legislative procedure is typically set forth in reinforcive rules. Thus, it might seem that if a rule-oriented approach can flourish anywhere, this must be in regard to procedure. Still, a form-oriented analysis is required in the first place before any reinforcive rules in effect prescribing form and complementary material and other components can even be drafted. Also, whereas a form-oriented analysis

Section Six: The Procedural Feature 125

takes procedural rules into consideration, such an account goes well beyond this. For example, a reinforcive procedural rule may merely prescribe in very general terms that statutes must be adopted "by majority vote." The contents of any such rule fail explicitly to differentiate between formal and other facets, and thus fail to address, as explained above, how formal features, procedural, preceptual, and other, make majority vote meaningful and possible. Or, a reinforcive procedural rule may be very sketchy. For example, it may merely provide for "debate," leaving open one or more major issues such as what parts of a proposed bill are subject to debate, when, by whom, how, for how long, and so on. Here the contents of relevant procedural rules may be only a very imperfect guide.

As we have seen, rule-oriented analysis is more sophisticated if it takes account of the purposive rationales of the reinforcive procedural rules. Yet the explicit contents of such rules commonly omit rationales, though these are necessarily part of purposive form as treated here. Study of the form of a functional unit in light of its rationales advances understanding. For example, the purposive rationales for the procedure of formal debate include deepening the grasp of legislative participants as to what is at issue. Thus debate is to serve rationality of deliberation. Another rationale for debate is to provide opportunity for improving the drafting of proposed statutes. This, too, serves rationality of another sort. Still another rationale for debate is that of securing informed voting, and this serves democracy as well as rationality.

A further inadequacy of any approach oriented merely to the contents of reinforcive rules specifying the procedural feature of legislative form is that such rules may be highly misleading as to the actualities. It is by no means true that all such rules are followed. For example, a procedural rule may require that no bill that treats more than one subject be eligible for consideration, yet in practice the body may regularly include "riders" on bills, which treat unrelated subjects and thus assure passage of "pork barrel" legislation. Or a rule ostensibly requiring referral of all major bills to a standing committee for study may, with some regularity, be invoked merely to kill bills. Here, a frontal form-oriented analysis of the overall procedure as it generally operates could advance understanding well beyond what such reinforcive rules say.

Furthermore, an analysis in terms merely of the contents of reinforcive rules purporting to prescribe formal procedure fails to address the credit due to well-designed form. Study of the contents of such reinforcive rules cannot alone reveal the credit due in part to form in terms of narrowing the issues, finding the facts relevant to the creation of law, securing fair and full debate, affording fair participation to the minority party, shaping a deliberative atmosphere, posing meaningful proposals in chosen words in fixed verbal sequence, providing a definitive decision-rule, and so on. Only an analysis addressed to form can reveal the credit due it.

Procedural, structural, and other formal features organize the roles of the complementary component of personnel in the legislative process, and insofar as being well-designed and duly operative, merit much credit for this, too. Each legislator has a very general role in the process by virtue of becoming a member of the body pursuant to the compositional feature of the institution. But there are many further specialized roles in most modern legislatures: presiding officers, committee chairs, leaders of floor debates on bills, chairs of party caucuses, and more. All these roles are to some extent creatures of the form – of the purposive systematic arrangement – of the institution, whether or not specified in reinforcive legal rules. Compositional, jurisdictional, structural, procedural, methodological, and preceptual features of form all contribute to defining and shaping these roles in diverse ways. The institutional existence and public recognition of these roles can even lead occupants to fulfill their roles with a heightened sense of mission. Here, to some extent, the overall institutional role itself may even inspire, and thus "make" the occupant, at least in some degree. Some credit must go to forms as sources of such inspiration, for these forms define and organize the institutional roles. It is true that reinforcive rules also figure in the creation and structuring of roles, and such rules may figure indirectly in the conscientious performances that these roles can themselves inspire. Yet as already seen, the roles themselves must be conceived prior to the drafting of the rules, and usually the very form of these roles is only partly prescribed in rules.

SECTION SEVEN: THE PRECEPTUAL FEATURE

I have deployed a form-oriented approach to elucidate features of a paradigm of the centralized legislative institution, and have contrasted this approach with a rule-oriented approach. Many legal theorists and other scholars have adopted a rule-oriented approach here. Hart even claimed that a system of law, despite all of its highly varied institutional, preceptual, methodological, enforcive, and other functional legal units, may be characterized "as essentially a matter of rules."[41] It is true that many aspects of the features of the overall form of the centralized legislative institution are prescribed to some extent in the contents of reinforcive rules. As I have explained, form-oriented analysis should have primacy here, nevertheless.

Yet I have conceded that an important feature of the overall form of an institution such as a legislature consists of precepts in the form of reinforcive rules having contents that in effect prescribe formal features and other facets of the institution. Some reinforcive rules are actually essential to the very existence of an institution. A modern centralized legislature, for example, could not exist if there

---

[41] H. L. A. Hart, *supra* n. 5, at 13.

Section Eight: Form and the Unity of the Legislature   127

were no rules prescribing to some extent the composition, jurisdiction, structure, and procedure of this institution. Such rules also provide "normative cement" that holds the institution together. That is, these rules bind legislators and other institutional participants who accept the rules as common public standards for the conduct of legislative activity. If legislators (and others) did not, in Hart's terms, accept such rules as binding standards, the institution would likely fall apart. In accepting and following reinforcive rules, legislators can also secure law-like regularity of legislative operations over time. Yet various other factors are at work, too, in holding a legislative institution together. These include the quality of training of institutional participants, the extent of alignment of form with customary practice, the effectiveness of criticism of departures from form, and the quality of the original organized form in the first place, especially its unifying facets.

SECTION EIGHT: FORM AND THE UNITY OF THE LEGISLATURE

A functional legal unit may be divided into parts and relations between parts. The main parts of a legislative unit consist of formal features and complementary material and other components, as defined and organized to serve purposes. The following chart indicates six of these parts:

Formal Feature	Complementary Material and Other Components
compositional	elected and other personnel; their required material resources; physical facilities; budgetary provisions; etc.
jurisdictional	subject matters of particular proposed laws; relevant documentary and other research materials; etc.
structural (internal)	officers of body; committee chairs and committee personnel; required material resources, testimony at hearings; research and other materials, etc.
structural (external)	personnel and material resources of other institutions, e.g., the executive and judicial, in structural relation with legislature
procedural	participating personnel; testimony at hearings; research materials; necessities for debate, etc.
preceptual	contents of reinforcive rules prescribing formal features and complementary material and other components

When I refer to a "part" of the whole of a legislature I refer to a formal feature of the whole *and* to the complementary material or other components that this feature specifies or arranges. There is more to the overall form and to the whole of a well-designed institution than what a mere listing of parts can reveal. This unified whole cannot be reduced, without remainder, to the mere sum of its parts. When parts are combined within the well-designed whole, synergistic effects will occur that exceed the sum of what would be the separate effects of each part alone. That is, here $1 + 1 = 3$! For example, when the procedural feature providing a stage in the process for study of draft statutes is combined with the committee structure for such study, the combined interactive effects of these and their complementary components exceed the total of what would be the separate effects alone of each of the two features with their own components.

I have so far not developed holistically the unified character of the parts of such an institution in any systematic way. I now turn to the unifying relations between parts as an avenue for advancing understanding of the whole. In so doing, I am guided by Immanuel Kant's famous injunction: "There is another thing to be attended to . . . namely to grasp correctly the idea of the whole and from there to get a view of all those parts as mutually interrelated."[42]

It is a primary attribute of any functional legal unit at all well-designed that it takes an overall form that is a unified whole. That is, the unit is itself systematically arranged as a whole to serve its purposes. The makeup and unity of this whole is perhaps best understood by way of contrast with several possible ways in which such a whole could lack unity. It might lack unity because the purposes of the systematic arrangement as a whole are conflicting and unprioritized. For example, the purposes of democracy and operational efficiency might not be duly prioritized. Institutional architects, purportedly to serve the purpose of "representative democracy," might misguidedly compose the legislature with a large and unwieldy membership fatal to operational efficiency. As a result, the whole would lack sufficient unity in this regard.

Further, the unit might lack all the parts necessary to be a functional whole. For example, a legislative institution might lack the jurisdictional feature, or the structural feature, or the procedural feature (along with complementary components). Without such part or parts, the whole would simply be incompletely formed and thus to an extent dysfunctional, given that each formal feature presupposes other formal features.

Moreover, even if complete in parts, that is, even if versions of all features of form and their complementary material and other components are present, some of these parts might still be ill-designed. For example, designers of a legislature might misguidedly seek to import a dialogic procedure appropriate to a court into a legislative procedure for the creation of statutes.

Finally, although existing parts might be potentially unifiable into a working whole, the designers of the institution might fail to specify the necessary integration. For example, they might create a two-chamber legislature, with both

---

[42] I. Kant, *Critique of Practical Reason and Other Works*, 95 (T. K. Abbott trans., 6th ed., Longman's, London, 1909).

Section Eight: Form and the Unity of the Legislature 129

chambers having responsibility for the making of laws, yet without providing for how the two chambers are to reconcile differences over proposed new statutes.

All four of the foregoing possible sources of disunity have been manifest in the institutions of legal systems. Merely to contemplate them is to see the importance of securing unity through choices of well-defined and organized form. In a unified institution, the purposes of the systematic arrangement will be duly formed, and where conflicting, duly prioritized. The whole will also be complete enough in its parts to be sufficiently functional, with each part itself duly designed and integrated into the whole. The foregoing choices of well-designed form, with complementary material and other components, unify the whole. This unifying function of form is explicitly recognized in technical usage, and in English lexicons, in very general terms, as that which "holds together the several elements of a thing."[43]

In legislative and in other major institutions, the main parts of the make-up of the whole are complex, and these main parts may have further complex counterparts at lower levels within the whole, all of which are to operate in tandem. For example, the whole legislative body has a compositional feature with its complementary components. If the body is a two-chamber legislature, then each chamber has its own composition. The committees within these bodies have their own composition. Likewise, the whole institution has a jurisdictional feature. If there are two chambers, one or both may have special jurisdiction. So, too, with regard to the jurisdiction of committees, and of any committee of the whole. Further, the whole institution has an overall internal structure. Again, if there are two chambers, there will be an internal structure for each, and a specified structural relation between them. Within each chamber, there will be specified relations between officers of the whole and individual members, and within and between committees there will be a specified structure. In addition, the whole has a procedural feature, and if there are two chambers there will be procedures for interactions between the two, procedures for operations of each, and procedures for the committees of each.

The foregoing makeup and unity comprise a complex and interdependent inner order, and no one feature can be effectively designed without regard to one or more of the others. The extent, density, complexity, and overall coherence of the definitive organization required in a well-designed institution such as a centralized legislature represents a great feat of overall form – a great feat of purposive systematic arrangement of the whole – a truth captured only in holistic perspective. In all this, form has a certain primacy over material and other components of the whole. Form defines and organizes roles to be fulfilled and pathways to be followed by personnel, as duly equipped with material and other resources for the conduct of institutional activities, all to serve purposes. The overall form and its constituent features define and organize who is to do what, when, how, and

---

[43] *OED, supra* n. 17, vol. 6, at "form," I.4.d.

by what means to serve purposes. Coherence is an essential purpose of form, and permeates the whole. To see how all this is so is to further one's understanding of the makeup, unity, mode of operation, and instrumental capacity of such an institutional unit.

Plainly one highly important way a legislature serves purposes is through its capacity to create valid statutes that are then implemented. It advances understanding to grasp, through the study of form, how each feature of overall legislative form jointly figures with other features and with complementary components in the creation of valid statutes. Thus, legislators voting for a bill creating a statutory rule must be properly elected (compositional), the statutory subject matter must fall within legislative power (jurisdictional), the bill must be considered for adoption in the form of a draft bill (methodological), studied in committee (structural and procedural), debated, subjected to possible amendment, and adopted by majority vote (procedural). Also, the bill must have any required assent of an executive branch where independent of the legislature (structural and procedural), the bill must generally be in the form of a rule that is sufficiently prescriptive, general, definite, and complete (preceptual), and the bill must be in printed form (expressional) and be duly promulgated (procedural). This summary account indicates the variety, complexity, interrelatedness, and general functions of required formal features.

This account also reveals how the foregoing formal features and their complementary material and other components can have effects that, when duly combined, contribute to the creation of statutory law. It also advances understanding to grasp how the creation of a statute is itself a synergistic effect of the foregoing complex combination. Thus, this combinatorial effect is greater than the mere sum of the individual effects of each of the formal features and their complementary material or other elements. Indeed, some of the individual effects could not even occur at all if the features and their complementary components were not so combined within a whole. Democratic enactment of a statute is just such an effect. For this to occur at all, at the very least compositional, jurisdictional, and procedural effects must be duly combined in the legislative processes involved. Well-designed form defines and organizes the makeup and unity of these very processes, and this inner order synchronizes formal features and complementary components to serve purposes. The resulting institution thus has characteristic modes of operation, special instrumental capacity, and distinctive identity as well.

In developed Western societies, legitimate democratic government under the rule of law requires the assent or voluntary acquiescence of the population over time. A population cannot meaningfully express such assent merely as assent to some general idea or abstraction. People can only express assent to, or acquiescence with respect to, concrete and public ways of doing things that are sufficiently definite and stable. This assent or acquiescence must extend at least to the broad outlines of the major institutions of democratic law-like governance. These broad

Section Nine: Skepticism about Institutional and Other Form

outlines include the overall forms and formal features of these institutions. For example, the overall form of a legislature and its features provide generally who is to do what, how, why, by what means, and with what effects in the making and implementation of statute law, and in the conduct of the other activities of a legislature. Though multi-faceted, the manifestations of such form and its features, are sufficiently concrete and public, at least in broad outline, to be objects of meaningful assent or acquiescence on the part of the populace or its representatives. Without such definite and stable form, there could be no meaningful assent to, or acquiescence in, what we know to be law-like governance, and this governance could not be legitimate.

A merely rule-oriented account, could not draw all of the foregoing together, although some of it might be pieced together from the contents of various particular rules purporting to be reinforcive of a democratic legislature. A form-oriented account is purposive and draws all of the foregoing together. It is, therefore, holistic and reveals the unity of inter-relations of formal features and of complementary components. It thus goes well beyond the contents of any particular reinforcive rules that merely prescribe various features of legislative form. It also reveals in general terms how the makeup and unity of the various formal features of the centralized legislative institution and the components complementary to these features make valid statutory enactment possible. As we have seen, operative effects of all of the foregoing features of overall legislative form figure directly or indirectly in satisfying the criterion of legal validity applicable here: "duly enacted by the legislature." This simple sounding phrase thus takes on new and complex meaning. It is overall legislative form and its features that define and organize a legislature and how it operates. Officials, citizens, and others must apply the foregoing criterion of validity (and in some systems, still other criteria) to differentiate a valid statutory rule from one that is not valid.[44] This source-oriented criterion is formal. Yet it presupposes scope in the legislative process for the exercise of democratic will, and for rational scrutiny of the form and content of proposed law. It also allows for relative certainty and predictability of particular judgments of officials and others to the effect that a designedly valid statute really is legally valid – essentials of the rule of law.

SECTION NINE: SKEPTICISM ABOUT INSTITUTIONAL AND OTHER FORM, AND RESPONSES THERETO

In this chapter, I have presented a description not of a thin version, but of what might be called a robust version of the overall form of a centralized legislative institution, and the constituent features of this form. This account reveals how

---

[44] Validity of a rule in a particular system could depend not only on form but also on some element of content. A statutory enactment the content of which infringes on a Bill of Rights could be invalid on that ground.

form purposively defines and organizes the resolution of compositional, jurisdictional, structural, procedural, and preceptual issues about who is to do what, when, how, and with what means, in the activities of participants in a democratic legislative institution. This mode of analysis also applies, *mutandis mutatis* to other functional legal units, noninstitutional as well as institutional.

One variety of form-skeptic might take the position here that nearly all of what I call legislative form here is not really form, but is rather the material or other components of a legislature. On this view, form is so thin that it barely exists as a possible avenue for advancing understanding or as an object of due credit for purposes realized. According to this form-skeptic, provision for selection of legislators is not really a formal compositional feature in any significant respect. Rather, it consists of very little more than the material component of personnel. Similarly, on this view, conferral of jurisdiction to legislate with regard, for example, to the subject matter of criminal law, is at best only very thinly formal, and consists in the main of the component of jurisdictional content, in this example, adoption of criminal statutes. Likewise, a two-chamber legislature, for example, is not essentially a formal structural feature, but again, essentially a complex material or other component – two houses rather than one. Similarly, provision for committee study and floor debate of bills is not essentially a formal procedural feature. Rather, it consists mainly of activities of personnel, a material or other component of the whole.

The general position of this form-skeptic leaves no, or very little, room for overall form and its constituent features, and leaves no, or very little, room for much except personnel, physical artifacts, and other material components. This position thus verges on denying that functional legal units – even institutional ones – take definitive forms at all or are organized at all as unitary wholes. The position of such a truly radical form-skeptic is simply not credible. Although it is certainly true that, in addition to form, an institution requires material or other components, we could not even know which such components a projected institution requires until we first determined the projected purposive systematic arrangement of the institution as a whole – its overall form, be it that of a legislature, or a court, or an administrative body, or some other institution.

Material components, such as personnel and physical facilities, are essential, but, as demonstrated in this chapter, it is form that specifies, defines, organizes, and regiments these components into an effective functional legal unit to serve purposes. Persons are merely persons. A building is simply a building. The nature and place of the material and other components within a functional unit depends on the overall form and formal features that define and organize these components, and on the imprints and other effects that such form leaves on these components. For example, legislators, in being duly elected and thus qualified to sit in the legislature bear this very imprint of compositional form. Far from material or other

Section Nine: Skepticism about Institutional and Other Form

components of a unit swallowing up or eclipsing form, as the skeptic might have it, it is overall form that purposively and systematically arranges these very materials or other components within a functional unit of the system. The robustness of the required overall form and its constituent features is especially plain in the legislative example.

A less radical form-skeptic might embrace a conception of the overall form of an institution that is not quite so thin. On this conception, the scope left for what would truly be features of overall form could still be small, however. Such features might, at most, only be highly abstract and skeletal resolutions of very general definitional and organizational issues as to composition, jurisdiction, structure, procedure, or methodology. Taken together, these still relatively thin formal features could, at most, amount to no more than a highly schematic general arrangement that goes only a very limited bit of the way to determining who the legislators are to be, to indicating merely that they are to have jurisdiction of some vague and general sort, and to providing that legislators are merely to operate within some kind of very abstract and indefinite structural and procedural set-up. Such features of overall institutional form would be indeterminate, anemic, and mostly very bare bones with little flesh. They could barely reveal, if at all, any institutional attributes such as the makeup and unity of the unit, its special instrumental capacity, and its distinct identity. This skeptic's highly thin version of form simply could not suffice. It would be an eviscerated version that fails to capture well-designed form's richness of purpose, robustness of systematic arrangement, *and overall efficacy of means-end relations*. How robust must form be to fulfill its essential defining and organizing purposes?

First, if an overall form is truly to be the purposive systematic arrangement of a functional legal unit such as a legislature, then it must at least be sufficiently robust to define and organize this functional unit so that it can serve its founding and other purposes, and thus have the instrumental capacity required for its characteristic functions, here law-making, oversight of administration, confirmation of official appointments, and so on. It cannot, as in the foregoing highly thin conception, be a merely skeletal abstraction relatively devoid of any instrumental or constitutive organization. Form so thin simply could not sufficiently specify, define, and organize the functional unit so that it could serve relevant purposes. Consider, for example, a highly thin compositional feature of a legislature consisting of no more than that "there be personnel." Such a feature would be so thin that it would specify no determinate makeup of personnel and thus would leave little by way of imprints upon the component of personnel. It could provide no specific answers to such essential questions as: Elected personnel? Personnel qualified to serve what purposes? Legislative law making? What else? How many legislators? From where, and what length of term, and so on? Or consider, for example, a highly thin procedural feature, namely one that consists of no more than a generality to the effect that the body "shall operate to create laws." Such a feature would be devoid of any meaningful specification of mode of operation or of the relevant instrumental capacity, and thus would not be at all organizationally definitive. As thus meagerly specified or otherwise ill-defined, it would simply be too thin to serve the purpose of making laws or to serve other legislative purposes.

To elaborate briefly, a legislature must, for example, have the organized capacity to consider and adopt statutory law. I have shown here how this requires, among other things, detailed procedural and other features of form, including written and fixed verbal features of statutory proposals, and a formal decision-rule, such as "adoption by majority vote." These and related formal features must be relatively robust rather than thin. Without procedural features, and without formal compositional, jurisdictional, and structural features, duly defined and organized, individual legislators could not themselves know what the contours of their own institutional *roles* would be, and would lack defined institutional *pathways* to follow in the conduct of their activities. Form defines and organizes these roles and pathways. Also, without such form, other members of the society at large could not even determine when institutional actors could be said to be duly acting on their behalf.

Second, overall form must at least be robust enough to provide criteria of identity for a functional legal unit so that we may discern and understand what is truly distinctive about the unit. That form is the primary source of such identifying criteria is a position traceable at least to the ancient Greeks. Such criteria allow for identification of the functional unit, and for its differentiation from another of the same sub-type, thereby also advancing understanding of the unit. On a highly abstract and thin conception of form of the kind the skeptic embraces, the imprints of form on other formal features and on material or other components would be so slight that it would not even be possible to tell whether an institution is of the legislative sub-type or of the judicial sub-type, or of the administrative sub-type, or of some other. A sufficiently robust conception of form is required to specify, define, and organize the purposive systematic arrangement of the functional unit, including its more particular purposes, so that it has its distinct identity. Plainly, the material and other components cannot give the unit such an identity. Thus, several people ("personnel") sitting in a room ("material resources") discussing possible alternative rules ("content") and expressing their preferences for one rule over another (choices) could hardly be identified on such skeletal bases as a legislature. The distinct identity of such an institutional unit (or, indeed, any unit) can be determined only by reference to a sufficiently robust version of its overall form with its constituent features and distinctive defining and organizing purposes. The special overall makeup, unity, mode of operation, instrumental capacity, and other facets of distinct identity presuppose basic differences of institutional definition and organization – differences of form in these very respects.

Section Nine: Skepticism about Institutional and Other Form

Third, it is only through sufficiently robust definitional and organizational forms that diverse functional legal units, such as legislatures and other institutions, rules and other precepts, interpretive and other methodologies, sanctions and remedies, and still other functional units, can be coherently combined, integrated, and coordinated within general operational techniques for creating and implementing law. To be so integrated and coordinated effectively, these diverse functional units must be sufficiently defined and organized on their own and also in light of the other units with which they are to be integrated, so that they can fulfill their own distinctive roles within these general operational techniques. These techniques, to be studied in Chapters Ten and Eleven, themselves take fundamentally different forms: the penal technique, the grievance remedial technique, the administrative-regulatory technique, the public-benefit conferral technique, and the private-arranging technique. Mere material and other components, such as physical facilities and personnel, simply cannot account for the distinctive operational coherence of discrete functional units as integrated and coordinated within any such technique. Nor can a thin conception of form. As Jhering implied, institutional and other legal forms must be robust. They cannot be "bare and thin."[45]

Finally, I have so far merely assumed that robust form must be purposive, and that these purposes are value-laden in developed Western systems. A form skeptic or other proponent of thin form might object that these assumptions "load up" or "bloat" form beyond all recognition as form that merely defines and organizes functional units. Thus, the purposes here, for example, rational legislative functions, democratic composition and operation, the fundamental political value of legitimacy, and the rule of law, are all heavily value-laden and import a veritable panoply of substantive values into form. According to the skeptic, form is no longer merely form, but is heavily value-laden.

In response, it is sufficient to say that if form in legal ordering is to be rationally defined and organized to serve purposes, then it *must* become value-laden at least insofar as those purposes themselves implicate values (as they typically do). It would be impossible, for example, to define and organize, i.e., give form to, a democratic legislature without regard to what a legislature ought to be if it is to be a legislature and without regard to what a democratic legislature ought to be if it is to be such a legislature. Indeed, form cannot be designed at all in a purposeless vacuum devoid of all value. This is not to say, however, that just any form is necessarily good in objective terms. Nor is it to say that value-laden form cannot be deployed to serve bad purposes.

---

[45] R. Jhering, *supra* n. 15, vol. 2, at 478.

5 ∿ FORMS OF PRECEPTS – RULES

"What a multitude of things there are . . . in a law."   – Bentham[1]

SECTION ONE: INTRODUCTION

Legal systems recognize varied functional units that are preceptual in nature, including rules, principles, maxims, and general orders. Each variety takes its own overall form. When well-designed, such purposive systematic arrangements can contribute to the realization of policy or other preceptual content. As Jhering held, there can be no realization of such content without form.[2] Due form in rules can also serve general values of the rule of law, and these values may even conflict with, and justifiably over-ride, policy or other content to an extent, a truth I stress here. Form in rules can contribute as well to the realization of democracy, justice, freedom, security, rationality, and other fundamental political values. As we will see, the form and formal features of rules leave major imprints and other effects on the contents of rules. Here, too, much of what may already be familiar will be presented anew in the idiom of form and the formal.

Rules have long occupied legal theorists and other scholars.[3] Rules may be said to be the "workhorse" precepts of legal systems and are worthy of extended attention. Yet despite the long history of legal studies, the overall form of rules and its constituent features have not received their due. It will be sufficient to

---

[1] J. Bentham, *An Introduction to the Principles of Morals and Legislation*, 311 (J. Burns and H. L. A. Hart eds., Clarendon Press, Oxford, 1996).

[2] R. Jhering, *Geist des Römischen Rechts: auf den verschiedenen Stufen seiner Entwicklung*, vol. 2, at 473 (Scientia Verlag, Aalen, 1993).

[3] See generally, G. H. von Wright, *Norm and Action* (Routledge and Kegan Paul, London, 1963). Among the many prior works, two recent and illuminating treatments are F. Schauer, *Playing by the Rules: A Philosophical Examination of Rule-Based Decision-Making in Law and in Life* (Clarendon Press, Oxford, 1991) and L. Alexander and E. Sherwin, *The Rule of Rules* (Duke University Press, Durham, 2001). None of these works concentrates frontally, systematically, and comprehensively on the formal features of rules as such.

Section One: Introduction

concentrate here on a common paradigm of the overall form of a statutory rule, the constituent features of such form, complementary content, and how all these are unified. The focus will be on regulative rules governing primary conduct of addressees on the frontiers of human interaction rather than on those rules, here called reinforcive, which prescribe features of other functional legal units such as legislatures, courts, contracts, interpretive methodologies, and sanctions. Still, much of the analysis of form here can be applied to reinforcive rules, too.

In many developed Western systems, statutory rules are by far the most important species of preceptual law. Even in Anglo-American common law systems, statutory rules today play very large roles. The creation of statutory rules poses the full range of choices of form in rules. Most of the analysis here applies to form in nonstatutory rules as well. Some of the analysis also applies, *mutatis mutandis*, to form in preceptual units other than rules, such as principles, maxims, and general orders.

The overall form of the paradigm of a statutory rule to be considered here is as follows. This form has diverse purposes. Its founding purpose is simply that of bringing the functional unit of a rule into being. Its immediate purpose is to prescribe to its addressees that specified action must, or may, or may not occur. A rule that so prescribes usually does so "as a rule" – that is, as a regular matter in recurrent circumstances.[4] The constituent features of the overall form of a rule consist of its prescriptiveness, completeness, generality, definiteness, internal structure, manner of expression, and mode of encapsulation. The overall form of a rule is more than the sum of its constituent features. It also includes the inter-relations between such features and an all embracing conception of the form of the unit as a whole including the features and their inter-relations.

The ultimate purposes of the overall form and complementary content of well-designed rules are these: to contribute, in combination with other functional units, to the realization of (1) policies and similar social ends, (2) general values of the rule of law, and (3) fundamental political values. The foregoing array of founding, immediate, and ultimate purposes can inform the form and content of even the simplest proposed rule. A proposed rule is to be evaluated for its form, for the quality of the ends aimed at, the efficacy of the means prescribed, the costs to be incurred in terms of conflicting ends foregone, and the costs of the means. Thus, reason has many points of entry here. Indeed, the commitment to purposive rationality in constructing the form and content of well-designed rules must be pervasive.

---

[4] Similarly, R. Collingwood once said: To make a rule is to adopt "a generalized decision to do many things of a specific kind on occasions of a specific kind. . . ." R. Collingwood, *The New Leviathan or Man, Society, Civilization and Barbarism*, 216 (Revised ed., D. Boucher ed., Clarendon Press, Oxford, 1992).

As John Finnis once observed, the making of a well-designed legal rule is almost never a mere "repromulgation" of a generally accepted policy norm or of a recognized moral or other social rule.[5] Rather, the making of such a legal rule is irreducibly creative, and is not arbitrary. Given the founding purpose to create a rule, reason dictates adoption of the overall form of a rule. When it comes to the immediate and ultimate purposes to be served, reason enters into the choices of these very purposes – ends – and into the choices of features of form and content as means to serve them. Such choices are seldom arbitrary. They call for identifying and articulating reasons for and against alternative choices of form and content, and for the weighing and balancing of such reasons.

The overall form of a statutory rule should not be conceived as in the nature of a ready-made, and thus pre-existing, mold into which content is poured, with this overall form having no effects on the content, and the content having no effects on this form. As I will show, the design of a rule requires choices of form that can affect whatever complementary content the rule is to have. Usually, imprints or other effects of form may be identified all over this content. Moreover, content can interact with and shape form in the construction of a rule.

Given the fundamental nature and wide importance of rules, it is hardly surprising that several principles of the rule of law, in effect, specify general desiderata of form in rules. Among other things, these principles require that rules be general, definite, and clearly expressed – three features of the overall form of a rule. Tenets of the rule of law such as fair notice and equal treatment favor the construction of rules that are prescriptive, complete, and relatively determinate rather than open-ended – basic choices of form.

We will consider not merely the capacity of rules as instruments of external policies or of other ends derived from independent sources. We will also explicate their other attributes of makeup and unity – their "inner order." As Jhering would have put it, form is rooted in the "innermost essence" of rules.[6] We will also address the attributes of mode of operation, determinateness, and distinct identity of a rule as a functional legal unit. We will focus on a well-designed rule as a source of legal reasons for determinate action or decision on the part of its addressees. In these ways, we seek to advance understanding of the attributes of rules.

The aim is also to determine the general credit due form for ends realized. Why give credit to well-designed form? All the credit here should not go to material or other components of the rule, such as policy content and addressees. Form and the quality of its design contributes, too. The focus on credit due well-designed form also facilitates the formulation of general standards for critical evaluation of actual or proposed forms and can lead to improvements in design.

---

[5] *The Oxford Companion to Philosophy*, 471 (T. Honderich ed., Oxford University Press, Oxford, 1995).
[6] R. Jhering, *supra* n. 2, at 479.

Section One: Introduction

The constituent features of the overall form of a rule are its prescriptiveness, completeness, generality, definiteness, internal structure, manner of expression, and mode of encapsulation. Although Plato identified all of the foregoing features, he did not always keep them distinct, and he did not develop a stable nomenclature with names for each.[7] In naming them here, my intent is to introduce a felicitous and stable vocabulary, one that also sharpens awareness of these features, their distinctiveness, their inter-relations, and the imprints and other effects of these features on each other and on the contents of rules.

A "rule" that uncertainly prescribes, is incomplete, lacks due generality, is unduly indefinite, lacks internal structure, is unclear in expression, or lacks appropriate encapsulation, does not have the overall form – the purposive systematic arrangement – of a rule that is well-designed, and such a rule is certain to merit less credit for any ends served. Even in developed legal systems, examples of malformed, and therefore instrumentally deficient, rules are not difficult to find.

The purposes of a rule go far to determine its form and content. However, the internal features of the overall form of a rule, such as generality and definiteness, are by no means determined solely by ultimate purposes consisting of policy aims or the like. As we will see, each feature has an integrity of its own as a necessary or salient feature of a rule, which can exert its own shaping influence on complementary content.

Throughout this chapter, I apply a form-oriented approach to advance understanding of rules and to attribute credit due to their overall form and constituent features thereof. A merely rule-oriented analysis of the form of such rules is not really possible in systems of law known to me. For a merely rule-oriented analysis to be possible, there would at least have to be a more or less comprehensive set of reinforcive rules of positive law with content prescribing the formal features of rules of the system. In the systems known to me, there are simply no such sets of rules. It is true that in some systems, there are isolated legal doctrines that do purport to prescribe one or two of the formal features of some rules. For example, in American constitutional law, the "void for vagueness doctrine" requires definiteness in some rules,[8] and the "equal protection" clause requires some generality.[9]

Rationality in the construction of a rule is a primary focus here. Just as there can, for example, be good reasons for choosing one version of policy over another version in the content of a proposed rule, there can be good reasons for choosing between different possible features of the overall form of a given proposed rule,

---

[7] *The Dialogues of Plato*, vol. 2, The Laws, 407–703 (B. Jowett trans., Random House, New York, 1937). Plato also did not provide a systematic analysis.

[8] See, e.g., *Lanzetta v. New Jersey*, 306 U.S. 451 (1939) and *Kolender v. Lawson*, 461 U.S. 352 (1983).

[9] See, e.g., *McLaughlin v. Florida*, 379 U.S. 184 (1964); see also, L. Fuller, *The Morality of Law*, 46 (Revised ed., Yale University Press, New Haven, 1969).

too. Choices between alternative versions of nearly all formal features, can be of immense significance. A choice, for example, between high definiteness and low definiteness must be manifest in complementary content of the rule and thus leave a significant imprint on that content. For example, high definiteness is an imprint of a formal feature manifest in the content of a rule allowing persons to vote "at age 21," as opposed to "at age of maturity." Ultimate purposes consisting of policy or other ends frequently conflict, and these, in turn, may conflict with general values of the rule of law and with fundamental political values. For example, traffic rules purporting to secure safety can conflict with fundamental values of free choice and citizen self-determination. Study of a draft rule such as "Drive no faster than 65 mph" for some roadways reveals how the formal feature of high definiteness can be adopted to resolve such a conflict so that the rule can have relatively stable, uniform, and meaningful content for addressees. A mere "drive reasonably" rule would leave the driver relatively free in the first instance to resolve such conflicts ad hoc, and leave open possibilities of quite inconsistent resolutions by the same driver on different occasions and as between different drivers on similar occasions. Again, as Jhering would have put it, the formal feature of definiteness can prioritize here as between conflicting ends and thus "fix fluid substance."[10]

As we saw in Chapter Four, the proposed content of a statutory rule, when in duly definitive and written form, can also be more effectively studied, debated, amended, and adopted by the legislature than can mere generalized statements of policy.[11] Further, the drafter of statutory rules who understands the complex anatomy of the overall form of a rule, and who is methodologically conscientious, that is, duly sensitive to the principles of a sound drafting methodology, is certain to be a better drafter and thus contribute more effectively to the creation of statutory rules. Moreover, if a legislature adopts a rule with well-designed features of overall form, this will later facilitate efforts of addressees of the rule to interpret the rule faithfully, and thus construct authoritative reasons for determinate action thereunder, and then act accordingly. Thus, much credit can be due to choices of formal features here. An addressee can faithfully construct and act on a reason for determinate action under a formally well-designed rule without being conscious that, or conscious of precisely how, features of form make this possible. It is likely, for example, that few citizens who abide by a rule specifying a deadline for filing their tax returns, are conscious, for example, that a high degree of definiteness is a *formal* feature of the rule at work here.

As we have seen, not all rules are "regulative." In Chapter Four, we focused on examples of that other class of rules that are "reinforcive" insofar as they prescribe features of the form of a functional legal unit, such as, for example, the

---

[10] R. Jhering, *supra* n. 2, at 471–8.
[11] See *supra* Chapter Four, at Section 6.

Section Two: Internal Formal Features of Rules

composition, structure, and procedure of a legislature, or prescribe its complementary material or other components. "Regulative" rules on the other hand, are far more numerous and are mainly addressed to and regulate, primary behavior of citizens in affairs of daily life. Many regulative rules prescribe actions that serve general policies such as the maintenance of community peace, the facilitation of traffic flow, the provision of potable water, the regulation of food and drugs, the judicial redress of torts and breaches of contracts, and so on. Some regulative rules and their overall forms are also means of serving such fundamental political values as rationality, freedom, democracy, legitimacy, and justice. Here, as Jhering put it, form can be "the sworn enemy of the arbitrary, and the twin sister of liberty."[12] Many regulative rules and their form also serve general values of the rule of law such as certainty and predictability, the dignity and efficiency of citizen self-direction under law, equality before the law, dispute avoidance, and dispute settlement. All the foregoing values are commonly recognized as concerns of law but they are not so often recognized as concerns of form in law.

SECTION TWO: INTERNAL FORMAL FEATURES OF RULES

There are many varieties of legal rules in any legal system. However, all of the following are true of most individual rules:

(1) the rule has various components of subject matter content,

(2) the rule prescribes components of content in that it directly or indirectly prohibits, permits, or requires action of addressees or ordains a state of affairs, and is, therefore, neither merely descriptive nor merely precatory,

(3) the rule prescribes components of content within the overall form of a rule, that is, it prescribes content complementary to constituent features of the overall form of a rule – completeness, definiteness, generality, and internal structure – the primary focus of the present chapter,

(4) the rule inter-relates and unifies the prescriptiveness, completeness, generality, definiteness, and internal structure of the overall form and complementary content of the whole rule, the overall unity of which comprises a whole greater than the sum of the parts of the rule,

(5) the overall form and complementary content of the rule is partly based, directly or indirectly, [a] on empirical generalizations about relations between means and policy or other ends, or [b] on reasoned hypotheses about how law can organize and facilitate some end such as the democratic election and accountability of political leaders, or [c] on general moral or social principles, or [d] on a conception of the essential or appropriate

---

[12] R. Jhering, *supra* n. 2, at 471. Many regulative rules also serve fundamental political values and values of the rule of law, as well.

form of an institution, precept, methodology, sanction, or other type of functional legal unit, which may or may not be set forth in law,

(6) the rule also has a formal expressional feature that is relatively explicit, usually in writing (or printing), and in appropriate grammar, syntax, and vocabulary of a common language of the system, at least when the rule is state-made, as opposed to privately made,

(7) the rule is also embodied in a formal encapsulatory feature, be it a constitutional provision, a statute, an administrative regulation, the common law, custom, a contractual form, or some other recognized authoritative form,

(8) the rule, if state-made, can usually be found as set forth in annual legislative compilations, official reports, or other authoritative sources.

When well-designed, each formal feature is distinct and independently significant, yet inter-related with the others in a unified whole. Each such feature serves the ends of the rule and can even leave major imprints or other effects on the content in which it is manifest. A grasp of these truths sharpens awareness of formal features and of their distinctness, and advances understanding of rules. This also makes it possible to see much more of what there is to a rule than if preoccupied merely with the policy or purported end-serving actions prescribed in components of content in a particular rule. The analysis here enables one to appreciate more fully the importance of particular choices of formal features in rules and the many kinds of good reasons that may justify such choices – itself a special avenue for advancing understanding of the attributes of a rule as a functional legal unit.

This analysis also positions us to see more clearly how a share of credit must go to the overall form of a rule and its features for whatever is achieved through the rule. For example, without due definiteness, it would not be possible, in the drafting of a rule, to prioritize firmly as between conflicting policies (such as the trade-off between safety and efficiency in a highway speed limit rule). Without due definiteness, it would not be possible to give addressees of such a rule fair advanced notice of what is required of them. Without due definiteness, it would not be possible for addressees to construct determinate reasons for action or decision under the rule – reasons that pre-empt conflicting moral, economic, and other practical considerations. Similar truths apply with respect to other features of the overall form of a rule.

This is not to say that choices of complementary content are not of vital import as well. Indeed, only after choice of some possible projected content, however tentative, can there even be occasion for choices of form. These choices cannot be made wholly independently of content. Choices of most formal features commonly implicate a choice or choices of complementary content. Rational choices of these features cannot be made without regard to their effects on this content.

SECTION THREE: THE FEATURE OF PRESCRIPTIVENESS

The most common legal rules have the feature of prescriptiveness. That is, such rules prescribe that an action or decision of a certain type is prohibited, permitted, or required. Many governmental communications are not prescriptive. Instead, they are merely precatory, hortatory, or descriptive. Hence, they cannot be rules according to the conception considered here. Language that is precatory merely recommends, entreats, or perhaps advises action or decision, as with advice to officers for the driving of police cars. Language that is merely hortatory exhorts or urges action or decision, as with calls for military volunteers. Language that merely describes represents in factual terms an action or decision or some related aspect or aspects. Of course, a rule, in prescribing, must include some terms that are descriptive, too.

There is sufficient reason to characterize the prescriptiveness of rules as formal. If a precept is to take the overall form of such a rule, it must in some way prescribe that a purported end-serving action or decision occur (under relevant circumstantial or other conditions), or prescribe that an action or decision not occur, or prescribe that such action or decision is permitted. A purported "rule" that fails to prescribe at all cannot be a rule of the common type considered here. It cannot direct, forbid, or permit action or decision and, therefore, serve the immediate purposes of the systematic arrangement of such a rule.

Thus, prescriptiveness is not only a feature, but a necessary feature of the overall form of the highly common type of rule considered here. It is one of several constituent features that together satisfies our general definition of form, as refined here to fit rules. Our general definition, as the purposive systematic arrangement of a functional legal unit, was introduced and defended in Chapter Two.[13]

Prescriptiveness is manifest in language of a rule specifying what actions or decisions "must," or "may not," or "may" occur and thus leaves a major formal imprint on the content of the rule. Prescriptiveness is to be contrasted with the complementary content of the prescription – the purported end-serving action or decision of specified addressees (and any relevant circumstances or conditions). The distinct identity of this formal feature can be readily discerned even though this feature is manifest in the very content of the rule. That is, this feature can be seen to answer to the concept of formal prescriptiveness, and can be isolated, described, and differentiated from complementary components of content in the rule.

Prescriptiveness, then, is not reducible to the content it prescribes. Any given prescriptive feature, such as language imposing a duty to take action, can apply to highly variable content – highly variable end-serving actions or decisions that addressees are to take. Moreover, the standards for determining formal

---

[13] See pp. 39–42.

prescriptiveness as duly end-serving, and the standards for evaluating content as duly end-serving, are not the same. Formal prescriptiveness consists of appropriate modal language: "must," or "may not," or "may," or synonymous expressions. A choice of this language could be duly prescriptive, yet the action or decision of the rule's addressees – the content so prescribed – fail to suit means to end, as with, for example, a speed limit rule that sets the limit too high. Or although the action itself be an apt means to the end in view, the language of the rule might not duly prescribe such action – it might be merely descriptive, hortatory, or precatory.

The mere fact that the prescription in the rule itself names or specifies content such as the end-serving action or decision subject to the prescription, does not signify that the actual content so named or specified is also to be classified as formal. The formal prescription in a rule must itself name or specify some content as the relevant end-serving action or decision. If merely so naming or specifying any facet of the make-up of a rule signifies that this facet is formal, it would follow that any rule is all form and no content, which would be false.

Many rules categorically prescribe that action must occur, or prescribe that action not occur. A rule of this nature affords addressees an authoritative, i.e., legal, reason for action or decision. This legal reason may conflict with competing moral, economic, or other social considerations emergent in the particular circumstances to which the rule applies. Seldom does any such legal rule include an explicit provision stating that the rule pre-empts any or all such competing moral, economic, or other social considerations. Nevertheless, in developed systems of law, categorical prescriptiveness in a legal rule is generally considered to pre-empt all such competing considerations, both for addressees who are officials as well as for private parties. As H. L. A. Hart once put it, a legal rule characteristically "makes a general claim to priority over other standards."[14] Without prescriptiveness, addressees of a "rule" could not take it to be a pre-emptive reason for action or decision. Here, too, major credit is due the formal feature of prescriptiveness, and such credit is in no way contingent on particular facts derived from empirical inquiry.

Some rules grant permissions or liberties. A rule of this type is still prescriptive. It explicitly directs that certain actions or decisions are permitted. Without more, it usually implicitly prescribes that interference by others with those who take permitted actions or decisions is not allowed. For example, a rule that grants me the right to drive my car not only means that I may drive if I choose, but also implicitly directs officials and others not to interfere with my choice, except insofar as I may drive impaired in some way, or drive a dangerous vehicle, or drive a vehicle I have no right to drive, or the like. Although such a rule does not, as such, give me a reason to drive on any particular occasion, it does direct others

---

[14] H. L. A. Hart, *The Concept of Law*, 249 (2nd ed., Clarendon Press, Oxford, 1994). This is not, however, the same as to say there is a moral obligation to obey all pre-emptory law, regardless of its content. See further *infra* n. 15 and accompanying text.

Section Three: The Feature of Prescriptiveness

not to interfere when I do decide to drive. It generally pre-empts countervailing reasons others might think they have to interfere.

To learn what all is prescribed in a rule, and learn which conflicting considerations it generally pre-empts, it is necessary also to turn to other features of form and complementary components of content that, together with prescriptiveness, enable addressees to determine the legal reasons for action or decision that arise under it. A purported prescription in a rule cannot be effectively directive in nature, and cannot effectively pre-empt conflicting considerations if the rule itself does not give rise to a reason for determinate action (or decision). A rule might fail to do so because it is incomplete, or over-general, or indefinite, or lacks coherent internal structure, or lacks clear and unambiguous expression. Yet when duly designed formal features are present in a rule that duly prescribes, the rule will give rise to reasons for determinate and pre-emptive action or decision.

Different rules may have differing degrees of pre-emptiveness. For example, at one polarity, a given rule may categorically and determinately prohibit or require action, and be construed as absolutely pre-emptive in legal terms. Such a rule would give rise to reasons for determinate action or decision that *in law* conclusively over-ride other legal reasons, equitable considerations in the particular case, and other countervailing moral, economic, or other reasons.[15] A very high degree of pre-emptoriness may be essential. This is true, for example, of rules prohibiting certain crimes, rules governing highway traffic, rules against contaminating water supplies, and many other regulative rules.

At the opposite pole, a rule, although otherwise duly determinate and directional, may only quite conditionally require behavior and thus have a low degree of pre-emptoriness. There are many such rules in the law. For example, some rules merely require a particular action or state of affairs provided that the affected private parties have not chosen, or do not choose, otherwise! This is true, for example, with respect to many general rules of law governing the content and performance of contracts – rules that apply only when the contracting parties have not provided otherwise, as, for example, with a rule providing that a seller of goods, unless otherwise agreed, discharges the duty to deliver the goods to the buyer merely by making the goods available to the buyer at the seller's place of business.

---

[15] This is not to say that under such a rule there is an absolute moral obligation to obey, regardless. In the analysis I offer here, from the fact that a legal rule is determinate and pre-emptory – even highly so, it does not follow that its addressees have a moral obligation to obey it. A legal duty is not necessarily a moral duty. Legal pre-emptoriness imposes a legal duty to follow what the law requires, even in disregard of competing moral, economic, personal, or other motives. It does not – indeed, it could not, impose a legal duty that over-rides any and all moral considerations to the contrary. For treatment of other complexities of pre-emptoriness, see P. Atiyah and R. Summers, *Form and Substance in Anglo-American Law: A Comparative Study of Legal Reasoning, Legal Theory, and Legal Institutions*, 16–17 (Clarendon Press, Oxford, 1987).

The language actually used to express prescriptiveness may not be wholly clear, and may call for interpretation. Various interpretive aids may then become relevant. For example, when a sanction or other such disincentive is in the offing if an addressee fails to act in some way, this will usually signify prescriptiveness. However, even language that on its face appears to be prescriptive may turn out not to be, all things considered. Consideration of adjacent law, or applicable interpretive or other principles, may ultimately yield the conclusion that seemingly prescriptive language is not really prescriptive after all, but is merely a precatory communication, or the like.

To summarize: in the most common type of rule, prescriptiveness requires, prohibits, or permits action (or ordains some institutional or other state of affairs). The imprint of prescriptiveness is ordinarily manifest in the language expressing the form and content of the rule. Prescriptiveness is a necessary feature of the overall form of such a rule – its purposive systematic arrangement. It is a positive feature of the rule, albeit a feature of its form. It is actually present in the rule, though it can be isolated for separate analysis, description, and evaluation, and is susceptible of affirmative characterization on its own terms.

This is not to say that prescriptiveness, as such, is the only feature of the overall form of a rule that can motivate action or decision in accord with the reasons that arise under it. Nor is it to say addressees act on such reasons merely because they are legal in nature. A general sense among addressees that "what the law says" is for the common good may also be a factor. Another possible factor is a felt duty to follow whatever the law says. Among still other factors is this. Addressees may be induced to act by communicated claims of right by those who would be adversely affected by nonfulfillment of a prescribed duty.

A system of law is not merely an aggregation of functional legal units duly systematized. It is also a vast network of extant legal relations between persons, between entities, and between persons and entitites. Most of these extant relations derive from rules. Prescriptiveness figures centrally with respect to all such relations. For example, many rules prescribing that persons must act or refrain, in effect prescribe duties and thus confer corresponding rights. Rules prescribe still other relations that take their own forms, too. For example, rules confer powers on persons, with other persons subject to the exercise of those powers. Many rules may be said to carve out "protected spaces" in which individuals exercise freedom and autonomy in the conduct of their affairs. Existing legal relations, including their own forms, are not to be equated with, or reduced to, the contents of such rules. Only if we go beyond the contents of rules and also deploy a form-oriented analysis, can we identify, describe, and differentiate types of extant legal relations and their forms, and trace them to rules or to other laws in force.[16]

---

[16] See W. Hohfeld, "Some Fundamental Legal Conceptions As Applied in Judicial Reasoning," 23 *Yale L.J.* 16 (1913); A. Corbin, "Jural Relations and their Classification," 30 *Yale L.J.* 226 (1920).

Section Four: The Feature of Completeness 147

To understand the most common type of legal rule, then, we must at least understand its prescriptiveness – a feature of its overall form. Without prescriptiveness, a rule could not serve the ends of such a rule, either. Prescriptiveness necessarily figures in the make-up, unity, and instrumental capacity of such rules. Also, without prescriptiveness, we could not have the vast network of legal relations extant in Western societies. Thus, much credit is due this formal feature.

SECTION FOUR: THE FEATURE OF COMPLETENESS

Completeness of rule may seem simple. It is, however, highly complex and extensive. Standard lexicons define something as complete if it has "all its parts or elements."[17] Here, I conceive a possible rule abstractly as having "spaces" for components of content, all of which must be fully "filled" to be totally complete, that is, to have "all of its parts or elements." The extent of completeness is a matter of degree and depends on how many spaces are filled and how far they are filled. Different types of rules have "spaces" that differ in nature and number. For example, a complex rule of the criminal law might have the following spaces for components of content: (1) scope, (2) addressees, (3) action, (4) requisite mental state of actor, (5) circumstances of acting, and (6) effects of action. A simple rule regulating how pedestrians cross the street would have fewer spaces. Thus, completeness is relative to type of rule.

There are sufficient reasons to characterize completeness of rule as a formal feature, even though it must be accompanied by complementary content in the relevant space or spaces. For a functional unit to take its form, it must be in some degree complete in the form it purports to take. The overall form of a totally complete rule has all of its spaces filled with content. With no degree of completeness, a purported rule simply could not take the overall form of a rule. At least a minimally sufficient degree of completeness is a necessary feature of the overall form of a rule. Completeness is one of several features that together satisfy the general definition of overall form, as duly refined to fit a rule. This general definition – the purposive systematic arrangement of a functional legal unit – was introduced and defended in Chapter Two. Standard English lexicons also designate completeness as a feature of form.[18]

Completeness is necessarily manifest in complementary components of content occupying spaces in a rule. A rule the spaces of which are filled with content will be complete in content and, therefore, also in form. Assume that the content of a given rule is to consist of components of scope, addressees, end-serving action, relevant circumstantial conditions, and any specified effects. The formal feature of completeness would manifest itself in complementary content filling these very

---

[17] *The Oxford English Dictionary*, vol. 3, at "complete," 1.a (2nd ed., J. Simpson and E. Weiner eds., Clarendon Press, Oxford, 1989), hereinafter *OED*.

[18] *Id.*, vol. 6, at "formal," A.3.b.

spaces. The formal imprints of completeness are necessarily dependent on such complementary content, and cannot be divorced from that content. A change in degree of completeness must manifest itself in the addition or subtraction of content from one or more spaces. The extent of completeness in a rule is a matter of degree. However, if a rule is not complete, it could be so dysfunctional that it would not even count as a rule. In the framework of analysis here, a rule that is incomplete in content necessarily has two deficiencies. It is deficient in this very content, and it is, therefore, also deficient in form, that is, lacks completeness in a space or spaces within the overall form of the rule.

Despite the intimacy of formal completeness and complementary content, the two are not the same. In virtue of having components of content in all its spaces, a complete rule is still not reducible to "all content and no formal completeness." It is still possible to isolate and differentiate the formal feature of completeness from the content in which it is instantiated. A conception of what counts as a complete rule of the type at hand – a feature of the overall form of such a rule – is required. The *spaces* to be filled with content in order for a rule to be complete are distinctly identifiable as answering to the conception of formal completeness applicable to a rule of the type at hand. The spaces in this conception can themselves be isolated, described, and also differentiated from any contents that happen to occupy such spaces.

Rules of different types vary somewhat in their overall form, and, therefore, vary in possible spaces for content. To know what content a type of rule requires to be complete, we must first determine what spaces there are to be filled in a rule of this type.

Completeness in spaces, as a feature of the overall form of a rule, then, is distinct from the complementary and contrasting components of content of the rule – from, for example, the prescribed addressees, actions, circumstances, and so forth, in the rule. This distinctness can be seen in further ways. It is often true that one or more spaces in the same rule can be instantiated in quite different ways, that is, with highly varied content. For example, the very same space in a rule about when to require workers to retire can be filled with a bright-line ("retire at age 60"), or a discretionary standard ("when no longer fit"), or some combination. In addition, the criteria for judging completeness and the criteria for judging quality of content are not identical. A space may be filled in some degree, although not aptly so.

As we saw, merely because completeness in the spaces within a rule requires complementary content in those spaces, it does not follow that completeness as a formal feature is reducible to the content in its spaces so that the rule becomes "all nonformal content" without any feature of formal completeness. Even when filled with content in all spaces so that the rule is complete, the spaces so filled remain independently identifiable as formal place-holders for content, and it will

Section Four: The Feature of Completeness

often also be easy to imagine that these "place-holders" could have had rather different content from what they actually have. Moreover, in an incomplete rule, some spaces are not filled with content, yet these spaces still exist as unfilled form.

A rule complete in form and content can, from its date of adoption, be a fecund source of full-fledged legal reasons for its addressees to take determinate action, assuming the rule is otherwise duly formal and well-designed. If well-designed to serve ends, the actions of addressees in accord with such reasons will, so far as feasible, further the policy or other social ends in the content of the rule, further relevant rule of law values, and further fundamental political values implicated.

Completeness in spaces, as a feature of form, must itself receive credit. It is a handmaiden of effective implementation of policy or other social ends in the content of the rule through addressee self-application. The credit due to the formal feature of sufficient completeness can be considerable. This is not an empirical claim. Sufficient completeness is one formal feature necessary for determinateness of rule. Without it, addressees could not construct reasons for determinate action under the rule. Completeness, however, is not alone enough for this. Other formal features such as generality and definiteness are required as well.

A rule complete in content upon adoption does not require the addition of further legal content at point of application in order for an addressee to construct from the rule a full-fledged legal reason for determinate action. (Due application of the rule may also require fact-finding and interpretation). Consider, for example, a simple yet complete (and otherwise duly formal) statutory rule designed to secure safety and quiet in major public parks. Assume the statute provides that "no vehicles may be taken into public parks." This statute may, once communicated, and even in the span of a few minutes after its inception, give rise to numerous and varied authoritative reasons for different addressees to act, including:

- "Since my motorbike is a vehicle, it is prohibited."
- "Since my pony is not a vehicle it is permitted."
- "Since my battery-driven wheelchair is a vehicle, it is probably prohibited."
- "Since my motorized hot dog vending machine is not a vehicle, it is probably permitted."[19]

One rule may have a higher degree of completeness than another. Two rules having the same set of spaces for content may easily differ in the degree to which those spaces are filled. One rule may have full content in all spaces, whereas the

---

[19] This rule may be said to "under-include" because objects other than vehicles may interfere with park safety and quiet. It "over-includes" because some vehicles do not so interfere, for example, a battery-driven wheelchair. Even though the completeness of such a rule under- and over-includes in relation to its aims of securing quiet and safety in parks, this completeness nevertheless contributes to the determinateness of the rule. An alternative rule, for example, "no unreasonable objects allowed in the park" would not, as such, under- or over-include, but would be highly indeterminate and therefore could not give rise to as many faithful reasons for determinate action or decision on the part of addressees.

other lacks content in one or more spaces, as with a rule purporting to lay down all qualifications for issuance of a driver's license but omits any reference to age.

Whatever the explanation, rule-makers sometimes unjustifiably adopt an incomplete rule – a rule lacking content in one or more spaces. If the rule is so incomplete that its addressees cannot construct reasons for determinate action thereunder, an official may step in and issue particular orders, if this is possible.

Suppose a park were regulated by the following rule: "The park superintendent may exclude objects therefrom in his or her discretion." If we were merely to consider the spaces recognized in the linguistic form of this rule, which would consist of subject, verb, object, etc., we might say that it is complete on adoption. Yet such a rule does not recognize all spaces that ought to be filled, given its intended function, and is thus functionally incomplete, even though not linguistically so. Here, the rule maker should make the rule functionally complete and thus "applicationally self-sufficient" from date of adoption. Addressees would then be able to apply the rule to many instances on their own. Thus, for example, we may readily imagine a list of objects that could be prohibited, such as motor vehicles, explosives, and other dangerous objects. Under this functionally more complete rule, addressees would then have far more direction and guidance, and could, in many circumstances, act on their own to serve the policy goals of the law, that is, park safety and quiet, without the necessity for official intervention. This would also serve the freedom, dignity, and efficiency of addressee self-direction. It would serve the rule of law as well, for it would provide for fair notice and equal treatment. It would save administrative costs, too, because constant official intervention would not be necessary. Such examples can be replicated throughout the legal system. It is evident in such examples that much credit is due the formal feature of completeness, along with its complementary content (assuming other features of form and complementary content are duly present).

It follows that one criterion for judging completeness of content in a rule at inception is whether the creator of the rule has chosen to provide for and fill all spaces that can and should be rationally filled in advance of occasions when primary addressees of the rule must apply it. Thus, it follows that we must differentiate two senses of completeness: (1) "linguistic completeness" – the extent to which spaces for content recognized in the actual linguistic form of the rule as created are filled, and (2) "functional completeness" – the extent to which the spaces for content that ought to be recognized in such a rule, given its proper function, are so recognized and filled.

In the foregoing example: "The park superintendent may exclude objects therefrom in her or his discretion," the rule is linguistically complete, but not very complete functionally. By merely linguistic criteria, there is no identifiable open space in the rule as created, so it is complete in a linguistic sense. Certainly the sentence expressing the rule is grammatically and syntactically complete. Yet the

Section Four: The Feature of Completeness 151

rule is not functionally complete. Given its intended function, it ought to recognize further spaces and fill them at least with various types of proscribed objects, such as motor vehicles, fireworks, and other dangerous objects. This would enable many addressees to administer the rule on their own at least in certain recurring circumstances.

It is true that functional incompleteness of a rule at inception is sometimes justified as a concession to necessity. Some rules cannot rationally be made fully complete in functional terms in advance of occasions for their application. Yet a rule should be as complete in form and content at inception as is possible in light of the nature and purpose of the subject matter and of what is foreseeable. When a rule is left justifiably incomplete at inception, courts or other officials may thereafter add content at point of application, either implicitly, via their own authoritative reasons for decision in disputed instances, or explicitly, via cumulative reformulations of the rule itself.

We will now consider illustrative scenarios in which incompleteness of content at inception may be justified. Consider a newly adopted rule providing that "custody of a child of a couple being divorced is to be awarded in accord with the best interests of the child." Although judged solely by linguistic criteria the rule is not incomplete, the rule is functionally rather indeterminate, and thus incomplete in this sense. Here, courts must, over time, determine the types of factors relevant to the best interests of children in awarding custody, a matter of legal content that will cumulatively fill the relevant space. In any particular case, the court will consider what is legally relevant under the "best interests" standard and then inquire into the correspondingly relevant facts, weigh and balance any conflicting interests, and award custody. Judicial infusions of content by way of specification of relevant factors and determination of their relative weight will be required at point of application. At inception, such a rule is far from complete in content and therefore in form. This, however, is justified insofar as it is not feasible at inception to fill out the rule for all types of cases that may arise.

Yet, unlike in my park regulation example, the failure of the incomplete custody rule at inception to give rise to determinate reasons for addressees to act outside of, and prior to, any court action, *may* be relatively inconsequential in many cases. This is because the decisions and actions under a rule of this type are usually to be taken by judges or other officials at point of application anyway and not at some prior point by private addressees who would have to decide how to act outside of court on their own. The occasion to apply a rule of this type commonly arises only when a dispute arises (here, over custody) itself calling for judicial action. Thus, the justified incompleteness of such a rule at inception could rest not only on the unforeseeability of all relevant interests at inception, and on the necessary weighing and balancing of these interests in light of particular facts at point of application, but also

152   Forms of Precepts – Rules

on the general lack of need for advance "out-of-court" guidance prior to judicial ruling.[20]

In a second type of case, incompleteness in the rule at inception can be justified, even though addressees of the rule must generally act prior to any judicial or other official intervention. Here, the failure of the rule to afford addressees full-fledged reasons to act from inception would be consequential, that is, would fail to provide needed guidance, yet countervailing considerations could still justify the incompleteness at inception. The wide-ranging general rule imposing civil liability in tort for negligent acts or omissions is illustrative. In some systems of law, if an auto accident occurs involving two vehicles and the driver of one vehicle is sued for negligently causing damage to the other, a court may decide (with or without the aid of a jury) that this driver was negligent in failing to take precautions, and in so doing, the court may add legal content to the applicable standard of care embodied in the rule, for example, "always slow down at a blind turn." Insofar as such an addition to a rule is required before it can be applied, and this may frequently be so, the rule may be said to lack a "part or element." Hence the rule is incomplete in content and therefore in form, prior to the addition.

Here, the incompleteness cannot be justified on the ground that the policy at stake generally calls for judicial administration anyway in light of the particulars of cases after the fact, as in the award of child custody. In fact, it is desirable that drivers be able to self-administer the rule against negligence to avoid accidents in the first place. The justification for incompleteness at inception here is simply that the rule against negligence governs infinitely varied situations, and not all of these are foreseeable enough to allow for complete articulation of the applicable standard of care in advance for each type of situation. As a result, the law cannot be completely formulated in advance to afford drivers reasons for fully determinate action so that they can avoid liability for negligence in all types of situations. This state of affairs has been explained as follows:[21]

" . . . [I]t is that we are unable to consider, before particular cases arise, precisely what sacrifice or compromise of interests or values we wish to make in order to reduce the risk of harm. Again, our aim of securing people against harm is indeterminate till we put it in conjunction with, or test it against, possibilities which only experience will bring before us; when it does, then we have to face a decision which will, when made, render our aim *pro tanto* determinate."

Thus, incompleteness in the content of a rule at inception, and therefore in this respect in the form of the rule, is not always unjustified, even though, in

---

[20] I do not claim that in such a case, no occasion could ever arise in which advance notice of the interests to be weighed could have no effect on out-of-court or pre-court action of potentially affected parties. For example, A and B may be considering a divorce. If B is a recovering alcoholic, he might not press for a divorce, knowing that the court would not award him custody.

[21] H. L. A. Hart, *supra* n. 14, at 133.

Section Four: The Feature of Completeness 153

general the ideal rule is one that addressees can apply to themselves on their own. Incompleteness at inception, then, can be a concession to necessity under the circumstances.

Generally, however, completeness is possible and desirable from inception. Completeness contributes to the fecundity of reasons for determinate action that arise for addressees under the rule. Completeness also contributes to the dignity and efficiency of addressee self-direction, to serving relevant policies such as public health and safety, and to realization of general legal values associated with the rule of law, such as fair notice and official evenhandedness. Completeness may also serve fundamental political values such as freedom, security, and justice. The features of the overall form of a rule include completeness, and, when the rule is sufficiently complete, due credit in this respect should also go to form.

Of course, rules complete at inception and in proper form still should not be applied mechanically. Some interpretive or other applicational reasoning will frequently be required. Also, some fact-finding may be required before the rule can be applied, and this may call not only for the finding of "brute facts," but also for more qualitative fact-finding, as in negligence cases where it is commonly recognized that whether an actor was negligent is a "mixed question of law and fact."

The nature and the number of spaces, and so of the "parts or elements" of the content complementary to the formal feature of completeness in a rule, are relative to the type of rule involved. There are many different types of rule, each with different possible "spaces" to be filled. For example, the crime of burglary requires that spaces be filled with respect to scope, addressees, conduct proscribed, causal relation between act and consequence, mental element of the actor, and so on. In contrast, a basic rule specifying requirements for the formation of valid bilateral contracts may call only for spaces to be filled with respect to offer, acceptance, consideration, and possibly some written memorial. Thus, although an omission as to a specific mental element would ordinarily make a criminal prohibition incomplete, such an omission would not make a contract formation rule incomplete.

A further important complication is this. A rule may be a member of a discrete set of rules, and its completeness relative to its assigned function within the set. Thus, what appears to be an incomplete rule, given that only one or two spaces appear to be filled, could turn out to be a complete rule, once it is seen that the function of this rule within the set is only to fill those two spaces, with another rule or rules filling the other spaces. A rule of the criminal law may impose liability for burglary but only state two elements of the offense, such as that of (1) a wrongful taking of (2) another's property, whereas a second rule in the set defines the mental element, and a third rule in the set defines still further elements, such as the circumstances of the taking. Here we have a discrete set of rules, with each filling a space in a single complete *law*. Here a holistic form-oriented approach captures the various constituents of the set and their unifying inter-relations.

Completeness is not merely a frequently recurrent feature in rules; it is a constituent feature of the overall form of a rule. A given candidate for status as a rule could easily lack completeness to such an extent, that is, lack an especially important "part or element," or simply lack so many "parts or elements," that it would not merely be a bad rule, but could not count as a rule at all (unless its function happened to be a limited one within a discrete set). On the other hand, total completeness of content at inception is not required for a rule to exist. In my "best interests of the child" example, and in my negligence example, even considerable incompleteness of content in a rule exists from inception, yet the precept remains a rule. In such cases, the rule is not applicationally self-sufficient for primary addressees at inception. Rather, it requires the addition of legal content at point of application in order to give addressees reasons for determinate action.

The analysis required to determine whether a particular actual or proposed rule is or is not complete in legal content requires several steps. There is a wide variety of rules, for example, criminal prohibitions, rules imposing tort liability, rules specifying criteria for the validity of contracts, rules of tax law, and so on, all with differing spaces for content. At the least, the analysis must consist of two basic steps. First, one must bring to bear criteria of completeness of content appropriate to the type of rule under consideration. As we have seen, different types of rules have different typologies of parts. For example, the terms of a statutory rule prohibiting a species of the crime of theft may simply provide: "A person is guilty of theft if the person unlawfully takes, or exercises unlawful control over, movable property of another."[22] A rule of this type, let us assume, requires that at least the following spaces be filled to be complete:

- scope
- addressees
- prohibited actions or forbearances
- consequences of such actions or forbearances
- causal relation between such actions or forbearances and consequences
- mental element of actors
- attendant circumstances

A rule of the foregoing type that, for example, omitted the mental element would be prima facie incomplete. As I have indicated, we cannot, however, merely look to the face of such a rule to determine completeness. We must go beyond the face of the rule. It may be a member of a set with another rule of the set filling the

---

[22] Cf. *Model Penal Code*, Official Draft and Explanatory Notes, at §223.2(1) (American Law Institute, Philadelphia, 1985).

Section Five: The Feature of Definiteness

space. Thus, although my theft statute is, on its face, incomplete in not specifying a mental element, this missing "part or element" – this apparently unfilled space – could be filled by: (a) a generally presumed (in the law) mental element, unless explicitly negated, (b) a particular adjacent rule supplementing all such rules (e.g., a "general part" of the criminal law), (c) a general principle running through the system, or (d) a definitional provision, or some other source. Thus, ultimately, a statutory rule may be judged complete, although this is not evident from the face of the rule.

At the same time, a rule of a given type may appear incomplete in light of the typology of parts appropriate to such a rule, yet not be so because the rule-creating body has chosen to create an exception. For example, the legislature might choose to impose strict liability for a given theft offense, and thus create an exception to the general rule requiring the filling of a space for a mental element for commission of such an offense.

Judgments of completeness in form and in complementary components of content, then, presuppose a relevant typology of "parts or elements" for the rule at hand. Moreover, where a rule is a member of a discrete set, judgments of completeness must be holistic – they must take into account the content of other rules or law in the set. Further, judgments of sufficient completeness at inception must also be made in light of possibly justified incompleteness. A rule may be considered sufficiently complete at inception even though it is significantly incomplete, provided this is for good reason.

Completeness as manifest in content in spaces is a positive feature of the rule, though a formal one that leaves rather more of an effect on content than a mere imprint. This feature may be said to be actually present in the rule, yet it can be isolated for analysis, description, and evaluation. It is therefore susceptible of characterization on its own.

Completeness is a distinct feature of the overall form of the most common type of a rule and, as we will see, must be understood on its own and in relation to other formal features if the overall form of such a rule is to be understood. A grasp of completeness is required to understand the makeup and unity of a rule. Completeness is required if a rule is to afford addressees reasons for determinate action from inception. If the rule is well-designed, and the ends of the rule valuable, completeness should receive some of the credit for any realization of value. Completeness contributes instrumental capacity.

SECTION FIVE: THE FEATURE OF DEFINITENESS

As Plato said: "unless you are definite, you must not suppose that you are speaking a language that can become law."[23] Aristotle was of like mind: "Now, it is of

---

[23] *The Dialogues of Plato, supra* n. 7, at 491.

great moment that well-drawn laws should themselves define all the points they possibly can.... "[24] Definiteness is defined in English as a degree of "fixity and specificity."[25] Much credit can be due the formal feature of definiteness in a rule. Definiteness in some degree is required in order for a rule to prescribe action, proscribe action, permit action, or ordain features of an institution or other legal phenomenon. Definiteness is required to prioritize between conflicting considerations in constructing a rule. Definiteness is also required for meaningful completeness, and thus may be thought to overlap with completeness to an extent. An indefinite rule leaves content relatively open in some respect or respects, and thus incomplete.

Like prescriptiveness and completeness, definiteness contributes to the determinateness of a rule, and thus to its fecundity as a source of reasons for action or decision. In so contributing to determinateness, definiteness tends, in turn, both to enable, and to influence, addressees to comply with the rule, thereby serving the policy or other content of a well-designed rule. In sum, the imprints of formal definiteness on the content of a rule can be considerable, and their effects wide-ranging.

Even though a highly definite rule may restrict behavior to an extent, its overall effect may even be to enlarge and protect freedom. For example, on many types of roadways, freedom of vehicular movement overall is better served by a definite and, therefore, restrictive speed limit rule of say, "drive no faster than 75 mph," than by a rule that says "drive reasonably." Under the latter, because different drivers have different conceptions of reasonableness, some would, for example, drive too fast, thereby frightening others into driving "defensively," or into not driving at all, thereby impairing their freedom of movement.

Well-drawn definiteness furthers the rule of law, especially in giving addressees fair notice of the law's requirements, in facilitating ease and accuracy of application of law, and in securing like treatment of like cases. Other things equal, definiteness also tends to render an otherwise well-designed law more respectworthy, too. Major credit must often go to the formal feature of definiteness for the ends realized. An understanding of definiteness is required to understand the form and content of rules.

There are good reasons to characterize a degree of fixity and specificity – definiteness – as formal. Some degree of definiteness is a necessary feature of the overall form of a rule – of its purposive systematic arrangement. Without some degree of fixity or specificity, a phenomenon could not be a rule. The feature of definiteness, together with other features, satisfies the general definition of the overall form of a functional legal unit, as further refined to fit the unit of

---

[24] *The Basic Works of Aristotle*, 1326 (R. McKeon ed., Random House, New York, 1941).
[25] *OED*, *supra* n. 17, vol. 6, at "formal," A.4.a.

Section Five: The Feature of Definiteness 157

a rule. This definition – the purposive systematic arrangement of the functional unit as a whole – was introduced and defended in Chapter Two.

Definiteness remains formal even though it must be manifest in complementary policy or other content and cannot be divorced from such content. Even as so manifest, definiteness does not lose its identity as a formal feature. Rather, definiteness in a rule can be seen to satisfy the concepts of fixity and specificity, and is thus susceptible of description as formal on its own. The designation of definiteness as formal is recognized in standard English lexicons as well.[26]

A rule, then, is not reducible to "all content and no formal definiteness." "Content" in a purported rule without any degree of definiteness – any fixity and specificity – would be formless in this regard. Jhering stressed that formless content cannot exist, at least for legal purposes.[27] Definiteness leaves a major imprint on content. Different degrees of definiteness leave different imprints and other effects on complementary policy content of a rule. For example, high definiteness (retire "at age 65") necessarily affects the policy or other content of the rule differently from low definiteness (retire when "no longer fit").

Though the formal feature of definiteness in a rule necessarily affects content, this feature and its complementary content are not identical. That is, the distinction between formal definiteness and complementary policy or other content of the rule survives the impact of form on content. Such content is the relevant subject matter of the rule, including any duly named or specified end-serving action or decision. This content is distinguishable from any particular degree of definiteness manifest in it. Although this content may bear major imprints of definiteness, these formal imprints may appear only within some of the subject matter of the rule. These imprints are not to be equated with the subject matter in which they appear. In the foregoing simple example, the subject matter content of the rule is a retirement policy that, among other things, hypothesizes a rational relation between a general age range and the time for retirement, fixes this relation, and specifies the scope of the rule. Definiteness, as manifest in subject matter content, is far from identical with the whole of that content. Also, two rules can plainly have the same general degree of definiteness, yet apply to very different content, as with "retire no later than 60 years of age" and "drive no faster than 60 mph." Further, the same rule can be definite in some spaces, yet indefinite in others, with subject matter content similar in all spaces.

The standards relevant to the evaluation of degree of definiteness and the standards relevant to the evaluation of complementary policy or other content in a rule are not the same. Appropriate definiteness is a justified degree of fixity and specificity in relevant spaces of the rule. A given degree of fixity and specificity

---

[26] *Id.*, at A.5.
[27] R. Jhering, *supra* n. 2, at 473.

may or may not be justified in light of a range of relevant considerations, including effects on the firmness of prioritization of conflicting policies in the content of the rule, on fair notice of this content to addressees, on ease of interpretation of the terms of the rule, on ease of any required fact-finding to apply the rule, on the determinateness of the legal reasons for action or decision arising under the rule, and on the scope for official arbitrariness and lack of even-handedness in the application of the rule. The definiteness of a rule could itself be appropriate, yet the complementary content of the rule itself still be deficient in some way.

Consider this example. The content of a rule for retirement of police officers might include the formal feature of bright-line definiteness specifying the age of 65, and this might be duly definite in light of all of the foregoing considerations, but age 65 could still be too high, given the policies at stake.[28] Thus, a rule could have undesirable policy content yet be duly definite, or the rule could have desirable policy content, yet not be duly definite in some respect (as with "retire when no longer fit"). The mere existence of complementarity between the formal feature of definiteness and corresponding content does not guarantee that either the form or the content is well-designed.

Degree of definiteness is likewise a positive feature of a rule, albeit a formal one. As such, it is manifest in the content of the rule, and, as we have seen, can leave major imprints on policy or other complementary content. Degree of definiteness can be identified and isolated for analysis, description, and evaluation. Thus, it is susceptible of affirmative characterization. Plainly, differences in the degree of definiteness of two rules can be isolated and described, even when the basic policy or other content is largely the same.

The inner order of a well-designed rule consists of its formal features and complementary components of content, all as unified within a coherent whole. To understand this inner order, it is necessary to grasp the relations between the formal completeness of a rule, and its other formal features, such as definiteness. A rule may be highly definite in all the relevant "spaces" making up a complete rule, or a rule may not be highly definite in any such space, or it may be highly definite in some spaces, but not in others, and all such variation still be justified. Two highly complete rules on the very same subject may easily differ in degrees of definiteness. For example, a highly definite and complete statute of limitations rule could bar lawsuits as untimely when "brought more than four years after the cause of action arose." A much less definite yet relatively complete rule might bar lawsuits brought an "unreasonable length of time after the cause of action accrues, having regard to continued availability of evidence and possible staleness

---

[28] Similarly, just because some precise rate of speed would be duly definite for a speed limit, it hardly follows that any particular rate necessarily constitutes appropriate policy content.

Section Five: The Feature of Definiteness

of evidence."[29] Because so indefinite, such a rule might not be justified. If not, then form would not leave a salutary imprint on content.

One might characterize the foregoing "unreasonable length of time" rule as not merely indefinite, but also as incomplete because it postpones determination of the full legal content of "unreasonable" to point of application when a judge authoritatively adds the relevant content, at least for the case at hand. If we so characterize the rule, it is both indefinite and incomplete at inception. An even clearer example of a rule that would be both indefinite and incomplete is a rule that fails to include *any* subject matter content in an essential space, as with a "rule" that imposes a tax on incomes at specified rates, but omits any definition of income. Without more, the rule would be both indefinite and incomplete. One might even say this rule would be indefinite because it is incomplete.

A rule can even be relatively complete in that it has all of its parts or elements, yet not be very definite, as in my statute of limitations example barring lawsuits brought "an unreasonable length of time after the cause of action accrues, having regard mainly to continued availability of evidence or its possible staleness." An incomplete rule cannot, of course, be definite in the precise respect in which it is incomplete. Indefiniteness in a particular rule can be so extreme that it is not, for all practical purposes, distinguishable from incompleteness. Also, a rule complete in all respects – one that has all its parts or elements – could still be indefinite in some degree in all these respects. Of course, a rule can be incomplete in a space, and thus not very definite or not definite at all in that space, yet be highly complete and definite in all other spaces.

Both completeness and definiteness contribute to the fecundity of a rule as a source of determinate reasons for action and decision in light of the applicable methodology of interpretation or application, and in light of any required fact-finding. Here, as well, sound choices of completeness and definiteness must receive due credit. However, as Aristotle suggested, even a complete rule can be definite only insofar as its subject matter permits.[30] For example, it is possible to define the duty of a merchant to collect a 29% sales tax on all sales of books, but it is impossible, without being quite unduly restrictive, to define the criminal offense of selling "obscene" books so definitely. Sometimes the very nature of the subject matter is such that we can have a rule about it only at the price of low definiteness. Some degree of indefiniteness may, of necessity, have to pass as tolerable, even if it leaves a somewhat indeterminate imprint on content. Here, though, some credit must still be given to form, if such an indefinite feature qualifies as a tolerable concession to necessity.

---

[29] The French Civil Code of 1804, still to an extent in force in some places, had such a rule.
[30] *The Basic Works of Aristotle, supra* n. 24, at 936.

A low degree of definiteness may overlap with incompleteness that is likewise a concession to necessity. The "best interests of the child" rule for the award of custody of children in a divorce case is an example. Here, the low degree of definiteness at inception overlaps with the incompleteness of any such rule. Similarly, incompleteness and indefiniteness in a rule prescribing liability for "negligent" behavior arise because we are "unable to consider, before particular cases arise, precisely what sacrifice or compromise of interests or values we wish to make in order to reduce the risk of harm".[31]

Thus, a low degree of definiteness, which also overlaps with incompleteness, may be justified not because desirable as such, but as a concession to necessity. Frequently, however, the rule-maker will rationally choose a relatively high degree of completeness, and a relatively high degree of definiteness. As we have seen, these formal features leave major imprints or other effects on content. This contributes to the fecundity of the rule as a source of reasons for determinate action or decision. If the rule is well-designed to serve ends, and if the ends are valuable, such action or decision will serve values. No amount of definiteness can dispense with the necessity of some interpretation (or other applicational reasoning) in some cases. Nor can even high definiteness dispense with all necessity for fact-finding. Yet we must credit definiteness with facilitating faithful interpretation and fact-finding, and thus with ultimately contributing to the construction of reasons for action or decision faithful to the terms and purposes of the rule.

Just as with completeness, a rule that on its face appears even quite indefinite may turn out to be much more definite when the analyst consults further authoritative definitions, general presumptions, adjacent rules, the bearing of general principles, relevant purposes, authoritative interpretive method, and still other law. Also, a rule definite on its face may turn out not to be definite in the final analysis in light of such further sources, as, for example, when a definite phrase is authoritatively defined in another rule in a way that introduces indeterminacy. For this reason, too, a holistic and form-oriented approach may reveal more than a rule-oriented approach that focuses merely on the contents of a particular rule.[32]

To grasp definiteness, the imprints or other effects that this formal feature leaves on policy or other content, its relation to other formal features of the rule, and its overall significance, is to advance one's understanding of rules. It is to understand part of their makeup, unity, and inner order. It is also to understand a major source of their instrumental capacity. Definiteness is often entitled to some credit for whatever is achieved through rules. In some rules, it is even entitled to much credit.

---

[31] H. L. A. Hart, *supra* n. 14, at 133.

[32] I use "holistic" here to refer to the bearing that all relevant parts of a whole may have on one or more parts. I also use it to refer to the relations between parts.

SECTION SIX: THE FEATURE OF GENERALITY

A law has some degree of the formal feature of generality if the law applies to more than one instance within any of its spaces. If a law applies to only one instance, it cannot be a rule, though it might be a legal ruling or a legal order. A legal rule is necessarily general, and this in itself is another imprint of form on content. Indeed, this imprint may be major. A given rule might have numerous spaces within which it is applicable to many more than one instance. A rule could be highly general in one, or in all of its spaces. Or the rule could be far less general in all spaces, or not be general at all in one or a number of spaces. Plainly, there can be great variation here.

Generality is a formal feature of a rule. It is one of the necessary features of the overall form of a rule and is, therefore, a constituent feature of that form.[33] A law without any generality could not be a rule. It would lack an essential feature of the purposive systematic arrangement of a rule. It would fail to satisfy the general definition of the overall form of a functional legal unit, as that definition is refined to fit a rule. This general definition was introduced and defended in Chapter Two. A formal feature of generality must be manifest in the content of a rule, yet it is not reducible to that content. It is formative of a facet of that content, and leaves a major imprint on this very content. Aristotle characterized some particular laws as mere "decrees," because they were not at all general in extent.[34] Consider a statute providing that an official shall bury a particular person's remains in a specified place of honor. This totally particular law lacks generality in all spaces and is therefore not a rule. Rather, it is an order – one that only gives rise to a single occasion for a single addressee to act. A precept that barely applies to more than one instance in only one space still has some generality, and is, therefore, at least marginally a rule, as with a precept providing for one person to bury two persons over time in a place of honor.

A law that is duly prescriptive, complete, definite, and general, can be highly efficient. Such a law, as a determinate rule, may enable many addressees to classify particular circumstances as falling under its general terms, and thus readily apply the rule without the direction of any official.[35] Particular orders of a particular official would usually be far less efficient. Generality of rule is not only more efficient; it conceives of citizens and other addressees as autonomous self-directing persons, rather than as objects to be ordered around by officials ad hoc. Generality is a formal feature that can leave a major imprint on content and even merit major credit for what is achieved through the rule.

---

[33] Generality is also designated as "formal" in standard English and other lexicons. *OED, supra* n. 17, vol. 6, at "form," I.11.a; see also *id.*, vol. 6, at "form," I.7.

[34] *The Basic Works of Aristotle, supra* n. 24, at 1213.

[35] H. L. A. Hart, *supra* n. 14, at 124. Further on generality, see K. Greenawalt, *Law and Objectivity*, Chapter 8 (Oxford University Press, New York, 1992).

It is one thing for a rule to be minimally general, that is, barely to apply to more than one instance, and another for it to be appropriately general. Almost any sound policy or other content to be embodied in a rule should be implemented not merely in one instance, but in all like instances. It might even be said that a policy really cannot be a policy at all if it applies to only one or two instances. The generality of a well-designed rule commonly extends to the full reach of its policy or other content, and thus applies to many instances. Usually, this generality also contributes to the realization of general values of the rule of law such as fair notice to all affected and like treatment of like cases. By and large, a rule should be drafted so that it is as general in scope (a) as its policy or other content requires in the standard instance of its application, and (b) as is required by treatment of like instances in like fashion. The formal feature of well-designed generality in a rule, then, may merit major credit for the realization of policy or other ends. Though the foregoing claims on behalf of generality are partly empirical, they are hardly controversial.

Rule-makers sometimes adopt highly definite "bright line" rules that over-include or under-include in relation to policy, and thereby also fail to treat all like cases in like fashion. Even so, such rules may still be justified. Whatever is lost in policy efficacy and in like treatment of like cases may be more than made up for because such bright-line rules better serve other general values of the rule of law such as fair notice, ease of administration, and dispute avoidance. On this, more later.

Generality, like completeness and definiteness, is a matter of degree. Rules vary greatly in generality. Such differences of degree can often be easily explained. Some policies or other ends simply require a high degree of generality, others not so high. Also, tradeoffs between policies or ends may justify different degrees of generality.

Generality is but one of several formal features in the paradigmatic legal rule considered here, and we must grasp this feature both on its own, and in relation to other such features, if we are to understand the overall inner order of a rule. Generality differs from prescriptiveness. Prescriptiveness directs that the addressee must, may not, or may take an action or a decision. Generality has to do with the extent to which a precept applies to more than one instance. Yet even an ungeneral law that applies to only one instance is prescriptive.

Generality also differs from completeness. Completeness pertains to how many and how far spaces are filled with subject matter content. A law could be highly complete, yet not general in any respect, and so not a rule. For example, a law might prohibit the entry into France of Mr. Pierre Washe because he participated in war crimes elsewhere. This law would be entirely complete, yet not general. Or a law could be incomplete, yet be highly general. Thus, a statute could provide

Section Six: The Feature of Generality 163

for registration of all motor vehicles, yet omit any reference to the method of registration.

Generality differs from definiteness, too. A law could easily have no degree of generality at all, yet have a high degree of definiteness, as with my example of a law excluding Mr. Washe from France. Such a law would simply not be a rule. A law could be highly general and thus in this respect qualify as a rule, yet also be low in definiteness. As we saw, an "age 60" retirement rule and an "unfitness" retirement rule are both highly general yet the latter is much less definite than the former.

So far, I have discussed the type of rule that purports to regulate the conduct of lay persons or officials in, say, retiring police officers, or having their motor vehicles inspected, or the like. In such examples, we can readily see what is, and what is not, general. But what of reinforcive rules that prescribe and, thus, ordain features of governmental institutions or processes? For example, a law may require that a single legislature in the society be bicameral. Although complete and definite, such a law is highly specific on its face and may seem to lack all generality. It seems merely to prescribe features of institutional phenomena. There are many such apparently ungeneral laws. It is possible that one might faithfully reconstruct some of these laws as general rules. A law ordaining a bicameral legislature might be faithfully reconstructed as a rule that implicitly provides that those responsible for establishing and maintaining a legislature ensure that it regularly function through a bicameral structure.

A rule is not necessarily as general as the mere use of a "class" term in the rule alone might suggest. The meaning of a class term in a rule could be highly general, yet there might be only one actual member of the class. For example, a generally worded rule might, in actual operation, accord only one corporation a specified tax advantage, there being only one actual member of the class term specified in the rule. Such a rule might, for at least some purposes, not be considered general at all, and, indeed, might be subject to constitutional invalidation as discriminating in favor of an entity. Here, too, a holistic form-oriented approach would again reveal these realities more faithfully than a mere rule-oriented approach.

With respect to completeness and definiteness, we have seen that relatively high degrees of such features in a law are usually appropriate. As for generality, a high degree in some spaces may not be appropriate. First, the policy or other content may not require it. Many statutes are not very general in scope, in addressees, in action required, or in some other spaces. Indeed, the statute books include laws that are even totally particular and thus apply to only one case. Much state-made law even takes the form of particular orders and the like, not rules. Much privately created law also lacks generality and thus does not consist of rules. Many contracts and wills are of this nature. A second reason that high generality in a law may not be appropriate is simply that this will render the law too indefinite to be workable. Here, there can be tension between two formal features – generality and definiteness.

Despite the relation of complementarity between generality and the policy or other content of the rule, the feature of generality and the components of content in which it is manifest remain distinguishable. The imprints of generality manifest in content can be distinctly identified as answering to the concept of generality, that is, as applying to more than one instance. Moreover, there is much more to the policy or other content of a rule than merely that facet of content in which generality is manifest. Also, two rules can be general in the same degree in the same spaces, yet the rules have totally different content. Compare: "all passenger vehicles . . ." with "all non-fiction books . . . " Further, a rule addressed to a given content can be highly general in some spaces and of low generality in others.

Plainly, a rule can be duly general (so far as possible) and yet highly deficient in content as with "all drivers of vehicles shall drive no faster than ten miles per hour." Or a rule can lack due generality yet be, so far as it otherwise goes, appropriate in content as with "all drivers of vehicles except motorcyclists shall observe the speed limit."

At the same time, variations in degree of generality necessarily affect content, as in the change from a requirement that "all motor vehicles" to "some motor vehicles, that is, passenger cars," be inspected annually. The same applies in reverse from lesser generality to greater. Again, the imprint that generality leaves on content can be very great. The degree of generality, like the content affected, is a positive feature of a rule, albeit a formal one. Degree of generality can be characterized as such and isolated for analysis.

To grasp the generality of rules is to advance one's understanding of another major constituent of the overall form of rules. As with prior features so far considered, this feature has its own facets, its own inter-relations with other features, and its own interactions with complementary policy or other content. In grasping the foregoing, one advances one's understanding of the makeup, unity, and inner order of rules. Also, upon grasping the formal feature of generality, given the significance of its imprint on complementary content, one can readily understand how this feature, when well-designed, can be entitled to major credit for ends served through a rule. Generality, like other formal features, thus contributes to the instrumental capacity of the rule.

SECTION SEVEN: THE FEATURE OF STRUCTURE

Structure is standardly defined as a relation or relations between parts within a whole.[36] Structure therefore presupposes parts of a whole, and these parts in turn

---

[36] *OED, supra* n. 17, vol. 16, at "structure," 3.

Section Seven: The Feature of Structure

presuppose the spaces for the parts. The structure of a rule has to do with: (1) the relations between its parts, (2) the relations between its parts and the whole of the rule, and (3) any relations between internal elements of any single complex part. Well-designed structure is part of the make-up of a rule, secures its unity and inner order, and contributes to its instrumental efficacy.

The structure of a rule is formal. It is a necessary feature of the overall form of a rule – its purposive systematic arrangement. This feature, together with other features, satisfies the general definition of overall form, as refined to fit a rule. Without some structure, a precept simply could not be a rule. Also, one meaning of the word "formal" is simply that which pertains to the structure of a thing or of an abstract object.[37] Further, the structure manifest in the make-up of a rule is not reducible to the content of the rule. That content consists of subject matter in which structure and other formal features such as prescriptiveness, completeness, definiteness, and generality are also embedded. Moreover, there is much more to such content than the imprints of these formal features.

Different types of rules have different parts arranged differently to form a whole, and the structure of a rule thus varies accordingly. Here is a summary of various component parts of at least many legal rules:

(1) the purposes which, or at least traces of which, may appear on the face of the rule, or are plainly implicated therein,
(2) scope, that is, conditions of applicability,
(3) addressees (expressly or impliedly specified),
(4) prescribed action and circumstances of action, or ordained institutional feature,
(5) the prescribed legal consequences of action or feature in accord with, or not in accord with, (4),
(6) any explicit exceptions to, or extensions of (2), (3), or (4), closed-ended or open-ended.

Most parts of a rule have relations "part-to-whole," and "part-to-part."

A rule-maker may face a number of major choices of structure. We will illustratively consider only three. First, a rule-maker must often choose a structural relation of instrumental "fit" between: (1) the purposes that the rule is to serve, which, let us assume, comprise one part of the rule,[38] and (2) various other parts of this rule such as scope, or prescribed actions, or their consequences, and so on. The rule-maker may choose a structural feature of "close fit" between purposes on the one hand, and the other parts of the rule on the other hand. A rule may even

---

[37] *Id.*, vol. 6, at "formal," A.1; *id.*, vol. 6, at "form," I.5.a.

[38] Purposes may even be explicitly a part, as where a statute has a preamble stating its purposes. Often, purposes are merely implicit in a rule and how they are to be formulated may be controversial.

be one that serves its purposes in the totality of instances to which it applies, as with a rule requiring all airline pilots to have at least 20-20 vision. Such a rule has something like "perfect fit" between purposes and the rest of the rule, assuming that fitness to fly (so far as vision is concerned) requires at least 20-20 vision.

Where there is some degree of "loose fit," the rule either over-includes or under-includes or both in relation to its purposes. For example, to prevent annoyance to patrons, a rule may prohibit dogs in all business premises open to the public. Yet, assuming annoyance to be due only to misbehavior, such a rule would over-include as to very well-behaved dogs, such as seeing eye dogs of blind patrons. With respect to some rules, someone may, at point of application, have some power to remedy any lack of initial fit through the creation of exceptions or extensions. Also a degree of "loose fit" may even be justified. For example, the considerable costs of checking on the spot to determine whether seeing eye dogs really are well-behaved, might in the end justify a rule flatly prohibiting all dogs in stores despite the loose fit between purpose and conditions of applicability.

A second major type of structural feature of many rules concerns the relation between the part of a rule consisting of a prescribed action or nonaction or a grant of permission, and the part specifying the legal consequences of action in accord with, or not in accord with, what is prescribed. Many rules specify such consequences, and those that do not are often members of a set that includes a further rule specifying such consequences. A major example concerns the relation between any prohibited action and the legal consequences of its occurrence. Such consequences may be specified as more or less automatic, or they may be specified as dependent on the exercise of further discretion by an official, or a lay addressee. For example, a rule consisting of a criminal prohibition may automatically specify a given penalty for its violation, as with certain highway speeding rules. Here, well-designed structural form merits credit for ends thus served.

In many penal rules, however, the relation between prohibition and penalty is not so structured. That is, for a serious offense, the imposition of any penalty may even be subject to a substantial further inquiry into the personal history of the offender and any special aggravating and mitigating circumstances. When so, the legal consequences of noncompliance are far from automatic. Any discretion conferred on a judge or other official to decide the consequences thus limits the capacity of addressees to know likely legal consequences in advance of any prohibited action or inaction, and therefore limits predictability for addressees. This may, among other things, impair the deterrent effect of a law. However, such a discretionary structural feature may still merit credit for some ends served, including, in this very example, a more context-sensitive exploration of factors relevant to sentencing of an individual offender.

A third major structural feature in many rules pertains to how a part of a rule such as a proviso, an exception, an extension, a qualification, or the like, operates

Section Seven: The Feature of Structure

to modify the scope, the prescribed action, consequences of compliance, or still other parts of the rule. For example, a proviso may modify the scope of a rule, or may reduce its over or under-inclusion, or may qualify its operation. A common proviso in a speed limit rule generally allowing drivers to drive up to, say, 75 mph, is that other exceptional factors, such as the condition of the roadway, may require that drivers drive below the limit.

Often, the structural relations between different parts of a rule are explicitly specified. Whether or not this is so, judges or other officials may have discretion to modify it at point of application. In such an event, a holistic form-oriented analysis provides a fuller account of the structural relation between parts than an approach focusing only on the contents of any rules specifying structure.

In a rule with an elaborate structure of relations between parts, we can readily differentiate this feature of internal structure from prescriptiveness, completeness, generality, and definiteness of the rule.[39] As we have seen, such structure pertains to relations between parts, including: (1) the degree of fit between purposes and the implementive parts of the rule, (2) the extent prescribed legal effects are "automatic," and (3) the extent provisos, exceptions, extensions, and qualifications modify the scope or conditions of applicability of the rule, and so on. Robustly articulated relations between parts is at the same time a set of structurally formal features susceptible of distinctive analysis and description, in addition to, and thus, beyond such features as prescriptiveness, completeness, generality, and definiteness.

Internal structural form, then, has significance independently of other constituents of the overall form of a rule, a truth that can be demonstrated in still another way. We may easily imagine two rules having the same components of content, with both rules satisfying the minimum requisites of prescriptiveness, completeness, generality, and definiteness, yet the two rules could still have quite different internal structural features.

Compare once again a rule prescribing that persons "drive reasonably" or be fined, with a rule prescribing that a "75 mph" speed limit be observed, or a fine will be imposed. These rules differ in the relations between the part requiring action and the part specifying legal effects, with the latter rule enabling the motorist in advance to determine with certainty, the legality of projected driving speeds – a major difference. This difference can be perspicuously represented by resort to the concept of structure. In this example, the change from a "reasonableness" rule to a "75 mph rule" is not merely a change in content. Nor is it merely a change in formal definiteness. It is also a change in the formal structural relation between

---

[39] If relations between parts is considered to be one type of space within a rule, then structure could be collapsed into completeness. Yet such completeness would be distinctively concerned with relations between parts, i.e., structure.

a part of the rule prescribing action and a part specifying legal consequences – a change that increases the degree of advance determinability of violation of the rule.

That the foregoing change is achieved through a change in the definiteness of the rule and in its complementary content is no objection to my account of it as also a change in structure. Merely because there is a change here in definiteness and so in complementary content, and merely because definiteness itself affects the structural relation between parts of a rule, it does not follow that structure has no independent significance as a realm of organization within the rule.

The structure of a rule may be simple or complex. The highest simplicity consists of simple, rather than intricate relations, between few, rather than many parts, with these parts each being simple and irreducible, rather than complex.[40] The highest complexity consists of numerous and intricately inter-related parts, which themselves consist of intricately inter-related sub-parts. Each part, whether there be few or many, could itself be complex and thus reducible into further parts, or itself be simple and so not reducible. Further, each part, whether itself simple or complex, might or might not be intricately inter-related with other parts and thus be complex or simple in this regard.

Simplicity of structure, although formal, can leave major imprints or other effects on content. It can also deserve much credit for contributing to the realization of ends. The simpler the rule, the easier it will be for its addressees to interpret it and construct reasons for determinate action or decision under it and the easier it will be for others, such as officials and nonofficials, to decide whether addressees have acted as the rule requires. In general, the simpler the structure, the fewer issues of interpretation it will pose, and the fewer facts must be found to determine its applicability.

Simplicity of rule is a matter of degree. One rule may be far simpler than another. A given rule may be simple in all respects or simple in only one or a few respects. For example, one rule may be simple only in the number of its parts, and another rule may be simple not only in the number of its parts, but also in the inter-relations of these parts.

A high degree of simplicity (or complexity) on the face of a rule is one thing, but its simplicity (or complexity) in light of further external factors quite another. A rule may be simple on its face, yet complex in light of adjacent rules that modify it. For example, an adjacent rule may add elements to a rule otherwise simple on its face, as where a rule in the "general part" of a criminal code adds a mental element to a rule prohibiting theft. Subsequent judicial modifications of a facially simple rule may also add complexity. A holistic form-oriented analysis reveals structural

---

[40] I am concerned here with simplicity (or complexity) of the structure of a rule, not simplicity (or complexity) of its *expression*, which I take up *infra* Section Nine.

Section Seven: The Feature of Structure 169

and other complexity more fully than an analysis oriented solely to the particular contents of the rules.

Simplicity, including simplicity of structure, differs from the formal feature of completeness. As we saw, "completeness" goes to whether the rule has "all its parts or elements." A rule may be highly simple in structure, yet not be at all complete. Or a rule may be highly complete, yet not at all simple. A detailed rule of priority resolving conflicting claims of creditors against a debtor in bankruptcy is highly complete, yet not simple. However, a rule generally requiring motorists to drive on the right is highly complete, yet simple.

Simplicity of structure also differs from definiteness. As we saw, definiteness is a degree of fixity and specificity in the rule. A rule could be highly definite, yet not simple, as in the aforementioned detailed and complex rule governing the priorities of claims of different classes of creditors in bankruptcy. Or a rule could be highly simple, yet not very definite, as with a rule that merely bars untimely lawsuits based on "stale" claims. A rule could also be both definite and simple, as in a rule prescribing retirement at age 60.

Simplicity of structure also differs from generality. Generality exists when a law applies to more than one instance. A law could be highly simple, yet lack all generality, as with a statute passed for a special case, such as a law relieving a single business entity of a tax. A law could be highly general, yet not simple. For example, a highly general rule could accord prima facie priority to all secured creditors over other creditors in a bankruptcy proceeding, subject to a complex set of exceptions.

The extent of simplicity of structure in well-designed rules varies. Where a rule depends for its efficacy primarily on the capacity of lay addressees to construct reasons for determinate action thereunder, a high degree of simplicity is often appropriate.[41] Sometimes a complex definition of a key term may be required, as in an income tax law allowing a reduced rate for "capital gains." Here legal advice may have to be sought.

If a rule is quite simple (or complex), its content will bear imprints of such form that fully reveal as much. Although the formal feature of structure in a rule thus necessarily affects content, such form and complementary content are not identical. Simplicity (or complexity) of structure does not lose its identity as a formal structural attribute when manifest in content, and simplicity (or complexity) is not to be equated with the content in which it is manifest. Plainly, two rules can have the very same degree of simplicity (or complexity) and yet have highly different content.

The evaluative standards applicable to simplicity (or complexity) on the one hand, and to content on the other, also differ. Plainly, a rule may have an appropriate degree of simplicity, yet be badly flawed in subject matter content. "Driving

---

[41] H. Jones, *The Efficacy of Law*, 18–19 (Northwestern University Press, Evanston, 1969).

over 75 mph shall be an offense" is duly simple, yet it may be highly flawed in content, as where 75 mph is far too fast for driving in the residential areas involved.

SECTION EIGHT: THE ENCAPSULATORY FEATURE

The formal features and the complementary content of a state-created rule may appear in any one of many formal modes of legal "encapsulation," including:

- a constitution
- a court opinion interpreting the constitution, or filling a gap in it
- a statute
- a court opinion interpreting the statute or filling a gap in it
- a court opinion creating, developing, or applying common law
- a regulation adopted by an administrative agency or official
- an opinion of an administrative agency creating, developing, or applying agency adjudicative law
- an opinion of a court interpreting or filling a gap in the law of an administrative agency[42]

The encapsulatory feature of a rule, as I conceive it here, pertains to: (1) the nature of the authoritative source of the rule and (2) the corresponding manner of incorporating both form and content within a rule deriving from such an authoritative source. For example, the authoritative source of a statutory rule is legislative enactment. The corresponding manner of incorporating form and content within a statute encompasses: (a) formulation in a chosen set of words in a fixed verbal sequence, and (b) formulation in writing, that is, in print. The first of these, that is, formulation in a chosen set of words in a fixed verbal sequence, is authoritative not only in source but also in formulation, whereas the second of these, formulation in writing, that is, in print, merely refers to the mode of communication of the rule – say, printed rather than oral, though this mode, too may be prescribed in law. As Plato put it, "the true legislator ought ... to write his laws ... " in a chosen set of words in a fixed verbal sequence.[43] A common law rule, on the other hand, is explicitly or implicitly set forth in a written (printed) judicial opinion in which the judge rules on a general point in issue between the parties on a given state of facts. Unlike a statute, common law is not considered here to be authoritatively formulated in a chosen set of words in fixed verbal sequence, even though judicial opinions are printed.

---

[42] The foregoing is not a comprehensive inventory of all types of formal encapsulatory features known to the law. For example, it does not include particular judicial or administrative orders and rulings, and it does not include privately created nonpreceptual forms, such as contracts, wills, and various property arrangements. It also does not include customary practice. The focus in this section is on preceptual law in the form of rules and their encapsulation, especially in statutes.

[43] *The Dialogues of Plato, supra* n. 7, at 576.

Section Eight: The Encapsulatory Feature 171

In general, a valid legal rule must derive from a distinct authoritative source, and must be correspondingly encapsulated in a statute, or in common law, or other such source.[44] Some authoritative encapsulation is a necessary feature of the overall form of any valid legal rule, and thus is formal. Moreover, authoritative encapsulation is also recognized as formal in standard lexicons.[45] It contrasts with the policy or other content so encapsulated, and is thus formal in this contrastive sense, too.

Yet mode of encapsulation is affirmatively characterizeable not only in terms of type of authoritative *source*, but also in terms of *manner* of encapsulation, that is, (a) whether it is a chosen set of words in a fixed verbal sequence and (b) whether it is in writing (in print). Mode of encapsulation does not lose its identity as such in the subject matter content it incorporates. Mode of encapsulation retains its distinct identity apart from content in the nature of the authoritative source involved, and in terms of the manner of encapsulation involved.

Today, all of the foregoing listed types of state-created rules take "written," that is, printed, form in developed Western systems. The requirement that, apart from custom, law generally be encapsulated in written or printed form is not surprising. Given the needs of a developed Western society, most of its laws of general application could not be oral. To determine whether a claimed statute, regulation, common law rule, or other written law allegedly created in the past really was validly created, and so continues to be law in the present, it is generally necessary to have a written and authentic formal record of prior purported law-making actions. Reliance merely on the memories of "law-givers," or of witnesses as to the contents of oral laws allegedly made in the past, could not be adequate to show in the present that an asserted law was, in fact, created in the past and has not been altered over time. This profound contribution of formal records is generally unnoticed and taken for granted.

Once stated, the point is also obvious that printed encapsulation facilitates formulation of features of rules: prescriptiveness, completeness, definiteness, generality, and structure. Moreover, writing, i.e., print, itself invites more explicit prescriptiveness. Writing also invites and facilitates inspection of a rule for completeness. Writing militates against the ungeneralized individuality of oral decrees, and is pregnant with potential for generality in ways that oral law is not. Writing allows for more refined definiteness, that is, more fixity and specificity than oral law. Writing permits more structural and other complexity than oral law, and complexity is often needed. Writing invites harmonization of new law with recorded written law. Writing facilitates choice of vocabulary and precise expression.

---

[44] This is not to say that the whole of any given law must be set forth in any one encapsulatory form. Part of a rule may be in a statute, and other parts of it in case law, for example.

[45] In English, one standard use of the word "formal" is simply to refer to encapsulation of content. *OED*, *supra* n. 17, vol. 6, at "formal," A.1, A.5; *id.*, vol. 6, at "form," I.12a. and b.

Writing is more susceptible to focused scrutiny prior to adoption, as well as correction of mistakes. Still, the choice of written rather than oral encapsulation is a choice of a formal feature. It is also one that can directly and indirectly leave many imprints on complementary content! Writing (print) is a formal feature entitled to much credit for the quality and efficacy of the rule ultimately created, though the virtues of writing, too, are often taken for granted.[46]

Indeed, there is still more here by way of form that often is also too obvious to be noticed. Written laws can be readily disseminated via authentic copies and other means instead of being passed orally by word of mouth subject to vagaries of memory, embellishment, and the like. Well-formulated written laws are far more communicable and learnable by addressees. They also serve as better sources of reasons for determinate action and decision than oral laws. Their official application is also more predictable. They are more effective, too, as means of control over officials. Officials subject only to the limits of oral laws would be less likely to observe the rule of law.

Also, disputes are less likely to arise over the applicability of a well-designed written rule than over a well-designed oral one. Of course, many disputes do arise under written rules. For this and other reasons, there must be adjudicative institutions. Such institutions of any complexity could not exist under modern conditions without some reinforcive written rules prescribing at least the outlines of facets of such institutions. Merely oral composition, oral jurisdiction, oral structure, oral procedure, and oral methodology would not be workable under modern necessities and could not inspire confidence or a sense of legitimacy.

Having rules in writing also facilitates objective determination of conformity or departure in particular cases, facilitates consistency and like treatment of like cases over time, provides fair notice in advance of the requirements of law, facilitates out-of-court dispute settlement, and much more. Oral adjudications of particular disputes are generally inferior to written adjudications. Over time written opinions can be drawn together and harmonized in ways that a series of merely oral "decrees" cannot. Developed Western systems of law are highly viable partly because, when legal disputes do arise, the parties can usually settle them on their own. This possibility exists partly because of the predictability of judicial resolution should any such matter go to court. Such predictability is facilitated by the existence of printed law and prior adjudications to which the parties and courts can turn in resolving disputes. It is also facilitated by written tenets of an interpretive methodology that courts can faithfully and consistently apply. Under an oral system, the level of predictability would be far lower.

---

[46] The importance of writing was not taken for granted in the early Greek city states, and when introduced there, it gave those legal systems a great shot in the arm in most of the ways alluded to previously. See generally, M. Gargarin, *Early Greek Law* (University of Cal. Press, Berkeley and Los Angeles, 1986).

Section Eight: The Encapsulatory Feature

Written, that is, printed encapsulation of law is indispensable under most conditions. Though it tends to be taken for granted, vast credit must go to this formal feature. If all, or even a significant part, of state-made law had to be oral, a modern legal system could not flourish. Insofar as this is an empirical claim, it can hardly be controversial.

As we have seen, encapsulation also encompasses another major facet, namely, whether the form and content of the rule is formulated in a chosen set of words in a fixed verbal sequence, as in a statute, or an administrative regulation, or the like. Merely having the law in writing, or in print, is not the same as having the law in a chosen set of words in a fixed verbal sequence. The due encapsulation of a statute, or an administrative regulation, not only takes the form of (a) a printed feature, but also (b) a chosen set of words in a fixed verbal sequence. Such a fixed verbal feature of form is canonical, and is to be contrasted with the discursive and far more "fluid" form of a written opinion of a common law court. Even if the judge writing a common law opinion explicitly formulates a rule in what becomes a printed opinion, this rule will be subject to reconstruction by subsequent judges in light of the facts of the case, the issues ruled on, and the reasoning of the court. On the other hand, a chosen set of words in fixed verbal sequence as, for example, in a statute, is not thus subject to reconstruction (at least not in the hands of conscientious judges). Other varieties of "fluid" law that do not have this feature of a chosen set of words in fixed verbal sequence, include judge-made case law interpreting or filling gaps in constitutional texts, case law interpreting or filling gaps in statutes, case law interpreting or filling gaps in administrative regulations, and case law as set forth in opinions of administrative adjudicators.

A chosen set of words in fixed verbal sequence, duly reduced to print, as in a proposed or adopted statutory rule, has many functions. For example, it goes far to secure that those who vote for, and those who vote against, a proposed law will be voting on the *same* proposition. This goes far to make enactment of a proposed statute by majority vote possible. The overall significance of the imprint on content that form – a chosen set of words in fixed verbal sequence – makes here can hardly be overstated. Major credit to form is due. This is an empirical claim to a limited extent, and it is not really controversial.[47] It generally goes unnoticed, and is taken for granted.

The content of a proposed rule may be of such a fundamental nature that it should be encapsulated in a constitution where it will be "entrenched" and thus relatively immune to change, and also take priority over all conflicting laws. Or the content of a proposed law may require for its legitimacy that it have the encapsulatory feature of a statute adopted by legislative representatives of the

---

[47] See *supra* Chapter Three, at 70–71.

people, as with a widely applicable rule of tax law. Or resolution of a law-making problem may require accumulated experience and expertise, and hence call for "delegated" legislation by a specialized administrative body and thus for the encapsulatory feature of an administrative regulation. Or general legal values of the rule of law may require that a given subject matter be removed from exclusive common law development case by case, and instead be laid down in advance in the encapsulatory form of a statute or regulation in order to give fair notice to addressees and more effectively serve the policies at stake.

Notable debates in the history of law have occurred over fundamental choices between alternative types of formal encapsulatory features. In the nineteenth century, William Blackstone and Jeremy Bentham debated the merits of common law versus statutory encapsulation.[48] Blackstone favored common law partly on the ground that, in his view, it was intrinsically more reasoned. Bentham colorfully denied this.[49] He also argued that statute law is far more intelligible ("cognoscible") than common law, partly because the language of statute law is in a chosen set of words in fixed verbal sequence. Bentham argued, too, that this fixed verbal feature of statute law renders it far more accessible than common law, because the determinative holding in a common law case must always be dug out of the facts, rulings, and reasons of a judicial opinion or out of several related judicial opinions that may even have to be duly synthesized, which is a complex and uncertain art.

Bentham also argued that statute law is more "truly law," because it is entirely prospective, whereas common law is partly retrospective. In addition, Bentham argued that statute law is more predictable in application and usually is duly general, whereas a common law rule must often be uncertainly constructed from the particulars of a decided case or from a series of decided cases. Moreover, Bentham argued that statute law is generally more coherent than common law, that statute law is usually a more decisive reconciliation of conflicting considerations and so less subject to judicial manipulation, that statute law has more authoritative status, and that common law is too easily changed by judges.

According to Bentham, the capacity of rules of law to give rise to reasons for determinate action depends heavily on whether the law is encapsulated in a statute rather than in a common law opinion or opinions. Whatever the merits of

---

[48] W. Blackstone, *Commentaries on the Laws of England* (Wm. S. Hein and Co., Buffalo, 1992); J. Bentham, *A Comment on the Commentaries and A Fragment on Government*, (J. Burns and H. L. A. Hart eds., University of London, The Athlone Press, London, 1977).

[49] "If, on any one point whatsoever, any advantage, how slight soever, could with any colour of reason be ascribed to *common* in comparison with *statute* law, it would be on the ground of the sort of *argumentative* matter of which the mass of common law is composed, and which has no place in statute law.... As in a dunghill here and there a grain of corn, so in a volume of common law here and there a grain of genuine reason...." *Jeremy Bentham's Works*, vol. 4, at 494 (J. Bowring ed., Simkin and Marshall, London, 1843).

Section Eight: The Encapsulatory Feature

Bentham's overall position, it remains true that how far a given law can effectively serve as an instrument of policy, of the rule of law, of fundamental political values, or of other ends, depends partly on its mode of encapsulation – a formal feature. Here, too, major credit must go to well-designed form.

Mode of encapsulation differs from preceptual form. A rule, for example, takes one type of preceptual form, and a rule may be set forth in any encapsulatory mode: constitutional, statutory, regulatory, common law, customary law, and so on. By the same token, to say that a given law is, for example, encapsulated in statutory form, or in common law form, is not also to say that this law takes a given type of preceptual form.

In general, the same content can be encapsulated in any of several ways. It could even be encapsulated in a constitution in one jurisdiction, in statute law in another jurisdiction, in common law in a third, and in customary law in a fourth. Also, the content of a single rule could be expressed partly in a statute and partly in a common law case. One type of encapsulatory feature might be more appropriate to a given subject matter than another. For example, it is today widely recognized that criminal prohibitions should always be encapsulated in a statute rather than in "common law." This is partly because statutory encapsulation assures that those charged with offenses may have fair notice of what exactly they must answer to. Also, statutory encapsulation limits the power of prosecutors to make up crimes against an accused. Again, important credit must go to choices of an appropriate encapsulatory feature here.

Plainly, the chosen feature of encapsulation could be entirely appropriate for the type of content involved, yet the particular content itself be highly flawed. For example, a rule requiring a seven-eighths majority for legislative adoption of an ordinary statute might be encapsulated appropriately in, say, a chosen set of words in fixed verbal sequence in a printed constitutional provision. Yet, this very rule would be highly flawed in content, because it grossly impairs majority rule and legislative fecundity.

A mode of encapsulation may even leave a massive imprint or have other major effects on content. Many examples of this may be drawn from the experience of Anglo-American common law systems in codifying their law. For example, in the United States commercial law early on took the common law form of encapsulation, was later cast in the form of various "uniform statutes" duly adopted, and finally was ultimately codified in the Uniform Commercial Code in the second half of the twentieth century. Formulating the law in code form thereby systematized the law and rendered it far more accessible.[50] It also provided occasions for wide-ranging reforms of content.

---

[50] See generally, J. White and R. Summers, *The Uniform Commercial Code*, 4 vols. (4th ed., West Group, St. Paul, 1995).

176   Forms of Precepts – Rules

Despite the significant imprints and other effects of statutory and other modes of encapsulation on the contents of rules, the distinction survives as between formal encapsulation and the content so encapsulated. Many different contents can be encapsulated in the same form, and the very same content can be encapsulated in different forms.

SECTION NINE: THE EXPRESSIONAL FEATURE

In Section Five of this chapter, I treated definiteness – a degree of fixity and specificity – as a distinct feature of the preceptual form of a rule rather than as merely expressional. In the immediately preceding section of this chapter and for the reasons given there, I treated as encapsulatory the formulation of a rule (1) in a chosen set of words in fixed verbal sequence within a statutory, regulatory, constitutional, or other set text and (2) in written, that is, printed form. Scope still remains for recognition of a further major feature of the overall form of a precept or other species of law. I call this further feature expressional.

The expressional feature of the overall form of rules is complex and includes:

- how far the terms of the rule are explicitly expressed rather than left implicit,
- whether the rule is expressed in accepted technical or other specialized vocabulary rather than in lay vocabulary,
- the extent to which the expression of the rule is rigorously organized in its grammar and syntax,
- the extent of resort to new technical terms, duly defined,
- how far lay and other terms used are well-defined,
- the extent to which all terminology is consistently used,
- the degree of harmonization with modes of expression in related rules,
- the degree of conciseness,
- the degree of simplicity (of expression),
- the overall degree of precision.

If a rule is to exist at all, it must be somehow expressed. A drafter of a statutory rule must address various expressional choices of the foregoing kinds. There are good reasons to characterize mode of expression as formal. An expressional feature is a constituent of, and necessary to, the overall form of a rule. Hence it is formal. Without this feature, duly designed, we could not have rules. Mode of expression, in many of its facets, is also recognized as formal in various standard usages in English and other languages. These standard usages of "form," include explicitness, type of vocabulary, syntax, orderly arrangement, and the like.[51] This feature of form expresses content, but is not reducible to that content. Indeed, the

---

[51] *OED, supra* n. 17, vol. 6, at "formal," A.1.c, A.3.b, A.5.

Section Nine: The Expressional Feature 177

same content can often be expressed differently and different contents can usually be expressed in the same fashion.

Much credit can be due the imprints and other effects of well-designed expression on the content of a rule. To exist, a rule must be somehow expressed. Appropriate expression can also contribute to careful consideration of a proposed rule in the first place. Plainly, due expression can make a rule more intelligible as a basis for addressees to formulate determinate reasons for action, which when acted on, serve the ends of the rule.

In many complex fields, such as tax law, the law of negotiable instruments, and the law of bankruptcy, an expressional feature that is quite technical is desirable. In other areas, such as rules of the road, technical language is far less appropriate. Factors relevant to such choices include whether the primary addressees of the law are ordinary lay persons or are specialists of some kind, the nature of the policy content at stake, and the need for fair advance notice of the content of the law. For example, if the primary addressees are lay persons, the use of lay vocabulary can significantly improve levels of compliance. Although these are empirical claims, general evidence supports them.[52]

The mere fact that all constituent features of the preceptual form of a rule must be somehow expressed does not, however, make all these features expressional! The expressional feature differs from, for example, prescriptiveness. It is true that the feature of prescriptiveness in the usual rule requires the use of modal terms: "must," "may not," and "may," or their equivalents. How these terms should be expressed in terms of explicitness, vocabulary, syntax and grammar, and so on is a further question.

The expressional feature also differs from completeness. A rule can be complete in the sense that its contents incorporate all of its "parts or elements," yet these very contents may not be duly expressed. For example, the rule may not be set forth in a vocabulary appropriate for its addressees. A rule may even be complete in all its spaces, yet not be well expressed in any of those spaces.

Definiteness is another constituent feature of the overall form of a rule that is intimately related to mode of expression. The expressional feature frequently contributes to fixity and specificity, that is, to the definiteness of rule, but no single facet of mode of expression is equivalent to definiteness. For example, an exception to a rule can be expressed explicitly and in lay terms, yet still be highly indefinite as with: "Retire all police officers at 65, except the most valuable who are still fit." Or a rule may be duly definite, but be set forth in technical vocabulary quite inappropriate for its lay addressees.

Generality can also be readily distinguished from due expression. A rule can be general, yet its mode of expression quite inappropriate in some respect or respects.

---

[52] See H. Jones, *supra* n. 41, at 18–19. See also the discussion of the foodstuffs labeling example at 68–71 of Chapter Three.

For example, a rule might be colloquially expressed, when technical vocabulary would be far more appropriate, given the subject matter and addressees.

Likewise, the internal structure of a rule differs from its expression. Internal structure pertains to the relations between the parts of the rule, as such. The expressional feature pertains to how such parts and relations are expressed.

Mode of expression can usually be determined from the face of a rule. However, judicial and other interpretive practices may alter its facial expression. Or an adjacent rule may, for example, provide a term not itself explicitly set forth in the rule. Or an adjacent rule may import lay or technical vocabulary.

Degree of explicitness, the use or nonuse of specialized vocabulary, rigor of syntax, and the other facets of formal expression must be manifest in complementary content. Changes in an expressional feature do not necessarily signify changes in content, however. When they do, this is not usually to the same extent that most changes in other features of the form of a rule bespeak changes in content. For example, a change in the generality of a rule necessarily changes its content, but a change in the expression of a rule that merely renders it more explicit could leave the rule with exactly the same content. Similarly, a rule originally formulated in lay terms, and now for the first time in technical vocabulary, could still have the same content. Of course, a purported change in expression may affect content.

Once proposed rules are expressed in a highly intelligible fashion, this may sharpen the analytical focus of law-makers and prompt them to pose questions that lead to improvements in the form and content of the rule. Also, changes in manner of expression, although not affecting content, can make the rule more intelligible to its addressees, which is a matter of great importance. That is, alternative imprints of form of expression on the same content can be highly consequential.[53]

The mere fact that facets of expression must be manifest in content does not signify that these merge with content and lose their identity as expressional. As indicated here, expressional facets manifest in the content of a rule can be separately identified and characterized. Two rules can even have the same content yet differ considerably in explicitness, type of vocabulary, and certain other expressional facets.[54]

Again, the expressional feature of a given rule can be well-designed overall, even though the content of the same rule is deeply flawed in some way. Due expression is hardly a guarantee of good quality content. A rule may even express perfectly what is a grossly faulty means-end hypothesis as to what actions will serve desired

---

[53] See Chapter Three at 68–71.

[54] Also, it may be noted that, in English, when it is said that manner of expression is formal, we may also mean to contrast it not with content, but with an informal mode of expression. For example, we may mean that the explicit is formal, whereas the implicit is informal or that specialized vocabulary is formal, whereas the colloquial is informal.

Section Ten: Responses to Objections

179

ends. The quality of expressional features in a rule and the quality of its content are to be evaluated by different, yet related, standards.

The expressional feature differs from the encapsulatory feature. For example, to say that the encapsulatory feature of a law is statutory is not to reveal anything about what I here classify as its expressional feature. It is to say that this law, as a statute, is in a chosen set of words in fixed verbal sequence, and is in print. This same statute could, for example, lack explicitness, lack appropriate specialized vocabulary, lack rigor of sentence structure, or otherwise be quite flawed in terms of mode of expression. Also, to say that a law exhibits appropriate expressional facets, such as explicitness or the use of lay rather than technical vocabulary, or rigor of syntax, is not to say that it has any particular encapsulatory feature either. The various facets of an expressional feature might be set forth within statutory, common law, or some other mode of encapsulation. Yet some modes of encapsulation are more congenial to some facets of expression than to others. For example, statutory encapsulation invites explicitness.

SECTION TEN: RESPONSES TO OBJECTIONS

"Law-is-policy" reductionists and form-skeptics, or, as some might call some of them, "the substantivists," may assume that the overall form of a rule, and its constituent features, really reduce to policy or other "substantive" content in the end. Let us test this position merely with respect to definiteness. Consider a rule on retirement of employees, which may provide either for retirement "at age 65" or "when no longer fit." The policy reductionist and the form-skeptic might even concede that the "bright-line" definiteness in the first alternative, as abstractly conceived, has distinct identity as formal, at least prior to its incorporation in complementary content. However, once this feature is fused with policy content in a concrete rule, the reductionist and the form-skeptic may assume that this formal feature becomes part of the content of the rule and thus loses its identity as formal. Hence any distinction between form and policy or other content vanishes, and only content survives the fusion. It follows, on this view, that any credit due for value-serving effects of the rule must, therefore, be due only to what survives this fusion, that is, policy or "substance," not form.

There are several responses here. First, in taking their position, the policy reductionist and form-skeptic merely *assume* that any formal feature such as definiteness loses its distinct identity as such a feature on being fused with complementary policy content of the rule. No argument is advanced as to why this must be so. In truth, in our example, the concept of the formal feature of definiteness – some degree of fixity and specificity – still readily applies to an identifiable feature within the final version of the rule, namely, retire "at age 65." This feature therefore does not at any point lose its identity as a degree of definiteness – a formal feature, and is thus still readily classifiable as such. Its evident manifestation in content still fully answers to the concept of definiteness (a degree of fixity and specificity). As thus isolatable, with its identity as formal intact, this feature survives the fusion with policy content in the rule and not only retains its distinct identity, but continues to be susceptible of further characterization on its own as formal in terms of whether it is a relatively high, medium, or low degree of definiteness.

Second, the position of the reductionist and the skeptic is not merely conceptually and descriptively erroneous. This type of position is, again, vulnerable to a *reductio ad absurdum* argument. A rule, as a preceptual functional legal unit, must take an overall form with necessary and salient features including some degree of definiteness. Yet, if the general position of the reductionist and skeptic is correct, not only definiteness but prescriptiveness, completeness, generality, and all other constituent features of the basic form of a rule similarly become fused with complementary policy content and thus lose their identity as formal as well. Hence, on this view, the whole of a fully formed rule becomes all content and no form. Yet this would be absurd. Without formal features necessary to the overall form of a rule, a rule could not exist at all, yet plainly many rules exist.

Third, the reductionist and skeptic also ignore the extensive imprints and other effects of formal features that the contents of the rule and formal features come to bear once the rule is formed. These imprints and other effects underscore the import of form. Throughout this chapter, we have identified numerous examples of such imprints and other effects of formal features on content and on other formal features. Once a rule is formed, its complementary contents bear distinctly identifiable imprints of prescriptiveness, completeness, definiteness, generality, internal structure, manner of encapsulation, and mode of expression. Formal features also have imprints and other effects on other formal features, too. These imprints and other effects cannot be reduced merely to policy or other components of content. Nor can they be dismissed by the skeptic as nonexistent. They contribute to advancement of our understanding of what a rule is. They, too, must have due credit for what is achieved through the rule.

The policy-reductionist and the form-skeptic may adopt a further and related position. According to such critics, the choice of the rule-maker to adopt one rather than another degree of a formal feature, for example, high rather than low definiteness – as in "retire at age 65" rather than "when no longer fit" – itself reduces solely to a policy choice that necessarily converts this formal feature into policy content. There are two responses here. First, this position confuses a formal feature with one of its possible rationales. Even if the rationale for choice of the feature of high definiteness were its superior policy efficacy, the formal feature so chosen would nevertheless remain a feature of the form of a rule. The reductionist and skeptic fail to see that a feature and its rationale are simply not identical. A feature of definiteness remains a formal feature even when the choice of this

Section Ten: Responses to Objections

feature is driven partly or exclusively by a policy that it serves – a policy rationale. If the existence of a policy rationale for a choice of a feature of form converts such a choice into one of policy, then choices of many features of form in many rules become choices of policy because the rationales for many features of form in many rules are at least partly ones of superior policy efficacy. Yet it would be absurd to say that such rules therefore have no form, and consist solely of content – policy content.

Second, and relatedly, there are also nonpolicy rationales for many choices of formal features. For example, the formal feature of definiteness in a rule can also serve general values of the rule of law such as fair notice and equal treatment. If a feature is to be classified as formal if it primarily serves rule of law values, but classified as policy content if it primarily serves policy, the very same feature, for example, high definiteness, would lack stable identity. In some rules it would be formal, in others, it would be nonformal content.

6 ∼ FORM AND CONTENT WITHIN A RULE – CONTINUED

"[A] body of law is more rational and more civilized when every rule it contains is referred articulately and definitely to an end which it subserves, and when the grounds for desiring that end are stated...."
— O. W. Holmes, Jr.[1]

"[I]rrationality of form continually breeds irrationality of substance..."
— R. Pound[2]

SECTION ONE: INTRODUCTION

In this chapter I continue to concentrate on one type of preceptual form – the overall form of a legal rule – that workhorse precept in all developed systems. First, the purposes of rules and of their overall form are summarized. We then analyze more fully how choices of features within this form contribute to the creation of a rule, and how in the course of this, two-way interactions occur between such choices and choices of policy or other complementary content. Form leaves its imprints and other effects on content, and content in turn shapes form. These interactions, which are set forth throughout in the idiom of choices, are analyzed to advance understanding of the attributes of legal rules, including their makeup, unity, instrumental capacity, and distinctive identity. This will also lay bare more fully the credit due to choices of form in rules for the realization of ends and values.

The role of rationality in the construction of rules will be addressed throughout. Given the founding purpose of creating the functional unit of a legal rule, reason obviously requires adoption of the overall form of a rule. Also, we will see more fully how reason may favor or oppose possible purposes that the form and content of a rule might be designed to serve. We will stress that it is sometimes justified to sacrifice certain formal features, and complementary levels of policy or other ends, in favor of different formal features that serve general values of the rule of law more fully. Some of the analysis in this chapter is intricate – unavoidably so.

[1] Oliver Wendell Holmes, Jr., *Collected Legal Papers*, 186 (Harcourt Brace and Co., New York, 1920).
[2] R. Pound, *Jurisprudence*, vol. 3, 735–6 (West Publishing Co., St. Paul, 1959).

Section Two: General Purposes of the Form and Content of Rules

SECTION TWO: GENERAL PURPOSES OF THE FORM AND CONTENT
OF RULES — A SUMMARY

The most obvious purpose of the overall form of rules is to provide a model for the design of rules. Without recognition of such an overall form, law-makers could not even entertain the intention to create rules. The overall form of a rule, constituent features, and complementary content bearing imprints and other effects of those features, can contribute to the realization of a wide variety of purposes. These purposes include creating and maintaining a legal system as such, serving policy and related ends, implementing the rule of law, and serving fundamental political values. In light of prior chapters, it is now possible to draw together and summarize concisely the foregoing purposes. These purposes explain the ubiquity of rules, both reinforcive and regulative.

The Purpose of Creating and Maintaining Discrete Functional Legal Units and a Legal System as a Whole. Without resort to the overall form of reinforcive rules, including their features of prescriptiveness, completeness, generality, definiteness, and internal structure, it would not be possible to create and maintain functional legal units within a legal system, as known in developed Western societies. Mere resort to general principles or to particular orders simply could not suffice. The credit due the overall form of reinforcive rules here is, therefore, considerable. The form as well as the content of such rules prescribes formal features and other facets of the makeup, unity, instrumental capacity, and other attributes of legislative and other institutions, of preceptual units, of nonpreceptual units, of interpretive and other methodologies, of sanctions, and more. The overall form of reinforcive rules also prescribes various systematizing features of a legal system, a topic considered extensively in Chapter Ten.

The Purpose of Formulating and Implementing Policy and Similar Social Ends. A legal system adopts and implements countless policies including the maintenance of community peace, the facilitation of safe and efficient traffic flow, the purification and maintenance of water supply, and so on. The workhorse unit here is the regulative rule, but reinforcive rules come into play here as well.

Those who would draft and adopt a well-designed regulative rule must, among other things, think through the due generalizability of projected standard instances to which the rule is to apply. Legislators and drafters frequently begin with a draft of a rule the general terms of which reflect tentative choices of form and content. These choices would dispose of some standard instance to serve ends. The question will then arise whether such disposition is justified, a question partly about the merits of the proposed formal feature of generality of rule and its complementary policy or other content. A well-designed rule is appropriately general, and in this respect leaves a definitive imprint on content. A well-designed rule applies to all instances sufficiently similar to the standard instance.

The degree of generality to be chosen is partly a question about the design of form. Again, we can answer this question partly by hypothesizing possible instances and testing the generality of the terms of the proposed rule to see if it is broad enough to include relevantly similar instances, yet narrow enough to exclude the relevantly dissimilar ones. If the generality does not include all relevantly similar instances, it should, in the absence of other considerations, be adjusted upward. If the draft includes dissimilar ones, the generality should, without more, be adjusted accordingly. A well-formed rule must also be duly prescriptive, definite, complete, and internally structured.

An analysis merely oriented to policy or other contents of rules cannot alone sufficiently reveal formal features and in this way advance understanding of rules.[3] The contents of typical rules do not explicitly differentiate between form and content. A theory of form is required for this. We have seen how in order to advance understanding of the nature of rules, the overall form of rules and the constituent features of rules must be subjected to frontal, systematic, and comprehensive form-oriented analysis.

Moreover, an analysis oriented merely to the policy or other contents of an existing rule cannot, as such, focus on the credit due to form for realization of ends. When credit is due to a rule as a whole, we should consider the extent of credit due to its form. This credit can be very great. At the same time, any bad choices of form must share blame.

The Purpose of Serving the Rule of Law. A rule appropriately prescriptive, complete, general, definite, structured, well-expressed, duly encapsulated, and sound in content, will be a rule that can be readily applied to the standard instances for which it is designed, and to other instances sufficiently similar. These formal features and content can serve rule of law values, such as like treatment of like cases, fair notice to the law's addressees, and predictability.

The formal features of a well-designed rule make it superior to most other varieties of law for many purposes. It is true, for example, that particular orders are more definite, but such orders are too particular for efficient discharge of many legal tasks. Principles, on the other hand, are often not sufficiently precise or determinate. In between are rules that are well-designed in formal features such as prescriptiveness, definiteness, generality, and clarity of expression that leave imprints and other effects on content that commonly enable addressees to interpret the rules as needed, and to classify facts to which the rules apply, all with any required private legal advice, yet often without the need for official

---

[3] "Good content" here might mean good ends, good means, or both.

Section Two: General Purposes of the Form and Content of Rules

intervention.[4] Even lay addressees can often themselves construct reasons for determinate action under many rules. When so, the rules are highly efficient and may serve the policy or other ends of the rules, rule of law values, democratic will, freedom and dignity of addressee self-direction under the rules, and still other fundamental political values. Citizens and other addressees are thus not treated as mere objects to be ordered around by officials. Rather, they may act as autonomous self-determining human beings responsible for their actions.

Knowledge of law and fact are required for the rule of law. This knowledge must figure in all kinds of operations with law, including identifying valid law in light of criteria of validity, determining what facts are legally relevant to application of the law, finding these facts, interpreting the law, and applying the law so interpreted. Law in the form of well-designed rules is more knowable, more effectively disseminated, more readily interpreted, and more readily learned for purposes of application than all varieties of state-made law except simple orders.

The overall form of a rule and its constituent features can also be used to resolve substantive and other issues that arise in the creation of law. Hence, rules can secure a definitive rule of law. This is of great importance, especially given conflicting policies or other conflicting values, which is very common. No other preceptual form is similarly resolutive of conflicting ends.

The imprints or other effects on content of choices of duly formal features of rules can, along with this complementary content, also reduce scope for arbitrariness and lawless abuse of discretion by officials that might occur under more open-ended law. It is true that law in the form of discretion exercisable in accord with general principles may allow decision-makers to engage in somewhat more context-sensitive exploration of the merits of alternative decisions in varied sets of particular circumstances. Yet, as Professor Schauer has emphasized, this must always be weighed against the extent to which a formally more definitive rule would delimit scope for the misjudgment, prejudice, bias, ignorance, and other faults to which discretionary decision-makers may be subject.[5]

The Purpose of Serving Fundamental Political Values. Rules well-designed in form and content are an indispensable species of law for the realization of fundamental political values such as democracy, legitimacy, rationality, freedom, security, justice, and efficiency in governance. The overall form of rules is generally far better suited to these ends than the forms of general principles, maxims, or the like. The powers of legislatures, courts, and administrative bodies are typically conferred in reinforcive jurisdictional rules. What legislators, judges, and other officials are authoritatively empowered to do can be readily measured against

---

[4] H. L. A. Hart, *The Concept of Law*, 124 (2nd ed., Clarendon Press, Oxford, 1994).
[5] F. Schauer, *Playing By the Rules: A Philosophical Examination of Rule-Based Decision-Making in Law and in Life*, 149–55 (Clarendon Press, Oxford, 1991).

the specific terms of such rules, provided these rules are well-designed. If well-designed in form, this will leave appropriate imprints or other effects on the content of jurisdictional rules. Such rules legally empower personnel to act, and contribute legitimacy as well. Such rules also specify limits on official power that can serve as bulwarks against official arbitrariness, official abuse of power, and official interferences with freedom. If means of enforcement are available, rules known in advance that are appropriate in form and content can readily deter official excesses, and provide bases for redress. Precepts in the form of vague general principles or maxims could not serve such purposes nearly so well.

The structures and procedures of legal institutions, private and public, must also be set forth to some extent in reinforcive rules duly designed in form and content. Rule-prescribed structures and procedures, when duly designed, manifest profound commitment to rationality in the creation and implementation of law. They call for fact-finding, for formulation of law in light of facts and relevant purposes, and for exclusion of irrelevant considerations. Overall, these structures and procedures facilitate objectivity in legal decision-making. Although they cannot guarantee that reason will prevail, their very existence tends to keep this primary end in view, and also tends to motivate vigilance and surveillance on the part of those affected.

Reinforcive rules well-designed in form and content are indispensable to effective democracy. Elections and elected legislators would be impossible without duly definite and explicit imprints of form on the contents of required rules. Formal features of these rules, with complementary content, are required to define and organize what counts as a valid vote, provide for definitive tabulation of votes for and against the same candidates, provide for meaningful votes for and against the same propositions, and establish and provide for enforcement of the institutional arrangements within which elected legislators function. Institutional and preceptual forms necessarily interact here. Reinforcive rules, and so the form of such rules, are required for the very creation and operation of those institutions that, once created, are then necessary for the creation and implementation of regulative rules with the form and content required to serve policy and other purposes.

Moreover, the regulative and reinforcive rules that elected legislators and other law-making agencies adopt must be carried out by citizens, officials, judges, and others. Democracy is not merely a matter of who makes the law or how the law is made. It also requires that the law be implemented. Formally well-designed rules facilitate this. Such rules also enable others to tell readily whether the law is being duly followed and applied. This contributes legitimacy and tends to induce voluntary compliance.

Rules are required for the realization of free choice and freedom more generally. Extensive use of the overall form of a rule is required if private citizens and other addressees of the law are to be free to choose to create and to implement privately

Section Two: General Purposes of the Form and Content of Rules

made law on their own (with advice as needed). Consider these examples. The form as well as the content of rules confers freedom on private persons and entities to enter, perform, and enforce contracts, and to acquire, use, and transfer property. Freedom to contract is not merely the absence of interference by others with one's attempts to create contracts. The legal system must also delimit, define, and organize what constitutes a valid contract. Freedom to enter contracts depends on rules with definitive form and content specifying what steps must be taken to exercise this freedom and thereby create contracts that are legally valid. As the great German poet, Göethe, himself a lawyer, once stressed, the law here frees by limiting.[6]

Similarly, freedom to own property is not merely the absence of interference by others. Rules definitive in form and content must define what can be the objects of ownership, specify who owns what, and provide how ownership can be acquired. Without such rules, we could not even know what constitutes interference. Such rules are also required if citizens are to be free to own and transfer property rights to others.

Consider, too, the fundamental freedom of movement. For example, formally definitive "rules of the road" are required if persons are to be able to coordinate the driving of vehicles and thereby exercise freedom of movement on the roadways. All the foregoing freedoms, and many others, could not be left merely to precepts in the form of general principles or maxims, or to open-ended discretion. Much law must be in the definitive form of rules with complementary content if it is to demarcate and order the "spaces" required for, and provide the facilities required for, the effective exercise and protection of such freedoms as the foregoing. Law limiting the power of officials and others to interfere with the exercise of such freedoms must be similarly definitive in form. Again, as Jhering put it, "form is the twin sister of liberty and the sworn enemy of the arbitrary."[7]

Another fundamental political value is security. The criminal law goes far to protect security of person and property, though this is not the only type of law at work here. The criminal law is to a large extent a law of regulative rules in form and content. Regulative rules with required content in which form has also left imprints of due prescriptiveness, generality, definiteness, and clarity are necessary to prohibit socially undesirable behavior.

Justice is yet another fundamental political value realized in part through form. Societies use legal rules to provide for rectification of injustices. Without the form

---

[6] J. Göethe, *Selected Poems*, 164–5 (C. Middleton ed., M. Hamburger et. al trans., Suhrkamp/Insel Publishers Boston, Inc., Boston, 1983). The poem includes these lines in German: "In der Beschränkung zeigt sich erst der Meister/Und das Gesetz nur kann uns Freiheit geben" *id.*, at 164. As translated: "None proves a master but by limitation/And only law can give us liberty" *id.*, at 165. (Göethe studied law at Leipzig and Strasbourg and then practiced law for a time in Frankfurt.)

[7] R. Jhering, *Geist des Römischen Rechts: auf den verschiedenen Stufen seiner Entwicklung*, vol. 2, at 470–1 (Scientia Verlag, Aalen, 1993).

of rules, societies would be much less effective in these efforts. This is not to say that rules as such guarantee justice. Rules can have unjust or even evil content. Although the foregoing is far from an exhaustive account, it is a sufficient summary of major illustrative uses of rule-like form and complementary content to serve fundamental political values.

SECTION THREE: INITIAL CHOICES OF POLICY OR OTHER CONTENT AND OF FORMAL FEATURES IN A PROJECTED RULE

A proposed choice of policy or other content for a regulative or other rule could not be tentatively formulated at the outset, except in terms of at least minimal degrees of prescriptiveness, completeness, generality, definiteness, internal structure, and mode of expression. Otherwise, the "proposal" would be significantly formless in some respect or respects, and could not serve as a sufficiently determinate object of rational legislative scrutiny. As legislators move a tentative initial proposal on toward final formulation, choices of content and of form often interact. Also, tentative initial choices of form are driven not only by policy or the like, but also by general values of the rule of law, such as fair notice and equality of treatment. Indeed, this chapter is emphatic that the need to serve values of the rule of law may even justify significant sacrifices of policy in formulating and implementing a rule. Fundamental political values, too, may drive a choice of form, and justify some sacrifice of policy.

In Chapter Five, we saw that many choices of formal features must be made in the course of drafting and adopting statutory rules. Given the imprints and other effects that such choices of form can have on content, much can be at stake. In the present chapter, I take this theme further. Here I focus on policy content and form, and contend that: (1) although the rational proponent of a draft statutory rule to serve policy does not at the outset make an "all-determining" and final choice of relevant ends and means of policy, this proponent does often make a tentative choice of such policy at the outset, (2) this proponent also makes tentative choices of formal features at the outset, choices themselves not necessarily driven solely by prior or concurrent choices of policy, and (3) this proponent may subsequently make new or modified choices of formal features that intervene between the initial and the final policy choices, and that may have important effects on the final policy and its efficacy. Again, in this overall process, choices of policy content and of form interact. The policy content ultimately chosen – the final prescriptions of content and of other facets of the rule – reflect not only choices of ends and means of policy, but also the imprints and other effects of choices of formal features of the rule.

In this and the next section, I will isolate, identify, and clarify choices of formal features, and then demonstrate how their imprints and other effects can figure in the final draft of the rule, and thus can ultimately contribute to the nature

Section Three: Initial Choices of Policy or Other Content

and efficacy of the policy served, to general values of the rule of law, and to the realization of fundamental political values.

In what follows I will not attempt to provide an overall calculus for determining the best combinations of choices of formal features and of policy and other content, with their attendant sacrifices of conflicting ends.[8] It is enough to demonstrate that choices of formal features must figure in any such calculus, that these choices, when well-made, merit some credit for what law achieves, and that the overall analysis advances understanding of the makeup, unity, instrumental capacity, distinct identity, and other attributes of rules.

I will hereafter posit a realistic yet schematic law-making episode in which legislators make choices of policy or other content and choices of formal features in a statutory rule. Enough choices of formal features will be identified and differentiated to illustrate their extensive and varied importance. These will be presented in a realistic sequence, although in actual statutory law-making, the sequence frequently varies.

Statutory law-making occurs in response to a perceived need for some policy or other end to be implemented. Thus, at the outset, some person or group may propose that relevant actions be prescribed in a law. Let us imagine a society building its first public highways. Assume all agree that there should be a general policy favoring safe and timely traffic flow, a policy to be realized, at least partly, by means of regulating the actions of drivers, yet with due regard for free choice of drivers. Let us suppose that this initial policy choice is made by a legislative committee. Although in need of refinement, a general orienting policy choice cast in some form at the outset is usually of major import in setting the stage for further interactions between form and content that follow in a statute-making process.

The first type of initial choice of form, also one that legislators would likely take for granted at the outset, is the choice of the preceptual form of a rule over, say, that of a mere principle, a maxim, an order, or some other preceptual form. Various alternatives might be considered here. Consider, for example, a proposed statute providing:

A person operating or driving any vehicle on a Class A public highway of this state shall drive the vehicle at a rate of speed no greater than 70 mph.

Most legislators in many developed Western societies would likely consider some such proposed rule to be at least tentatively appropriate.[9] Law in the preceptual form of orders, for example, would plainly not be appropriate here. Nor would law in the form of a very general maxim. We will later focus more precisely on choices within the preceptual form of a rule. For now, we can see how the formal

---

[8] Nor have I sought to do so before. But see L. Lidsky, "Defensor Fidei: The Trevails of a Post-Realist Formalist," 47 *Fla. L. Rev.* 815, 827–8 (1995).

[9] In some systems, this definiteness of rule might even be required to be constitutional. See, e.g., *State v. Stanko*, 974 P. 2d 1132 (1998).

choice of one type of precept over another leaves an imprint on content that can be appropriate.

A second type of choice at the outset is that between a statutory, regulatory, common law, or customary form. Let us assume that legislators choose to use the encapsulatory form of a statute for the projected regulation of highways, rather than leave this to an administrative agency by way of a regulation, or to the development of judge-made common law, or merely to the evolution of customary practices. This choice of statutory encapsulatory form will leave its own imprint on content, too. What might support this initial choice? A statute consists of chosen words in fixed verbal sequence, and a law with this formal imprint on content can be more readily disseminated and learned than can a common law precedent. It may also be said that a law affecting so many people in their daily lives should have general democratic backing if it is to be legitimate.

A third type of initial choice of form implicit in our illustration – one that legislators, legal theorists, and others might take for granted at the outset – is that any such law have a well-designed expressional feature. Among other things, the content of the law would have to be relatively explicit and in a vocabulary appropriate to its addressees, both major imprints on content.[10] As we have seen, drafting in suitable preceptual, encapsulatory, and expressional form facilitates the very legislative processes of scrutinizing, debating, amending, and adopting a statute. Such drafting also facilitates learnability of the law and the pre-emptoriness of those legal reasons for determinate action that arise for addressees under the statute. All this, in turn, should contribute to realization of democratic will. It should also serve the end of fair notice to addressees, and still other values of the rule of law. Accordingly, the foregoing *initial* choices of form merit important credit. These, and still *further* initial choices of formal features, can also merit credit, as we will now see.

SECTION FOUR: FURTHER INITIAL CHOICES OF FORMAL FEATURES

In addition to the foregoing initial choices of preceptual form, of encapsulatory form, and of expressional form, further initial choices should also be made so that a statute in the preceptual form of a rule is:

(1)   duly prescriptive,
(2)   sufficiently complete,
(3)   duly definite,
(4)   as general in scope as is required by (a) its policy or other content in the standard instance of its application and (b) like treatment of sufficiently like instances, and
(5)   as simple in internal structure as reasonably feasible.

[10] *Supra* Chapter Five, Section Nine.

Section Four: Further Initial Choices of Formal Features

The preceptual form of a well-designed statutory rule with complementary content such as a 75 mph limit for Class A highways, would be preferable here to a mere general principle such as "Drive safely" also because, among other things, such a rule can be more fully prescriptive and determinate, and thus provide its addressees with more guidance. That is, addressees can more readily construct reasons for determinate action under a well-designed rule, reasons which, when acted upon, should serve policy ends of the rule. Action under such a rule should also serve values of the rule of law, including fair notice, and like treatment of like cases. In addition, action under such a rule should to an extent serve fundamental political values, such as freedom of choice, legitimacy, rationality, and democracy. The formal feature of prescriptiveness, then, is of wide-ranging import here. It also renders the rule pre-emptive, and thus resolutive of conflicts with external considerations.

It will be sufficient merely to treat illustratively in some depth only *one* of the previously listed further initial choices of a formal feature within the overall form of a rule, namely due definiteness. Due definiteness has some claim to special status among the various features of the overall form of a rule. Plato was emphatic that a purported law that is not sufficiently definite cannot really be a satisfactory law.[11] The general analysis of definiteness now to be presented can be applied, *mutatis mutandis*, to all further relevant choices of formal features in a rule as well. It is also true that choices of all the various features of the form of a rule, and not merely choices of definiteness, leave imprints and other effects on content.

Assume that the following two drafts of a proposed statutory rule are presented to the relevant legislative committee: a draft incorporating an indefinite standard of behavior, that is, "Drive reasonably," and a draft incorporating a highly definite bright-line, which let us assume, is framed in two alternatives the legislature is to consider: "Drive no faster than 75 mph," and "Drive no faster than 60 mph".[12]

The choice of form in our illustrative episode is that between different degrees of the same feature within the same preceptual form – here a higher versus a lower degree of definiteness. The very possibility that an issue as to such a choice of form can arise presupposes an initial orienting choice of policy content – here safe and timely traffic flow, with some regard to driver free choice. Indeed, a meaningful choice of definiteness can usually arise only with respect to alternative degrees of definiteness of the same type of complementary content, as in our example of "drive reasonably" (low definiteness) versus "drive no faster than 75 mph" (high definiteness). The differing imprints of the alternative formal features on content here are plain.

---

[11] *The Dialogues of Plato*, vol. 2, at 491 (B. Jowett trans., Random House, New York, 1937).

[12] I am mindful that some statutes combine some version of each. Such statutes both limit speed to a maximum rate and also require reasonableness in driving at any rate below the limit. For example, the New York statute so provides. See Chapter 71 of the *Consolidated Laws of New York*, Title VII, Article 30, Sections 1180 and 1180-a.

The fact that a choice between two versions of the formal feature of definiteness also presupposes two complementary policy contents in which this choice must necessarily manifest itself does not, however, convert or collapse this choice of formal feature solely into a choice of policy content as such. As we saw in Chapter Five, the choice of high, rather than low, definiteness still retains its identity as a formal choice between different degrees of definiteness, even though the effects of the choice are necessarily differently manifested within complementary policy contents. Definiteness thus retains its own conceptual autonomy – its own fixity and specificity – as well as its own identity, even though necessarily manifest in content. If we were to make the test of what counts as a choice between alternative formal features of definiteness that it be a choice wholly divorced from, and without any imprints or other effects on, policy or other content in the projected rule, there could be no choices of definiteness, nor of most other formal features in any rule, and no overall form of such rules, and, therefore, no such rules at all! Any choice between alternative versions of a formal feature such as definiteness, generality, or almost any other formal feature, manifests itself in, and thus leaves its imprint or other effects upon some projected content. As we have seen, a rule, if it is to be a rule, cannot be "all content and no form."[13]

Let us now identify major types of considerations that would be relevant to a choice of one rather than another version of the formal feature of definiteness in a rule. Here, we will also see how choices of form interact with complementary policy content in the course of constructing a rule, and how what are partly choices of form may in the end be entitled to much credit for ends realized. First, what need, if any, is there for a choice that firmly prioritizes between conflicting policies of safety on the one hand, and timeliness of traffic flow and other relevant considerations that may be implicated such as driver free choice on the other? A bright-line rule here could prioritize definitively between such conflicting policies or any other considerations, whereas a rule embodying an indefinite standard could not and would leave resolution of such conflicts largely up to ad hoc choices of individual drivers. Any formal prioritization as between policies is, *in part*, a choice of policy content as well as a choice of form. For example, "Drive no faster than 75 mph" definitively prioritizes efficiency of traffic flow and driver free choice up to 75 mph over safety (at least on some roadways), whereas "Drive reasonably" does not definitively prioritize as between these competing ends. A definite bright-line would be preferable, assuming that some prioritization between competing ends is preferable to leaving this to ad hoc driver choice on the type of roadway involved.

---

[13] A somewhat different story here applies to different versions of the expressional feature. The imprints are in terms of expression, which may not affect content. Yet, there must be some mode of expression, and there is scope for great variety. In addition, some variations will affect content. See *infra*, text accompanying n. 26.

Section Four: Further Initial Choices of Formal Features

Such prioritization would qualify as a major imprint or effect of the formal feature of definiteness on rule content.

Second, *assuming* addressees could learn and apply both rules with equal effectiveness, which rule with its degree of the formal feature of definiteness and complementary content would best serve relevant policies and other ends? A highly definite rule at, say, 75 mph, may over-include in relation to one or more policy purposes (for example, some speeds in some circumstances will still be safe above the bright-line limit) and under-include in relation to one or more policy purposes (for example, some speeds will be unsafe at or below the limit in unusual road conditions). However, law-makers might, in light of available factual data, conclude that any such losses in policy efficacy attributable to over- and under-inclusion would still be less than losses attributable to the mistakes drivers would make in exercising judgment entirely on their own, thereby going too fast or too slow under a less definitive "drive reasonably" standard. If the factual data shows that the more definite bright-line would have greater policy efficacy, this would favor legislative choice of high definiteness, which, again, would leave a major imprint on complementary policy content, as driven by considerations of form and of policy content together.

Third, which rule could the addressees more effectively learn and apply to serve the policies implicated and also any other relevant ends such as driver free choice? Under the more definite bright-line rule, such as a 75 mph limit, drivers could more effectively learn the rule, interpret the rule, ascertain relevant facts, and faithfully apply the rule, than would be possible under a less determinate "drive reasonably" rule. Rules highly dependent on addressee self-direction for whatever efficacy they have, and there are many such rules, require sufficient definiteness to enable addressees themselves to construct reasons for determinate action under the rule. Such bright-line rules are also more readily enforceable by police and courts. These considerations here generally favor high definiteness that, depending on the data, may, however, also impair policy efficacy somewhat through over-inclusion or under-inclusion, as explained. Again, any such choice of bright line would leave its imprint, or reinforce other imprints on content, and would be, in part, a choice of form and, in part, a choice of complementary policy content.

Fourth, which rule would serve values of the rule of law better? As briefly suggested earlier, the choice of a more highly definite formal feature in our example may be justified on the ground that this feature would serve general values of the rule of law more fully than a less definite feature. For example, a bright line gives addressees fairer notice of the law's requirements than a vague standard. It may also be that a bright line secures a greater likelihood that, in general, despite under- and over-inclusion, more similar cases will be treated alike by officials, than under a vague standard. Fairer notice is worth having for two reasons. It is a means to more effective addressee self-direction for purposes of serving relevant policy or other ends. It also affords such addressees due notice in advance that, in exceeding the limit, they become subject to adverse legal consequences.[14] Unlike policies such as road safety and timeliness of traffic flow, and unlike the end of driver free choice, the principle of the rule of law requiring fair advance notice defines a major aspect of law-like governance. Also different from such policies, and from the end of driver free choice, is the further principle requiring like treatment of like cases – another general value of the rule of law.[15] Under an indefinite standard in a rule, it may be more likely that like cases will be treated differently than under a bright line rule (again, despite under and over-inclusion). The more definite rule, then, *may* be justified here on rule of law grounds as well as the postulated superior efficacy of the more definite rule in serving the policy of safe and efficient travel.[16]

Consider now a second basic type of illustrative law-making episode, one posing a choice between two alternatives. The first alternative consists of a rule incorporating an indefinite standard, for example, "drive reasonably," that we will *now assume*, in light of hypothetical data, yields *more* realization of policies such as safety, timeliness, and more driver free choice than the more definite rule "Drive no faster than 75 mph," yet *less* realization of general values of the rule of law than this more definite rule. The second alternative consists of a bright-line rule "drive no faster than 75 mph" that we *now assume* in light of such data, yields *less* realization of policies of safety and timeliness and of driver free choice than the less definite rule in the first alternative, yet *more* realization of general values of the rule of law such as fair notice and equal treatment than this less definite rule. To confront the realistic possibility of such a choice, we need only to assume the data reveals that circumstantial conditions prevail in which the bright-line rule in the second alternative under- and over-includes with regard to the policy of safe and timely traffic flow to a considerable extent, yet drivers exercising their own judgment under a "drive reasonably" rule, given relevant road conditions, would make very few errors of judgment. For example, drivers might be quite good, and road conditions very good, so that drivers would make relatively few errors of judgment with respect to safety and timeliness under the "drive reasonably" standard on the first alternative, and would have considerable free choice.

Even if we assume that the rate under a "drive no faster than 75" rule would itself be approximately right *as a fixed rate* in terms of safety and timeliness of flow, still, a rule specifying such a fixed rate would, we are now assuming, significantly under- and over-include in relation to the policy of safe and timely traffic flow. That is, in

---

[14] See case cited *supra* n. 9 that is illustrative of many in which such an issue arises.

[15] Still other principles of the rule of law are relevant, including the principle requiring predictability.

[16] I do not claim that more definiteness is always the appropriate form, even in the type of circumstances hypothesized. Under some types of circumstances, as where the roadway is not straight but highly variable, a less definite "drive reasonably" rule might be the more appropriate formal feature.

Section Four: Further Initial Choices of Formal Features

a significant proportion of instances, drivers could safely go faster than 75 mph, and would do so under a "drive reasonably" standard. Further, in some proportion of instances, 75 mph would be too fast, given general road conditions, yet some drivers, we assume, would "chance it" and drive up to the limit under a 75 mph rule, whereas, we are assuming, under a "drive reasonably" standard, these drivers would slow down. Thus, in such general circumstances, a bright-line rule would have less policy efficacy than a "drive reasonably" rule, and would allow less driver free choice.[17]

Here in this second basic type of law-making episode, if legislators were to decide on the appropriate degree of the formal feature of definiteness *only* by reference to how this would serve policy efficacy and driver free choice, then the less definite "drive reasonably" feature would be the appropriate choice of form and complementary content. However, rational choices of form and content in the creation of law are not driven only by policy efficacy or by fundamental political values, such as driver free choice, but are driven also by general values of the rule of law. Rational legislators would, therefore, also inquire which rule would better serve values associated with the rule of law, such as fair notice and like treatment of like cases. Law-makers could decide, in my hypothetical circumstances, to sacrifice some level of policy efficacy and driver free choice realizable through the less definite "drive reasonably" standard in favor of a higher level of realization of general values of the rule of law, such as fair notice and like treatment, realizable through the more definite bright-line rule.[18] Such a preference contemplates a certain level of interaction between form – here, a degree of definiteness – and policy content in the creation of a rule. The resulting policy content would bear the imprint of the formal feature of high definiteness, and the overall effect of this on the ultimate policy content (and on free choice) in the rule would be significant.

Thus, in this second basic type of law-making episode, which is representative of many that arise in lawmaking, the final choice of appropriate definiteness – a formal feature – is not rationally driven if driven solely by policy or other ends such as driver free choice. To be rationally driven, it must also be driven by general values of the rule of law. These general categories of ends – policy and free choice on the one hand, and general values of the rule of law on the other – are often highly compatible, as postulated in our first basic type of law-making episode. This general compatibility is most fortunate for the law! However, as we have just seen in this second basic type of law-making episode, when the degree of the formal feature of definiteness required for realization of general values of the rule of law is incompatible with some higher level of desired policy efficacy, it is not always the case that this higher policy efficacy should take priority, even when

---

[17] Of course, general road conditions in a given region could go either way. Highly variable road conditions could argue for a standard "drive reasonably."

[18] For a recent case in which these very arguments were made, see *supra* n. 9.

combined with a further political value such as driver free choice. That is, contrary to law-is-policy reductionists and form-skeptics, policy efficacy is not an absolute. It is not the "be all and end all" of legal ordering, even when combined with the further desideratum of a fundamental political value, such as driver free choice.

General values of the rule of law, such as fair notice of the law and equality before the law, are, therefore, purposes that may even drive a choice of a formal feature that, in effect, subordinates policy realization to some extent. When this occurs, we may call it the "rule of law priorial effect."[19] This is an effect that underscores the over-riding credit for serving rule of law values that can be due to choices of formal features independently of policy and other ends, such as free choice. Indeed, the credit due to choices of form as manifest in complementary content here is profound. Without choosing a highly definite formal feature here, it would simply not be possible to fix and prioritize the rule of law values at stake over conflicting policy. The word "imprint" alone may seem too anemic to describe this effect of a choice of form. The "rule of law priorial effect of form" is better.

At this point, if not earlier, at least some law-is-policy reductionists and form skeptics might make the following move: "General values of the rule of law are really policies. Thus, rule of law policies trump other policies here, which is nothing new." Rule of law values are not, however, the same as policies. First, the realization of general values of the rule of law, such as fair notice of the law's requirements and like treatment of like cases, is definitive of law-like governance (though not exhaustively so). The mere implementation of any particular policy, such as safety or timely traffic flow, is not, as such, definitive of law-like governance, even in part. Second, and relatedly, the scope for serving any given value of the rule of law is far greater than the scope for serving almost any policy. Presumptively, every use of law should, at least to some extent, serve the values of the rule of law implicated in that use. Yet it can hardly be said that every use of law can and should serve a given policy, such as road safety! Third, the realization of many values of the rule of law, including fair notice and equal treatment, is valuable as such, without regard to the desirability of any particular proposed policy to be concurrently implemented. The desirability of implementing a proposed policy, however, is not valuable as such. Rather, its desirability depends entirely on the quality of the particular policy, the need for it, and the costs of it, including any sacrifice of other values it entails such as diminished realization of rule of law values.

However, for the sake of argument, let us concede that general values of the rule of law can be reduced to policies. It would still remain true that an appropriate choice in the rule of the formal feature of definiteness, in light of the data, would be

---

[19] For discussion of this priorial effect in quite another context, see R. Summers, "How Law is Formal and Why It Matters," 82 *Cornell L. Rev.* 1165, 1219 (1997). The sacrifice of general values of the rule of law that pursuit of a policy might entail may even be so great as to justify nonadoption of the policy altogether.

Section Four: Further Initial Choices of Formal Features

required to specify and fix the most justified balance of such conflicting "policies." It would also remain true in the end that this balance could, as hypothesized earlier, favor that degree of definiteness required to serve values of the rule of law rather fully, whether called policy or something else. Moreover, the formal feature of definiteness in rules has other key roles to play besides trumping policy to serve values of the rule of law.

To summarize: when policy, other ends of free choice and the like, and general values of the rule of law are not really in conflict but fully compatible, as in the first basic law-making episode we hypothesized, the higher degree of definiteness would be the appropriate formal feature, given that it duly serves policy efficacy, ends of freedom and the like, and values of the rule of law. As we saw, a highly definite 75 mph limit, for example, might involve no sacrifice of overall policy if we assume the over- and under-inclusion of a bright line would generally be offset by driver errors of judgment in driving too fast or too slow under a "drive reasonably" rule. Here, the higher degree of definiteness would be appropriate given that it would involve no sacrifice of policy, would duly serve values of the rule of law, and would only very limitedly sacrifice driver free choice because, at the higher speeds, the value of driver free choice is itself attenuated. Further, in the second basic type of law-making episode hypothesized here, we saw how values of the rule of law may take priority, at some level, over policy and other ends and, thus, justify choice of a formal feature of definiteness that even sacrifices some level of policy realization. We called this the "rule of law priorital effect."

Though in the foregoing discussion we treated an important freedom – driver free choice, we still have not put everything in the scales. The choice of a higher degree of the formal feature of definiteness can be supported, in many cases, not only by the absence of any significant sacrifice of policy efficacy as combined with the increase in realization of values of the rule of law that this choice brings, but also by fuller realization of still other fundamental political values, such as democracy, rationality, and legitimacy in law-making. Consider democracy, for example. With the adoption of a "drive reasonably" standard, we really do not know fully whether the legislative "majority" was truly of like mind because we do not know what individual legislators had in mind when they voted for a standard of reasonableness. Half of the majority may have thought that 60 mph to 75 mph was reasonable for general highways, whereas the other half may have had roughly 50 mph to 65 mph in mind, or something else altogether. However, with the adoption of a bright-line rule, at say, a limit of 75 mph, there is necessarily more of an objective "meeting of the minds" among the majority, and thus more by way of a truly democratic choice. This is not to say that somewhat vague statutes are never justified.

Still a third important type of law-making episode may be hypothesized. In this episode, we can see that the postulated "priorital effect" of general values of the rule of law favoring high definiteness in the second law-making episode is not an absolute. The extent of sacrifice of policy and other ends, such as driver free choice, that would result if high definiteness were chosen could be very considerable. If the data show that the sacrifice of policy and other ends due to high definiteness (with its under- and over-inclusion) would simply be *too great*, the less definite "drive reasonably" rule would be better, even though it involves some sacrifice of rule of law values, such as fair advanced notice and like treatment of like cases. In this third type of law-making episode, we would have what might be called a "policy priorital effect." The choice of a lower degree of definiteness would implement this trade-off, and this formal feature would merit some credit, too.

There is also a fourth possible type of law-making episode. Sometimes the inherent nature of the subject matter of the policy or other end at stake allows only low degrees of a given formal feature such as definiteness, and so limits the extent to which general values of the rule of law can be realized at all. Consider, for example, the general policy favoring the exercise of due care in the various activities of social life. As we have seen, it is not feasible to define fully and in advance what constitutes due care.[20] There are many other examples of important policies that cannot be defined with high degrees of definiteness in advance of occasions for their implementation. In such cases, the nature of the policy content involved generally limits the possible formal choices to lower degrees of definiteness because higher degrees would introduce intolerable over or under-inclusion or both. Some sacrifice of values of the rule of law is, therefore, required not so much because these values are outweighed by the extensive policy to be realized through the lower degree of definiteness, as in cases of the third type mentioned earlier, but as a concession to necessity if there is to be any such law at all. It is true that, in some of these instances, general values of the rule of law will not be significantly at stake, anyway. For example, the general value of advance notice of the law's requirements to persons possibly acting out on the frontiers of human interaction is far less important, or not relevant at all, where it is simply the case that no one or only very few may be so acting, as is true of parties in court cases in which judges award child custody case-by-case on the basis of the "best interests of the child."

The foregoing analysis of form in the formation of a rule is not exhaustive. It merely dwells illustratively on the feature of definiteness without considering other formal features. A comprehensive analysis would be even more telling as to the vital role of form, and far more complex, if all of the various formal features in a rule were similarly considered systematically and in relation to each other. Still, the limited focus here on definiteness itself advances understanding of the

---

[20] See *supra* Chapter Five, at 160.

Section Five: Final Choices of Form and Final Choices of Policy

makeup, unity, and instrumental capacity of rules and illustrates that much credit can go to a formal feature.

SECTION FIVE: FINAL CHOICES OF FORM AND FINAL CHOICES OF POLICY AND OTHER CONTENT

As we have seen, in the process of creating a statutory rule, initial choices of formal features figure in tentative formulations of the rule at the outset. At the same time, an initial and tentative choice of policy or other content also occurs. Thereafter, revised choices of formal features and of policy or other content often occur. When so, these may contribute significantly to what becomes the final choice of formal features and complementary content. We will now elaborate on this truth, for it also advances practical and theoretical understanding of the makeup, unity, instrumental capacity, and other attributes of rules. In one variation of our highway speed illustration, we saw how the desirability of a high degree of definiteness to serve values of the rule of law could justifiably influence law-makers in the end to sacrifice some complementary policy content of a draft rule. That is, law makers could rationally refine the rule from an initial general reasonableness standard to a definite rate for driving on open highways, say 75 mph, even though this would sacrifice some policy realization.

The choice of the formal feature of a definite rate of 75 mph over, for example, a rate of 60 mph is necessarily, in part, also a choice of complementary policy or other content. This is so in at least two respects. First, it is a choice between different policy trade-offs of safety and traffic flow at these two rates. Second, it is a choice favoring more, rather than less, driver free choice (although at the higher rates of permissible speed, there is less interference with such choice). Even though the choice is, in these two respects, in part a choice of policy and other ends, the choice also remains one of high definiteness (at some rate). Such a choice of formal feature leaves a major imprint on content thereby also serving policy or other ends. This imprint may better serve values of the rule of law, as well.[21]

Assume legislators have chosen not to have a general standard, that is, not to have a "drive reasonably" rule, but instead to have a bright-line rule. Assume they have determined that such a rule better serves general values of the rule of law, and they believe the line can be drawn to serve policies of safety, timeliness, and free choice better as well. A question that could still be left open to an extent is this: "What should the exact rate be in that bright-line?" I will now render explicit a conflict between policies heretofore left largely implicit. Assume the

---

[21] A choice of content can serve the rule of law, too, as where a choice is made to adopt content that is itself susceptible of a high degree of definitiveness.

circumstantial conditions are such that a choice of 75 mph as a speed limit rate serves timeliness of traffic flow, but that this is, to some extent, at the expense of safety. Similarly, assume that 60 mph as a speed limit rate serves safety well, but that this is, to some extent, at the expense of timeliness of traffic flow. The choice to be made here between the rates should be based on data and related evaluative analysis outside the parameters of this book.[22] Even so, the formal choice of degree of definiteness can rationally contribute to this final choice of rate – a choice of policy and of form, in interaction. Let us see how.

First, the alternatives in this further hypothesized choice are already defined partly in terms of identical formal features, that is, two bright-line rules (75 mph and 60 mph) with different complementary policy contents. This very identity of the formal imprint on content of the two alternatives – two bright lines – itself casts the difference between complementary policy contents into bold relief and facilitates their rational scrutiny.[23] This prompts the question: "Just what rate, in policy terms, is the better rate, or more nearly so, and why?" Thus, form organizes the focus of legislative study and scrutiny in terms of different rates expressed with the same degree of definiteness, in light of relevant data and evaluative analysis. Rationality of deliberation, a fundamental political value, is thus served because the sameness of the bright-line definiteness provides objects for scrutiny that are more comparable. That is, we have a choice between the same feature of form in the two alternatives, that is, two bright-lines that differ only in complementary content (75 mph and 60 mph). This clarity is a significant contribution of form to rationality of deliberation over ends and means and merits credit.

Secondly, a choice of a high degree of definiteness is necessary if the legislature is definitively to prioritize one of the two conflicting policies over the other in each of the two alternatives now to be compared and considered: safety to some extent over time at one specified rate (60 mph), or time to some extent over safety at another specified rate (75 mph). We are assuming the law-maker has already decided there is to be a prioritizing bright-line rule, rather than a rule granting discretion that leaves the trade-off to the driver's own judgments of reasonableness in particular circumstances.[24] Different choices favoring one policy over the other appear in each alternative, and bright-line definiteness in each prioritizes one policy over another, a major imprint of form on content. Without the bright-line – a feature of form – it would not be possible to express such definitively prioritized alternatives and, thus pose a definitive choice of one policy over another in the two alternatives. Form merits major credit here.

---

[22] Again, for the purposes of the type of analysis I present here, it is not necessary to provide a calculus, let alone any data.

[23] It might be said that form here reduces these to a "common denominator," thereby facilitating scrutiny of the alternatives on equal terms.

[24] It may be noted that the priority choices are merely relative to these alternatives – the prioritization of policy choices is reversed if the alternative bright line choice is 85 mph.

Section Five: Final Choices of Form and Final Choices of Policy   201

Thus, as in our illustration, revised choices of formal features within the overall form of a rule may, in the course of constructing a rule, intervene *after* the initial and tentative choices of policy content and form, yet *before* the final choices and, thus contribute ultimate refinement of proposed policy. An interactive process of this nature can occur in our illustration somewhat as follows: (1) the initial and tentative general policy is chosen favoring safe and timely highway travel and the preceptual form of a rule is also chosen at the outset to embody this policy; (2) these choices lead to a further choice within the overall form of a rule, not of an indefinite general standard, but instead of a *possible* bright-line at a possible rate of speed; and finally (3) the choice of some possible bright-line leads to choice of an actual bright-line, itself definite enough to specify one rate of speed over another, thereby at the same time prioritizing one conflicting policy over another at that rate – timeliness over safety or the reverse.

The initial and tentative general choice of policy content at the outset – the choice to regulate traffic flow in the interest of safe and timely travel and other values such as driver free choice – is thus ultimately transformed and refined on the "anvil" of legal form. In the process, considerations of appropriate form not only figure in initial and tentative choices at the outset, but also intervene after the initial and tentative choice of policy content and of the rule-form, and yet before the final choices of form and complementary content. These intervening considerations make their own contributions to the form and complementary content of the final rule, in light of considerations of policy content and its efficacy, of efficacy to serve general values of the rule of law, and of efficacy to serve any fundamental political values implicated, such as driver freedom of movement.

We have identified tentative choices of the formal feature of definiteness that not only may figure in *initial* policy formulations, but also intervene *after* the initial and general orienting choice of policy and form in a proposed rule to regulate traffic flow and serve other ends. There are other choices of features within the overall form of a rule besides definiteness such as completeness and generality. Formal choices of encapsulation and of mode of expression also figure. All formal choices retain their own identity and significance distinct from policy as such.

Among the features within the overall form of a rule, we have illustratively concentrated on the choice of degree of definiteness, and we have said this choice presupposes a complementary choice of policy. Thus, in our illustration, we have:

(A) The choice of a formal feature of degree of definiteness as between:
1. "Drive reasonably" – the form of an indefinite standard in a rule, with necessary complementary policy content, versus:
2. "Drive no faster than a specified rate, e.g., 75 mph v. 60 mph" – the form of a definite bright-line rule with complementary policy content, yet to be specified,

(B) If (A) (1) is not adopted, and we have identified "rule of law" and other reasons why it might not be, the remaining choice of policy content, which is to be made within the form in (A)(2) above, would be between:
1. The policy of timeliness prioritized to some extent over the policy of safety in the complementary form of a bright-line rule: "drive no faster than 75 mph" (for example) versus:
2. The policy of safety prioritized to some extent over the policy of timeliness in the form of a complementary bright-line rule: "drive no faster than 60 mph (for example)."

In constructing a statutory rule, then, the final choice of policy content presupposes choices of (1) a type of preceptual form (whether a rule, principle, etc.), (2) features within the chosen preceptual form such as, in the case of rules: prescriptiveness, definiteness, generality, completeness, and internal structure, (3) a formal feature of encapsulation, and (4) a formal expressional feature.

Again, contrary to the form-skeptic and the law-is-policy reductionist, a statutory rule, as ultimately created, never becomes "all policy content and no form." Whether or not all choices of formal features are explicitly disentangled from each other and from content and recognized for what they are, rational legislative law-making commonly involves a complex combination of interacting choices of form and policy content. For example, in (A), above, both the formal feature of definiteness and the complementary policy content differ in each of the two alternatives in (A). That is, each of the two in (A) presents a different fusion of formal feature with complementary policy content. In (B), the two formal features are the same (bright-lines), but the complementary contents of the policy trade offs between safety and timeliness differ (as does the degree of sacrifice of driver free choice). That is, in (B), each alternative represents a fusion of the same formal feature with different complementary policy content. Even so, the alternatives in (B) presuppose both choices of form and of policy content, in interaction.

The differences of form in (A)(1) and (A)(2) cannot be explained without reference to the differences in types of complementary policy content as between (A)(1) and (A)(2). Yet the differences of form in (A)(1) and in (A)(2) define and focus these very differences of policy content. A choice of policy content in (A) simply cannot be made independently of form, and is, therefore, *not solely a choice of policy*. Moreover, nonpolicy considerations, including general values of the rule of law, are importantly relevant to the alternative choices of formal features of definiteness in (A)(1) and (2). As we have seen, other nonpolicy considerations, such as freedom of choice, democracy, rationality, and other fundamental political values, may enter the analysis, as well. The sameness of form in (B)(1) and (B)(2) isolates and sharply reveals the differences in complementary policy content in the two alternatives. Thus, form has functions here, too.

Section Six: General Interactions and Other Inter-Relations 203

In law-making, if form is not at least an equal partner of policy content, it is still an important partner, given its imprints and other effects on content and its interactive bearing on policy and other content, and given its own instrumental significance, as illustrated here merely with regard to formal definiteness. When a legislative choice involves differences both of form and of policy content, as in (A), form is even more important as a partner of policy. When further choices of encapsulatory, expressional, and other features of preceptual form besides definiteness, are fully taken into account, it becomes apparent that form is still even more important as a partner of policy.

SECTION SIX: GENERAL INTERACTIONS AND OTHER INTER-RELATIONS BETWEEN CHOICES OF FORM AND CHOICES OF CONTENT

Bad choices of form beget bad content, sometimes necessarily. For example, a rule that is insufficiently complete – a formal feature – is necessarily deficient in complementary content. A rule that is not duly definite in its content necessarily manifests this formal flaw in complementary content. A purported rule that is not duly general necessarily manifests this formal deficiency in complementary content that is too narrow.

Yet careful consideration of a choice of a formal feature may rationally support a complementary choice of content that is salutary. For example, where the drafter gives careful consideration to generality – a necessary feature of the form of a rule, the drafter may come to see that an existing draft of the rule should be more general if it is to serve the full reach of the policy content of the rule, and also treat like cases alike. To see this is to see that such a choice of form – greater generality in my example, also entails a particular complementary policy content. Thus, assume that a draft of a proposed rule, which is to implement a general policy of highway safety, provides for "annual inspection and certification of the safety of trucks, with regard to brakes and steering mechanisms." If the policy content in the proposed rule is to be extended to its full reach, then we can see that the rule must be redrafted with greater generality. The rule should apply to all motor vehicles for highway use, not merely trucks. The formal feature of generality and its complementary content, then, together serve the relevant ends when well-designed.

The analysis here also renders explicit the truth that a formless rule cannot exist. As Jhering stressed, a purported rule can have no realizeable content without form.[25] We can readily summarize the general nature of a "formless rule." It would be unprescriptive, highly incomplete, highly indefinite, grossly over or under-general, without internal structure, expressionally opaque, and devoid of

---

[25] Jhering, *supra* n. 7, at 473.

any encapsulation. Plainly, a fully "formless rule" could not exist. Yet formlessness does vary in degree. A "rule" could even be relatively formless in some of its features, yet duly formal in others. Also, it would not be rational to posit a high degree of all formal features as ideal. The policy purposes and other rational dictates of the form and content of rules are variable and falsify any such ideal.

The effects of choices of some formal features of rules, and the effects of a change in some formal features necessarily affect complementary policy or other content. For example, a change in a speed limit rule from high to low definiteness necessarily affects complementary policy content in the rule. However, the effects of changes in some formal features on complementary policy or other content are contingent and, therefore, may not occur at all. For example, a change in mode of expression from oral to written law may involve no change in complementary content. Likewise, a change in mode of encapsulation from common law form to statutory form may involve little or no change in content.

As indicated, some choices of form in a rule tend to beget good policy or other complementary content and can serve general values of the rule of law. Thus, definiteness and clarity of expression in a draft rule facilitate scrutiny and may lead to improvements in content. On the other hand, bad choices of form can translate into, or beget, bad content, and thus disserve policy and other ends. A highly incomplete rule entails considerable absence of content, and thus is both bad in form and in content. Moreover, just as due form in a rule makes it a source of reasons for determinate action and so a better means to realization of its policy or other content, flawed form can impair this very determinateness and efficacy. Choices of form can include formal flaws of inadequate prescriptiveness, of incompleteness, of indefiniteness, under- or over-generality, deficient internal structure, and inappropriate encapsulation or expression. Choices of content can be bad policy, as well.

A draft of a rule may have, on its face, many formal features that appear to be well-designed. This appearance can be no guarantee, however, of good content. For example, a prescriptive, complete, general, definite, structurally apt, clearly expressed and well-encapsulated rule may in its content even discriminate against a minority group.[26] Furthermore, despite generally well-designed form, the content of a rule may unduly sacrifice one policy to another, as with a duly definite speed limit set at a rate too low that, although purportedly in the interest of safe travel,

---

[26] A formal feature must be manifest in complementary content, and if the form is appropriate, then it may be thought that the complementary content must, as such, be good, too. This, however, does not follow, at least with respect to most features of form. For example, high completeness is usually appropriate, but it does not entail good content. High definiteness is often appropriate, but it does not entail good content, as with a fixed speed limit on certain highways that is set too high or too low. Relatively high generality is usually or often appropriate, but it does not entail good content. It may simply cover too much. Appropriate expressional form does not entail good content. Appropriate encapsulation does not entail good content.

Section Six: General Interactions and Other Inter-Relations

unduly sacrifices timeliness of traffic flow and driver free choice. Also, a rule generally well-designed in form may purport to embrace a desirable policy end, yet the prescribed action in the rule may not really be an effective means to that end, as with a formally clear and definite speed limit rule in which the limit is set too high, a major type of bad content.

In addition, whereas well-designed form can make a rule a more effective means to realization of fundamental political values implicated in its content such as freedom, democracy, legitimacy, justice, and rationality, deficient form can also subvert these very values. For example, a broad grant of discretion to drivers to "drive reasonably" is not a feature of form that always furthers freedom. It may actually invite some to drive aggressively, and this may constrain the freedom of other drivers. It may also invite highway police to intervene excessively.[27]

It is now possible to summarize four main types of possible combinations of form and of content in a rule. These are:

(1) Well-designed form in all respects combined with good policy or other content. An example would be a speed limit rule in due form set at a rate that best serves conflicting policies, general values of the rule of law, and fundamental political values, overall.

(2) Poorly designed form combined with potentially good policy or other content, so far as this is possible. Such form may be poorly designed in that it is insufficiently prescriptive, or incomplete, or indefinite, or unclear, or otherwise ill-suited as means to policy, general values of the rule of law, or fundamental political values. An example would be a criminal statute purporting to define a genuine offense yet in unduly vague terms, such as: "A person who causes harm to another shall be guilty of a felony." Such opaque or otherwise deficient form can also invite, and serve as a cloak for, official arbitrariness in particular cases.

(3) Well-designed form combined with bad policy or other content. Form may be generally well-designed as a means to whatever the policy or other content is. The pre-Civil War American Fugitive Slave Act is illustrative.[28] This Act fully satisfied nearly all standards of well-designed form, yet aptly illustrated that well-designed form does not guarantee good content.

(4) Poorly designed form combined with bad policy or other content. Alas, there have been many examples of this, including some vague criminal statutes that grossly impair freedom and facilitate official injustice.

In these combinations, different forms and formal features interact with variant content in rules. Plainly, the best type of combination is (1). The worst possible

---

[27] See case cited *supra* n. 9, at 1137–8.
[28] See Chapter 60, 9 Stat. 462 (1850).

combination is (4). The only real competitor to (4) for status as the worst is (3), and in (3) it is true that form can be designed as a highly effective means to evil, though it may still serve such general values of the rule of law as due notice and equal treatment – dubious values where content is evil! Yet (3) as compared to (4) does limit scope for official arbitrariness within the purview of the statute. Poorly designed form plus bad content – (4) above – is worse than (3) because poorly designed form, for example, vague discretionary power, may allow leeway to officials for evil or maladministration well beyond the bad policy or other content of (3).

A choice of ill-designed form in a rule, for example, insufficient definiteness, even when policy or other content is potentially good, as in (2) above, can render the rule ineffective, as when it is too indefinite to provide guidance. Form-oriented analysis reveals how credit would be due form if better designed. In a case of type (3), form is partly to blame, for it serves as a means to realization of bad content. In (3) the choice of bad content is plainly also to blame.

A choice of bad policy content may be either a choice of a bad policy end or a choice of a bad policy means. To illustrate the former, let us consider a hypothetical choice of a 45 mph rather than a 75 mph speed limit for open highways. The choice of 45 mph would unduly favor safety over timeliness of traffic flow and driver free choice. It would thus subvert these latter values. These effects of such a law would not be attributable to a choice of form – to the high degree of definiteness of the rule, for example. It is not this formal choice that subverts sound policy, driver free choice, and related values. Rather, it is the policy choice – a bad choice of a trade-off between safety on the one hand, and timeliness of travel and driver free choice on the other – a trade-off that is fixed at a rate of 45 mph for open highways rather than, say, 75 mph.[29]

The best rule is a combination of well-designed formal features with good policy (or other content), as in (1). Even the best rule, however, can itself be of limited efficacy, and in several major ways. First, how far features of form can approximate the best is limited by the content involved. For example, where the content consists of inherently vague subject matter, such as with prohibition of obscenity in publications, the extent to which formal definiteness and mode of expression can yield reasons for determinate action is inherently limited. This is another major interaction between form and content. Here content limits form.

Second, even granting close approximation to the ideal combination of due form and good complementary policy or other content in a rule, what such a rule alone can achieve is always subject to major limits. To be effective, the ideal rule, as

---

[29] It is also question-begging to say that a definite rate and so a formal feature, necessarily subverts freedom, as, for example, with a rule that forbids persons to drive above 75 mph in built-up areas. The very question at issue is whether people should have such "freedom" in the first place. We should not say that denial of the "right" to kill people or expose them to severe risk is an invasion of freedom; rather, it is license.

Section Seven: Further Responses to Objections 207

in (1), must be disseminated, learned, and applied by its addressees. This usually calls for further auxiliary rules and other implementive functional units. These may not sufficiently exist. If they do, form figures in them as well, and it may or may not be well-designed.

Third, even when we have well-designed form, along with good policy or other complementary content, as in (1), and even when we have well-formed auxiliary rules and other functional units required for implementation, the personnel involved, be they officials or private parties, may still fail to follow the rule. Here, too, we are up against inherent limits of law. Neither good form nor good policy (or other content) in rules, even when duly combined and deployed with other required functional units, can guarantee that addressees will act to implement the law.

By now what I have been saying about the nature of form in rules, and the credit due such form may seem obvious. Yet even if obvious, many have only an intuitive understanding of it. The systematic study of form can provide more articulate understanding, more detailed understanding, more holistic understanding (of relations of parts within a whole), and more appreciative understanding.

SECTION SEVEN: FURTHER RESPONSES TO OBJECTIONS

Again, a form-skeptic or law-is-policy reductionist might advance any or all of the following further objections. First, the most radical may say that, compared to content, form in rules is so thin and insubstantial that it can account for very little of what law achieves. This disregards the major organizational and other imprints and effects of form treated here and was also analogously responded to at the end of Chapter Four. Second, even if form in rules is not so thin and insubstantial, the critic might revert to the view that any choices of form must themselves be driven essentially by policy content, and therefore, choices of form must be of minor import. I provided a brief response to this at the end of Chapter Five. Third, the critic may urge that even if form is not thin and insubstantial, and even if it is not driven entirely by policy content, its reality in a rule cannot be separated from policy content and, therefore, cannot be studied except as an integral part of the whole rule. Hence, to try to identify and evaluate separately the role of form – give it "due credit" apart from the rest of the rule – is simply an artificial and fruitless exercise. I now turn to the second objection. Thereafter, I will take up the third.

Form in Rules Is Dictated Solely by Policy or Similar Ends – Further Response.
Critics may view form as dictated entirely by policy or other ends, and, therefore, conclude that form, as such, is only of minor and derivative significance. Although briefly considered in Section Two, we revisit this issue here because, in light of the intervening discussion, more can now be meaningfully added.

I will now develop the point that after some initial orienting, and even sound, tentative choices of policy early on, major scope can still remain for significant choices of form. Let us assume that the law-makers, as an initial matter, choose to regulate driver speed on open highways mainly through a general speed limit rule rather than by, say, regulating the manufacture of vehicles. As already shown, even this relatively means-determining choice of policy and this choice of pre-ceptual form do not themselves *dictate* a further choice of degree of definiteness to regulate through a bright-line rule rather than through a rule embodying a general standard of reasonableness. If they did so dictate, once a society chose a driver speed regulation policy, the society would not even perceive that there is a further choice between resort to a bright line or a discretionary standard. Yet such a further choice often looms large. This choice must depend at least on fur-ther factual inquiry into the likely efficacy of these two alternatives to serve policy, and into the general values of the rule of law and the fundamental political values stake. Thus, there could be much scope for further significant choices of form and complementary content here relatively independently of the initial choice of policy and preceptual form.

Far from a choice of a formal feature such as a degree of definiteness always itself being dependent upon, and so following automatically from, an initial choice of a policy or other end, such a formal choice may itself be indispensable to an ultimate imprint upon, or refinement of, such policy or other end that proves desirable in constructing the rule. That is, the dependency here may actually run the other way. Content specifying action as a means to policy ends may even be dependent on, and thus a derivative of, form, at least in major part. As I explained earlier, a more refined policy choice favoring a speed limit at some definite rate would be impossible without the imprint on content of the formal definiteness required to prioritize safety over time at this definite rate. Here, the choice of a high degree of definiteness – a formal feature – would be indispensable as a tool to prioritize as required by the policy choice, and so would be worthy of special independent credit for whatever law ultimately achieves. Here, some credit must be given to a choice of formal feature in forming the very content of the policy finally chosen – timeliness of flow and driver free choice over safety at the definite rate of 75 mph on open highways.

Thus, the common conception that law-makers initially make a wholly inde-pendent choice of policy end, and thereafter choose the policy means, including formal features, without any concurrent or subsequent refinement of policy or related end, is a misconception. Commonly, the finally refined ultimate choice of policy or other end simply cannot be made at all, except via some formal choice with its imprint on complementary content, for example, a choice of a bright line at a specified rate of speed. There can be no wholly "form-free" choice of the final refined policy or other end. That refined end is itself partly a formal choice. This is true *a fortiori* where form is not merely instrumental, but is also to a large extent

Section Seven: Further Responses to Objections

constitutive of the end – defines and organizes it – as with an electoral system securing democratic voting and majority rule.

In the lawmaking process, an initial choice of policy or other content in a proposed rule may itself be rationally influenced, even at the earliest stage, by the general awareness legislators have of various versions of formal features that may be available as means to implement the policy. A legislator will, at the beginning of a law-making episode, consider what form a proposed law should take, and the basic preceptual form of a rule will most often be the answer. Here, the legislator's awareness at the outset of the overall form and constituent features of rules (whether or not so called) could even affect the legislators' initial choice of policy end. When so, legislators do not make even their initial choice of policy or other end wholly independently of their knowledge of what features of the form of a rule may be available and apt. For example, legislators considering a regulatory policy as to highway speed will simultaneously think both about policy and relevant degrees of generality and definiteness of rule, whether or not they call these features formal. This truth further undermines those policy-imperialists who are disposed to hold that an initial orienting choice of policy, wholly devoid of any form, always automatically and solely determines all other further choices, including choices of form.

Attributing Credit to Form As Such Is Not Artificial. A further possible objection of form-skeptics and law-is-policy reductionists is that, even if features of the form of a rule are really not thin and insubstantial, and even if initial choices of policy do not dictate all concurrent or subsequent choices of formal features within the form of a rule, and even if such choices of formal features themselves affect ultimate policy or other content, it remains impossible, without undue artificiality, to disentangle form from policy or other content in a legal rule and give credit to form for realization of ends. We have earlier conceded that in a rule most choices of form cannot be divorced from all policy content. A choice of form must be manifest in complementary content of a rule, and frequently leaves a significant imprint or other effect on that content. The overall content of a rule is rationally formed in interaction with its formal features.

However, as already demonstrated, it is possible to analyze a rule and identify its formal features such as prescriptiveness, completeness, definiteness, generality, internal structure, manner of expression, and mode of encapsulation. It is also possible to disentangle these features from each other, and to separate them from the policy or other content of the rule. Some such disentanglement and separation of form and content is necessary if we are to give form any credit for values realized. In our highway speed illustration, the ultimate achievement would be the creation of an effective policy of regulating safety and timeliness of traffic flow, all largely in accord with general values of the rule of law, and in a fashion that also duly serves any fundamental political values implicated such as driver free choice. Not all credit for such an achievement should go to choices of policy or other similar content. Form is not anemic.

Even theorists who wish to downplay form must themselves single form out, at least implicitly, from policy or other content. In seeking to give due credit to form, I, too, must single it out (albeit more whole-heartedly). At the same time, I concede that the credit to be given duly designed form in such a rule must always be credit that presupposes policy or other content. Also, it is not possible to apportion credit to form in a precise quantitative fashion. Yet justified claims of credit due to form can often be made. Indeed, without relevant overall forms and formal features, no ends could be reliably and consistently served at all through law. Also, it is possible to make comparative judgments that certain formal features would serve the ends in view better than alternative formal features. Although many claims to credit on behalf of form are empirical, many are not controversial.

A major source of skepticism about the significance of legal form may be rooted in spurious conclusions drawn from a "form v. content" contrast as applied to rules, or rooted in spurious conclusions drawn from the wider "form v. substance" contrast as applied not only to rules, but to other functional legal units, as well. Here, it is enough to respond to two conjectures. First, some skeptics may conclude that because content is distinct from form, and because, in their view, content is robust and end-serving, it follows that form must somehow be anemic and, thus, itself devoid of any significant end-serving contribution. That is, because form is not content, form must be relatively devoid of significance. Yet, as argued here, nothing inherent in form requires that it be anemic and so without capacity to share in serving policy or other ends of the rule. On the contrary, a formal feature can leave major imprints on content (and on other formal features), and as demonstrated in this and prior chapters, the overall form of rules and the constituent features of that form can be robustly organized instrumentally, and constitutively, to contribute to the realization of ends. Form, as well as the content of rules, is end-serving. Moreover, without the imprints and other effects of formal features on content, the contributions of content would be much diminished.

Second, at least the radical form-skeptic may believe that it is the true province of content alone to incorporate or serve ends, with form merely an insignificant or even dispensable appendage, that is, "merely formal." However, form and content are interdependent, with form indispensable as well. A rule cannot be formless. Moreover, imprints and other effects of form are to be found all over the content of any rule. As Jhering stressed, without the form of a legal rule, the content of a legal rule could not even exist.[30] Formal features as affecting each other, and as manifest in the content of a well-designed rule themselves merit credit as end-serving.

---

[30] R. Jhering, *supra* n. 7, at 473.

7 ~ FORMS OF NONPRECEPTUAL LAW – CONTRACTS AND RELATED PROPERTY INTERESTS

Legal facilitation of contract and property is "the most important hallmark of modern society."
— A. Giddens[1]

SECTION ONE: INTRODUCTION

The freedom to enter into and realize the benefits of legally valid contracts is a fundamental freedom recognized in all developed Western societies. Without this freedom, countless choices in the planning and conduct of economic and other activities of life would simply not be open. Individuals would be far less autonomous. Scope for individual self-realization would be vastly diminished. Goods, services, real property, and much else could not be bought and sold in the ordinary ways. Free market economic activity could not flourish.

Contracts and property interests are major functional units in Western legal systems. They are species of nonpreceptual law, and take their own overall forms. As we will see, these forms are very different from the forms of rules and other preceptual law. The forms of contracts and property interests also differ greatly from the institutional forms of legislatures and of courts. Here, then, we focus not on contracts and property as branches of substantive law, but rather on the distinctive overall forms of these two important types of nonpreceptual law. Because many see such "law" as consisting only of substantive content without form, a major corrective is required here, too.

The legal systems of developed Western societies fully recognize discrete contracts. Regulative and reinforcive rules allow individuals and entities to enter into contracts, prohibit interferences with freedom to contract, specify requirements of valid contracts, protect the performance of contracts, provide for enforcement of contracts, and grant judicial remedies for breach. As we have seen, such rules

---

[1] A. Giddens, *The Constitution of Society*, 269 (Polity Press, Cambridge, 1984).

take the overall form of rules. But the roles of form hardly end there. Form also defines and organizes contracts and leaves its own imprints and other effects on particular contracts.

Not just any agreements can be legally valid contracts. Overall forms – purposive systematic arrangements – define and organize what counts as valid contracts in a Western system. There are various types of contracts, but the most common is the valid bilateral contract between two parties. Such a contract may involve a present exchange, a future exchange, or a mix of these. Here we concentrate on negotiated bilateral contracts for future exchanges. The primary features of the overall form of such a valid bilateral contract require promissory undertakings and the exchange of such undertakings with mutual assent. These requirements and constraints of the bilateral contract form leave their own imprints and other effects on the contents of particular contracts. Freedom to contract could not exist without such requirements and constraints. Together, they free the parties to create contractual obligations, as we will see.[2]

In developed Western societies, then, the major species of law are not confined to preceptual phenomena such as rules, principles, maxims, or the like. Rather, law also takes nonpreceptual forms, including the overall form of bilateral contracts as made by private individuals, and by other entities, corporate and noncorporate. When two private parties validly exercise freedom to contract, their contract becomes binding law for those parties. As will be explained, this privately made law often binds third parties, too, especially when property interests are affected. Public entities make contracts as well, but it will be enough to concentrate on contracts made by private parties, and on some of the property interests that may be affected.

Law consisting of the totality of the terms of all of the valid bilateral contracts of private parties in a Western society at any given point in time vastly exceeds the totality of law in the form of rules and other law made by legislatures, courts, governmental agencies, and other officials. The law that two private parties make and embody in a discrete contract consists of a whole structure of rights and duties. The entry of such parties into, and their performance of, valid contracts in due form serves the purposes of freedom of choice, individual autonomy, promise-keeping integrity, economic exchange, and efficiency. A market economy could not exist without freedom to contract. Some of the foregoing purposes are realized primarily in the course of the processes whereby parties enter contracts, whereas others are realized primarily through the outcomes of these processes. Given the

---

[2] Contract then, is not "content unconstrained." Again, it is appropriate to cite Göethe: "In der Beschränkung zeigt sich erst der Meister/Und das Gesetz nur kann uns Freiheit geben." (None proves a master but by limitation/And only law can give us liberty.) "Nature and Art," in J. Göethe, *Selected Poems*, 164–5 (C. Middleton ed., M. Hamburger et al. trans., Suhrkamp/Insel Publishers, Boston, Inc., Boston, 1983).

Section One: Introduction

founding purpose of allowing parties to create valid bilateral contracts, reason dictates legal recognition of their overall form. Without this, valid contracts could not be formed. The credit due to form here is great.

Study of the overall form and constituent formal features of a bilateral contract is also a major avenue for advancing understanding of it as a discrete type of functional legal unit. As we will see, form plays major roles in facilitating the creation of a valid contract, in the specification of contract terms and the rights and duties arising therefrom, in the interpretation and performance of terms, and in the provision of judicial remedies for contract enforcement.[3]

The overall form of the valid bilateral contract is a major form in the typology of forms of discrete functional units treated in this book. Such form differs fundamentally from the preceptual form of a legal rule. Although both a statutory rule and a bilateral contract are prescriptive, they differ in what is prescribed. The typical statutory rule does not prescribe an exchange of objects of value, whereas this is the primary function of the bilateral contract.

Moreover, statutory or other rules differ from most bilateral contracts in various other formal features. One of these is generality. Most rules apply to classes of persons in recurrent circumstances over time, whereas discrete bilateral contracts apply only to two contracting parties in limited circumstances (with some major exceptions, to be considered later). Bilateral contracts also typically include more highly definite terms than most statutory rules – another major imprint of form. Also, parties to many contracts choose not to specify terms beyond the essentials of the exchange.[4] Contracts and statutory rules differ in internal structure, as well. A bilateral contract provides for reciprocal undertakings of the parties, whereas there is no comparable internal "exchange" structure in a typical statutory rule.[5] The formal encapsulatory features of a contract and of a statutory rule also differ. The contents of all statutes are encapsulated in legislative enactments in fixed verbal sequence in print. Although many contracts are written or printed, these terms are not in fixed verbal sequence in the fashion of a statute, and many contracts are oral. Although some contracts read somewhat like statutes, the formal expressional feature of most contracts also differs in vocabulary and style from that of most statutes. In sum, the formal features of a bilateral contract differ in major ways from the formal features of statutory rules.

---

[3] Justice Oliver Wendell Holmes, Jr. once remarked that "the whole doctrine of contract is formal." G. Gilmore, *The Death of Contract*, 21 (Ohio State University Press, Columbus, 1974). At least on one interpretation of Holmes, his is not my position here. My position is that the functional unit of a bilateral contract takes an overall form with constituent formal features as manifest in, and thus combined with, complementary material or other content of particular contracts.

[4] Gap fillers from general contract law may often be invoked to fill spaces that the parties leave open and thus save the validity of the contract. See, e.g., J. White and R. Summers, *Uniform Commercial Code*, vol. 1, at 3–5 through 3–10 (4th ed., West Group, St. Paul, 1995).

[5] This is not to say that nothing analogous to trading ever occurs in the legislative process itself!

Contractual exchanges and statutory rules also differ greatly in material and other components of content. The essential content of the typical bilateral contractual exchange consists of at least two objects of value reflecting preferences of two private parties, whereas the essential content of a statute sets forth the position of a legislative majority, usually by way of a general rule as to policy or other public subject matter.[6] Also, the duration of most bilateral contracts is far more limited. It ends when the parties perform their reciprocal promises. The duration of a statutory rule, however, is not usually specified at all and generally continues to be valid law until it is amended or falls into desuetude. Of course, bilateral contracts may include some rules, as in those contracts that govern relations between the parties well into the future.[7] For example, a contract of employment may incorporate rules as to safety in the work place.

Institutionalized legislative processes differ in major ways from private contracting processes. Yet contracting parties have often been characterized as "private legislators," and there are some general analogies here. On analogy to the formal compositional feature of a legislature that specifies qualifications of legislators, terms of office, and mode of selection, private contracting parties must at least be of the age of majority and of sound mind. On analogy to the formal jurisdictional feature of a legislature, contracting parties must have legal power to enter into contractual relations of the type at hand. For example, they must own or lawfully control any subject matter to be exchanged or be agents of those who do. On analogy to the formal feature of procedure in a legislature for proposing, evaluating, voting on, and thus adopting a statute, private parties who exercise freedom of contract must do so in accord with certain criteria for the validity of contracts, some of which are procedural in a broad sense. For example, to be valid and enforceable, promises must not be deceptively induced, and must be free of unconscionable bargaining.

As we saw in Chapter Four, the instrumental capacity of a legislature to make valid statutory rules is dependent on various features of overall legislative form. We also saw that a form-skeptic may deny or refuse to acknowledge this, and deny or fail to notice how the creation of a statutory rule necessarily requires important choices of formal features – of prescriptiveness, completeness, generality, definiteness, internal structure, mode of expression and encapsulation. We also saw that the form-skeptic tends to conclude, erroneously, that such formal features lose their identity in the content of statutory rules.

Here, the form-skeptic may make similar claims, and fail to notice or downplay the formal choices involved in creating a valid contract. The form-skeptic might

---

[6] I will later have occasion to soften one or two of these contrasts.

[7] Of course, legal rules bear on particular contracts in many ways beyond the scope of this chapter. For the American system, see, e.g., E. A. Farnsworth, *Farnsworth on Contracts* (3rd ed., Aspen Publishers, New York, 1999).

Section Two: Choices of Form and of Complementary Material

also hold that any initial orienting choices of contractual content that the parties tentatively make at the outset of negotiations must necessarily dictate any and all concurrent or subsequent choices of formal features. According to this view, the final form of the contract merely follows directly from the initial orienting choices of subject matter content. Thus, any choices of form, implicit and explicit, must be insignificant here, too. The form-skeptic who so concludes fails to give due credit to the effects of contractual form in the process, and fails to give due credit to the imprints of form on the subject matter of the exchange, thereby over-crediting the initial orienting choices of contractual content in determining the final form and content of a contract.[8]

Here, we treat the overall form and complementary content of valid negotiated bilateral contracts from an external point of view as instruments of exchange and economic efficiency – external purposes. We also study this form and content from an internal point of view, too. As Jhering would have said, form is the "innermost essence" of contracts, and without studying form, we could not understand the makeup, unity, instrumental capacity, determinateness, and distinct identity of contracts. Indeed, without such study, contracts could not be adequately understood as instruments of free choice, autonomy, promise keeping integrity, economic exchange, and efficiency, all of which are purposes realizeable either through the very processes of creating and performing contracts, or through the outcomes of these processes, or both.

Contracts, too, are not independent and self-sufficient functional units that operate entirely apart from other legal units. Contracts are integrated and coordinated within the overall form of one of a legal system's major operational techniques, namely, the "private-ordering" technique, which is characterized in detail in Chapter Ten as one of several major devices organizing functional legal units into an operational system. Besides the general legal framework of rules for creating valid bilateral contracts, and besides particular such contracts, methodologies of drafting and of interpretation, various legal rules, remedies for breach, courts, and other functional units are integrated within the private-ordering technique as well.

SECTION TWO: CHOICES OF FORM AND OF COMPLEMENTARY MATERIAL OR OTHER COMPONENTS OF CONTENT IN A CONTRACT

Assume that a party wishes to buy a car. This person will formulate at least tentative preferences with respect to the nature of the car to be bought, and with respect to how much to pay for such a car and on what terms. The car dealer involved will also have, or come to formulate, preferences with respect to how much money to ask

---

[8] See *infra* pp. 217–218.

for the car, on what terms, and other matters. In ultimately reaching an agreement, the parties will make final choices of contract content. Reduced to simplest terms, the buyer will choose to give up money for the car, and the dealer choose to give up the car for money. These choices of subject matter – these preferences expressed in terms of the subject matter of the exchange – will make up the primary non-formal content of the resulting contract. Such content also includes the named parties in the contract who are to perform their duties under it.

In the course of negotiations, the parties, implicitly or explicitly, make choices of particular features of contractual form that play significant roles in the overall process. These choices ultimately affect the content of the resulting contract. The contract will not only have content – the objects of the exchange named in the contract and the named parties thereto – but also the overall form required for creation of a valid bilateral contract. Form purposively and systematically arranges this functional unit. The fundamental purposes of this form include the realization of free private choice, individual autonomy, promise-keeping integrity, and free market exchange.

In developed Western societies, many millions of persons utilize the bilateral contract form regularly in daily life, and perhaps even only half consciously in regard to some affairs. Even in our car purchase illustration, a large transaction for most people, the parties might be puzzled if someone were to tap them on the shoulder and tell them that they are making use of an overall contractual form – that of the bilateral contract. They might be further puzzled if told they are also making choices that are in part choices of formal features. Yet, in all such deals, the parties make such choices, though very likely without classifying these choices as, in part, choices of form. Rather, they are much more likely to think their choices consist solely of "choices of content," in the sense of subject matter preferences. In our illustration, these preferences would extend to type of car, color, price, etc.

We are, of course, assuming that the parties are not adopting the "gift form." In the standard form of a gift, one party transfers an asset to another without bargaining for anything in return.[9] The car dealer's choice to utilize the bilateral contractual form rather than the gift form is itself a choice of form, and may be analogized to the legislature's choice of the form of a rule over other preceptual forms such as a principle.[10]

In a contract negotiation, as in a legislative process, the relevant choice of overall form – in the one case typically that of a bilateral contract, and in the other, typically that of a statutory rule – is made, however implicitly, alongside initial, orienting, and tentative choices of complementary content. Moreover, just as the initial choice of legislators to use the overall form of a statutory rule

---

[9] Various formal requirements may have to be met to make the gift valid. See, e.g., 62 NY Jur. 2nd *Gifts* §5.

[10] The choice of a bilateral contractual form over the gift form is a choice of form even though there are also complementary differences of subject matter content, too.

Section Two: Choices of Form and of Complementary Material 217

requires still further choices within that form such as degrees of generality and definiteness, so too, the choice of two contracting parties to utilize the overall form of a bilateral contract requires still further choices of formal features within this contractual form. Also, just as features of the overall form of a rule, such as generality and definiteness, manifest themselves in, and thus leave imprints and other effects upon complementary policy or other content, features of overall contractual form manifest themselves in, and thus leave imprints and other effects upon complementary content.

If the prospective contracting parties merely happen to come to have subject matter preferences that "match," this state of affairs cannot alone constitute a legally valid contract.[11] In my example, the prospective buyer might actually prefer to have the car rather than the purchase money, and the prospective seller at the very same time might actually prefer to have the prospective buyer's money rather than the car. Yet, to give rise to bilateral contractual obligation, the parties must explicitly or implicitly communicate their subject matter preferences in the overall form of a valid bilateral contract as required by the general law of contract. To illustrate, I here draw mainly on rules of Anglo-American law, although much other Western law is similar in most major respects.[12]

The choices of particular features of overall bilateral contract form – of the purposive systematic arrangement of such a contract as made by contracting parties – will be manifest in, and thus leave imprints or other effects upon, complementary contract content. In my highly simplified example as set forth above, these features of form may seem to be hidden. Yet in this example, the parties make choices of form with complementary material or other components, as follows:

(1) The prospective buyer of the car chooses to promise and does promise to the seller, expressly or impliedly, to pay the price on or by a given date. That is, the buyer expresses a preference to the seller for having the car rather than the money, and the buyer expresses this preference in the form of a promise to the seller to pay the money for the car (using the language of promise or its equivalent): B prefers C over M and promises to S accordingly – *a formal promissory feature prescribing the buyer's undertaking.*

(2) The prospective seller of the car chooses to promise and does promise to the buyer, expressly or impliedly, to transfer title to the car on or by a given date. That is, the seller expresses a preference to the buyer for having the money rather than the car, and the seller expresses this preference in the form of a promise to the buyer to transfer the car for the money

---

[11] However, an invalid contract may still give rise to some legal obligations, such as the duty of restitution under the law of unjust enrichment.

[12] See, e.g., B. Markesinis et al., *The German Law of Obligations*, vol. 1, Chapter 2, §§1, 2, 3 (Clarendon Press, Oxford, 1997); B. Nicholas, *The French Law of Contract*, Chapter 3 (2nd ed., Clarendon Press, Oxford, 1992).

(using the language of promise or its equivalent). S prefers M over C and promises to B accordingly – *a formal promissory feature prescribing the seller's undertaking.*

(3) Each party in (1) and (2) is *induced* to make his or her respective promise to the other in exchange for the promise of the other, so that there is *mutual assent* to an exchange in the *structural* form of an agreed bargain: B and S make their promises of M and C, each in exchange for the other – in reciprocal promissory form, thereby manifesting *the formal feature of mutual assent to a bargained for exchange of promissory undertakings.* (This might also be characterized as "internal structure." It is independent of (1) and (2) because the promise by one and the promise by the other do not necessarily induce each other, as in (3)).

(4) The parties choose to formulate their agreed promissory exchange with sufficient specificity and fixity, at least with respect to the essentials of the bargain – *the formal feature of due definiteness.*

(5) The parties choose to formulate the terms of their agreement with sufficient completeness – *the formal feature of sufficient completeness.*

(6) The parties choose the formal encapsulatory feature of a writing, or of a printed document, or of a merely oral form if permissible; choice of the oral form may not be permissible, for the general law may require that a contract of the type involved be evidenced by some written or printed form – *the encapsulatory formal feature.*[13]

(7) The parties choose to express their overall agreement with sufficient explicitness and overall clarity, in the vocabulary they prefer, in the syntax and grammar they prefer, with the conciseness, etc. they prefer – *the expressionally formal feature.*

In general, the foregoing seven features are necessary constituents (except as qualified above) of the overall form of a bilateral contract in Anglo-American systems, and apply to a considerable extent in other Western societies, too. These features, as refined here, together satisfy the general definition of overall form as the purposive systematic arrangement of the functional unit of a bilateral contract. Several of the foregoing constituent features are also specifically recognized in English as formal.[14]

Each of the foregoing seven features is a *distinct* constituent of the overall form of a bilateral contract. Although each feature must be manifest in complementary contractual content, each feature is not reducible to this content and remains

---

[13] What I have elsewhere called the fixed verbal feature of form in regard to statutes is not generally present here. See *supra* Chapter Five, Section Eight.

[14] *The Oxford English Dictionary*, vol. 6, at "form," I.5.a. (2nd ed., J. Simpson and E. Weiner eds., Clarendon Press, Oxford, 1989), hereinafter *OED*. This is true, for example, of definiteness and of structure. See *ibid.*, vols. 4 and 16 at "definiteness" and "structure."

Section Two: Choices of Form and of Complementary Material 219

separately identifiable. Without at least some minimal version of each feature, the form could not sufficiently arrange the functional unit purposively and systematically.

Moreover, each feature is formal by way of contrast with the particular subject matter in which the feature is manifest. The named objects of the exchange and the named parties to the exchange are material or other components of content. (Some objects of the exchange may themselves take a "component form," as with the money, i.e., legal tender, in our illustration.) Each formal feature can also be characterized affirmatively as a positive feature of the overall form of a bilateral contract, rather than merely as something that contrasts with material or other components of content.

Choices of formal features define and organize a particular contract, and thus leave formal imprints or other effects on its complementary content. The subject matter preferences of the parties and their rights and duties are set forth in this contractual form and content. The formal features and complementary content thus comprise the makeup and unity of this particular functional unit, account for its instrumental capacity, and give it its distinct identity.

In Anglo-American systems, and to a large extent in other Western systems, the legal criteria of bilateral contractual validity generally track the foregoing formal features. The first four are generally required for a contract to be valid and thus legally enforceable. As for the fifth, if any incompleteness is significant, and the general law provides no "gap-filler," the agreement may not be a valid contract. As for the sixth, validity may require a writing or other formal record. What may be called *prima facie* validity usually arises from satisfaction of the foregoing formal requirements. Yet any such requirement might be negated, and thus not satisfied. For example, the formal requirement of mutual assent might not be satisfied because negated by specific proof of duress, fraud, mutual mistake, procedural unconscionability, or the like.

Even if all formal requirements are satisfied, the *prima facie* valid contract that results could still not be *ultimately* valid. That is, in our illustration, the *prima facie* obligations to pay money and to deliver the car that arise from satisfying the foregoing formal requirements are still "defeasible." That is, they could still be subject to any one of various possible content-oriented defenses such as illegality of content, conflict of content with public policy, substantive unconscionability of content, and the like.[15] When any such content-oriented defense is available, the contract, although we may say it is *prima facie* valid, is not ultimately valid.

The distinction is straightforward as between the features of bilateral contractual form on the one hand, and, on the other, the material or other components of

---

[15] See generally H. L. A. Hart, "The Ascription of Responsibility and Rights," 49 *Proceedings of the Aristotelian Society* 171, 175 (1948–9).

the content of the contract. The latter consist of the expressed and definite preferences in the contract for the car and for the money, and the named parties to this contract who are to perform it. The mere fact that the objects of the exchange and the parties thereto are specified and described in the features of the overall form of the contract of the contract does not signify that these objects and parties, too, are formal. If that were so, the distinction between the formal and the material or other components in a contract would vanish because features of the overall form must necessarily refer, expressly or implicitly, to such components. The features of a promissory undertaking by each party, (1) and (2) presented earlier, are features of the overall form of a bilateral contract. These formal features require complementary components of content to create a legally binding contract. In this illustration, this content consists essentially of the promises with respect to the car and the money – C and M in (1) and (2), and the named parties who are to perform.

These very components of content reappear in the exchange mutually assented to in (3). Yet, this mutual assent to the bargained for exchange of subject matter in (3) is not itself the subject matter content, but is a further feature of the overall form of a bilateral contract, as manifest in relation to this complementary content. This feature requires content in the form of reciprocal inducement: the car *for* the money *and* the money *for* the car. Bilateral contract form, as such, neither requires nor presupposes any *particular* subject matter content, and can accommodate highly varied content. The overall form of a prima-facie valid bilateral contract, then, generally consists of a mutually agreed exchange of promises that is duly definite, complete, encapsulated, and expressed.

The discrete functional unit of a bilateral contract, then, takes the overall form of such a contract, with features of form manifest in complementary content, and with form presupposing content and content presupposing form, as Jhering emphasized.[16] In our illustration, the material and other components of the contract include content in which one party promises a particular car in return for the other party's promise of a sum of money, and the other promises a sum of money in return for the promise of a particular car. These promises, and these inducements require, of course, not only the car and the money, but also the promising parties. The objects of the exchange and the parties thereto are material or other components, both as specified in the terms of the agreement, and as concretely identified in the actual exchange.

A merely rule-oriented analysis here is not sufficient. Although the general requirements of a valid bilateral contract in a given system are stated in reinforcive legal rules, a grasp of the contents of these rules of contract law cannot alone

---

[16] R. Jhering, *Geist des Römischen Rechts: auf den verschiedenen Stufen seiner Entwicklung*, vol. 2, at 473 (Scientia Verlag, Aalen, 1993).

Section Three: Due Credit to Form

enable us to understand the form and content of bilateral contracts. The contents of reinforcive rules could not even be formulated in the first place without prior understanding of the features of bilateral contract form involved and of the purposes that shape this form. Moreover, the contents of reinforcive rules themselves merely prescribe features without explicitly differentiating between the form and the material or other components in a contractual arrangement. Thus, what is prescribed requires form-oriented analysis to be fully understood. For example, the nature of the formal feature of a promissory undertaking is not self-elucidating. A frontal account differentiating the form of the promissory undertaking from its complementary content is necessary. A mere rule stating that some action is required does not itself so differentiate.

Furthermore, an account of the overall form of a bilateral contract and its constituent features requires a holistic form-oriented analysis. In such an analysis, relations between parts, and between parts and the whole, are among the central objects of consideration. Such relations are structural and therefore formal. A form-oriented analysis addresses the bilateral contract as a whole, and focuses on how its formal features inter-relate, fit together, and thus form a unity. For example, in a particular bilateral contract, the mere existence of two promises is not enough. If one person promised to transfer money to a second person, and that person promised to transfer a car to the first person, a contract would not necessarily be formed. The promises must be reciprocally inducing. That is, there must be a bargained relation (in Anglo-American and certain other systems).

In addition, the contents of reinforcive rules governing the validity of contracts are themselves typically silent with respect to their purposive rationales. Yet a grasp of the rationales for these rules is required to understand fully how form is a means to ends, and is thus entitled to credit. These rationales, as we will see, are largely cautionary and evidentiary. Form-oriented analysis addresses these purposive rationales and the credit due to form, whereas an analysis merely of the contents of the usual reinforcive rules does not even reveal these rationales.

In the absence of specific efforts explicitly to give contractual form its due, explained heretofore and in what follows, form might not get its due. Rather, it might get lost in the details and in the material and other components of contracts. It might even be swallowed up by contractual content. The types of credit due to form themselves call for special articulation without which the credit involved might not be seen at all.

SECTION THREE: DUE CREDIT TO FORM

What the parties are to exchange, the possible terms of the exchange, and any alternative opportunities, are not the only factors influencing the ultimate subject matter preferences of the parties as expressed in the final terms of the bilateral contract to which they finally agree. In negotiated agreements, the overall form of a bilateral contract itself, and the criteria of contractual validity tracking this form, also play important roles, directly and indirectly, in determining final contract content. Pursuant to, and within this overall form and these formal criteria, the parties make various choices of contractual form and complementary content. In the end, form leaves significant imprints and other effects on content.

When the parties do form a bilateral contract, and then duly perform it, this serves the purposes of freedom of choice, private autonomy, and the integrity of promise keeping, all of which may be classified as internal ends in the sense that they are realized partly in the course of the very processes of creating and performing a contract. Without the availability of the overall form of such a bilateral contract, parties would realize far less free choice and private autonomy, and there would be many fewer occasions to vindicate the integrity of promise-keeping as well.

Contracting within well-designed bilateral contract form also tends to beget good content, which may be defined as content in line with preferences of the parties. When possible terms are clearly expressed, this enables parties to bargain, facilitates their efforts to realize preferences, and thus may ultimately increase satisfaction through choices made. This also serves external purposes of economic exchange and efficient allocation of resources as determined by prices in a free market. The imprints and other effects of form on particular contracts are therefore considerable.

The promissory undertakings of the parties, and their reciprocally induced mutual assent to the exchange, are the central formal features of the purposive systematic arrangement of the discrete functional unit of a bilateral contract. This stable purposive core of overall form contrasts with the highly varied material and other components of particular exchanges. Without this form, there could be no bilateral contracts valid in law. In most developed Western societies, nearly all of the foregoing features of the overall form of a bilateral contract translate into criteria for determining the legal validity of particular contracts, thus providing a great social facility. Here, much credit must go to form.

Meaningful freedom of contract requires more than mere grants of rights to parties to enter contracts and general prohibitions against interference with exercise of such rights. Equally fundamental, freedom of contract requires legal criteria for determining when efforts of parties to exercise freedom of contract result in contracts at least *prima facie* valid in law. Such criteria are largely formal in developed Western systems.

Just as a legislature cannot create a valid statute without complying with some established formal criteria of valid enactment, neither can contracting parties create a valid contract without satisfying formal criteria for the making of a valid bilateral contract. Contract law distinguishes between mere preliminary

Section Three: Due Credit to Form

negotiations and final entry into a valid contract. Negotiating parties usually understand the difference between a mere declaration of intent as to future action or a mere recital of expectation and entry into a genuine *promissory undertaking*. Typically, final entry occurs when two parties duly make reciprocal promissory undertakings to each other, as in our illustration involving the sale and purchase of a car. The parties can usually know when they have crossed the line from mere preliminary negotiations and entered into a valid contractual relation. This is because they generally understand the relevant validating contractual form. (This is not to say they must consciously classify the validating features as *formal*.) At the least, both parties understand what it is to give the other reciprocal promissory assurance, and thus express mutual assent.

In Jhering's terms, it is form here that marks a vital line, and thereby *channels* efforts of parties either to contract or not to contract.[17] Form thus shapes this process. In consequence, the parties are likely to feel more free to enter contracts, and to feel more secure in doing so. A party is much less likely to feel free to contract when that party cannot discern clearly what would constitute the exercise of freedom to enter a contract. Also, one feels more free to enter negotiations knowing that one is highly unlikely to bind oneself inadvertently.

Accordingly, the formal criteria for entry into *prima facie* valid contracts are readily understandable and relatively certain in application. Prospective contracting parties can themselves usually apply such criteria effectively on their own, and can usually be highly certain that they have, or have not, entered into an arrangement satisfying these criteria. Contract formation dependent primarily on satisfying formal criteria is also relatively nondisputatious and this saves costs. All this makes it more likely parties will freely enter into contract negotiations.

Merely formal criteria for the formation of *prima facie* valid contracts allows for vast freedom of contract, in contrast with possible nonformal criteria that might, for example, permit persons only to enter contracts having specified content, or allow only persons who are members of certain groups to enter contracts. For this reason, too, credit should go to form.

Form must receive still further credit. In the negotiation of bilateral contracts of any significance, the prospect of promising a performance to someone can be sobering, and calls for exercise of careful judgment. A promise takes the form of a present undertaking by the promisor to render performance to another in the future. The promisor must be aware that this requires a commitment to give up time or other resources necessary for performance and in so doing also to pass up other possible opportunities now or in the future. Each party knows, too, that one cannot without consequences, make a half-considered deal and then back out on discovering the deal to be inconsistent with one's preferences. Each party

---

[17] *Id.*, at 494–5.

usually also knows that once a proposed exchange of promises is assented to, one party may justifiably rely on the promise of the other, perhaps immediately as by incurring expenditures. Each, therefore, usually realizes that a promise is not to be made lightly. In a matter of any significance, the sobering effect of thinking over whether to commit oneself and one's resources tends, as Fuller stressed, to lead a party to think more carefully about one's preferences, about the extent of one's own resources, and about possible alternative opportunities.[18] In the end, a prospective promisor may be led to negotiate for and, thus, ultimately agree to contractual content that is aligned more closely with the promisor's preferences and resources, or, indeed, may even be led not to enter a particular proposed contract at all, given that an alternative appears preferable.[19] Again, form is a factor that can leave deep and indelible imprints and other effects on contract terms as finally negotiated.

In the foregoing ways, in all but routine matters, the very form of bilateral promise-making activity tends, along with complementary content, to influence many promisors to be more mindful of what is at stake, to be more cautious in making commitments, and in the end to make contracts better for them than they might otherwise. Of course, these more immediate purposes of form can be no guarantee against improvident judgment and can be no guarantee of good contract content. Yet it is plain that some credit is due overall contractual form here for the nature, number and quality of particular contracts that negotiating parties enter into. It is not merely that without some such contracting framework with its formal criteria of validity, the parties could not even know whether and when they have made a valid contract. It is also that negotiating within this framework tends, as Jhering and Fuller emphasized, to foster considered deliberation and a cautionary frame of mind. This serves the purposes of free and rational choice, autonomy, and the integrity of promise keeping – all ends to be realized internally in the course of contract formation and performance, as well as through outcomes of these activities. At the same time, overall bilateral contract form also serves external purposes of facilitating free market exchange and economic efficiency.

The final choice of a party to promise and thus commit resources is a choice to enter into a contract the overall form of which includes a reciprocal exchange of promises. The prospect of such a choice fosters deliberation in all but routine matters. The making of such a choice tends to focus the mind of the prospective promisor on the *relation* between what that promisor is to give up and is to get in return. This, more than simple promise-making as such, can be an especially sobering exercise for the parties, and may induce a party to bargain further for content better aligned with one's preferences and with resources. As the English

---

[18] *Id.*, at 495–8. See also L. Fuller, "Consideration and Form," 41 *Colum. L. Rev.* 799, 800–4 (1941).

[19] This is not to say contract negotiations are wholly rational, even judged subjectively! See L. Fuller, *Anatomy of the Law*, 104 (Greenwood Press, Westport, 1976).

Section Three: Due Credit to Form

theorist John Austin once put it, each such party is "contracting for his own pecuniary advantage; contemplating a quid pro quo; and therefore being in that circumspective frame of mind which a man who is only thinking of such advantage naturally assumes."[20] The foregoing claims crediting form for its influence on the final contents of contracts are largely empirical, yet not really controversial. Although contracting parties will be influenced differently here by the overall form of the valid bilateral contract, many will be influenced as hypothesized by Austin.

As suggested earlier, the position of contracting parties may be considered that of "private legislators," with contractual form affecting them similarly to how institutional form affects legislative processes. As we saw, procedural and structural features of overall legislative form, and features of the overall form of a proposed statutory rule such as definiteness and mode of expression, facilitate the efforts of legislators rationally to scrutinize and debate the form and the policy or other content of a proposed statutory rule. Similarly, the overall form of a proposed bilateral exchange, with its various constituent features, tends to concentrate the minds of prospective contracting parties on the contents of the proposed exchange, on what each is giving and getting, and on relative values involved for each party.

A further type of formal choice also tends to beget good subject matter content in the course of contract negotiations. As already indicated, choices of sufficient definiteness – of sufficient specificity and fixity of complementary content – are generally required for the legal validity of a contract. The parties to a proposed contract may even choose to make its terms more definite than required for contractual validity. Definiteness in proposed contract content, like definiteness in a rule under legislative consideration, facilitates rational scrutiny by the parties to the proposed exchange at the negotiating stage. This may lead to refinements of the terms and as a result, they may be more acceptable to both parties. As with the formal feature of definiteness in statutory rules, contractual definiteness contributes reasons for parties to act determinately under the contract and thus perform their contractual duties faithfully. Definiteness of terms also facilitates ascertainment of any breach, and enables the parties to know more fully what judicial remedies may be available in event of breach. Those remedies commonly require determination of the prospective value to the aggrieved party that contract performance would have had in order to award damages for loss of expected gain. If the promised performance is too indefinite, this lost expectation cannot be effectively measured. The formal feature of definiteness, then, leaves its imprints on content, and here, too, merits major credit for contractual efficacy. Again, to the extent these claims are empirical, they are hardly controversial.

---

[20] J. Austin, *Lectures on Jurisprudence*, vol. 2, at 907 (5th ed., R. Campbell ed., John Murray, London, 1911).

Related claims can be made for the effects of the requirement of contract completeness, a formal feature with complementary content. A proposed contract with significant gaps may not be a satisfactory basis for making rational commitments, nor an adequate guide to required performance, nor a basis for grant of remedy. An incomplete agreement may not even be a valid contract if the general law cannot fill the gaps.

Another choice of form of importance in many contracts is whether to leave the contract in oral form or instead put it in writing (or in print). For the validity of some contracts, a formal record may even be required. The oral form is a much less firm and reliable mode of encapsulation. A proposed contract in writing or in print can be subjected to close scrutiny – all the more so if duly definite and complete. This, too, tends to beget good contract content, as judged by the parties' own lights. Also, fewer serious problems of interpretation will arise. This, too, facilitates efforts of parties to perform in complying fashion. The reduction of terms to written or printed form provides evidence of contract content, as well. This forfends against disputes over terms and facilitates the negotiated resolution, and also any litigated resolution, of disputes over terms that do arise. Again, much credit is due various features of form here for wide-ranging imprints on content.

A contract in writing or in printed form is more likely to be complete, and thus minimize disputes over whether the parties agreed to further terms not included in the writing. In some systems, a specific legal rule, which in Anglo-American law is called "the parol evidence rule," generally precludes a party to a written contract from attempting to prove in court any alleged term extrinsic to the written contract, thereby preventing alteration of the writing.[21] Under such a rule, if the alleged term is inconsistent with the writing, it simply may not be proved. Even if consistent, the alleged term may not be proved if the writing is adjudged a complete and exclusive embodiment of the contract. Indeed, the agreement may explicitly recite that it is complete and exclusive and thus bind the parties here. Such a rule protects the written or printed encapsulatory form and content of the contract and, therefore, also the corresponding subject matter preferences of the parties as set forth therein. All this, in turn, also serves general values of the rule of law including certainty and predictability. Again, credit is due form for its imprints and its exclusionary effects.

The analysis here also applies to standardized contracts in printed encapsulatory form. These are common and frequently involve little or no negotiation. Most contracts between businesses and consumers in some Western systems occur pursuant to printed standardized agreements.[22] Except for a few blank spaces to be filled in, these contracts set forth the terms of a standardized promissory exchange

---

[21] See, e.g., *Restatement (Second) of Contracts* §213 (1981).

[22] D. Slawson, "Standard Form Contracts and Democratic Control of Lawmaking Power," 84 *Harv. L. Rev.* 529 (1971).

Section Three: Due Credit to Form

and are expressed in definite and relatively complete terms. Mutual assent to each printed term in such a contract rarely occurs, and a rule of contract law in some systems may be invoked to invalidate any printed term that unfairly surprises a party.

Standardized printed agreements can be efficient, which, of course, is supposed to be one of their functions. Such agreements usually include terms that strongly favor the party who drafted the form. The other party is often faced with a "take it or leave it" deal and may even have little opportunity to read the form. Also, where the subject matter in question is a material necessity, the quality of the other party's "choice" may be eroded by intensity of need or be nonexistent if there is a monopoly. Yet this other party still has the choice of whether to enter the contract at all and may also have a choice between standardized agreements of competing offerors.

To return to negotiated bilateral contracts, these may include salient formal features beyond what formal criteria for validity require. Generality, for example, is a formal feature not usually required for contractual validity. Yet a particular contract may be quite general. For example, the two parties may agree not to a "one-shot" discrete exchange but to a "relational" contract, which is to govern their interactions well into the future. Contracts of this nature are common and include contracts of employment, contracts of brokerage, and contracts of lease. They often also include rules governing the interactions of parties over time, and thus are far more general than "one-shot" exchanges. Two parties to a contract may even agree to general terms that extend to third parties. For example, when a party sells land or goods to another, the transferee acquires ownership rights not only against the seller, but against third parties as well. Here, the totality of effects of a contractual exchange may even exceed the effects that some statutory rules have. Some contracts even extend to many parties, as with collective bargaining agreements between employers and unions.

Many contracts also have a structurally formal feature that is itself salient, yet not usually required for the legal validity of a contract. A contract may include only a few simple parts with correspondingly few and simple inter-relations, or it may have many complex parts with many complex inter-relations. Some executive compensation contracts, for example, have many complex inter-related provisions. Indeed the internal formal structure of some contracts is as complex as the structure of even the most complex statutory rule. An appropriate formal feature of structure can serve important ends. A formal feature, such as complex structure, high generality, or high definiteness, need not be a criterion of legal validity to be entitled to important credit.

Like other types of law, contracts can be analyzed in terms of their expressionally formal feature, a feature that can leave significant imprints on expressed content. Contracts vary greatly in explicitness, in the extent their vocabulary is technical, in their syntactical and grammatical structures, and in other facets of expression. The credit that can be due to mode of expression is seldom inconsequential. For example, clarity is essential to rational scrutiny of proposed terms at the formation stage, minimizes later disputes, facilitates ready interpretation, delimits the necessity for fact-finding, and facilitates the ready construction of reasons to perform in determinate ways.

SECTION FOUR: FORMAL *PRIMA-FACIE* VALIDITY AND FURTHER CREDIT DUE TO FORM

Nearly all choices that are in part choices of form in my schematic illustration of the sale and purchase of a car are also choices required to satisfy formal criteria for the legal validity of bilateral contracts in many developed Western systems, too. Such choices of formal features can be made with respect to subject matter highly varied in complementary content. These features include, as we have seen: the choices to make promissory undertakings, to exchange such undertakings by reciprocally induced mutual assent, to so deal with due definiteness and completeness, all in written, printed, or oral form, and in any due expressional form as well.

There are major advantages to Anglo-American and other Western systems in which the *prima facie* validity of a contract is recognized merely when formal criteria of validity are met, even though, in some circumstances, still further content-oriented criteria of validity may turn out not to be satisfied. One major advantage is that the formal requirements of contract formation can be readily learned and are relatively simple and easy for most lay persons to implement. This is true of all features of the overall form of standard bilateral contracts: promissory undertakings, bargain reciprocity and mutual assent, due definiteness, sufficient completeness, written or printed encapsulation for some transactions, and due clarity of expression. In Jhering's terms, these formal features allow for, and facilitate, efforts of parties to "channel" their particular intentions and understandings into contracts that are *prima facie* valid when these features are met.[23] In relatively few cases will there be evidence of duress, fraud, mistake, procedural unconscionability, or the like, to negate or defeat *prima facie* validity. Moreover, *prima facie* legal validity typically turns out to be equivalent to *ultimate* legal validity. This is because any content-oriented defenses such as illegality, conflict with public policy, or substantive unconscionability, very seldom arise.

The confinement of *prima facie* validity largely to satisfaction of formal requirements also facilitates free and ready formation of contracts, and tends to minimize instances of nonperformance. Parties to such *prima facie* valid contracts can readily see formal validity, readily feel resulting obligation, and readily perceive

---

[23] On the channeling function of form, see R. Jhering, *supra* n. 16, at 495.

Section Four: Formal *Prima-Facie* Validity and Further Credit Due to Form   229

self-interest in performance. Moreover, formal *prima facie* validating requirements such as due definiteness, sufficient completeness, written or printed terms, and clarity of expression, along with any tacitly understood background practices, such as usages of trade and course of prior dealing, leave imprints and other effects on content that lend special determinateness to the exchange. Hence, both parties can more readily grasp what performance requires, form justified expectations, and formulate justified claims of right to performance and cooperation, should that prove necessary. Of course, the nature of contract content can contribute here, too. All this makes it more likely that performance and cooperation will follow in the usual case, and that disputes will be less frequent.

When disputes do arise with respect to satisfaction of *prima facie* validating requirements that are formal, which is unusual, then a full-fledged judicial inquiry may be required to determine, for example, whether duress, fraud, mistake, procedural unconscionability, or the like operated to negate a formal criterion such as mutual assent. Even here, there may still be a more firm basis for settling such disputes out of court than would be true if *prima facie* validating requirements also included matters of content, such as legality of content, conformity to public policy, or substantive conscionability.

Another function of contracts taken individually and in the aggregate is that of facilitating free markets. Formal criteria of *prima facie* validity maximize the freedom of contracting parties to express their preferences in competitive markets establishing prices for land, goods, services, and more. Compared to officials in a command economy, private parties know better what they need and prefer. In a command economy, officials in effect impose goods and services on people to "satisfy" their *assumed* wants and preferences. Such officials must often act in the dark, except as to minimum subsistence needs. Even if officials could somehow learn what choices private parties would make, officials could seldom satisfy these as cost effectively as a free market. Moreover, the free play of market forces in the setting of prices generally allows resources to be allocated to their highest valued uses, as determined by the willingness of contracting parties to pay for these objects of value.

Choices of form pursuant to formal criteria of *prima facie* validity can also serve general values of the rule of law. One of these values is the freedom and dignity of citizen self-direction in choosing the formal features (however implicitly) and the complementary content that, in effect, satisfy relevant criteria of legal validity. Formal criteria of *prima facie* contractual validity track features of overall contractual form generally understood by the laity in developed Western societies. Business parties and consumers who enter valid bilateral contracts generally do so entirely on their own, without guidance from judges, officials, or even lawyers! As already indicated, given formal criteria of validity, parties can usually tell with certainty whether they are making a valid contract, and thus usually tell when they have incurred legal duties of performance and acquired corresponding rights thereto. In addition to serving as formal criteria of *prima facie* validity, due definiteness and completeness in the contract, and due encapsulatory and expressional features of form, enable the parties to determinate what is required to perform the contract. This not only facilitates and induces hitchless performance. It also serves certainty and predictability – general values of the rule of law. Again, much credit is due form here.

The fact that parties in developed Western systems can so effectively enter contracts that are at least *prima facie* valid, without conscious awareness, or with only limited awareness, of specific legal criteria of validity as such, is actually a high tribute to the formal character of these criteria. These criteria capture and express general ideas already familiar to such parties: ideas of promise, of bargain reciprocity and mutual assent, of due definiteness, of sufficient completeness, and of the utilities of having something in writing, duly expressed. It is not merely that these formal features reinforce concepts already familiar. Sheer repetition of contractual negotiations and interactions over time pursuant to bilateral contract form generates further familiarity with both the legal and the social versions of these features. This enhances the effectiveness of contractual interactions far beyond what they would be if *prima facie* validity had to be determined case by case on the basis of content-oriented criteria of validity.

The easy familiarity of most contracting parties with formal criteria of contractual validity enables them to enjoy the dignity of individual self-direction by effectively evaluating and deciding to enter most contracts on their own, or largely on their own. This value goes beyond freedom of contract as such. It is one thing for a legal system to allow wide freedom of contract, and quite another for the system to provide for the valid exercise of this freedom by individuals with the certainty that formal criteria of *prima facie* validity allow. Again, this high certainty is an important value of the rule of law.

Indeed, in the usual case, contracting parties can, with relative ease, make choices that satisfy formal criteria of *prima facie* legal validity. Ease of application of legal criteria of validity by parties and by courts is another important value of the rule of law. It is not only that these criteria are easily understood. Usually, they require little fact-finding, tend to be inexpensive to satisfy, and thus make contracting cheap. In the unusual dispute over validity that does go to court, judges and juries must, of course, decide validity in light of evidence purportedly negating satisfaction of one or more criteria, as, for example, in cases in which it is claimed that duress, fraud, mistake, or substantive unconscionability negates the formal criterion of mutual assent.

Some formal criteria of *prima facie* validity, such as the requirement of writing for certain types of exchanges, also fulfill an evidentiary function that facilitates due performance and contributes to dispute avoidance – another value of the rule

Section Four: Formal *Prima-Facie* Validity and Further Credit Due to Form   231

of law. The parties may create their own writing for the exchange at hand, or one of the parties may propose a printed standardized contract. Printed form contracts, though often somewhat one-sided, themselves usually reflect and satisfy most formal criteria of bilateral contractual validity: promises, reciprocity, definiteness, and completeness, as well as any requirement of a "writing." (Mutual assent may be another matter.)

Furthermore, formal criteria of *prima facie* validity confer relatively less discretion on the judge who is to resolve any issues of formal legal validity in the infrequent event that a dispute arises over whether, say, fraud, duress, mistake, or procedural unconscionability negates mutual assent. This limited discretion, in itself, contributes to dispute avoidance, and is highly efficient. It is certain that if judges were entirely free to pick and choose which particular deals are to count as *prima facie* valid contracts, parties would dispute over validity far more often. Furthermore, if the *prima facie* validity of all contracts had to be decided *ad hoc* by the exercise of judicial discretion in accord with a general method of "weighing and balancing all conflicting considerations," disputes would multiply, the "rule of contract law" would flounder, thousands more judges and lawyers would be needed, and market economies might collapse!

Formal criteria of *prima facie* validity serve the rule of law in still a further major way and at the same time serve freedom of contract. Judges applying these criteria must respect the subject matter preferences of the parties as expressed in contractual content. Formal criteria of *prima facie* validity are neutral as between the contract content bargained into the deal by each party. These criteria do not authorize judges to rewrite such content, and thereby substitute their own preferences or some assumed ideal set of preferences. When citizens rely on their agreements, they can also rely on the fact that at least the *prima facie* legal validity of their agreement is mainly formal, so that no judge will have much, if any, power to import his or her own personal views with respect to the content or equality of the bargain, in the course of deciding any issues of *prima facie* validity. Instead, the rule of contract law prevails.

Although *prima facie* validity ordinarily translates into ultimate validity, as I have said, the two are not identical. Contracts *prima facie* valid in light of formal criteria not negated by fraud, duress, mistake, procedural unconscionability, or the like, may nevertheless still be invalidated on such grounds as that their content is illegal, is in conflict with public policy, is substantively unconscionable, or the like. These content-oriented grounds, however, arise only in exceptional cases, and thus generally leave in tact the credit due to form for relatively hitchless contracting processes whereby formal criteria of validity are satisfied, and the parties perform without hitch. That form is entitled to credit here is not at all controversial.

Conformity of an agreement to formal requisites of *prima facie* validity is, of course, no guarantee against ultimate invalidity because of illegal content, content in conflict with public policy, content that is substantively unconscionable, or the like. Yet conformity to formal requisites can help guard against these, too. Awareness of the parties borne of formal definiteness, completeness, explicitness, and clarity of expression, and the requirement of an arms-length bargain, for example, can figure prominently here to forefend against bad content.

SECTION FIVE: CONTRACTUAL FORM AND RELATED PROPERTY INTERESTS — STILL FURTHER CREDIT TO FORM

The effects of the use of bilateral contractual form, and the credit due this form, extend far beyond the foregoing. At that, we will now consider only the wide-ranging and continuing effects of bilateral contractual form in relation to property interests. Here, too, the under-crediting of form is commonplace, if we are to judge from the sheer absence of its acknowledgment.[24]

As stressed in Chapters Five and Six, a law in the preceptual form of a statutory rule may be a law that binds all of its addressees. Such addressees could be highly numerous. By virtue of this and other differences between state-made rules and privately made contracts, some might think such state-made rules are "more truly law," and far more important than privately created contracts which, so far as we have now seen, appear to bind only two parties. We have concentrated so far mainly on the type of contract between two parties in a discrete transaction that terminates with performances of each party. The effects of such a contract are usually far narrower in scope and far shorter in duration than the effects of the usual statutory rule. In addition, state-made rules often affect private contractual relations. For example, under contracts of employment, certain state-made regulatory rules apply to employers and employees as classes. One common rule requires the employer to provide a safe place to work, a requirement that contracting parties may not legally obviate. Indeed, state-made rules often prevail when in conflict with terms of a private contract.

Yet, the terms of many private agreements entered pursuant to the overall form of a bilateral contract are frequently much more far-reaching in scope, and have legal effects much longer in duration, than my general account so far indicates. It is not merely that some contracts are themselves multi-party contracts of lengthy duration, such as collective bargaining agreements that themselves also typically incorporate rules. It is also true that what seems initially to be merely a simple two-party private contract can turn out to be very far reaching in scope and in duration. I will now demonstrate how this is so, as confined merely to one major category of legal relations much affected by seemingly simple two-party contracts, namely ownership rights in property.

---

[24] Again, exceptions are R. Jhering, *supra* n. 16, at 493–9 and L. Fuller, *supra* n. 18, at 800–4. Here Fuller explicitly drew on Jhering.

Section Five: Contractual Form and Related Property Interests

The functional legal units of ownership interests are highly varied, largely nonpreceptual, and take their own overall forms. Yet such interests are often significantly affected by the terms of seemingly simple two-party contracts. The terms of many such contracts often have binding effects on many parties, and for lengthy durations, and this makes such contracts much more like statutory rules in their generality and in certain other respects.

A. M. Honoré has said of the paradigm case of a full-fledged ownership interest in a thing that it consists in "those legal rights, duties, and other incidents that apply, in the ordinary case, to the person who has the greatest interest in the thing admitted by a mature legal system".[25] Many private contracts relate to ownership interests in discrete proprietary units. These units take distinctive forms of their own, but it is not necessary to explicate these here. It is enough merely to identify many of them. It is familiar that Anglo-American systems recognize such ownership interests as those in:

land	bonds
leasehold and other limited interests in land	bank accounts
mortgagee and other creditor interests in land	money
interests in residential and manufacturing structures,	negotiable instruments
goods, including fixtures	licences, transferable and non-transferable
leasehold and other limited interests in goods, including equipment	copyrights
bailor and bailee interests in goods	stocks and bonds in corporations
security interests in goods	patents

The foregoing ownership interests have counterparts in other developed Western societies. Ownership interests that individuals or entities acquire through exchanges via the use of the overall form of the bilateral contract encompass major sets of private rights. A party who acquires these rights generally holds them against all third parties, too, and far into the future. For example, ownership interests in land and goods frequently include:

the right to possession (of tangible property)
the right to be secure in possession, including the right to exclude others
the right of use or management
the right to any income or other fruits of the property

---

[25] A. Honoré, "Ownership," in *Oxford Essays in Jurisprudence*, 107 (A. Guest, ed., Oxford University Press, Oxford, 1961).

234 Forms of Nonpreceptual Law – Contracts and Related Property Interests

the right to transform the property or combine it with other property
the right to consume
the right to modify, sell, or otherwise transfer

The bilateral contract form has many uses here. Many bilateral contracts are used to transfer an ownership interest in its entirety from one party to another. Still other such contracts are concerned with the formation, combination, transformation, or re-creation of ownership interests into new interests taking their own forms, as in contracts for construction of buildings, manufacture of cars, preparation of foods and medicines, creation of patentable inventions, writing of books that are copyrighted, and so on. For many persons and entities, the most important right of ownership in property, after the right to sell and to use, is the right to create, through contract and other ways, new or different property.

When a contracting party transfers an ownership interest to a purchaser, the rights of the purchaser are, under the general law, usually valid against the seller and all third parties for an indefinite duration. Thus, when, in our earlier illustration, the buyer utilizes the bilateral contract form to purchase the car from the seller, the buyer's ownership rights to the car are valid not only against the seller but also against neighbors, coworkers, and everyone else in the world, and continuously so. Such a contract of purchase thereby creates in the purchaser major new legal rights and duties wide in scope and lengthy in duration.

This resulting legal state of affairs is only in part the creation of contract, however. Beyond the terms of the contract for the sale and purchase of the car, statutory rules, case law rules, and other varieties of state-made law already exist and define in general terms the rights and duties of ownership. For example, under existing state-made law, the buyer of a new car gets title against all others. Moreover, statutory and other rules actually contribute to the very creation of some forms of intangible property that become the subject matter of private contracts. Familiar examples are copyrights in books and patents of inventions.[26] The contents of state-made rules in effect define and organize the very forms that such interests take. State-made rules provide that ownership interests in such property may be acquired by purchase or otherwise, set forth general rights of such owners, specify protections for such rights, and so on.

In our purchase and sale of a car illustration, we saw how the parties used the overall form of a bilateral contract to transfer ownership rights under state-made rules. Once a party acquires ownership of property, that party can, depending on the nature of the property, transform it into other property, as when a buyer of a pick-up truck converts it into a van. All this may occur not through one contract, but through many contracts. Again, the creator of such new property interests

---

[26] Such intangible forms are creatures of law that add greatly to the "ownership menu" in developed Western societies.

Section Five: Contractual Form and Related Property Interests

ordinarily also has rights of ownership in it valid against third parties, and of unlimited duration.

Privately made law created through the use of the overall form of a bilateral contract is all the more consequential if we take into account the cumulative legal position of a contracting party who has purchased properties, transformed the properties, or otherwise modified property relations, not merely over a short time span, but over a number of years. At any one time, an owner may exercise ownership rights purchased, modified, or transformed pursuant to many past contracts that have been fully executed and are, as such, entirely in the past. Ownership rights of an individual or entity thus contractual and proprietary in origin, may cumulate and come to comprise a large body of privately created law and rights that are valid not merely against prior original contracting parties, but against third parties generally. Again, these accumulated rights may not only be wide-ranging, but extend far into the future.[27] Ownership interests in lands on which owners have constructed buildings over time are aptly illustrative.

The credit due to form can thus be compounded, often many times over. The overall form of the bilateral contract not only serves the ends associated with a privately made two-party bilateral contract discussed earlier. This form also serves further special ends when contract subject matter consists of ownership interests in property. When the ownership rights that parties acquire and accumulate through the overall form of bilateral contracts, and through proprietary forms, are recognized and protected, parties enjoy free choice and security of ownership – fundamental political values. The full realization of such values frequently involves further creative activity. The exercise of rights of ownership acquired through bilateral contracts is a special type of autonomy for owners. Also, when parties freely buy and sell ownership rights in the same free market, they realize their preferences, and resources are allocated to their highest valued use in the market.

Freedom of ownership depends on far more than the rules empowering individuals and entities to acquire and own property interests, and on far more than the rules protecting against interference by others with the exercise of ownership rights. Freedom of ownership presupposes adequate legal definition and recognition of possible *objects* of ownership in the first place, including those various types of objects identified earlier.[28] All such proprietary units take their own overall forms and have their own material or other components, too. For example, interests in land consist of far more than the material component of the soil itself. These interests take their own defined and organized forms – purposive systematic arrangements. Usually, the legal identity of an interest in a piece of land is

---

[27] It is true, as well, that much of the property law applicable to the particular interests in these accumulations is also partly state-made.

[28] *Supra* p. 233.

geographically located, plotted, measured, and registered within specified territory, all in relation to adjoining lands, too. In turn, the nature and extent of the interest in this land, and in other objects on the land also take defined and organized forms specified in law. For example, full ownership of land is distinguished in the law from many lesser interests, including leasehold interests.

Freedom of ownership also presupposes the legal definition and recognition of modes of acquiring ownership. As we have seen, the valid bilateral contract is one major mode of acquiring ownership. If the law did not define and recognize this contractual form – this purposive systematic arrangement, a legal system would lack its most important legal facility for the transfer and acquisition of ownership.

At any given time, the complex social order of a developed modern society includes a vast array of extant legal relations between persons, including relations of a contractual and proprietary nature. Particular contracts, especially those involving property interests, may even create vast structures of rights and duties as between the contracting parties, and as between such parties and third parties. These relations cannot themselves be reduced to rules, though rules govern the creation, nature, and change of such relations. An analysis oriented to the overall forms of the contractual and related property interests themselves is essential if we are to understand such relations.[29] This is true not merely with respect to entry into contractual and proprietary arrangements, but also with respect to the implementation of such arrangements.

SECTION SIX: IMPLEMENTATION OF CONTRACTUAL AND RELATED PROPERTY LAW — CREDIT TO FORM CONTINUED

Of the activities devoted to implementation of law of all kinds in most developed Western societies, far more are devoted to implementation of privately created law than to state-made law. One explanation for this is simply that there is far more privately created law. This law includes countless contract terms and related property interests, as shaped by form. Moreover, the implementors of privately created law consist overwhelmingly of private individuals and private corporate and other entities. Such individuals and entities vastly exceed in number and roles the various agencies of the state, other officials and judges – important though all these are – in the implementation of law. Furthermore, even most state-made rules of law are themselves not implemented by officials, but by private parties, and the formal features of rules loom large in this.

Private parties who exercise the power to contract, and invoke the overall form of the bilateral contract, usually voluntarily implement the respective sides of their

---

[29] W. Hohfeld, "Some Fundamental Legal Conceptions as Applied in Judicial Reasoning," 23 *Yale L. J.* 16 (1913).

Section Six: Implementation Of Contractual and Related Property Law 237

own contracts. We have seen that overall contractual form must have due credit here, and not only for its validating effects. Generality and definiteness of terms, appropriate expressional form, and still other formal features leave imprints and other effects on contract content that enable parties to interpret, to construct, and to act on, contractual reasons for determinate performance and other implementive actions. Every day, in countless instances, the terms of contracts created by private parties are privately implemented without any intervention by officials of any kind. This is also true where the subject matter of a contract consists of ownership rights, although officials may sometimes be called upon to recognize and protect the interests involved.

The processes of private administration and implementation of contractual and related law often require interpretation of contracts. All developed Western systems have the functional legal unit of a formal methodology of contract interpretation. Such a methodology may be applied by a contracting party or by a party purporting to exercise a right of ownership acquired through contract. Of course, if a dispute arises, and if it goes to court, a judge will be called upon to apply the formal interpretive methodology, too.

A valid contract may not be performed at all, or not be performed properly, and this may lead to a dispute in which the aggrieved party ultimately seeks the judicial remedy of damages or a judicial order requiring performance.[30] If the contract is not sufficiently definite and complete – formal features, a court cannot measure the lost expectation of the aggrieved party, or frame a decree requiring specific performance. The court granting any such remedy is an institution that itself takes an overall form, and this form and its constituent features contribute extensively to its capacity for serving ends and values.[31]

Most of the law of most developed Western societies, then, consists not of statutory rules, or of state-made law of other kinds, but of terms of private contracts, including the effects of these on proprietary interests. Every person of legal capacity makes valid contracts, often many. Contracts are typically formed and performed without the intervention of state officials, something that, as we have seen, well-designed form facilitates.

It is true that the overall form of a bilateral contract and constituents of that form are manifest in complementary contract content. For example, reciprocal promises take their own form with complementary content. Such form and content may be characterized as implementing the policy of freedom of contract, or to put it another way, the policy of facilitating the realization of preferences of contracting parties. Even so, contrary to the form-skeptic and the law-is-policy reductionist, bilateral contract form, once manifest in particular contract content, still does

---

[30] See *infra* Chapter Nine.
[31] See *infra* Chapter Eleven.

not lose its identity as form, or lose its efficacy *as such*. Moreover, choices of form in particular contracts, as implemented along with complementary content through contract performances, contribute to the realization of many important purposes, and are entitled to major credit. This credit is magnified by the aggregate importance of contracts in general, especially in market terms, and is magnified also through numerous contracts dealing with proprietary interests affecting third parties over lengthy periods.

SECTION SEVEN: RESPONSES TO FORM-SKEPTICS AND
LAW-IS-POLICY REDUCTIONISTS

As I have indicated, a form-skeptic or a critic disposed to reduce all form to policy might assume or assert that overall contractual form, at least once manifest in content, loses its identity as form, and thus disappears within the subject matter content of the contract.[32] Bilateral contractual form and its constituent formal features such as promissory undertakings, mutual assent, and due definiteness do not, however, lose their identity once manifest in the specific contents of particular contracts. They still answer to the relevant concepts of form and can be readily seen to do so. Moreover, if such a feature were to lose its formal identity in this way, then so would all features of bilateral contract form, and a particular bilateral contract would then be "all content and no form." This would be absurd. Contracts must take a form to exist at all.

It is true that contractual form, together with complementary content, serves policies of general contract law, for example, exchange and economic efficiency. Yet contrary to law-is-policy reductionists, from the fact that form serves such policies, it does not follow that form loses its identity as form. Well-designed contractual forms are necessarily purpose-serving. As we have seen, promissory undertakings, the requirement that such undertakings be reciprocally inducing with mutual assent thereto, and that there be due definiteness and completeness, all as manifest in complementary content, are necessary features of the overall form of the bilateral contract. Without these, the resulting arrangement simply could not take the overall form of a bilateral contract.

To be sure, choices by legislators and courts to adopt and implement a general policy, such as freedom of contract, and the choices by private parties of contractual content that is realizable, also merit vast credit for private and social ends ultimately served through contract. Likewise, material and other components such as the personal capacities of individuals in performing contractual duties deserve major credit for realization of values through contract. Even given sound legislative or judicial choices of policy, such as wide freedom of contract, and even given the

---

[32] Compare Chapter Five at 179.

Section Seven: Responses to Form-Skeptics and Law-Is-Policy Reductionists 239

disposition of contracting parties to agree on realizable content, and even given the extensive capabilities of individuals to perform their contracts, much scope still remains for things to go wrong because of poorly designed contractual form. For example, formal criteria of contractual validity in a particular system might not be well suited to implementation of the policies and the contractual content at stake. These criteria might be formalistic, as would be so were the law to require parties to resort to ritualistic forms of specific words for validity, with the parties often failing to use such words. Or, inappropriately formal criteria might even fail to require sufficient mutual assent to promissory exchange, as when a party is treated as contractually liable despite mutual misunderstandings for which that party is not really responsible.

Even if form-skeptics and law-is-policy reductionists were to concede that what I call form here is truly form, and that form deserves some credit for what is realized through contract, such critics still might argue that the contribution of *legal* form is relatively minor. This cannot follow, however, given the significance of the various imprints and other effects of form on contractual content without which a contract could not even have intelligible identity, let alone serve ends.

A skeptic or reductionist might also maintain that the overwhelming share of credit for values realized through contracting should go not to *legal* form, but rather to popular general understanding of the corresponding *socio-moral* form – to socio-moral ideas of promise, bargain, mutual assent, definiteness, completeness, and of "getting it in writing" – these being ideas already widely understood in developed Western societies perhaps even before legal systems adopted largely formal contractual forms. The eighteenth century philosopher, David Hume illuminatingly treated the socio-moral idea of promise and related features of moral promissory obligation.[33]

Let us concede that citizen awareness of a pre-legal or of an a-legal socio-moral form of promissory obligation has been and is today a significant factor that helps account for the realization of benefits through legally valid contracting. It still would not follow that the corresponding *legal* requirements of bilateral contractual form I have identified here should receive no credit or relatively little credit for what is realized through contract. Without legal reinforcement of the socio-moral ideas of promissory form, such ideas would very likely lose much of their own vitality. The overall form of the discrete and legally organized bilateral contract remains highly important even though this form closely tracks general socio-moral ideas of promissory obligation. At the very least, this legal form gives definitive body to, and authenticates such socio-moral ideas. At the same time, legal form, duly instantiated in a particular contract, contributes its own justified

---

[33] D. Hume, *A Treatise of Human Nature*, 516–525 (L. Selby-Bigge, ed., Clarendon Press, Oxford, 1960). *See* also, P. Soper, *The Ethics of Deference*, esp. 134–9 (Cambridge University Press, Cambridge, 2002).

and determinate legal bases for contract performance by the parties, its own bases for claims of legal right to such performance as asserted by the parties, and its own legal standards for criticism by parties of prospective failures to perform.

Further, the legal system provides judicial and other functional units for the resolution of disputes arising over contractual form and complementary content, and provides legal remedies for breach of promise. These remedies presuppose established legal measures such as lost expectation and lost reliance expenditures. These measures cannot be calculated and applied unless contractual promises are duly definite and sufficiently complete – legal requirements of contractual form. The form and content of legal rules and of legally valid contracts also legitimize the resort of an aggrieved contracting party to the powers of a court. General contractual norms merely of a socio-moral nature could not be adequate substitutes here. Thus, legal form here continues to have major significance independently of highly congruent and supportive socio-moral form.

The claims to credit set forth here on behalf of the law's bilateral contractual form are not really controversial. It is true that we cannot, without artificiality, separate and allocate credit with precision as between legal forms and socio-moral forms here, given that these are so closely intertwined. We can, however, be virtually certain that without the backing of legal form the foregoing socio-moral norms could not adequately secure the foundations of contractual exchange. Moreover, it is highly likely that, over time, legal form itself has substantially influenced and reinforced socio-moral promissory form.

8 ∽ FORMS OF LEGAL METHODOLOGIES – STATUTORY INTERPRETATION

"[T]he words used, even in their literal sense, are the primary, and ordinarily the most reliable, source of interpreting the meaning. . . . " – L. Hand[1]

"There is no surer guide in the interpretation of a statute than its purpose when that is sufficiently disclosed. . . . " – L. Hand[2]

SECTION ONE: INTRODUCTION

A legal methodology may be defined as a systematic general approach to the duly purposive and consistent execution of a recurrent type of major task arising in the making or application of law. A methodology is thus a special type of functional legal unit. A legislature may adopt tenets of a methodology more or less all at once or a highest court may evolve tenets of a methodology case by case over time. A methodology may not be fully developed in a jurisdiction at a given time.

In many jurisdictions within developed Western systems, generally authoritative methodologies are recognized in some measure for the duly purposive and consistent execution of at least the following major types of tasks: interpreting statutes, interpreting contracts, and interpreting written constitutions. Methodologies may also exist for the application of case-law precedent, and for the drafting of statutes, and of contracts.

The use of a methodology for the duly purposive and consistent execution of a major and recurrent type of task arising in the making or application of law is to be contrasted with purported execution of such a task without resort to any methodology. The principal differences are twofold:

First, a methodology is constructed on the basis of theory and experience as to what steps are generally most likely to lead to the duly purposive execution of the

---

[1] *Cabell v. Markham*, 148 F.2d 737, 739 (1945).
[2] *Federal Deposit Insurance Corp. v. Tremaine*, 133 F. 2d 827, 830 (1943).

241

task. A well-designed methodology is purposively and systematically arranged for effective execution of the task, and thus takes an overall form. Nonmethodological execution of such a task involves no resort to a purposive systematic arrangement, and is therefore relatively formless.

Second, those who follow a well-designed formal methodology take the *same* general approach – a *uniform* approach – to execution of the task as it arises. Those who purport to execute a task nonmethodologically are much less likely to take a uniform approach and are much less likely to execute the task in consistent fashion over time.

To explicate the overall form and constituent formal features of a methodology and thereby advance understanding of such a functional unit, and to attribute credit to the form of such a unit for purposes served, it will not be necessary here to address any particular methodology in any given system. It will be enough to concentrate merely on a schematic paradigm of the overall form of, constituent features of, and complementary material or other components of, one major type of methodology. For this purpose, I have chosen to offer a schematic analysis of a paradigm of a methodology for interpreting statutes. Such a methodology exists in varying degrees in all developed Western systems. Interpretive methodologies vary somewhat from system to system, and thus converge differently on the paradigm. The schematic mode of analysis offered in this chapter can be applied to the overall forms of particular interpretive methodologies for statutes in particular systems, and can also be applied, *mutatis mutandis*, to other types of interpretive methodologies for other species of law, such as those for contracts and constitutions. The functional legal unit of an interpretive methodology presupposes the existence of other units, including, of course, the very statutory, contractual, or other legal units to be interpreted.

In all Western legal systems, statutory interpretation is an important and recurrent task.[3] The purposes of the overall form and other components of a methodology for interpreting statutes include objective, reasoned, faithful, consistent, predictable, efficient, and purpose-fulfilling interpretation. A well-designed interpretive methodology is a systematic means to realization of the policy or other immediate purposes of statutes. It is also a systematic means to the realization of more ultimate purposes such as democracy, legitimacy, and the rule of law. Thus, such a methodology is "purpose-built" and its purposes inform its overall form and constituent features. This form defines and organizes how interpretive

---

[3] For a systematic general study of interpretive methodologies for statutes in Western systems, see D. N. MacCormick and R. S. Summers eds., *Interpreting Statutes: A Comparative Study* (Dartmouth Pub. Co. Ltd., Aldershot 1991). Much of this chapter derives from this study. Not all statutes operate in ways posing the usual interpretive problems. Some statutes merely confer vast power on courts to create and develop whole branches of the law. See generally, G. Lovell, *Legislative Deferrals – Statutory Ambiguity, Judicial Power, and American Democracy* (Cambridge University Press, Cambridge 2003).

Section One: Introduction

reasoning is to be formulated and brought to bear to resolve particular issues of interpretation.[4]

An interpretive methodology for statutes is a functional legal unit. Its overall form and the constituent features thereof define and organize the unit. Given the founding purpose to create such a methodological unit in the first place, reason dictates adoption of this overall form and its constituent features. The main constituent features of the overall form of a duly designed methodology for the interpretation of statutes are: (1) a primary criterion of the faithfulness of interpretations to the form and content of the statute being interpreted, for example, conformity to standard ordinary, technical, or special meanings of the statutory words in light of purpose and context, (2) recognized types of interpretive arguments implementive of the foregoing primary criterion, or if applicable, implementive of a secondary criterion and (3) principles prioritizing such arguments.

Judges, officials, lawyers, and still others in a developed Western system generally seek to interpret statutes in accord with an authoritative methodology. I will now contrast an interpretive approach that takes an overall methodological form with an approach that is not methodological. I develop this contrast primarily to advance understanding of the nature of a methodological approach and to show how major credit is due well-designed methodological form here.[5]

The most important defining and organizing purposes of the overall form of a particular interpretive methodology are to serve the policies and other ends of statutes through consistent and predictable interpretations supported by objective and reasoned interpretive argument faithful to the form and content of the statutes.[6] To understand how an interpretive methodology can honor such purposive methodological commitments, it is necessary to lay bare the makeup, unity, instrumental capacity, and distinct identity of a schematic paradigm of this type of functional legal unit.

A specific jurisdiction within a developed Western system generally strives to develop and follow a single methodology for interpreting statutes.[7] The schematic methodological paradigm I now set forth is abstracted from common features of actual methodologies in use in developed Western systems.[8] From this realistic paradigm, we can readily see what is formal about particular interpretive methodologies. We can also see how a grasp of the overall form and constituent features of such a paradigm can advance understanding of particular methodologies

---

[4] As we will see, another purpose is to facilitate effective legislative drafting.

[5] I do not claim that just any particular methodological approach is necessarily good. A methodological approach could be quite ill designed.

[6] For an extended argument that a methodology can structure the rational exercise of judgment and thus make it more objective, see K. Greenawalt, *Law and Objectivity* (Oxford University Press, New York, 1992).

[7] See MacCormick and Summers, *supra* n. 3.

[8] This is based largely on the extensive study cited *supra* n. 3.

operative in particular jurisdictions. We can see, as well, how duly designed overall form and its constituent features in particular methodologies should, when applied, have some credit for ends served through the statute.

Contrary to those theorists who embrace rule-oriented analysis, the best way to study the overall form, constituent features, and material or other components of a particular interpretive methodology, or of a paradigm of such a methodology, is not to study merely the contents of any reinforcive legal rules purporting to prescribe its makeup. Although some facets of a methodology for statutes can be prescribed in rules and such a methodology is typically so prescribed to some extent in particular systems, a form-oriented analysis must have primacy here, too, and for several reasons.

First, the purposes of an interpretive methodology, its overall form, and the constituent features of this form, must be formulated before anyone could even draft legal rules purporting to prescribe this overall form and its features. This requires the articulation of purposive rationales for such overall form, and, as we have seen, rules are generally silent as to these. A specification of the desiderata of form, which we will soon take up, is logically prior to the formulation of any rules purporting to prescribe such form.

Second, some of the constituent features of the overall form of a methodology consist of very general principles or maxims and, therefore, cannot be felicitously formulated as rules. For example, when interpretation requires resolution of conflicts between interpretive arguments, many courts first seek to invoke general priorital principles or maxims, rather than rules. When no such principles or maxims apply, or when they conflict, interpretive reasoning may take the form of weighing and balancing of interpretive arguments, a process that also cannot be specified at all fully in rules, yet can be meaningfully described partially in terms of form, as we will see.

Third, a form-oriented analysis is more holistic than a rule-oriented one. A form-oriented approach embraces not only the constituent features of the overall form (and complementary material or other components) of an interpretive methodology, but also the various inter-relations between each of these features and between features and components. These inter-relations together make the methodology an integrated whole that is more than the sum of its individual parts. For example, and as we will see in detail, a language-oriented criterion of the faithfulness of an interpretation to statutory form and content is a major formal feature that, together with recognized types of language-oriented arguments – another formal feature, figures in such an integrated whole.

Fourth, a form-oriented approach frontally addresses the issue of due credit to the overall form of a methodology, whereas a merely rule-oriented analysis does not. Indeed, a rule-oriented analysis does not even differentiate, within the contents of rules, between overall form and material or other components of a

Section Two: Sources of Needs for A Well-Designed Methodology 245

methodology, and therefore cannot attribute general credit to methodological form as such.

Fifth, and as will be explained, a form-oriented analysis, unlike a rule-oriented one, reveals how an interpretive methodology interacts with a drafting methodology in synergistic ways.

SECTION TWO: SOURCES OF NEEDS FOR A WELL-DESIGNED METHODOLOGY TO INTERPRET STATUTES

If a statutory rule is to serve its purposes, the addressees of the statute – officials, judges, lawyers, and private parties – must be able to interpret it and construct reasons for determinate action or decision under it that are faithful to its form and content.[9] Even when a statutory rule is as well-designed and well-drafted as feasible, this cannot prevent doubts and disputes from arising about the meaning of the statute in application to some particular circumstances. Indeed, issues of interpretation can arise even with respect to the most perfectly drafted statute.

It is true that an ill-designed methodology may yield interpretations that resolve interpretive issues. As we will see, however, an approach in accord with a well-designed interpretive methodology, not only can resolve interpretive issues, but can resolve them in a more objective, more reasoned, more faithful, more consistent, more predictable, more efficient, and more purpose-fulfilling fashion. When a genuine issue arises, appropriate interpretive arguments should be constructed, and the issue resolved in light of these. A well-designed interpretive methodology, purposively and systematically arranged, is needed to construct these arguments, to resolve any conflicts between them, and, ultimately, to facilitate the formulation of a reason for determinate action or decision under the statute that is faithful to its form and content.[10]

Interpretive issues may arise even under a well-drafted statute. Here, a well-designed interpretive methodology still meets needs although it may not be necessary for the interpreter to invoke the methodology at all elaborately. I will draw a number of my illustrations here from penal statutes, but the lessons will be more widely applicable. Consider, for example, one type of case of an offense arising under a penal statute, a case to which the statute can be seen clearly to apply even without elaborate invocation of a methodology. Assume that a statute imposes a penalty, not merely for stealing a vehicle, but also a further special penalty upon one who "steals a vehicle and knowingly drives it across the border from one state within a federal system into another state of that system." Assume the drafter of this penal statute justifiably assumed that interpreters under the particular

---

[9] In interpreting a statute, these addressees may or may not need the advice of lawyers. Much depends on the nature of the statute.

[10] The essential commitment to reasoned resolution is central. On this, much more later.

interpretive methodology in force would generally be required to interpret such a statute in accord with the leading principle that standard ordinary meanings of ordinary words in a *penal* statute, as construed in light of text and context, must control. In accord with this methodological principle, the foregoing statute would clearly be violated if the facts were that the wrongdoer stole an automobile and knowingly drove it across the border. Thus, such a clear case of an offense would give rise to a highly determinate reason for a driver to conclude in advance that he or she may not steal and drive the vehicle across the border in the first place, without incurring the special penal liability under the statute. This would also afford a prosecutor a clear basis to prosecute and afford any jury or court a clear basis to impose the special further penalty for such action.

Under such a statutory rule well-designed in prescriptiveness, generality, definiteness, clarity of expression, and other formal features, nearly all types of possible addressees of the statute could, in light of the foregoing leading interpretive principle for interpreting penal statutes, readily classify the foregoing facts as falling within the ordinary meanings of the terms of the rule. In such a clear case of an offense under the statute, the need for a discrete functional legal unit consisting of a well-designed interpretive methodology to guide addressees in constructing determinate reasons for action or decision under the statutory rule might not seem all that pressing. Yet even in such a clear case, the foregoing leading interpretive principle, as incorporated in a known and binding interpretive methodology, would as applied to the case, at least serve the important, although limited, purpose of providing further authoritative justificatory confirmation of the conclusion that an offense had been committed. Especially where the power of the state to punish is being exercised, this further confirmation deriving from application of the authoritative methodology itself to the statutory language and the facts, still serves an important purpose. An "interpretation" derived from an ill-designed methodology would very likely not serve this limited confirmatory purpose.

Many types of less clear cases of statutory applicability often arise, and in these cases, a more pressing need arises for resort to an interpretive methodology. Suppose the defendant, as the alleged thief, had testified that his son was actually doing the driving, albeit under orders from the defendant, and, therefore, argued that he, the defendant, did not "drive" the vehicle across the state line as that word appears in the statute. Under our schematic interpretive methodology, this case would still be a clear case of violation, though marginally not quite as clear as the one in which the actual driver was the defendant. After all, even in standard ordinary usage, one can still be said to "drive" a car through someone over whom one is exercising control. Here our hypothesized methodological principle for interpreting penal statutes also fulfills a need. That is, a conclusion that an offense had occurred in this marginally less clear case (the defendant driving through a defacto agent

Section Two: Sources of Needs for A Well-Designed Methodology 247

under the defendant's control), would at least be reinforced by application of an interpretive methodology incorporating a principle calling for interpretation of a penal statute in accord with standard ordinary usages of the words in the text of the statute, taken in context. A nonmethodological interpretation could provide no such reinforcement here, yet with penal liability at stake, such reinforcement has special importance.

Not all cases of an asserted offense, even under a very well-drafted statute, will in the end be so clear. Rather, some will be significantly borderline, and these may even frequently occur. For example, what counts as a stolen "vehicle" under our statute? A stolen automobile is a clear case. But is a stolen horse-drawn carriage? A stolen bicycle? A stolen airplane? Not even the most imaginative and accomplished legislative drafter can anticipate and dispose of all borderline cases in advance through use of suitable general language, and statutes drafted with sufficient detail to address all such particular cases on their own would be unwieldy and might even be confusing. This reveals a further basic source of the general need for an interpretive methodology, namely, the inevitability of significantly borderline cases calling for the kind of well-justified resolution that resort to a methodology can provide.

A well-designed interpretive methodology can explicitly incorporate, for example, not only a basic principle authorizing resort, in penal matters, to standard ordinary meanings of statutory words that in light of context readily resolve or confirm the resolution of relatively clear cases of liability, but also a further principle authorizing resort to *immediate* statutory purposes evident from the face of the statute and context, as a further aid in resolving borderline cases arising under it. Indeed, all well-drawn statutes may be said to be freighted with such immediate purposes. Let us assume that these immediate purposes in our statute making it a special crime to steal and drive a car across a state line include: (1) prevention of highway trafficking in stolen vehicles and (2) prevention of escape of wrongdoers using the highways. These immediate purposes would afford some systematic guidance to interpreters in the foregoing borderline cases. For example, in light of the second of these immediate purposes, the statute would cover the horse-drawn carriage, although probably not the stolen airplane flown over state lines. "Interpretation" without regard to the interpretive principle embracing resort to the immediate purposes of the statute evident from text and context could not provide the further guidance or justificatory grounds to dispose of such cases.[11]

The borderline nature of some of the cases that inevitably arise under the terms of ordinary language in a statutory rule is not the only further fertile source of the need for guiding and justificatory principles of the kind that the discrete

---

[11] This is not to say that such a methodology can be applied mechanically, obviating all need to exercise judgment.

functional unit of a well-designed interpretive methodology embraces. Even a tolerably well-drafted statute may include a technical word that has two technical meanings, or a technical word with no settled meaning, or a technical word the meaning of which is in process of change in the relevant realm of usage at time of drafting. Also, a statute may be well-drafted on its own terms, yet fail to mesh well with pre-existing yet still valid statutes on the same subject. Furthermore, a well-drafted statute may come into conflict with a general legal principle widely recognized in the law. And more. Accordingly, further methodological principles are required here. It is not possible for good drafting to eliminate all sources of interpretive issues. Indeed, that some interpretive issues later arise is not even inconsistent with drafting of the highest quality.

Methodological principles or tenets, then, are needed to guide the formulation of interpretive arguments, to specify their general scope, and to prioritize as between types of conflicting arguments. As we will see, a methodology well-designed in form and in its other components incorporates such further interpretive principles and tenets. In light thereof, the interpreter can usually construct reasons for determinate action or decision under a statutory rule far more faithfully to its form and content than would be possible on a nonmethodological or merely *ad hoc* approach.

Still another major source of the need for a well-designed interpretive methodology is that some statutes are poorly drafted. A statute can be plagued with unduly vague terms, elliptical expressions, syntactical ambiguity, internal inconsistency of usage of the same term, inept punctuation, gaps, and a host of other sources of interpretive issues familiar to all who have had any extensive experience with interpretation. Interpretation without regard to a well-designed methodology also affords little or no systematic guidance with respect to such statutes. Although a well-designed interpretive methodology cannot resolve all cases involving poor draftsmanship, it can often be highly useful. For example, it can incorporate interpretive principles calling for resolution of issues of vagueness under statutory language by reference to what would qualify as a clear standard case for application of the statute in light of its linguistic and factual context, in light of its immediate purposes, and in light of how far the case at hand is similar to (or different from) the features of what would be a clear standard case for application of the vague language. Or, for example, if the statute includes an elliptical expression, the methodology may incorporate an interpretive principle calling for resolution of the ellipsis in light of evidence of how ordinary or other users of the language in related contexts would resolve such ellipses.

Earlier, I suggested that there is still a further major source of the general need for a well-designed interpretive methodology, one often overlooked. Without being able to predict the methodology that interpreters would apply to a proposed statutory rule in course of being drafted, legislative drafters could not themselves

Section Two: Sources of Needs for A Well-Designed Methodology

know best how to draft such a rule well in the first place. A drafter needs to be able to draft with a special eye to the prevailing methodology that judges in the jurisdiction would apply to resolve issues of interpretation under the statute. For example, if the drafter knows that official addressees of a penal statute will, under the authoritative interpretive methodology, generally be required to give a relevant ordinary word in the statute the ordinary meaning it would have in light of context, then the drafter will know that such a word can be reliably used in the statute in a given way for the purpose of drafting its form and content. Since significant variations in interpretive methodologies are possible, there is special need for a *single* authoritative methodology, and the jurisdictions in developed systems have gone far in this direction.[12]

If, however, interpreters of statutes were to interpret without regard to the principles and tenets of a well-designed interpretive methodology, a drafter who would otherwise be methodologically self-conscious would have little to go on when drafting statutory rules, and many more interpretive issues would arise for addressees. Yet if drafters do their work in light of a well-designed interpretive methodology, interpreters aware of this influential drafting methodology can interpret more faithfully. In this synergistic interaction, one plus one equals three, and the overall forms of the two methodologies in combination should have more total credit than if operating alone and without coordination. Numerous examples illustrate this. A simple and schematic one is this. If, according to the governing interpretive methodology, the primary criterion of faithfulness of a particular interpretation of a criminal statute is conformity to the standard ordinary meanings of the words used in light of the context, a legislative drafter who knows this will be in position to draft more effectively than a drafter who is in the dark about any such primary criterion, and, of course, far more effectively than a drafter who is consigned to drafting for interpreters who have no definite and consistent interpretive methodology to follow at all. At the same time, an interpreter aware of the methodology applied in drafting the statute is in a position to interpret more faithfully.

Interpreters who must interpret without regard to a well-designed methodology may even be at sea as to the primary criterion of interpretive faithfulness, whether it be conformity to the language of the statute, the intent of the legislature, or whatever. An ill-designed methodology may be devoid of any authoritative primary criterion for judging the faithfulness of a possible interpretation, or may not provide authoritative formulations of recognized general types of interpretive arguments implementive of such a criterion. It might give interpreters no guidance at all in the construction of such arguments. It may not prioritize, even in presumptive fashion, as between conflicting types of arguments.

---

[12] See MacCormick and Summers, *supra*, n. 3, especially Chapter Four on the German system.

With many different official and other addressees and, therefore, with many different interpreters of the same statute at the same time and over time, a methodological approach is far superior in securing faithfulness to the policy or other content of the statute, and in securing objective, reasoned, consistent, predictable, efficient, and purpose-fulfilling interpretations. Also, there are many other ends that only a well-designed methodological interpretive approach can serve well. These include the ends of the rule of law, and other fundamental political values as we will see. An ill-designed interpretive methodology could be devoid of any purposive systematic arrangement of overall form and its constituent features. These truths also remind us of the considerable credit that can be due to the form of a well-designed interpretive methodology.

SECTION THREE: STUDY OF THE OVERALL FORM OF
A PARTICULAR INTERPRETIVE METHODOLOGY AS
AN AVENUE FOR ADVANCING UNDERSTANDING

In a given jurisdiction within a Western legal system, the main principles and other tenets of the functional legal unit of an interpretive methodology may be explicitly and authoritatively set forth in one place in a constitution, in a general code, or in a special statutory scheme. When the principles and other tenets of a methodology are generally recognized, but are merely left scattered through general case law interpreting particular statutes, the authors of treatises or of encyclopedias may draw these principles and other tenets together and systematize them into a coherent whole purportedly faithful to the overall form of the methodology. In the absence of such a treatise or encyclopedia, an interpreter must work directly with the case law on method.[13]

I will now identify the main constituent features of a schematic paradigm of the overall form of a methodology of statutory interpretation. On the basis of such a paradigm, particular counterpart methodologies in jurisdictions within Western systems can be readily identified. The overall form, constituent formal features and complementary components, may be characterized in terms of makeup, unity, instrumental capacity, distinctive identity, and other attributes. In light of this schematic paradigm, one can also identify, analyze, and advance understanding of, a particular counterpart methodology within a jurisdiction of a given Western system. One can also readily see how its overall form and constituent features, if well-designed, leave major imprints or other effects on particular interpretations. These imprints, in turn, contribute to objective, reasoned, faithful, consistent,

---

[13] Simply because a methodology in a given system has to be constructed from bits and pieces of case law, it does not follow that the methodology does not truly take an overall form, that is, a purposive systematic arrangement. A highest appellate court is capable of coherent action here over time. Scholars can render explicit the overall form and constituent features as expressed in the case law.

Section Three: Study of Overall Form of A Particular Interpretive Methodology 251

predictable, efficient, and purpose-serving interpretations of statutes in a particular system. Thus the analysis can also reveal the general nature of the credit due to well-designed form here.

In the schematic paradigm, the constituent features of the overall methodological form – the purposive systematic arrangement of a functional unit for interpreting statutes – consist of the following:

(a) a primary criterion of the faithfulness of an interpretation e.g., conformity to statutory language, or conformity to the "intent of the legislature," etc., and any secondary such criteria, duly ranked,

(b) recognized types of interpretive arguments implementive of (a),

(c) "procedural" prescriptions for the construction of such arguments,

(d) priorital principles that at least presumptively resolve conflicts between recognized types of arguments in particular circumstances,

(e) due generality of the scope of the methodology,

(f) internal structural coherence,

(g) sufficient definiteness, and

(h) provision for the filling of statutory gaps.

These features, as constituents of the overall form of the schematic paradigm of a methodology, can each be elaborated much more fully. These features have counterparts in constituents of the overall forms of particular interpretive methodologies actually in use in jurisdictions within developed Western systems.

There are at least three reasons to characterize the foregoing features as formal. First, all of these features (except perhaps (c) and (h)) may be said to be necessary features of the overall form of an interpretive methodology. Together, these features satisfy the general definition of overall form in this book, as refined here to fit the functional unit of a methodology for interpreting statutes. This general definition of overall form as the purposive systematic arrangement of a functional unit was introduced and defended in Chapter Two. Without the foregoing necessary features, a particular interpretive methodology could not serve its central purposes, namely, objective, reasoned, faithful, consistent, predictable, efficient, and purpose-fulfilling interpretation. Second, ordinary English (and other) usage specifically recognizes that constituents of this general nature, as taken together, are formal, for they comprise a "set . . . or prescribed way of doing anything."[14] That is, they are "regular . . . [and] methodical."[15] Third, such features differentiate a functional methodological unit from a merely *ad hoc* approach, which takes no methodological form.

---

[14] *The Oxford English Dictionary*, vol. 6, at "form," I.11.a. (2nd ed., J. Simpson and E. Weiner eds., Clarendon Press, Oxford, 1989), hereinafter *OED*.

[15] *Id.*, vol. 6, at "formal," A.4.a.

A discrete methodology for interpreting statutes within a jurisdiction in a particular Western system may not explicitly specify all features of the foregoing schematic paradigm. Yet, as one major study indicates, a methodology in a particular jurisdiction can usually be reconstructed to do this.[16] For example, overall form requires specification of a primary criterion of interpretive faithfulness such as conformity to standard or technical ordinary meanings of words, in light of immediate and other purposes evident from text and context. If not explicitly specified, some such specification can usually be formulated on the basis of existing practice. The overall form of the unit also requires other features, including recognized types of interpretive arguments implementive of the primary criterion, and if such types of arguments are only implicit in a methodology, they can usually be explicitly formulated on the basis of relevant practices.

Although the overall form of a methodology for interpreting statutes in a jurisdiction within a particular system must have all the features in the foregoing schematic paradigm to be fully complete, I do not claim that in the jurisdictions of every Western system, the prevailing methodology is thus fully complete, or fully articulated. The methodologies in some American state jurisdictions, for example, are not fully explicit or complete. Nor do I claim that the foregoing schematic paradigm captures all of the richness of detail within actual methodologies of some particular systems.[17]

Also, methodologies vary somewhat from system to system. For example, the jurisdictions of one legal system might generally adopt, as primary, a language-oriented criterion of interpretive faithfulness. According to this criterion, a faithful interpretation is the one that accords most fully with standard ordinary or technical meanings of the words used, especially in light of immediate purposes as evident from text and context. Jurisdictions in another legal system might adopt as the primary criterion of interpretive faithfulness that interpretation that conforms most closely to the subjective intentions of a legislative majority as manifest in authentic materials evidencing the legislative history of the statute. Jurisdictions in still another system might adopt a primary criterion consisting of that interpretation that best serves some more ultimate purpose of statutory policy or the like, where that purpose may be gleaned either from the face of the statute or from other authoritative sources. Also, some systems, in effect, adopt all such criteria but rank them in some rough order, thus specifying which criterion is to control when the primary one, or the next in order, is not applicable.[18] Although

---

[16] See MacCormick and Summers, *supra* n. 3.

[17] Various methodologies in developed Western societies are set forth and explained in MacCormick and Summers, *supra* n. 3. Again, the German methodology is exceptionally systematic and fully articulated. See *id.*, at Chapter 4.

[18] All the foregoing possibilities are illustratively treated, though not so conceptualized, for the American and the English systems in W. Eskridge, Jr., P. Frickey, and E. Garrett, *Cases and Materials on Legislation*, Chapters 7, 8 (3rd ed., West Group, St. Paul, 2001). See further, R. Summers, "Interpreting Statutes in

Section Three: Study of Overall Form of A Particular Interpretive Methodology 253

the jurisdictions within a system have adopted one criterion as primary, these jurisdictions may later move toward another instead.

Different judges in different jurisdictions of the same system or even different judges in the same jurisdiction in a given system may not all follow the same methodology. For example, some judges may follow a language-oriented primary criterion of faithful interpretation in light of text and content, while other judges follow a legislative intent criterion (as manifest in legislative history). Such variations forfeit major benefits of a uniform methodology such as consistency, predictability, and the synergistic interaction between interpreting and drafting. Some variations in formal criteria of faithfulness, in the ranking of such criteria, and in other methodological features may not be explicitly formulated, yet be manifest in interpretive practices.

To apply a methodology to resolve particular interpretive issues, the interpreter must deploy the methodology and bring into play the various material or other components complementary to its overall form. Here we must also distinguish within a formal methodology between the abstract and general specification of components on the one hand and particular such components actually figuring in applications of the methodology on the other hand. I will now, merely for illustrative purposes, cite examples of such complementary components.

One formal feature is the primary criterion of faithfulness of an interpretation. This criterion may, for example, be conformity to the ordinary or technical meaning of the words used, in light of purpose evident from text and context. The complementary material component of this criterion here would be the relevant particular ordinary or technical meanings of the words. The formal criterion plainly leaves its imprint here, insofar as it determines that these particular meanings govern. Or, for example, if the primary criterion is conformity to the intentions of a majority of legislators, the complementary material component of this criterion would be the specific evidence of those intentions. Again, formal imprints on the resulting interpretation would be evident.

The foregoing analysis thus preserves the basic contrast between formal features and complementary material or other components in an operational interpretive methodology. Thus, form hardly swallows up all. In the end, each formal feature has complementary material or other components in which there are imprints or other effects of form. Ultimately, each formal feature may ultimately leave an imprint or other effect on a particular interpretation.

An interpretive methodology in operation, then, is not wholly formal. Just as with the functional legal unit of a rule, which has material policy or other content

Great Britain and the United States – Should Courts Consider Materials of Legislative History?," in *The Law, Politics, and the Constitution: Essays in Honour of Geoffrey Marshall*, 222 (D. Butler, V. Bogdanor, and R. Summers eds., Oxford University Press, Oxford, 1999). See also MacCormick and Summers, *supra* n. 3.

even though formal features of the rule such as generality and definiteness are manifest in that very content, so, too, the form of a functional unit of an interpretive methodology, as applied, has complementary material or other components in which formal features also leave imprints.

The interpreter of a statute who applies a single interpretive methodology uniformly prevailing in the jurisdiction invokes it in particular circumstances as part of an overall process. The process begins with a doubt or doubts on the part of addressees about the meaning of the statutory rule to be interpreted. A further facet of the process consists of the particular state of facts to which the statutory rule may be applicable, depending on how it is interpreted. This state of facts can lend concreteness and sharpen the interpretive issues. Another facet of the process consists of the various formal features of the interpretive methodology itself. A fourth facet consists of the various complementary material and other components specified within the methodology and how they figure in applications of the methodology. This fourth facet encompasses resources of language usage – ordinary and technical, the general context of the statute, evidence of statutory purposes, analogies to related statutes, and more, as we will see.

The overall interpretive process itself requires multiple steps. Though seldom consciously identifying all the steps as such, the careful interpreter, and this includes judges, other officials, and also lawyers advising clients, will:

(1) read and study the statute in light of the facts to which it may be applicable,
(2) frame the issue or issues of interpretation in terms of the particular statutory language in which the issue arises, in light of the facts,
(3) review the principles and tenets of the governing interpretive methodology as set forth in constitutional law, statutory law, case law, the works of treatise writers, or some combination,
(4) determine the primary (or other applicable) criterion of faithfulness of an interpretation as specified in the interpretive methodology,
(5) identify possible types of relevant interpretive arguments as authorized in the interpretive methodology to implement the criterion of faithfulness,
(6) construct these arguments in light of relevant materials,
(7) resolve any conflicting arguments in light of the primary (or other applicable) criterion of faithfulness and of any applicable principles of priority specified in the interpretive methodology, and
(8) where different criteria of faithfulness, in light of available interpretive arguments, point to the same conclusion, marshall all the supportive arguments accordingly, and
(9) formulate interpretive conclusions as reasons for action or decision in the circumstances.

Section Three: Study of Overall Form of A Particular Interpretive Methodology 255

I will now treat, in schematic and summary terms, the major constituent features of the overall form of a more or less complete interpretive methodology for statutes, with emphasis on how these features can figure in particular interpretations. I will begin with an extended account of the criterion of interpretive faithfulness.

Methodological Form – Primary and Secondary Criteria of Interpretive Faithfulness. Interpretive methodologies for statutes in particular systems adopt, with varying degrees of explicitness, a primary criterion in effect specifying the type of interpretation, among competing ones, that is most faithful to statutes. This criterion is primary in the sense that, if a proposed interpretation satisfies it, then we may assume, absent any significant contrary indication, that this interpretation controls, even though an alternative interpretation may satisfy some secondary faithfulness criterion. If no interpretation satisfies the primary criterion, as when, for example, the conditions for constructing arguments satisfying the primary criterion do not exist, then the interpretation that satisfies the next highest ranked secondary criterion should generally control. The primary criterion of interpretive faithfulness in a given system might, for example, be:

(1) the interpretation that conforms most closely to the relevant standard ordinary, or relevant standard technical, or relevant special, meaning of the language adopted in the statute, in light of immediate purposes of the statute evident from text and context (language-oriented), or

(2) the interpretation that best accords with reliable evidence of the applicational intentions of individual legislators, or of major committees of legislators, or of sponsoring legislators speaking on the floor of the legislature, etc. (intent-oriented), or

(3) the interpretation that best implements the ultimate general purpose or purposes justifiably attributable to the legislature in adopting the statute, (ultimate purpose-oriented), or

(4) the interpretation that best implements a policy judges themselves wish to implement, believe the legislature may have espoused, and believe to be achievable in the circumstances, (policy-oriented), or

(5) some other criterion.

I will now briefly illustrate the possible significance of differences between the foregoing candidates for status as a formal "primary criterion" of statutory faithfulness. In this, I will use a highly simplified example. Assume a statute provides: "No vehicles may be taken onto pathways in public parks." Assume that a defendant takes a horse onto the pathways and is arrested. On a language-oriented primary criterion, there would, at least, be a real question whether a horse is a "vehicle" even in light of context. On an intent-oriented primary criterion, evidentiary materials of legislative history might specifically reveal that a majority of legislators specifically did not intend to prohibit horses. On an ultimate purpose criterion, the interpreter might discern from this statute, and related statutes, that the ultimate purpose of such a statute is to make the park pathways safe for children, for the elderly, and for the infirm, and accordingly also interpret the statute to prohibit horses. On one possible judicial policy-oriented criterion, the interpreter might favor a policy of keeping the pathways clean, and thus free of horse debris, and interpret the statute to exclude horses. It follows from the foregoing differences that the resolution of an interpretive issue can depend on which criterion of faithfulness is considered primary.

Once a jurisdiction adopts a formal criterion as the primary criterion of interpretive faithfulness to the statute, the other criteria of faithfulness listed become secondary or tertiary, etc., and in a fully specified methodology, these would be ranked, although not necessarily in rigid fashion.[19] Here are various overlapping considerations that are relevant to a choice of one interpretive criterion of faithfulness as primary within a given legal system:

(a) the extent to which the criterion is genuinely interpretive in nature, that is, generally favors those conclusions based on purposively reasoned interpretive arguments supporting plausible meanings of specific words and phrases actually used in statutes,

(b) the criterion for which it is most feasible to design methodological principles and tenets for systematic construction and prioritization of those purposively reasoned arguments that interpreters (nonjudicial as well as judicial) can, thereafter, effectively and efficiently deploy to support conclusions that satisfy the criterion,

(c) the extent to which the criterion can effectively limit scope for manipulative "interpretation" by strong-willed judges of the left, right, or middle who might be disposed to substitute their policy or other judgment (consciously or unconsciously) for that of a legislative majority, either in the guise of interpretation, or perhaps, even more openly,

(d) the criterion that generally best serves other related interpretive ends and values at stake, including consistent and predictable interpretations (as specified and elaborated in Section Four later).

(e) the criterion that provides the best guidance to legislative drafters, that is, which enables them, when drafting, effectively to take into consideration how draft versions of the statute would be interpreted.

---

[19] I do not mean to imply that legal systems have, all at once, constructed such explicitly specified and complete methodologies.

The foregoing types of considerations generally favor adoption of a language-oriented criterion as the primary criterion of interpretive faithfulness. This formal criterion may be phrased as that interpretation which conforms most closely to the relevant standard ordinary, or relevant standard technical, or relevant special meaning of the language adopted in the statute, in light of immediate purposes of the statute as evident from text and context. This criterion also appears to be the one most widely espoused, although with varying degrees of rigor and consistency, in the actual methodologies in the jurisdictions of most developed Western systems with which I am familiar.[20] That this formal language-oriented criterion is most widely chosen as primary is not difficult to explain.

First, this criterion is the one that is most genuinely interpretive in nature. A genuine interpretation must be of *authoritative language*. The language of a valid statute is the only language that the legislature has adopted as law. Indeed, as we have seen, a legislature can only adopt, as a statute, a chosen set of words in fixed verbal sequence, and a legislature typically does this quite purposively to achieve purposes.

Second, experience indicates that it is feasible to formulate workable methodological principles and tenets for systematic construction and prioritization of those purposively reasoned arguments required to implement a language-oriented criterion. It is generally less feasible to do this for implementation of any other criterion.[21]

Third, a language-oriented criterion is relatively more constraining than any of the other criteria and, thus, forfends more effectively against any strong-willed judges of the left, right, or middle, who may be disposed to substitute their own judgment as to policy or other content for that of the democratically elected legislature as expressed in the ordinary or technical language used. If, for example, a criterion of conformity to legislative intent were adopted, a judge could look to the usual conflicting versions of the legislative history of the statute in the process and merely adopt the one that is closest to the judge's own personal leanings.

Fourth, the methodological principles and tenets that can be constructed to implement the language-oriented criterion are also the ones that are likely to serve best other related ends and values usually at stake, including furtherance of (1) authoritative legislative policy or other statutory content, (2) general values of the rule of law including fair notice and consistent treatment of like cases, (3) fundamental political values, especially democracy, rationality, legitimacy, and justice, and (4) rational and duly coordinated drafting technique.

---

[20] See generally, MacCormick and Summers, *supra* n. 3.
[21] Other things equal, a system should favor the methodology that can yield the interpretive practices that are most methodological.

Fifth, a language-oriented criterion is most likely to accord with the interpretive approach to which most intended addressees of a statute are naturally inclined.[22] At the very least, they will first turn to the language of the statute and seek to ascertain the meaning of the relevant words.

Yet in times past in some systems, including in the American federal jurisdiction, some have advocated conformity to subjective legislative intention of a majority of the legislators as manifest in materials of legislative history as the primary criterion. Still others have advocated serving some ultimate purpose arguably attributable to the statute as primary. Still others have favored the criterion of serving most effectively the best possible policy in the circumstances, as viewed by the judges. Of course, some of these overlap.

Plainly, the choice of one criterion as primary will leave major imprints on resulting particular interpretations. I will now elaborate on the special claim to primacy here of the language-oriented criterion of faithfulness. Although, of course, many statutes have words with technical or special meanings, I will for illustrative purposes assume the statute uses ordinary words, and address implementation of this criterion through that most common type of interpretive argument, namely, the argument from the ordinary meaning of the statutory words used in light of immediate purpose evident from text and context. The resources in Western systems for construction of such "language-oriented" argument are wide-ranging and deep,[23] far more so than many observers assume. Most of the words of nearly all proposed statutes are ordinary words in ordinary language. The language in all proposed statutes is in the syntax of ordinary language. Also, the language used in committee study, legislative deliberation, and debate on the floor of the legislature is overwhelmingly ordinary language. Absent special circumstances, it is, therefore, more than a fair inference that most legislators who studied and who voted in favor of any statute drafted in ordinary language also understood the statute in terms of ordinary meanings of ordinary words in it as evident from text and context. Most addressees of the new statute would likely understand it in similar fashion, for they, too, would be conversant with such meanings. Although ordinary words can have more than one ordinary meaning, the immediate purpose evident from text and context will usually provide guidance as to which meaning is meant. It should be clear from the points made earlier that reliance upon the resources of ordinary language argumentation is not to be equated with mere "literalism" or the "formalistic," a matter to which I return in the last section of

---

[22] I am indebted to Philip Soper here.

[23] See *infra* text preceding n. 26. Also, see R. Summers and G. Marshall, "The Argument from Ordinary Meaning in Statutory Interpretation," 43 *N. Ireland L.Q.* 213 (1992). Later, I also consider statutes using technical words, and also ordinary words used with special meanings. See, e.g., n. 26 *infra* and accompanying text.

Section Three: Study of Overall Form of A Particular Interpretive Methodology 259

this chapter. Indeed, as I will show, the resources of ordinary language argumentation, as implementive of a language-oriented criterion, are sufficient to rule out the merely literal and the formalistic and still leave intact the distinction between such a primary criterion and other criteria.

A mode of argument that appeals to the ordinary meanings of ordinary words insofar as used carefully in the statute is usually also highly determinate, and thus relatively susceptible of even-handed application across time and space in the hands of different interpreters, whether they be judges, other officials, or lay addressees, as duly advised. This is true partly because this mode of argument is such common property. In contrast, "legislative intent" arguments are not so susceptible of even-handed application. Also, they derive from materials of legislative history that are often unformed, conflicting, sometimes superceded in the legislative process, unknown to many legislators voting on the text, and, in these and other ways, not as legitimate in origin as language-oriented arguments.[24] Much the same is true of so called "ultimate purpose" arguments and at least of those "policy" arguments that are free-wheeling in nature.

Furthermore, statutory drafters cognizant of the interpretive methodology that would be applied to a statute being drafted can more effectively draft the statute if they know it will be interpreted in accord with arguments from ordinary meaning in light of immediate purpose evident from text and context, than in accord with evidence of intentions of legislators as set forth in legislative history, or in accord with some general notion of ultimate legislative purpose, or in accord with judicially preferred policy outcomes.

The authoritative methodologies for interpreting statutes in particular Western systems do not all explicitly accord primacy to what I call the language-oriented criterion, or all rigorously rank the different criteria. The courts of a few systems may not accord general primacy to any one criterion, and different criteria may hold sway, even in the same time period. Even so, interpretive practices here are far from unmethodological or simply *ad hoc*. According to one extensive and recent study, in most major Western systems the practices are generally methodological, and most of these systems generally follow a single criterion as primary, with the language-oriented one most common.[25]

Of course, alternative possible primary, and any secondary, criteria as implemented via argument, do not necessarily support conflicting interpretations in particular cases. For example, under a language-oriented criterion, the very same ordinary meaning might be supported not only by the resources of ordinary language argumentation but also by evidence of legislative intent from

---

[24] I develop this point in the essay cited *supra* n. 23.
[25] See MacCormick and Summers, *supra* n. 3.

materials of legislative history, and by, say, judicially preferred considerations of policy.

Methodological Form – Recognized Types of Interpretive Arguments. Another complex feature of overall methodological form consists of recognized types of interpretive arguments implementive of primary criteria of statutory faithfulness. Here, too, the imprint of a choice of methodological form can be profound. An interpretive methodology is committed to resolution of interpretive issues via reasoned arguments supporting interpretations authorized by the primary criterion of faithfulness. The primary criterion adopted in the methodology of a particular system therefore largely determines the types of interpretive arguments that are, in the first instance, to have sway. For example, a criterion calling for interpretation in accord with ordinary meanings of statutory language in light of immediate purposes, as evident from text and context, calls for language-oriented argumentation. By way of contrast, a legislative intent-oriented criterion, for example, calls for argumentation focused upon materials of legislative history, or other evidentiary sources that indicate the actual intentions of at least some legislators in adopting a statute.

Language-oriented argument, where the words in issue are ordinary words, may be defined more fully as argument from that meaning or those meanings that a competent, knowledgeable, purposeful, and informed user of the language would give to the words in issue on the basis of the resources of ordinary language including context. Consider again the simple example of a statute providing that "no vehicles may be taken into the park." Language-oriented arguments used here – the words in issue being ordinary words – to resolve an issue of whether a horse is a vehicle, include reference to a standard dictionary definition of vehicle, which states that a vehicle is any means of carriage with wheels, runners, or the like. However, the resources of ordinary language argumentation are very rich. These resources go far beyond lexicons, and include grammar books, the bearing of a general context, general knowledge of the typical language user, the immediate purposes of usage insofar as evident from the text and context, usage in parallel circumstances in ordinary life, special factual knowledge fairly attributable to the language user, reminders of factual considerations already familiar, the use of hypothetical case analysis testing the scope of usage, usages of analogous words, standards of linguistic consistency, systematic reflection on relevant usages across a range of contexts, and construal of words to rule out absurd consequences as not compatible with legislative use of language. Each of the foregoing, which I have merely identified, is itself a considerable resource of ordinary language argumentation and is susceptible of extended elaboration.[26] A similar account

---

[26] See *supra* n. 23. So called "canons" of interpretation often encapsulate recognized types of interpretive argument.

Section Three: Study of Overall Form of A Particular Interpretive Methodology 261

can be provided for argumentation with respect to technical or special meanings of ordinary words and with respect to technical meanings of technical words.[27]

By contrast, a primary faithfulness criterion calling for interpretation in accord with specific evidence of the applicational intentions of individual legislators or of a key legislative committee, is a rather different criterion. It draws only indirectly on language-oriented resources and invites the interpreter to resort to actual historical evidence consisting, for example, of committee reports, and records of floor debates to establish what appear to have been the actual intentions of particular legislators in adopting the statute.[28] With regard to the "no vehicles in the park" example, an argument from legislative history as to whether a horse is a vehicle might well take note of the fact, if true, that, in legislative debate prior to enactment, only motorized transportation was mentioned. (It is true that an intent-oriented argument, for example, reliance on a quotation in a committee report or in other legislative history, may also sometimes support a particular language-oriented argument, as when such a quotation reveals in which of two ordinary senses the law-makers may have used a given word or phrase in the statute.)

A primary faithfulness criterion may call for interpretation in accord with the ultimate purpose of the statute. This purpose may be explicitly set forth in a preamble to the statute. If meaningfully set forth, the remaining task for the interpreter will be to determine which interpretation best serves that explicit purpose. The ultimate purpose may not be explicitly set forth, too. In that event, the ultimate purpose criterion invites many types of arguments, including language-oriented ones, intent-oriented ones, policy-oriented ones, and still others, with the only common thread being that the arguments somehow support attributing a given ultimate purpose to the statute, and perhaps also support one interpretation as more fully implementive of that purpose than others. These different types of arguments may or may not converge here. For example, if the ultimate purpose of a statute prohibiting "vehicles on park pathways" is to secure safe pathways, then an interpretation that precludes the riding of horses on the pathways would implement the ultimate purpose, even though the ordinary meaning of "vehicles" does not include horses and even though some legislators may have specifically intended to allow horses. As in this example, in which different types of arguments do not converge, an interpretive methodology is all the more important insofar as it provides for resolution of such conflicts, and consistently so. Interpretation devoid of method itself is far less likely to resolve such conflicts consistently.

A primary faithfulness criterion calling for interpretation in accord with the best possible policy the judges think the statute might serve is a criterion that

---

[27] Judicial opinions interpreting statutes in Western systems reveal all of the foregoing modes of argumentation in considerable abundance. Whole books could be written on the resources of ordinary language argumentation.

[28] See MacCormick and Summers, *supra* n. 3, at 416–417.

requires construction of policy arguments, of which there are also many types. The resources of such arguments can even be highly complex, as with those that draw on economic analysis that some may attribute to the legislature. Again, arguments may be made to support the attribution of one policy (or policies), rather than another (or others), to the statute as adopted. Once duly attributed, the statute is then interpreted to serve the policy.

Some types of interpretive arguments can be articulated and formulated in far more determinate terms than others. Arguments oriented to ordinary or technical language of the statute are often the most determinate in their bearing on interpretations. Intent-oriented arguments based on evidence in materials of legislative history, such as committee reports and floor debates, are often much less determinate, given the frequent conflicts within such materials, and the varying weight to be attributed to them.

A methodology, then, may be said to specify and structure how interpretive reason is to be brought to bear on the issues. An authoritative methodology in which interpretation is to be largely a matter for argument, can if well-designed, go far to serve objectivity, rationality, faithfulness, consistency, predictability, efficiency, purpose-serving efficacy, democracy, legitimacy, and the rule of law in the application of statutes. In contrast, interpretation devoid of method can contribute far less.

Methodological Form – Procedural Prescriptions for Constructing Arguments.
A comprehensive interpretive methodology would also prescribe in general terms the main steps for constructing major types of interpretive arguments. These steps could be set forth in general "procedural prescriptions." Though seldom called by this name, such prescriptions are frequently found in scholarly treatises on interpretation. For example, one procedural prescription for constructing an argument appealing to the appropriate ordinary meanings of statutory words in issue requires: (1) canvassing possible ordinary meanings of the words, (2) identification of the generally recognized context of usage for each of these meanings (taking into account relevant purposes; the subject matter, and also the grammar and syntax of the sentence in which the word or words appear), (3) determination of which general context of usage most closely matches the context of usage envisioned in the statute at hand in light of its purposes, and (4) adoption of that meaning that most closely matches the statutory context of usage. The resources of ordinary language argumentation are considerably more extensive than this schematic example indicates, and call for many other procedural prescriptions for the construction of arguments.[29]

---

[29] See MacCormick and Summers, *supra* n. 3, at Chapters 2, 11, and 13. See also R. Summers and G. Marshall, *supra* n. 23.

Section Three: Study of Overall Form of A Particular Interpretive Methodology 263

In a full-fledged and well-articulated methodology, prescriptions would be specified for construction of all major types of language-oriented arguments including those for technical words, and for technical uses of ordinary words, in the statute. For example, if a technical word is defined in the statute, the methodology will prescribe construction of an argument from this definition and this will usually be controlling. Or, if the statute does not define a technical word or words, yet uses a word or words having an established common law meaning, as with "in loco parentis" in a child custody statute, the methodology will prescribe construction of an argument from the common law meaning.

A comprehensive methodology would also include prescriptions for constructing the major types of nonlanguage-oriented interpretive arguments as well. Such prescriptions are seldom set forth in statutes, constitutions, or other written law. Many can be found in judicial opinions, in scholarly treatises, and in essays on the nature of legal reasoning. Such procedural prescriptions call for and facilitate effective and efficient construction of particular interpretive arguments. Here, too, the imprints of form on particular interpretations can be considerable.

Methodological Form – Principles of Priority. The overall form of a methodology usually embraces more than one formal criterion of interpretive faithfulness. Though this may not be very explicit, one criterion can often be adjudged to be primary. However, in a particular case, the resources required to construct arguments implementive of that primary criterion may simply not be available, given the statute and the context. For example, the ordinary meaning of the words may not be workable as a primary criterion because of semantic or syntactic ambiguity in the statute, ambiguity which arguments cannot clear up. Thus, it may be necessary to turn to a secondary criterion.

With more than one faithfulness criterion, conflicts may arise between arguments implementive of the differing criteria. For example, it is not uncommon that language-oriented arguments conflict with policy-oriented arguments in the interpretation of a statute. If the language-oriented criterion is generally ranked as primary, the language-oriented argument will usually take priority.[30] Not all conflicts between types of interpretive arguments are resolved by reference to what might be considered the ranking of differing criteria of faithfulness. Indeed, such ranking itself may not be explicit, or sharply on-off, and thus may call for exercise of judgment. But ranking and its effects, even when implicit, can leave major imprints of form on the interpretations that prevail.

Conflicts may also arise as between two arguments implementive of the *same* criterion of interpretive faithfulness. A comprehensive and well-designed interpretive methodology will include formal principles that generally accord at least

---

[30] See MacCormick and Summers, *supra* n. 3.

presumptive priority to one of two types of argument implementive of the same criterion. Consider the following schematic illustration. Assume the criterion is language-oriented and that a given argument favors one ordinary meaning of a statutory word, whereas another argument favors a generally recognized technical meaning of the same word. For example, assume a statute makes it a crime to "steal or take property by fraud." The defendant knowingly infringed a copyright. Here let us assume that the ordinary meaning of "steal" is limited to physical property, but that in some contexts "steal" has a technical meaning that could be extended to infringing a copyright. If the force of these arguments is roughly equal (a matter for analysis and judgment), a priorital principle may provide that the argument favoring the ordinary meaning takes priority. One rationale for this could be that, in the absence of an argument convincingly favoring the technical meaning of the word in issue, the ordinary meaning should control because this is the more widely prevailing meaning, and thus the one that legislators most likely embraced. Such priorital principles are usually only presumptive, and thus rebuttable. A more elaborate methodology may even explicitly specify authoritative ways of rebutting a merely presumptive principle of priority.

Further, with regard to conflicting arguments implementive of the same criterion, a jurisdiction may generally embrace a formal priorital principle that accords priority to that argument which supports the interpretation that better serves general values of the rule of law at stake. That is, if an interpretation supported by one argument would also yield a statutory rule the form of which is more law-like than the rule supported by another argument, the more law-like interpretation would prevail, for it would better serve general values of the rule of law. Interpretations can differ in law-like form in several ways. One of the reasoned interpretations may make for a more determinate, more certain, more reliable, and therefore more law-like rule than would a competing interpretation. Or one reasoned interpretation might yield a rule more appropriately general in treating like cases alike than another. Or one reasoned interpretation might be preferable as having prospective, and therefore more law-like effect, whereas the competing one could even have retrospective effect, and thus upset justified reliance. Or one reasoned interpretation might be more in accord with the rule of law because it gives a prospective wrongdoer fair notice whereas another interpretation does not. In the above example involving a statute making "stealing of property" a crime, a mere copyright infringer, even a deliberate one, might well not have fair notice that infringement could constitute stealing.

Another principle of presumptive priority may favor that reasoned interpretation most consonant with appropriate judicial role. For example, a reasoned interpretation that does not require any judicial rewriting of the statute should generally take priority over an interpretation that requires such rewriting, for it is

Section Three: Study of Overall Form of A Particular Interpretive Methodology 265

not the usual role of courts in effect to rewrite statutes. Arguments from ordinary meaning generally require less rewriting than arguments from legislative intent, for example. Still another principle of presumptive priority favors that interpretation over another where the other rests on an argument susceptible to a reductio ad absurdum.

Jurisdictions differ in the extent to which formal presumptive priorital principles are explicitly laid down. Such principles most often appear in judicial opinions and in scholarly treatises. When found in judicial opinions, they still may not be set forth clearly. That is, it may be necessary to reconstruct the text of the opinions. In the end, when two interpretive arguments implementive of the same criterion conflict, no formal priorital principle may be applicable, and the interpreter may be left simply to "weigh and balance" conflicting arguments – an approach that is generally less determinate and less predictable.

Methodological Form – Generality, Structure, and Definiteness. The overall form of a methodology for interpreting statutes must be sufficiently general to accommodate the highly varied contents of statutes. A methodology that is insufficiently general is not merely imperfectly implementive. It is also less valuable as a methodology. Special provisos may, however, limit the scope of an otherwise general methodology. For example, a proviso may require construal of penal statutes, if not narrowly, then in favor of the accused when the case is a close one. Such interpretive imprints may afford fairer notice, and also restrict prosecutorial discretion, thereby serving values of the rule of law.

The overall form of a well-designed methodology for interpreting statutes also has a structural feature and is thus formal. This feature coherently relates parts within an integrated whole. For example, it may as we have seen, specify primary, alternative, and perhaps even tertiary faithfulness criteria. Such ranking may be only presumptive, or it may be subject to exceptions. Moreover, structural form may prescribe a coherent general approach for implementing faithfulness criteria. As I have explained, this approach should include: authorized types of interpretive argument, procedural prescriptions for constructing and evaluating such arguments, and principles that presumptively prioritize types of conflicting arguments. A methodology so structured leaves imprints of its own on prevailing interpretations.

A well-designed methodology is also formulated with sufficient definiteness. An indefinite methodology cannot be very effective, for interpreters cannot follow it at all closely, and cannot apply it consistently. The more definite the methodology, the more meaningful the obligation of addressees, including judges, to follow it. Here, the best combination is a duly definite interpretive methodology, and duly definite statutes, with both as clearly expressed as possible. This combination also yields imprints of form on resulting interpretations. These imprints forfend against those few judges who would impute ambiguity or vagueness merely in order to inject their own views.

Again, jurisdictions in developed Western systems vary here. Some honor due generality of scope, due structure, and due definiteness in interpretive method rather highly, others less highly.

Methodological Form – Preceptual Feature. We saw in Chapter Four that some formal features of institutions can, and should, be prescribed in reinforcive rules. We saw in Chapter Five that reinforcive rules may prescribe certain formal features of regulative rules. Similarly, some formal features of methodologies can, and should, be prescribed in rules. For example, the adoption of a primary criterion of faithfulness should be formulated in a general rule, as should the general ranking of other criteria, whether or not presumptive. The authorization of types of interpretive argument may also be prescribed in a rule or rules.

Much that is important in a methodology, however, cannot be formulated in categorical rules and must take the preceptual form of principles or very general procedural prescriptions. This is generally true with respect to precepts specifying presumptive priority as between two competing arguments, both of which satisfy the primary criterion of statutory faithfulness. This is also true of procedural prescriptions for the construction of arguments. It is true, as well, with respect to methodological generality, structure, and definiteness.

Through study of the overall form and complementary material and other components of a particular methodology, it is possible to provide an account of the purposes and makeup of an interpretive methodological unit, to explain its unity and inner order as an integrated whole, to lay bare its complexity, elucidate how it is designed and organized to serve ends – its instrumental efficacy – and explicate its distinct identity. Understanding of this nature can also serve well those who wish to create a methodology, or improve an existing one.

SECTION FOUR: THE GENERAL CREDIT THAT MAY BE
DUE THE OVERALL FORM OF AN INTERPRETIVE
METHODOLOGY FOR STATUTES

The consistent implementation of a primary faithfulness criterion through well-designed methodological principles and tenets serves important purposes. Interpreters implement the primary criterion and any applicable alternative ones by constructing authorized supporting arguments, and by applying presumptive priorital principles to arrive at interpretations that serve as legal reasons for determinate action or decision. Given the potency of a well-designed interpretive methodology, and given the imprints and other effects of methodological form on particular interpretations, the credit due methodological form for the realization

Section Four: The General Credit That May be Due the Overall Form

of ends can be extensive, especially when the statutes themselves are duly designed to serve valuable ends and are drafted with an eye to the prevailing interpretive methodology. Indeed, the very existence of an interpretive methodology susceptible of adoption requires the form that defines and organizes it.

The general nature of the credit due to overall methodological form can be seen clearly if, for each category of the relevant values to be served, we briefly compare a well-designed methodological approach with a nonmethodological approach. In regard to each, we will assume the same statute, the same material and other components for construction of interpretive arguments, and the same trained drafters and interpreters.

A well-designed methodology in a particular jurisdiction that is duly applied to well-designed statutes, enables interpreters regularly to formulate those reasoned interpretations that, under the prescribed primary criterion of faithfulness, as supported by arguments, duly prioritized, qualify as most faithful to the statutes in question. These interpretations bear imprints of formal features: the imprint of the primary criterion of faithfulness, imprints of recognized interpretive arguments, imprints of principles of presumptive priority of certain arguments over others, and imprints of generality, structural coherence, and definiteness. When a statute is well-designed in form and content, reasoned interpretations bearing the foregoing imprints, in turn, become for addressees of the statute, legal reasons for determinate action or decision, and such action or decision implements the particular policy or other end involved, serves general values of the rule of law such as fair notice, predictability, and equality before the law, and serves fundamental political values, including democracy, legitimacy, rationality, and justice in the application of law. It is also a central purpose of the overall form of an interpretive methodology to define and organize every interpretation from beginning to end as a process of objective and reasoned argumentation.

A nonmethodological approach to interpretation simply cannot leave truly methodological imprints on particular interpretations.[31] The nonmethodological interpreter is always entirely free in any particular case to adopt any one of several possible criteria as the governing criterion of faithfulness of an interpretation to the form and content of the particular statute at hand. This interpreter is, therefore, not subject to the disciplining force of consistently having to satisfy, so far as feasible, the same primary criterion of interpretive faithfulness in each particular case. This interpreter can even choose not to follow any given principle or tenet of a general interpretive methodology, no matter how implementive. The most radical such interpreter does not bring *interpretive* reason to bear at all, and might even decide solely on the basis of relatively unconstrained and unarticulated intuitions

---

[31] This is not to say that interpreters applying a well-designed methodology can dispense with the exercise of judgment. Sound methodological interpretation is not and cannot be mechanical.

as to the "merits" of each particular interpretive issue arising in the application of a statute. A judge so "interpreting" statutes provides others little or no basis on which to predict how statutes will be applied. Also, this "interpreter" could not consistently serve other rule of law values such as equality before the law, either.

Of course, nonmethodological interpreters could differ in degree here. A less radical one might even decide to try to apply some criterion of faithfulness in some particular case. Yet, nothing would really constrain such an interpreter from shifting around from one interpretive criterion of faithfulness to another, case by case, or even issue by issue, in the same case. The interpreter would not be committed to any criterion of interpretive faithfulness at all and could simply adopt that interpretation which seemed to be intuitively "the best result" in light of all the facts of each particular case, perhaps with little serious attention to the language of the statute itself.

Free-wheeling "interpretation," in disregard of any methodology and even of the statutory language sometimes actually occurs.[32] Merely seeking what a judge or judges believe to be the "best policy result" or the "best result in terms of the merits" all in the guise of interpretation is hardly equivalent to implementing the statute adopted by the legislature in the first place. The legislative majority simply may not have espoused this "best result" in adopting the statute, and the language simply may not bear this "interpretation." If this is so, then, such an "interpreter" usurps the democratic role of the legislature. In this, and in other ways, nonmethodological "interpretation" is utterly noninterpretive, and almost certainly begets inconsistency, and so is unpredictable as well.

On a less extreme version of nonmethodological interpretation, let us assume the interpreter seeks to implement a recognized faithfulness criterion in each case. This interpreter still might choose a different faithfulness criterion from case to case. Or, although adhering to the same faithfulness criterion from case to case, this interpreter might still feel free in any particular case to invoke just any type of argument to "implement" it, no matter how marginal its relevance and force. Similarly, even if our interpreter were to adopt the same criterion, and were to invoke only arguments truly implementive of it, the interpreter still might not consistently follow any priorital principles in resolving conflicts between arguments that arise. Again, the process could not yield consistent and predictable results.

On the other hand, if an interpreter were to apply a duly designed and appropriately formal methodology, this methodology would embrace a single criterion as generally primary for judging whether an interpretation is faithful to the statute,

---

[32] See, e.g., *Welsh v. United States*, 398 U.S. 333 (1970) (holding that a personal moral code was a religion within the meaning of the statute despite statutory language expressly to the contrary); *Friends of Mammoth v. Board of Supervisors*, 502 P. 2d 1049 (Cal. 1972) (holding the California Environmental Quality Act applicable to private development despite clear language to the contrary).

Section Four: The General Credit That May be Due the Overall Form 269

and when satisfied, this criterion would control. The legislature could then be aware of this and could act accordingly when drafting, debating, and adopting statutes. The effort of the methodological interpreter to implement such a criterion systematically, also via implementive arguments and priorital principles, would then constitute a rational and consistent effort to serve the expressed democratic will of the legislative majority and would also provide legislators with a firm basis on which to draft statutes.

Such general adoption of one primary criterion would also be more legitimate than *ad hoc* selection of one or another criterion from case to case. It would be more predictable and consistent and, thus, serve general values of the rule of law better as well. That is, adoption of interpretations implementive of the same primary criterion of interpretive faithfulness, for example, conformity to ordinary (or technical) meanings of words in the statute in light of text and context, would be far more predictable, consistent, and reliable than, say, *ad hoc* invocation of this criterion in one case, of the criterion of legislative intent manifest in materials of legislative history in the next case, and of the criterion of serving policy or ultimate purpose in a third case, and so on. General adoption of one criterion as primary would leave major imprints of methodological form on particular interpretations for which much credit could be due.

Moreover, a system adopting a well-designed formal methodology would (1) choose not only to adopt a single criterion of faithfulness as primary, but also adopt the best primary criterion, and (2) follow that criterion, so far as feasible, in all cases. In most jurisdictions in Western systems, it would be agreed that the best such criterion is the one most consonant with the actions of the democratic majority of the legislature as manifest in the ordinary (or technical) language of valid statutes, that is, the language-oriented criterion.[33] Such a primary criterion might, however, not always be fully implementable. For example, if the language of the statute at hand is quite ambiguous, the interpreter must try to implement a secondary criterion. Yet here, too, the methodological interpreter would be far more constrained than a nonmethodological interpreter, and this should lead to results that are more objective, reasoned, faithful, consistent, predictable, efficiently realized and purpose-serving. Again, much credit would be due to the imprints of methodological form on the resulting particular interpretations.

Furthermore, a well-designed methodological approach can effectively implement a primary criterion of interpretive faithfulness, whereas a nonmethodological approach cannot. Let us assume an interpreter chooses to try to implement a given faithfulness criterion, but without otherwise being methodological – that is, without systematically constructing arguments implementive of this criterion,

---

[33] Earlier I canvassed at pages 257–258 general considerations that favor choice of a language-oriented criterion as primary.

and without applying the same presumptive priorital principles when arguments conflict. Here such a nonmethodological interpreter could implement the criterion only haphazardly. On a methodological approach, however, the interpreter would construct and invoke those arguments implementive of the relevant primary criterion, and this would yield more faithful interpretations. Moreover, the interpreter following a methodology would get better and better at it. Practice would tend to "make perfect," and the benefits of well-designed form would be compounded.

In following a formal methodological approach that is well-designed, the interpreter formulates and utilizes interpretive arguments implementive of a primary faithfulness criterion. In this way, the interpreter arrives at reasoned interpretive conclusions which can then be deployed as reasons for determinate action or decision under the statute. On a nonmethodological approach there is no similar assurance of objective, reasoned, faithful, consistent, predictable, efficient, and purpose-serving interpretive decision-making. Consider, for example, the arguments of the methodological interpreter applying a language-oriented criterion of faithfulness. The interpreter constructs arguments addressed to the language of the statute in light of text and content. Such arguments must be ones that support plausible meanings of that language. This, in itself, imposes highly important discipline. That language, although itself the very source of the issue to be resolved, nevertheless constrains the possible alternative interpretive conclusions and reduces them to perhaps two which qualify as truly plausible. The methodological interpreter is further constrained by the types of interpretive argument authorized in the methodology. For example, a language-oriented criterion of faithfulness authorizes, defines, and itself prioritizes those arguments that favor interpretations faithful to the wording of the statute, in light of text and context. A nonmethodological approach does not. Again, the imprints of methodological form on particular interpretations can be considerable.

Such a combination of specified criterion, and of argumentation implementive of the criterion, can beget far greater determinateness of interpretive conclusions than nonmethodological interpretation. This combination also facilitates the efforts of officials, citizens, and other interpreters (with any needed legal advice) to apply a statute reliably to their own circumstances *from the time of its inception* without having to wait until later for judicial pronouncements on meaning, which may not come until long after the addressees have had to act under the statute. The addressees of most statutes are individuals and entities who must interpret and apply statutes *from inception*, and thus act well before any dispute over meaning can be taken to a court, though they may have advance advice of lawyers. A methodology incorporating a language-oriented criterion of faithfulness implemented via arguments from ordinary (or technical) meaning in light of text and context, enables addressees reliably to interpret and apply most statutes

Section Four: The General Credit That May be Due the Overall Form 271

from inception. A nonmethodological approach cannot provide such guidance. A well-designed methodology also takes account of the special linguistic context of all statutes in which language is used for the special purpose of creating *law* – a purpose that favors interpretations that are rule-like, determinate, and prospective, thereby serving the rule of law. Again, well-designed methodological form merits much credit for resulting interpretations in which these imprints of form can be seen and acted upon.

The judiciary of a given system consists of many judges. If they all were to interpret nonmethodologically, or were to apply diverse methodological approaches, the results would be chaotic, unpredictable, illegitimate, and undemocratic. On a well-designed methodological approach, judges are supposed to apply the same general methodology. This is not to say they always do. Yet it is absolutely certain that an approach in accord with a duly-designed methodology prescribed for all judges would, if followed over time, yield far more objective, reasoned, faithful, consistent, predictable, efficient, and purpose-serving interpretations than would occur if an array of various judges were to take nonmethodological "approaches" to interpretation. A well-designed methodology focuses the argumentation of different interpreters on the same things, and these interpreters should generally arrive at similar outcomes. Such an approach excludes merely *ad hoc* decision making "on the merits" with no regard for consistency or integrity of interpretive argument. A duly methodological approach rules out deciding relevantly similar cases differently, and relevantly different cases similarly. It rules out, as well, decision-making that fails to ground the result in authoritative language. Methodological consistency serves the ends of fair notice, justice and equality before the law, rationality in the application of the law, and legitimacy – all general values of the rule of law. The credit due to uniform methodological form, then, can be very great, and reveals itself via imprints on particular interpretations.

As I have explained, methodological interpretation also synergistically serves methodological drafting and vice versa. Together, these two types of methodologies implement democratically adopted content. Nonmethodological interpretation cannot consistently contribute to these ends. The credit due form and its imprints on interpretations does not end here, however.

The general adoption of a formal interpretive methodology in a constitution, code, or statute also invites the creation in particular jurisdictions of more specific principles and tenets of *methodological case law* that further define, organize, and elaborate the methodology. The fact that some features of overall form here come to be quite specifically prescribed in principles, tenets, and other law, and are thus also recognized *as case law*, can have important effects of several different kinds. Interpreters will take the principles and tenets of the methodology more seriously than if not recognized in case law. This also sharpens the focus of criticism that lawyers, judges, professors of law, and the informed laity can bring to bear on any particular judicial acts of interpretation that depart from principles or tenets of a fully specified methodology not only in statutory or other written law but also recognized in case law. Such specific legal recognition of methodological principles and tenets thus extends the rule of law in more concrete terms, and lends determinacy to conceptions of what is good or bad about interpretive practices. Appellate judges assume responsibility not only to recognize but also to refine these very conceptions as they review, and affirm or reverse, interpretive decisions of lower courts. Of course, such refinements in the case law must be consistent with the principles and tenets of the methodology laid down in any constitution, code, or statute. If there be no such written law, the case law then becomes all the more important.

Specific judicial application of the principles and tenets of a methodology also invites concentrated attention on their adequacy and coherence. Any judge-made methodological law duly reported and published also preserves legal experience with types of interpretive problems, and invites scholars and judges to reflect on the adequacy of interpretive practices. Over time, this can lead to improvements in the overall form and in the material and other components of the methodology, and could even lead to legislative adoption in a generally well-defined, coherent, and readily accessible code for interpretation. So encapsulated, such a code could be the object of continuous improvement over time. A nonmethodological approach simply cannot lead to any of the foregoing. Again, the credit due form here can be vast.

Judicial deployment of an objective, reasoned, faithful, consistent, predictable, efficient and purpose-serving methodology can also lead to improvements in the quality of the form and content of statutes being interpreted. A well-designed methodology, duly applied, can reveal flaws in statutes that can then be remedied by the legislature. A methodology may even contribute to the coherence of the substance of case law under statutes being interpreted. Also, legislators may more reliably predict how a draft statute would be interpreted in light of the prevailing interpretive methodology, and be led to make desirable changes prior to adoption.

It is true that, within the same jurisdiction, there may be significant variations within a methodological approach, as applied by different judges. For example, it might even occur that some judges will adopt a language-oriented criterion, others an intent-oriented criterion, others an ultimate-purpose criterion, and so on. If the legislature does not enter, and if the highest court in the jurisdiction does not generally settle on one such criterion, then interpretive practices, though to an extent methodological, may, nevertheless, vary significantly, even in an otherwise unitary system. In a federal system in matters of state law, without a single highest court applying an interpretive methodology for all the states, there could be significant methodological variations from state jurisdiction to state jurisdiction. Also, even a highest state court might, over time, change from one

Section Five: Other Related Factors of Form

methodology to another. To the extent variations or changes occur, this would render the system less methodological, with all the sacrifices this entails.[34]

SECTION FIVE: OTHER RELATED FACTORS OF FORM

We saw in Chapters Five and Six that a statutory rule well-designed in form is duly prescriptive, general, definite, complete, internally coherent, duly expressed, and well-encapsulated. We also saw that these features all leave their own imprints or other effects on the content of a rule, and contribute to the determinateness of the reasons for action or decision that interpreters may faithfully construct under the statute. Indeed, a statutory rule that, for example, is indefinite, incomplete, or not clearly expressed very likely cannot be reliably and uniformly interpreted at all, and therefore cannot yield determinate reasons for action and decision. Thus, to grasp the full credit due to form, one must at least consider holistically how the form of the statutory rule and the form of the interpretive methodology together interact synergistically. As we will now see, there may not only be "double" but "triple" or "quadruple" synergies here.

As explained earlier, when drafters can rely in drafting statutes on a well-formulated interpretive methodology, they can do a better job of drafting in the first place. Well-designed structural and procedural features of institutional form provide for, and facilitate, legislative activities, such as referral of draft statutory rules to committees for study, floor debate, amendment, and further review of the whole process by a second legislative chamber. All this can contribute in synergistic fashion to the quality and efficacy of the final form and content of a statutory rule. Although formal legislative structures and procedures cannot guarantee well-designed statutory rules, they can influence legislators and drafters in ways that tend to improve form and content. This, in turn, can contribute to the efficacy of an interpretive methodology, because a well-drafted statute is much more readily and faithfully interpreted than a poorly drafted one. A well-drafted statute, duly interpreted, in light of a well-designed methodology, gives rise to interpretive reasons for determinate action and decision, which, when acted upon, serve relevant ends and values.

In addition, the overall institutional form of a court, when well-designed, can contribute to the effectiveness of the very interpretive methodology that the court applies to resolve issues of interpretation. Due qualifications of judges, as specified in the compositional feature, the independence of judges as secured through a structural feature separating governmental powers, and procedures guaranteeing robust adversarial interpretive argument, contribute to reasoned judicial

---

[34] In Chapter Ten on what is systematic about a legal system as a whole, uniformity of interpretive method is treated as one major systematizing device.

applications of an interpretive methodology. The experience that qualified and independent judges accumulate over time in the course of applying an interpretive methodology also tends to improve their skill and judgment in this very activity. Here, too, synergistic interactions between types of form can occur.

Of very great importance here is a well-designed procedural feature of the overall form of a court which duly defines and organizes the court's adversarial and dialogic processes. These processes facilitate the sharpening of issues of interpretation and enable participants to focus the interpretive methodology on the issues with more exactness. This, in turn, invites robust articulation of the competing arguments authorized by the methodology. Also, the tri-partite structural form of the court itself tends to secure impartiality and, thereby, facilitate objective application of the principles and tenets of the methodology.

Throughout the processes in which an interpretive methodology is applied, the principles of the rule of law, which are all form-oriented, exert their own force, too. One principle of the rule of law requires the addressees of statutory rules, including judges, to take seriously the principles and tenets of an applicable interpretive methodology embodied in the law.[35] If these tenets are well-designed, they will, when taken seriously, tend to secure fair notice, predictability, and equal treatment under the law being interpreted.

Due credit must, of course, also go to various complementary material or other components, including the general quality of personnel such as legislators, administrators, judges, and lawyers, all of whom bear some imprints of formal qualifications, too. The quality of lawyers plainly affects levels of interpretive performance. Good lawyers faithfully interpreting statutes in accord with a well-designed methodology serve the laity, serve corporate and other entities, and serve officials, the courts, and the system at large. Yet, even otherwise outstanding lawyers can do far less well if forced to interpret in a non-methodological fashion.

Also of major importance are various other resources that figure in the effective workings of an interpretive methodology. Without resources required to construct the particular interpretive arguments implementive of a faithfulness criterion, methodological efficacy would be vastly diminished. For example, the resources required to construct language-oriented arguments include official drafting manuals, legal dictionaries, general lexicons of the language, treatises on grammar, and evidence of parallel authoritative use of the language in question in related statutes. Materials for construction of policy-oriented arguments authorized by the methodology include authentic policy studies, relevant data, and testimony of experts. Other resources provide interpreters access to related statutes and to how they have been interpreted, and access to the legislative history of the statute being interpreted, if relevant under an interpretive methodology. Still other resources consist of general linguistic sophistication and skill at interpretive argumentation.

---

[35] See principle No. 14, *infra* Chapter Ten, at 335.

Section Six: Formalistic Statutory Interpretation

An interpretive methodology simply works better with regard to statutes sound in content – sound in means and ends. We saw in Chapters Five and Six how attention to well-designed form in a draft statutory rule can even tend to beget good policy or other content in the final version of the rule. Statutory content and methodological form can even function synergistically. Statutes deficient in quality of ends to be served, or deficient in the means prescribed to serve those ends, are not sound in content and may be difficult to interpret in accord with any methodology. For example, it may be difficult to judge whether a proposed interpretation of a statute incorporating conflicting policies, which the legislature has not duly prioritized, satisfies the specified criterion of faithfulness. It is simply more difficult, in regard to such a statute, to determine whether an interpretation counts as faithful to statutory form and content.

SECTION SIX: FORMALISTIC STATUTORY INTERPRETATION

The vice of formalistic statutory interpretation occurs in all developed Western systems. This vice includes but is not limited to wooden literalism, deductivist conceptualism, undue assimilation of the distinguishable, and the drawing of distinctions without justified differences. The criticism that a given interpretation is objectionable because "formalistic" is familiar, especially in the American system. Judges from time to time even express this criticism of other judges.[36] Many American professors of law and of legal theory are ready, and sometimes eager, to voice this criticism of judges.[37] The vice of formalistic interpretation, is not the only type of vice in the interpretation of statutes. Among various others is what might be called the opposite vice – "substantivistic" interpretation.[38] Yet, American professors of law voice this criticism much less often and rarely use the word "substantivistic," although it is very likely applicable to criticize interpretations at least as often as "formalistic."

I take up formalistic interpretation here for a special reason. Professors of law and legal theorists generally agree that such interpretation is bad, and that is my own view, as well. Yet some appear to think that it is simply not possible for a legal academic to be an advocate of well-designed *form* and the *formal* in statutes, and of well-designed *form* and the *formal* in an interpretive methodology, without somehow embracing, or at least encouraging, *formalistic* statutory interpretation. Some well known critics of formalistic interpretation of statutes have failed to

---

[36] See, e.g., *Paragon Jewel Coal Co., Inc. v. Comm'r of Internal Revenue*, 380 U.S. 624, 639 (1965) (Goldberg, J., dissenting); *Bindczyck v. Finncane*, 342 U.S. 76 (1951) (Reed, J., dissenting at 92); *New York v. Owusu*, 93 N.Y. 2d 398, 406 (1999) (Bellacosa, J., dissenting).

[37] See, e.g., C. Sunstein, "Regulating Risks after ATA," 2001 *Sup. Ct. Rev.* 1, 4 (2001); D. Klein, "Revenge of the Disappointed Heir: Tortious Interference with Expectation of Inheritance – A Survey with Analysis of State Approaches in the Fourth Circuit," 104 *W. Va. L. Rev.* 259, 283 (2002).

[38] See illustrative cases cited *supra* n. 32.

distinguish satisfactorily between form, the formal, and the formalistic.[39] It may be that such critics assume that when a truly formalistic interpretation does occur, this must somehow be attributable to the overall form or to formal features of the statutory rule itself, or to the overall form or to formal features of the interpretive methodology being applied, no matter how well-designed these forms and formal features may be. Yet, any such position cannot stand up, and it is important now to demonstrate as much. Form, including well-designed form in statutory rules and in interpretive methodologies, ought not to have a bad name simply because judges sometimes interpret statutes in formalistic fashion, just as policy or other content in a statute should not have a bad name merely because some such content is ill-advised. Also, one who urges the importance of form in statutory rules and in an interpretive methodology should not be taken thereby to encourage or endorse formalistic interpretation. This would be like saying that one who urges the importance of policy content in a statute should be taken thereby to encourage or endorse bad statutory content.

To address this vitally important topic in a meaningful fashion, it is necessary to illustrate formalistic interpretation in concrete terms. What I call "wooden literalism" may be the most common variety. (It is sometimes mislabeled merely as interpretation based on "plain" meaning of statutory words.) It will be sufficient here to consider only a single example of wooden literalism – a classic case mentioned by Blackstone – that seems to be truly ancient, deriving it appears from Cicero.[40] This case, as modified here, is also illustrative of many modern instances of wooden literalism.

In the case apparently posed by Cicero, we may assume that a marine "salvage" statute provided somewhat as follows: "Owners of a ship who forsake the ship when it is in distress shall forfeit ownership of it to any person or persons who stayed with the ship if it is later safely moored." We are also to assume that a sailor on board a ship in distress because of a storm, was then in sick bay by reason of illness, and thus unable to escape when all the others abandoned ship. The ship, however, happened to float to safety later with this lone sailor still on board in sick bay. This sailor later claimed ownership of the ship under the salvage statute. In a dispute between the ship's owner and this salvage claimant, we are to assume that the court awarded the ship to the salvage claimant, giving as its reason that this claimant had "stayed with the ship" within the meaning of the language of the salvage statute. In my view, this would be an instance of wooden literalism in the interpretation of the words of a statute, and so one variety of the formalistic.

I concede that the sick claimant "stayed with the ship," but only in a woodenly literal sense of that phrase, namely, that of continuing to be on board. However,

---

[39] See, e.g., R. Posner, *The Problems of Jurisprudence* (Harvard University Press, Cambridge, 1990); D. Kennedy, "Legal Formality," 2 *J. Legal Stud.* 351, 358–9 (1973).

[40] R. Summers and G. Marshall, *supra* n. 23, at 215.

Section Six: Formalistic Statutory Interpretation

according to: (1) a general language-oriented criterion of faithful interpretation, (2) the corresponding implementive arguments from ordinary meaning in light of the context of use of the words "stayed with the ship," and (3) the evident immediate purpose of this use of statutory words, all of which, let us assume, are provided for in the applicable interpretive methodology, the sick claimant did not by choice "stay with the ship" in order to save it, could not thereby have contributed to saving it, and so should not receive the ship under the statute as a reward for effort to salvage it. The sick person was unable to do anything other than involuntarily remain on board, and thus deserved no salvage reward under a proper interpretation of the statute.

All considered uses of ordinary words and phrases are ones with an immediate purpose or purposes determinable in light of context and subject matter. The use of words and phrases in a statute is typically a considered use, all the more so where the statute is drafted via a well-designed drafting methodology. It is true that many words and phrases in ordinary language have, in the abstract, more than one possible meaning, and thus they may have more than one possible immediate purpose in being used, as any major lexicon will reveal. However, when an ordinary word with two (or more) possible standard meanings is used in a statute, this use is typically freighted with a particular immediate purpose that, if not explicit, is usually discernable from the specific context of usage. This context includes the other words in the particular statute, the subject matter of the statute, and often more. In light of the context, the interpreter can usually determine faithfully to the statute which of the two (or more) standard meanings should be attributed to the language user. This is true in Cicero's case, as we will now see.

Which possible immediate purpose should be attributed to the legislative language user here – "stayed" merely in the sense of continuing to be on board, or "stayed" by choice to try to save the ship? In Cicero's case, we are assuming the court awarded the ship to the sailor and not the erstwhile shipowner because, on the court's interpretation, the sick sailor "stayed with the ship," albeit merely in the sense of continuing to be on board, and not in the sense of staying by choice in order to save the ship. This interpretation was incorrect. The court should have interpreted the statute in light of the immediate purpose of the legislators evident from this context. In adopting such statutory language, the evident immediate purpose of the legislators was to reward efforts to salvage and thereby conserve valuable property. Here, the sick sailor made no such efforts and could not have done so. The court should, therefore, have given the statutory words "stayed with the ship" the ordinary meaning these words would have in this context, that is, as so purposively used, rather than a woodenly literal and therefore formalistic meaning in disregard of the immediate purpose evident from the context of usage.

Some might also think that actual wooden literalism in statutory interpretation, perhaps because it is thought to be felicitously called "formalistic," must somehow derive from some defect of *form* in the statutory rule. Yet, the statutory rule here appears to have taken the overall form of a rule and to have been sufficiently prescriptive, complete, definite, general, internally structured, and well-expressed. Hence it had no real formal deficiencies. It is true that the statute could have been more explicit with respect to its immediate purpose. For example, it could have been drafted to read: "stayed with the ship by choice in order to salvage it." Under this less elliptical version of the statute, a court would almost certainly not have interpreted the statute in favor of the sick sailor. But accepted standards of appropriate drafting do not require that statutory rules be so explicit as to preclude the various possible woodenly literal or other erroneous readings. Here the language and subject matter indicate plainly that this is a salvage statute. Hence, a reasonable drafter could not be expected to foresee such a woodenly literal interpretation and explicitly provide against it.

Moreover, a statute is seldom drafted to include specific negations of possible interpretations that would be erroneous. There are good reasons for this. The basic operative language of a well-designed statute, as distinguished from possible mis-interpretations that the legislators might also identify and specifically rule out, is sufficient to serve the ends at stake when duly interpreted in light of a well-designed methodology. Also, the drafters might not foresee all possible such mis-interpretations, and if the drafters should choose to rule out one or more of those that they do see, this might then lead judges and others to conclude erroneously that only those specifically ruled out are excluded.

Nor does wooden literalism, as one version of the formalistic, necessarily derive from the overall form of the interpretive methodology. Such a methodology could be in due form, yet an interpreter still *misapply* it to yield a woodenly literal interpretation. Merely because a statute is thus formalistically interpreted, it hardly follows that this is necessarily the fault of a methodology with its formal features. Let us assume that those features of the form of the interpretive methodology to be applied here are complete and include: a general language-oriented criterion of statutory faithfulness to be implemented primarily via the general argument from ordinary or from technical meaning, in light of context, including the evident immediate purpose. The methodology would, in this regard, be well-formulated, even though it does not explicitly negate types of formalistic "interpretations" including wooden literalism. Nevertheless, a court might still *misapply* the methodology, as in Cicero's case, and adopt a woodenly literal and hence formalistic interpretation.

Although well-designed form in the drafting of a statutory rule, and well-designed form in an interpretive methodology may forfend against formalistic interpretation, such forms cannot guarantee against its occurrence. Given that formalistic interpretation can still occur even though there is no deficiency of form in the drafting of the statute or in the interpretive methodology, it follows that

Section Six: Formalistic Statutory Interpretation 279

we should not blame well-designed form for formalistic interpretation. The other things to blame for formalistic interpretation are numerous. To be least charitable, these include in ascending order: disregard of obvious contextual implication, disregard of the implications of immediate statutory purpose evident from the language and the subject matter, obtuseness with respect to basic nuances of language, impatience with complexity, general incompetence, and haste. Thus, the material component of personnel – judicial and other – can be entirely to blame, with form blameless.

A critic of formalistic reasoning who attributes the formalistic vice of wooden literalism or other varieties of the formalistic to the very presence of form in statutory rules or interpretive method, even when such form is well-designed, might also believe that we could somehow have statutory rules and interpretive methodologies without formal features of any kind, and might even think that we ought to have such rules and methodologies. This, however, would not be possible. Such overall forms and their constituent features are necessary to the very existence of these functional units.

Critics of formalistic interpretation (and I am, of course, one of them), all assume that judges and lawyers can choose to avoid formalistic reasoning. In my example, the judge could have readily interpreted the statute in favor of the shipowner rather than the person who "stayed" with the ship, and I have shown how a well-designed formal methodology with complementary content would actually call for this very interpretation. Yet if critics of formalistic reasoning attribute (incorrectly) such reasoning merely to the very presence of form in statutory rules or merely to form in interpretive methodologies, even when appropriate, then some, perhaps much, formalistic interpretation would simply be unavoidable in any developed Western legal system, for such forms are necessarily widely at work. If simply unavoidable, it would then follow that formalistic reasoning in the interpretation of statutes could not even be a rational object of criticism! In truth, however, formalistic interpretation is not unavoidable, and is simply not to be attributed to the presence of well-designed form in statutory rules or in an interpretive methodology.

If the source of formalistic interpretation is truly to be form, and not some aberrant disposition or approach of the interpreter, then this culprit would have to be some version of ill-designed form in the statutory rule or in the interpretive methodology. Yet, no lawyer or legal theorist known to me has ever knowingly advocated ill-designed form in statutory rules or in an interpretive methodology. So far as I know, no lawyer or theorist can be charged with favoring ill-designed form because it is the mother of formalistic statutory interpretation, even if it be assumed that this is what it is.

It might be that an imaginative thinker could show that the very presence of form in a statutory rule, well-designed or not, and the very presence of form in an interpretive methodology well-designed or not, tends somehow to lead interpreters of statutes to interpret formalistically in some proportion of cases. If this be so, then to avoid all formalistic interpretation, we would have to abandon statutory law and interpretive methodologies altogether, given that these simply cannot exist without form. No self-styled antiformalist has, to my knowledge, ever proposed abandoning these.

It is my view that well-designed form in a statutory rule and in an interpretive methodology actually forfends against, rather than caters for, or somehow "mothers," formalistic interpretation. Let us return to Cicero's salvage statute mentioned by Blackstone and the methodology to be applied there. Though, as I have conceded, the statute could, in terms of formal expression, have been somewhat more explicit ("stayed with the ship by choice in order to save it"), the preceptual form of the statutory rule is itself expressed with due definiteness. Thus, the drafter used the words "stayed with the ship." These words have sufficient fixity and specificity. Likewise, we are assuming the methodology that the interpreter was to apply incorporated a language-oriented faithfulness criterion and authorized the interpreter to resort to the argument from ordinary meaning as implementive of this criterion. I have already explained that a knowledgeable user of English, mindful of the context, mindful of the subject matter, and mindful of how the immediate purpose of salvage freights this particular use of ordinary language with meaning, would certainly have interpreted the statute in a nonformalistic fashion.[41] That is, the interpreter would have interpreted the words "stayed with the ship" to mean so stayed "in order to save it." Such a methodology is entirely uncongenial to formalistic interpretation. Again, here the form of the methodology, as well as the form of the statutory rule, can hardly be to blame for formalistic interpretation.

It is also important to distinguish between a formalistic statute and a formalistic interpretation. What I call a formalistic statute is not interpretively so. Let us assume the content of a statutory rule is itself deficiently drafted in a fashion such that its very content can be characterized as formalistic. (Again, no lawyer or legal scholar would advocate such drafting.) Let us assume the wording of this statutory content assimilates disparate types of instances on the basis of insufficient similarity. That is, the very content of the rule therefore treats quite different instances in the same way. To return to Cicero's example, assume the content of the statute there explicitly provided for a reward for salvage, yet also explicitly made plain that a person could qualify as a "salvor" entitled to a share of the reward not only by seeking to save the ship, but also merely by staying on board, as in the case of this sick person, until the ship came to port. As a result, the

---

[41] This resort to immediate purpose in context is not a departure from ordinary meaning argumentation. Most uses of ordinary words are freighted with immediate purpose discernable from context.

Section Six: Formalistic Statutory Interpretation 281

judge interpreting the statute, let us assume, granted the sick person a share of the value of the ship along with a share to a healthy person who actually stayed with the ship to save it. I concede that a statute that gives such a sick person a share could be characterized as a formalistic *statute*. The judge's interpretation would not, however, be a formalistic *interpretation* as such. This would be because the interpretive result is rooted in a formalistic assimilation *embedded in the content of the statutory rule itself*, and not in an interpretive methodology or its application.

The form of the interpretive method would therefore not be in any way to blame for such a formalistic result. Because this is supposed to be a "salvor's" statute, a person who merely continued to be on board due to illness should not get a share. Merely continuing on board as such is not sufficiently similar to the standard case of one who, in remaining on board, made efforts to salvage. The legislators, in erroneously assimilating the two instances, adopted a statute that *in its content is formalistic*. The blame here must be attributed to the work of the legislators – to formalistic assimilation of disparate instances in the very language of the statute itself. At bottom, the culprit here cannot be the interpreter or the form of the interpretive methodology. The culprit is not even the form of the statute, but its content! More particularly, this flaw in statutory content is a failure to draw justified distinctions in that very content between possible types of claimants of a salvage award. Thus, just as good preceptual form cannot rescue a statute with poor policy content, neither can well-designed methodological form rescue a statute with poor policy content. Hence, it is "policy content" or "substance," those great paragons of inherent legal and moral virtue in the eyes of some antiformalists, that are to blame!

I concede that an ill-designed form of a methodology could be responsible for formalistic interpretations. We might, for example, imagine a formalistic methodology which included a tenet that explicitly prioritized woodenly literal interpretations over all others! This would, however, be ill-designed form.

I also concede that the ill-designed form of a statutory rule, as distinguished from its policy or other content, could be partially responsible for formalistic interpretation. A feature of a statutory rule might lack explicitness to a considerable degree – an expressionally formal feature – and this could, in particular circumstances, tend to invite or regularly lead to formalistic interpretation. Again, the overall form of a rule does not, however, call for ill-designed form. In sum, form is not to be equated with the formalistic, even in matters of interpretation. Indeed, well-designed form can even be said to forfend against the formalistic, which is yet another type of credit due it.

The danger of formalistic interpretation arises also for those interpreters who would interpret *nonmethodologically*. On such an approach, the interpreter would lack the benefit of a well-designed methodology and would therefore be more likely to fall into interpretive error of all kinds.

SECTION SEVEN: METHODOLOGICAL FORMS AND OTHER FORMS

In Chapters Four, Five, Six, and Seven, we have encountered fundamentally different types of functional legal units within a legal system and therefore quite different types of overall forms of such units: the institutional (legislative), the preceptual (rules), the nonpreceptual (contracts) and the methodological (interpretation). This selective typology of forms is not merely classificatory. That is, it is more than merely taxonomic in significance. The forms in this selective typology are highly variegated. If the truth of my central theses about form as an avenue of understanding, and as an object of credit, holds over such highly variegated terrain, this testifies to the significance of these theses. All such units are formal in major ways. Each takes its own distinctive overall form, which, with its constituent features, is the central key to understanding the nature of this unit. The overall form of each unit is also entitled to significant credit for what is achieved through the unit. Indeed, form is required for such a functional unit even to exist. Credit due for this can hardly be more fundamental.

It is true that a radical form-skeptic might seek to question the very existence of interpretive methodologies on the ground that they are not always explicitly recognized, or fully developed, or consistently followed in Western legal systems. Certainly they are not fully developed in some systems. There are also variations in methodologies within and between systems. Yet in no jurisdiction within any Western system known to me is statutory interpretation essentially nonmethodological, even though the methodology in a given system may not be fully developed or wholly uniform. In some systems, such a methodology is even enacted, at least partially, in a code or in a statute.[42] Even in so-called common law systems, there are many statutes, an accumulated body of interpretive case law addressed to these statutes, and elaborate treatises in which the authors discern and record major methodological patterns in the cases interpreting these statutes.[43]

---

[42] See MacCormick and Summers, *supra* n. 3.
[43] *Id.*, at Chapters 10 and 11.

9 ⁓ FORMS OF SANCTIONS AND REMEDIES

"[J]ustice may need to be secured by force. . . ."   – J. Finnis[1]

"Civilization involves subjection of force to reason and the agency of this subjection is law."   – R. Pound[2]

SECTION ONE: INTRODUCTION

Law in due form must be created, but once created, it is not self-implementing. This is true of law in the form of precepts such as statutory rules and common law principles, nonpreceptual species of law such as contracts and property interests, and all other varieties of law, whether state-made or privately created. Law must be implemented by its addressees. These include private individuals and entities, and public officials and bodies of all kinds. The law to be implemented must be validly made in the first place, and we have seen how form can figure in this. Valid law must also be accessible and duly communicated, and form is essential here, too. For addressees to implement valid law effectively it must be in form and content suitable for implementation.

In earlier chapters, we saw how form defines and organizes law creating institutions and processes. We also saw how formal records facilitate reliable determinations that purported law to be applied today was validly created in the past. We also saw how choices of well-designed form in rules, in contracts, and in other species of law thus validly created, can contribute to the capacity of addressees to formulate reasons for determinate action and decision arising under such law. We also saw how choices of form in an interpretive methodology can facilitate objective, reasoned, faithful, consistent, predictable, purpose-serving, and efficient interpretations. In addition, choices such as formal definiteness and clarity

---

[1] J. Finnis, *Natural Law and Natural Rights* 260 (Clarendon Press, Oxford 1980).
[2] R. Pound, "The Future of Law," 47 *Yale L.J.* 1, 13 (1937).

of expression in a law can also facilitate interpretation and fact-finding required for the application of law.

Most law is implemented in developed Western societies through voluntary self-direction by addressees – private citizens, entities, officials, and others – in accord with reasons for determinate action or decision that these addressees have constructed under statutes, contracts, and other species of law.[3] When addressees voluntarily so act, there is no need for the state to impose sanctions, remedies, or the like then and there. Legally well-informed addressees who voluntarily implement the law may be the most important material components of any system.

In tolerably well-ordered societies, a major factor that influences addressees voluntarily to act in accord with rules and other valid law is the general respect they have for the law, and for the pre-emptive force of particular legal reasons for determinate action and decision that can be seen to arise under the law. In regard to most laws in these societies, such respect derives largely from the sense that addressees have that law is for the common good, that particular laws themselves are justified, and that the system of law and its manner of operation are acceptable. Relatedly, addressees also respect general duties of societal membership, many of which are recognized in law. One of these duties is simply the duty to abide by the law, though this is not an absolute duty. Still another factor is this. Those who might be adversely affected by nonperformance of a legal duty often stand ready to assert claims of right, thereby inducing compliance.

Various nonlegal factors also account for voluntary compliance in a tolerably well-ordered society. Perceived self-interest in following the law is one such factor. Officials readily perceive that it is in their interest to do their jobs according to law. Ordinary citizens and other inhabitants perceive that voluntary compliance with law is not merely a way of staying out of trouble, but generally enables all to live and let live in pursuit of their own interests. Further nonlegal factors influencing voluntary compliance include the fear that others will criticize noncompliance, and the fear that those adversely affected by noncompliance may retaliate.

So far, I have identified many of the factors that influence voluntary compliance. I have characterized most of these as largely nonlegal. Yet, well-designed form in functional legal units contributes in various ways to the efficacy even of some of these largely nonlegal factors. We have seen how form leaves imprints

---

[3] See generally H. L. A. Hart, *The Concept of Law*, 124 (2ⁿᵈ ed., Clarendon Press, Oxford, 1994):

'In any large group general rules, standards, and principles must be the main instrument of social control, and not particular directions given to each individual separately. If it were not possible to communicate general standards of conduct, which multitudes of individuals could understand, without further direction, as requiring from them certain conduct when occasion arose, nothing that we now recognize as law could exist. Hence the law must predominantly, but by no means exclusively, refer to *classes* of person, and to *classes* of acts, things, and circumstances; and its successful operation over vast areas of social life depends on a widely diffused capacity to recognize particular acts, things, and circumstances as instances of the general classifications which the law makes.'

Section One: Introduction

on material and other components of these functional units, many of which are deep and indelible. For example, the better defined a legal rule, the more clearly it is expressed, and the better it is publicly disseminated, all of which are wholly or partly matters of form, the more likely addressees will understand the rule, and, in turn, respectfully comply. Also, the more understandable a rule (including its rationale), the more focused and intense will prospective criticism or other social pressure be that could ultimately induce voluntary compliance. The foregoing are, in part, empirical claims on behalf of well-designed form, yet they are not really controversial.

Still, if a legal system had no capacity to coerce potentially recalcitrant persons through, for example, threats of sanctions for crimes, or threats of sanctions for administrative violations, or through prospective grants of judicial remedies for breaches of contract, for torts, or for other civil wrongs, it is certain that a higher proportion of persons would commit crimes, break contracts, or otherwise take advantage of others in disregard of legal duties. It is also highly likely that any such lawlessness, if widespread and continuous, would eventually erode the general cooperative spirit and morale of many persons who would otherwise fulfill their legal duties.[4] In that event, the social order might even degenerate, as Thomas Hobbes most famously put it, into a war of "all against all" in which life becomes "solitary, poor, nasty, brutish, and short."[5]

Thus, in addition to duly formed and validly adopted rules and other law, formal promulgation and other methods of communicating or making law accessible, formal interpretive and other methodologies and the pre-emptive reasons for determinate action and decision arising thereunder, and the non-legal factors tending to induce voluntary compliance, legal systems must also have state sanctions, state remedies, and other enforcive units. Without these, some persons could not be motivated to act in accord with even the clearest and most highly pre-emptive reasons for determinate action that arise under law. Indeed, some persons can be motivated to comply only insofar as they learn of, and come to fear, a state imposed sanction, remedy, or the like. Still others can be motivated to comply only by some combination of (1) the threat of a legal sanction, remedy, or other adverse state action, and (2) various nonlegal factors such as fear of criticism, or of retaliation by a victim or someone else adversely affected.

State sanctions, remedies, and other discrete enforcive legal units, then, are necessities. Justice and other ends of civil society must be secured to some extent

---

[4] *Id.*, at 197–9.

[5] T. Hobbes, *Leviathan*, 82 (M. Oakeshott ed., Basil Blackwell, Oxford, 1960). In the American Federalist Papers (no. 15) published in 1788, it was said: "It is essential to the idea of a law, that it be attended with a sanction.... If there be no penalty annexed to disobedience, the resolutions or commands which pretend to be laws will, in fact, amount to nothing more than advice or recommendation." A. Hamilton, "The Federalist No. 15," in A. Hamilton et. al, *The Federalist: A Commentary on the Constitution of the United States*, at 91 (Random House, New York, 1950).

by force. Enforcive units are socio-legal creations and due form is required for their very existence and operation, as well. Yet, these units are neither free-standing nor self-sufficient. Sanctions and remedies, like other functional legal units, must be integrated and coordinated within operational techniques for the creation and implementation of law.

In this chapter, it will be sufficient to treat the overall forms, constituent features, and complementary material or other components of only two major types of functional legal units that are enforcive: the sanction of state imprisonment for crime, and the judicial grant of compensatory damages as a remedy for breach of contract. I will also identify further ways that form and formal features enter into the overall coercive capacity of a legal system.

My primary focus will be on how study of the overall forms of imprisonment and of contract damages advances understanding of the makeup, unity, instrumental capacity and distinct identity of these units, and on how credit is due these forms for ends realized. Some of the claims to credit I assert here on behalf of form are, like others in this book, partly empirical, yet not controversial. Still other claims I assert are not empirical at all. For example, without sufficiently well-designed form, sanctions and remedies could not be defined and organized as functional legal units. Hence, they could not exist at all.

I have given enforcive units a place in the typology of functional legal units selected for consideration in this book for two main reasons. First, sanctions and remedies are different from the other types of functional units so far considered. For example, the sanction of imprisonment is far from equivalent to any specific rule of the criminal law, e.g., against theft, that may be broken and for which such a sanction may be imposed. Also, a compensatory damages remedy for breach of contract is far from equivalent to the contract term that has been broken. More-over, sanctions and remedies are plainly far from equivalent to the very judicial institution required to impose sanctions or grant remedies, and far from equivalent to the legislative or other institutions that may have created such enforcive units in the first place. Thus, sanctions, remedies, and other enforcive units have their own autonomy, although they, too, are not functionally independent. They presuppose legislatures, criminal prohibitions, courts, contracts and contracting processes, and still other functional units.

Second, enforcive units are essential to the viability of a legal system. One influential legal theorist even claimed that a legal system, in its entirety, is a "coercive order."[6] Although in this chapter, I draw illustratively from Anglo-American systems, the major types of enforcive legal units in developed Western systems are broadly similar.

---

[6] See generally H. Kelsen, *General Theory of Law and State* (A. Wedberg, trans., Harvard University Press, Cambridge, 1945).

SECTION TWO: THE FORMS OF ENFORCIVE FUNCTIONAL UNITS — GENERAL

State-administered enforcive units are numerous and varied. They include imprisonment, fines, capital punishment, compensatory remedies, orders requiring specific action, disgorgement of gain, forfeiture of property or other rights, revocation of licenses, and so on. Each enforcive unit takes its own overall form – its own purposive systematic arrangement – and has its own complementary material or other components. Yet most share several formal features that go to the very essence of enforcive units. These shared features together comprise the key to understanding such units. These features and complementary components also serve policies and other ends of the specific laws at stake, general values of the rule of law, and fundamental political values including legitimacy, rationality, and justice. Here, much credit is due enforcive forms.

Before turning to the specific formal features that leading enforcive units share when suitably designed, I will identify the primary facet that figures in all such functional units. This primary facet is, in its nature, *adverse* to the addressee and is state-imposed. For example, imprisonment or other restriction of liberty is adverse. A fine is adverse. A court judgment requiring that a party pay money damages is adverse. Official confiscation of property to pay damages is adverse. And so on. Of course, many varieties of action by private persons can be similarly adverse, too. For example, a private victim of serious harm might thereafter seize and lock the wrongdoer up in a room. This would not, however, be state-imposed imprisonment, though its adverse character could be highly similar in impact. A private victim of a breach of contract might simply grab property of the contract breaker as recompense. This would, likewise, not be a state-imposed remedy, yet the immediate adverse effects on the contract breaker could be very much the same.

In a well-designed system, an element of adversity must be combined with various formal features and other complementary components before the unit can qualify as a state-imposed sanction or a state imposed remedy. First of all, the overall form of a state sanction or remedy provides that the specific adversity it entails can generally be authoritatively imposed only by state officials (often only judges), and not by the party harmed. The rights of a harmed citizen to impose a sanction or to exercise a remedial power of "self-help" are severely limited in all Western legal systems with which I am familiar. For example, the family of a victim of a criminal assault cannot lawfully lock up the wrongdoer in a room, nor can the victim of even a serious breach of contract lawfully confiscate property of the wrongdoer against the latter's will. Also, a victim cannot lawfully hire another private party to "impose a sanction" for an offense, or "exact a remedy" by way of taking the wrongdoer's assets as compensation. Such acts would be unlawful and illegitimate. The overall form – the purposive systematic arrangement of an enforcive functional unit – typically provides that the adversity of a state sanction or a state remedy can only be imposed by authorized officials of the state. The roles of such officials are themselves defined and organized by institutional form.

Second, the overall form of a state-imposed sanction or remedy requires a recognized *legal* rationale for such adverse official action. The act of locking someone up in a room, or the act of taking someone's property is certainly adverse to the party affected and without an appropriate legal rationale, it would be lawless and illegitimate, even though imposed by officials of the state. In a well-ordered society under the rule of law, not even the state can act adversely to inhabitants without a legal rationale. The imposition of what is truly a legal sanction, remedy, or other enforcive device thus cannot be simply an "act of hostility" toward an individual, as Hobbes put it.[7] The lawful imposition of a state sanction or remedy presupposes a rationale to the effect that the individual to be adversely affected has in some relevant way been *legally errant.* The overall forms of such discrete enforcive units as sanctions and remedies share the feature that state-imposed adversity of this nature can only be an *authorized response* to a party's wrongful action or other failure to fulfill a recognized legal duty arising under a rule, a contract, or other law.

Third, the overall form of a sanction, remedy, or other enforcive unit also generally has the further feature that the core adversity involved is characteristically delimited. It is not amorphous, open-ended, ill-defined, or otherwise indeterminate. That is, in general this adversity is not unlimited constraint, arbitrary confiscation of any amount of property, or the like. Nor, generally is the adversity to be disproportionate to the wrong. The adversity of the duly designed sanction, remedy, or other enforcive unit is characteristically determinate and proportionate. The purposive systematic arrangement of the unit – its overall form – defines, specifies, circumscribes, and de-limits the adversity to be imposed, in advance of any such imposition. Without this constraining feature, the adversity could easily, in the hands of state officials, become an illegitimate and lawless instrument of arbitrariness, injustice, inhumanity, or even tyranny. Developed Western systems generally do not recognize an uncircumscribed element of "state coercive power" that may be freely imposed adversely. With one general exception to be considered later, a developed system has only well-designed highly organized sanctions, remedies, and other enforcive units that are duly defined, duly circumscribed and duly de-limited in scope.

Fourth, another feature of the overall form of an enforcive functional unit is that those authorized to impose the adversity involved can, in general, only do so pursuant to due process of law, which is itself defined and organized through form.

---

[7] T. Hobbes, *supra* n. 5, at 204. See also J. Bentham, *Of Laws in General*, 134 (Athlone Press, London, 1970).

Section Three: The Sanction of State Imprisonment for Criminal Offenses

In general, a sanction, remedy, or other enforcive unit can be imposed against the will of a person only after a public proceeding, usually in a court of law, in which the alleged criminal or civil wrongdoer has a fair opportunity to contest the law and the facts as to the occurrence of the asserted wrong and to contest the law and the facts as to the appropriateness of any given sanction or remedy.

Fifth, the foregoing features of the overall forms of enforcive functional units and their complementary material or other components are also generally prescribed in reinforcive and other rules in due form laid down publicly in advance. This is not to say that these rules are explicitly formulated in the language of form. They seldom are. Still, to be rules at all, they must take the overall form of rules. It is also difficult to believe that enforcive legal units could effectively exist and operate if not provided for in writing (or print), a formal feature.

Each discrete enforcive sanction, remedy, or other device, then, takes its own overall form, with the foregoing constituent features. The above five features of the overall form of an enforcive sanction, remedy, or other device, together satisfy the general definition of overall form as refined to fit such a unit. Again, this general definition was introduced and defended in Chapter Two. Each discrete enforcive unit is thus purposively and systematically arranged and has its own complementary material or other components. Some features of this overall form are also independently recognized in our lexicons as formal. This is true, for example, of the feature of authoritativeness.[8] It is true of the feature definitively circumscribing each unit.[9]

SECTION THREE: THE SANCTION OF STATE IMPRISONMENT FOR CRIMINAL OFFENSES

Apart from punishment by death, the most drastic enforcive phenomenon in developed Western societies is the punitive sanction of imprisonment for the commission of a serious crime. Such imprisonment may be for life or for a shorter term. The judicial imposition of imprisonment of offenders, duly publicized, not only punishes the offenders but also makes the general threat of such imprisonment credible as a deterrent, and limits the capacity of the persons to commit further offenses during the period. Publicizing the proceedings has a legitimizing effect, as well.

The sanction may be said to *enforce* the relevant criminal prohibition – the legal precept at stake. For this, and for other reasons, the sanction as a whole is entitled to some credit for the realization of security, justice and other ends and values at stake. The overall form of the sanction, along with its material and

---

[8] *The Oxford English Dictionary*, vol. 6, at "form," I.11.a (2nd ed., J. Simpson and E. Weiner eds., Clarendon Press, Oxford, 1989).

[9] *Id.*, vol. 6, at "formal," A.5.

other components must share in this credit. Study of this form also advances understanding of the sanction.

Imprisonment for a serious crime presupposes many major varieties of functional legal units: institutional, preceptual, methodological, and others. Furthermore, it is integrated and coordinated with other functional units within that overall operational technique I have denominated the penal technique, a subject treated in Chapter Ten.

The discrete functional unit of imprisonment for serious crime is to be analyzed in terms of its overall form and the constituent features of that form. It is also to be analyzed in terms of complementary material and other components. These components include all resources required for imposition of the adversity involved, that is, the duly circumscribed deprivation of liberty: prisons, prison officials, various material resources such as weapons and other equipment required by prison officials, food and water to provide sustenance for prisoners, and so on. The overall form of this unit defines, organizes, and renders intelligible the sanction of imprisonment for crime. There is, then, far more to this functional legal unit than merely the "sheer force" of state prison walls, armed guards, and other material components.

Generally, a state sanction could not even exist without being purposively defined and organized as such – without taking a duly designed overall form with constituent features. This is one major variety of credit due to form, and this claim is not empirical in nature. The overall form of the sanction of imprisonment for serious offenses in developed Western societies generally consists of well-defined and duly organized *provision* for judicially ordered deprivation of the liberty of a convicted offender at the hands of authorized state officials within quarters maintained by the state. The constituent features of this purposive systematic arrangement – of this overall form – typically provide for:

(1) the organized adversity involved, that is, duly circumscribed, determinate, and proportionate deprivation of liberty for a period of time pursuant to court order,

(2) of a person who has violated a nonminor criminal statute,

(3) who has been duly convicted thereof in a public proceeding in a court of law, after fair opportunity of the alleged offender to contest (or waive) the officially asserted applicable law and facts found,

(4) who has been duly sentenced to prison pursuant to court order after a sentencing hearing in public at which the offender has had the opportunity to contest (or waive) the lawfulness and appropriateness of the penalty, and with,

(5) the foregoing being subject to appeal for errors of law or fact,

(6) the foregoing being prescribed in rules in due form and content.

Section Three: The Sanction of State Imprisonment for Criminal Offenses   291

The overall form of the sanction of imprisonment is thus systematically arranged. The founding purpose informing this overall form is that of defining, organizing, and bringing such a discrete sanctioning unit into being so that it can, in turn, serve its further purposes. With a duly organized arrangement for imprisonment of offenders in existence, the imposition of this sanction in particular cases serves the further immediate purpose of enforcing criminal law rules for the breach of which sanctions are provided. Without the reality of, and without the threat of, such punishment, the ultimate and more external purposes that criminal law and its sanctions are to serve would be in dire jeopardy. These purposes include reinforcement of the general sense that certain conduct is wrong, general deterrence of wrongdoers, preservation of the sense of security against murder, violence, theft, fraud, and so forth, and encouragement of citizens to exercise the freedoms of daily life in a well-ordered society.

Another purpose of the foregoing systematic arrangement of the discrete sanction of imprisonment is one that may also be considered ultimate and external, namely, that of publicly demonstrating in particular cases the legality, legitimacy, and justice of any state sanctioned incarceration of those particular individuals so imprisoned. Here, provision within the arrangement for various procedures such as public hearings, and for publicly announced imposition of the penalty, serves such purposes. This feature of overall organized form and complementary content limits and regulates the exercise of the coercive power of the state to restrict the freedom of citizens through imprisonment. Here, form also serves general values of the rule of law.

Other purposes of the overall form and complementary content of the sanction may be considered internal in the sense that they are to be realized primarily through the workings of the sanction itself during the time it is being imposed. Among the important internal purposes served here are: vindicative justice for the victim of the crime and for relatives of the victim, the meting out of just deserts to the offender including not only the deprivation of freedom but also the moral opprobrium attaching to the conviction, incapacitation of the offender, and rehabilitation of the offender. Again, the very realization of such purposes depends (1) on the availability of the sanction, which is itself, in part, dependent on form, and (2) on the correctness of the imposition of the sanction, which in turn, is partially dependent on the formal features listed above. Form that is not well-designed simply cannot sufficiently serve the foregoing purposes.

Again, a sanctioning unit, like all discrete legal units, is not independently functional. It functions within, and is dependent upon, that overall operational technique of a system of law identified in this book as the "penal technique."[10] The imposition of a criminal sanction pursuant to this technique presupposes that a

---

[10] See *infra* Chapter Ten, Section Six for a general account of this technique.

crime has been committed. Crimes are prohibited by rules and, as we have seen, rules take a distinctive preceptual form. The formal features of rules, studied in Chapters Five and Six, define and organize the contents of many laws, including criminal prohibitions. Without these prohibitions, the sanction of imprisonment for crime could not be imposed. Furthermore, a legislative institution typically enacts the rules that prohibit crimes, and we have seen how due form is required for the very existence of a legislature. We have also seen how the formal procedural, structural, and other features of a legislature can contribute to the quality and efficacy of the form and content of statutory rules generally, including those prohibiting crimes.

In addition, imposition of the sanction of imprisonment pursuant to that overall legal modus operandi here called the penal technique presupposes the existence of judicial institutions, which must also be defined and organized through form. Courts could not exist without duly designed form. In developed Western societies generally, only an authorized judge can order the sanction of forcible deprivation of liberty for commission of a crime. Also, this can, in general, only be done after a procedural determination by fair process that the offender has, in fact, committed an imprisonable offense, and only after opportunity for a fair sentencing hearing at that.[11] In order for a person to function as a judge (or a juror), the relevant features of judicial institutional form must be present, including the compositional, the jurisdictional, and the procedural. Insofar as these features are well-designed, they will contribute to the quality of the processes involved and the quality of the exercise of judgment by judges and any jurors. Given the judicial role in the penal technique, the features of overall judicial form with their complementary material and other components, take on major importance here, too. Furthermore, form facilitates judicial fact-finding in many ways. The more definite the basic criminal prohibition in question – a formal feature – the more focused the fact-finding. When the procedural feature of the form of a court is well designed to provide for the testing of proferred evidence, the truth is more likely to emerge.

The quality and efficacy of the procedural feature of overall judicial form has special importance here. When well-designed, procedure assures fair notice, fair opportunity of the accused to defend, and fair determination of issues of guilt or innocence. In a well-formed and otherwise rational sentencing process, due consideration will be given to such factors as the nature and circumstances of the offense, the history and circumstances of the defendant, the seriousness of the offense, what is required for just punishment including consistency with similar past dispositions, deterrent efficacy of proposed sentences, and rehabilitation of the offender. How sentencing discretion is structured is itself a formal feature that can contribute to rational exercise of this discretion.

---

[11] In the American federal system, see 18 U.S.C. §3553 (2000).

Section Three: The Sanction of State Imprisonment for Criminal Offenses 293

The functional legal unit of punishment by imprisonment is sometimes simplistically reduced to such complementary material components as armed guards, prison walls, and various other state symbols of "sheer force." Yet, imprisonment is better viewed not as "force-backed" law, but as "form-backed" and "law-backed" force.[12] Due form lawfully backed, tends to secure legitimacy here. It is true that armed guards and high prison walls are necessary. Yet to be legitimate, even the guards must be duly authorized, and the prison facility duly authorized. As I have explained, various features of form define and organize the whole of this punitive functional unit, and rules, which take their own overall form, prescribe imprisonment. This does not mean this enforcive unit is reducible to such rules. A duly functioning prison is not a rule, or even a set of rules.

Study of the overall form of the sanction of imprisonment is required to advance understanding of the nature of this enforcive functional unit as a whole. Form defines, organizes, and renders intelligible the make-up, unity, instrumental capacity, and distinct identity of the unit. A form-skeptic might object that what I call the very core of the overall form of this sanctioning unit – the organized provision for imprisonment of offenders – is in truth, not formal at all. According to the skeptic, this core should be characterized as nonformal, along with the related material components such as the prison-facilities themselves, the required personnel such as jailers and the judges, the necessary material resources for the maintenance of the facilities, and the provision of food and medical supplies for the imprisoned. Here, the form-skeptic errs in reducing overall form to complementary material components. The form-skeptic also fails to see the proper place of the deep and indelible imprints of formal features on these components and on imprisonment as such.

What the skeptic considers to be the "core" of the phenomenon – the *definitively organized provision* for imprisonment of offenders – is really the core of the overall form of the functional unit as a whole. Without this organized provision for authorized imprisonment, the form of the unit could not exist, and, as I have demonstrated, without this form, the functional unit of imprisonment could not exist. The form of any such unit must have purposes that inform its systematic arrangement. Here, the founding purpose is that of bringing into being the organized provision for authorized imprisonment of offenders. The resulting purposive systematic arrangement qualifies as the core of this overall form. We can easily imagine the complementary material and other components "standing alone." A building with people in it being watched over by armed persons could exist, but that would hardly make it a state prison. A state prison is not a pre-legal or an a-legal phenomenon. It requires an overall organized form. This form providing

---

[12] See also, R. Collingwood, *The New Leviathan*, 180 (Rev. ed., D. Boucher ed., Clarendon Press, Oxford, 1992), where this is said to be the greatest discovery (a discovery by Hobbes it is said) in political science since Aristotle's many discoveries.

for authorized imprisonment of offenders, together with complementary material or other components, makes up the whole of the functional legal unit of state-sanctioned imprisonment.

Let us imagine that state officials capture an individual, even one who has admittedly committed a crime, and merely lock him up in a room and feed him from time to time. Without the defining and organizing features of overall form described above, and their due operation, such state intervention in the life of an individual could not qualify as lawful punishment by authorized imprisonment. Unless the detention is somehow justified as temporary pending further legitimate investigation or proceedings, this detention could only be naked coercion, and in Hobbes' terms, an "act of hostility." Any person so held might consider himself or herself to be imprisoned, but this still could not be legitimate state imprisonment.

My account of overall form is not so broad that it swallows up the material or other components of the unit and thus obliterates the distinction between form and these other components. Although I classify the foregoing "core" of organized provision for authorized imprisonment of an offender as a matter of form, much remains that consists of material or other components of the whole, including the prison facilities, necessary material resources, and various personnel, including jailors.

Even if we were to take an extremely narrow view of the overall form of state-imposed imprisonment and thus exclude from it the core organization of the unit, namely the definitively organized provision for lawful deprivation of the freedom of an offender, much scope for form would still remain. There would still be the formal features of all the rules that govern imposition of the sanction, many of which have contents that in effect prescribe the form of the sanction. There would also be the compositional, jurisdictional, structural, procedural, methodological, and other institutional features of judicial form. And more.

Plainly, then, here we have, firstly, the realization of the founding purpose of bringing into existence duly organized provision for imprisonment of offenders. This is not to be credited solely to material or other components such as the existence of buildings called prisons, to persons wearing badges who operate the facilities, or the like. Nor should these components get all the credit for the realization of more immediate and internal purposes to be served thereby including legitimate incapacitation, punishment, and rehabilitation. Nor should these components get all the credit for the realization of more ultimate and external purposes such as general deterrence, preservation of security in the community, and encouragement of citizens to exercise freedoms of daily life. Nor should applicable legal rules get all the credit here. Rather, much credit must also go to the overall form that defines and organizes the functional legal unit of state-imposed imprisonment for offenses. This overall form and complementary material and other components, comprise the whole of the unified, intelligible, and rationally

Section Four: Remedies for the Private Wrong of Breach of Contract

justified functional unit of judicially ordered imprisonment of offenders. Again, the imprints of form here on the whole are deep and indelible.

This overall form, in combination with complementary material and other components, marks the fundamental difference between this legitimate phenomenon on the one hand, and mere acts of state hostility through forcible deprivation of liberty of individuals on the other. This legitimate functional unit is duly defined and organized as an operational whole through form. Without the deep and indelible imprints of form on the whole unit, the resulting constraint of offenders certainly could not be legitimate. Moreover, this constraint would very likely be amorphous, open-ended, arbitrary, disproportionate, and inefficacious. The whole might even so lack determinateness that it could not even be identified as a discrete functional legal unit at all.

Without form, the discrete sanction of imprisonment simply could not exist. With well-designed form, much credit must go to form itself for the efficacy of this sanction. Form is thus a major avenue for understanding the sanction itself.

Despite the emphasis here on official action, it should not be assumed that the effectiveness of the sanction of imprisonment is in no way dependent on private action. Private parties, by their own actions, may deter crimes. They may also alert police to actual or prospective crimes. They may testify as witnesses, and more.

Beyond the foregoing, some legal systems also authorize the exercise of somewhat less well-defined and more open-ended coercive powers of police and other state officials. Some of these powers are to take actions to pre-empt prospective behavior such as terrorist acts, which if allowed to occur, would ultimately be criminal. Such generalized coercive power is not itself reducible to, or equivalent to, the power of officials and the judiciary to impose discrete sanctions for crimes actually committed. Yet, even here, the purposes for which such pre-emptive power may be exercised are, in most developed Western systems, largely confined and limited to the pre-emption of those prospective activities which, if they were ultimately to occur, would constitute discrete crimes for which discrete sanctions could be imposed.

SECTION FOUR: REMEDIES FOR THE PRIVATE WRONG OF BREACH OF CONTRACT

There are many types of private wrongs, including breaches of contract and various torts or "delicts," all of which can cause serious harm to others. Developed Western legal systems provide remedies for such private wrongs, and these remedies are available to enforce the law of contract, the law of tort, and other law. Here, I focus illustratively on the standard remedy for breach of contract consisting of a court judgment for a monetary sum to be paid by the contract breaker as compensatory damages for losses caused. This remedy may be said to implement separate legal rules to the effect that a party who enters a valid contract incurs a legal duty to perform it, and must pay damages for the losses.

This remedy for contract breach, unlike imprisonment for criminal offenses, is not essentially punitive, but is instead compensatory.[13] In developed Western systems, this remedy requires the contract breaker to pay a court judgment for money, and also confers power on the state, in effect, to compel such payment from assets of the contract breaker if that person does not voluntarily pay the judgment. Unlike conviction and imprisonment of a party who has committed a crime – processes undertaken and administered by state officials – the aggrieved party to a broken contract must take steps to secure a court judgment against the contract breaker for monetary compensation. In many systems, the aggrieved party must seek enforcement of any unpaid judgment against assets of the judgment debtor.

In developed Western societies, just as the overwhelming majority of private parties voluntarily choose to abide by the rules of the criminal law, so too, the overwhelming majority of contracting parties voluntarily perform their contractual obligations. In light of contract terms, the parties themselves construct reasons for determinate action thereunder and voluntarily act to perform. As already explained in Chapter Seven, the definitive overall form of a contract, and the form of a methodology of contract interpretation, enable those who have entered a duly formulated contract to construct pre-emptive reasons to take the determinate actions that constitute contract performances. Major credit is due such forms when contracts are voluntarily performed, as is usually the case.

Such voluntary performance occurs because each contracting party thereby gets what was bargained for from the other, or because this preserves reputations for being reliable, or because of fear of criticism of contract breach in the particular instance, or because of a general sense of legal obligation, of a sense of justice, of moral duty, or because of some combination of the foregoing. Some of these factors are legal and some are not, yet form figures directly or indirectly in all. For example, the overall form of a bilateral contract defines and organizes the very legal obligations that the parties incur in the first place.[14] If the terms of contracts are well-formulated in accord with due definiteness and other formal features, the obligations to perform under these terms will be readily determinable. Formal definitiveness thus sharpens the sense of legal obligation, sharpens the sense of moral obligation, affords a firm basis for claims of rights to performance on the part of each party, and provides well-focused standards for criticizing a prospective or actual breach. Here, the overall form of a bilateral contract, especially the formal features of definiteness, and of mode of expression, as manifest in the explicitness and clarity of contract language, shares credit with non-formal economic,

---

[13] Or, in some systems, the remedy may call for the defendant to perform specifically, on pain of being in contempt of court.

[14] See *supra* Chapter Seven.

Section Four: Remedies for the Private Wrong of Breach of Contract 297

moral, and other motivations that explain why so many performances voluntarily occur.

A judicially awarded judgment that a contract breaker must pay money to an aggrieved party to compensate for losses caused serves a variety of purposes. The founding purpose informing the overall form of this general remedy is simply that of bringing this type of remedial functional unit into being. Particular such remedies are designed to serve further immediate purposes. The first type of such purpose served is that of inducing the recalcitrant party to perform. The general threat of a judicial grant of a particular remedy against a prospective contract breaker is a factor that can induce performance in some proportion of instances. A particular judicial grant of the remedy renders the general threat credible in other instances and affords just compensation to the aggrieved party for losses sustained from the breach. The standing availability of such a remedy also facilitates settlement of contract disputes by the parties themselves. Insofar as contract duties are well-defined, a feature of form, this, too, facilitates settlement. Contracting parties are far more likely to settle their disputes on their own in the shadow of a likely court remedy than if no such remedy were available.

Without the threat, and the actuality, of judicial remedies of damages for breach of contract, further more ultimate purposes could not be satisfactorily realized. These further purposes include the freedom of choice that the right to contract recognizes and implements, private planning for, and the just satisfaction of, individual wants through contract, the efficient allocation of resources through markets, and private autonomy generally.

Still further more ultimate purposes are served through the discrete and well-designed overall form and complementary material and other components of the remedial phenomenon of damages for breach, and through the law and the procedures governing this remedy. One such purpose is that of securing an orderly process for awarding damages. The power to grant such a remedy is confined to the state acting through the judiciary and generally precludes private self-help by the aggrieved party to grab assets of the breaching party as compensation. Among other things, such self-help would be freighted with potential for violence and injustice. In all of the foregoing ways, the general values of the rule of law are served, as well. Fundamental political values of legitimacy, freedom, justice, and security of contractual expectations are served, too.

The realization of the foregoing purposes through such judicial judgments awarding damages is not to be credited solely to material or other components of the remedy, that is, to the existence of valuable assets owned by the breacher that may be used to pay compensatory damage claims, to personnel called judges who enter judgments for damages, to administrative officials who may seize some of these assets to pay the claimant's damages, to buildings to office such personnel, or the like. Much credit must also go here to the defining and organizing effects of the overall form of the damages remedy. This overall form and its constituent

298   Forms of Sanctions and Remedies

features, as combined with complementary material and other components, is
what marks the difference between the legitimate functional unit of judicially
awarded and enforced contract damages and the naked grabbing of a breaching
person's assets by the person aggrieved by a contract breach. This functional unit
is duly defined and organized through form. This, too, is not an empirical claim
to credit for form. Without the defining and organizing features of overall form
here, no such remedy could exist at all. Here, too, the imprints of form on material
and other components of the remedy are deep and indelible. Much credit must
also go to the institutional and related forms of functional units such as courts
that also figure in provision of this remedy.

The absence of a well-formed damages remedy for losses due to contract
breaches would certainly make contracting far more precarious. Not only would
aggrieved parties have to swallow more losses due to breaches, but some contracting parties would be forced to expend further resources on security deposits and
other costly devices to enhance the likelihood of performance in many circumstances.

The remedy of a coercive judicial judgment against the breaching party requiring that party to pay damages compensating for losses due to breach is available
in all developed Western systems. This remedy is not a free-standing functional
unit that operates independently of all other legal units. It presupposes institutional, contractual, methodological, and preceptual units. It is integrated and
coordinated with these other types of functional units within the overall operational technique I denominate the private-ordering technique.[15] This technique,
like the penal technique, incorporates and integrates in its own distinctive way
most of the major functional units studied so far in this book: institutions such
as legislatures and courts which make law, the rules and other varieties of law
so made, the very framework whereby private parties enter contracts, particular
valid contracts, interpretive and other methodologies, courts that grant remedies
for breach of contract in particular cases, and sheriffs and other officials who
enforce judgments pursuant to court order for money damages against assets of
the contract breaker to compensate for breach.

The constituent features of the overall form, that is, of the purposive systematic
arrangement of the standard judicial remedy of compensatory damages for breach
of contract, at least in most developed Western systems, may be summarized as
follows:

(1) the discrete organized adversity involved, that is, entry of a court judgment
     for a monetary sum,
(2) against the contract breaker,
(3) who has been duly adjudged by a court to be in breach of a valid contract,

---

[15] See *infra* Chapter Ten, Section Six, for a general account of this technique.

Section Four: Remedies for the Private Wrong of Breach of Contract

(4) for compensatory reparation of loss duly measured and proven in court to have been caused by the breach in the amount adjudged,

(5) such judgment, if not voluntarily paid, being enforceable by officials against assets of the contract breaker,

(6) the foregoing being provided for in reinforcive and other rules or other law appropriate in form and content, and subject to appeal for errors of law or fact.

Study of the overall form of the remedy of money damages for breach of contract is an essential avenue for advancing understanding of the very nature of this discrete enforcive functional unit as a whole. This form defines, organizes, and renders coherent and intelligible, the makeup, unity, instrumental capacity, and distinct identity of the damages remedy for breach of contract. The coercive capacity of the state, and the compensatory sums awarded, are essential material components. So, too, the required implementive personnel, and the assets of the contract breaker required to pay the damages award. Nevertheless, the overall form of this functional unit and the imprints of this form on provision of the remedy, are plainly entitled to a share of the credit for purposes realized through judicial grants of remedies, and through the standing availability of such remedies. Thus, there is far more here than the sheer force of the state and the assets of the contract breaker. Well-designed overall form – the well-organized provision of a damages remedy and its imprints – are major parts of what more there is.

I will now consider briefly the bearing of the institutional form of the remedy-granting court, and also of relevant preceptual and methodological form. In most Anglo-American systems, a judgment against the breaching party for monetary damages can only be granted by a judge. This can only be after the judge's determination (with or without a jury), in accord with substantive law and procedure and via applicable fact-finding and law-applying methodologies, that the breaching party committed an unexcused breach for which the law provides a remedy. Typically, this determination, too, may only be made after opportunity of the alleged contract breaker to contest the law and the facts as to breach and as to remedy.

Various rules govern the measurement of compensatory contract damages, and the breaching party typically has an opportunity in court to challenge the application of any such rule as well. Depending on the circumstances and the law, the aggrieved party may be entitled to: (1) damages measured by lost expectancy – those required to put the aggrieved party in the position that this party expected to have been in had the breaching party performed, or (2) damages measured by expenditures incurred by the aggrieved party in relying on the prospect of performance, or (3) damages measured by the amount of any benefit conferred by the aggrieved party on the other party, or (4) some combination of the foregoing.

Unlike the ends of criminal punishment, the ends of contract remedial law are, in general, not punitive. Rather, they are reparative. A breach of contract remedy that repairs the wrong is generally considered sufficient. The general assumption is that anything more would put the contracting party in a better position than this party would have been in had the contract been performed and, thus, unjustifiably provide a windfall. Form is of major importance here, too. If the terms of the expected contractual performance are not sufficiently definite, it will simply not be possible to measure lost expectancy.

Well-designed form defines and specifies the contours of the duty broken, and defines and organizes the remedies that would likely be granted in court. Form also defines and organizes the judicial institution itself. Disputing parties bargaining in the shadow of this institution and the likely remedies it would grant, can often resolve the matter voluntarily on their own. That is, the facts and the applicable law will be such that the parties will voluntarily settle their dispute out of court for any damages due.

The alleged breaching party may, however, choose to answer in court and defend against an aggrieved party's claim, and if proved liable for breach, only then pay damages. The contract damages remedy is also better viewed not as "force-backed" law, but as "form-backed" and "law-backed" force. Features of form define and organize the remedial unit as a whole. These features are prescribed to an extent in reinforcive rules that have their own formal features. The remedy of compensatory damages is not, however, reducible to these rules. This remedy is not itself a rule or even a set of rules. It is a discrete functional unit with its own form and material or other components, some of which are prescribed in rules, though not explicitly in such terms. Again, to be effective, many of these rules must be duly drafted, another feature of form.

In sum, the judicial award of a compensatory damages remedy for breach of contract takes an overall form and is thus systematically arranged to serve various purposes. This functional unit is dependent on institutional functional units such as courts and administrative entities, and presupposes the breach of an actual obligation arising from the phenomenon of a distinct contract. Despite this dependence upon and overlap with other legal units, the remedy of a compensatory damage award for breach of contract itself remains a circumscribed and relatively discrete type of unit.

Again, the form-skeptic may object that the foregoing analysis classifies too much here as formal. The skeptic may argue that the very core of what I here call the overall form of this functional legal unit, namely, the organized provision of judicially awarded damages against a contract breaker whose assets may, to the extent necessary, even be subjected to coercive confiscation by state officials to pay the judicial award, is not really formal at all. Rather, or so the skeptic may argue, this core is to be characterized as consisting essentially of material or other

Section Four: Remedies for the Private Wrong of Breach of Contract 301

components. That is, this core really consists of the contract breaker's assets, the judicial personnel, the courthouse, and the administrative officials who may be called upon to enforce a judgment against a contract breaker's assets. Again, there are answers to this objection similar to those set forth in answer to the parallel objection in regard to the sanction of imprisonment for a crime.

First, the purposively and systematically arranged character of this phenomenon – the *organized provision* for judicial imposition of a remedial duty on the contract breaker to pay damages – is, itself, the core of the overall form of this remedial unit. Without this organized core, the overall form of the unit of a damages remedy simply could not exist, and therefore the unit could not exist. This remedy is not a pre-legal or an a-legal phenomenon. This remedy taken as a whole is a creature of form, of material and other components, and of law. It is easy to imagine a promise that is broken thereby causing loss, and easy to imagine the possibility of an aggrieved party having some moral right to a sum of money from the promise breaker's assets as just reparation. Here we would have some putative ingredients of a damage remedy, but we would still not have organized provision of that functional unit as such. We would lack the required overall form – the purposive systematic arrangement of the unit as a whole. We would also lack the complementary material or other components of the unit, as duly organized with formal imprints, and would lack relevant rules and other law prescribing facets of the formal and the nonformal here.

Second, my account of overall form and its constituents here does not swallow up the material and other components, and thus obliterate the distinction between form and the nonformal. If the *organized provision* for the remedy of compensatory damages is classified, as I contend it should be, as a matter of form, much remains here that would still count as material or other components, including the parties to the contract, the assets of the contract breaker from which the compensatory sum is to be paid, the person of the judge entering a judgment for that sum, the sheer coercive power of the state, and still other components.

Again, even if we were to take a narrow view of the overall form of the functional unit of the contract damages remedy, and exclude the organized core, namely the provision for this remedy, we would still be left with much that qualifies as formal. We would be left with the formal features of all the rules that govern the remedy, many of which themselves have content prescribing form. We would also be left with the aforementioned compositional, jurisdictional, structural, procedural, methodological, and other features of judicial form. Thus, whether we take a narrow view of form and exclude the organized core of the unit, or take a broader view of form and include this core within the overall form itself (as we should), much of the unit is formal, and much credit goes to these formal facets both (1) for what study of them contributes to understanding by way of rendering the makeup, unity, instrumental capacity, and distinct identity of the functional unit coherent and intelligible, and (2) for what these formal facets contribute to the realization of the ends of the remedy of damages for breach of contract.

In addition to imprisonment for crimes and award of damages for breach of contract, legal systems "put teeth" in laws in still other important ways. A further such implementive unit is that of licensing and the revocation of licenses. This device and several others will be illustratively considered in Chapter Eleven. All such implementive units are integrated wholes that must be analyzed in terms of their forms, constituent features of these forms, and material or other elements, and also in terms of the contributions to the realization of various ends. In a well-designed system, all such enforcive units are relatively well-defined, discrete, and determinate and are, therefore, not amorphous or open-ended. Also, they can typically be invoked only against sufficiently well-defined wrongs.

PART THREE

THE OVERALL FORM OF
A LEGAL SYSTEM AND
ITS OPERATION

10 ∽ THE OVERALL FORM OF A LEGAL SYSTEM AS A WHOLE

"The concept of law includes . . . two elements; a system of *purposes*, and a system of their *realization*."
— R. von Jhering[1]

SECTION ONE: INTRODUCTION

The legal system of a developed Western society includes a vast heterogeneous array of what may be called "first-level" functional legal units. These varieties take their own overall forms, and have their own constituent formal features, with complementary material and other components. In Chapters Four through Nine, we considered a selection of major varieties of such functional units: institutions of a legislative nature, precepts consisting of rules, nonpreceptual law including contracts and certain property interests, interpretive methodologies, and sanctions and remedies. We now turn to how what I will call various "second-level" systematizing devices organize these first-level units (and still others) into the overall form of a legal *system* as a whole. The overall form of this resulting system is itself a highly complex purposive systematic arrangement designed to govern in accord with law a population typically residing in a geographically contiguous area. The system-wide material and other components of this complex system include this population and this geographical area. H. L. A. Hart stressed that such a system as a whole includes a characteristic minimum of first-level "primary" rules in due form with content protecting persons, property, and promises.[2] As I have emphasized, Hart should have stressed that the first level here also characteristically includes many other major varieties of functional legal units besides rules.

The major varieties of first-level functional units in a developed Western system consist of all of the various units identified in Chapters Four through Nine of this

[1] R. von Jhering, *Law As a Means to an End*, 56 (I. Husic trans., Boston Book Co., Boston, 1913).
[2] H. L. A. Hart, *The Concept of Law*, 193–200 (2nd ed., Clarendon Press, Oxford, 1994).

305

book, and many others. A partial list is as follows:

(1) arrangements for the election or appointment of legislators, administrators, and judges;
(2) a legislature or legislatures;
(3) an executive body, administrative agencies, and other public entities;
(4) courts;
(5) private entities such as corporations, partnerships, private persons, all with legal "personality," etc.;
(6) frameworks and processes for the creation and administration of contractual and other privately made law;
(7) interpretive, drafting, and other methodologies for creating and applying state-made law, and privately created law;
(8) state-made rules and other precepts of substantive law;
(9) state-made rules and other precepts of procedural law;
(10) contractual terms, property interests, and other privately created non-preceptual species of law;
(11) sanctions, remedies, and other implementive devices;
(12) the institution of the family;
(13) a legal profession; and
(14) more.

Each of the foregoing varieties of first-level functional units takes its own overall form – its own purposive systematic arrangement, and has complementary material or other components. In the usual system, there are numerous instances of some varieties of first-level functional units such as substantive legal rules, contracts, and property interests. There are far fewer instances of certain other varieties of first-level units. For example, there may be only one legislature. In a well-organized system with a unitary jurisdiction, there will be only one interpretive methodology for statutes.

The vast first-level multiplicity and heterogeneity of discrete functional legal units can be readily explained. Most units have come into being over time in response to the highly varied and numerous tasks to be performed in the making and implementation of law. Neither law nor a legal *system* could be said to exist if the discrete functional units consisted of only one institution, or only one rule!

In preceding chapters, we have seen how even a seemingly simple functional legal unit such as a rule or a contract takes a complex overall form that defines and organizes its makeup and also unifies its formal features and complementary material or other components into a coherent whole with distinctive instrumental capacity. The unity of each first-level functional unit is one thing, and the second-level systematization of all such first-level units into a unified legal system is quite another.

Section One: Introduction

A mere heterogeneous array of numerous first-level functional units could not qualify as a legal *system*. Various formal second-level systematizing devices are required to organize instances of discrete first level units into the overall form of a legal system. One of the most important traditional problems of legal theory is that of providing an adequate account of how a legal system is systematized. In his relatively monistic account, H. L. A. Hart emphasized only one major second-level systematizing device, namely, the "rule of recognition," which purports to systematize first-level and other rules into a system. In the similar account of Hans Kelsen, the emphasis is on only one major second-level systematizing device, namely the "basic norm." Hart's rule of recognition and Kelsen's basic norm mainly specify criteria by reference to which first-level legal rules can be identified as valid laws of a given system.[3] For Hart and Kelsen, who conceived of first-level functional units as consisting essentially of regulative and reinforcive rules, and who largely applied an analysis oriented to the contents of applicable reinforcive rules to elucidate institutional units such as legislatures and courts, systematization is concerned mainly with how first-level rules become valid law of the system, and with how valid rules are prioritized when in conflict. In the form-oriented account I offer here, those discrete first-level functional units consisting of rules are systematized in other important ways besides those which result from satisfying criteria of validity specified in a "rule of recognition" or a "basic norm." For example, such units are also integrated within operational techniques which take distinctive forms. In the account I offer, first-level functional units also consist of far more than rules, and these other units are duly systematized as well. For example, first-level functional units of an institutional nature such as legislatures and courts are not reduced to reinforcive rules, and are duly systematized in accord with various devices, such as centralization and hierarchical ordering.

Various formal second-level systematizing devices unify diverse first-level functional units into the coherent whole of an operational legal system. Study of these devices can advance understanding of the systematic nature of a legal system – a fundamental formal characteristic. In Jhering's idiom, the effects of such formal systematizing devices account for the innermost essence of a *system* of law. To explicate these second-level systematizing devices and their effects, that is, the resulting systematized features of a legal order, is to advance understanding of how first-level functional units are unified into a system, and of what is systematic about a legal system.

---

[3] H. L. A. Hart, *supra* n. 2, at 95–8. See also H. Kelsen, *Introduction to the Problems of Legal Theory*, 55–64 (B. Paulson and S. Paulson, trans., Clarendon Press, Oxford, 1992); H. Kelsen, *General Theory of The Law and State*, Chapters 10 and 11 (A. Wedberg, trans., Harvard University Press, Cambridge, 1945). Hart and Kelsen would, in my terms, also see major deficiencies in a mere "regime of instances of first-level functional units."

In nearly all of the subsequent sections of this chapter, my general approach will be as follows. I will first sketch a hypothetical state of affairs in which selected first-level functional units are unsystematized in some important way because a required second-level systematizing device is assumed to be absent. I will then introduce that device and show how it goes far to systematize the relevant first-level units. I will then explicate the systematizing effect of the device – the resulting systematized feature – which, in turn, comprises a complex feature of the overall form of a legal system. The main second-level systematizing devices to be considered are:

(1) the centralization and hierarchical ordering of legislatures, courts, administrative bodies, and other entities operating *within* their own jurisdictional spheres, i.e., systematization of such first-level institutions that make law, apply law, render lawful decisions, and conduct other legal functions;

(2) specification of systematic priorital relations *as between* first-level legislative, judicial, administrative and other jurisdictional spheres in (1), thereby also specifying how general types of conflicts between otherwise valid rules, between other law, and between official and other actions are to be resolved;

(3) codification, consolidation, or other continuing systematization of first-level rules and other law, in one field after another, into coherently ordered bodies of law;

(4) adoption of *uniform* interpretive, drafting, and other first-level methodologies;

(5) allocation of coordinated and thus systematically ordered judicial and other authority to impose first-level sanctions, to grant first-level remedies, or to bring into play other first-level enforcive units;

(6) the special combination, integration, and coordination of required first-level units within five systematic operational techniques for the creation and application of law; and

(7) the law-like functioning of each operational technique in (6) as systematically specified by second-level principles of the rule of law.

The foregoing systematizing devices are all formal. Each in its own way purposively arranges, and thus systematizes, discrete first-level functional units that as we have seen, all take their own forms. Each device also depends in part on rules, and rules take their own form as well. Each also orders relations between parts within larger wholes, and thus is structurally formal. The systematizing effects of these devices together define and organize the overall form of a legal system, as I will explain.

No single one of the above systematizing devices alone systematizes the whole legal system. Indeed, contrary to certain claims of Hart and Kelsen, no single device whether it be a "rule of recognition" or a "basic norm," or an analogous

Section One: Introduction

device can begin to account for the systematized character of a whole legal system. Rather, the effects of each device, above, merely systematize a complex facet of the whole. Together, the devices severally (and synergistically) systematize the whole, thereby largely accounting for its overall unity and distinct identity *as a system*.

As a result of the systematizing effects of each device, a highly complex, yet duly systematized feature of the legal system comes into being. Law-making and law-applying institutions and entities operating within the same jurisdictional spheres are centralized and hierarchically ordered. The relations between institutions and entities operating in different jurisdictional spheres are generally prioritized. General types of conflicts between otherwise valid rules, other law, and official actions are thereby resolved. Discrete bodies of valid law are codified, consolidated, or otherwise duly ordered. Interpretive and other methodologies are rendered more or less uniform within the relevant jurisdiction or jurisdictions. Exclusive authority to impose sanctions and grant remedies is coherently assigned. Various first-level functional units are duly combined, integrated, and coordinated within complex operational techniques, which in turn operate in law-like fashion in accord with principles of the rule of law. As we will see, various features of the highly complex overall form of a legal system result from the effects of systematizing devices.

As I will explain, the absence of the systematizing effects of any one of the foregoing second-level systematizing devices would have major adverse consequences. For example, without centralization and hierarchical ordering of institutions, the legislators, judges, officials, and others in a system could not know the scope of their jurisdictional roles, and addressees of the law could not know what counts as valid law of the system.

Without duly designed formal second-level systematizing devices, the ends and values to be achieved through a legal system simply could not be sufficiently realized. The credit due to appropriate systematizing form here is therefore profound and wide-ranging. This credit extends to far more than, as Hart argued, clearing up uncertainty, facilitating legal change, and remedying inefficiency.[4] Hart is hardly the only legal theorist who failed to address and to give due credit to the effects of the diverse second-level devices (1) for the resulting systematized features of the overall form of a system of law as a whole and (2) for the extent to which these systematized features in turn contribute to the realization of ends and values.

I will now take up the principal systematizing devices and their effects in developed Western systems, although I do not claim that these devices are identical in all systems or have identical systematizing effects in all systems. Overall systematization is a complex matter of degree in particular systems, and some systems are rather more fully systematized than others. A major version of each one of the second-level systematizing devices to be treated here is, however, be found in each developed Western system. Prior to treating each device and the resulting

---

[4] H. L. A. Hart, *supra* n. 2, at 91–96.

feature of the overall form of the system deriving from effects of each device, it is useful to identify the devices and the major systematized features that result from deployment of each device as follows:

First-level functional units	Second-level formal systematizing devices	Resulting systematized feature of overall form of system as a whole
1. Legislative, judicial, and administrative institutions, and contractual and other private-ordering entities within their own jurisdictional spheres	**1.** Within each type of jurisdictional sphere, e.g., legislative, judicial, administrative, contractual, and other private-ordering, etc., the ultimate authority of law-making and law-applying institutions and entities involved is centralized and ordered hierarchically	**1.** A centralized hierarchical order of ultimate authority *within* each jurisdictional sphere – legislative, judicial, administrative, contractual, and other private-ordering spheres
2. Institutional and other entities systematized within jurisdictional spheres, as result of devices in 1. above, but not yet systematized *as between* spheres	**2.** *As between* two or more jurisdictional spheres, the actions of an institution or entity in one sphere are prioritized over conflicting actions in another sphere or spheres	**2.** General prioritized relations *as between* jurisdictional spheres, thereby, among other things, resolving general types of conflicts between otherwise valid rules, other law, various official actions, and private actions
3. Valid individual rules and other related laws within discrete fields	**3.** Codification, consolidation, or other systematization of related rules and other laws within discrete fields	**3.** Duly unified bodies of related rules and other laws within discrete fields
4. Approaches to basic legal tasks such as interpretation and drafting	**4.** Adoption of methodologies for the conduct of interpretive and other recurrent legal tasks susceptible of methodological regimentation	**4.** Uniformity of interpretive and other methodologies within relevant spheres
5. Sanctions, remedies, and other enforcive devices	**5.** Conferral on courts, among the institutions and entities of the system, of final authority to impose coercive sanctions or remedies for violations of law or legal wrongs	**5.** Legitimate and coordinated institutional and other resort to sanctions, remedies, and other enforcive devices
6. All the foregoing and other relevant first-level functional units, as required	**6.** Integration and coordination of units within a relevant basic operational technique, e.g., penal, grievance-remedial, administrative-regulatory, for creation and implementation of law	**6.** Units duly integrated and coordinated within operational techniques for creation and implementation of law
7. All the foregoing and other relevant first-level units, as required	**7.** Operational techniques are deployed to create and implement law, each in law-like fashion as defined and organized by principles of the rule of law	**7.** Coordinated operation of all techniques of the *system* in law-like fashion in accord with principles of the rule of law

Section Two: Systematization of Institutions and Entities 311

The founding purpose of the overall form of a legal system is simply that of bringing such a complex systematized whole into being. Each second-level systematizing device may be thought of as contributing a resultant feature, as above, that figures in the complex purposive systematic arrangement of this whole, that is, of the overall form of a legal system. In turn, this overall form of the systematized whole, its constituent features, and its material and other components, once in being, may be deployed to serve the purposes of a system of law.

Many Western legal systems have written constitutions. Depending on their form and content, these constitutions may include reinforcive rules prescribing systematization. For example, written constitutional rules may define the jurisdictional spheres of basic institutions such as legislatures, courts, and administrations, and prioritize the relations between these institutions. A written constitution is also a major mode of encapsulating fundamental law. Some encapsulation is necessary. If encapsulation is set forth in a written constitution, the effect is not merely a systematizing one; it also provides the legitimacy of fundamental law.

Before turning to more detailed treatment of formal systematizing devices and their effects on a legal system, a general caveat is in order. Legal systems, even developed Western ones, differ significantly in degrees of overall systematization. Perhaps no actual system could ever be fully systematized in every respect. If, for example, the rules of a system are generally tightly drawn in form and content, and if formal methodologies of interpretation and application are uniform and precisely specified, a system may not be very dependent on periodic external infusions of considerations of reason and value, at least in the short run. Other systems may be more open to such infusions and thus more adaptable to change as well. At the same time, these other systems may sacrifice some coherence and certainty of operation as well as some equality in the application of law over time. The overall form of a legal system can be structured either way, and there are gains and losses either way. Not all systems are equally open to change, either.

SECTION TWO: SYSTEMATIZATION OF INSTITUTIONS AND ENTITIES — CENTRALIZED AND HIERARCHICAL ORDERING *WITHIN* EACH MAIN TYPE OF JURISDICTIONAL SPHERE: LEGISLATIVE, JUDICIAL, ADMINISTRATIVE, AND PRIVATE-ORDERING

No developed Western legal system exists and operates through a single, multipurpose, institution or entity that performs all law-making, law-applying, and other functions. Nor could it. In all such systems there are diverse institutional units and other discrete entities at the first level. Each has one or more primary functions within its own jurisdictional sphere. For example, legislatures mainly legislate, although they also may select the government of the day, approve budgets, conduct administrative oversight, approve executive appointments, and do other things, too. Administrative agencies mainly administer, though they may engage in rule-making and even in versions of adjudication. Courts mainly adjudicate, although in the course of this, they administer and create law. Private entities, including individuals, and corporate bodies, create and perform contracts and other private ordering arrangements. The intrinsic requirements of these diverse primary functions, and the advantages of a complex division of legal labor in which differently formed institutions and entities specialize in the discharge of different functions, largely account for the number and varied nature of legal institutions and other entities at the first level.

This multiplicity and differentiation of institutions and entities is characteristic of developed Western legal systems, and serves numerous purposes, including: law-making fecundity, efficiency, policy-efficacy, expression and implementation of democratic will, freedom and free choice, legitimacy, rationality, and the rule of law. This very first-level multiplicity and differentiation of institutions and entities requires systematization in order to be effective. Only through required internal formal design and the effects of second-level systematizing devices can such first-level phenomena be coherently organized into an array of institutions and entities capable of operating together effectively. The unifying contributions of form here are fundamental, and often taken for granted.

I will begin with legislative institutions and will illustratively concentrate solely on law-making, though these units fulfill many other functions, and problems of coordination and priority arise with respect to all of these. Let us suppose several different legislatures were to exist at the first-level, with each adopting different laws, and thereby asserting legislative jurisdiction over the same persons in the same geographical territory with regard to the same matters. Such a state of affairs would be profoundly dysfunctional, and could hardly be characterized as systematized legislative law-making.[5] Officials and the laity could not know which of several different statutes on the same subject, adopted by different legislatures, they must follow. Officials and the laity would frequently be confronted with conflicting legal reasons for action under statutes emanating from these different bodies. Consequently, officials and the laity could not rely on any of these statutes, the policies or other contents embodied in these statutes could not be well served, and the rule of law could not prevail. Nor could democracy, for the democratic organs would conflict, and there would be no clear lines of accountability to the electorate for statutes adopted. Such a state of affairs would lack a system.

One possible second-level systematizing device for use here would simply be to abolish all the legislatures except one, and thereby centralize authority to create statutes in one legislature for the territory involved. A familiar variation on this

---

[5] A fundamental body of law aptly illustrative of such failures to systematize was the United States Articles of Confederation, which went into effect in 1781 and was later superceded by the U.S. Constitution.

Section Two: Systematization of Institutions and Entities 313

is to have one centralized legislature with superordinate jurisdiction over law-making and other affairs of general interest, and establish local legislatures with subordinate jurisdiction limited to local affairs. If there are several states or several discrete locales within a whole territory, another familiar variation is to set up one centralized and super-ordinate federal legislature having supreme jurisdiction over law-making and other matters deemed federal, with each state or designated locale within the federation also having its own single, yet subordinate, centralized legislature for its own nonfederal matters. In all this, private ordering through contract and other functional units is left to private entities.

The formal systematizing device that many developed Western legal systems rely on here consists of the centralization of ultimate legislative authority in a single legislature designated as supreme in the territory, with one or more of the foregoing duly subordinated "local" variations. This resulting feature of the overall form of the system as a whole thus systematically arranges the relations between legislative institutions within the system. Centralized hierarchical ordering, then, is one major type of formal systematizing device. Without it, the relations between multiple legislative institutions within a society could not be coherently systematized.

The foregoing problem of first-level institutional disunity that can arise from uncentralized and unsubordinated legislative institutions can arise with respect to institutions within the judicial sphere as well. It is hardly surprising that developed Western systems have, in similar fashion, established centralized and hierarchically ordered judicial institutions. If, for example, there were more than one court in the same territory resolving with finality identical legal issues in different ways, this would be highly dysfunctional and contrary to the rule of law. The resulting arrangement could not really qualify as a *system* in this sphere. It is familiar that, even in developed systems, lower courts in different locales within the same territory sometimes resolve disputes of the same type differently. When this occurs an appeal can be taken to a centralized higher court with authority for the entire territory. This court is, in effect, charged with overseeing the uniform application and development of case law throughout the territory. Though today entirely taken for granted, this is a feature of the overall form of the system as a whole, a feature resulting from the second-level systematizing device of centralized hierarchical ordering of ultimate judicial authority within the judicial sphere.

Similarly, and merely to continue illustratively with law-making and law-applying functions, if different administrators of various state agencies and officialdoms residing in different locales within the same territory were to create different regulations for similarly situated persons, or to apply the same law differently to different persons in similar circumstances, this would be profoundly dysfunctional and contrary to the rule of law. Again, some centralization and hierarchical ordering of ultimate administrative authority, with appeals within the administrative hierarchy (and further appeals to courts), is the typical second-level systematizing device used to resolve this problem. Although we take it for granted, the resulting effects of such a device comprise an indispensable feature of the overall form of the system as a whole.

The device of centralized hierarchical ordering of authority, then, is required for the systematization of institutional and other relations *within each main type of jurisdictional sphere.* Such first-level functional units are thus duly subordinated and coordinated, and the potential for operating in conflict greatly reduced. The resulting centralized hierarchical order is one necessary feature of the overall form of a legal system – of the purposive systematic arrangement of this complex whole. In this resulting order, relations between parts within a whole are thus systematized. The resulting systematization is therefore also structural, and hence formal in this standard usage, too.[6] In each of the legislative, judicial, and administrative jurisdictional spheres, the resulting centralized order is hierarchical in the sense that the highest central institution in a given jurisdictional sphere has superior and binding final authority in law-making and other functions over lower-level institutions in that same sphere: the superordinate legislature over subordinate legislatures, the superordinate court over subordinate courts, and the superordinate administrative body or official over subordinate such bodies or officials.

The systematizing device of centralized hierarchical ordering within a jurisdictional sphere usually requires the introduction or recognition of further parallel functional units at the second level, such as a centralized legislature above local ones, an appellate court above trial courts, and a highest administrative agency over lower ones.

There is also a separate sphere of private-ordering in which private persons and entities have power to make and apply contracts or create other private legal arrangements. Allocation of final authority between state institutions on the one hand, and private parties or entities on the other, is also required if the relations between these spheres are to be duly systematized. How this is done in different systems also embeds or reflects different concepts of the individual citizen.

In sum, if the first-level institutions or other functionaries within the same jurisdictional sphere – the legislative, the judicial, or the administrative, were not subjected to the second-level device of centralized and hierarchical ordering of ultimate authority, a legal *system* would be impossible. Here we see that the credit due form is not limited to form in first-level functional units. Credit is also due to form in further formal systematization, and in the further units that figure in this. As between functionaries in the same jurisdictional sphere, who has power

---

[6] *The Oxford English Dictionary,* vol. 6, at "form," I.5.a (2 nd ed., J. Simpson and E. Weiner eds., Clarendon Press, Oxford, 1989), hereinafter *OED; id.,* vol. 16, at "structure."

Section Three: Systematization *as between* Jurisdictional Spheres of Institutions 315

to do what, when, and how must be duly specified, and must be prescribed in rules, so far as feasible. However, such reinforcive rules could not even be drafted without first conceiving and settling upon the desired centralized and hierarchically ordered feature of the system. The rules adopted here (often constitutional in nature), must also have appropriate features of form, especially due prescriptiveness, completeness, generality, and definiteness.

Without the systematizing effects of centralized and hierarchically ordered authority, institutional actions within the same jurisdictional spheres could not be duly ranked and coordinated and thus would be far less predictable. Even what counts as the valid exercise of state power to make or apply law would be highly uncertain. With multiple institutional functionaries at the first level and nothing more, there could be no criteria for identifying valid law purportedly created within the legislative sphere, or within the judicial sphere, or within the administrative sphere. The laws within the same territory would almost certainly not be uniform in content or applied uniformly. Addressees could not know which of conflicting legal reasons for action arising under different laws would be binding. Policies could not be effectively adopted and served through law. General values of the rule of law could not be realized. Nor could fundamental political values such as legitimacy, democracy, and freedom.

In sum, centralized hierarchical ordering of ultimate authority, along with introduction or recognition of further required functional units at the second level, such as appellate courts within the judicial sphere, is a formal second-level systematizing device, and the resulting systematization is a necessary feature of the overall form of a legal system. We may call this resulting systematized feature the centralized hierarchical ordering of ultimate authority for institutions and entities operating within the same sphere. As we have said, this centralized hierarchical feature is also structural. It specifies relations between parts within the same sphere and is thus formal in this sense, too. Its effects on the whole legal order are deep and pervasive. What I assert here by way of credit due to form is not an empirical claim. It is a claim of necessity. Without this ordering, at least in substantial degree, a legal *system* simply could not exist. As we will see, however, much further formal systematization is also required, and much credit is due form for this, too.

SECTION THREE: SYSTEMATIZATION *AS BETWEEN* JURISDICTIONAL SPHERES OF INSTITUTIONS AND PRIVATE ENTITIES — PRIORITIZATION

In the preceding section, I assumed that, in the end, one institution either continuously existent or newly introduced – within each jurisdictional sphere – legislative, judicial, or administrative – at least has, by virtue of the second-level systematizing device of centralized hierarchical ordering, superordinate jurisdiction to make or to administer law binding on other bodies or entities within its own sphere. As a result, each such centralized institutional body has supreme authority within its own type of institutional sphere, so that the rules, rulings, decisions, and the like duly made by this body are valid and, thus, binding within its sphere. Thus, merely to focus on the law-making function, the statute law of a centralized and hierarchically ordered legislature would, so far as applicable, be valid and binding on all local legislatures. The case law of a supreme court would be valid and binding on all other courts within its sphere. Decisions of a supreme administrative entity would be valid and binding on all other administrators within its sphere. Similarly, private parties and other entities making and performing contracts and carrying out other private-ordering activities left to them by the system would have final authority in these matters.

An overall arrangement within each such institutional and other jurisdictional sphere that *merely* so provided, however, would still lack major systemic unity and would, therefore, be profoundly dysfunctional, and inimical to the rule of law and other values, as I will now explain. The systematization resulting merely from centralized hierarchical ordering of ultimate authority *within* each of the foregoing institutional and other spheres – legislative, judicial, administrative, and private ordering – important though this hierarchical ordering is, would still leave us without fundamental unity within the system as a whole. For example, there would still be no provision for resolution of conflicts arising *between* applicable laws, rulings, decisions, or the like *as adopted or made by two or more* institutions each of which operates within a *different* jurisdictional sphere. In the most extreme possibility, although the statutes adopted by a supreme centralized legislature would be binding on local legislatures, these statutes would, *without more*, not be binding on courts or administrators, given that these institutional functionaries operate within jurisdictional spheres different from the legislative. Similarly, although the precedents adopted by a centralized supreme court would be binding on lesser courts, these precedents would not, *without more*, be binding on agencies or officials within the jurisdictional sphere of administrators, or on legislators within their jurisdictional sphere. There would be similar conflict and confusion with respect to the other functions of the state besides law-making.

A further basic second-level systematizing device is, therefore, required: prioritization as between spheres with respect to any conflicting laws, rulings, decisions, or other matters emanating from the different spheres. To provide this, it is familiar that developed Western systems adopt formal priorital rules that leave profound and far-reaching effects on the system as a whole. At least as to the law-making function, such rules rank the basic spheres as follows: constitutional, legislative,

Section Three: Systematization *as between* Jurisdictional Spheres of Institutions 317

judicial, administrative, and other, generally in that order.[7] In general, then, constitutional law generally prevails over all contrary law, statutes generally over all remaining law, ordinary judge-made law generally over most administrative rulings, authorized state law mandatory in nature over private contract, and so on. As a result of such priorital ranking, the law's addressees (with any needed legal advice) can then know which of two or more conflicting laws, rulings, decisions, etc. created by institutional or other functionaries operating in different jurisdictional spheres, yet applicable to the same subject, is ultimately binding. When disputes arise over the application of priorital rules, a court or other body can resolve these disputes with finality. The law's addressees can knowingly construct legal reasons for determinate action that ultimately take priority. Again, though we tend to take formal prioritization as between institutional and other spheres for granted, the credit due to such form for the resulting systematized feature of the overall form of a legal *system* here is profound. It is true that legal rules with priorital content are required for this. Yet this is form-prescriptive content, structural in nature. Moreover, without appropriate features of form in these general priorital rules such as due prescriptiveness, completeness, definiteness, generality, and clarity of expression, these rules simply could not fulfill their systematizing function.

Like centralization and hierarchical ordering of authority *within* a sphere, such prioritization *as between spheres* is a necessary feature of the overall form of a legal *system* – of the purposive systematic arrangement of this complex whole. Prioritization orders the relations between parts of the whole, that is, between the various institutional and other sources of valid law, rulings, decisions, and other official actions in the system. As such, this prioritization is structural and, therefore, formal in this sense, too.

Inconsistencies between laws, rulings, decisions, and other actions calling for prioritization arise not only because there are different types of law-making bodies and entities, that is, different institutional and other jurisdictional spheres. Inconsistencies also arise over time as between laws, rulings, decisions, and acts of the *same* law-making body or jurisdictional source. For example, inconsistencies may arise as between two statutes adopted by the same legislature at different times, or between two rules of judge-made law laid down by the same highest court at different times. The foregoing systematizing device of priorital ranking of law, rulings, decisions, and actions emanating from *different* types of law-creating and other institutions cannot forfend against or resolve inconsistencies of this nature. Yet, some systematization is possible here, too, and modern systems have formal

---

[7] Here Hart's "rule of recognition" and Kelsen's "basic norm" provide due prioritization but only as to law-making. See *supra* n. 2 and 3. See also M. Eisenberg, *The Concept of National Law and the Rule of Recognition*, 29 Fla. State U. L. Rev. 1229 (2002).

prioritizing devices that go far to achieve this. For example, resolution of conflicts as between different statutes of the same legislature may be sought through such formal techniques as judicial espousal of more recent statutes over earlier ones, and of more specific statutes over more general ones. Resolution of conflicts as between different case law precedents may occur partly through formal judicial construal of case law so that, for example, the more recent supersedes the earlier. More fundamental and far reaching systematic coherence in related statute laws and related case law precedents can be achieved also through codification of whole fields of law, as we will see.

In systematizing between institutional spheres, the foregoing second-level devices, priorital in nature, in turn serve fundamental ends and values. These include: uniformity in the implementation of law throughout the territory, legal certainty and predictability, equality before the law as between similarly situated persons within the same territory, and the overall systemic integrity that derives from consistent and coherent creation and implementation of law applicable within the same territory. All these are also general values of the rule of law. The foregoing unifying effects of different second-level systematizing devices can also serve the various particular policies embedded in the contents of laws, and serve fundamental political values such as legitimacy, justice, freedom, rationality, and democracy itself. A superordinate democratic legislature would have final say with respect to all law-making, subject to constitutional limits. A generally subordinate system of courts and administrators would seek to implement this democratic will.

Again, though we tend to take the foregoing second-level devices for granted, their resulting systematizing effects contribute major features of overall systemic form – of the purposive systematic arrangement of the legal system as a complex whole. Without these devices, a legal *system* would simply not be possible, and important ends and values could not be satisfactorily realized. Again, the credit due to well-designed form for the resulting unity of the system is profound and far-reaching.

This credit is all the more significant if we also take into account that both (1) centralization and hierarchical ordering of authority *within* the same institutional spheres, and (2) prioritization as between *different* spheres, have major systematizing significance beyond the allocation of law-making and other authority, and beyond unification and ranking of the general criteria within the system for identifying putative law as valid law. The foregoing systematizing devices and their resulting formal features also centralize, coordinate, and prioritize with respect to various nonlaw making activities of institutions, too. That is, at least in a well-designed system, these devices generally specify who is to do what, how, when, and by what means, not only in regard to law-making functions, but also with respect to many other functions of government as well, including who is to appoint

Section Four: Systematization of Valid Laws within Discrete Fields

executive officials, who is to conduct investigations of administration, who is to conduct foreign policy, how such functions are to be carried out, and more.

SECTION FOUR: SYSTEMATIZATION OF VALID LAWS WITHIN DISCRETE FIELDS

Within a developed Western society at a given time, one may find a great multiplicity and diversity of first-level preceptual and nonpreceptual species of law. Indeed, the heterogeneity here can be truly vast. The same general subject matter can even be governed by a vast array of valid rules, principles, maxims, rulings, and orders. As we have seen, such diverse forms of law may emanate from diverse institutional sources. In a given field, constitutional law, statute law, common law, administrative rulings and regulations, and custom may all deal with aspects of the same general subject matter. In Anglo-American "common law" systems, a whole field of law may consist largely of a complex admixture of common law, isolated bits of statute law, various administrative regulations, and even particular administrative rulings. Such law may not only be diverse in preceptual and other species, but diverse in features of encapsulatory form as well. It may be diverse in its expressional features, too. Law on the same general subject may not even be coherently organized. Indeed some laws may simply not fit well together.

In complex modern systems, there can be no single systematizing cure here – no single second-level device that can banish all such disunities, and secure overall coherence within and between bodies of law. The nearest to anything like a sweeping solution to most of the varieties of disunity here is known in developed Western systems as the codification of relatively discrete fields of statutory or other law.[8] Here the legislature, or a codifying commission set up by the legislature, reconciles and draws together in systematically ordered statutory form, the relevant rules, principles, and other law within a discrete field, such as commercial law, or criminal law, or property law. Although confined to a discrete field (which may, nevertheless, be very large), such a codification qualifies as an important second-level systematizing device that secures a formally unified body of related rules and other species of law for a given field, or even a set of related fields. Insofar as codification is replicated from field to field, the law of a society is thus systematized all the more. Western legal systems vary greatly in the extent to which they have resorted to codification, and some systems have not resorted to it very fully. Some

---

[8] See, e.g., A. Mehren and J. Gordley, *The Civil Law System*, 43–95 (2nd ed., Little, Brown and Co., 1977); R. Schlesinger et al., *Comparative Law*, 530–96 (5th ed., Foundation Press, Mineola, 1988); R. C. van Caenegem, *Judges, Legislators and Professors*, Chapters 3 and 4 (Cambridge University Press, Cambridge, 1987). See also E. Patterson and R. Schlesinger, "Problems of Codification of Commercial Law," in Report of the New York Law Revision Commission, vol. 1, No. 65A, at 50–1, 57–61 (1955). See also O. Behrends, "Die europäische Kodifikation und die Kontinuität der Rechtswissenschaft ünter besonderer Berücksichtigung des BGB," 23 *Zeitschrift für Neuere Rechtsgeschichte* 295 (2001).

have employed still other systematizing devices such as statutory consolidation. Even when the law itself is not thus formally systematized, scholars may put the law of a field in some order through systematically organized treatises.

I will now explain the nature of codification, its formal character, and the contributions it can make to the systematization of a large body of law, and to the ends and values of a legal system more generally. The legislatures of some developed Western societies have frequently adopted, not one sweeping code for all of their law, but various codes for various relatively discrete, yet major fields of law. Codification is a European idea (albeit with ancient roots), and is widely implemented in Europe. Even Anglo-American common law countries have enacted some major codes for certain fields. The most prominent example in the United States is the Uniform Commercial Code – the "UCC," which was enacted mainly in the 1960s in all fifty of the American states, and for federal matters, by the federal Congress (and has since been revised). In what follows, I draw on the American experience with the UCC merely to illustrate the nature of codification as a major systematizing device in certain developed Western societies.[9]

The encapsulatory feature of the overall form of a code is statutory and, therefore, is set forth in a chosen set of words in fixed verbal form. Unlike isolated statutes, however, a code is a comprehensive revision, reformulation, rearrangement, and enactment of the rulings, rules, principles, and definitions that have theretofore made up a whole field of law, or even several related fields.

Ideally, the expressional feature of the overall form of a code consists of relatively explicit, well-defined, concise, and consistent terminology that also draws on duly defined technical terms used in the field involved. For example, the UCC in the United States purported to codify via state by state legislative enactment, the whole of several related areas of commercial law, including the law of sale of goods, of negotiable instruments, and of security interests in goods and other personal property. In so doing, the UCC displaced much pre-existing statutory and common law. The preceptual form of any such code consists primarily of rules, but it also includes general principles, definitions, and coordinating provisions. For example, the UCC has provisions that incorporate various general equitable principles and also the general principle of good faith (sec. 1-203).[10]

A well-designed code also has a rationally ordered internal structure that systematizes the general form and content of the discrete body of law involved. The UCC for example, is arranged in a coherent fashion so that its major segments comprise an interlocking and integrated body of law. Each major subdivision of

---

[9] See generally J. White and R. Summers, *Uniform Commercial Code* (4th ed., West, St. Paul, 1995). The chief drafter of the American Uniform Commercial Code, Professor Karl N. Llewellyn, studied in Germany, and drew heavily on European experience with codification.

[10] See Summers, "Good Faith in General Contract Law and the Sales Provisions of the Uniform Commercial Code," 54 *Va. L. Rev.* 195 (1968).

Section Four: Systematization of Valid Laws within Discrete Fields

a code, in the UCC, called an "Article," is organized in accord with principles of structural form. For example, Article Two of the UCC, on the sale of goods, adopts a "stage-oriented" structure whereby each major "part" of the Article follows after the next in accord with the main chronological stages of a standard transaction for the sale of goods. Thus, after an introductory Part One, there follows Part Two on form and formation of the contract of sale, Parts Three and Four on obligations arising therefrom for the parties and third parties, Part Five on performance of these obligations, Part Six on breach, and Part Seven on remedies.

A code, such as the UCC, generally subsumes provisions dealing with aspects of the same topic under the same general heading – another contribution of structural form. For example, all provisions on the sale of goods are set forth in one "Article," and provisions relating to the same sub-topic within the law on sale of goods are set forth in a separate "Part" of that Article. Thus, sections dealing with "Form, Formation, and Readjustment of the Contract" for sale of goods are set forth in Part 2 of Article Two, beginning with section 2-201 on "Formal Requirements; Statute of Frauds," and ending with section 2-210 on "Delegation of Performance; Assignment of Rights." Nearly all exceptions to, and qualifications of, a rule or of a principle are generally stated within or adjacent to the rule or principle or are duly cross-referenced. One finds after each section a set of cross-references to defined terms and to related sections in the same or other parts.

A body of statutory law may also incorporate methodological principles on how this law is to be interpreted. For example, the UCC includes several major interpretive principles, and these contribute to unity of form and content as well.

A codified body of law can be formal in several major ways: in preceptual, encapsulatory, expressional, structural, and in methodological features. All these formal features, as well as the formal systematizing device of codification itself, contribute to the systematized character of the body of law as a whole, and thus to the systematic character of a legal system overall. A body of law thus systematized is also worth having for what it contributes to coherence of form and content. It purges inconsistencies, and integrates and synchronizes the law as well.

A codified or otherwise duly systematized body of law is formal in still other valuable ways. It is far more accessible to the addressees who must identify and construct reasons for determinate action under the law. When a code is introduced to displace a vast body of common law, or a series of isolated statutes, or some admixture, the new law in the form of a systematic code can be found far more readily. Such a code will be well-organized, relatively comprehensive with respect to the field or fields involved, and periodically updated. Law organized in accord with principles of due subordination and with like subject matter placed with like, is far more accessible and conveniently usable than law not so organized. Moreover, new code law, being statutory law laid down in advance is, unlike new common law, prospective rather than retroactive, and so can be found in advance of occasions for its application – a further important facet of accessibility. Code law is more accessible than common law in still another way. Code law is usually formulated in explicit rules and principles duly stripped of the bulk of factual circumstances, specific issues and rulings thereon, supporting reasons, and procedural context that make up so much of judicial opinions in common law cases.

Also, the applicability of a common law case or series of cases is always contingent in a way that a code is not. An explicit code rule or principle has a formal feature of fixity of scope that cannot be "distinguished" away in common-law fashion in light of new facts or other material in a subsequent case. By contrast, the bearing of language in a prior common law case is highly contingent. That is, when the facts and issues in a new case relevantly differ, the language of an otherwise applicable prior case law precedent can often be "distinguished" away, thereby leaving a gap or gaps in the law. A code purports to pre-empt the field and leaves far fewer gaps. The common law lawyer must, except for analogies, regularly "run out of law" in a way that the code lawyer need not. Code law, then, is generally more comprehensive.

Furthermore, because the provisions of a new code are usually drafted over the same time period by the same persons, the various rules and principles of that code can be aligned, coordinated, and synchronized in form and content by those who draft these provisions. Case law, however, is generally created by different courts at different points in time, often far apart. Even in a system that seeks to follow precedent, there is less opportunity for different judges over time to align, coordinate and synchronize the law they are creating on a case by case basis than there is opportunity for code drafters to align, coordinate and synchronize the code law they are creating then and there.

Many fields of law are complex, but when a complex field is left to isolated and diverse common law cases, or to a series of isolated statutes, the complexity can be compounded. When put in code form, however, it is often possible to reduce complexity through systematic use of various devices, such as disentanglement and separate formulation of a complex rule in several rules, coherent aggregation of related rules under the same sub-division, explicit specification of priorities between potentially conflicting rules, explicit definition of relevant terms in rules, and the use of cross-references to any closely related rules. These systematizing steps also make the law far more accessible.

Putting the law of a field into code form is also an occasion to reformulate the law in coherent, consistent, well-defined, and rule-like terms, thereby improving its overall form. At the same time, putting the law into code form can be an occasion to improve the substantive content as finally embodied in the code. A proposed rule in a body of law being duly drafted in code form is a highly fit object for legislative scrutiny, and this, in turn, can lead to revisions and amendments that, in the very process of adopting the code, improve its content. Concurrent scrutiny

Section Five: Systematization through Uniformity of Interpretive Method 323

of a proposed set of related rules can contribute specially to the improvement and integration of overall content, as well. The preparation and adoption of a code requires focus on the coherence of all related parts of the whole code. This can lead to improvements in content, as well as form.

In sum, codification is one major second-level systematizing device the results of which can render accumulated first level rules and other law more coherent in form *and* content in the discrete field, or fields, involved. The more fields of law that are codified, the more this mode of systematization is extended across the system, and thus becomes a systematized feature of the whole system. Here, form affects content, too. That is, law that is made more coherent, accessible, intelligible, prospective, and suited to its ends – all in part contributions of code form – serves relevant policies better, serves fundamental political values such as legitimacy, rationality, and democracy better, and serves predictability, equal treatment, and other values of the rule of law better. All this credit to codifying form is not really controversial.

SECTION FIVE: SYSTEMATIZATION THROUGH UNIFORMITY OF INTERPRETIVE AND OTHER METHODOLOGIES, AND IN REGARD TO SANCTIONS AND REMEDIES

Even if the first-level institutions *within* their own jurisdictional spheres are duly centralized and hierarchically ordered, and even if there is due prioritization *as between* spheres that, among other things, specifies which conflicting laws, rulings, decisions, and actions are valid and binding, and even if the many and diverse species of first-level law within discrete fields are codified or otherwise *unified* for those fields, a purported system of law might still not be duly systematized in other major respects. For one thing, even if the accepted ways of interpreting a major type of law, such as statutory rules, qualify as methodological, different judges, other officials, and private addressees in the same system still might apply different interpretive methodologies rather than one uniform one, as we saw in Chapter Eight. Similarly, different judges and other officials in the same system might not apply the same methodologies in determining what is binding in judicial precedents, or apply the same methodologies for interpreting contracts, and so on. In these major respects, first-level interpretive and other applicational practices would lack methodological unity – another important feature of the overall form of a duly systematized legal order.

If first-level interpretive and other applicational practices are not methodologically uniform within the society, then it is virtually certain that some, perhaps many addressees will interpret and apply the same laws in diverse and inconsistent ways. If this unsystematized state of affairs is sufficiently extreme, the system might even be quite dysfunctional. Let us merely consider statutes as an example

324   The Overall Form of a Legal System as a Whole

of a major type of law requiring a uniform methodological approach throughout the system. The sources of interpretive issues are numerous and diverse. These include:

(1) linguistic and related sources (e.g., ambiguity, vagueness, ellipsis);
(2) incongruities between statutory language and apparent purposes of the statute;
(3) conflict of the statute with an accepted general principle of the system;
(4) internal structural issues arising from asymmetry, inconsistency, or other internal incoherence of the statute;
(5) uncertain "mesh" between the statute at hand and other statutes;
(6) inadequacies of basic statutory design, for example, mistaken assumptions about means, faulty ends, bad drafting; and,
(7) post enactment changes in knowledge, technology, generally accepted values, or obsolescence affecting the form and content of the statute.

In the absence of a *uniform* methodology for resolving such issues, different interpreters – judicial, administrative, and private – would often interpret the same statutory language differently. They would take the same statute in similar circumstances to generate quite different conclusions, and thus to give rise to reasons for quite different action or decision. This deficiency of methodological uniformity would impair the efficacy of many statutes to serve their purposes and limit the extent to which law's other ends and values could be served, including fair notice, consistency, equality before the law, other values associated with the rule of law, and various fundamental political values at stake.[11]

As we saw in Chapter Eight, the scope for differences in an interpretive or applicational methodology is vast. In the absence of uniformity of general methodology, judges and other interpreters might even adopt differing criteria of interpretive faithfulness. For example, some judges might give great weight to the standard ordinary or technical meanings of statutory words, others might emphasize evidence of intentions of legislators as found in materials of legislative history, whereas still others might construe the statute in light of an ultimate statutory purpose. All of these (and other) major methodological variations would usually show themselves in inconsistent interpretations of the same laws.

A major, yet still partial second-level cure for such methodological disunity at the first level is for the legal system to prescribe that the methodology of statutory interpretation be *uniform* throughout the entire system. In Chapter Eight, I formulated a schematic version of the overall form that a first-level interpretive methodology may take in many developed Western systems. When such a methodology is well-designed in the first place to secure uniformity of interpretations as

[11] L. Fuller, *The Morality of Law*, 33–94 (Rev. ed., Yale University Press, New Haven, 1969).

Section Five: Systematization through Uniformity of Interpretive Method 325

to similar issues, and is then also uniformly prescribed throughout the jurisdiction or jurisdictions of a legal system, this very requirement of uniformity qualifies in the analysis here as a major second-level systematizing device. Even though such prescribed uniformity may seem to be a relatively simple systematizing device as such, the resulting systematization can add a major feature to the overall form of the system as a whole, especially if the methodology itself is well-designed to serve its purpose. Of course, this resulting formal feature of methodological unity cannot guarantee that all judges and others will always interpret the same statutes in the same way. Nothing can.

Also, as I stressed in Chapter Eight, a statute that is drafted in light of a well-designed interpretive methodology can be drafted more effectively, and can be interpreted more uniformly, than a statute drafted without regard to such an interpretive methodology. Such interpretation furthers the policy or other ends of the statute and democracy itself. A well-designed and uniform interpretive methodology can go far to enable addressees to construct the same determinate reasons for action under the same law, facilitate voluntary self-application of well-designed law, and thereby also serve the dignity of citizen self-direction (with any needed legal advice). This serves general values of the rule of law, including certainty and predictability, fair notice, equality before the law, dispute avoidance, and private dispute settlement. Again, though these general claims to credit on behalf of a well-designed and uniform methodology are to some extent empirical, they are not really controversial.

What I have said here with respect to interpretive methodologies for statutes applies to other major types of methodologies as well, including those for interpreting contracts and for applying a common law precedent or series of precedents. That is, form is entitled to much credit when a well-designed methodology for any given type of recurrent legal task is adopted and *uniformly* applied throughout the geographical reach of the legal system. Without form, a methodology simply could not exist at all. Without a requirement of methodological uniformity – a formal systematizing device, the same methodology, whether interpretive or other, would almost certainly not prevail throughout a given jurisdiction. Hence, the legal system would lack a formal systematized feature of major significance.

Sanctions and remedies are also first-level units of special significance, as we saw in Chapter Nine. Second-level systematizing devices are required for the due and consistent imposition of sanctions and remedies. The authority to impose coercive sanctions and exact remedies is not distributed haphazardly in developed Western systems. This authority is generally conferred exclusively on courts, and then only for violations of law or legal wrongs duly proved in court after due process of law, and subject to appeals that can secure general uniformity.

With few exceptions, private parties may not "take the law into their own hands." Rather, in a well-designed system, the authority to impose sanctions and

326   The Overall Form of a Legal System as a Whole

exact remedies is concentrated in the hands of judges and other state officials acting in accord with formally well-defined and well-organized powers duly set forth in rules and principles. Moreover, different judges and officials in the same territory generally do not have power to pile sanctions on, or exact remedies from, the same individual for the same acts. Appeals lie to higher courts on a variety of grounds, including failure of proof of the wrong, excessiveness of sanction or remedy, and inconsistencies with prior cases. All the foregoing can have significant systematizing effects.

SECTION SIX: FURTHER SYSTEMIZATION OF FUNCTIONAL LEGAL UNITS THROUGH BASIC OPERATIONAL TECHNIQUES

There is still another fundamental way that institutions, bodies of related law, methodologies, sanctions, and still other discrete first-level units may lack systematization. No individual unit can effectively function independently of other units. It must be combined, integrated, and coordinated with other units to create and implement law in a coherent linear fashion. To consider only the array of units addressed in this book, let us assume that the law-making and law-applying institutions and other entities within the same jurisdictional spheres are duly centralized and hierarchically ordered, that the relations between different institutional spheres are duly prioritized, that the varied laws within bodies of law are duly codified or otherwise coherently organized, that interpretive and other methodologies are uniformly adopted and uniformly applied to discharge interpretive and other recurrent tasks, and that the various enforcive sanctions and remedies are duly defined and organized.

Such a purported legal system still would not, however, qualify as a full-fledged legal *system* if it did not also coherently combine, integrate, and coordinate first-level functional legal units within second-level techniques operating in coherent linear fashion to create and implement law. These techniques – these organizational modalities – take their own overall forms, and are essentially reducible to five in number. I have named these the "penal," the "grievance-remedial," the "administrative-regulatory," the "public-benefit conferring," and the "private-arranging" techniques.[12] Each distinctively organizes various institutional, preceptual, methodological, enforcive, and other discrete first-level units into operational wholes. Important as these techniques are, and important as their overall

---

[12] See further R. Summers, "The Technique Element in Law," 59 *Calif. L. Rev.* 733 (1971) in which the major choices in the construction of these techniques are identified. For a later treatment drawing extensively on the foregoing article in basic concepts and in terminology, see J. Raz, "The Functions of Law" in *The Authority of Law*, 163 (Clarendon Press, Oxford, 1979). See also, R. Summers, Kevin Clermont, Robert Hillman, Sheri Johnson, John Barceló, and Doris Provine, *Law, Its Nature, Functions, and Limits*, 3rd ed. (West Publishing Co., St. Paul, 1986).

Section Six: Further Systemization of Functional Legal Units

organizational forms are, they, too, have not yet received their due in studies of what is systematic about legal systems.

The foregoing operational techniques are essential second-level systematizing devices. As we will see, each version of an operational technique is a distinctive "compound" of discrete first-level and still other functional units specially organized for the creation and implementation of law. Not all the same units figure in each technique, and some serve somewhat differently even when they figure in the same techniques.

No discrete functional unit is ever deployed solely on its own. Even an isolated stop sign, which itself signifies a rule, as duly posted at crossroads on a lonely prairie, is not deployed solely on its own. It is integrated with other functional units within an overall operational technique I call the administrative-regulatory. This technique is deployed to secure safety on highways, and incorporates in addition to stop signs, many other regulative rules, the licensing of drivers, an administrative officialdom including police, judicial institutions, and discrete sanctions – all suitably integrated and coordinated within the technique.

A first-level functional legal unit, then, is not combined with other functional units within an operational technique in a merely ad hoc, haphazard, or patternless fashion. Such a unit is rationally combined with other first-level units within one or more of the five overall forms of operational techniques. Each technique operates linearly and is a complex social construction that takes its own overall form. Only through study of its distinctive overall form can the nature of each technique be adequately understood. Major credit for the efficacy of each technique is attributable to its well-designed overall form.

Whatever is achieved through law occurs via deployment of one of the foregoing techniques, or some readily recognizable variant or some combination. The various functional legal units and thus the activities of law-makers, administrative officials, citizens, judges, and others are organized to operate within these techniques, as deployed in linear progressions from initial creation of law to ultimate implementation. The discrete units, as operational within these techniques, are necessarily dynamic. Moreover, any such operational technique in action is itself more than the sum of its parts – more than the mere sum of the effects of the various individual units involved. This is because the form of each technique duly combines and coordinates the individual units within what becomes an integrated whole that operates with synergistic effects.

The resulting synergistic effects can be considerable. Here, that one plus one equals three may be seen many times over. An operational technique, as a complex organized whole, can be designed and deployed to serve any ends realizable through law – ends as varied as crime control, the regulation of highway travel, the provision of potable water, and the conferral of free public education. Discrete individual units, deployed alone, could never serve such purposes, except perhaps haphazardly. The forms of relevance here are of two types: (1) the various overall forms of individual first-level units and the forms of various systematizing devices, and (2) the five overall forms of the second-level operational techniques in which discrete first-level and other units are appropriately combined, integrated and coordinated. Any such technique is to be analyzed as a "compound" of individual units otherwise duly systematized, yet also organized in accord with the overall form of this technique to be operational in accord with the distinctive linear ordering of this technique.

To understand the five techniques, and thus understand a further major category of systematizing devices known to the law, it is essential to grasp the overall form of each technique and how discrete first-level functional units are combined and deployed in it to serve ends. When well-designed, these techniques are, themselves, major means to the realization of ends. It will be sufficient for my purposes merely to provide schematic accounts of the five techniques and their overall forms.

The first is the "penal" (also "correctional") technique. This technique typically takes an overall operational form in which initially a legislature adopts statutes prohibiting socially undesirable conduct, i.e., crimes; police, prosecutors, courts, and punitive and correctional officials are duly appointed and constituted; actions such as regular police patrols are taken to deter would-be criminals, and criminals are caught, prosecuted, punished, and possibly rehabilitated. Thus, a wide variety of discrete functional units, including institutions, statutory and other rules, interpretive and other methodologies, and sanctions and other enforcive devices, must be integrated and coordinated within this type of overall technique if it is to be effective to deter crimes and punish offenders. No single functional unit, institutional, or otherwise, could alone serve such purposes.

A second technique may be called the "grievance-remedial." In its most common version, this technique takes an overall operational form in which legislatures, courts, and administrative entities create bodies of tort and other law defining what constitutes a recognized grievance to an individual or entity, as caused by another individual or entity. Courts, or in some types of cases, administrative entities, then grant remedies to the aggrieved for harm caused when duly proved. The effective operation of this technique discourages individuals and entities from causing such grievances in the first place. This type of technique integrates and coordinates some of the same law-making and law-applying institutions and other phenomena as does the penal technique, yet the overall forms of these two techniques are far from identical. Among other things, the penal technique operates through dissemination of knowledge and understanding as to what conduct is prohibited as wrongful, through systematic policing and also through credible threats of sanctions for crimes, whereas the grievance-remedial technique operates primarily through the threat and the actuality of providing redress for victims

Section Six: Further Systemization of Functional Legal Units 329

of torts and other wrongs, as proscribed in rules. This technique is more reparative than preventative.

A third overall form of operational technique is the "administrative-regulatory." In this technique, the legislature and administrative bodies create and lay down standards of behavior designed to serve regulatory policies. These standards are addressed to discrete classes of persons who are required to follow them in the conduct of what are generally wholesome activities such as the driving of automobiles, food manufacturing, construction of buildings, radio and television programming, and the provision of airline transportation. Administrative officials then take steps in advance through publicity, licensing, periodic inspections, and the like to secure compliance with regulatory standards on the part of those who conduct the relevant activities. This technique is more preventative than reparative. The generally wholesome activities to which regulatory standards are addressed must be contrasted with the intrinsically wrongful behavior that the penal technique is largely designed to deter and punish. Administrative bodies and courts impose sanctions, including the revocation of licenses and fines, on any violators of regulatory standards, thereby securing the credibility of these standards. In the overall form of this technique, cadres of administrative officials usually have special roles in creating, monitoring, and applying the regulatory standards. Legislatures and courts can have important roles here, as well. (The operation of this technique is illustrated in depth in Chapter Eleven.)

In a fourth overall form of operational technique, a governmental body confers public benefits. In this "public-benefit conferring" technique, legislatures and administrative bodies use law to authorize, define, and confer public benefits such as, for example, public school education, public health services, the public provision and maintenance of roadways, and public provision of potable water. Governmental agencies and authorized private contractors confer these benefits, and legislatures and administrative bodies impose taxes or otherwise secure resources required to finance the conferral of such benefits by public agencies or via contracts with private parties or entities.

The fifth basic form of operational technique may be called the "private-arranging" technique, and although it has a coherent core, it is more heterogeneous than the others. In the core use of this technique, private parties, often within markets for goods, realty, services, etc., voluntarily enter and fulfill various legally recognized types of private arrangements, including contracts and property relations. Rules and other functional units facilitate entry into contracts and other arrangements in various ways. Courts provide remedies for those harmed by breaches of contracts or by other wrongs here, too. Administrative agencies may provide remedies as well.

Frequently, two or more of the foregoing five techniques are jointly deployed to serve the same general ends and values. Thus, for example, the penal technique and the grievance-remedial technique are used against some actions that may be both a crime and a civil wrong. As a second example, consider how the public-benefit conferral technique provides for the construction of safe public highways for travel, whereas these facilities are at the same time further regulated through the administrative-regulatory and the penal techniques to secure highway safety.

The foregoing five second-level systematizing techniques are formal in several ways. First, each technique takes the overall form of a basic organizational modality. It distinctively combines, integrates, and coordinates functional legal units within an operational whole. Second, each technique is also derivatively formal because it is a compound of various functional units each of which takes its own form, with its own complementary material or other components. Third, each technique is formal in a well recognized special meaning of "formal" in standard lexicons of the English language. That is, each technique "holds together the several elements of a thing,"[13] and thus qualifies as another major variety of structural form.

In Western systems, all law (except some constitutional law) is created and implemented via one or more of the foregoing operational techniques, or via some readily recognizeable variant thereof. That is, when the legal system operates to create and implement law to serve purposes, it almost always does so through one or more of the foregoing five basic operational techniques. Each of the five forms of technique thus combines and integrates diverse first-level and other legal units into an operational whole for deployment in a linear progression to serve purposes. For example, as we saw in the account of the penal technique, legislatures at the outset prohibit antisocial conduct by adopting criminal prohibitions in the form of rules; these prohibitions are duly publicized or otherwise communicated; punitive and correctional facilities are established; police, prosecutors, courts, and punitive and correctional officials are recruited and organized to deter would-be criminals from violating these prohibitions; police and other officials arrest alleged criminals (often with the aid of private citizens); these arrested are then arraigned in court and tried, and if convicted, sanctioned and/or rehabilitated; and so on.

Many different first-level functional units may be combined and integrated in varying ways within one of the five second-level operational techniques in order to create and implement law. Each technique integrates some of the same first-level units. All usually resort to the legislative institution in some way, though the legislature may not be the primary law-maker in a given technique. For example, in some systems, administrative agencies, rather than legislatures, create most of the law in the administrative-regulatory technique. In the private-arranging technique, private contracting parties are the primary law-makers, for they are the ones who create the terms of contracts. Courts and administrative officials

---

[13] See *OED, supra* n. 6, vol. 6, at "form" I.4.d.

Section Six: Further Systemization of Functional Legal Units 331

figure in all techniques, though in quite differing ways. All techniques incorporate and integrate rules. All techniques deploy interpretive and other methodologies. All techniques resort, though in differing ways, to sanctions or remedies, and the like. The sanction of imprisonment, however, is largely limited to the penal technique.

At the same time, each technique presupposes and draws upon systematized features of the legal system as a whole, such as the accepted general criteria for identification of valid law of the system, criteria that in turn presuppose the existence of legislatures, courts, and other sources of valid law, and presuppose centralized hierarchical ordering and prioritization of these sources.

We have already seen major ways that a discrete first-level functional unit might itself lack unity. The overall form of an institution might be poorly designed internally, and therefore not even be susceptible of being effectively combined, integrated, and co-ordinated within the overall form of a given type of operational technique in the first place. For example, the procedural decision-rule of a legislature might require a three-fourths majority for any legislation to pass, with the result that the legislature would be neither democratic nor fecund, and, therefore, would regularly fail to make needed law that a majority favors. Or, for example, a rule, or a methodology, or a sanction could simply fail sufficiently to take the overall form required for it to qualify as such a functional unit at all.

Even if discrete first-level functional units are formally well-designed on their own, legal architects could still fail somehow satisfactorily to combine, integrate, and co-ordinate institutional or other functional units within the overall form of an effective operational technique. This would be a further kind of failure of systematization – a further way a legal order could fail to be a full-fledged legal *system*. For example, a system might choose to deploy the administrative-regulatory technique in a fashion that leaves the initiative to enforce regulatory standards for the manufacture of food and drugs solely to injured private citizens acting *after* the fact of injury. That is, the technique might fail to assign any responsibility to administrative officials to take action *in advance* to set and enforce standards of quality for the manufacture of certain food and drugs, and thus prevent bad food and drugs from being marketed in the first place. This would, in major part, be a failure of overall form – a failure to combine, integrate, coordinate, and thus systematize first-level and other functional units within the administrative-regulatory technique so that it could operate in an appropriately preventative fashion to serve relevant ends.

Let us consider a second, somewhat less dramatic, example of failure to combine, integrate, coordinate, and thus systematize the deployment of first-level units within a second-level operational technique – one that is penal in nature. Different governmental agencies jointly concerned, for example, with enforcement of criminal laws against terrorism might fail to share vital information which, if shared, would lead police or administrators to detect terrorist plots in advance. Or, also in a technique that takes the penal form, the courts might sentence recidivist offenders to lengthy imprisonment, only to have prison officials be forced to release them within far shorter time spans because of legislative failure to provide funds for construction of sufficient prison space.

Still another possibility is that two or more operational techniques might not themselves be well *coordinated as between* each other, though the potential of both to serve the same general purposes is considerable. For example, what I have called the public-benefit conferral technique might be utilized to confer the benefit of public highways, yet the highways themselves not be built in a fashion to facilitate effective highway policing efforts pursuant to the administrative-regulatory and the penal techniques.

In a well-designed legal system, the five basic operational techniques will themselves be well-designed. Thus these techniques will duly combine, integrate, and coordinate discrete first-level and other functional legal units. The resulting systematized feature of the overall form of a legal system, then, will reveal itself in duly integrated and coordinated law-making and law-implementing activities that, in linear progressions, serve purposes. In this operational fashion, too, the legal system will be systematically functional and dynamic. The central lesson here, then, is this. Even though a legal order is otherwise duly systematized, it may remain significantly unsystematized if it fails to combine, integrate, and coordinate discrete first-level and other units into operational techniques that function to create and implement law. As we will now see, a legal order can also remain significantly unsystematized if, though it operates to an extent through such techniques, these fail to operate in law-like fashion.

SECTION SEVEN: OPERATION OF BASIC TECHNIQUES IN CONFORMITY WITH PRINCIPLES OF THE RULE OF LAW

I here classify principles of the rule of law as second-level principles. That is, the principles of the rule of law largely prescribe, albeit in general terms, how first-level functional units are to be combined, integrated, and coordinated to operate within basic techniques for creation and implementation of law. It is one thing for various discrete first-level and other functional units to be *somehow* combined, integrated, and coordinated within one of the five second-level operational techniques. It is something further for these, even as somehow combined, integrated, and coordinated within basic operational techniques, not merely to operate together, but also to operate in accord with second-level principles of the rule of law. For example, a first-level functional unit of a legal rule, may even when duly combined with other units in that operational technique here called the penal, still fail, as drafted, to treat similarly situated addressees equally. Indeed, a penal rule might, as drafted,

Section Seven: Operation of Techniques in Conformity with Rule of Law

even discriminate against a minority group. A penal technique incorporating such a rule would fail to conform to an important second-level principle of the rule of law requiring equal treatment of similarly situated persons. Or, to cite a second example, the penal technique, even though it duly integrates required first-level functional units consisting of rules expressly applicable to similarly situated persons, still might, as administered, fail to conform to one or more other principles of the rule of law, as when an accused criminal is not afforded fair opportunity to confront and cross-examine prosecuting witnesses at trial.

As the foregoing examples indicate, although the combination, integration, and coordination of functional legal units within an operational technique may be systematizing in its own way, the technique still may not operate in due conformity with second-level principles of the rule of law. When the technique does operate in such conformity, however, the technique is, itself, not only further systematized, but its operation is also, at the same time law-like, thereby serving general values of the rule of law.

The principles of the rule of law prescribe form. That is, they prescribe that those who create and implement law through any of the five second-level operational techniques: (1) make required choices of form, content, and other complementary components in first-level and other functional units to begin with, and (2) combine, integrate, and coordinate these units within operational techniques in ways that also systematically secure, so far as practicable, the law-like operation of these techniques. Such systematic law-like operation, that is, operation in conformity with principles of the rule of law, is a further complex feature of the overall form of an operational legal *system*. Principles of the rule of law not only apply to define and organize the law-like operation of law's five basic techniques. Some of these principles, as the two foregoing examples from the penal technique also indicate, may also apply directly to, and organize facets of first-level functional units such as rules as well. In this respect, too, the principles of the rule of law qualify as complex "second-level" systematizing devices addressed to such first-level units.

We have here, then, a further major and wide-ranging second-level systematizing device insofar as duly implemented through the design of first-level and other functional units, and also as duly implemented through the operation of techniques combining, integrating, and coordinating such units. The resulting systematizing effects of these principles of the rule of law render the operations of the system law-like, a further fundamental feature of the overall form of a legal system as a whole. Developed western legal systems usually operate in law-like fashion, that is, in general conformity with principles of the rule of law.

I will now consider in more extended fashion how second-level principles of the rule of law define, organize, and systematize this further fundamental feature of the overall form of an operational legal system. The analyses to follow best come here, after a representative selection of first-level functional units and of various second-level systematizing devices have been intensively studied. These analyses will advance understanding of a legal system as a highly complex whole that both operates in accord with basic operational techniques, and operates in a complex law-like fashion in conformity with principles of the rule of law. The analyses will also explain more fully how such law-like operation generally serves values of the rule of law.[14]

H. L. A. Hart conceived of a system of law as a system of rules, and Hans Kelsen conceived of a system of law as a system of norms. Both deployed an essentially rule-oriented approach in order to elucidate the characteristics of a system of law. One consequence was that they failed to provide a frontal and holistic account of that complex feature of the overall form of a legal system that I here call its systematically law-like operation. Indeed, in his highly important book, *The Concept of Law*, Hart devoted less than one page to principles of the rule of law.[15] Yet these principles are extensive, complex, and functionally of great importance. They pertain to the very nature of a duly operational legal system, as well. I will now merely identify numerous second-level principles of the rule of law nearly all of which are widely recognized in some degree in all developed Western societies. Some systems conform in their operation relatively fully to principles of the rule of law, others less so.

Some principles of the rule of law specify certain requirements of first-level and other functional units, as well as define and organize the complex *law-like* operation of the law's techniques. The principles of the rule of law are far more numerous and far more complex than is often assumed. The contents of most of these principles are largely form-prescriptive, though not always categorically so. These principles require:

(1) That all institutional and other recognized sources of valid law be sufficiently determinate and stable;

(2) That all purportedly valid species of law be duly authorized, and thus satisfy applicable source-oriented and any content-oriented criteria for the identification of valid law;

(3) That the criteria for determining the validity of law generally be clear and determinately applicable, and also provide for priority as between any conflicting valid law;

(4) That state-made law, so far as feasible, take the form of general rules applicable to classes of persons, acts, circumstances, etc.;

---

[14] See *The Dialogues of Plato*, vol. 2, at 407–712 (B. Jowett trans., Random House, New York, 1937); G. Morrow, "Plato and The Rule of Law," 50 *Phil. Rev.* 105 (1941). See also Chapter Two of the present book at p. 45.

[15] H. L. A. Hart, *supra* n. 2, at 207. Kelsen similarly neglected many of these principles. See, e.g., the two works of Kelsen cited *supra* n. 3.

Section Seven: Operation of Techniques in Conformity with Rule of Law 335

(5) That state-made law on any given subject be uniform within the relevant boundaries;

(6) That, in general, state-made law, and other law as appropriate, be in some printed or other written form, and be duly promulgated, published, or otherwise accessible to its addressees;

(7) That state-made law and other law, when appropriate, generally apply to lay persons and officials alike;

(8) That all rules, principles, orders, contracts, proprietary interests, and other species of valid law be clearly expressed with sufficient clarity to be determinately applied;

(9) That, in application, all rules, principles, orders, contracts, proprietary interests, and any other species of valid law give rise to pre-emptive reasons for determinate action or decision that generally over-ride competing nonlegal considerations emergent in particular circumstances;

(10) That newly created law, and changes in existing law, generally be prospective rather than retroactive. (See also (14) and (15));

(11) That the behavioral requirements of any variety of law be within the capacity of its addressees to comply;

(12) That the law on a subject, once made and put into effect, not be changed so frequently that its addressees cannot readily conform their conduct to it, or cannot feasibly plan for future relationships and contingencies;

(13) That changes in the law generally be made by due notice and by duly authorized institutions, officials, persons, or other entities, and in accord with known procedures;

(14) That law be interpreted or otherwise applied in accord with a well-designed, uniform (for that type of law), and determinate interpretive or other relevant applicational methodology – itself a methodology duly respectful of the expressional and encapsulatory features appropriate for the type of law;

(15) That any possible remedy, sanction, nullification, or other adverse consequence of failure to comply with a type of law, be known or knowable in advance of the relevant occasions of addressees for action or decision under that law;

(16) That in cases of legal or factual dispute over the applicability of law, a politically independent and impartial system of courts, administrative tribunals or other official bodies as appropriate exist and have power, [a] to determine the validity of the law if in dispute, [b] to resolve issues of fact, [c] to apply valid law in accord with appropriate interpretive and other applicational methodologies, and [d] to authorize application of any sanction, remedy, or other implementive device, all in accord with relevant procedural and substantive law;

(17) That when, in a particular instance, an interpretive or other applicational methodology yields a given outcome in light of the facts and antecedent law, yet a court or other appropriate tribunal is urged to modify or otherwise depart from this outcome, such courts or tribunals shall have only quite limited and exceptional power thus to modify or depart from what would otherwise be binding antecedent statute, precedent, or other law, so that any reasons for action or decision which arise under valid law, duly interpreted or applied, are generally pre-emptive for the law's addressees, including the courts and other tribunals;

(18) That any exceptional power of courts or other tribunals to modify or depart from antecedent law at point of application under (17) be a power that, so far as feasible, is itself specified and duly circumscribed in general rules, so that this is a power the exercise of which is itself law-governed;

(19) That a party who is a claimed victim of a crime, or of a regulatory violation, or of a tort, or of a breach of contract, or of wrongful denial of a public benefit, or of wrongful administrative action, or of any other legal wrong, shall be entitled to seek appropriate redress before an independent and impartial court or other tribunal with power to compel the alleged wrongdoer or allegedly errant official to answer for such wrong, if such wrong be established;

(20) That, except for minor matters, no significant sanction, remedy, or other adverse legal action shall be imposed on a party, against his or her will, for any alleged legal wrong, criminal or civil, without that party having advance notice thereof, and a fair opportunity to contest the legality and the factual basis of any such sanction, remedy, or other adverse legal action before an independent and impartial court or other similar tribunal;

(21) That a private party who fails to prevail before such court or other tribunal pursuant to (19) and (20), whether an alleged victim or an alleged wrongdoer, shall have the opportunity to seek at least one level of appellate review, in a court, as a check against legal or factual error in the proceedings below;

(22) That the legal system and its institutions and processes be generally accessible. That is, [a] that there be a recognized, organized, and independent legal profession legally empowered and willing to provide legal advice, and to advocate causes before courts, other tribunals, and other institutions as appropriate, and [b] that at least where a party is accused of a significant crime or similar violation, denies wrongdoing, and is without financial means to pay costs of defense, such party be entitled to have defense provided by the state.[16]

---

[16] This set of principles is more extensive than, and differs significantly from, that of Lon L. Fuller as set forth in his fine book, *The Morality of Law, supra* n. 11, although there is overlap.

Section Seven: Operation of Techniques in Conformity with Rule of Law 337

The foregoing second-level principles of the rule of law prescribe, in general terms, only some of the features of the forms of first-level rules and other law, and also prescribe only some of the features of the forms of other first-level functional legal units addressed in the typology of units treated in this book. For example, principle (16) is addressed to institutional form, whereas principles (14) and (17) are addressed to interpretive or other applicational form, and principle (20) is addressed to the forms of enforcive devices. Although the contents of principles of the rule of law are largely form-prescriptive and thus go far to define, specify, and organize law-like operation of a system, these principles do not, however, go very far to specify the specific formal features of institutions, of rules and other species of law, of interpretive and other applicational methodologies, of sanctions and remedies, or of any other first-level functional legal units. Yet, as explained at pages 45–6 of Chapter Two, it is a striking fact that the main requirements of nearly all the various types of functional legal units, and thus also of their overall forms, are largely deducible from widely accepted principles of the rule of law.

All of the foregoing second-level principles of the rule of law are formal, and most of these principles are formal in the same general respects. Nearly all of these principles have form-prescriptive content, though some have other content as well. These principles prescribe various formal features of institutions, precepts, methodologies, sanctions, and other first-level functional units. Standard lexicons also justify characterization of these principles as formal, for most of their content is broadly methodological. That is, this content generally pertains to the "manner, method, way, or fashion" in which law and its techniques are to operate in order to be law-like.[17] Furthermore, almost all of the form-prescriptive principles of the rule of law are formal in procedural terms. They prescribe aspects of the very procedures by which law is created and implemented. Again, "of or pertaining to procedure" is itself a well-recognized meaning of formal in the English language.[18]

Moreover, a number of major principles of the rule of law are also "jurisdictionally" formal. That is, they recognize, organize, and limit the conferral of jurisdiction and thus pertain to legal validation. In lexical idiom, "of or pertaining to validity" is a recurrent meaning of formal in English.[19] The form-prescriptive contents of some principles of the rule of law also prescribe structural features of legal institutions and other functional units. For example, several principles, in effect, require of a court that it have a tripartite adjudicative structure in which the judge has an impartial role as between opposing litigants. Such structural principles order relations between parts within a whole, another standard meaning of formal.[20]

---

[17] See *OED*, *supra* n. 6, vol. 6, at "form," I.10 ("manner, method, way, fashion (of doing anything)").

[18] *Id.*, at vol. 6, at "form," I.11.a ("a set, customary, or prescribed way of doing anything, a set method of procedure according to rule (e.g., at law); formal procedure").

[19] *Id.*, at vol. 6, at "formal," A.5.

[20] *Id.*, at vol. 6, at "form," I.5.a.

As indicated, principles of the rule of law, as second-level principles, may be implemented both through the design and operation of first-level functional units, and also through the design and operation of other second-level systematizing devices. For example, not only must first-level units such as rules be designed in sufficiently definite fashion to afford addressees fair notice – a major value of the rule of law, but other second-level systematizing devices such as the uniformity of a methodology for interpreting statutes must secure, so far as feasible, equal treatment under the same statutes throughout the jurisdiction – also a major value of the rule of law. By far the most all-encompassing other second-level systematizing device consists of the five operational techniques, which are to operate in law-like fashion, as defined and organized in accord with second-level principles of the rule of law.

Not all of the foregoing principles of the rule of law are explicitly set forth in the positive constitutional or other law of all developed Western systems. Most, however, are so embodied to some extent, and when not, they tend nevertheless to be widely accepted as public standards for critical evaluation of the law-likeness of the operations of the law's techniques in most of these systems. Judges, officials, members of the legal profession, law professors, the news media, and many others may invoke these principles as standards for evaluating the creation and implementation of law and for evaluating other first-level functional legal units as deployed within law's five basic operational techniques. Such evaluative standards, in a healthy legal order, can, when invoked as normative principles of law-like operation, have important influence of their own, even when not explicitly embodied in positive constitutional or other law.

The credit due to form, as prescribed in the contents of widely observed second-level principles of the rule of law, is vast. In thus systematizing the operations of a legal system in law-like fashion, many values are served. What now follows is in the nature of a summation of most of the major types of credit due form here. Some of this credit has already been identified in general terms in this book, though not in the name of principles of the rule of law as such.

Consider, first, the fundamental political value of legitimacy. Principles of the rule of law require that institutional sources of law such as legislatures, courts, and administrative agencies, be operationally determinate and stable. This contributes to their legitimacy. An indeterminate or unstable source of law lacks legitimacy. Those related principles of the rule of law requiring that valid rules and other law derive from determinate and duly authorized sources, and that any changes in them be duly authorized, likewise prescribe law-like operation, and serve legitimacy.

Principles requiring that a law not only be duly adopted and promulgated, but also be clear in meaning and provide fair notice in advance of the law's requirements, are principles of law-like operation. These serve legitimacy, too.

Section Seven: Operation of Techniques in Conformity with Rule of Law 339

The same is true of principles requiring consistent administration. These can serve justice and fairness, and this furthers legitimacy. Persons faced with an unclear law, or faced after the fact with an interpretation that diverges sharply from the dictates of accepted interpretive method, are denied fair opportunity to conform their conduct to the requirements of the law in the first place.[21] This deprives them of a meaningful and fair basis on which to plan and order their affairs, is not law-like, and erodes legitimacy. Further, a law is at least *prima facie* unjust if it is over-general or under-general, and thus fails to treat like cases alike. The formal principle calling for due generality in rules is a principle of the rule of law. Its violation is not law-like and forfeits legitimacy to an extent.

In the event of a dispute before a court, or before another official body, denial of due process violates a further principle of law-like operation. Such denial deprives the citizen of a fair chance to present a case. As such, it is unjust and delegitimizing, as well as not law-like. Due process is also denied to a party before a court or other tribunal when the content of the law is quite unclear or indeterminate, a violation of another requirement of form. Such a party cannot determine the meaning of the law to be applied, cannot know what arguments and evidence will be relevant, and so cannot effectively prepare and respond in a legal proceeding. This is neither law-like, nor legitimate.

Violations of principles of the rule of law may also deny addressees the dignity of self-direction under law, another fundamental political value. For example, a system that generally operates not primarily through rules laid down in advance that addressees are to apply to themselves, but largely through the form of *ad hoc* official orders, is not law-like and treats its inhabitants as mere subjects to be ordered around – with little capacity to determine and exercise rights or to fulfill duties on their own power.

Principles of the rule of law, in operation, also serve the fundamental political value of freedom and individual autonomy. Consider, for example, a first-level rule with contents that protect freedom of movement within the society. Although the principles of the rule of law do not prescribe this content as such, these principles generally require that the contents of such a law be set forth in the form of clear and sufficiently definite rules and thus be law-like. This form in itself serves as a bulwark against official interferences with this very freedom. The very fact that freedom of movement is authorized in the form of clear and definite rules makes it less likely that officials or others will invade this freedom. They know their conduct will be measured against these known and determinate rules, and that this will very likely reveal the interference.[22] Clear and definite rules – requirements of form – may

---

[21] See L. Fuller, *supra* n. 11. See also J. Raz, "The Rule of Law and its Virtue," 93 *L. Q. Rev.* 195 (1977); R. Summers, "The Place of Form in the Fundamentals of Law," 14 *Ratio Juris* 106 (2001).

[22] "Form is the sworn enemy of the arbitrary and the twin sister of liberty." R. Jhering, *Geist des Römischen Rechts: auf den verschiedenen Stufen seiner Entwicklung*, vol. 2, at 471 (Scientia Verlag, Aalen, 1993).

even affirmatively enhance the quality of the freedom involved. For example, clear and definite rules for highway use facilitate safe and efficiently coordinated actions by drivers and thereby improve the very quality of their freedom of movement. These rules organize and thereby enhance the extent and quality of freedom. Such freedom is not the mere absence of constraint; it must be affirmatively organized before it can be duly operational. Well-designed form is required for this.

The principles of the rule of law may even exert influence upon law-makers to adopt law the very content of which favors freedom. These principles favor law in the form of rules and these are law-like. Some generality is a required formal feature of a rule. A proposed rule the contents of which restrict freedom would have to apply generally. It might even have to apply to law-makers in their own private capacity! Democratic law makers will, without more, tend to be less inclined to adopt any such laws.[23]

Insofar as principles of the rule of law, as manifest in the operations of the system, secure limited government, they also tend to secure the freedom and dignity of citizen self-direction and individual autonomy. A given first-level rule may limit governmental power in some specific and explicit way. Beyond this, any clear and definite rule, duly interpreted and applied, itself implicitly limits government. For example, a definite law requiring that persons drive no faster than seventy miles an hour also implicitly limits, at least to some extent, the power of police to arrest persons driving under seventy. Officials are not to act unless authorized by law. Insofar as persons drive under seventy, such a law generally leaves them to enjoy the freedom and dignity of citizen self-direction in the absence of special circumstances. If, however, departing from principles of the rule of law, the primary speed limit law for major roadways were, without qualification, left relatively indefinite, as for example, in a general rule that simply reads "drive reasonably," many police might purport to invoke this law inconsistently and rather readily, which would not be law-like and would impair freedom. Thus, formal features that are not duly definitive can undermine limited government and, at the same time, also deny addressees the freedom and dignity of self-direction under law.

The principles of the rule of law also facilitate realization of fundamental political values of democracy and rationality in the operations of self-governance. Among other things, these principles require definiteness in election laws so that what counts as a valid vote can be readily determined, and prospective legislators and other officials can be definitively declared the winners (or losers) of an election.[24] These principles also require definiteness in the statutory rules that duly elected legislators adopt. This formal feature serves rationality of deliberation of

[23] See *supra* Chapter Three, Section Three.
[24] See, e.g., *Bush v. Gore: The Court Cases and the Commentary* (E. Dionne Jr. and William Kristol eds., Brookings Institution Press, Washington, D.C., 2001).

Section Seven: Operation of Techniques in Conformity with Rule of Law   341

elected legislators in the legislative process. It is easier for legislators to evaluate and improve a draft statute when it is definite. Moreover, the electorate can more readily hold legislators accountable for a statute when it is definite. Most important, a definite statute is more clearly an expression of the will of the democratic majority that can be meaningfully implemented. It is not enough, however, that there should be democratic elections and democratic participation in law-making activities, or that elected legislators be held accountable periodically. The laws duly made must also be implemented if there is to be democratic and law-like governance. Without due definiteness in a statute, its addressees cannot formulate reasons for determinate action under the statute, and disputes over applicability will be more frequent. Without due definiteness in a statute, it is also much more difficult to tell whether it is truly effective once it has supposedly gone into "effect."

Adherence to formal principles of the rule of law, then, can serve fundamental political values of legitimacy, justice, freedom, dignity, democracy, and rationality in the course of law-like operations of the law's techniques for the creation and implementation of law. As we have seen, such adherence serves general values of the rule of law, as well. These values are numerous and complex, and overlap somewhat with fundamental political values. General values of the rule of law include rationality in the administration of the law, "learnability" of the law, fair notice of the law's content, predictability as to how the law will be applied, equality before the law for those similarly situated, and freedom from official arbitrariness. A single episode violating one or more principles of the rule of law is not only unlawlike but can dis-serve several such values all at once. For example, unclarity in the law itself, or lack of public promulgation, or retrospectivity of a newly adopted law can, at one stroke, defeat or grossly impair the realization of nearly all of the foregoing values of the rule of law.

Law-like operation in accord with principles of the rule of law serves the general value of rationality *in the administration* of first-level law. Often, there is scope for reasoned argument with respect to the proper interpretation or application of a law, and with respect to what the relevant facts really were, or are. Adherence to principles of the rule of law can channel such argumentation, and thus serve rational administration. For example, when interpreters apply a legally recognized methodology of statutory interpretation, they must construct and deploy interpretive arguments of the types recognized in the methodology. Thus, when a dispute arises in court, both litigants will usually strive to construct arguments recognized in the methodology, such as arguments that appeal to the ordinary or technical meanings of the statutory words, in light of purpose, text, and context. In this way, the litigants seek to instantiate a relevant general mode of argument, thereby bringing rationality, as so recognized in the law, to bear.

It is true that principles of the rule of law have content prescribing form and, therefore, do not as such specify the policy or other substantive content of first-level functional units such as regulative rules. It is certainly possible for those who govern to adhere to principles of the rule of law, and yet at the same time adopt some rules with bad or unsound policy content. However, adherence to various principles of the rule of law, although themselves merely form-prescriptive in content, generally *tends* to beget good policy or other substantive content in the first-level law being adopted in the course of law-like operations. That is, the rule of law tends, and in more ways than one, to beget the rule of good law.

As we have seen, one basic principle of the rule of law requires that law be validly made – that it be authoritative. This formal principle requires not only that the law-maker have jurisdiction to make the law at hand, but also that the law-maker follow procedures required for making the kind of law involved. It is true that formal procedures cannot themselves prescribe the particular policy content of proposed first-level law, yet such procedures would not even count as procedures for making law if they were wholly indifferent in their operation to the quality and likely efficacy of the policy or other content of proposed laws. As we saw in Chapter Four, legislative procedures are not thus indifferent. They generally require legislators to draft and introduce a bill in the form of a rule, determine any legislative facts relevant to the content of their proposed law, study and hold public hearings on the proposed law at which facts and arguments are considered, engage in deliberation and public debate on the proposed law, and consider possible amendments – all prior to the time when the statute is finally voted on and adopted. Legislators required to follow such formal procedures and thus act in law-like ways are called upon to bring rationality to bear in law-making processes on the content of the proposed laws. Here, appropriate procedural form in the law's operations tends to contribute to good policy content in the law as finally made. It is not, of course, a guarantee of good content.

There are still other major ways in which adherence to second-level principles of the rule of law tends to beget good policy or other content in first-level law being created. One principle of the rule of law, applicable to state-made law generally, favors adoption of the preceptual form of a rule, rather than, say, that of a principle, maxim, or general order, at least so far as a rule is feasible. As we have seen, the overall form of a rule has various constituent features: prescriptiveness, definiteness, generality, completeness, internal structure, and modes of encapsulation and expression. Again, consider definiteness. Among other things, specific defects in a draft of a definite rule can be quite obvious, far more so than in an indefinite rule. Because legislators can more effectively bring rationality to bear on a draft of a definite rule, such a rule, as ultimately revised, is more likely to be good in content. Consider also the generality of a rule. The drafter who gives due attention to generality will carefully consider the appropriate range of persons, citizens, and circumstances the rule should apply to, if it is to serve effectively as a

Section Seven: Operation of Techniques in Conformity with Rule of Law   343

means to the proposed policies at hand. A system thus operating in law-like ways, as prescribed by principles of the rule of law, can serve many important ends. Indeed, there is happily here, a confluence of factors that both serve the rule of law and the rule of good law.

Another principle of the rule of law requires that any duly adopted first-level rule or other law be thereafter promulgated and publicized, and thus rendered accessible to its addressees. A system so operating not only serves the effectiveness of the policy of such a law. It also serves quality of content of the law being made. Legislators who wish to be free of serious public criticism and wish to be re-elected, are likely to work harder to make the content of the law they create better if they know that this content, once adopted, will be publicized and that citizens will immediately learn of it. Here again, adherence to principles of the rule of law tends to beget good content in the law being made.

The principles of the rule of law are not merely means to policy or other ends served by first-level law. If these principles had merely to do with efficacy, then their violation would signify that the system would merely be less effective as a means to the policy or other ends of the law. However, a violation of one of these principles usually signifies also that a given use of law is not really law-like. Such a violation might even deny addressees a meaningful basis on which to act. A rule that is unclear in its meaning, for example, is not merely less effective. It can hardly be law-like in its operation. In the absence of special circumstances, a retroactive statute is not really law-like. A law that is not sufficiently publicized is not law-like. Official administration that is not even-handed is not law-like. In all such instances, not only is the efficacy of law sacrificed, but general values associated with the rule of law are sacrificed as well.

As we have seen, principles of the rule of law, in the course of law's operations, do contribute instrumentally to many ends, including the realization of general values of the rule of law. But this is not all. The form-prescriptive contents of these principles are also constitutive of some of these very values. Consider, for example, processual fairness, as served by principles of the rule of law requiring fair notice of a criminal charge or of an adverse claim, and requiring fair opportunity to respond in court. The form-prescriptive contents of these principles go far to define the very nature of such fairness. Here form is constitutive and not merely instrumental.

On a larger scale, the formal and highly complex law-like operation of a legal system is not an end wholly external to the second-level principles of the rule of law, with these principles merely serving as instrumental means to this end. Nor is the end of law-like operation of the system a natural pre-legal, or an a-legal end like public safety or clean air. Rather, law-like operation is itself a socio-legal end that form-prescriptive principles of the rule of law define and organize. Such

344   The Overall Form of a Legal System as a Whole

principles are constitutive of this highly complex end. Appropriate form here is not merely instrumental.[25] At this point, the reader may wish to return to the chart at pp. __ *supra* for a summary.

SECTION EIGHT: THE ROLES OF FURTHER SYSTEMATIZING FACTORS

I have considered various formal second-level systematizing devices in this chapter, and how these organize first-level functional units and other phenomena of law into features of the overall form of a legal system. Still further factors have their own systematizing effects, too. For example, that the system operates within a discrete geographical region contributes a special type of unity. It can even engender a general sense of unity among the populace within that region. Integrated systems of communication and similar material resources may also secure a sense of unity among the citizenry and the officialdom of a given region. A shared political culture, shared history, shared language, and shared sense of identity also have unifying effects.

To extrapolate from the theory of H. L. A. Hart, one of the most significant factors contributing to the systematic character of a legal system consists of well-informed and well-trained personnel – legislators, judges, other officials, lawyers, legal and other scholars, and representatives of the media who: (1) generally accept the authority of the system, (2) understand the various second-level systematizing devices as required to unify first-level functional units and other features into an integrated whole, and (3) treat these devices and the resulting systematized features as sources of common public standards of what is desirably systematic in a legal order. In so treating these features of form, the foregoing types of personnel stand ready to act, and do act, in the name of systemic unity, though they rarely express themselves in these terms.[26]

For example, legislators, judges, and administrators are generally aware that they are supposed to act only within their own jurisdictional spheres, and they often cite rules and other law formally allocating jurisdiction to legislate, adjudicate, or administer, as reasons for so confining their actions. If their jurisdiction is

---

[25] It is sometimes suggested that because the contents of principles of the rule of law themselves serve such "substantive" ends as moral legitimacy, fundamental fairness, and individual autonomy, these contents are not form-prescriptive, but "substantive." See P. Craig, "Formal and Substantive Conceptions of the Rule of Law: An Analytical Framework," 1997 *Public Law*, 467, 481. In response, consider the following. First, the foregoing argument proves too much. On this argument, we could seldom meaningfully distinguish form-prescriptive content from substantive content, for all well-designed form-prescriptive content serves ends and values many of which may also be characterized as "substantive." Yet the distinction between the contents of principles of the rule of law prescribing formal features of precepts and of other phenomena on the one hand, and the contents of legal rules that incorporate policy or the like, on the other hand is a readily intelligible distinction. Second, we do in fact regularly distinguish form-prescriptive content and substantive policy or other such content.

[26] Cf. H. L. A. Hart, *supra* n. 2, at 88–91, 98–9.

Section Nine: Formalness As One Major Characteristic of a Legal System 345

challenged, they can also be expected to assert, in defense of their law-making or other actions, the relevant formal allocation of jurisdiction. In the face of prospective acts of others that would exceed jurisdiction, individuals may be expected to invoke such systematizing features as binding standards to oppose and condemn acts that exceed jurisdiction. Hart called the foregoing factor contributing to systemic unity an "internal point of view" – an essential attitude that officials and certain others take toward the overall form of the system. Hart's own emphasis was on such an internal point of view toward rules prescribing facets I here independently classify as formal. Without this internal point of view, widely disseminated at least among officials, especially the judges, Hart believed a legal system would fall apart.[27] The internal point of view is partly borne of, and bears the effects of, the way the system is set up, which includes its overall form and its duly systematized features. Before the systematizing features of unifying form can become, from the internal point of view of officials and others, common public standards, they must first be constructed and understood as such. That is, the first-level and other facets of the system must first be organized and integrated into the overall form of a legal system. The system as a whole must be unified in accord with the various formal unifying features identified in this chapter.

Another major factor that has some systemic unifying effect is simply the wide acceptance of the system and the general sense of allegiance of the citizenry and other inhabitants. Indeed, perhaps the most important asset of a legal system overall is a cooperative and legally sensitive populace. Again, such a populace accepts the system partly for what it is, and this includes its overall form. For example, formal principles of the rule of law serve predictability and fairness, and these can go far to inspire the populace to accept the system in the first place.

SECTION NINE: FORMALNESS AS ONE MAJOR CHARACTERISTIC OF A LEGAL SYSTEM AS A WHOLE

As already suggested, the first-level functional units and other facets of a duly systematized legal order comprise a system, with inter-related general characteristics. These general characteristics are numerous and complex and may be succinctly identified and categorized here as follows:

(1) A system of law in a developed Western society is characteristically designed to serve and does serve human interests, and to the extent it fails to do so, it is, as Plato suggested, less truly a system of law.[28]

(2) It is characteristic that such a society recognizes and accepts as legitimate an authoritative, relatively autonomous, exclusive, and organized system

---

[27] *Id.*, at 88–91.

[28] See *Plato*, 2 Dialogues of Plato 486–7 (B. Jowett trans. 1937).

for making and implementing legal rules and other devices of social facilitation and control.

(3) This recognized and accepted system includes a characteristic set of first-level functional units including a legislature, courts, bodies of law, interpretive methodologies, sanctions, and so on, some of which are highly complex.

(4) These functional units are, in turn, characteristically organized systematically: institutions and other entities are centralized, hierarchically ordered, and duly prioritized; bodies of law are codified or otherwise duly unified, interpretive and other methodologies are made uniform throughout the boundaries of the system, and first-level functional units and systematizing devices are characteristically combined, integrated, and coordinated within various general operational techniques: penal, grievance-remedial, administrative-regulatory, public-benefit conferring, and private-arranging, for the creation and implementation of law.

(5) Through these functional units and systematizing devices as organized in (4), and as operative through the foregoing general techniques, official personnel, lawyers, private citizens, and other legal entities characteristically fulfill law-making and law-implementing roles in accord with a systematic division and specialization of legal labor, itself defined and delimited by law.

(6) Characteristically, most of the law made by state organs is in the form of general rules reduced to some written form, i.e., statute, regulation, judicial opinion, etc., whereas law created by private parties and entities may or may not be written, and takes more varied overall forms, e.g., contracts, property arrangements, and wills.

(7) The totality of the bodies of state-made law characteristically has a minimum substantive policy content encompassing at least basic protection of the bodily integrity of human beings, the protection of property, and of promises, and thus serves corresponding values.

(8) Valid law publicly or privately created is characteristically regarded as generating, in accord with prescribed uniform interpretive and other applicational methodologies, authoritative reasons for citizens, other inhabitants, other entities, and officials, to take determinate actions or to make decisions accordingly.

(9) The addressees of the law characteristically act or decide, more or less voluntarily, in accord with the authoritative reasons for action or decision so generated by valid law and relevant interpretive or other applicational method, and the system is thus generally efficacious.

(10) The system, however, characteristically has the capacity to coerce or sanction any persons or entities who do not act in accord with the authoritative reasons so generated.

Section Nine: Formalness As One Major Characteristic of a Legal System 347

(11) The system characteristically provides for orderly modes of change in the content and form of the law, in functional legal units, and even in features of the system as a whole.

(12) The system characteristically operates, to a large degree, in accord with principles of the rule of law, and in accord with various limitations on governmental power, and thus characteristically serves corresponding values.

(13) The system is characteristically dependent for its efficacy on a common language, on the dissemination of legal and other knowledge, on trained personnel, on various material resources, and most important of all, on social acceptance and social attitudes.

(14) The system is characteristically formal in rules and other law, in other first-level legal functional units, and in core features of the system as a whole.

This last general characteristic may be considered the formalness of a legal system, overall. To recapitulate briefly: rules of law are formal in that they conform to the overall form of a rule with its constituent formal features. A similar yet modified analysis can be deployed to explicate the formality of rulings, principles, maxims, and other species of law. All other first-level functional units such as the institutions of legislatures and courts, interpretive and other methodologies, and sanctions and remedies are formal in their conformity to the overall forms of such units. The system as a whole is also formal in all the ways considered in this chapter.

Formalness is merely one of the basic characteristics of a legal system. Yet for several reasons, this formalness has a *special primacy* among all of the foregoing characteristics of a legal system. First, it figures in each of the other characteristics. Functional legal units figure directly or indirectly, in each of the system's other characteristics, and we have seen that all units are formal in major respects. For example, regulative or reinforcive rules figure in all of the characteristics, and rules are formal in several major ways. Moreover, many varieties of form contribute directly and indirectly to the incorporation and organization of the material or other components of all functional legal units. These components include substantive policy content, official personnel, material resources, specialized knowledge, and more. Here, form not only leaves its own imprints on and has other effects on these components, but is a kind of binding that ties all together.

Secondly, the formal character of a legal system has special primacy among the characteristics of such a system because it is required for the very existence of a legal system as a whole. To exist, a legal system requires first-level functional units such as a legislature, courts, bodies of rules, interpretive methodologies, sanctions, and more. Yet even with such first-level units, we would not have a system of law without the formal systematizing devices considered here that account for the systematic arrangement of the system as a whole.

Thirdly and relatedly, the formal character of law has special primacy among law's characteristics because it is indispensable to the very existence of duly constituted and legitimate civic authority. Such authority is foundational. The most fundamental of all political values is that of securing within a society legitimate political authority to make and implement law. Duly designed form is indispensable to authoritative public decision-making – to the very existence of legitimate authority. Without duly constituted authority, there could be no valid rules or other law, and no authoritative, interpretive, and other applicational method, and no legally authoritative reasons for citizens, officials, and others to take determinate action. Without such reasons, there is no law. For authority to make law to exist, the "authors" who make law must be authorized. This authorization cannot exist if law-making is ad hoc and haphazard. It must be organized and regularized through the adoption and implementation of formal rules establishing law-making roles and conferring law-making power on occupants of those roles. Moreover, such authority must be similarly established for those who interpret and apply rules in cases of dispute.

The very efficacy of legitimate processes for making and applying legal rules and other law is therefore heavily dependent on duly designed forms. Without such forms, and without the established mandatory force of legally authoritative reasons for action and decision that validly created law and its operational techniques generate, there could be *no social objects* of sufficient determinateness and constancy through time to which the people of a society could express or imply their assent, acceptance, or acquiescence – the primary sources of legitimacy in modern systems. And without such legitimacy, the levels of voluntary compliance in accord with the formal reasons for action and decision that law generates could not be sustained. Because the efficacy of the coercive apparatus of such systems is itself heavily dependent on such legitimacy, this apparatus could not, without such legitimacy, alone secure sufficient levels of compliance.

Fourth, as Jhering taught us, any characteristic that goes to the very *identity* of a particular legal system as such has a claim to special primacy. A primary measure of the very identity of any particular legal system is the nature and extent of its formal character, overall. One way to test this view is to imagine that a number of basic changes in the functional legal units of a given system (with changes in complementary material or other components) take place over a given period of time, and then to pose the issue of whether that system might be said to have lost its very identity and to have taken on a new one. Suppose that the system is changed from one of open-ended rules to highly definite ones. Suppose that the system is changed from one in which law is interpreted ad hoc and rather freely merely in light of substantive ends and means implicated in particular cases to one in which law is interpreted and applied in light of a more refined and uniform interpetive methodology. Suppose that the system is changed from one in which

Section Nine: Formalness As One Major Characteristic of a Legal System 349

courts have vast power to modify antecedent law at point of application to one in which they have only very restricted power to do so. Now, if such changes were cumulatively to occur, a system so changed in these *formal* respects, with their complementary manifestations in material or other components, would no longer be considered the *same* legal system. If this be doubted, many more such changes, major in nature, could easily be imagined.

Moreover, the distinctive identity of a particular legal system is determined not only by its functional units, but also by reference to what is special about how it is systematized. No two particular systems are systematized in precisely the same fashion. It should hardly be surprising, given the importance of formal systematizing devices, that the distinctive identity of a particular system can be determined, in part, by reference to what is special about how it is formally systematized. For example, a system may fail to separate at all sharply the legislative, executive, and judicial spheres of governmental activity. Its legislature and its executive might actually be fused, as in England. A system may not codify fields of law but leave them largely in common law form systematized only by scholars. A system may rely heavily on the penal, the grievance-remedial, and the private-arranging techniques, and much less heavily on the public-benefit conferral and administrative-regulatory techniques. Its techniques may also fail to operate very consistently with principles of the rule of law. All such differences pertain to basic modes of systematizing the form of a legal order. We can readily see how such differences in systematized features may reveal much of what is important about the distinctive identity of a given legal system, as a system.

Fifth, a system of law in due form not only creates and implements policy or other similar content. The contours of the system's very institutional and pro-cessual forms, characteristically define, express, enshrine, symbolize, radiate, and reinforce legal commitments having special primacy in the society. These are com-mitments to such fundamental political values as democracy, justice and fairness of process, rationality of decision-making, principles of the rule of law, liberty, limited government, and still more. Duly designed form is indispensable for these purposes. Let us close with the example of democracy.

Duly designed form in the law's institutional architecture and daily functioning is required to define, express, enshrine, symbolize, radiate, and thus reinforce the fundamental value of democracy. Without such form, there could be no suffi-ciently well-designed electoral processes and no elected legislature. Appropriate form here requires not only the minimal forms required for the mere organized existence of an electoral process and of a legislature, but also various duly designed elaborations on these if they are to be effective. Many of these elaborations are preceptual, structural, methodological, and procedural, and so formal in all these ways. An electoral process is a highly rule-defined process. It includes rules that prevent ineligible persons from voting, rules that prescribe how votes are to be counted, rules that prevent persons from voting twice, etc. Further, the legislature has to be formally organized so that the results of democratic elections can, in turn, be implemented in law-making and other processes. Moreover, in order for democracy to be realized, structural, methodological, procedural, and other formal limits must be imposed on still other institutions of the legal system, and these must take appropriate encapsulatory (often constitutional) form. For instance, courts and other authoritative institutions must not have a general power, even in the name of interpretation, simply to amend and thus undo statutes adopted by the democratically elected legislature.

11 ∼ CUMULATIVE AND SYNERGISTIC EFFECTS OF LEGAL FORMS – A SCHEMATIC PRACTICAL APPLICATION

"Laws, like houses, lean on one another. . . . "   – E. Burke[1]

"With the right combinations, one and one can make three."   – S. Kimble [2]

SECTION ONE: INTRODUCTION

A highly concrete, felicitous, and revealing way to draw together, summarize, and highlight major contributions of duly designed form in a standard modern use of law that has itself been highly successful, is: (1) to present a synoptic overview of the main stages in an illustrative linear progression in which functional legal units are deployed concurrently or in sequence to create and to implement law to serve a standard legal policy, (2) to identify how systematizing devices, and resultant formal features of the legal system as a whole, contribute in this overall process, focusing especially on how various legal units are, at these main stages, combined, integrated, and coordinated within one or more of the law's five basic operational techniques for the creation and implementation of law, all in accord with principles of the rule of law, (3) to identify and review how major choices of form and of complementary material or other components in discrete legal units, and how major choices of form in the formation of the system as a whole, contribute by way of imprints and other effects to the operation of this progression at each stage, and (4) to consider the cumulative and synergistic effects of such choices of form and complementary material and other components, at each stage and at subsequent stages of the progression, as these imprints and other effects converge and add up in the processes and outcomes involved, and thus ultimately contribute to the realization of purposes.

---

[1] E. Burke, *The Writing and Speeches of Edmund Burke*, vol. 9, at 453 (R. B. McDowell ed., Clarendon Press, Oxford, 1991).
[2] *N.Y. Times*, Oct. 4, 1984, p. D1, col. 5.

What here follows, then, is what will be called a "linear progression analysis" mainly of the choices of forms in functional legal units and in systematizing devices, and of the types of imprints and other effects of these choices, as these converge and cumulate from stage to stage. This mode of analysis puts duly designed forms and their effects into an overall operational framework, and underscores the dynamic character of a system of law.[3] In a linear progression, legal units and systematizing devices are deployed in appropriate sequence to create and implement law. However, legal units and systemizing devices do not always operate in an order that follows a single sequential pattern. As we will see, they also sometimes operate concurrently, and sometimes they function even out of what would be the usual sequence.

My general aim is to utilize this linear mode of analysis, as applied in an illustrative American context, to reveal and summarize main types of contributions of choices of form and of complementary components in first-level units and in second-level systematizing devices. This analysis identifies choices of form made, or carried forward, at each stage of the linear progression, shows how choices made earlier can affect later ones, and demonstrates how the combined imprints and other effects of the various choices can synergistically interact, either simultaneously or sequentially. Thus, the analysis lays bare in broad terms the overall cumulative imprints and effects of choices of form and of complementary material and other components. Though the illustrative materials here are drawn from an American context, most of what they reveal about form has counterparts in other developed Western systems.

The linear mode of analysis presented here is explicitly form-oriented, whereas an analysis merely in terms of the contents of the relevant reinforcive rules is not. My ultimate focus continues to be on form as a key to understanding, and on the credit due form as instrumental to ends, and even as constitutive of some ends.[4] I do not, however, equate linear analysis as such with form-oriented analysis. Most form-oriented analysis so far in this book has not been presented in linear terms, though it could have been so treated.

Toward the end of this chapter, I also present a major supplement to Chapter Four on institutional form. That is, I treat, albeit summarily, general contributions of various choices of form to the existence, operation, and effects of those

---

[3] Linear progression analysis is also to be contrasted with other varieties of essentially form-oriented analysis treated in this book. It is to be contrasted with the type of "anatomical" and "structural" analysis presented in the various chapters on types of functional legal units. A linear progression analysis does not focus on a single stage. It focuses on all stages in a linear sequence from creation of law to ultimate implementation. Such linear analysis is also to be contrasted with the type of "two-level" vertical analysis considered in Chapter Ten.

[4] This chapter presupposes the accounts of forms earlier in the book, and those forms will only be summarily identified. It would also be tedious to repeat in detail here all the various bases for attributing credit to choices of appropriate form identified as such in earlier chapters. Yet I will often remind the reader in general terms of credit due.

Section One: Introduction

institutional units consisting of trial courts (and, to an extent, appellate courts) as they resolve disputes over the applicability of law, and bring that law to bear on facts. Trial courts in due form are actively in play most significantly toward the very end of most of the linear progressions to be considered here. Yet, the standing availability of well designed trial courts, and their potential for intervention at the behest of a party or an official, can have operative effects at much earlier stages, as I will explain.

An analysis of the contributions of form as displayed at the various stages of a linear progression demonstrates yet another advantage of a form-oriented approach over an approach oriented solely to the contents of reinforcive rules. A form-oriented approach addresses and underscores in general terms the imprints and other effects of choices of form in functional legal units and in systematizing devices at all stages of a law-making and law-implementing progression, whereas a rule-oriented approach presupposes that such choices have been made, and does not itself focus frontally upon their imprints and other effects at the various stages in the overall process. In fact, a rule-oriented approach provides no account of such cumulative imprints and effects. A form-oriented approach addresses imprints and other effects of choices of form, as these choices are made at the earliest stages, on the institutions and other entities that are to make the law, on how this law is to be made, on the ultimate form and content of that law in which imprints and other effects of form also appear, and also on implementation at later stages. A form-oriented approach is therefore in temporal terms also more holistic than a rule-oriented approach. The whole treated here is thus an operational whole extended in time. A form-oriented approach lays bare the "physiology" as well as the "anatomy" of legal units as they function within an operational technique. A rule-oriented approach does not.

In the functional and dynamic perspective of a linear progression, it is possible to understand more fully how choices of form at one stage can have imprints or effects at that stage and at later stages, and also how these imprints and effects can cumulate and converge as we proceed from stage to stage, thereby contributing, along with complementary material and other components, to the realization of various purposes and values in the very course of the process as well as through ultimate outcomes. In this perspective, it is possible to see how the various contributions of choices of well-designed form "add-up" from stage to stage. If we assume, say, two factors, one or both of these may not be as effective alone as when combined with the other, and this combination may occur simultaneously or sequentially. Any resultant enhanced imprint or effect of either or both factors merely in virtue of the combination (one plus one equals three or four), is here designated as a synergistic effect.

A synergistic effect occurs when two factors, as operative in combination, interact to produce a sum total of effects that is greater than the sum total of what would be the effects of each of these factors if operative alone rather than in combination. Thus $1 + 1 = 3$ or more! The two "factors" may be highly varied, a truth also of major importance in the general theory of form. Thus, they may consist of (1) two different features within the overall form of the same functional legal unit, (2) two different features and complementary components within the overall form of the same functional unit, (3) the formal features and complementary components of two different functional units, (4) two different operational techniques with their own forms and components, (5) a functional legal unit and a moral or social counterpart, and (6) other factors.

For the purposes of this chapter, and its linear progression analysis, a concrete context is required. I have chosen, from countless possibilities, to treat the cumulative and synergistic imprints and effects of choices of form in the various functional units and systematizing devices, as deployed within operational techniques, to combat an illustrative public health problem. Although the problem I have selected is common to all developed Western systems, I will treat in very general and schematic terms the problem as it arose in New York City in the late nineteenth and in the twentieth centuries. The problem I have selected is that of preventing occurrence of the potentially fatal disease of cholera mainly by, among other things, creating and implementing binding legal standards of quality for drinking water, and policing against discharges of pollutants into the watersheds from which the drinking water is to come. Here I do not purport to treat this example in very much historical detail. Rather, I use it more as an authentic context to illustrate in very general terms how form in the law should have its due as an avenue of understanding and as a means to ends.

My choice of example can be defended as follows. If the central thesis of this book is correct about the many important contributions of form in the workings of a legal system, then we should, in linear progression, be able to see form's imprints and other effects all over a highly successful use of law such as its use to eliminate the public health threat of cholera. In this chapter, we will see how this hypothesis is borne out. We will identify the imprints and other effects of form in this use of law, and we will see that these are significant. Along the way, this focus on form will prove to be a major avenue for advancing understanding of the relevant functional units and systematizing devices, in operation. This focus will also reveal the very great credit that can be due to choices of form – credit here for contributing to the almost total elimination of a major health hazard in modern Western societies. At the same time, we will also see how adverse in its effects flawed form can be.

Cholera (*Vibrio cholerae*) is a bacterial disease that appears to infect only humans. The disease is contracted largely through food and drink as contaminated by human waste. When most acute, cholera can be fatal, and many have died in various countries from the disease. It has been recorded that one of the

Section One: Introduction

most famous victims was Peter Iljitch Tchaikovsky (who died on November 6, 1893). When the disease goes untreated, the fatality rate is generally between 40% and 60%, and death can occur in four to five days. Cholera, once contracted, is extremely resistant to medical measures. However, through scientifically informed purification of the water supply in accord with law, through scientifically informed legal regulation of sewage disposal, and through scientifically informed legal protection of watersheds, cholera has been stamped out entirely in many places.

Despite this great progress, cholera still persists in certain areas. In 1961, a cholera pandemic surfaced in the Pacific Islands and spread rapidly throughout Asia. It reached Bangladesh in 1963, India in 1964, and Russia, Iran, and Iraq in 1965. Cholera struck West Africa in 1970. During the 1970s and 1980s, major outbreaks occurred in the Far East and in South America. In 1992, a different serogroup of the bacteria caused another large outbreak in Bangladesh.[5]

Through well-designed choices of form and of complementary material and other components of functional legal units, and through due deployment of these functional units and well-designed systematizing devices, many developed countries have virtually obliterated the once persistent public health hazard of cholera. The first main cholera outbreak in the United States occurred in 1832 in New York City.[6] The New York legislature and other bodies responded quickly, but because cholera was not well-understood at that time, the response was largely limited to imposing a quarantine on persons and on vessels entering the state from cholera-infected areas, and to ordering cities and villages to create local boards of health.[7] New York City already had a Board of Health, but the Board only met during the summer months, and was comprised only of the Mayor and City Aldermen.[8] The Board also operated as one of a confusing and overlapping tripartite arrangement of agencies which also included the City Health Office and the City Inspector. There was no comprehensive sanitary program in the City in 1832.[9] Nor was any organized provision made for systematic gathering of data. These factors, and general ignorance as to causes of cholera and how it was spread, led officials to take misguided, albeit earnest, actions. The resulting failures were in part failures of form.

Rather than adopting a preventative approach primarily through systematic deployment of a formally well-designed administrative-regulatory technique, officials limited themselves largely to combating any outbreaks through various ad hoc

---

[5] See World Health Org., Fact Sheet N107, (Rev. March 2000), available at http://www.who.int/inf-fs/en/fact107.html

[6] C. Rosenberg, *The Cholera Years: The United States in 1832, 1849, and 1866*, 13 et seq. (University of Chicago Press, 1962).

[7] Ch. 333, 1832 N.Y. Laws 581–4.

[8] J. Duffy, *A History of Public Health in New York City 1625–1866*, 280 (Russell Sage Foundation, New York, 1968).

[9] *Id.*, at 282.

actions.[10] Officials were not merely ignorant of the nature of the disease. They were also ignorant of the proper operational techniques of the law to employ. Moreover, at the time when New York was first dealing with cholera epidemics in the City and elsewhere, the New York legal order did not have anything approximating a developed administrative-regulatory technique, let alone a full understanding of its distinctive overall form and its preventative potential. At this stage in the evolution of the American legal order, the overall form of this technique simply had not yet been invented, in part a failure of form.

Even with a proper knowledge of the causes and nature of the disease, it is unlikely that New York officials would have battled the epidemic very effectively, given that this knowledge would very likely have been misdeployed. This can be seen in the actual reaction of City officials during the cholera epidemic in 1832. Some did speculate as to what caused the disease: some type of "miasma" – an evil force in the atmosphere, or a merely "spontaneous generation" from garbage or sewage.[11] The City had not then even adopted comprehensive public regulatory standards as to garbage and sewage disposal. Nor had the City encouraged private self-regulation. The City simply did not have in place any adequate general preventative methods – the essence of the administrative-regulatory technique. The City had empowered the Board of Health to build hospitals and to do anything else that it deemed advisable to "alleviate and prevent the cholera."[12] Thus, even though officials thought that they knew the source of the disease (which they were in fact mistaken about), they still did not understand what would be the most appropriate operational technique of the law required to combat the disease. As indicated, American legal architects simply had not yet invented the basic form of the administrative-regulatory technique, with its distinctive preventative efficacy.

Here we will see in some detail how deficient understanding of the potential of relevant form and its complementary components – of the potential of that operational technique here called the administrative-regulatory – accounted for early failures of uses of law to combat cholera. At the same time, we will also see how the potential credit due form was very great, especially once some of the relevant forms were invented and duly defined, designed, and organized.

Subsequent outbreaks of cholera occurred in New York City in 1849 and 1866. During these two epidemics, the number of reported cases dropped. This was due to a better understanding of the disease itself, to legislation reforming the public health system in New York City,[13] and to a developing understanding of

---

[10] *Id.*, at 291.

[11] See also N. Longmate, *King Cholera: The Biography of a Disease* 67 (Hamish Hamilton, London, 1966).

[12] J. Duffy, *supra* n. 8, at 283.

[13] See, e.g., Chapter 187, 1849 N.Y. Laws 282 (consolidating all public health authority in the City Inspector rather than in the tripartite structure); Chapter 275, 1850 N.Y. Laws 597-613 (vesting the powers of the board of health of New York City in the mayor and common council, setting the powers and duties of the board and the city inspector, establishing public health regulations, and establishing guidelines for

Section One: Introduction 357

the essentials of the administrative-regulatory technique and its special preventative efficacy. The discovery that cholera could be spread by drinking contaminated water (1855) and the discovery of the cholera bacterium itself (1884), enabled officials to combat cholera more effectively through regulation of waste disposal in watersheds, through construction of sanitary sewer systems, through adoption of water quality standards for officials and citizens to abide by, and, as we shall see, through development and deployment of the law's administrative-regulatory technique to set and enforce these water quality standards. Even so, there were five major outbreaks in New York City from the late nineteenth to the early twentieth century. The last significant cholera epidemic in the United States occurred in 1910. Today, the disease is, for practical purposes, dead in New York, dead in the rest of the United States, and dead in nearly all developed Western societies.

This, like many other major public health successes, is a great credit partly to law and legal form. Successful cholera-prevention in New York required many well-designed choices of form along with complementary material and other components. In addition to demonstrating how such choices can serve the basic policy of improving public health, the materials here, which are drawn from the New York experience, also illustratively reveal how form can contribute to the realization of fundamental political values such as democracy, legitimacy, and rationality, and also to the realization of general values of the rule of law. In these concrete materials, we will address schematically the cumulative and synergistic effects of choices of form throughout the various stages of a linear progression, emphasizing use of the administrative-regulatory technique as the primary form of technique to prevent cholera.[14]

It will be sufficient to treat merely in broad outline the creation of various institutions, the passage of state and local laws, administrative adoption of health rules and regulations, general implementation of these by both public and private parties, and enforcement through both administrative and judicial action. The general illustration here is reflective of choices of legal form made widely elsewhere in New York State, in the United States, and in other Western societies. Though the schematic illustration focuses on cholera, and mainly on one locale, New York City, it is generalizeable, with modifications, to many other public health

the quarantine of persons and vessels); Chapter 74, 1866 N.Y. Laws 114-44 (creating an independent public health authority in New York City).

[14] This illustrative and schematic example of the role of form in a regime for the prevention of cholera in New York City draws on various diverse sources of law. Sources of law for the state of New York include state potable waters statutes, N.Y. Pub. Health Law §§ 1100, 1101, 1102, 1103, 1107 (Consol. 1987), and Drinking Water Supplies regulations, N.Y. Comp. Codes R. & Regs. tit. 10, §5-1 (1998). Sources of law for New York City include general public water supply provisions, N.Y. Comp. Codes R. & Regs. tit. 10, §§ 128-1.4, 128-2, 128-5.1 (1998). Federal sources include Environmental Protection Agency Water Quality Standards, 40 C.F.R. § 131.3(b) (2002).

problems, and to many other problems requiring preventative action that have confronted and continued to confront developed Western systems.

When cholera became a problem in New York, that state already had a *legal system* of its own in place (also a part of the U.S. federal system). For the state of New York, then, most of the choices of second-level devices systematizing the overall form of a legal system discussed in Chapter Ten had already been made. These choices definitively allocated primary law-making and law-implementing jurisdiction to the New York state legislature, which itself had power to delegate some of that jurisdiction. Choices of jurisdictional form in the New York constitution generally prioritized state legislative action over judicial and other official action, and also empowered the state legislature to delegate responsibility to state-wide administrative bodies and to local administrative, legislative, and other entities, including municipalities such as New York City. The law-making and administrative functions of the relevant institutions were thus hierarchically ordered and duly prioritized. The resulting systematization determined who could do what, as between institutions and entities, thereby reducing jurisdictional disputes between legislators, administrators, and judges to a minimum. Here, much credit was due well-designed structural and other form.

The New York Constitution recognized the protection and promotion of health as a matter of public concern and authorized the state legislature to take measures necessary to ensure public health. The state legislature enacted New York's Public Health Law. This law authorized the state Public Health Department, headed by the state health Commissioner, to make rules and regulations to provide and to protect potable water, and to address other health related concerns. The state Public Health Law also authorized the creation of local departments of health, such as the New York City Department of Health, headed by the City Commissioner of Health, and which included the New York City Board of Health. These local departments were charged with safeguarding the public health through adoption of regulations having the force of law within their jurisdiction. The state Public Health Department had to approve any regulations proposed for adoption by the City Board of Water Supply, and by other officials charged with maintaining the purity of all water from which the New York City water supply was to be drawn. Enforcement of statutes, rules, and regulations occurred through this hierarchical structure.

As mentioned, the first major intervention of the New York State Legislature occurred in response to the cholera outbreak of 1832. Over the years, as understanding of the disease improved, and as the law's five basic forms of operational techniques became more fully developed, the legislature chose two major techniques as the primary means of combating cholera through law: the administrative-regulatory and the public-benefit conferring techniques. Of these two, the administrative-regulatory was primary. These major choices of form

Section One: Introduction

were made in the course of the functioning of overall legislative form and its complementary material and other components already studied in Chapter Four of this book. As we saw, the main choices of features of legislative form include the compositional, jurisdictional, structural, and procedural.

The importance of the choice of the administrative-regulatory technique, as supplemented by the public-benefit conferring technique, cannot be comprehended without further consideration of the basic nature of these techniques and their alternatives.[15] We have seen that the five basic operational techniques of the law are: (1) the "penal" technique, whereby legislatures adopt statutory rules prohibiting antisocial conduct, these statutes and enforcement officials together deter the proscribed conduct, and criminals are caught and punished, with some also rehabilitated, (2) the grievance-remedial technique, whereby courts, legislatures, and other bodies define civil wrongs such as torts and provide judicial compensatory or other remedies for actual aggrieved parties, (3) the administrative-regulatory technique in which administrative agencies and legislatures preventively regulate activities through adoption and promulgation of regulatory standards in rules, and through licensing, inspections, testing for compliance, sanctions, etc., (4) the public benefit-conferring technique whereby legislatures and administrative agencies define public benefits such as highways, sewer systems, and water supplies, secure funding and other resources required for public conferral of these benefits, and distribute the benefits, and (5) the private-arrangement technique whereby private parties enter into arrangements, such as contracts, and property arrangements, to serve private and social ends. As we saw in Chapter Ten, within each of these five techniques, first-level functional legal units including institutions, rules, other species of law, methodologies, sanctions, and second-level systematizing devices, including prioritized criteria of legal validity, are all integrated and coordinated for the creation and implementation of law to serve purposes.

Each of the five overall forms of operational techniques, then, is a purposive systematic arrangement of various first-level and other devices as duly integrated and coordinated. Of all choices of form to be made in the course of a projected linear progression, the choice, at the outset, of one basic operational technique as primary with one or more further ones as supplemental is usually the most important choice of all. As we will see, such choices can be both wide-ranging and far-reaching in impact. Such choices can even be as important as choices of form in a basic rule or rules adopting a leading policy to be implemented.

As we saw in Chapter Ten, each of the foregoing five operational techniques takes an overall form. That is, each is a purposive systematic arrangement in which

---

[15] R. Summers, "The Technique Element in Law," 59 *Cal. L. Rev.* 733 (1971).

discrete first-level units and systematizing devices are duly combined, integrated and coordinated to serve purposes through law. These forms differ in major ways, only two of which I will now stress. First, there are important differences of primary purposes: prohibitive (penal), reparative (grievance-remedial), preventative (administrative-regulatory), distributive (public-benefit conferring), and facilitative of private choice (private-arranging). Second, there are major differences in features of internal organization – in *how* first-level phenomena are combined, integrated, and coordinated in the techniques. For example, the administrative-regulatory technique is organized primarily to operate *before* the fact of harm, and thus is organized to prevent harm. Regulatory officials deploying this technique formulate binding regulatory standards, communicate them in advance to a relatively discrete class of addressees, closely monitor compliance therewith through inspections, testing, and the like, and assume responsibility for policing and sanctioning noncompliance. Thus, such regulators need not generally depend on the penal technique for sanctioning. They do rely on administrative-regulatory sanctions, as we will see. Though there are similarities, the other techniques are not essentially so organized – so formed. It follows that the choice of the administrative-regulatory technique as primary leaves distinctive and far reaching imprints and other effects on the overall legal program. Indeed, this very choice is, in itself, a choice of basic organizational modality very different in overall form from the other operational techniques.

I will now present a schematic linear progression beginning with the creation of statutory and administrative rules in the administrative-regulatory technique. There will also be occasion to discuss rules as they come into play in other basic operational techniques. The main stages of the type of linear progression in the administrative-regulatory technique to be considered illustratively here are:

- determination, usually in a state or local legislative or administrative body, of the nature of the problem, and adoption of the administrative-regulatory technique, with any other techniques, in combination,
- invocation of legislative, administrative, or other law-making bodies to create or authorize primary and auxillary law, including regulatory standards of water quality, and regulations with regard to discharge of pollutants in watershed,
- creation of any further more detailed regulatory standards by an administrative agency or agencies,
- promulgation and dissemination of laws, and education of primary addressees, public or private, as to the form and content of laws,
- self-application of laws by addressees, including public and private providers of water, public and private dischargers of possible pollutants into the watershed, and various official regulators,

Section One: Introduction 361

- any administrative inspection, administrative testing, administrative licensing, administrative sanctioning, or other action to determine and secure compliance with regulatory standards,
- disposition of disputes arising in the operation of the regulatory program (not only between regulators and regulatees, but between courts and administrative officials).

At all of these stages, a variety of choices of well-designed form, and of various complementary material and other components of functional units must be made. Each choice of form may affect later choices of form. One choice of form at an early stage in the progression may even exclude other choices of form later in the progression. The credit here, or lack thereof, due to form can be very great. For instance, if the State of New York had erred fundamentally here, and had ultimately chosen only the grievance-remedial technique (reparative), rather than chosen to develop the administrative-regulatory technique (preventative) as the primary technique for preventing cholera, this choice of form would have greatly limited the efficacy of further choices of form at almost every later stage of the linear progression. Although a law-making body, such as a legislature, could still have been involved, the primary law thus created by that body or by the courts would have very likely merely been a reparative principle of tort law providing the aggrieved party or relatives money damages (or other remedies) for the harm or death actually caused by cholera. Though the remedying of particular grievances can have considerable deterrent effect, this technique does not operate in an essentially preventative fashion in the way the administrative regulatory technique does. As already indicated, implementive devices of the administrative-regulatory technique include adoption, promulgation, and dissemination of regulations prohibiting supply of nonpotable water, official inspections and testing of water for potability, various injunctive or other remedies, and administrative penalties. These devices are essentially preventative, whereas nearly all tort remedies largely operate after the fact of harm and are essentially reparative rather than preventative.

Alternatively, the state legislature could have similarly erred fundamentally in its main choice of a form of operational technique hereby invoking the private-arranging technique as primary. For example, the state legislature might merely have specified in a statute the terms on which public bodies could enter contracts with private parties who would provide potable water. The remedies available under the private-arranging technique for failure to provide such water would differ from those available in the administrative-regulatory technique. Under the private-arranging technique the remedies would largely consist of judicial awards of monetary damages for breach of contractual agreements. Again, here these remedies would largely come into play after the fact of harm, and are essentially reparative not preventative.

The foregoing analysis again reveals major differences that a choice of form at the very outset – choice of the form of one basic operational technique rather than another as primary – may have on later stages of the linear progression. Plainly, it is far better to prevent cholera in the first place than seek merely to provide remedies after the fact to persons who come to suffer from the disease, yet survive somehow. The lack of a sufficiently developed administrative-regulatory technique in due form during the early cholera outbreaks greatly limited the possible responses of the legal system here.

The early choice of a form of an operational technique, then, can either augment, or undermine, the purpose-serving effects of later choices of form in a linear progression. When the form of an operational technique is well chosen at the outset, its effects may contribute: (1) to the quality and efficacy of legislated and other policies embodied in the law, for example, the convenient provision of potable water, (2) to the realization of general values of the rule of law such as fair notice and equality before the law, and (3) to the realization of fundamental political values such as democracy, rationality, and legitimacy.

It is not enough, however, merely for legislators and other officials, within a duly systematized legal order, to choose the basic form of the best possible operational technique (or combination of techniques). Plainly, discrete first-level functional units such as rules and other law to be made and implemented via the chosen technique must also be well-designed in form and complementary content, with form leaving its essential imprints and other effects on this content. If, for example, the administrative-regulatory technique is adopted at the outset, yet the rule on water quality adopted at the outset is not sufficiently definite, in that it only prescribes the provision of "drinkable water," or "water free of pollutants," officials and citizens could not sufficiently determine what the statute actually requires! The indefinite form of such a law simply would not inform official and private addressees as to what they are to do. Hence, the efficacy of the policy would be vastly diminished.

Also, in order for democracy to be effective, the democratic will must be formulated by legislatures, or by legislatures and administrative agencies together, in terms sufficiently definite to be implemented. In the absence of this, democratic will, rationality in the formulation of policy and other purposes, and overall legitimacy could not be realized. General values of the rule of law could not be well served, either. For example, addressees could not even have fair notice of what they are to do, and similarly situated providers of water might be treated quite differently by the regulatory body. The formal feature of due definiteness in a proposed rule synergistically interacts here with due expressional form. The more definite a proposed rule, the more clearly it can be expressed. Thus, the two together – a definite and clear rule – "make three," not merely two.

The stages of the linear progression, then, begin with recognition of the nature of the problem and choice of form of primary operational technique (or techniques),

Section Two: Choices of Forms of Basic Operational Techniques   363

all against a background of a duly systematized and prioritized institutional set-up. Along with the choice of primary operational technique, usually by a legislative or administrative body, further choices must be made, either in a legislative process whereby the form and content of proposed statutory rules are debated and finally adopted, or in an administrative rule-making process in which regulations implementative of a general statute are adopted as delegated legislation by an administrative agency. We saw in Chapter Four how choices of well-designed institutional form are required if a law-making body is to function sufficiently well. For example, choices of formal structure and procedure can function synergistically to bring essential facts and reason to bear in studying the problem and formulating proposed law. A formal "decision rule" in a legislature – e.g., adoption by majority vote – is required if proposed statutory law is to be adopted at all. In turn, reason can be more effectively brought to bear on the proposed content of a duly defined and well-expressed draft of a rule, still another synergy of good drafting and good procedure, both partly matters of well-designed form.

The linear progression continues on with duly adopted law being formally promulgated and disseminated, with relevant addressees, including public officials and private parties learning the law, and thereafter, in a healthy legal order, generally abiding by it – (that is, voluntarily complying with its requirements, in which event, no harm occurs.) Again, with rules bearing formally well-defined and expressed imprints and other effects, formal promulgation and dissemination of these rules can be more effective, too, still another synergy. In any such linear progression usually only a small proportion of trouble cases will arise in which sanctions are threatened or imposed, with an even smaller proportion finally ending up in administrative adjudication or in courts of law.

Different things do not always occur at each stage of a linear progression. Education, for example, may occur at nearly all stages. So, too, dispute resolution of various kinds. Nor do I claim that the same institutions or other types of functional legal units all come into play at the same or similar stages of each operational technique. In the penal technique, for example, police regularly come into play at very early stages, but this is not so of police in the other operational techniques.

SECTION TWO: CHOICES OF FORMS OF BASIC OPERATIONAL TECHNIQUES

As we have seen, choices of form can leave major imprints and other effects on the policy or other content of the law and its efficacy. When confronting a problem, such as the major public health problem of providing potable water and protecting it against contamination, the choice of one or more forms of basic operational technique at the outset reflects the view of policy makers as to the best general approach to the problem.

The choice of a basic form of operational technique necessarily includes resort to a combination of first-level functional units: institutional or other entities, preceptual or nonpreceptual species of law, methodologies, sanctioning and other implementive devices, and still other units. The choice of operational technique also embraces modes of combining, integrating, and coordinating the foregoing first-level functional units in order to create and implement law. For example, choice of the grievance-remedial technique entails that the courts will have a large role. Choice of the penal technique entails that criminal law enforcement agencies will play a large role. If the private-arranging technique is chosen, such agencies will have much less of a role. Administrative agencies and officials have large roles in the administrative-regulatory and public-benefit conferral techniques, but little role in the private-arranging technique. Because the nature of the problems with which the law is to deal varies, and because the suitability of techniques varies, the credit that can be due here for choice of technique is considerable.

Various criteria are relevant to the choice of form of operational technique or techniques. These criteria include: (1) preventative efficacy, as opposed to efficacy that is largely remedial and therefore "after the fact" of harm, (2) the necessity to bring any scientific or technological expertise to bear, (3) requirement of specially qualified institutional personnel, (4) strictness or flexibility of required procedures, (5) strong political accountability as opposed to relative isolation from the political process, (6) cost-effectiveness, and (7) any special limits on the use of a technique that may be applicable, for example, the penal technique not only does not work well against addressees unaware their conduct is morally wrongful, but is not appropriately used against most such addressees, either.

With regard to some problems, each of the five techniques may have a role. In dealing with the public health problem of cholera, although policy makers have concentrated on the administrative-regulatory technique, as primary, and the public-benefit conferral technique as supplemental, all five basic forms of operational techniques have been deployed. For example, the New York City Sanitary Code provides that the city may enforce the Code through criminal actions.[16] The penal technique has thus been used as an important adjunct to deter the knowing or reckless contamination of water. At the state level, the New York Consolidated Laws, Section 1103, provides for criminal prosecution for any violation of Article 11 of the New York Public Health Laws on pollution of potable water supplies in the state as, for example, by dumping or discharging human waste into a watershed that drains into a source of public drinking water. The Code makes it a misdemeanor to violate Article 11, punishable by a fine, not to exceed $200 per violation, or a year in prison, or both. Choices in rules that are partly choices of form allocate responsibility and provide for cooperation as

---

[16] N.Y. Comp. Codes & Regs. Title 10, §128-5.1(b) (1998).

Section Two: Choices of Forms of Basic Operational Techniques 365

between agencies at the state and local levels. Such coordinating and systematizing form, with its synergies, is thus entitled to credit here, too.

Cholera has also been addressed partly through the grievance-remedial technique. The New York City Sanitary Code provides for public enforcement of water potability regulations by civil actions in tort of private parties as well as by public officials against polluters. For example, courts have held companies and individuals liable in tort for harm caused when they have discharged pollutants into the water or watershed. The possibility of incurring tort liability for high compensatory damages doubtless deters some entities from discharging pollutants. Yet, this technique is less preventative than remedial, and over-reliance on it may be characterized as in part a flawed choice of form.

Additionally, parties might seek to ensure water quality partly through the private arranging technique. For example, a municipality may enter into a contract with a waste disposal company to ensure clean drinking water, or a contract with private companies for filtration and chlorination of drinking water. Courts in some systems have invoked the implied warranty of habitability or fitness to hold a builder-vendor liable for breach of contract where the vendor sells a building that lacks a clean water supply.[17]

However, New York decision-makers have relied mainly on two techniques here, the administrative-regulatory, and the public-benefit conferring, with the former primary. As we saw, the administrative-regulatory technique is itself essentially preventative. It imposes water quality standards in advance that suppliers of water, public and private, must meet before supplying the water. This technique also creates and disseminates regulations against pollution of the watershed by those who dispose of sewage. The public-benefit conferring technique is, in effect, used to prevent cholera mainly through direct governmental supply of some of the required potable water financed through the tax rolls. The benefit to be conferred here is itself defined in terms of a potable water standard.[18] Vast governmental resources of the state of New York and New York City have been invested in providing potable water supplies. Authorized private suppliers have entered here, too. New York State law and New York City law also require all suppliers of potable water to chlorinate water as a minimum treatment.[19]

In considering the cumulative effects of choices of form, we will concentrate primarily on the administrative-regulatory technique. In this basic form of operational technique, a legislature itself adopts rules, or delegates to an administrative agency the authority to make rules that set standards of water quality to prevent

---

[17] See also *Rogers v. Lewton*, 570 N.E.2d 133 (Ind. Ct. App. 1991) (septic system illegally discharged pollutants into lake); *Hoye v. Century Builders, Inc.*, 329 P.2d 474 (Wash. 1958) (house was unfit for habitation due to continual discharge of raw sewage).

[18] N.Y. Pub. Health Law §1100 (Consol. 1987).

[19] N.Y. Comp. Codes R. & Regs. tit. 10, §5-1.30 (1998).

cholera and other related diseases, and to protect potable water generally. The primary policy objective is to secure water quality *in advance* so no one is harmed. Essentially preventative methods are deployed before anyone gets cholera, and so that no one gets it. The efficacy of these methods depends heavily on general willingness of official and private addressees to cooperate in carrying out the regulatory program. Where public health is obviously at stake, many private addressees willingly cooperate, once duly informed of what they are to do.

Even though most potable water is actually supplied through the public-benefit conferring technique rather than through private sources, use of this technique alone could not be sufficient. The water supplied must be concurrently subjected to the essential methods of the administrative-regulatory technique to secure that the benefit to be conferred itself meets prescribed standards. Generally, public suppliers of water pursuant to the public-benefit conferring technique are also subjected to the regulatory standards of quality of the administrative-regulatory technique, just as any private suppliers are. At the same time, other private parties are subjected to the administrative-regulatory technique to prevent them from discharging pollutants into the watersheds near sources of supply, whether these sources be public or private. Such regulation precludes dumping of waste, requires public and private construction of suitable sewage disposal systems, and more.

The credit due to choices of forms of primary operational techniques at the outset can be demonstrated most convincingly if we merely hypothesize, in the spirit of Jhering,[20] that the legal system chooses, as primary, a *wrong* technique here such as the grievance-remedial or the penal. The preventative resources of the administrative-regulatory technique, either alone or as combined with the public-benefit conferring technique, are vastly superior here. It is the very function of the regulatory technique to prevent cholera (and other water borne diseases) in the first place, rather than to provide compensation after the fact to harmed persons or to relatives of deceased victims as in the grievance-remedial technique, or to impose penalties on knowing polluters after the fact, as in the penal technique.

The effective functioning of any of the five operational techniques depends not only on well-designed form, but plainly depends on complementary material and other components too, including: the contents of laws consisting of appropriate choices of policy, various trained personnel, material resources, technology, communication devices, periodic inspections, enforcive capacity, and more. Another vital nonformal element that figures in its own way in each of the techniques is an alert, informed, legally sensitive, and cooperative public. Usually, if people know their health is at stake, they will be ready to cooperate. A choice of well-designed technique can harness this cooperative spirit.

---

[20] R. Jhering, *Geist des Römischen Rechts: auf den verschiedenen Stufen seiner Entwicklung*, vol. 2, at 480 (Scientia Verlag, Aalen, 1993).

SECTION THREE: CHOICES OF FORMS IN LEGISLATURES, ADMINISTRATIVE BODIES, OR OTHER ENTITIES

Legislators and administrative bodies do not choose operational techniques, or make related choices of formal design in rules and other discrete phenomena, all in a formless institutional vacuum. The very existence of legislatures, administrative agencies, and other entities required to make relevant law presupposes that appropriate choices of form and complementary material and other components have been made and implemented to create such bodies in the first place. In Chapter Four, we saw that an institution such as a legislature is formally composed of persons having specified qualifications, and these differ from qualifications of other institutional personnel. We also saw that each variety of institution also has different formal features of jurisdiction that authorize it to deal with certain subject matters, geographical areas, types of individuals, or entities. Each also has different formal features of internal and external structure, of procedure, and of methodology. All the foregoing features of form, if well-designed, can leave important imprints or other effects on law made and applied.

Choices of a compositional feature in an institution or other entity are made partly with an eye to incentives. As we have seen, pursuant to the formal feature of democratic composition, legislators and administrators who are to make laws will often be making laws from which they, themselves, will benefit (or suffer) in their own daily lives. For example, it would be contrary to the interests of law-makers to create an overly burdensome water quality standard, given that these law-makers will drink water, and will also be affected by the costs of complying with the standards that are set. At the very least, the choice of how to compose a legislature or an administrative body in turn affects many policy choices that such personnel will make, including choices of form and content in the laws that the body adopts. Plainly, democratic compositional form must receive significant credit (or blame) for the quality (or lack of quality) of laws ultimately adopted. Because democratic legislators and other officials themselves are to benefit from the very quality of the laws they create, they plainly have special incentive in matters of this type to adopt laws good in policy content. Moreover, legislators who wish to be re-elected also have incentive to adopt such laws.

In our illustrative New York episode, state legislators adopted and promulgated a very general statute providing for protection of the public from any contamination of public supplies of potable water.[21] The statute delegated to the state

---

[21] The 1987 statute reads as follows: N.Y. Pub. Health Law §1100(1) (Consol. 1987):

> The department may make rules and regulations for the protection from contamination of any or all public supplies of potable waters and water supplies of the state or United States, institutions, parks, reservations or posts and their sources within the state, and the commissioner of environmental protection of New York may make such rules and regulations subject to the approval of the department for the protection from contamination of any or all public supplies of potable waters and their sources within the state where the same constitutes a part of the source of the public water supply of said city.

Department of Health, and to other officials, the authority to make further regulations for the protection of the water supply of New York City, all subject to legislative supervision and review. State and local regulations were promulgated, including the New York City Sanitary Code, a body of law administered and enforced by administrators, private parties, and the courts. Private parties also have played large roles herein, for example, alerting officials to instances of nonconformity with potability standards and to instances of wrongful watershed discharge.

The first major stage in the typical linear progression in which the relevant law is created and implemented, then, is that of introducing, studying, debating, amending, and adopting a basic legislative program for regulating supply of water. In the course of this, a choice of form of operational technique or techniques will be made, and the relevant laws adopted. As we saw in Chapter Four, choices of procedural form in the initial design of the legislature can contribute to the quality of this law-making process, and so to the quality and efficacy of the form and content of particular laws that legislators adopt in the process of evolving an overall regulatory program. The procedures required for the creation and promulgation of valid regulations by the Department of Health in our current example are likewise important.[22] The procedures of such an administrative body can provide a forum for soliciting the best proposed solution via "notice and comment" rule-making whereby prospective regulatees and other interested parties may contribute factual and other data. The foregoing choices of form, of course, have many effects and leave many imprints, either necessarily or contingently.

As we also saw in Chapter Four, choices of structural form in a legislature, including that of an appropriate committee system for the study of legislative proposals, can bring facts and reason to bear on a proposed water quality law. To the same effect are choices of appropriate methodological form with regard to drafting and interpretation of proposed statutes in appropriate procedural contexts of legislative action. Moreover, appropriate choices of structural, methodological, and procedural forms in an administrative agency will have many of the same types of effects and imprints on regulations proposed, studied, and adopted by that agency. Here, too, synergies occur.

Again, as we saw in Chapter Four, when a proposal is drafted with clarity and precision, a proposed law is more susceptible of effective study, debate, and amendment – a major synergistic effect of the combination of formal features, preceptual and procedural. When committees or agencies deploy an appropriate fact-finding methodology for ascertaining basic "legislative" facts establishing the nature of the problem, including any essential technological aspects, this can contribute vitally to the quality of the form and the policy content of the law finally

---

[22] N.Y. Pub. Health Law §1100(2) (Consol. 1987).

adopted, and to its efficacy. This is not to say that choices of well-designed forms guarantee good policy content. But they tend to beget such content, and synergistically as well. At the same time, choices of ill-designed compositional, jurisdictional, structural, procedural, or methodological form in law-making institutions and entities can frustrate legal objectives and wreak havoc.

SECTION FOUR: CHOICES OF PRECEPTUAL AND RELATED FORMS
AT THE LAW-MAKING STAGE

In the course of choosing the primary technique – here the administrative-regulatory, and the main supplementary technique – here the public-benefit conferring, the relevant law-making bodies make tentative choices of preceptual form at the law-making stage in our linear progression. Among the possible preceptual forms to be chosen from are: general principles, rules incorporating general standards, highly definite rules, general orders, or some combination. Choices of formal encapsulatory features must also be made and these can be highly important. So, too, choices of formal expressional features.

Imprints and Other Effects of Choice of Formal Encapsulatory Feature. The subject matter of possible law here might be put in statutory form, or in the form of administrative regulations, or in the form of case law developed in courts, or left to the form of customary practice, or some combination. The choices of forms here differ profoundly and leave their own distinctive imprints and other effects on complementary content.

Statutory rules and administrative regulations express the view of a legislature or an administrative agency in chosen words in fixed verbal sequence duly set forth in print. Here, for a general water quality law, the choice of statute, or of regulation, is most appropriate. The fixed verbal feature of these encapsulatory choices is required in the first place if there is to be legitimizing enactment by a legislature or due adoption by an authorized administrative agency. This fixed verbal feature is also stable and certain. Law in the form of a fixed verbal feature can also be readily promulgated and publicized. Various synergies of combined forms thus occur here.

Purported regulatory standards, merely as laid down by courts in case-law form, would also be inappropriate here. Courts generally lay down new law only after disputes have arisen and the disputants have brought the matters before the court. Yet, if standards are to be regulatory they must be laid down in advance of such disputes. Furthermore, the technological and scientific expertise available to legislatures and administrative bodies might not be available to courts. Such expertise is essential to due formulation of the content of many regulatory standards, including those for water potability. Finally, the discursive nature of court opinions makes many of them more difficult for most addressees to apply than well-formed statutory rules or administrative regulations.

Law in the encapsulatory form of custom is often inappropriate, too. Customary law takes time to evolve, whereas the nature of the cholera problem, and many other problems, required immediate preventative action. Also, custom cannot respond quickly to developments in modern science. Further, customary practices lack the authoritative definiteness necessary for water quality standards in due form.

Imprints and Other Effects of Choices within the Form of a Rule. Assuming that the legislature chooses the preceptual form of some version of a rule or rules in which to set forth authorization of a basic regulatory program, the legislature will also make further choices within this form. As we have seen, the features of the overall form of a rule: (1) are prescriptive, and directly or indirectly permit, require, prohibit, or otherwise guide action, or ordain a state of affairs, (2) have some level of generality, (3) are definite in some degree, (4) are at least minimally complete in their parts, (5) are in structured relation as between parts, (6) are duly expressed, and (7) duly encapsulated. Thus, many formal choices are required here. Imprints and other effects of such choices will be manifest in the form and the complementary content of the rules.

An administrative agency to which the legislature delegates power to set regulatory standards in rules must similarly choose features of the form of such rules. The mere fact that a rule minimally qualifies conceptually as a rule, and therefore has, for example, some level of definiteness, generality, and clarity hardly signifies that such minimal formal features will be appropriate for the task at hand. Usually, further focused choices of formal features, with complementary content, will be required.

The initial orienting choice of a law-making body to adopt a general legal policy of cholera prevention is not itself primarily a choice of form as such. Yet, this choice of policy is of necessity a choice that must occur prior to, or simultaneously with ascertaining the features of form that should define and organize the required rule or rules. This initial policy choice will have to be made by resolving conflicts between health considerations on the one hand, and such other considerations as cost effectiveness, freedom to use natural water sources, and the rights of property owners in the watershed to use their lands. Concurrently with this initial choice of a general orienting policy, choices of constituent features within the overall form of a rule will be required.

Having selected the form of a rule as encapsulated in a statute authorizing, among other things, an administrative-regulatory program for controlling cholera, the New York legislators had to determine the degree of definiteness and formal features in the required law. In the end, legislators decided to delegate the formulation of regulatory rules to a specialized administrative agency. To

Section Four: Choices of Preceptual and Related Forms 371

modern eyes, the usual rationales for such delegation were plainly applicable. Such an agency could be much closer to the problem. Here, agency officials had been accumulating experience with the problem. Hence, they could bring concentrated scientific and technological expertise to bear more readily than a legislature. By delegating the formulation of regulatory rules to an agency, interested parties, including possible commercial and other polluters, could also participate fully in the processes of fact-finding and rule formulation, which in turn could facilitate dissemination of the new rules, and could elicit cooperation of interested parties.

In fact in New York, the administrative officials responsible for drafting rules on water quality ultimately came to prefer a highly definite, general, and clear primary rule. Drafts of such a rule enabled administrators to focus on, deliberate over, and amend the rule as desired, in light of relevant data. The choice of the form of a rule over a mere general statement of policy, and the choice of a more definite, general, and clear rule over one lacking these qualities, illustrate choices of form that at least render the form and complementary content of the proposed law more fit objects for rational deliberation, one of many effects or imprints of form. A definitive choice rather than one that is less so, is likely to induce more careful consideration of the question whether that choice is appropriate – a truth that applies generally to all issues as to form and content in a rule.

A more definite, general, and clear rule poses fewer issues of interpretation and focuses required fact-finding prior to application. Such a rule is less likely to provoke disputes that must be resolved in court, as well. In those disputes that do go to court, such a rule will pose fewer problems of interpretation and fact-finding. The combined effects and imprints of the foregoing choices of form are synergistic and thus exceed the mere sum of effects as taken separately.

Given the foregoing considerations of form, and especially given the relevant policy, it should be no surprise that the legislative and administrative drafters of the New York State Sanitary Code, after study and deliberation with regard to the scientific and technological aspects of the problem, eventually adopted a definite, general, and clear set of basic rules as the centerpiece of the regulatory program at hand. These rules included the following:

Raw water fecal coliform concentrations must be equal to or less than 20 colonies per 100 milliliters or total coliform concentration must be equal to or less than 100 colonies per 100 milliliters in at least 90 percent of measurements made over the previous six months that the system was in operation. Monitoring shall be conducted in accordance with section 5-1.52 table 11A of this Subpart. If both fecal and total coliform analyses are performed, the fecal coliform results will take precedence.[23]

Plainly, a law requiring that there be no more than "20 colonies per 100 milliliters," would be vastly preferable to an indefinite formulation such as "no toxins in

---

[23] N.Y. Comp. Codes R. & Regs. tit. 10, §5-1.30(c)(1)(1998), as it currently reads.

unsanitary amounts."[24] The imprints and effects of formal definiteness, generality, and clarity in this law synergistically enhance the objectivity of fact-finding of administrators who must apply such a law.

Formal definiteness and other features also leave imprints and effects that minimize issues of interpretation, and in this way, facilitate efforts of administrative addressees and private addressees to construct pre-emptory reasons for determinate action under the rule. Under an indefinite rule, for example, some cautious addressees, not wanting to risk sanctions, might not wish to exercise their full powers. A private addressee, for example, might choose instead to discharge fewer pollutants than the law allows. This could throw off a careful balance between benefits and costs that law-makers intended. Indeed, such an addressee might even incur substantially greater costs that could cause it to go out of business, or at least to raise the price of any goods being made and sold.

The policy content of a proposed rule may be distinctively improved through careful choices of appropriate generality, a formal feature that leaves its own imprint or effect on a rule. As we saw in Chapter Five, law-makers drafting a proposed rule must think through the degree of generality required by the policy at hand. Suppose, for example, that the generality of a related type of water quality rule, as initially proposed, limits the discharge of pollutants within a given watershed area, except that the draft includes an explicit exception for Company X which, under the terms of the proposed rule, would be allowed to discharge more freely. Here, let us assume, however, that all dischargers, including Company X, fall within the policy of the proposed rule. If the actions of Company X are not rationally distinguishable from what would be the more stringently regulated actions of other dischargers, due generality would, without more, require that the drafter abandon the exception and include Company X. In the end, the scope of the duly revised rule would extend to its full policy reach. Here the synergy between due generality, a formal feature, and justified content, is also plain.

Again, policy efficacy is not the only end at stake in these choices. For example, such undergenerality as that hypothesized with regard to Company X, would not only fail to serve policy but would also fail to treat like cases alike,[25] a general value of the rule of law. A general perception that an exception is unjustified would also diminish the legitimacy of the regulation in the eyes of addressees. Choices of due generality can instill in addressees a sense of confidence that similarly situated parties are being treated the same. The appearance of equality and fairness is

---

[24] 40 C.F.R. §131.3(b) (2002) does permit criteria to be "expressed as . . . narrative statements," but presumably these must be duly definite.

[25] Cf. *Thompson Water Works v. Diamond*, 356 N.Y.S.2d 130, 133–4 (App. Div. 1974) ("Plainly, the public health should not be used as a pretext to aid one [water] supplier in competition with others to provide potable drinking water to the residents of the [v]illage. . . . ").

Section Four: Choices of Preceptual and Related Forms 373

a factor that tends to lead addressees to recognize the rule as legitimate, and these together tend to foster a spirit of cooperation – major contributions of well-designed form and content in a rule, also an additional synergy.

To determine due generality of a regulatory scheme, law-makers must focus on the scope of the regulatory policy, on the identity of possible addressees, and on the language appropriate to name these addressees. For example, the addressees of a given water quality law inhabiting a watershed area that drains into a drinking water reservoir could be quite diverse. These could include private individuals who might pollute, private corporations or other entities who might pollute, and public or private water suppliers who might pollute. Sometimes, a single rule would justifiably apply to all of the above addressees. At other times, different rules should be devised to apply to different types of addressees. Section 5-1.30 of the New York State Sanitary Code applies to public suppliers of drinking water, and requires them also to develop a filtration and disinfection system that guarantees water potability. The New York City Sanitation Code also applies to private entities who discharge pollutants into the watershed and requires them to obtain prior approval for such discharges. The Code provides that the activities of "all persons undertaking, or proposing to undertake"[26] discharges to which the Code applies "be planned, designed, scheduled, and conducted in such manner as not to constitute a source of contamination to, or degradation of, the water supply," and requires that any person undertaking such activities apply in advance to the City Department of Health for approval.[27]

Choices of internal structural form in a rule can have their own important effects, here, as well. Internal structure orders the relations between parts of a whole. For example, a state program for regulation of water quality will include a rule that specifies water quality requirements. The program may also include a rule that specifies the scope of the foregoing rule. If so, this latter would be a choice in the name of structural completeness. The choice of whether to make a fine for violation automatic, rather than discretionary, is also an internal structural choice in the sense that it is a choice about the relation within a proposed rule as between the part that specifies water quality, and the part that specifies the consequences of failing to meet those requirements. At the same time, this choice is also a choice of prescriptiveness, that is, whether the fine "must" or only "may" be imposed. The ends and values at stake in such structural and prescriptive choices go beyond the efficacy of the policy of cholera prevention, and include minimization of scope for official arbitrariness, equality before the law, and fair notice of possible adverse legal consequences – all general values of the rule of law. Well-designed formal features of internal structure can thus serve these values, too.

---

[26] N.Y. Comp. Codes R. & Regs. tit. 10, §128-1.4(a)(1998).
[27] *Id.*, at § 128-2.1(a).

Choices of Expressional Features. The creator of a law must make important choices in mode of expression and these are choices of form. As we saw in Chapter Five, these choices pertain to the degree of explicitness of the rule, to the extent it is appropriately set forth in lay or specialized vocabulary, to the nature of its grammar and syntax, to how its relation to other rules is specified, and more. These choices leave imprints and have other effects that can "make or break" the rule.

Laws should be explicit. This facilitates the effective dissemination of the rule and the ease with which its addresses can learn its content. Choices of appropriate vocabulary, for example, as between technical and lay terms, are also especially important. Similarly, simplicity of structure in the syntax of the rule, and in any of its exceptions or qualifications facilitates learnability. Here, too, there is internal synergy between other features of a well-formed rule and the feature of its expression.

Whether a law should employ technical or lay vocabulary often depends upon the subject matter of the law and its addressees. Although a speed limit law must be communicated in a lay vocabulary, for example, "drive no faster than 75 miles per hour," many laws, including some provisions of a water quality law, must use specialized vocabulary, for example, "coliform concentrations must be equal to or less than 20 colonies per 100 milliliters." When the addressees are industrial or highly specialized parties, technical vocabulary is appropriate for this reason, too. For lay addressees it may be necessary, for example, to explain in a three-page document expressed in lay terms what could be easily stated in a half-page of technical terms for expert addressees.

For example, one part of the New York City Sanitation Code addressed to private citizens simply states that no person shall discharge pathogenic materials, hazardous substances, human waste, etc. "without first obtaining written approval from the department."[28] The law then lists, in lay terms, what documents and information must be supplied to the department. For example, the law requires the applicant to describe the activity, location, and topography of the area, and to identify any existing structures at the location.[29] In contrast, when the relevant New York law is addressed to officials who are to supply public water, it requires that the official water supplier monitor the water to ensure that the following requirements have been fulfilled:

(1) Raw fecal coliform concentrations must be equal to or less than 200 colonies per 100 milliliters or total coliform concentrations must be equal to or less than 100 colonies per 100 milliliters in at least 90 percent of measurements made over the previous six months...

---

[28] *Id.*, at § 128-2.3(b)(1).
[29] *Id.*, at § 128-2.3(c)(1).

Section Four: Choices of Preceptual and Related Forms 375

(2) Raw water turbidity levels must not exceed five nephelometric turbidity units...

(3) Disinfection must be sufficient to ensure at least 99.9 percent inactivation of *Giardia lamblia* cysts and 99.99 percent inactivation of viruses, between a point where the raw water is no longer subject to recontamination by surface water runoff and a point downstream before or at the first consumer...[30]

Indeed, when the state health code is addressed to civic water suppliers, the definitions section defines some thirty-five terms, including jargon such as "CT,"[31] "diatomaceous earth filtration,"[32] "first draw tap sample,"[33] "gross alpha particle activity,"[34] and "man-made beta particle and photon emitters."[35] When the New York City Sanitation Code is addressed to private citizens, it simply uses lay vocabulary.[36]

Other Imprints and Effects of Form on Addressee Self-Direction. The efficacy of a regulatory rule frequently depends upon the capacity of its addressees, lay and official, for self-direction under the terms of the rule without further "on the spot" guidance from officials. Here, legislators and administrative agencies must be cognizant of the effects of choices of form at the law-making stage on behavior of addressees at a later stage. The general conditions for effective addressee self-direction under a rule, such as one prescribing a water quality standard, include:

(1) advance notice of the content of the rule,

(2) "learnability" of the rule,

(3) susceptibility of the rule to faithful interpretation in light of an interpretive methodology,

(4) ready ascertainability of the facts to which the rule applies,

(5) sufficient ease of compliance,

(6) pre-emptoriness of the reasons for action arising under the rule,

(7) duly specified sanctions for noncompliance.

None of these conditions can be satisfied without choices of well-designed features of form at the lawmaking stage. Well-designed features of form in a rule or rules synergistically enhances all of the foregoing. That is, the overall effects of these choices, when operative together, exceed the mere sum of the

---

[30] N.Y. Comp. Codes R. & Regs. tit. 10, §5-1.30(c) (1998).

[31] *Id.*, at § 5-1.1(j).

[32] *Id.*, at § 5-1.1(o).

[33] *Id.*, at § 5-1.1(w).

[34] *Id.*, at § 5-1.1(y).

[35] *Id.*, at § 5-1.1(af).

[36] N.Y. Comp. Codes R. & Regs. Title 10, §128 (1998).

individual effects that would separately occur. Moreover, the more appropriate these choices, and thus the better designed the form, the greater the opportunity for, and the greater the likelihood of, effective addressee (official as well as private) self-direction, and hence the greater policy efficacy of the rule, assuming that the means-end hypothesis embodied in the content of the rule to be sound in the first place.

Public health laws imposing water quality standards depend heavily for their efficacy upon the self-direction both of addressees who are officials and addressees who are private parties. To that end, any public and any private water suppliers or pollutant dischargers must have advance notice of any rule imposing such standards. The constituent features of the overall form of a rule – its prescriptiveness, definiteness, completeness, generality, simplicity of rule structure, and expressional clarity, all in their own ways, enable addressees to interpret and learn the rule, find relevant facts, and apply it.

Definiteness not only helps to render the rule "learnable," but prioritizes conflicting policy considerations such as desired level of health versus costs of water purification techniques. A definite rule, for example, one that provides that raw water coliform concentrations not exceed "20 colonies per 100 milliliters" prioritizes health over cost in terms of that degree of definiteness. At least any further reduction of concentrations would cost more. A vague rule, for example, "no toxins in unsanitary amounts," would not efficiently prioritize at any exact degree. Other features of expressional form also contribute to prioritization here, especially explicitness, appropriate vocabulary, and rigorous syntax. Again, the combined effects of all these formal features taken together synergistically exceed the sum of the effects of each that would occur alone.

As we have seen, efficacious addressee self-direction on the part of officials, as well as private parties, requires choices of features of the form of a rule that, as interpreted, render it a source of reasons for determinate action or decision. A "no toxins in unsanitary amounts" rule would be rife with issues of interpretation and would be intolerably indeterminate. The very same formal features in our "20 colonies per 100 milliliters" rule that make it readily learnable also minimize interpretive issues. Even so, there is still need for application of a duly formed interpretive methodology for those interpretive issues that do arise. Choices of duly designed form are required to define and organize any such methodology, as we saw in Chapter Eight.

A further condition of efficacious addressee self-direction under rules is the ready ascertainability of the facts to which the rule applies. The rule applier must be able to determine the meaning of the rule, and then ascertain and classify the relevant factual circumstances as ones that do, or do not, fall under the rule. The lawmaker may choose a highly definite, general, and clear "bright-line" rule, and so a particular limit, for example, "20 colonies per 100 milliliters." These formal

Section Five: Choices of Form at the Stage of Public Promulgation

features and complementary content (along with requisite filter and water quality testing technology) greatly facilitate the fact-finding required for the addressee to comply.

A further related functional legal unit to be considered at the law making stage consists of the possible sanction for non-compliance that the law-maker may wish to create and prescribe. In Chapter Nine, we considered formal choices that define and organize the unit of a sanction. There, we saw that a sanction could not even exist without choices of due form. Further choices must also be made as to what sanction should be available to punish noncompliance and to induce future compliance.

SECTION FIVE: CHOICES OF FORM AT THE STAGE OF PUBLIC PROMULGATION

After the law-making stage, we come to a further major stage in the unfolding linear progressions of the administrative-regulatory technique, and of the public-benefit conferral technique – the two main techniques treated here. Usually, the policy or other content of a law cannot be learned and thereafter implemented by its addressees unless the law is somehow publicly promulgated. Here, too, the imprints and other effects of form are fundamental. In general, a statute or administrative regulation cannot even be lawfully binding on its addressees unless duly promulgated.[37] Also, if such law is not duly promulgated, it is not likely to be an adequate basis for addressee self-direction, or for effective enforcement. Various features of the form of a rule, including its expressional feature, function synergistically here with promulgation, also largely a formal matter.

In our illustration, Section 1100 of New York's Public Health Laws require every new rule or regulation for the protection of potable public waters from contamination to be "published at least once in each week for two consecutive weeks, in at least one newspaper of the county where the waters to which it relates are located."[38] The statute requires the costs of publication "to be paid by the corporation, municipality, state, or United States ... [or] institution ... benefited by the protection of the water supply."[39] It also provides that "the affidavit of the printer, publisher, or proprietor of the newspaper in which such ... regulation is published ... shall be conclusive evidence" on the question of publication.[40] So, this law clearly requires public promulgation, though it does not include any statement of the effects of failure to do so.

---

[37] Cf. M. Lohmüller, *Canon Law Studies, The Promulgation of Law,* 7 (Catholic University of America Press, Washington, DC, 1947).

[38] N.Y. Pub. Health Law §1100(2) (Consol. 1987).

[39] *Ibid.*

[40] *Id.*, at § 1100(3).

Plainly, a law must be accessible to its addressees. Promulgation of the law is a major stage in linear progressions of several of the law's basic operational techniques. We have seen that accessibility is dependent on major prior choices of features of form including printed over oral, the explicit over the implicit, lay language over technical (where appropriate), and so on. Promulgation renders the contents of legal duties and rights accessible to addressees. It may also include relevant rationales for the law. In the case of public health programs, such as cholera prevention, clear communication not only of relevant legal duties, but also of the rationales for such duties can elicit voluntary cooperation.

An existing administrative agency with regulatory responsibility usually has jurisdiction to promulgate whatever new law is adopted. Such an agency itself takes an overall institutional form with various features constitutive of this form, including composition, jurisdiction, structure, and procedure. In the exercise of jurisdiction not only to make, but to promulgate law, more specific formal choices may have to be made by the responsible agency. Promulgation must be in some form of writing or print and clearly expressed. Oral promulgation could be feasible only rarely.

The public promulgation of a law not only serves policy or other purposes, but also satisfies principles of the rule of law. The principles of the rule of law require, among other things, that law be authorized, that it generally be in the form of rules (so far as feasible), that the law be clear and learnable, that it be duly promulgated, that it be prospective in effect, that it be relatively constant through time – all so that people can abide by it, and so that those against whom it may be adversely applied can have fair notice and "due process."

The formal requirement of promulgation rendering the law known and accessible is an obvious necessity in our illustration of a law regulating water quality. Such a law could itself be highly learnable, yet its addressees not even know of its adoption by the legislature, or by an administrative agency. In a system duly attentive to well-designed form, failures of public promulgation rarely occur. Legislatures and official agencies take steps to convey the law they adopt to addressees via one or more of a variety of promulgative devices. As I have explained, Section #1100 of the New York Public Health Law requires that every new rule pertaining to the supply of potable water be published once a week for two consecutive weeks in at least one newspaper in the relevant county.[41] In many developed Western societies, new legislation is published in annual volumes of official statutes. New administrative regulations must be duly published too. Beyond this, official agencies responsible for the administration of an important new law commonly disseminate it through annual booklets, through trade-association channels, and through the news media. Sometimes a law can be duly communicated in public

---

[41] *Id.*, at § 1100(2).

Section Six: Form and the Stage of Addressee Self-Application 379

places, such as by posting a sign near a reservoir to announce that specified types of pollutants may not be dumped in the area without a permit. It is familiar that highway traffic laws and many other laws are similarly communicated through strategically located signs. As a further signal to addressees to take notice, many signs and related devices are uniform in size and shape.

SECTION SIX: FORM AND THE STAGE OF ADDRESSEE SELF-APPLICATION

The next major stage in most linear progressions whereby laws are duly created and duly implemented, is the stage at which the addressees learn of the law, interpret the law, ascertain any relevant facts, and apply the law. Both state-made and privately created law are generally implemented by addressees who take the law as providing legal reasons for actions or decisions. Thus, nearly all that has so far been said about the roles of well-designed form at such prior stages as the law-making stage and the promulgating stage anticipates the law-applying stage. Choices of form have major cumulative effects at this stage, and some of the combined effects function synergistically here, as well. Due form in the law itself is required in the first place if addressees are to have the capacity to comply with and implement any law. If, for example, a given rule is too indefinite, or too deficient in expression to be faithfully interpreted and understood, or is not duly promulgated and disseminated, then its addressees will not be able to apply the law to their own circumstances and act accordingly. Few cumulative imprints and other effects of bad form could be more dysfunctional. The relation between well-designed form and required addressee understanding of what the law requires is an intimate one.

A well-formed law, for example, a duly prescriptive, complete, and definite rule that is also duly general, clearly expressed, and duly promulgated, can along with its complementary content, even inspire a general spirit of cooperation among its addressees. In our illustration, addressees will know the purpose of the law. They will also know that all other water suppliers or potential polluters must comply with the same rule or rules, and that their competitors will not be getting an economic advantage from failure to comply with the law. On the other hand, a law might, for example, be under-general and thus not applicable to certain private addressees who also supply water. Other private suppliers to whom the law does apply might well come to resent the law because they view it as drawing unfair distinctions between themselves and other similarly situated water suppliers. This, in turn, could undermine any spirit of voluntary cooperation.

A public or a private water supplier, or a party who discharges pollutants via an inadequate sewage disposal system, should have little difficulty applying the law, assuming it is set forth in the form of a determinate rule or rules, is expressed in terms readily understandable by its addressees, and insofar as it calls for factual inquiries, these can be readily made in light of filter or other technology. Because the law is in prescriptive and determinate form, it will also be pre-emptory, and its addressees should generally not let other countervailing considerations over-ride the legal reasons for action or decision arising under it. For example, a public entity supplying water should reason as follows: we must act to limit "coliform concentrations to no more than 20 colonies per 100 milliliters." The law when promulgated and thus acted upon, serves policy and other purposes, and is, as we have seen, itself formal in several ways. The legal reason for action or decision that the law gives rise to here is also formal in its pre-emptoriness and in its determinateness. The various formal features of the rule: its prescriptiveness, completeness, generality, definiteness, and internal structure, contribute here. So, too, do the formal expressional and encapsulatory features. Again, the imprints and other effects of these features of form come into play as well. All these contributions of form add up.

In the type of linear progression at hand, the addressee of the law, whether public entity or private party, is expected to interpret the law, find any relevant facts, and faithfully apply the law. Various features of form and their imprints and other effects facilitate this in many ways. In our water quality example, the clarity and precision of the rule, which are attributable partly to its formal expression and definiteness, along with any prescribed testing technology, simplify any interpretive and fact-finding tasks. To facilitate regular determinations of whether water quality has, in fact, been compromised, state administrators can also post tables that specify maximum contamination levels, specify the type of sampling required, specify the location or types of water that must be sampled, and specify the regularity with which such samples must be taken.[42]

Thus, in our illustration, toward the end of the various stages in our overall linear progression from rule creation, to rule promulgation and dissemination, and to rule implementation through addressee self-application, we can see how choices of well-designed form at all these stages can contribute to the quality of policy content, to policy efficacy, to rule of law efficacy, and to the realization of fundamental political values. Our simple illustration reveals many choices of form that drafters of such a law must make and the types of imprints and effects that those choices can have when they occur, and at later stages of the linear progression. Poor choices early on can preclude appropriate choices later, or make them more costly. Good choices early on can synergistically interact with other choices at the same time and with later choices.

In the type of illustration I have posed, private parties and officials can apply well-designed rules effectively out on the frontiers of human interaction in the

---

[42] N.Y. Comp. Codes R. & Regs. Title 10, §5-1.12(b), 5-1.52 Table 11A (1998).

Section Seven: An Exceptional Yet Important Stage   381

vast majority of instances. Such effective regulatory rules, and many others like them, thus lead their lives primarily out on these very frontiers, and only quite secondarily inside judicial or administrative adjudications. The lives of these rules effectuate democracy as well as policy and other purposes. Again, democracy is not merely a "processual" value whereby majorities of elected representatives merely participate in the making of laws. Democracy is an "outcome" value, too. When laws are created by a democratic legislature, or their creation is delegated to an administrative agency, and these laws are thereafter implemented, democratic will is effectuated through actual outcomes, too.

The specific contributions of each of the major types of choices of form in the course of our linear progression, from initial creation of a law to its ultimate implementation, cannot be isolated, disentangled, and measured with precision. Yet, the total cumulative contribution of all these choices of well-designed form must plainly be a major factor in the efficacy of any such use of law, stage by stage in linear progression, from initial creation of law to its ultimate implementation via any relevant operational technique or techniques. Concededly, any rule created must also have appropriate material or other components such as policy content. In our example, this content should include policy duly mediating between health on the one hand, and efficiency and other ends on the other. Effectiveness also requires complementary and other material components such as trained and informed water purifiers, trained and informed waste dischargers, and technology for modern filtration and testing systems. Even though it is not possible to disentangle and measure the relative contributions of form and these complementary material and other components with precision, it is plain that choices of well-designed form are indispensable. These choices define and organize the functional legal units, and leave major imprints and other effects. These choices also combine, integrate, and coordinate these units within an overall operational technique or techniques that operate dynamically from stage to stage. Effective working law can never be formless. Content without form in a law is not even a possibility. Also, what it would be like to have material and other components in a formless "functional unit" can hardly be imagined, and such a "unit" could have little efficacy. Apt choices of form are essential here to define and serve the policies of public health, to serve general values of the rule of law, and to serve fundamental political values including democracy, legitimacy, and rationality.

SECTION SEVEN: AN EXCEPTIONAL YET IMPORTANT STAGE — ADMINISTRATIVE INTERVENTION

Let us assume that the immediate addressees of a legal regulatory program consist solely of private persons or private entities, a state of affairs that frequently obtains. If the creation and implementation of law in the administrative-regulatory technique is well-designed and executed, trouble cases will not be frequent in the course of linear progressions. When they do arise, administrative officials may be authorized to intervene, and they may even have power to take immediate remedial action, including the imposition of sanctions, on due notice.

Let us return to our illustrative context. The New York Public Health Law authorizes the New York City Commissioner of Environmental Protection to enter and inspect any private property within the relevant watershed to determine if the regulations have been or are being violated.[43] The formal definitiveness of the water quality standard prescribed in regulations, and the existence of reliable testing technology readily facilitate such official determinations. If the Commissioner or an agent thereof determines that a private party is guilty of a violation and finds that this would contaminate the water supply of the City, the Commissioner may "summarily enforce compliance with such . . . regulation and may summarily abate or remove the cause of the violation . . . and to that end may employ such force as may be necessary and proper."[44] Such a summary procedure is itself formal, though, of course, it has complementary material and other components. Also, the very existence of such an administrative body or official is itself defined and organized by features of institutional form, such as the compositional, jurisdictional, structural, and procedural. Without such form, there simply could be no duly defined and organized institution or entity such as a Commissioner of Environmental Protection, a Commissioner of Public Health, or a Department of Public Health.

Let us assume, contrary to likely fact, that today an actual outbreak of an infectious disease known to be waterborne, such as cholera, occurs.[45] The State Department of Health (usually in cooperation with local or federal authorities) would investigate the quality of water sources in the area, sources that may even include some private ones. Pursuant to that investigation, let us assume the State Health Commissioner determines that a contractor built a subdivision without following regulations as to sewage disposal, that the water supply became polluted, and that this was the source of the disease. The State Health Commissioner could then order the municipality that controls the water supply to: (1) require reconstruction of the sewage disposal system, or (2) discharge chlorine into a reservoir or other source of supply to kill existing bacteria, or (3) take daily samples of the water supply to check for further signs of the bacteria, or (4) impose a timetable for the construction of an adequate water treatment facility, or (5) some combination of these.[46]

---

[43] N.Y. Pub. Health Law §1101 (Consol. 1987).

[44] *Id.*, at § 1102(3)(a).

[45] This illustration takes its factual underpinnings from *Rome v. New York State Health Dept.*, 411 N.Y.S.2d 61 (Sup. Ct 1978).

[46] *Id.*, at 63. (Authority to grant such an order derives from N.Y. Pub. Health Law §1107. (Consol. 1987)).

Section Eight: Ultra-Exceptional Stage – Trial and Appellate Court Action

In all these, and in still other ways, potable water policies are effectuated with regard both to private polluters, and to public municipalities responsible for water quality. Without due form of any one of the kinds heretofore considered, and especially without the prescriptive definitiveness and clarity of the water quality standard, effectuation of these policies would be problematic, or be far more at risk.

The formal features heretofore considered also delimit the scope for potential disputes. This is perhaps most dramatically so of definiteness and clarity of expression in bright-line rules. The availability of complementary material components such as electronic or other mechanical measuring devices for determining water quality, and of duly trained personnel also drastically delimits scope for disputes. There is synergy here, as well, between the formal and the nonformal, because the rules can themselves be drafted effectively to take account of available technology and trained personnel, thereby making administrative intervention at this stage even more effective.

The policies of the statute, efficiency of implementation, and the avoidance of disputes, are not the only immediate values to be served by well-designed form in such cases of official intervention and coercive enforcement. Such form contributes to ease of administration. Also, a determinate and clear law enforced by an official in what is, and is perceived to be, a highly objective fashion, induces voluntary compliance by others, serves the rule of law, and lends rationality and legitimacy to the entire enforcement process. Such a law delimits scope for official arbitrariness in determining the existence of any violation in particular cases, and this, too, serves rationality and legitimacy. Again, the imprints and other effects of well-designed form can be deep and indelible.

SECTION EIGHT: ULTRA-EXCEPTIONAL STAGE – TRIAL AND APPELLATE COURT ACTION

In what would be an ultra-exceptional stage arising in a linear progression of the administrative-regulatory technique, let us assume that an alleged private violator chooses to dispute an administrative determination of violation and under the law demands a judicial determination of the facts and applicable law. Thus, for example, assume an alleged supplier of polluted water, or an alleged discharger of pollutants in the watershed refuses to comply, or complies under protest, with an order from the State Health Commissioner or other official to cease alleged polluting activities, and wishes to appear before a trial court to challenge the order. Much can be at stake in such a dispute for the accused, including the possibility that the accused may lose a license to discharge some pollutants, have to pay a fine, or even in an extreme case, be incarcerated. (An alleged violation could also be litigated in a civil case for its bearing on tort liability to others.)

384 Cumulative and Synergistic Effects of Legal Forms

In this final, and ultra-exceptional stage of our illustrative linear progression, after any required administrative steps have been exhausted, a trial court may then be called upon to decide issues of law and of fact, and to decide whether any sanction (or remedy in a civil case) may be imposed.[47] A trial court takes its own overall form, and as we have seen, its constituent formal features are compositional, jurisdictional, structural, procedural, methodological, and preceptual. After a trial, the loser may appeal to an appellate court, a body that also takes its own overall form.

Such cases before trial courts are ultra-exceptional in administrative-regulatory matters in the American and various other systems, both because significant disputes seldom arise under such duly formed law, and because those disputes that do arise are usually resolved through administrative action without judicial intervention, or if there is judicial intervention, it may be solely by appellate review of administrative agency or other action. Let us assume that rather than admit wrong, or negotiate some other resolution, our alleged wrongdoer challenges the foregoing administrative order in a trial court. (In various Western systems, such cases comprise a very small proportion of the total instances occurring within any similar linear progression.)

Here, in some systems, two fundamental principles of appropriate institutional form converge. First, and as we saw in Chapter Nine, there is a formal structural principle that the function of implementing a sanction against a violator is to be separated from the function of determining, with finality, in a contested case whether a violation subject to sanction has occurred. Second, there is the formal procedural principle of the rule of law that before any such sanction is imposed, the party to be adversely affected shall be entitled to due process, that is, have notice and a fair opportunity to contest the facts and the law on which any such sanction (or remedy) may be premised before an independent and impartial court (or other tribunal).

In our illustration, let us assume the State Commissioner of Health (or some other agency) takes the dispute to a court for a finding of violation, an injunctive order restraining the wrongdoer, and for imposition of penalties.[48] In court, the alleged wrongdoer may pursue a number of avenues. For example, this party may argue that the Commissioner's order suffers from procedural flaws. Or the alleged wrongdoer may argue that the actions of the Commissioner exceeded statutorily prescribed authority. Or the alleged wrongdoer may contend that no violation, in fact, occurred.

In the American and various other Western systems, in cases arising in the standard linear progression involved in our illustration, actions of trial courts are unusual. It does not follow, however, that courts play no role in the implementation

---

[47] Of course, courts could come into play much earlier. In our illustration, they might be involved at the very outset, as when someone became ill from drinking water and sued in court for the harm caused.

[48] N.Y. Pub. Health Law §1102(2)(b) (Consol. 1987).

Section Eight: Ultra-Exceptional Stage – Trial and Appellate Court Action   385

of such law except in those unusual cases in which they are called upon to take action. The mere standing availability of independent and impartial courts before whom administrative bodies, prosecuting officials, and others may summon those who refuse to admit, or dispute, that their actions constitute regulatory, penal, or other wrongs, operates to serve the basic policy at stake here – the policy of providing and protecting potable water. Here, courts stand ready, on proper proof, to enforce the law and thus "back up" administrative bodies, or other officials, who can demonstrate they are in the right on the facts and the law. This standing readiness of courts is generally known to possible violators and lends further credibility to the law itself, thereby often inducing voluntary compliance.

Yet a court is not merely a "club" to be used only by an administrator or an administrative agency on the heads of primary addressees of the law. Private parties, too, can usually go to court to challenge the legality of agency actions at various stages of a linear progression. In some systems, such parties must first "exhaust administrative remedies."

Moreover, when a dispute over fact or law does arise between an administrative body on the one hand, and an addressee of regulatory law on the other, and the dispute is not satisfactorily resolved by the regulatory agency, the standing availability of a court to resolve it often induces the disputants to resolve the dispute on their own, especially when the law involved is in determinate form. In the overwhelming proportion of the small class of disputed cases that do arise at this stage in some systems, the opposing parties themselves typically settle through negotiation in the shadow of the law. In such instances, besides serving the policy involved, the standing possibility of judicial action also serves general values of the rule of law and fundamental political values, such as legitimacy, rationality, and justice. The possibility of judicial action even serves democracy insofar as the threat of it leads to implementation of the general policy enacted by a democratically composed legislature.

Although it is not necessary for my purposes to treat the forms of all types of functional units and systematizing devices, and although I have not frontally and systematically treated the forms of trial and appellate courts in this book, these units also take their own overall forms. The overall form of a court is a form of a major institutional unit with its own complementary material and other components. Thus a form-oriented analysis parallel to that applied to legislative institutions in Chapter Four also applies to courts. Although both types of institutions have compositional, jurisdictional, structural, procedural, methodological, and preceptual features of form, these differ importantly in the two types of institutions. In an earlier chapter, I illustrated one of the major differences relevant here, namely, the dialogic procedure of a typical court in contrast to the nondialogic procedure of a legislature.[49]

---

[49] See *supra* Chapter Two, at 56.

SECTION NINE: CHOICES OF FORM — SUMMARY OF MAJOR CUMULATIVE AND SYNERGISTIC EFFECTS

As we have seen, choices of form early on in a linear progression can have effects that cumulate with later choices, and together, carry forward synergistically to serve ends. The clear choice to allocate primary jurisdiction to a legislature to make, or to delegate the making of, the primary legal rules in our illustration generally minimizes conflicts with other institutional branches, tends to reduce false starts in a regulatory program, and tends to secure general uniformity in such a program. These effects also carry forward throughout the stages of a linear progression in the relevant form of operational technique, with different institutions generally contributing in accord with their own distinctive capacities and their own comparative institutional advantages.

As we saw at length in Chapter Four, important choices of form necessarily figure in the very construction and existence of institutions. The effects of these choices carry forward and affect the functioning of these institutions at various later stages of linear progressions in which the institutions are operational. Without choices of definitive features of institutional form, legislatures, administrative agencies, and courts could not even exist, let alone function appropriately in coordinated fashion at the various stages of a linear progression to create and implement law to serve ends.

The choice of an operational technique such as the administrative-regulatory, within which various first-level units and second-level systematizing devices are combined, integrated and coordinated, affects much that follows in the ensuing linear progression, including especially overall preventative efficacy. When the administrative regulatory technique is combined here with supply of water by public entities, that is, with the public benefit conferring technique, the overall synergistic effect is dramatic. The due combination of the two enhances the efficacy of each in the pair beyond the mere sum of what each would otherwise contribute separately. Choices of institutional composition, jurisdiction, structure, and procedure also interact with choices of form and content in rules, or in other law that is adopted. Indeed, such adoption of rules is actually borne of procedural form – a validating decision-rule such as "passage by majority vote." The early choices of form in the very rules and other law duly created carry through from initial adoption to subsequent implementation. Indeed, choices of such formal features as generality and definiteness of rule continue to be operative through all subsequent stages of the linear progression.

Formal choices in the creation of a rule or other law can also greatly facilitate promulgation, dissemination, and learnability of that very rule or other law at the later stage at which it is communicated to addressees. Here, the earlier choices of formal features of rules, including due definiteness and clarity of expression

Section Ten: The Roles of Form and Information in a Linear Progression   387

synergistically cumulate and converge with formal promulgation and dissemination to facilitate communication of the law to addressees who then learn it and later apply it to serve purposes.

All of the foregoing types of choices of form, as well as choices of form in an interpretive methodology of the kind studied in Chapter Eight and choices of forms of sanctions and remedies of the kind studied in Chapter Nine, cumulate with combined synergistic effects at the stage of addressee self-application: (1) to enable addressees to construct pre-emptory reasons for action or decision under the rules or other law, and (2) to motivate addressees to take action accordingly. It is not merely that the foregoing choices of form are alone facilitative, although they are that too. They are, many of them, indispensable to (1) and (2). Without most of these choices, duly designed, voluntary efforts of addressees to apply law would not be very effective. Of all the synergistic effects that occur in the linear progression, this is probably the most important. Voluntary addressee self-application presupposes prescriptive determinacy in the law to be applied, and when that is present, such voluntary compliance becomes far more likely, especially where the policy at stake is readily perceived to be in the addressee's interest, and more generally, as socially beneficial. Of course, in all of this, complementary material and other components of the relevant units must figure as well.

Finally, without enforcive entities such as courts and administrative agencies in the picture, some addressees at earlier stages of the progression would almost certainly not take the rules seriously at all. Another kind of synergy occurs here, too. Well-formed rules created at an early stage also provide a fair basis for the imposition of state sanctions at a later stage. Prospective violators realize this, too, and this adds motivational effect.

SECTION TEN: THE ROLES OF FORM AND INFORMATION IN A LINEAR PROGRESSION

Study of a linear progression affords opportunity to consider a further major type of credit due to form not yet systematically addressed, namely, the extent to which well-designed form can facilitate or otherwise affect the gathering and dissemination of information of importance to the creation and implementation of law. As Jeremy Bentham stressed, it is a major function of a legal system to concern itself with "the perpetual information and direction of all persons. . . . "[50] Although much of what follows may be too obvious to be noticed, and thus taken for granted, it is of very great importance and can easily be ignored, with prejudicial effect. Well-designed form plays many roles in securing information. Information is not just a one-way street. Officials not only convey information to

---

[50] J. Bentham, *A Fragment on Government*, Chapter 5, §2 (F. Montague ed., Oxford University Press, London, 1951).

the public, but receive information from the public as well. Form figures in both. It is not surprising that "form" and "information" share common linguistic roots, for they are closely related. The inter-relations between form and information are far too numerous to be treated comprehensively here, but their importance requires at least that we draw together some general reminders of this further major realm of credit due to form.

At each of the various stages of the linear progression presented so far in this chapter, and in all other such progressions, form requires that information be elicited and disseminated. For example, at the initial stage, the choice to use the administrative-regulatory technique to fight cholera is, as a rational choice of form, one that presupposes the gathering and consideration of information regarding the nature of the problem, and, among other things, information regarding the comparative means-end efficacy of each basic form of operational technique to deal with this problem. Plainly, rational choices of operational techniques cannot be made in an informational vacuum in which little is known either about the forms of these techniques or their comparative efficacy. The very nature of the problem of rationally suiting legal means to ends compels such informational inquiry at the outset.

At the next major stage in a linear progression, the law-making stage, form again requires that information be gathered and disseminated. For example, a valid statute simply cannot be adopted without information regarding what counts as a valid statute in the society, who has the authority to adopt it, and what the procedures are to be followed. This information is only available via knowledge of the overall form and constituent formal features of a legislative body and of a valid statutory enactment. Further, formal structural and procedural features of the form of a well-designed legislature themselves require informational input at various points, including at the initial policy formulation stage. Is there a water quality problem? If so, how large? Can we fix it? In the course of legislative fact-finding via committees, what are the available technologies? Do they do the job? What are the costs of improving water standards? During floor debates: will this bill work? What information do we need to answer this? Should the bill be amended? Do my constituents favor such a bill? Well-designed legislative form also requires the dissemination of information regarding what laws have been proposed so that those potentially affected may provide further information, and informed evaluation may then occur. Administrative agencies follow similar procedures when adopting rules.

Once a law is passed, or a rule adopted, the content of that law, as adopted, must be disseminated to the public. Without such information, addressees of the law simply cannot know what the law is, whether it applies to them, what it requires of them, or even that such a law was duly adopted in the first place. Formal promulgation must be well-designed to communicate or to provide access to the

Section Ten: The Roles of Form and Information in a Linear Progression 389

relevant information. The expressional and encapsulatory features of the form of a rule to be promulgated loom especially large here. Proper attention to these formal features during the law-making stage can ultimately make the law more learnable and accessible, with legal information being more effectively conveyed at the promulgation and dissemination stage. As we have seen, formal publication requirements, such as those found in Section 1100 of the New York Public Health Law, may require that information concerning the law be disseminated to the public.

At the application stage, addressees of the law, including, in our example, public and private providers of water, public and private dischargers of possible pollutants into the watershed, and various official regulators, all require information in order to act. The clarity of the law that is achieved through well-designed form, such as appropriate prescriptiveness, generality, definiteness, and mode of expression, enables addressees to inform themselves as to the form and content of the law, and thus reliably ascertain what is expected of them. Notice of a rule conveys information about the prescriptive contents of the rule (what must, may, or must not be done), and also conveys information as to any further information the addressee may need in order to comply with the rule. For example, due notice of a rule that permits "no more than 20 colonies per 100 milliliters" not only conveys information that water must meet that standard, but also that testing for the presence of those colonies is to occur. Violating addressees are also informed that by making appropriate changes they can be sure of compliance. Well-designed form and content also conveys information to addressees regarding possible sanctions for non-compliance and any available remedial processes if non-compliance occurs.

At the next stage, administrative inspection, sanctioning or other action to determine and to secure compliance also requires that information be elicited and disseminated. For example, state inspection and testing of water samples simply is the gathering of information regarding water quality. This information is then compared to other information – the water quality standards – to determine compliance. Well-designed form for a water quality law would include a readily administered procedure for inspections and, therefore, deserves credit for information gathered.

The final stage of the progression, the disposition of disputes, plainly requires information, too. For example, if an administrator sues an alleged violator of water quality standards, the institutional form of a court comes into play. This, of course, requires the parties to have information regarding what a court is and how it operates. Also, information, in the way of evidence and witness testimony, must be put before the court. The court considers the information and alleged information so presented, makes findings of facts, and issues an opinion, that contains and relates information regarding the disposition of the case, and/or an order, that informs the parties as to what actions to take (or to refrain from taking). Others, too, are informed of the result.

Without adherence to proper form, much of the information that is needed for proper consideration, adoption, promulgation, addressee application, and ultimate enforcement of the law simply could not be gathered or disseminated. Thus, we see another wide ranging way in which credit is due to form.

SECTION ELEVEN: THE LIMITS OF FORM AND ALSO ITS GENERAL POTENCY

Throughout this book, I have stressed the credits due to choices of well-designed form for the imprints and other effects of form. I have also stressed the debits that may be due to ill-designed form. Let us now consider the limits of form in general terms before returning to its general potency. First, functional legal units and systematizing devices are themselves inherently limited in their efficacy to serve purposes and values. It follows that the forms of such legal phenomena must also be so limited. For example, merely because Americans have obliterated the public health menace of cholera mainly through combined uses of the administrative-regulatory and the public-benefit conferral techniques, it does not follow that this success will inevitably hold against all forces of the wrong and the bad, now, or in the future. For example, terrorists could act in all sorts of imaginable ways to bring cholera back, at least for a time, and, during that time, with drastic consequences. Plainly, even well-designed form with its complementary components cannot stop all that may need to be stopped. Legal forms and their complementary components are inherently limited.

Second, my use of a public health illustration may actually obscure the bearing of another factor that can limit the efficacy of form and its complementary components in the law. In such an illustration, if high levels of success are achieved, this must be attributed partly to the ready understandability to all concerned of the vital importance of stamping out the health hazard, which is a hazard to everyone. This understanding and knowledge, once disseminated with clarity, tends to elicit high levels of voluntary cooperation among private parties and citizens, many of whom may even feel themselves threatened. It is true that law and form may play large roles merely in disseminating information required for such understanding. Beyond this, much of the *motivation* to implement and comply can come from the dissemination of knowledge of the nature of the threat itself. In certain other uses of law, the threat to addressees is not so clear or so stark, and levels of voluntary cooperation must therefore be more limited, with the result that the efficacy of such uses of law are therefore more limited.

Third, even well-designed form in functional legal units and systematizing devices only *tends* to achieve many of the ends that such units and devices are

Section Eleven: The Limits of Form and also Its General Potency

deployed to serve. For example, well-designed formal procedures only tend to influence legislators and other officials to bring rational scrutiny to bear on proposed laws. Indeed, Western societies have hardly been free, even in modern times, of barbarians who have hijacked the machinery of the state for evil ends. Compositional, structural, procedural, and other features of institutional form here can be no guarantee that the content of laws adopted will be salutary. Well-designed form cannot guarantee rationality, though it tends to promote it. Nor can such form preclude all unintended effects.

Fourth, form alone can do relatively little. As we saw in this and earlier chapters, material and other components, such as information and general scientific knowledge of cause and effect, physical facilities, material resources, technology, and personnel, are always required. Without these, functional legal units could not exist at all.

Fifth, and more fundamentally, there must be shared purposes, that is, shared policies, shared values of the rule of law, and shared fundamental political values. Without these, legal forms could not even exist, for forms are *purposive* systematic arrangements, and without the foregoing, which are the "stuff" of purposes, we could not even know what systematic arrangements to make.

Sixth, important limits of law and form derive from the limits of the wit of man and woman. Much is not yet known. For example, we frequently lack full knowledge of cause and effect. The early experience with cholera and much else tells as much. Also, humans have doubtless not yet discovered all possible types of formal devices for use in the law. It seems certain that we do not yet fully understand all that goes into the efficacy of law itself. This is a significant limit of law and so of form, although how significant, we do not know.

Finally, form cannot teach its own potential. Form cannot teach respect for itself. Some must understand this potential before they can teach it to those who use it, and before those who use it and, others too, can respect it. A general theory of form is required for this understanding. Even when form is well understood and respected, human beings in charge may still fail at design or implementation in many ways.

Even granting the foregoing major limits of form, the general potency of well-designed form is far greater than is articulately understood, and goes far to account for major achievements of law as a great societal resource serving the just and the good. Well-designed law duly implemented is heavily dependent on access to factual information at every stage of the law's linear progressions from initial creation of law to ultimate implementation, and form plays indispensable roles at every stage in this, as we have just seen in this chapter. Well-designed law and functional legal units are necessarily dependent not only on factual information but also on choices of good purposes for law to serve. Here, too, form is a means to the definition and organization of the very purposes to be served through law.

Form not only defines and organizes purposes but also organizes many of the very ends implicit or embedded in these purposes. Form is even to an extent constitutive of some of the most important of the very ends pursued in civil society, including democracy and rule of law values. Indeed, without duly designed form these very ends could not even be formulated in terms susceptible of legal implementation.

As I have also stressed, functional legal units and the systematizing devices of modern legal systems could not exist at all without duly designed form. Indeed, without due form, legal rules simply could not exist. Nor could determinate institutional sources of valid law, such as legislatures and courts. Without such determinate sources it would not even be possible to differentiate valid law from asserted law that is not really valid. It follows that such rule of law values as fair notice, equality before the law, and legal certainty could not be realized, either.

Even if form be minimally adequate for functional legal units and systematizing devices at least marginally to exist, these units and devices would serve purposes and values far more efficaciously if formally better defined and organized.

Then, too, there is need for coercive force in a system of law. Freedom, justice, and other fundamental political values could not be realized if the state had no power to enforce law through sanctions and remedies. Form is essential to the definition, organization, and legitimate existence and use of such coercive power.

Also, without due form, the cooperative spirit of the populace could not be harnessed. Pathways for cooperation simply could not be duly defined and organized.

NAME INDEX

Alexander, L., 25, 136
Alexy, R., 8, 34
Aristotle, 24, 155, 156, 159, 161, 293
Atienza, M., 13, 73
Atiyah, P., 23, 25, 53, 61, 145
Austin, J. L., 49, 62
Austin, J., 225

Barcelo, J., 326
Behme, K., 92
Behrends, O., 3, 12, 21, 51, 59, 74, 319
Bell, J., 91
Bellacosa, J., 275
Bentham, J., 16, 136, 174, 175, 288, 387
Blackstone, W., 174, 276
Bleckley, J., 12, 37
Bobbio, N., 28
Burke, E., 351

Cardozo, B., 7, 30
Cassirer, E., 17
Cicero, 276, 277, 278, 280
Clermont, K., 326
Cohen, M., 64
Coleman, J., 31
Collingwood, R., 44, 110, 137, 293
Corbin, A., 146
Craig, P., 344

Davidson, R., 91
Davis, K., 25
del Vecchio, G., 28, 40
Duffy, J., 355, 356
Dworkin, R., 74

Eckhoff, T., 28
Ehrlich, E., 12

Eisenberg, M., 317
Eskridge, W., 252

Fallon, R., 26
Farnsworth, E., 214
Finnis, J., 109, 111, 138, 283
Fowler, H., 63
Frickey, P., 252
Fuller, L., 10, 22, 25, 26, 27, 28, 40, 52, 103, 139, 224, 232, 324, 336, 339

Gargarin, M., 172
Garrett, E., 252
Giddens, A., 211
Gilmore, G., 213
Göethe, J., 187, 212
Goldberg, J., 275
Gordley, J., 319
Greenawalt, K., 26, 161, 243
Guastini, R., 76

Hacker, P., 76, 96
Hamilton, A., 26, 106, 285
Hand, L., 241
Hart, H., 3, 4, 8, 10, 16, 26, 27, 28, 55, 63, 64, 72, 73, 74, 75, 76, 77, 79, 82, 83, 84, 85, 86, 87, 93, 95, 96, 103, 105, 111, 126, 144, 152, 160, 161, 185, 219, 284, 305, 307, 308, 309, 317, 334, 344, 345
Hillman, R., 326
Hobbes, T., 285, 288, 293, 294
Hohfeld, W., 146, 236
Holmes, O., 3, 16, 182, 213
Homans, G., 16
Honoré, A., 233
Hume, D., 20, 21, 118, 239
Hyman, I., 24

393

Ilbert, C., 92

Jhering, R., 3, 7, 11, 12, 13, 14, 15, 18, 27, 28, 36,
    40, 47, 65, 72, 92, 101, 102, 121, 135, 136, 138,
    140, 141, 157, 187, 203, 210, 220, 223, 224,
    228, 232, 305, 307, 339, 348, 366
Johnson, S., 326
Jones, H., 169, 177

Kadish, M., 24
Kadish, S., 24
Kant, I., 128
Kantorowicz, H., 12
Kaplan, B., 26
Kelsen, H., 3, 4, 8, 10, 26, 27, 28, 73, 75, 79, 85, 93,
    286, 307, 317, 334
Kennedy, D., 12, 25, 29, 46, 276
Kenny, A., 83
Kimble, S., 351
Klein, D., 275
Koopmans, T., 93
Kopp, H., 28

Lidsky, L., 36, 189
Livingston, R., 91
Llewellyn, K., 16, 28, 29, 72, 96,
    320
Locke, J., 104, 106
Lohmüller, 377
Longmate, N., 356
Lovell, G., 242
Lucas, J., 21

MacCormick, D. N., 25, 26, 242, 243,
    249, 252, 253, 257, 259, 261, 262,
    263, 282
Macpherson, S., 25
Madison, J., 26, 106
Mann, B., 26
Markesinis, B., 217
Markwick, P., 47, 71
Marshall, G., 12, 32, 86, 91, 253, 258, 262,
    276
Mehren, A., 319
Morrow, G., 334

Nicholas, B., 217
Norton, P., 91, 93, 95

Patterson, E., 319
Plato, 21, 47, 139, 155, 170, 191, 334, 345
Pole, D., 25
Posner, R., 12, 25, 29, 276
Pound, R., 21, 28, 62, 182, 283
Provine, D., 326

Radbruch, G., 28
Raz, J., 326, 339
Reed, J., 275
Reed, T., 16
Rosenberg, C., 355
Ross, A., 28

Schauer, F., 25, 136, 185
Schlesinger, R., 319
Shapiro, M., 31
Sherwin, E., 25, 136
Simmel, G., 64
Slawson, D., 226
Smith, A., 24
Soper, P., 13, 239, 258
Stevens, A., 91
Stone, M., 31, 63
Summers, R., 8, 12, 13, 22, 23, 25, 26, 28, 29, 31,
    36, 45, 47, 53, 61, 67, 73, 76, 86, 96, 122, 145,
    175, 196, 213, 242, 243, 249, 252, 253, 257,
    258, 259, 261, 262, 263, 276, 282, 320, 326,
    339, 359
Sunstein, C., 275

Tchaikovsky, P., 355
Thaysen, U., 91
Trachenburg, M., 24

van Caenegem, R., 319

Waddams, S., 12
Waldron, J., 25, 93, 95
Washe, P., 162, 163
Weber, M., 28, 40, 62
Weinberger, O., 25
Weinrib, E., 25
Wheare, K., 59, 91, 113
White, J., 175, 213, 320
Wieacker, F., 28
Wittgenstein, L., 15, 16, 64, 77, 83
Wright, G., 136

SUBJECT INDEX

addressee self-direction
effects of form on, 193, 375
linear progression stage of, 379
need for sanctions and, 284–285
public promulgation stage and, 377
rule of law and, 184–185
administrative agencies
centralized-hierarchical ordering within, 311
choices of forms in, 367
form v. component arguments and, 60
rule-making by, 370–371
administrative-regulatory technique
choice of technique, 364
cholera example, 356–357, 358–359, 360–362,
365–366
credit due to form, 68–69
general description of, 329
law-making stage, choices at, 369
public-promulgation stage, choices at, 377
systemizing effects of, 6, 8, 326, 327

bilateral contracts. *See* contracts

cholera example, 354–390
choice of example, 354
general background of, 354–355
See also linear progression analysis; *specific units,
techniques*
codification
accessible to addressees, 321–322
case law and, 322
common law and, 320, 321–322
encapsulatory feature of, 320
expressional feature of, 320
as formal, 321–322
general description of, 319–323
internal structure and, 320
interpretive methdology and, 321

substantive content in code, 322–323
systematizing devices and, 308
Collingwood's formulation of rule form, 43–44
complementary components, 41, 130. *See specific
legal functional units*
completeness feature, 147
addressees and, 149–150
complementary content and, 148–149, 203,
204
constituent feature of form, 154
credit for purposes served, 149, 153
criminal law and, 147
criterion for judging, 150, 154–155
culmulative reformulations and, 151
definiteness and, 156, 158–160
degree of, 149–150
determinateness of rules and, 149
English lexicons and, 147
expressional feature and, 177
formal character of, 147
functional v. linguistic, 150–151
generality and, 162
holistic approaches and, 154
incomplete rules, examples of, 150
incompleteness at rule inception, 151–153
internal features of rules and, 141
political values and, 153
rule design, initial choices in, 190
rule of law and, 153
rule-rule interactions and, 153–154
spaces for content, 147–148, 153
structure and, 169
compositional feature
bill enactment process, 130
complementary components and, 103, 108,
127
credit due to for purposes served, 104–105, 108
design criteria, 102–103

395

Subject Index

compositional feature (*cont.*)
  elected legislatures and, 106, 107
  general description of, 97, 101–102
  major issues of, 101–102
  membership issues, 99, 102
  multiple political parties and, 104
  Parliament v. Senate, 103
  process values and, 108
  purposiveness of, 102, 104
  rationales for, 102
  reinforcive rules and, 106–108
  representational government and, 104–105
  valid-law criteria and, 104
conceptualistic deductivism, 36, 63, 275–281
constitutional law, scholarship on form in, 26
constitutive rules, 27. *See* reinforcive rules
contracts, 3–4
  breach of. *See* remedies
  communication requirement, 217
  complementary components and, 214, 215, 217–218
  completeness of, 218, 219, 226, 237, 238
  credit due form, 221, 228, 232, 236
  declarations of intent, 223
  definiteness and, 213, 216–218, 227, 237, 238
  as discrete functional units, 53, 213
  duration of, 214
  economic efficiency and, 215
  encapsulatory features of, 213, 218, 226–227
  exchange role, 215
  expressional feature and, 218, 227–228, 237
  first-level functional units and, 306
  form-content distinction, 219–220
  form of, choices, 215
  form skepticism and, 214–215, 237, 238
  formalism in, 29
  freedom of contract, 14, 45, 222–223, 238
  generality and, 213, 216–218, 227, 237
  implementation of law and, 236
  internal formal structure of, 213, 227
  interpretive methdology and, 237
  jurisdictional features and, 214
  law-is-policy reductionism and, 238
  mode of expression, 226
  mutual assent requirement, 218, 219, 222–223
  negotiations, 216–218
  negotiations, initial choices in, 216–218
  negotiations, sobering effects of, 223–224
  non-preceptual species of law and, 38
  one-shot v. relational, 227
  parole evidence rule, 226
  prima facie validity, 219, 223, 228–232

printed standardized agreements, 226–227, 230–231
  private administration of law, 237
  private-legislators analogy, 214, 216
  private ordering technique. *See* private ordering technique
  promissory feature, 217–218, 222–223
  property interests and, 232
  purposes of form of, 212, 216
  reinforcive rules and, 220–221
  rule of law and, 229–230, 231
  rule-oriented approaches, 220–221
  scholarship on, 26
  simplicity and, 227
  statutory rules and, 213
  third parties, 227
  in writing, 219, 226–227, 230–231
courts, 3–4. *See also* judges
  importance of form in, 18
  institutional functional legal units and, 38
customary practices, 7

definiteness, 141, 155
  addressee self-direction, 193
  administrative intervention stage and, 383
  cholera example, 370–372
  complementary content and, 20, 157, 192, 203, 204
  completeness and, 156, 158–160
  degree of, 20
  democracy and, 362
  determinateness and, 156
  English definition of, 156, 157
  evaluation of degree, 157–158
  evaluation of in holistic context, 160
  expressional feature and, 177
  facilitation of rule implementation, 21
  form skepticism arguments and, 30–31, 60
  formal characterization of, 156–158
  freedom protected by, 156
  generality and, 162, 163
  imprint of on content, 139–140
  justified fiat and, 118
  learnability and, 376
  pre-emptoriness, 372
  prescription-consequences relations, 167–168
  prioritizing ends, 140, 142, 156, 192–193, 200, 201–202, 208
  procedural features and, 118
  rationality of deliberation, 200
  rule design, initial choices in, 190–192, 195
  rule of law and, 156, 193–195, 196–200, 342–343
  structure and, 167–168, 169
  void-for-vagueness doctrine, 139

Subject Index

democracy, 21–22, 362
  participation, 31
  as a process value, 31
  See also rule of law; *specific legal functional units*
determinateness
  complementary content and, 204
  completeness and, 149
  jurisdictional features and, 110
  See also specific legal functional units

empiricist methodology, 93–94
encapsulatory feature, 142, 170
  administrative regulations, 174
  authoritative sources, 170–171
  Blackstone-Bentham debate, 174–175
  choice of, 369
  codification, 175. *See* codification
  common law systems and, 174–175
  communication modes, 170
  complementary content and, 204
  constitutions, 173–174
  definition of, 52
  expressional feature and, 179
  fixed verbal sequence, 369
  fixed verbal sequences, 170, 173–174
  law-making stage and, 369
  preceptual form and, 175
  printed, 204
  rule design, initial choices in, 190
  statutory law systems and, 174–175
enforcive units, 39, 285–286
  adverse to addressee, 287
  form-skepticism and, 293–294
  forms of, 287
  reinforcive rules and, 289
  state imposed, 287
  systematizing devices and, 308
  types of, 286
  See also sanctions
expressional feature, 31, 142, 176
  choices of, 369, 374
  complementary content and, 178, 204
  completeness and, 177
  context of adjacent rules, 178
  credit due to for purposes served, 177
  definiteness and, 177
  democracy and, 362
  encapsulatory feature and, 179
  evaluation of, 178–179
  formal characterization of, 176–177
  general description of, 176
  generality and, 177
  law-making stage and, 369
  legislative bill enactment process, 130
  parts of, listed, 176

  prescriptiveness and, 177
  rule design, initial choices in, 190
  structural feature and, 178
  technical language, 177

form
  ancient Greeks and, 134
  apolitical nature of, 35
  attributes of functional legal units and, 65–66
  authoritative refinement of policies and, 70
  component form, 58–59
  constituent features of rules and, 30–31
  container conception, 52–53
  contribution defined away, 35
  credit due for purposes served, 10–11, 14, 20,
    66, 67, 68, 69–71
  credit due, possible objects of credit, 67–68
  current potential for improvement in forms,
    33
  drafting of rules, 69–70
  efficacy of functional legal units and, 17
  English language meaning of, 48, 50–52
  existence of functional legal units and, 17, 63
  features taken for granted, 11
  functional legal units and, 19, 64
  general definition of overall form, 11, 39–42, 47,
    50, 54–55
  general potency of, 390
  humanistic disciplines focus on, 24–25
  importance to legal profession, 22
  imprints of, 7–8, 14
  key concepts in, 41–42
  key terms of, 40–41
  legal theorists v. practitioners, 33
  level of generality of, 54–55
  limits of, 387
  linguistic, 31–32
  as mark of mint to a coin, 47
  material components and, 11
  nonempirical nature of claims for, 69–71
  phenomenological fit, 50
  philosophical meaning of term, 47–48, 62
  physical-shape meaning of term, 50–52
  political values and, 23
  purposive systematic arrangements, 14–15
  rationales for, 47
  rationality and, 14–15, 21
  reasons for adopting, 39–40
  rule of law and, 23
  rules compliance and, 70–71
  scholarship neglect of, 11, 16, 24, 25,
    30–32, 33, 35, 65–66, 95. *See also* form
    skepticism
  scholarship on, 25, 26
  slow evolution of legal systems and, 33

398   Subject Index

form (*cont.*)
  special primacy of, 9
  technical meaning of term, 47
  types of claims for, 68
  types of purposes served, 42
  wide-ranging fit, 50
  See also form skepticism; form-oriented
    approaches
formal
  authoritative-source meaning, 53, 109
  design quality and, 6–7
  English usage of term, 48–49, 102, 109
  formal-formalistic distinction, 24, 27–28, 29,
    275–281
  mode-of-expression meaning, 53–54
  scholarship neglect of, 7
formalistic interpretation, 275
  formalistic statutes vs., 280–281
  ill-designed methodology and, 281
  ill-designed statutory rules and, 281
  nonmethodological interpretation and, 281
  well-designed form forfends against, 280
form-oriented approaches
  aims in adopting, 78–79
  as complementary to rule-oriented, 74–75
  general description of, xiii–xiv, 10
  importance of, 5
  main steps in, 77–78
  regulative rules and, 10
  reinforcive rules and, 10
  rule-oriented approaches and *See* rule-oriented
    approaches
form skepticism, 11, 131, 179, 196, 207, 238
  antiformal attitudes, 11, 12, 24, 28–29
  behaviorist approaches, 29, 93, 96
  definiteness and, 179
  form inseparable from content, 207, 209
  form v. material components, 61, 132–133
  formalism, pejorative use of term, 63
  formalistic term, 29–30
  imprints and, 180
  law-is-policy reductionism, 179, 196–197,
    202–203, 207
  policy content as primary, 180, 202–203, 207
  reductio ad absurdum arguments, 180
  rule of law and, 196–197
  socio-moral form, 239–240
  See also formalistic interpretation; rule oriented
    approaches; *specific functional legal units*
forms
  cumulative-synergistic effects of, 351
  fundamental questions in general theory of,
    listed, 72
  general theory of, 8–9
  importance of, 17

free-law movement (Freierechtslehre), 12
functional legal units
  attributes of, 65
  bilateral contracts, 38
  constituent features of, 41
  court procedures vs legislative, 56–57
  founding purposes, 43
  general definition of, 9, 39
  heterogeneity of, 306
  holistic approaches and, 80–81
  independent from material components, 60–61
  institutional, 38
  instrumental capacity of, 66
  integrated within operational systems, 8
  interdependence among, 6
  internal unity between features of, 6
  material components and, 57
  methodological, 39
  multiplicity of, 306
  necessity of overall form to, 8
  non-preceptual species of law, 38
  obviousness of, 15
  ordering of relations between. *See* systemizing
    devices
  origins of, 7
  overall form of units, 5. *See* form
  overlapping purposes, 43
  political values realized through, 45
  preceptual, 38
  predecessor systems of, 7
  priorital relations between, 308
  private ends of individuals and, 44
  purposes of, 5, 6, 7, 9, 44
  rationality, 46–47
  remedies, 39
  rule of law, 45–46
  rules and, 183
  sanctions and, 39
  sequential deployment of. *See* linear progression
    analysis
  study of, 15
  systemization and, 307, 308, 326
  as taking distinctive forms, 75
  typology of, 37, 54, 310
  unity within individual units, 66, 306
  vary from society to society, 55–56

generality feature, 161
  choosing level of, 372–373
  class terms, 163
  complementary content and, 164, 203
  completeness and, 162
  as constitutive, 161
  definiteness and, 162, 163
  degree of, 162, 163–164

Subject Index

efficiency and, 161
equal protection clause and, 139
expressional feature and, 177
initial choices in formulating laws, 190
prescriptiveness and, 162
reinforcive rules and, 163
rules, internal formal features of, 141
simplicity and, 169
structure and, 169
grievance-remedial technique, 8
choice of technique, 364
cholera example, 361, 365
general description of, 328–329, 359
systemization through, 326
Grundnorm, 8, 27

Hart, H.L.A.
background of, 76–77
on overall form, 26–27
rule-oriented approaches and, 72–88
systemizing devices and, 307, 309
Hart-Kelsen mode of analysis, 4
Heaven of Juristic Concepts, 36
Holmes, Oliver Wendell Jr., 16

imprisonment sanction, 289
authorized judges for, 292
complementary material and, 293
constituent features of, 290
penal technique. *See* penal technique
purposes of, 291
rule of law and, 291
unit not independently functional, 291–292
information, linear progression analysis and, 387
institutional forms, 31
mixed forms, 23–24
neglect of, 95
scholarship on form in, 25
institutional functional legal units, 38. *See specific
institutions*
internal structure of rules, 41, 141
interpretive methodology, 242
borderline cases and, 247
case law and, 250
complementary material and, 253–254, 274
completeness feature, 252
constituent features of, 243, 250–251
credit due form, 266
definiteness, 251, 265
faithfulness of interpretation, 251, 253, 255, 257,
259
filling of statutory gaps, 251
formal characterization of, 251
formalistic abuses of, 275
general principles and, 263–265

generality and, 251, 265
issues in, listed, 324
judicial role, 253, 263, 264–265, 271–272
jurisdictional features, 252–253
language-oriented criteria, 257, 259
methodological case law, 271
in operation not wholly formal, 253–254
ordinary English usage, 251
ordinary meanings of words and, 247
penal statutes and, 245
preceptual feature, 266
prescriptions for constructing arguments,
262
principles of priority, 263
priorital principles, 251
procedural prescriptions for, 251
purpose-built, 242
reductio ad absurdum arguments, 265
rule design and, 244, 249, 273
rule inception and, 270–271
rule of law, 274, 337, 339, 341
rule-oriented analysis and, 244–245
scope, 265
sources of needs for, 245
statute conflicts with legal principles, 248
steps of, listed, 254–255
structure and, 251, 265
study of as means for advancing understanding,
250
synergies, multiple, 273
systematizing devices and, 308
technical language, 248, 252
treatises for, 250, 274
types of interpretive arguments, 260
uniformity of, 308
vague language, 248
See also rule of law

Jhering, Rudolf von, 27–28
judicial institutions, centralized-hierarchical
ordering within, 311. *See also* interpretive
methodology
jurisdictional features, 108
complementary components, 127
democracy and, 110
determinateness and, 110
institutional legitimacy and, 110
legislative bill enactment process, 130
legislative compositional feature and, 41
legislature constituent features, 97
procedural features and, 109–110, 119, 120–121
reinforcive rules and, 111–112
rule-oriented approaches and, 111–112
two-chamber legislatures, 129
validity of law and, 111

jurisdictional spheres
  centralized-hierarchical ordering within, 308, 311
  hierarchical ordering of, 308
  prioritization among, 315

Kelsen, Hans
  on overall form, 26–27

legal forms. *See* forms
legal functional units
  constituent features of, 5
  as enriching possible ends, 21–22
  key questions about, 9
  list of, 3–4
legal positivism, 26, 34, 52, 88, 139
legal realists, 25, 28–29, 96
legal systems
  examples of disunity, 129
  first-level functional units, 305. *See* functional legal units
  formalness and, 344, 347–350
  general characteristics of, listed, 344
  gradual evolution of, 33
  major questions about, 305–311
  norms and, 73
  overall form of, 305
  rules and, 183
  rules prescriptiveness and, 146
  second-level systemizing devices, 305, 309, 331, 343–344
  as systems of rules, 3–5. *See* rule-oriented approaches
  unity of law, 146
  as vast network of extant legal relations, 146–147
legislative institutions, 91
  academic literature on, 93–94
  bicameral, 6
  bill enactment process, 130
  centralized-hierarchical ordering within, 311
  choices of forms in, 367
  coherence, 129–130
  compositional feature, 99
  constituent features of, 97–98. *See also specific features*
  constituent forms of, 97
  credit due to for purposes served, 20–21, 93–95, 101
  early Greeks and, 99
  executive branch relation to, 55
  first-level functional units and, 306
  functional legal units and, 3–4, 38
  general definition of overall form and, 40–42

holistic approaches and, 129–130
  inner order of, 92, 109–110
  key issues, 92
  legal validity criterion, 131
  lobbyists and, 108
  main parts of, listed, 127
  major purposes of, 97
  membership, 55, 74
  normative cement and, 96
  outside view of, 92
  overall form of, 18–19
  parts of, 96
  as purposive, 92, 98
  reinforcive rules and, 98, 99–100
  rule-oriented approaches, 131
  single legislature systems, 312–313
  structural form in, 368
  synergistic effects, 128
  two-chamber legislatures, 128–129
  unity of features, 127
linear progression analysis, 351
  administrative intervention stage, 381
  cholera example. *See* cholera example
  court-action stage, 383
  form-orientation of, 352
  information in, 387
  main stages of, 360–361
  public promulgation stage, 377
  rule-oriented approaches and, 353
  stages of, 362–363
  synergistic effects, 353–354

material components, 57
  credit due to, 11
  examples of, 57–58
  See also specific legal functional units
methodologies, 242
  combinations of, 249
  defined, 241
  forms of, 241
  as functional legal units, 241
  interpretive. *See* interpretive methodology
  legislative bill enactment process, 130
  major types of, 241
  purposive, 241–243
  uniformity and, 242, 324–325

neo-realists, 29
nonpreceptual law, 3–4, 211. *See* contracts; property interests
norm-oriented method, 73

operational techniques
  choice of technique, 363, 364, 368, 386
  compared, 359–360
  complementary material and, 366

Subject Index

credit due forms of, 366
early choice of rule forms and, 362
as formal, 329–330
function of, 6
jointly deployed, 329–330
listed, 326
rule of law and, 332
scholarship neglect of, 27
synergy between, 327–328
systematizing devices and, 308
systemization of functional legal units through, 326
See also specific techniques

penal technique
choice of technique, 364
cholera example, 364–365
general description of, 328
imprisonment and, 290, 359
presupposes judicial institutions, 292
systemization and, 8, 326, 331, 332
personnel
judges, importance of, 59
keeping units on-track, 6–7
legislative unity of form and, 127
roles organized by form, 126
See also specific institutions
policy priorial effect, 198
political values, 19–20, 23, 45, 185
See also democracy; rule of law; *specific legal functional units*
pre-realist formalism, 36
precepts, 3–4. *See* rules
preceptual feature, 126
choices at law-making stage, 141, 369
complementary components, 127
encapsulation and, 175
initial choices in law making, 189
legislative bill enactment process, 130
legislative institutions and, 98
normative cement and, 127
personnel training and, 127
procedural features and, 122–123
reinforcive rules and, 126–127
rule of law and, 122–123
prescriptive rules
legislative bill enactment process, 130
prescriptiveness feature, 141, 143
authoritative, 144
categorical, 144
choice of, 373
complementary material and, 143, 145
definition of overall form and, 143
expressional feature and, 146, 177
formal characterization of, 143, 144
generality and, 162

granting permissions-liberties, 144–145
hortatory language, 143
initial choices in rule design, 190–191
modal language of, 144
motivational, 146
pre-emptoriness, 144, 145
protected spaces of autonomy carved out, 146
structure and, 167
unity of law and, 146
private entities, systemization between, 315
private law, scholarship on form in, 25
private arranging technique
breach of contract and, 298
choice of technique, 364
cholera example, 365
contracts and, 215
general description of, 329
jurisdictional spheres and, 311
legislatures and, 361
scholarship neglect of, 326
procedural features, 116
accumulation over time, 122
authoritative decisions and, 121
clarity of expression and, 121–122
complementary components, 118–119, 127
contributes justified fiat to content, 118
credit due to for purposes served, 122–123
debate cloture, 119
decision-rules for, 118, 121
decisiveness in, 44
definiteness and, 118
dialogic, 128
as distinct, 119
elaboration of, 119
fixity of verbal formulations, 121–122
as formal, 116–117
gaps in reasoned content and, 118
general mode of operation of, 119
interactions with other features, 124
joint conference committees, 120
jurisdictional features and, 109–110, 119, 120–121
legislative bill enactment process, 121–122, 130
legislative institutions and, 41, 98
legislatures v. courts implementation of, 56–57
majority party potentially limited by, 119
majority voting, 118, 121
personnel and, 126
preceptual feature and, 122–123
process values and, 117
publicity and, 123
as purposive, 117
reinforcive rules and, 119, 120–121
role in history of progress of governance, 117
rule of law and, 122–123
rule-oriented analysis, 124–125

402 Subject Index

process values, 31, 45, 67, 108
property interests, 3–4, 306
  contracts and, 232
  credit due form, 232, 235, 236
  freedom of ownership, 235–236
  implementation of law, 236
  intangible property, 234
  major categories, listed, 233
  property rights, listed, 233
public-benefit conferring technique, 8
  choice of technique, 364
  choices at law-making stage, 369
  choices at public-promulgation stage, 377
  cholera example, 358–359, 365–366
  coordination between techniques, 332
  general description of, 329
  operational techniques, 326

regulative rules
  criminal law and, 187
  definition of, 4
  democracy and, 186
  form-oriented analysis and, 10, 19–20
  legitimacy, 186
  policies and, 183
  reinforcive rules and, 140–141
  voluntary compliance and, 186
reinforcive rules
  defined, 73
  democracy and, 186
  form and, 27
  form-oriented analysis and, 10, 74,
    75–76
  games and, 100
  general description of, 4, 5
  jurisdiction and, 185–186
  legitimacy, 186
  normative cement and, 76, 96
  policies and, 183
  political values and, 185–186
  preceptual features and, 126–127
  rationality in construction of, 186
  regulative rules and, 140–141
  rule-oriented analysis and, 11
  voluntary compliance and, 186
  See also rule-oriented analysis; *specific functional*
    legal units
remedies, 283
  breach of contract and, 295
  constituent features of, 298–299
  credit due form, 297–298
  damage measurement, 299–300
  definiteness and, 296–297
  form skepticism and, 300–302
  as functional legal units, 286

private ordering technique and. *See* private
  ordering technique
purposes of, 297
systematizing devices and, 308
uniformity of interpretive methodology and,
  323
voluntary performance and, 296
See also enforcive units
rule design
  choices within form of, 369
  court form and, 273–274
  definiteness, 199–200
  final choices, 199
  form-content interactions, 203
  free choice and, 195–199
  general categories of ends, 195–196
  initial choices in formulating laws, 190
  initial choices in formulation of, 188
  interpretive methdology and, 244, 249,
    273
  overall course of, 201
  policy ends, 195–199
  policy-form interactions, 200–201
  rule of law and, 195–200
rule of law
  acquiescence of population, 130–131
  addressee self-direction and, 185
  authoritative law, 342
  credit due form of, 338
  definiteness and, 342–343
  as desiderata of form for rules, 138
  discretionary powers of officials, 185
  due process and, 339, 384
  elections, 340–341
  enforcive devices and, 337
  formalness of principles of, 25
  functional legal units and, 338
  individual autonomy and, 339–340
  interpretive methodology and, 274, 337, 339,
    341
  jurisdictional spheres and, 337
  legitimacy, 338
  overall form and, 23
  preceptual forms of rules and, 342–343
  principles of, 337
  principles of, listed, 334–336
  priorital effect, 196, 197
  promulgation-publicizing of laws and,
    343
  public standards and, 338
  realized through form, 45–46
  rule-completeness and, 153
  rule design, initial choices in, 188
  self-direction under law, 339
  systematizing devices and, 308

Subject Index

systemization devices and, 332–333, 338
violations of principles of, 343
rule of recognition, 8, 27
rule-oriented approaches, 4, 72–88
  as complementary to form-oriented, 74–75
  holistic approaches and, 80
  institutional forms and, 95
  legal theorists on, 93
  as normative cement, 88
  reinforcive rules and, 11
  as a study in indirection, 79–88
  See also form skepticism
rule v. discretion theory, 25
rules, 3–4, 136–138
  addressees, 59–60
  adjudication, 4
  complementary components, 7–8, 59–60, 142,
    165–166
  composition feature of, 4
  constituent features of, 7, 19, 30–31, 59, 66, 137,
    139. *See specific features*
  credit due to for purposes served, 140, 142, 184
  desiderata of form in, 138
  drafting of rules, 183–184
  duty-imposing, 75
  enactment of statutes, 124
  form and, 137, 182
  form and content of, 183, 205–207
  formal features of, 141–142
  formless-rules, 203–204
  freedom and, 186–187
  freedom of movement, 187
  freedom to contract, 187
  functional legal units and, 183
  games and, 76–77, 100
  generality, level of, 20
  generality of, 183–184
  imprints of, 142
  internal features of, 139
  of jurisdiction, 4
  legal systems and, 183
  legal theorists on, 136–138
  legal validity v. serving values, 21
  legitimization of authority and, 186
  model for design of, 183
  overall form of, 59–60
  paradigm of statutory rules, 137
  policy content of, 59–60
  policy formulation and, 183
  policy implementation and, 183
  political values and, 185
  as pouring content into mold, 138
  power-conferring, 75
  primary, 75
  private law and, 186–187

of procedure, 4
property rights and, 187
purpose of overall form of, 183
purposes of, 139
purposive rationality in construction of, 137
rationality in construction of, 139–140, 182
regulative. *See* regulative rules
reinforcive. *See* reinforcive rules
rule of law and, 184. *See* rule of law
rule-oriented approaches to, 139
schematic law-making example, 189
scholarship on form in, 25
secondary, 75
substantive, 30
substantive content of, 30
systemizing devices and, 307
ultimate purposes of, 137
unifying effects of, 142
validity of, 307
See also rule of law; *specific rules*

sanctions, 283
  adversity characteristically limited, 288
  constituent features of, 287–289
  due process requirement, 288–289
  as functional legal units, 286
  imprisonment. *See* imprisonment sanction
  legal rationale requirement, 288
  rule of law and, 384
  state imposed, 287–288
  systematizing devices and, 308
  sytemization and, 323
  uniform interpretive methodology and, 323
  See also enforcive units
social-scientific methodology, 93–94
statutory rules. *See* rules
structural feature, 112
  British-American differences in, 112, 113–114
  choices of, 165, 373
  committee systems, 114–115
  complementary components and, 113, 127
  completeness and, 169
  credit due to for purposes served, 113, 114, 168
  definiteness and, 167–168, 169
  definition of, 164–165
  determinateness, 114
  discretionary powers of officials, 166
  distinctiveness of, 167–168
  expressional feature and, 178
  fit to purposes, 165–166
  formal character of, 112, 164, 165
  generality and, 169
  independence of judiciary, 114
  initial choices in formulating laws, 190
  legislative bill enactment process, 130

404   Subject Index

structural feature (*cont.*)
  legislative institutions and, 97
  part-to-part relations, 165
  part-to-whole relations and, 165
  political parties, 115
  political values and, 114
  prescription-consequences relations, 166,
    168
  prescriptiveness and, 167
  provisos, 166–167
  purposive, 113
  rule-oriented approaches, 116
  simplicity and, 168, 169–170
  systems of checks, 113
substantivists, 35, 36, 179, 275
synergistic effects, 386
systemization, 8, 9, 307
  basic norm, 307
  citizenry allegiance to system, 345
  codification. *See* codification
  constitutions and, 311
  degrees of systematization, 311
  devices listed, 310
  as formal, 308
  functional legal units and, 307, 326
  geographical regions, 344
  integrated communication systems and, 344
  interpretive uniformity and, 323
  jurisdictional spheres and, 315. *See*
    jurisdictional spheres
  main devices, listed, 308
  methodologies and, 323

  operational techniques and, 326
  prioritization and, 315
  purposes and, 309
  remedies and, 323
  rule implementation, 307
  rule of recognition, 307
  rule prioritization, 307
  sanctions and, 323
  shared political cultures and, 344
  of valid laws within discrete fields, 319
  values and, 309
  well-trained personnel and, 344–345

technological-scientific expertise, 369, 371
terrorism, 295, 331–332, 390

Uniform Commercial Code. *See* codification

valid law, criteria of, 18–19, 307, 317
values. *See also* purposes
  freedom, 19–20
  humanistic, 7, 17
  policy values, 19–20
  political values. *See* political values
  process values. *See* process values
  rationality, 19–20
  societal, 17

wills, 26, 29, 53
Wittgenstein, Ludwig
  influence on Hart, 76–77
  on seeing the obvious, 15–17